CHARTER JUSTICE

IN

CANADIAN CRIMINAL LAW

THIRD EDITION

by

DON STUART

B.A., LL.B., Dip. Crim., D. Phil.

FACULTY OF LAW
QUEEN'S UNIVERSITY
KINGSTON, ONTARIO

CARSWELL

A THOMSON COMPANY

National Library of Canada Cataloguing in Publication Data

Stuart, Don, 1943–
    Charter justice in Canadian criminal law

3rd ed.
Includes bibliographical references and index.
ISBN 0-459-26113-4

1. Criminal procedure — Canada. 2. Trial practice —
Canada. 3. Canada. Canadian Charter of Rights and
Freedoms. I. Title

KE9304.S78 2001   345.71'07   C2001-930289-4
KF9655.S78 2001

CARSWELL

A THOMSON COMPANY

One Corporate Plaza, 2075 Kennedy Road, Scarborough, Ontario M1T 3V4
Customer Service:
Toronto 1-416-609-3800
Elsewhere in Canada/U.S. 1-800-387-5164
Fax 1-416-298-5094

This book is dedicated to the Queen's law students who were so keen to see this project completed that they

did, on April 16, 1991, at the end-of-year P.O.I.T.S. party at Law House in the city of Kingston, in the county of Frontenac, conspire to break my ankle

and, lovingly, to Pamela Jane, who continues to bear the brunt of such family happenings.

Preface

The 1982 entrenchment into the Canadian Constitution of a *Canadian Charter of Rights and Freedoms* has had a considerable impact on criminal courts in Canada. Even though reform of the criminal law was clearly not uppermost in the minds of the politicians who achieved the passage of the *Charter*, our criminal justice system has been its main beneficiary. Encouraged by interventionist stances of the Supreme Court of Canada, courts at all levels have taken very seriously their *Charter* mandate to be guardians of the Constitution. The *Charter* has become a powerful vehicle for searching re-examination of many long established precepts of criminal law, whether these be matters of substance, procedure, evidence or sentencing.

The *Charter* has its detractors. Critics have suggested that the priority it accords individual rights is out of step with the modern State's recognition of collective interests. Some worry about an unjustifiable transfer of power from legislatures to non-elected judiciary and question the appropriateness and ability of judges to rule on difficult questions of value and policy.

In this edition I attempt to answer such views as expressed by Professors Michael Mandel and Christopher Manfredi in Chapter 1. I argue there that the assertion of *Charter* standards has resulted in some check by independent judges to the inexorable trend for politicians to pander to the expediency of making the criminal law ever tougher. Attacks on the judicial record under the *Charter* should be balanced by an equally determined critical review of the legislative process. Legislative records on the protection of minority interests, including rights of accused, have been woeful. The judicial system under the *Charter* may be far from perfect, but it provides some counterpoint to the tyranny of the majority. However the *Charter* is not a panacea and the Supreme Court record can be criticized for excessive complexity, inconsistency and sometimes setting *Charter* standards too low.

The aim of this book is to provide an accurate and critical review of how the Charter has been applied in the criminal courts. The major impetus came from my sabbatical experience during 1988-1989 as a full-time prosecutor in the city of Toronto. Especially when in the busy trial courts, one became immediately aware of the challenge and difficulty of having even the basic principles of the now voluminous *Charter* jurisprudence at one's fingertips. Often one seemed trapped in a mindless search for minor precedent which lost sight of the big picture.

What this book seeks to do, then, is to identify the central authorities and arguments concerning the *Charter* in the specialized context of the criminal trial and to point to some new possibilities. I have tried to be selective and not go over the old bones of precedent or argument now authoritatively rejected.

There may well be a tendency in criminal trials in Canada to place too much emphasis on *Charter* defences. This book focuses on the *Charter*, but I have tried to place it in the context of non-constitutional criminal law and practice. In some cases defence counsel would be much better advised to rely on a common law or statutory defence.

The structure of the book remains intact in this third edition but there has been substantial updating and revisions to every chapter.

Chapter 1 on "Basic Principles" includes analysis of the determination in *Mills* that there is a need for the Courts to engage in a "dialogue" with Parliament such that the Courts' determination of *Charter* standards is not necessarily the last word. This rhetoric allowed the Court to uphold Parliament's legislation of the minority position of L'Heureux-Dubé J. in *O'Connor* limiting defence access to therapeutic and other records of complainants in sexual assault cases. This appears to substantially weaken the notion that the Courts must be the guardian of the Constitution declaring minimum *Charter* standards subject only to section 33 overrides. In *Mills* and in *Darrach*, in which the Court confirmed the constitutionality of Parliament's rape shield, the Court also recognised enforceable section 15 equality rights for complainants in sexual assault cases. The dubious process of recognition without any consideration of the ten-part test the Court had earlier established in *Law* to assess section 15 claims is addressed, as are disturbing issues arising out of the recognition of such victims' rights. The first Chapter also reviews the latest approach to section one justification in the *Little Sisters* case and further developments in procedural issues arising in *Charter* applications.

As was the case with the second edition, a staggeringly large number of significant developments in section 7 *Charter* jurisprudence in just four years has necessitated major re-writing of Chapter 2. The residual protection of section 7 is clearly still in flux. Chapter 2 now analyses, for example, the Supreme Court's latest assertion of a principle against self-incrimination in *White* and its majority ruling in *Noble* that no adverse ruling may normally be made from silence of an accused at trial. These rulings are contrasted with the Court's recent re-interpretation of the common law voluntary confession rule in *Oickle*, which appears, over the sole dissent of Justice Arbour, to authorise a wide range of deceptive interrogation techniques by police in combination with polygraphs. Lower courts have been resistant to extending the pre-trial right to silence beyond the narrow limits of *Hebert* but note is also taken of decisions, such as that of the Quebec Court of Appeal in *Otis*, which would make that right more meaningful. The trend these last four years in the interpretation of trial rights has often clearly favoured the State. The Supreme Court in *Mills* and *Darrach* emphasises that an accused is not entitled to the most favourable procedure and that the right to a fair trial does not include the right to distort the truth. In the context of disclosure, the Supreme Court now appears to have limited the remedy of a stay to deliberate non-disclosure (*La, Vu,* distinguishing *Carosella)* and requires the defence to diligently pursue disclosure (*Dixon*). So too a stay for an abuse of process is now emphasised to be rarely required (see *Tobiass* but compare *Shirose and Campbell* and the Court's recent pronouncements in the extradition cases of *Cobb* and *Shulman*). The Court has also adopted, with little introspection, the narrow *Strickland* test to determine the right to effective assistance of counsel (*B.G.D.*). On the accused's side of the ledger, the Supreme Court in *Biniaris* requires Court of Appeal judges to give reasons in the interests of transparency and thus appears to be hastening its retreat from *Burns*, which should be squarely reversed to require reasons in all contexts of the criminal trial. In *White* the Court further extends its *Harrer* recognition of an uncertain discretion to exclude evidence to ensure trial fairness.

The publication of this book was held back to include consideration of the Court's blockbuster ruling in *Ruzic* that moral involuntariness is now a minimum *Charter* standard for any defence. The Court struck down part of the narrow *Criminal Code* defence of duress

Chapter 3 on the section 8 right to be secure against unreasonable search and seizure has also been substantially re-written to reflect major recent jurisprudence. The chapter traces a substantial and regrettable weakening of *Hunter* v. *Southam*. Through an undue emphasis on property rights for the triggering concept of reasonable expectation of privacy in *Edwards*, many Canadians, such as passengers in vehicles (*Lawrence and Belnavis*), no longer have section 8 protection. The unruly consideration of context often now results in much reduced section 8 protection, as in the case of school children (*M.M.R.*) or intrusive drugs searches in loo facilities at airports (*Monney*). Accused do appear to have gained more protection in the case of searches incident to arrest (*Stillman* and *Caslake*). However the Supreme Court's adoption in *Godoy* of a broad ancillary powers doctrine for *ex post facto* recognition of police powers may well extend far beyond its context of legalising emergency investigation of disconnected 911 calls and further weaken section 8. Ontario courts have, however, refused to extend the *Simpson* power to stop for articulable cause to a wholescale checkpoint stop of bikers (*Brown* v. *Durham*) or to pedestrian stops (*Powell*).

A further major change in this edition is a full analysis of the *Stillman* re-assertion of the Court's approach to the exclusion of evidence obtained in violation of the *Charter* under section 24(2). Like other commentators, I find the notion of *automatic* exclusion of conscripted evidence troubling. The *Stillman* distinction between conscripted and non-conscripted evidence is strange and difficult to draw and the doctrine of discoverability seems ill-considered. But I am equally troubled by a trend to automatic *inclusion* of non-conscripted evidence, particularly noticeable in section 8 drug cases. Unless there is a real risk of exclusion of evidence obtained through *Charter* violation, *Charter* rights for accused become meaningless.

There has been less major change in the remaining chapters. Chapter 5 on section 10 rights notes that the Ontario Court of Appeal adopted a much more pro-accused position to the meaning of detention in *Johns*. Chapter 6 on section 11 rights draws attention to the decision of the majority of the Supreme Court in *Stone* to reverse the onus of proof for the defence of sane automatism, even though no counsel raised that issue. The impact of *Stone* may already have been partially blunted by the Supreme Court's decision in *Ruzic*. Like other commentators I find that decision has little to commend it. Chapter 6 also analyses the rejection by the B.C. and Ontario Courts of Appeal (in *McDougall* and *Hall* respectively) of the section 11(e) Charter challenge to the new public interest ground for denial of bail under s. 515(10)(c) of the Criminal Code. It is suggested that the Courts should have confronted broader issues, including issues of systemic racism in bail detention recently documented in Ontario. Chapter 7 assesses the continued trend in Supreme Court jurisprudence to weaken cruel and unusual protection, most recently manifested in its approach in *Morrissey*, upholding a four-year minimum gaol provision for criminal negligence causing death by use of a firearm. The new *Law* test for section 15 discrimination is considered in Chapter 10, together with the latest pronouncement on analogous grounds.

Some of the material published in this edition first appeared in headnotes, comments and articles for the Criminal Reports. This work and many of the ideas in this book owe a great deal to the insight and help of my expert Criminal Reports and Queen's Law School partners, Ron Delisle and Allan Manson, and my new colleague, Gary Trotter. I am also indebted to the voice-activated computer technology of the Worddancer system, which much facilitates my work. Finally I would like to thank the staff at Carswell, particularly Jilean Bell, for her support and encouragement, and the content editor, Debbie Bowen, for another superb job.

Don Stuart
January 1, 2001

Table of Contents

Table of Cases

1

Basic Principles

1. STRUCTURE OF CHARTER

The Canadian Charter of Rights and Freedoms was entrenched by the Constitution Act[1] on April 17, 1982. The Charter, expressly made applicable to both provincial and federal laws,[2] sets out a number of rights and freedoms.

Of particular interest in the criminal[3] context are the "Legal Rights" contained in ss. 7 through 14. The broadest provision is that in s. 7, which reads,

> Everyone has the right to life, liberty and security of the person and the right not to be deprived thereof except in accordance with the principles of fundamental justice.

The Supreme Court of Canada sees ss. 8 to 14 as specific examples of the umbrella "principles of fundamental justice" to be asserted in the context of criminal or penal law:

> Sections 8 to 14 address specific deprivations of the "right" to life, liberty and security of the person in breach of the principles of fundamental justice, and as such, violations of s. 7. They are therefore illustrative of the meaning, in criminal or penal law, of "principles of fundamental justice"; they represent principles which have been recognized by the common law, the international conventions and by the very fact of entrenchment in the Charter, as essential elements of a system for the

---

[1] Enacted by the Canada Act 1982 (U.K.), c. 11, Sched. B. The Charter is Part I of the Constitution Act.

[2] Section 32(1) reads:

This Charter applies

    (a) to the Parliament and government of Canada in respect of all matters within the authority of Parliament including all matters relating to the Yukon Territory and Northwest Territories; and

    (b) to the legislature and government of each province in respect of all matters within the authority of the legislature of each province.

[3] "Criminal" is used throughout this book in its broadest, non-constitutional sense to include all federal and provincial prohibition and punishment of conduct.

administration of justice which is founded upon a belief in the dignity and worth of the human person and the rule of law.[4]

"Everyone" has the right to be secure against unreasonable search or seizure (s. 8), not to be arbitrarily detained or imprisoned (s. 9), and has certain rights on arrest or detention (s. 10), including the right to retain and instruct counsel without delay. Section 11 lists a number of rights for any person charged with an offence including the right to be tried within a reasonable time (subsection (b)) and the right to be presumed innocent (subsection (d)). Section 12 protects everyone from being subjected to cruel and unusual treatment or punishment. Section 13 protects a witness from self-crimination and s. 14 concerns the right to the assistance of an interpreter. Clearly, these various rights do not apply in every penal context, since they are dependent on triggering devices such as arrest or detention in the case of the right to counsel under s. 10(b) or charging an offence in the case of the various rights under s. 11. More general provisions that have also impacted on criminal trials are s. 2 dealing with fundamental freedoms such as those of freedom of expression (subsection (b)) and freedom of association (subsection (d)), s. 19 concerning the use of English and French in courts, s. 35 protecting existing aboriginal rights and treaties[5] and the equality protection given in s. 15.

It is quite clear that none of these rights are absolute. Part of the political compromise that made possible the entrenchment of a Charter was the recognition that Parliament or a provincial legislature could expressly declare a law to operate notwithstanding the Charter.[6] Furthermore, and far more significant in the context of criminal law, where no legislature has resorted to the notwithstanding clause,[7] is the so-called "Guarantee of Rights and Freedoms" in clause 1 of the Charter. The heading of "guarantee" is a misnomer because the section is designed to allow courts to recognize limits on rights and freedoms:

---

[4] *Motor Vehicle Reference* (1985), 48 C.R. (3d) 289 at 317 (S.C.C.) (per Lamer J.) — fully discussed in Chapter 2.

[5] See especially *Sparrow* (1990), 56 C.C.C. (3d) 263 (S.C.C.), in which it was held that in interpreting s. 35(1):

> "the government has the responsibility to act in a fiduciary capacity with respect to aboriginal peoples. The relationship between the government and aboriginals is trust-like, rather than adversarial, and contemporary recognition and affirmation of aboriginal rights must be defined in light of this historic relationship" (at 287) (per Dickson C.J.C. and La Forest J. for the Court).

See W.I.C. Binnie, "The Sparrow Doctrine: Beginning of the End or End of the Beginning" (1990), 15 *Queen's L.J.* 217.

[6] "Parliament or the legislature of a province may expressly declare in an Act of Parliament or of the legislature, as the case may be, that the Act or a provision thereof shall operate notwithstanding a provision included in section 2 or sections 7 to 15 of this Charter." The opting out must be renewed every five years: s. 33(3).

[7] The Quebec Government's attempt to use the notwithstanding clause to opt out of ss. 2 and 7-15 of the Charter for all Quebec laws (An Act respecting the Constitution Act, S.Q. 1982, c. 21) was held unconstitutional: *Alliance des Professeurs de Montréal v. Quebec (A.G.)* (1985), 21 C.C.C. (3d) 273 (Que. C.A.). For an argument for the abolition of the notwithstanding clause on the basis of conformity with Canadian constitutional theory and political practice see John D. Whyte, "On Not Standing for Notwithstanding" (1990), 28 *Alta. L. Rev.* 347.

The Canadian Charter of Rights and Freedoms guarantees the rights and freedoms set out in it subject only to such reasonable limits prescribed by law as can be demonstrably justified in a free and democratic society.

Unlike its predecessor, the Canadian Bill of Rights,[8] the Charter not only declares rights but expressly confers remedies for breaches. Under s. 24:

(1) Anyone whose rights or freedoms, as guaranteed by this Charter, have been infringed or denied may apply to a court of competent jurisdiction to obtain such remedy as the court considers appropriate and just in the circumstances.

(2) Where, in proceedings under subsection (1), a court concludes that evidence was obtained in a manner that infringed or denied any rights or freedoms guaranteed by this Charter, the evidence shall be excluded if it is established that, having regard to all the circumstances, the admission of it in the proceedings would bring the administration of justice into disrepute.

The availability of effective remedies for Charter breaches, particularly the possibility of exclusion of evidence under s. 24(2), undoubtedly accounts for the Charter's considerable impact on criminal justice in Canada.

Independently of s. 24, s. 52(1) makes it quite clear that the Charter is not just an interpretive device as was the Bill but a significant inroad on the principle of parliamentary supremacy. Section 52(1) mandates courts to measure legislation against the now entrenched yardstick of human rights and freedoms:

The Constitution of Canada is the supreme law of Canada, and any law that is inconsistent with the provisions of the Constitution is, to the extent of the inconsistency, of no force or effect.

2. "PURPOSIVE" INTERPRETATION

Prior to the decision of the Supreme Court of Canada in *Hunter v. Southam Inc.* (1984),[9] there were competing schools of thought amongst the judiciary as to the proper approach to interpreting the Charter. Some courts had accepted the validity in this context of Viscount Sankey's statement that the Canadian Constitution was "a living tree capable of growth and expansion" and that Constitutional interpretation had to proceed by "large and liberal interpretation" rather than "narrow and technical construction."[10] On the other hand, there had been powerful voices calling for restraint, as in Mr. Justice Zuber's oft-quoted remark in the Ontario Court of Appeal that "the Charter does not intend a transformation of our legal system or the paralysis of law enforcement."[11] In *Hunter*, the Supreme Court of Canada enrolled all Canadian judges in the broader school.

---

[8] R.S.C. 1985, App. III.
[9] (1984), 41 C.R. (3d) 97 (S.C.C.).
[10] *Edwards v. Canada (A.G.)*, [1930] A.C. 124 at 136-137 (P.C.). The "liberal" interpretation in *Edwards* was that "person" in the British North America Act includes women for the purpose of membership in the Canadian Senate!
[11] *Altseimer* (1982), 29 C.R. (3d) 276 at 282 (Ont. C.A.).

For a unanimous Court, Mr. Justice Dickson, later to be Chief Justice, first asserted a "purposive" approach which has been consistently asserted ever since:[12]

> The task of expounding a constitution is crucially different from that of construing a statute. A statute defines present rights and obligations. It is easily enacted and as easily repealed. A constitution, by contrast, is drafted with an eye to the future. Its function is to provide a continuing framework for the legitimate exercise of governmental power and, when joined by a bill or a charter of rights, for the unremitting protection of individual rights and liberties. Once enacted, its provisions cannot easily be repealed or amended. It must therefore be capable of growth and development over time to meet new social, political and historical realities often unimagined by its framers. The judiciary is the guardian of the constitution and must, in interpreting its provisions, bear these considerations in mind. Professor Paul Freund expressed this idea aptly when he admonished the American courts "not to read the provisions of the Constitution like a last will and testament lest it become one.
>
> The need for a broad perspective in approaching constitutional documents is a familiar theme in Canadian constitutional jurisprudence.
>
> . . . .
>
> [A] broad, purposive analysis, which interprets specific provisions of a constitutional document in the light of its larger objects, is also consonant with the classical principles of American constitutional construction . . .
>
> . . . The Canadian Charter of Rights and Freedoms is a purposive document. Its purpose is to guarantee and to protect, within the limits of reason, the enjoyment of the rights and freedoms it enshrines. It is intended to constrain governmental action inconsistent with those rights and freedoms; it is not in itself an authorization for governmental action.[13]

A skeptic might suggest that identifying a distinctive approach to Charter interpretation is mere semantics and rhetoric. Is the task of interpreting a written Charter really different from that of interpreting a statute? Although it is difficult to generalize about approaches to statutory interpretation, surely the best judicial approach would always do more than concentrate on ordinary grammatical meaning and find an interpretation that best achieves the objective of the provision? Even if this is so, the functional role for judges outlined in *Hunter* does indeed make the "purposive" approach distinctive. Under s. 52, every judge has a duty to declare inoperative any law that conflicts with one of the Charter's rights and freedoms. Vincent Del Buono[14] sees the implications as follows:

> When a Charter issue is raised now with respect to the existence of a statutory power or right or its exercise, the courts will no longer understand their role to be to ask what is the intent of the legislation; that is the language of Parliamentary supremacy and statutory interpretation. Rather, the courts will now talk in terms of reconciling the competing interests of government and the individual when considering government intrusions on Charter rights and freedoms: very much the language of public policy making in its widest sense.[15]

---

[12] See, for example, *Brydges* (1990), 74 C.R. (3d) 129 at 139 (S.C.C.) (right to counsel), discussed below, Chapter 5.

[13] Above note 9, at 110-111.

[14] "The Implications of the Supreme Court's Purposive Interpretation of the Charter" (1986), 48 C.R. (3d) 121.

[15] *Ibid.*, at 123-124.

The best illustration of the significance of a purposive approach is to be found in *Hunter* itself.[16] A combines investigator had searched the offices of a newspaper acting under authority of the appropriate Federal Act. The issue was whether this offended the right under s. 8 to be "secure against unreasonable search and seizure." Rather than focusing on the word "reasonable", the Court first explored what interest the section protected. It was found to protect people as well as property and, at the very least, to confer a right to privacy. This, the Court held, could only be adequately protected by asserting a minimum standard of prior authorization by one capable of acting judicially and based on objective grounds established upon oath. The combines search in question had been unconstitutional even though there had been a warrant.

In contrast, less than two weeks before *Hunter* was handed down, the British Columbia Court of Appeal in *Hamill* (1984)[17] decided that the anomalous power of writs of assistance in the Narcotic Control Act authorizing warrantless searches of dwelling houses did *not* offend s. 8. The absence of a warrant was of no constitutional significance. The proper approach was to analyze the words appearing in s. 8 and not to rely on a judge's subjective view as to what the law should be. Section 8 had said nothing regarding the procedures required in order to prevent unreasonable searches and that remained a matter for Parliament. The Court was not concerned with the interests that s. 8 sought to protect but rather with matters of law enforcement, not involving the Court in an inquiry it was not well equipped to make and with the dangers of introducing into criminal trials matters entirely unrelated to the question of guilt.[18]

Even accepting that the purposive approach is established for the Charter, there is no automatic guarantee of interpretations favouring civil liberties. As always there is room for considerable judicial discretion and caution. According to one judge "even the liveliest of living trees takes time to grow — it is a tree, not a weed."[19] In *Big M Drug Mart* (1985),[20] Chief Justice Dickson himself warned that, although the purposive approach aimed at a "generous rather than a legalistic" approach to fulfill the purposes of the Charter,

> it is important not to overshoot the actual purpose of the right or freedom in question, but to recall that the Charter was not enacted in a vacuum, and must therefore . . . be placed in its proper linguistic, philosophical and historical contexts.[21]

In developing its purposive approach to the Charter, the Supreme Court has been determined to examine old issues with fresh lenses. Pointing to the markedly different constitutional structure of the Charter, it has held that previous interpretations of the Canadian Bill of Rights are "not a reliable guide" to the interpretation of the Charter.[22] The Court has also refused to be bound by a clear

---

[16] *Hunter v. Southam* is fully discussed below, Chapter 3.

[17] (1984), 41 C.R. (3d) 123 (B.C. C.A.).

[18] *Ibid.*, at 139-140 (per Esson J.A., Taggart and Mcdonald JJ.A. concurring).

[19] *Public Service Alliance of Canada*, [1984] 2 F.C. 889 at 895 (Fed. C.A.) (per Mahoney J.A.).

[20] (1985), 18 C.C.C. (3d) 385 (S.C.C.).

[21] *Ibid.*, at 424.

[22] *Therens* (1985), 45 C.R. (3d) 97 at 124 (S.C.C.) (per Le Dain J.), refusing to follow a previous

understanding of the meaning of s. 7 by its drafters at the Committee stage of the passage of the Charter.[23]

At an early date, it declared that decisions of American courts interpreting the United States Bill of Rights[24] could not be determinative:

> We would, in my view, do our own Constitution a disservice to simply allow the American debate to define the issue for us, all the while ignoring the truly fundamental structural differences between the two constitutions.[25]

The Court noted that the United States Constitution has no s. 52 nor the "internal checks and balances of ss. 1 and 33."[26] In the context of a s. 1 analysis Chief Justice Dickson wrote:

> Canada and the United States are not alike in every way, nor have the documents entrenching human rights in our two countries arisen in the same context. It is only common sense to recognize that, just as similarities will justify borrowing from the American experience, differences may require that Canada's constitutional vision depart from that endorsed in the United States.[27]

The protections under the Charter might well have been diluted had our courts slavishly followed American jurisprudence when ascertaining the content of each right.[28] In the United States balancing of interests must inevitably take place when the court determines the boundary of a Constitutional right. Under the Canadian Charter, in the absence of internal modifiers such as "unreasonable", the balancing of the rights of the individual against other state interests should occur under s. 1 or at the point of deciding upon the appropriate remedy.[29] Our courts have generally[30] adopted a clear two-stage approach under which the

---

narrow interpretation of detention for s. 10(b): discussed below, Chapter 5. See too *Motor Vehicle Reference*, above note 4 and *Oakes* (1986), 50 C.R. (3d) 1 at 19 (S.C.C.).

[23] *Motor Vehicle Reference*, above note 4. The drafters thought that "fundamental justice" in s. 7 was limited to procedural justice and did not include substantive review. The Supreme Court did not find this "persuasive or of any great force." See discussion below, Chapter 3. The Court would have endorsed the view of the Earl of Halsbury in *Hilder v. Dexter*, [1902] A.C. 474 at 477 (H.L.) that "in construing a statute I believe the worst person to construe it is the person who is responsible for its drafting. He is very much disposed to confuse what he intended to do with the effect of the language which in fact has been employed."

[24] U.S. Constitution, Amendments I-X.

[25] *Motor Vehicle Reference*, above note 4, at 305.

[26] *Ibid.*

[27] *Keegstra* (1990), 1 C.R. (4th) 129 at 166 (S.C.C.). Dickson C.J.C. for the majority went on to hold that international commitment to eradicate hate propaganda and the special role given equality and multiculturalism in the Canadian Constitution necessitated a departure from the prevalent American view that suppression of hate propaganda was incompatible with free speech. For detailed consideration of the applicability of international rights see Anne F. Bayefsky, *International Human Rights Law in Canadian Charter Litigation: A Practical Guide* (1991).

[28] See too Paul Bender "The Canadian Charter of Rights and Freedoms and the United States Bill of Rights: A Comparison" (1983), 28 *McGill L.J.* 811.

[29] Canadian remedies under s. 24 allow for discretionary balancing: see below, Chapter 12. In the United States, Constitutional rights of an accused may be unduly qualified in view of the rule in that jurisdiction that all illegally obtained evidence has to be excluded.

[30] See especially *Oakes*, above note 22, at 26. However, balancing has occurred in defining "principles of fundamental justice" under s. 7: see below, Chapter 2; and the right to be tried within a reasonable time under s. 11(b): see below, Chapter 6.

content of the right or freedom is first defined in terms of the individual interest it was meant to protect. State objectives and other interests are only relevant once a violation has been found and the state is attempting to demonstrably justify the violation as a reasonable limit under s. 1. Balancing at the first stage weakens Charter protections in view of the state's heavy burden under s. 1.

3. DIALOGUE WITH PARLIAMENT

In *O'Connor* (1996), [31] a 5-4 majority of the Supreme Court through a joint judgment of Lamer C.J. and Sopinka J., with Cory, Iacobucci and Major JJ. concurring, declared a two-part test for granting an accused access to therapeutic and other records of complainants in sexual assault cases. This test balanced the accused's right to full answer and defence under s. 7 of the Charter of Rights and Freedoms against privacy rights of complainants under ss. 7 and 8. The dissenting opinion of L'Heureux-Dubé J., with La Forest, Gonthier and McLachlin JJ. concurring, agreed with a two-part test but would have also balanced equality rights for complainants under s. 15 and adjusted the tests to favour the rights of complainants. The majority, in not mentioning the s. 15 claim although it was fully argued, implicitly rejected it.

In *Mills* (1999),[32] a joint judgment by Justices McLachlin and Iacobucci holds constitutional the more comprehensive Parliamentary scheme for access to complainants' records in sexual assault cases, which had enacted word for word the minority approach in *O'Connor*. Of the *O'Connor* majority, only Lamer C.J. dissented in *Mills* and only on the issue of applying the balancing of complainants' rights approach to records in the possession of the Crown. Justice Cory chose not to participate before his retirement and Justices Iacobucci and Major no longer supported their *O'Connor* positions. One suspects that Justice Sopinka may well not have capitulated so easily.

The *Mills* decision is disturbing for some of its rulings on the records issues[33] but even more so for its broader pronouncements on the need for dialogue with Parliament and on its assertion of equality rights[34] for complainants without reference to current s. 15 tests or the implications of its ruling. At this point we will consider the Court's new discourse of dialogue with Parliament.

The Court addressed this issue in a number of pronouncements. Firstly the enactment of a legislative scheme different from that put in place by the Court in the absence of a statutory scheme was not necessarily unconstitutional:

> Parliament may build on the Court's decision, and develop a different scheme as long as it remains constitutional. Just as Parliament must respect the Court's rulings, so the Court must respect Parliament's determination that the judicial scheme can be improved. To insist on slavish conformity would belie the mutual respect that

---

[31] (1995), 44 C.R. (4th) 1 (S.C.C.).
[32] (1999), 28 C.R. (5th) 207 (S.C.C.).
[33] See below Chapter 2.
[34] See below notes 237-242.

underpins the relationship between the courts and legislature that is so essential to our constitutional democracy.[35]

There is nothing to be concerned about thus far. But the Court then proceeds to crumble in its resolve to uphold Charter standards. It speaks of a "posture of respect towards Parliament" and that

> if legislation is amenable to two interpretations, a court should choose the interpretation that upholds the legislation as constitutional. Thus courts must presume that Parliament intended to enact constitutional legislation and strive, where possible, to give effect to this intention.[36]

It is remarkable that the Court would invoke such a canon in a case where Parliament could not have been clearer in its intent to enact "in your face" legislation to overcome an unpopular Charter ruling. Until now such a presumption of constitutionality has existed only in the context of division of powers cases as distinct from the Charter, except for purposes of reading down.[37] The case of *Slaight Communications Inc.* v. *Davidson*[38] the Court relies on for this deferential canon is not on point. It dealt with the conferring of discretion on a labour adjudicator and held that the delegation of authority should be interpreted only to confer decision-making authority that did not infringe s. 2(b) of the Charter. It is not an appropriate precedent for deferring to Parliament in the context of the review of the legislative scheme in *Mills*.

The Court speaks of the need to see the relationship between the courts and the legislature as one of dialogue essential to democracy:

> To my mind, a great value of judicial review and this dialogue among the branches is that each of the branches is made somewhat accountable to the other. The work of the legislature is reviewed by the courts and the work of the court in its decisions can be reacted to by the legislature in the passing of new legislation (or even overarching laws under s. 33 of the *Charter*). This dialogue between and accountability of each of the branches have the effect of enhancing the democratic process, not denying it.[39]

The Court adds that there could be no dialogue if the common law were to be taken to establish the only possible constitutional regime and that, while the dialogue was "somewhat different" when the common law rule involves a Charter interpretation, it is to remain a dialogue.[40]

What a far cry from the vision of Chief Justice Dickson in *Hunter* v. *Southam Inc.*[41] that under the Charter the judiciary are the guardian of the constitution for the unremitting protection of individual rights and freedoms and that the Charter is to constrain not authorise, governmental action.

---

[35] At para. 55.

[36] Para. 56.

[37] See Peter Hogg, *Constitutional Law of Canada* (1998 student ed.) c. 35.5, p. 703. He relies on Beetz J. in *Metropolitan Stores Ltd.* v. *Manitoba (Attorney General)*, [1987] 1 S.C.R. 110.

[38] [1989] 1 S.C.R. 1038.

[39] Para. 57.

[40] Para. 57.

[41] Above note 9.

The Court in *Mills* chooses to de-emphasise the very nature of the entrenchment of a Charter of Rights and the existence of s. 52 of the Constitution Act that makes the Constitution the supreme law of the land. The entrenched compromise was to allow for demonstrably justified reasonable limits on Charter rights in s. 1 and an override provision in s. 33 which permits legislatures to opt out on a five year renewable basis. Once the highest Court has declared minimum Charter standards, absent a s. 33 override, the only dialogue in the courts should be whether responsive legislation meets those standards. The devastating impact of *Mills* is that it will encourage quick "in your face" legislation whenever a legislature does not like a Charter ruling[42] and that legislation is likely to survive any new Charter challenge. Why should politicians now bother with thinking about a s. 33 override? Given the law and order mood of the community, and the expediency of politicians and now the Court, the likely effect of *Mills* will be far less protection for accused.

Professor Kent Roach has advanced a similar criticism of *Mills*:

> The court in *Mills* gave Parliament much more respect than *O'Connor* received from the elected branch of government. . . .Faced with a direct repudiation of its earlier decision, the court not only blinked, but looked away. . . . Respect for the rule of law required more. The court should either have admitted that it had been wrong and overruled *O'Connor* or required Parliament to use its s. 33 override. . . .Stealth overrides by Parliament and stealth overruling of controversial decisions by courts do little to promote careful deliberation about complex and difficult questions of competing rights[43].

Hopefully the Court will collect its senses and be more mindful of its institutional responsibilities in subsequent Charter cases involving rights of accused.[44] Access to records of complainants in sexual assault cases was indeed a particularly controversial criminal law issue. The problem is that all criminal law decisions are controversial unless the Court favours the Crown. The Court should be independent and above law and order politics.

It is possible, but likely a stretch, that these broad pronouncements could be properly confined to issues of sexual assault. Any such ground of distinction would stem from the following passage:

---

[42] Parliament has already responded quickly with Criminal Code amendments to counteract Charter rulings striking down rape shield provisions, the extreme drunkenness defence to general intent crimes and the "public interest" ground for denying bail.

[43] Editorial, "Mills" (2000), 43 *Crim. L.Q.* 145.

[44] In *Little Sisters Book & Art Emporium* v. *Canada (Minister of Justice)* (2000), 36 C.R. (5th) 223 (S.C.C.), a gay and lesbian bookstore alleged discrimination by customs officials contrary to s. 2(b) and s. 15 in their interception and exclusion under the Customs Act of obscene material imported into Canada. Binnie J. for a 6-3 majority decided that, apart from a reverse onus which was to be declared unconstitutional, the problem was not the Customs Act but discriminatory enforcement. The majority further determined that any further remedy would be impractical and was up to Parliament. In arguing that more than the onus provision had to be struck down, Iacobucci J. for the minority (Arbour and Lebel JJ. concurring) relied on McLachlin J. in *RJR-MacDonald*, below note 106. While deference was appropriate, the Court could not "abdicate its duty to demand that the government justify legislation limiting Charter rights" (at para. 221). McLachlin C.J., the other author of *Mills*, here joined with the majority.

Courts do not hold a monopoly on the protection and promotion of rights and freedoms; Parliament also plays a role in this regard and is often able to act as a significant ally for vulnerable groups. This is especially important to recognize in the context of sexual violence. The history of the treatment of sexual assault complainants by our society and our legal system is an unfortunate one. Important change has occurred through legislation aimed at both recognizing the rights and interests of complainants in criminal proceedings, and debunking the stereotypes that have been so damaging to women and children, but the treatment of sexual assault complainants remains an ongoing problem. If constitutional democracy is meant to ensure that due regard is given to the voices of those vulnerable to being overlooked by the majority, then this court has an obligation to consider respectfully Parliament's attempt to respond to such voices.[45]

The notion of deferring to Parliament's wisdom in matters of sexual assault, given historic vulnerabilities of victims, is itself troubling given the Court's constitutional mandate to protect all minority rights, including those of all accused.

There are also serious concerns about the impartiality of the legislative process. Alan Gold, the President of the Criminal Lawyers Association, put it well in an early response to *Mills*:

Mr. Gold rejected the court's portrayal of Parliament as listening sagely to all sides before it created a kind of Solomonic compromise. He said the rights of the accused were simply washed away by a massive lobby of women's and victims' groups. "It is such a Polyanna-ish view of Parliament." Mr. Gold said, "With respect, if you are only listening to one side of an issue, it doesn't matter how long you do it; it doesn't make it any more of a consultation."[46]

Consider too the impact of granting intervenor status at the Supreme Court. In *Mills*, when intervenors for Attorneys General are factored in, there was a significant power imbalance with 16 lawyers taking the Crown side and only 5 speaking for the defence.

Whether there should be a special approach to sexual assault may well depend on the basis for the Court's further pronouncement that complainants in sexual assault cases have enforceable equality rights under s. 15. If confined to sexual assault, the Court may wish to distinguish *Mills* in other criminal law contexts where there are no competing rights to consider and return to its previously stated view in the section one context that

the courts will judge the legislature's choices more harshly in areas were the government plays the role of the "singular antagonist of the individual" - primarily in criminal matters - owing to their expertise in these areas.[47]

4. ENDANGERING DEMOCRACY THROUGH CONSTITUTIONALISING JUDICIAL VALUES?

The Charter has its detractors. Some suggest the priority the Charter accords individual rights is out of step with the modern state's recognition of collective

---

[45] Para. 58.

[46] *The Globe and Mail*, November 27, 1999.

[47] *Libman* v. *Quebec (Attorney General)*, [1997] 3 S.C.R. 569 (per curiam). That perspective was first introduced by Wilson J., dissenting in *Chaulk* (1990), 2 C.R. (4th) 1 (S.C.C.).

interests. Many political scientists and politicians express concerns about what is seen to be an unjustifiable transfer of power from legislatures to unelected judiciary and question the appropriateness and ability of judges to rule on difficult questions of value and policy. Such concerns will only be partly assuaged by the new Supreme Court stance in *Mills* of the need to dialogue with, and defer to, the legislative process.

Law professor Michael Mandel[48] sees the Charter as a powerful threat to the integrity of the very political system itself. The Mandel thesis continues to be that the Charter has legalized politics in the sense that legal values have become the most important ones and that the Charter' effect has been the antithesis of democracy both in form and content.[49] He is especially concerned with the transfer of power to judges, who represent the power elite, are not elected or accountable, are authoritarian and hide their political choices and ideology under the guise of neutral interpretation of the law.[50] He sees the constitutionalization of criminal procedure in Canada, as in the United States, as having performed

an essentially symbolic, legitimizing, or to put it bluntly, *public relations* function.[51]

Mandel reaches the depths of cynicism in a wild thesis that this constitutionalization of procedural rights legitimates the expanded repression of the criminal law evident in increasing imprisonment and probation rates.[52]

There is a rival thesis. We live in law and order times. There are constant and widespread calls in the media for toughening the criminal law, especially as it relates to violence against women and children. Voices favouring restraint have been drowned out. Instead there are pleas for "zero tolerance" and concern that criminals have too many rights at the expense of victims. Politicians of all stripes have been unable to resist the political expediency of pandering to the perceived need to toughen penal responses. There are no votes in being soft on crime. In this context it is fortunate that basic Charter rights have been entrenched and that the Supreme Court has been activist in its interpretation of rights for accused.[53] Given that the criminal law is inherently an exercise of massive state power against an individual, the predominant focus on individual rights under the Charter seems appropriate for the criminal process. The changes have not been revolutionary. With or without Charter rights, most accused are convicted. Yet we do have a system which is more just to accused and one in which state agents, including police and prosecutors, may be held to account. The criminal justice system is no longer, if it ever was, solely concerned with the pursuit of truth as to guilt and innocence. It is also a matter of constitutional imperative to review the legitimacy of state methods of obtaining that evidence by police or prosecutors. The Charter is not a panacea and the Supreme Court record can be criticized for

---

[48] *The Charter of Rights and the Legalization of Politics in Canada* (2nd ed., 1994).
[49] At p. 4
[50] Preface, pp. xi-xxii.
[51] At p. 192.
[52] At p. 225.
[53] See further Stuart, "An Entrenched Bill of Rights Best Protects Against Law and Order Expediency" (1998), 11 *S. African L.J.* 325.

excessive complexity, inconsistency and sometimes setting Charter standards too low. As Iacobucci J. put it in a recent dissenting opinion:

> Sometimes "constitutionality" means only that an unimpressive minimal threshold has been met.[54]

Given legal aid cutbacks and the low competence of some defence counsel, the right to counsel and other rights before and at trial may sometimes be purely formal. However Mandel's attempts to ridicule the judicial record of criminal justice under the Charter seems doggedly destructive and does not present a fair picture.

The Mandel perspective is also not objective in a different sense. Clearly he has no faith whatsoever in the judicial system. He damns all judges and all lawyers. Yet is there any reason to have blind faith in elected politicians? His attack on the judicial record under the Charter should be balanced by an equally determined critical review of the legislative process. Legislative records on the protection of minority interests have been woeful. The judicial system under the Charter may be far from perfect but it provides some counterpoint to the tyranny of the majority.[55]

A similar response may be offered to the concerns of Professor Christopher Manfredi.[56] His review of Charter jurisprudence concludes[57] with the lament that judges have expanded judicial supremacy by showing little restraint in asserting their pre-eminent authority and that there has been the "legal seduction of politics" such that the public and governments now assume that divisive issues are better resolved through the judicial rather than the political process. According to Manfredi, since majorities shift all the time on every issue:

> Judicial supremacy cannot be defended by characterising the legislative process as a continuous attempt by the majority to oppress the majority.[58]

A good response to such a position has been provided in a speech by Justice Rosie Abella of the Ontario Court of Appeal:[59]

> What Canada got with the Charter was a dramatic package of guaranteed rights, subject only to those reasonable limits which were demonstrably justified in a free and democratic society, a package assembled by the legislature, which in turn, it bears repeating, assigned to the courts the duty to decide whether its laws, politics or practices met the constitutional standards set out in the Charter.[60]

Professor Manfredi also expresses more ominous concerns[61] at

---

[54] *Little Sisters*, above note 44, para. 271.

[55] For more detailed description of, and responses to, the Mandel positions see my review of his second edition in (1995) 21 *Queen's L.J.* 261.

[56] *Judicial Power and the Charter. Canada and the Paradox of Liberal Constitutionalism* (Oxford University Press, 2nd. ed., 2001).

[57] At pp. 196-199.

[58] At p. 198.

[59] "The Judicial Role in a Democratic State", Faculty of Law, Queen's University, October 15, 2000.

[60] At p. 8.

[61] For far more strident critiques see Alex Macdonald, *Canada's Justice System on Trial* (Vancouver: Raincoast Books, 1999) and F.L. Morton and Rainer Knopff, *The Charter Revolution and the Court Party* (Broadview Press, 2000).

the development of a new form of constitutional politics in which special interests are satisfied by granting them preferred constitutional status and by providing a new set of constitutional rules that might be manipulated to advance their policy agendas.[62]

There may be some truths to be found in political trends in Supreme Court jurisprudence on value-laden issues but the problem here is Manfredi's apparent assumption that the political process is not also the subject of manipulative policy and value-laden agendas. Justice Abella offers a powerful retort to what she calls the "New Inhibitors" who have in the 90's

> turned the good news of constitutionalised rights, the mark of a secure and mature democracy, into the bad news of judicial autocracy, the mark of a debilitated and devalued legislature. They called minorities seeking the right to be free from discrimination, special interests groups seeking to jump the queue. . . .

> The whole story is that the Charter does not represent heterodoxy about democracy but rather its finest manifestation. People elect legislators who enact the laws they think the majority of their constituents want them to enact, and appoint judges who are expected to be independent from those legislators and impartial in determining whether the legislature's actions meet constitutional standards.[63]

What Parliament put in place with the entrenchment of the Charter as the supreme law is a distinctive system of constitutional checks and balances. Charter critics seem to have lost sight of the reality that neither the judges nor the legislatures were intended to have absolute supremacy. Under our constitutional system there should be tension between the legislatures and the judges.

5. DEMONSTRABLY JUSTIFIED REASONABLE LIMITS UNDER SECTION 1

An entrenched Charter would not have been politically attainable without the key compromise in s. 1. This "guarantee" of rights and freedoms reads:

> The *Canadian Charter of Rights and Freedoms* guarantees the rights and freedoms set out in it subject only to such reasonable limits prescribed by law as can be demonstrably justified in a free and democratic society.

No Charter right is absolute. Each is subject to the possibility that a limit can be demonstrably justified under s. 1.

(a) Oakes Approach

The authoritative blueprint for justifying limitations on Charter rights under s. 1 was established by Chief justice Dickson for a majority of the Supreme Court of Canada in *Oakes* (1986).[64] The onus of justification rests upon the party seeking

---

[62] At p. 199.

[63] At pp. 9 and 10.

[64] Above note 22. The seed may have been the scholarly judgment of Deschenes C.J.S.C. in *Quebec Association of Protestant School Boards v. Quebec (A.G.)* (1982), 140 D.L.R. (3d) 33 (Que. S.C.). Compare too *Central Hudson Gas and Electric Corp. v. Public Service Commission of New York*, 447 U.S. 557 at 566 (1980) (regulation on commercial speech is protected by the First Amendment if government interest is substantial and regulation is "not more extensive than is necessary to serve that interest").

to uphold the limitation. Although the standard of proof is the civil standard of proof on a preponderance of probability that test must be applied rigorously such that there would have to be "a very high degree of probability."[65] The Court asserts two central criteria: the objective of the limit has to be of sufficient importance to warrant overriding a constitutionally-protected right or freedom and the limit has to satisfy a form of proportionality. The measure will be proportional where the measure is carefully designed to achieve the objective, impairs the right as little as possible and there is proportionality between the effects of the measure and the objective.[66] There can be no doubt that this approach was carefully designed to preclude s. 1 becoming an easy avenue to the dilution of Charter protections.

In the fifteen years of jurisprudence since *Oakes*, s. 1 consideration has invariably started with a recitation of the *Oakes* approach, almost as if it were a legislative replacement of the words of s. 1. In *R.J.R. MacDonald Inc. v. A.G. of Canada* (1995),[67] the most recent major decision on s. 1, McLachlin J. reasserts for the majority that:

> The factors generally relevant to determining whether a violative law is reasonably and demonstrably justified in a free and democratic society remain those set out in *Oakes*. The first requirement is that the objective of the law limiting the Charter right or freedom must be of sufficient importance to warrant overriding it. The second is that the means chosen to achieve the objective must be proportional to the objective and the effect of the law — proportionate, in short, to the good which it may produce. Three matters are considered in determining proportionality: the measures chosen must be rationally connected to the objective; they must impair the guaranteed right or freedom as little as reasonably possible (minimal impairment); and there must be overall proportionality between the deleterious effects of the measures and the salutary effects of the law.[68]

(b) Minimum Intrusion Test is Key

Experience has shown, however, that the *Oakes* test is formalistic. Whether a limit can be demonstrably justified under s. 1 almost always[69] turns on what has become known as the "minimum intrusion" test in "section" 2(b) — does the limitation restrict as little as possible? It will be suggested here that the Supreme Court has, in its many applications of the minimum intrusion test in the context of criminal law, become far too receptive to arguments based on law enforcement expediency and has also been bewilderingly inconsistent.[70]

---

[65] *Ibid.*, at 29.

[66] *Ibid.*, at 30-31.

[67] [1995] 3 S.C.R. 199.

[68] At 329-330. The need to consider salutory effects was established in *Dagenais v. C.B.C.* (1996), 44 C.R. (4th) 1 (S.C.C.).

[69] See comprehensive surveys by Norman Siebrasse, "The Oakes Test: An Old Ghost Impeding Bold New Initiatives" (1991), 23 *Ottawa L. Rev.* 99 and Leon Trakman, William Cole-Hamilton and Sean Gatien, "*R.* v. *Oakes* 1986-1997. Back to the Drawing Board" (1998), 36 *Osgoode Hall L.J.* 83.

[70] Most analysis of the *Oakes* approval and subsequent jurisprudence has been highly critical. Consistent themes have been that the formal adherence to the *Oakes* test has hidden the inherent

In *Chaulk* (1990),[71] Chief Justice Lamer reduces the tests of minimum impairment to "whether Parliament could reasonably have chosen an alternative means which would have achieved the identified objective as effectively." This pronouncement represents the culmination of a clear trend of judicial deference to legislative choices. Four decisions are of particular note.

(c) Edwards Books: As Little as Reasonably Possible

In *Edwards Books* (1986)[72] the issue was whether a Sunday observance law was unconstitutional through a violation of the freedom of religion guaranteed by s. 2(a) of the Charter. In restating his *Oakes* test, Chief Justice Dickson stated that the nature of the proportionality test would "vary depending on the circumstances" and that, both in the articulation of the standard of proof and in the applicable criteria, the Court had been "careful to avoid rigid and inflexible standards."[73] In applying the test the Chief Justice saw the question as whether the Act abridged freedom of religion as "little as is *reasonably* possible."[74] Was there "some *reasonable* alternative scheme which would allow the province to achieve its objective with fewer detrimental affects on religious freedom?"[75]

The need for flexibility is even more evident in the separate judgment of Mr. Justice La Forest:

> [I]n describing the criteria comprising the proportionality requirement, the court has been careful to avoid rigid and inflexible standards. That seems to me to be essential. Given that the objective is of pressing and of substantial concern, the legislature must be allowed adequate scope to achieve that objective. It must be remembered that the business of government is a practical one. The Constitution must be applied on a realistic basis having regard to the nature of the particular area sought to be regulated and not on an abstract theoretical plane. In interpreting the Constitution, Courts must be sensitive to . . . "the practical living facts" to which a legislature must respond. That is especially so in a field of so many competing pressures as the one here in question.[76]

(d) Prostitution Reference: Legislative Scheme Need Not Be Perfect

In the *Prostitution Reference* (1990),[77] the Supreme Court agreed that s. 210 of the Criminal Code, which prohibits a person from communicating or attempting

---

normative and political values and choices raised by the s. 1 inquiry and led to inconsistencies. See, for example, Pamela A. Chapman, "The Politics of Judging: Section 1 of the Charter of Rights and Freedoms" (1986), 24 *Osgoode Hall L.J.* 867: Joel Bakan, "Constitutional Arguments: Interpretation and Legitimacy in Canadian Constitutional Thought" (1989), 27 *Osgoode Hall L.J.* 123; Robin M. Elliott, "The Supreme Court of Canada and Section 1 — The Erosion of the Common Front" (1987), 12 *Queen's L.J.* 277 and Roger P. Kerans, "The Future of Section 1 of the Charter" (1989), 23 *U.B.C. L. Rev.* 567.

[71] (1990), 2 C.R. (4th) 1 (S.C.C.) at 31.

[72] (1986), 55 C.R. (3d) 193 (S.C.C.). For early criticism see G.D. Creighton, "Edwards Books and Section 1: Cutting Down Oakes?" (1987), 55 C.R. (3d) 269.

[73] *Ibid.*, at 234. Chouinard and Le Dain JJ. concurred.

[74] *Ibid.*, at 237 (emphasis added).

[75] *Ibid.*

[76] *Ibid.*, at 259.

[77] (1990), 77 C.R. (3d) 1 (S.C.C.).

to communicate in any manner with a person in a public place for the purpose of prostitution, violates the guarantee of freedom of expression under s. 2(b) of the Charter. However, by a majority of four to two the Court found that the offence constituted a demonstrably justified reasonable limit on that freedom. Chief Justice Dickson for the male majority[78] put the minimum impairment question as "can effective yet less intrusive legislation be imagined?"[79] His Lordship held that it was legitimate to take into account the fact that earlier alternatives had been found to be less effective. To survive the alternative "need not be the perfect' scheme that could be imagined by this Court or any other Courts."[80] The Chief Justice re-asserted his earlier dictum in *Edwards Books* that:

> [It] is not the role of this Court to devise legislation that is constitutionally valid, or to pass on the validity of schemes which are not directly before it or to consider what legislation might be the most desirable.[81]

In contrast Madam Justice Wilson, joined in dissent by Madam Justice L'Heureux-Dubé, was much more demanding on the minimum intrusion test. These measures were not sufficiently tailored to the objective of preventing public nuisance by street solicitation. The prohibition was not confined to places where there would necessarily be numerous people offended or inconvenienced. It was not reasonable to prohibit all expressive activity conveying a certain meaning that takes place in public simply because in some circumstances and in some areas that activity might give rise to a public or social nuisance. The broad phrase "in any manner communicates or attempts to communicates" seemed to encompass every conceivable method of human expression. Making criminal the communicative acts of persons engaged in a lawful activity could not be justified by the legislative objective advanced in its support.[82]

(e) Keegstra: Need for Flexibility Given Context and Values of Free and Democratic Society

In Chief Justice Dickson's swan song judgment for the majority of the Court in *Keegstra* (1990),[83] he went out of his way to hold that it is "dangerously misleading to conceive of s. 1 as a rigid and technical provision"[84] and that it was "clear that a rigid and formalistic approach to the application of s. 1 must be avoided."[85] The Chief justice expressly approved of the description of La Forest J. of a "flexible" approach in *United States of America v. Cotroni* (1989):[86]

---

[78] La Forest and Sopinka JJ. concurred. Lamer J.'s concurring judgment was similar on the proportionality issue (*ibid.*, at 61-63).

[79] *Ibid.*, at 14.

[80] *Ibid.*, at 15.

[81] *Ibid.*

[82] *Ibid.*, at 74-76.

[83] Above note 27.

[84] *Ibid.*, at 162.

[85] *Ibid.*, at 163.

[86] [1989] 1 S.C.R. 1469.

In the performance of the balancing task under s. 1, it seems to me, a mechanistic approach must be avoided. While the rights guaranteed by the *Charter* must be given priority in the equation, the underlying values must be sensitively weighed in a particular context against other values of a free and democratic society sought to be promoted by the legislature.[87]

The issue in *Keegstra* was whether the Criminal Code offence under s. 319 of wilfully promoting hatred against an identifiable group was unconstitutional because of its violation of freedom of expression protected under s. 2(b) of the Charter. It was also urged that requiring the accused to prove a truth defence contravened the presumption of innocence in s. 11(d). The Court was unanimous in holding that ss. 2(b) and 11(d) *had* been violated but split on the question of whether the violations could be saved under s. 1. Chief Justice Dickson for the majority[88] held that both violations could be justified. In the course of his lengthy judgment he took into account Canada's international commitments to eradicate hate propaganda and the stress upon equality and multiculturalism in other sections of the Charter. Following a detailed assessment of the particular offence involved he held that the violation of the freedom of speech was narrowly confined and not too broad nor vague. The existence of other modes of combating hate propaganda did not make this criminal offence unjustified.[89] As far as the reverse onus was concerned its justification lay in the fact that it only applied once the Crown had proved beyond a reasonable doubt the intentional act of promoting harm-causing hatred and in the recognition that undue deference to the possibility of truth would undermine Parliament's objective.[90]

On the freedom of speech issue Madam Justice McLachlin concluded for the minority[91] that the violation of freedom of expression could not be justified under s. 1:

Section 319(2) of the *Criminal Code* catches a broad range of speech and prohibits it in a broad manner, allowing only private conversations to escape scrutiny. Moreover, the process by which the prohibition is affected — the criminal law — is the severest society can impose and is arguably unnecessary given the availability of alternative measures.[92]

Her Ladyship also held that the reverse onus could not be demonstrably justified under s. 1.[93] Only a countervailing state interest of the most compelling kind could have justified an infringement given that falsehood was an important element of the offence and the centrality of the presumption of innocence in criminal law.[94]

(f) Chaulk: Test of Effectiveness

In *Chaulk* (1991),[95] it was argued that the presumption of sanity in s. 16(4), placing the onus of proving the defence of insanity on the accused, was an

---

[87] *Ibid.*, at 1489-1490.
[88] Wilson, L'Heureux-Dubé and Gonthier JJ. concurred.
[89] Above note 27, at 169-202.
[90] *Ibid.*, at 205-208.
[91] La Forest and Sopinka JJ. concurred.
[92] Above note 27, at 260.
[93] Sopinka J. concurred.
[94] Above note 27, at 263.
[95] Above note 71.

unconstitutional violation of the presumption of innocence in s. 11(d). Chief Justice Lamer writing for himself and four other judges[96] held that there had been a violation but it could be justified under s. 1 The objective of the presumption was to "avoid placing an impossible burden of proof on the Crown."[97] Citing judgments of the Court[98] indicating that Parliament was not required to adopt the absolutely least intrusive means, Chief Justice Lamer saw the issue as "whether a less intrusive means would achieve the same' objective or would achieve the same objective as effectively."[99] The Chief Justice concluded that the alternative of an evidentiary burden requiring that the accused merely raise a reasonable doubt would not be as effective, accepting arguments by Attorneys General that it would be very easy for accused persons to "fake" such a defence and to raise a reasonable doubt. Parliament had chosen from a range of means which had impaired s. 11(d) as little as reasonably possible.

The sole dissenter on this point in *Chaulk* was Madam Justice Wilson.[100] Her first major difficulty was whether the object was of sufficient importance to warrant overriding the presumption of innocence given the absence of evidence of any historic experience with a purely evidentiary burden. She decried the majority's approach as a "prophylactic measure designed to fend off a hypothetical social problem that might arise if accused persons pleading insanity had to meet only an evidentiary burden."[101] Furthermore, the American experience did not support the contention that a full persuasive burden on the accused was indispensable. This was, in her view, not a case for relaxing the minimum impairment test. This might be done where a legislature, mediating between competing groups of citizens or allocating scarce resources, had to compromise on the basis of conflicting evidence. In *Chaulk* the state was acting as "singular antagonist" of a very basic legal right of an accused and the strict standard of review in *Oakes* should be applied. The government's objective could be quite readily met by a mere burden on the accused to adduce evidence that made insanity "a live issue fit and proper to be left to the jury."[102]

(g) What's Wrong with Test of Effectiveness?

Madam Justice Wilson's position in *Chaulk* is entirely persuasive. It is alarming that no other member of the Court was listening and that Wilson J. was the only judge to be consistently faithful to the *Oakes* standard in the criminal context. One can perhaps understand the need to dilute the *Oakes* test in the

---

[96] Dickson C.J.C., La Forest, Sopinka and Cory JJ. concurred.

[97] Above note 71, at 30.

[98] The Court referred to *Edwards Books*, above note 72; *Irwin Toy Ltd.*, [1989] 1 S.C.R. 927 and the *Prostitution Reference*, above note 77. His Lordship might also have referred to *Lee* (1989), 73 C.R. (3d) 257 (S.C.C.), in which there is a strong dissent by Wilson J.

[99] Above note 71, at 32.

[100] McLachlin J. (L'Heureux-Dubé and Gonthier JJ. concurring) found no violation of s. 11(d) and did not consider s. 1.

[101] Above note 71, at 59.

[102] Above note 71, at 75.

context of *Edwards Books* or the issue of mandatory retirement,[103] given the variety of competing interests there as stake. In *Edwards Books*, for example, as there were a variety of different provincial Sunday observance statutes, any mechanical application of the "impairment as little as possible" test would have meant that only the least restrictive provincial scheme could have survived. However, in the case of criminal law there is invariably only one federal statute to interpret and one common law tradition. The Charter's focus on the protection of individual rights against the power of the states is conspicuously well-suited to the criminal law and should be rigorously safeguarded, as the Court in *Oakes* originally set out to do. Whatever happened to the ruling in *Cotroni* — adopted in *Keegstra* — that Charter values are to have the highest priority? What of the *Oakes* standard of proof to a high degree of probability? The substituted test of efficacy accedes to mere arguments of law enforcement expediency, which seem a far cry from what should be needed to demonstrably justify a reasonable limit on an entrenched Charter right.

In criminal law it is trite that the policy interests are invariably those of civil liberties of the accused against the interests of enforcing the criminal law efficiently. If efficacy became the real test of s. 1 *any* Charter violation will be saved under s. 1. How could it, for example, ever be argued that a law without a reverse onus clause will operate as effectively?

(h) Laba: Stricter Section 1 Test in Criminal Law

In *Laba* (1994),[104] the issue was the constitutionality of a provision under s. 394(1)(b) of the Criminal Code requiring a person charged with possessing or selling minerals to establish the defence of ownership or lawful authority. Sopinka J., for a Court unanimous on this point, held that the Crown could not demonstrably justify this persuasive burden on an accused given a reasonable legislative alternative of an evidentiary burden. In the course of the judgment a reference to *Chaulk* is followed by the remark that:

> [It] is also important to remember that this is not a case in which the legislature has attempted to strike a balance between the interests of competing individuals or groups. Rather it is a case in which the government (as opposed to other individuals or groups) can be characterised as the singular antagonist of an individual attempting to assert a legal right which is fundamental to our system of criminal justice.[105]

This appears to endorse the minority Wilson position in *Chaulk*. Since the Court has changed its basis premise previous s. 1 rulings justifying various Charter violations in criminal cases, especially but not only those concerning reverse onus clauses, should be revisited and/or properly distinguished on fresh challenges.

---

[103] See *McKinney v. University of Guelph* (1990), 76 D.L.R. (4th) 545 (S.C.C.). Wilson J. even dissented against showing judicial deference in this context since younger academics had not been shown to be a "vulnerable" group (at 617).

[104] (1994), 34 C.R. (4th) 360 (S.C.C.).

[105] At 392.

(i) R.J.R. MacDonald: Context, Less Deference and Proof

In its very lengthy judgment in *R.J.R. MacDonald* (1995),[106] the Supreme Court held that a federal ban on advertising and promotion of tobacco without health warnings under the Tobacco Products Act violated freedom of expression guaranteed by s. 2 (b) of the Charter. The Court further held, 5-4, that the violation could not be saved under s. 1. The judgment turns on s. 1 with the degree of deference to be paid to Parliament the pivotal issue. The majority finds it crucial that the federal government did not tender evidence in support of the need for a total ban. The minority through Mr. Justice La Forest would have allowed Parliament considerable latitude in its decision that a total ban was appropriate. On minimum intrusion the Court again seems agreed that the issue is whether the measure restricted as little as reasonably possible.

One of the majority judgments by Madam Justice McLachlin (Major J. and Sopinka J. concurring) engages in the most wide-ranging and thoughtful consideration of *Oakes* since that decision. Unfortunately the extent to which she is speaking for the Court is unclear given a much shorter concurring judgement by Justice Iacobucci (Lamer C.J. concurring) which indicates that he differs "somewhat" with McLachlin J.'s s. 1 analysis. The extent of the disagreement is left unclear.[107]

McLachlin J. calls for a new stress by courts on the words "reasonable" and "demonstrably justified":

> While remaining sensitive to the social and political context of the impugned law and allowing for difficulties of proof inherent in that context, the courts must nevertheless insist that before the state can override constitutional rights, there must be a reasoned demonstration of the good which the law may achieve in relation to the seriousness of the infringement. It is the task of the courts to maintain this bottom line if the rights conferred by our constitutional are to have force and meaning. The task is not easily discharged, and may require the courts to confront the tide of popular public opinion.[108]

McLachlin J. agrees with La Forest J. that the *Oakes* test, being a fact-specific inquiry, must be applied flexibly having regard to the factual and social context of each case. However she warns that this should not undercut the obligation of Parliament to justify limitations on Charter rights by reasoned demonstration. She later warns that care must be taken not to overstate the objective of the measure under challenge:

> The objective relevant to the s.1 analysis is *the objective of the infringing measure,* since it is the infringing measure and nothing else which is sought to be justified. If the objective is stated too broadly, its importance may be exaggerated and the analysis compromised.[109]

---

[106] [1995] 3 S.C.R. 199.

[107] One clear disagreement is over the application of the rational connection test. Iacobucci J. joins La Forest J. to form a 6-3 majority ruling that a rational connection had been demonstrated. McLachlin J. disagrees.

[108] At para. 129.

[109] Para. 144. (emphasis by McLachlin J.).

On the degree of deference courts should show Parliament, McLachlin J. accepts that context is relevant. She gives a qualified answer to the question of whether a tougher approach should always be demanded in criminal law:

> It has been suggested that greater deference to Parliament or the legislature may be appropriate if the law is concerned with competing rights between different sections of society than if it is a contest between the individual and the state. . . . However, such distinctions may not always be easy to apply. For example, the criminal law is generally seen as involving a contest between the state and the accused, but it also involves an allocation of priorities between the accused and the victim, actual or potential.[110]

McLachlin J. also suggests that care should be taken not to extend the notion of deference to the point of relieving the government of its burden:

> Deference must not be carried to the point of relieving the government of the burden which the Charter places upon it of demonstrating that the limits it has imposed on guaranteed rights are reasonable and justifiable.

> To carry judicial deference to the point of accepting Parliament's view simply on the basis that the problem is serious and the solution is difficult, would be to diminish the role of the courts in the constitutional process and to weaken the structure of rights upon which our constitution and our nation is founded.[111]

For McLachlin J. the standard of proof is not to the standard required by science nor proof beyond reasonable doubt. The standard of proof on a balance of probabilities may be established by the application of common sense to what is known. However she determines that this standard must be applied at all stages of the proportionality analysis, including the demonstration of a rational connection.[112]

Her final general point relates to deference by appeal courts to findings by trial judges. There should be more deference to findings based on evidence of a purely factual nature, but less where the trial judge has considered social science and other policy oriented evidence.[113]

(j) Inconsistency

If one considers the results of the Court's applications of s. 1 in the context of criminal law the record has been one of stunning inconsistency. In each of the

---

[110] Para. 135. In *Ross v. Bruce*, [1996] S.C.R. 825, La Forest J., for the full Court, adopts the first part of this statement of McLachlin J. without reference to the further comment about victims. The need to "dialogue with Parliament" approach of Iacobucci and McLachlin JJ. in *Mills*, above note 39, appears to favour considerable deference to Parliament at odds with *R.J.R. MacDonald*. Perhaps the explanation is that that decision concerned the accused's right to discovery under s. 7 respecting access to therapeutic and other records of complainants in sexual assault cases and this was a special criminal law matter involving balancing of conflicting privacy and equality rights of complainants.

[111] At para. 136. This passage was relied upon by Iacobucci J., dissenting in *Little Sisters*, above note 44.

[112] La Forest J. would not have applied the onus at the rational connection inquiry.

[113] Para. 146.

decisions reviewed above the majority and minority judges did their very best to articulate their approaches and justify their conclusions. This is by no means always the case. Often lip service is still paid to the "impair as little as possible" test in *Oakes* but the Court appears in its application to be applying a far less demanding approach. This is particularly true in rulings relating to impaired driving that have justified a reverse onus clause,[114] a limit in the case of a demand for a roadside sample of breath on the right to counsel[115] and, finally, random vehicle stop powers in the absolute discretion of the police.[116] In these decisions little or no attention was given to the possibility of less intrusive alternatives.

On the other side of the ledger the Supreme Court[117] took less than a paragraph to hold that the violation of s. 7 by the constructive murder rule in s. 230(d) of the Criminal Code could not be saved under s. 1, and was similarly quick in its later holding that subjective foresight of death is constitutionally required for murder.[118] The majority gave no consideration to whether a murder law based entirely on a subjective standard would be less effective than the former approach. So too when it struck down the Criminal Code rape shield law the issue of effectiveness was ignored by the majority although pivotal to the minority.[119]

Very clearly in the impaired driving cases the Supreme Court was influenced by the evidence presented to it concerning the social dangers of drinking and driving. These are well-documented and worrisome. However, similar dangers could be easily established in the case of most crimes, especially those of violence.

It is to be hoped that the principled approach of McLachlin J. will become the consistently applied new test for section one justification in the criminal context. Her Ladyship commendably requires a high standard of justification. At least the Court appears to have settled on the minimum intrusion test of whether the measure restricts as little as reasonably possible. It may be that the essentially policy determination made under section one will never lead to consistency. Nevertheless the Supreme Court's record thus far is cause for considerable concern.

(k) Swain: No Judicial Deference in Case of Common Law

Although *Chaulk* was not mentioned in the Supreme Court decision in *Swain* (1991)[120] there was a re-consideration of the relaxation of the minimum intrusion test. Mr. Justice Lamer for the majority[121] held that the common law rule[122]

---

[114] *Whyte* (1988), 64 C.R. (3d) 123 (S.C.C.), discussed below, Chapter 6.

[115] *Thomsen* (1988), 63 C.R. (3d) 1 (S.C.C.), discussed below, Chapter 4.

[116] *Hufsky* (1988), 63 C.R. (3d) 14 (S.C.C.) and *Ladouceur* (1990), 77 C.R. (3d) 110 (S.C.C.) (which included a strong dissent), discussed below, Chapter 4.

[117] *Vaillancourt* (1987), 60 C.R. (3d) 289 (S.C.C.), discussed below, Chapter 2.

[118] *Martineau* (1990), 79 C.R. (3d) 129 (S.C.C.), discussed below, Chapter 2.

[119] *Seaboyer* (1991), 7 C.R. (4th) 117 (S.C.C.), discussed below, Chapters 2 and 11.

[120] (1991), 63 C.C.C. (3d) 481 (S.C.C.).

[121] Sopinka and Cory J. concurred. Gonthier J. (La Forest J.) concurred separately, voicing minor differences not in issue here. Wilson J. concurred, subject to major differences, and L'Heureux-Dubé J. dissented on the basis that the common law rule did not violate the Charter.

[122] *Saxell* (1980), 59 C.C.C. (2d) 176 (Ont. C.A.).

allowing the Crown to adduce evidence of insanity over and above the accused's wishes was not in accordance with principles of fundamental justice under s. 7 and could not be saved by s. 1 Lamer J., referring to the relaxation of the *Oakes* test to require merely that the violation infringed the rights as "little as is reasonably possible", however determined that consideration of judicial deference had no place respecting common law violations for which only the "least intrusive" alternative would do:

> In cases where legislative provisions have been challenged under s. 52(1) of the *Constitution Act, 1982* this Court has been cognizant of the fact that such provisions are enacted by an elected body which must respond to the competing interests of different groups in society and which must always consider the polycentric aspects of any given course of action. For this reason, this Court has indicated that Parliament need not always choose the absolutely least intrusive means to attain its objectives, but must come within a range of means which impair *Charter* rights as little as is reasonably possible. However, . . . in cases where a common law, judge-made rule is challenged under the *Charter* there is no room for judicial deference.[123]

The majority went on to fashion a new common law rule under which the Crown could raise evidence of insanity after the trier of fact had concluded that the accused was otherwise guilty or if the accused's own defence put the accused's capacity for criminal intent in issue.[124]

(l) Prescribed by Law

Since s. 1 is expressly designed to consider the possibility of reasonable limits "prescribed by law", it can never be used to justify unconstitutional conduct, for example by police officers. It is now well established that the prescription by law can be by statute or regulation, express or implied, or by common law.

> The limit will be prescribed by law within the meaning of s. 1 if it is expressly provided for by statute or regulation, or results by necessary implication from the terms of a statute or regulation or from its operating requirements. The limit may also result from the application of a common law rule.[125]

The Ontario Court of Appeal has held[126] that a non-binding set of broad guidelines promulgated by a pamphlet was not capable of being law and therefore could not be a s. 1 limit on the freedom of expression.

---

[123] Above note 120, at 514.
[124] *Ibid.*, at 516-517. Wilson J. dissented on the basis that s. 1 was not to be considered respecting a s. 7 violation and that the new common law rule violated s. 15. The majority also held that the automatic indeterminate detention following a verdict of not guilty but insane under what is now s. 614(2) of the Criminal Code violated s. 9 (discussed below, Chapter 4) and could not be saved under s. 1, as it did not restrict "as little as possible" (at 540). Once again, the Court shows vacillation on the test. Here there is no talk of restricting as little as reasonably possible!
[125] *Therens*, above note 22, at 126 (per Le Dain J.), adopted by a unanimous Court in *Thomsen*, above note 115, at 10.
[126] *Ontario Film and Video Appreciation Society v. Ontario Board of Censors* (1984), 38 C.R. (3d) 271 (Ont. C.A.).

Since the Supreme Court's decision in the *Prostitution Reference* (1990),[127] it has been clear that a Charter right of freedom cannot be subject to a reasonable limit prescribed by law under s. 1 if that law is too vague. The Supreme Court adopted the Federal Court of Appeal's[128] holding that a customs tariff on an immoral or indecent matter was so vague, ambiguous, uncertain and subject to discretionary determination that it was, for that fact alone, an unreasonable limit.

(m) Can Any Violation be Saved by Section 1?

In early Charter analysis, it was thought that there would be some rights or freedoms under the Charter which would not be subject to further balancing under s. 1 In *Hunter* (1984),[129] the Supreme Court of Canada specifically left open "the difficult question" of the relationship between the protection in s. 8 against unreasonable search or seizure and s. 1 and, in particular, "what further balancing of interests, *if any*, may be contemplated by section 1, beyond that envisaged by section 8."[130] Later, for the Ontario Court of Appeal, Mr. Justice Martin indicated that he would have "great difficulty" in concluding that an unreasonable search power was justifiable under s. 1 as a reasonable limit.[131] Likewise, it seems counter-intuitive to justify cruel and unusual punishment contrary to s. 12 or a denial of liberty contrary to principles of fundamental justice in s. 7. However, even in such cases it is now beyond question that the Supreme Court will consider demonstrably justifying violations.[132]

In the case of s. 7 violations various dicta suggest that such arguments should rarely succeed. In *Heywood* (1994),[133] the majority of the Court held the a loitering offence under what was then s. 179(1)(b) of the Criminal Code was contrary to s. 7 of the Charter on the basis of overbreadth and that the violation could not be justified under s. 1. Justice Cory for the majority noted that in the *Motor Vehicle Act Reference* case[134] the Court had previously expressed doubt whether any s. 7 violation could ever be justified except perhaps in times of war or national emergencies. He further held that overbroad legislation which infringed s. 7 would "appear to be incapable of passing the minimum intrusion branch of the s. 1 analysis".[135]

On the other hand, Lamer C.J. in *New Brunswick (Minister of Health & Community Services)* v. *G.(J.)* (1999)[136] appeared to contemplate that s. 7

[127] Above note 77, discussed below, Chapter 2, "Void for Vagueness".
[128] *Luscher v. Dep. Minister* (1985), 45 C.R. (3d) 81 (Fed. C.A.) See too *Robson* (1985), 45 C.R. (3d) 68 (B.C. C.A.) (provincial driving suspension too vague).
[129] Above note 9.
[130] *Ibid.*, at 122.
[131] *Noble* (1984), 42 C.R. (3d) 209 at 237 (Ont. C.A.).
[132] See, for example, *Smith* (1987), 58 C.R. (3d) 193 (S.C.C.) (s. 12); and *Vaillancourt*, above note 117 and *Swain*, above note 120 (both s. 7).
[133] (1994), 34 C.R. (4th) 133 (S.C.C.).
[134] Above note 4, at 321, discussed below Chapter 2, "Fault".
[135] At 163.
[136] (1999), 26 C.R. (5th) 203 (S.C.C.). See below Chapter 2.

violations could be justified under s. 1. However he again suggested[137] that they would not easily be saved for two reasons. The rights protected under s. 7 were very significant and could not ordinarily be overruled by competing social interests. Secondly, violations of principles of fundamental justice, specifically the right to a fair hearing, would rarely be upheld.

6. WAIVER[138]

The Supreme Court of Canada is in agreement on tests for whether an accused has waived a Charter right.

In *Clarkson* (1986),[139] Madam Justice Wilson for the Court[140] held that

> . . . any alleged waiver of this right by an accused must be carefully considered and that the accused's awareness of the consequences of what he or she was saying is crucial. Indeed, this court stated with respect to the waiver of statutory procedural guarantees in *Korponey v. A.G. Can.* . . . (1982), 26 C.R. (3d) 343 . . . that any waiver:
>
>> . . . is dependent upon it being *clear and unequivocal that the person is waiving the procedural safeguard and is doing so with full knowledge of the rights the procedure was enacted to protect and of the effect the waiver will have on those rights in the process.*[141]

She noted that there was a wealth of authority in the United States and that its Supreme Court had gone as far as to hold that the accused person must be aware not only of the consequences of a waiver of a constitutional right but also of the legal specifics of the particular case.[142] She concluded as follows:

> Whether or not one goes as far as requiring an accused to be tuned in to the legal intricacies of the case before accepting as valid a waiver of the right to counsel, it is clear that the waiver of the s. 10(b) right by an intoxicated accused must pass some form of "awareness of the consequences" test.
>
> . . . .
>
> While this constitutional guarantee cannot be forced upon an unwilling accused, any voluntary waiver, in order to be valid and effective, must be premised on a true appreciation of the consequences of giving up the right.[143]

---

[137] Para. 99.

[138] See Alan Young "Not Waving But Drowning: A Look at Waiver and Collective Constitutional Rights in the Criminal Process" (1989), 53 *Sask. L. Rev.* 47.

[139] (1986), 50 C.R. (3d) 289 (S.C.C.).

[140] McIntyre J. (Chouinard J. concurring) dissented on a non-Charter issue.

[141] Above note 139, at 301-302.

[142] A leading pronouncement of the U.S. Supreme Court (not referred to in *Clarkson*) is that in *Edwards v. Arizona*, 451 U.S. 477 at 482-483 (1981):

> It is reasonably clear under our cases that waivers of counsel must not only be voluntary, but must also constitute a knowing and intelligent relinquishment or abandonment of a known right or privilege, a matter which depends in each case "upon the particular facts and circumstances surrounding that case, including the background, experience, and conduct of the accused."

[143] Above note 139, at 302-303.

In *Korponey* (1982),[144] in which the issue was the possible waiver of a statutory right to a jury trial, the Supreme Court had ruled that a waiver can only be express and that mere silence or lack of objection will not be enough.[145] In *Manninen* (1987),[146] the Supreme Court however held that waiver, in that case of the right to counsel under s. 10(b) of the Charter, can be implicit although it asserted that "the standard will be very high."[147] According to *Manninen*, where the detainee has asserted the right to counsel, there is a right not to be asked questions by the police and the detainee must not be held to have implicitly waived that right simply because police questions were answered.[148]

When the Supreme Court has characterized the issue as one of waiver, it has repeatedly demonstrated its reluctance to find that there has been a waiver of a Charter right. This is particularly so of rulings respecting the right to counsel,[149] the right to be tried within a reasonable time[150], the right to trial by jury[151] and the right to an interpreter.[152]

The doctrine of waiver has no application to the s. 7 right of a detainee to remain silent, recognized by the Supreme Court in *Hebert* (1990).[153] For the majority, Madam Justice McLachlin pragmatically rejected an approach which assumed an absolute right to silence, capable of being discharged only by waiver. Such an approach would exclude all statements to undercover agents, as well as conversations with fellow prisoners overheard by the police and statements overheard through listening devices. The right to silence, held the majority, should not be extended this far.[154]

In *Richard* (1996),[155] the Supreme Court was unanimous in declaring that provisions for trials in absentia under the New Brunswick ticket scheme for provincial offences do not violate s. 11(d) because it is appropriate to assume a waiver of rights in the situations covered.[156] For the Court, La Forest J. indicated that the regulatory context could be considered in determining the manner and extent to which a right could be waived. The Court entered substantial caveats. The scheme in question could not lead to imprisonment even in default of payment

---

[144] (1982), 65 C.C.C. (2d) 65 (S.C.C.).

[145] *Ibid.*, at 73 (per Lamer J.).

[146] (1987), 58 C.R. (3d) 97 (S.C.C.).

[147] *Ibid*, at 105. See too *Bartle* (1994), 33 C.R. (4th) 1 (S.C.C.), further holding that waiver of the informational component of s. 10(b) would have to be express: fully discussed in Chapter 5.

[148] *Ibid.*

[149] See below, Chapter 5. The picture is, however, confused by parallel decisions on the duty to exercise the right with reasonable diligence. See *ibid.*

[150] See below, Chapter 6.

[151] *Ibid.*

[152] *Tran* (1994), 32 C.R. (4th) 34 (S.C.C.), discussed below Chapter 9.

[153] (1990), 77 C.R. (3d) 145 (S.C.C.), discussed below, Chapter 2, under "Right to Silence".

[154] *Ibid.*, at 188. Dickson C.J.C., Lamer, La Forest, L'Heureux-Dubé, Gonthier and Cory JJ. concurred. Only Wilson and Sopinka JJ. in separate concurring judgments favoured the application of waiver in this context.

[155] (1996), 3 C.R. (5th) 1 (S.C.C.).

[156] This is a new approach. There was a strong trend in lower courts to reject such challenges by resort to s. 1 justification: see, for example, *Newton*, Ont. P.D., August 16, 1996 (per Payne J.) and *Pilipovic*, Ont. P.D., August 29, 1996, not yet reported.

of a fine. A possibility of imprisonment would engage s. 7 issues. The scheme also had to provide full information of consequences for failure to act and a mechanism to review for events beyond the accused's control.

7. JURISDICTION[157]

(a) Section 24

(i) *Trial courts*

The primary remedy against a Charter violation in the criminal law is for the accused to bring a motion to the trial court under s. 24. Under s. 24, "Anyone whose [Charter] rights and freedoms . . . have been infringed or denied" may apply for a remedy to a court of "competent jurisdiction".[158] A trial court, as a "court of competent jurisdiction", may give an "appropriate and just" remedy (s. 24(1)) or exclude evidence obtained in violation of the Charter if admission would bring the administration of justice into disrepute (s. 24(2)).[159] The remedies issues are considered later in Chapter 11.

In *Mills* (1986),[160] the Supreme Court held that all criminal trial courts as defined by s. 2 of the Criminal Code, and thus including trials before provincial court judges, were "courts of competent jurisdiction" for the purpose of granting s. 24 remedies. This was not because s. 24 conferred a new jurisdiction but because those courts already had

> jurisdiction conferred by a statute over the offences and persons and power to make the orders sought.[161]

On the other hand, the Court unanimously ruled[162] that a justice at a preliminary inquiry was *not* a court of competent jurisdiction for the purpose of granting Charter remedies under s. 24. Their jurisdiction under what is now Part XVIII of the Criminal Code was limited to considering whether there is sufficient evidence to put the accused on trial. Even though rules relating to the admissibility of evidence apply at preliminary hearings, the majority of the Court further held that there is no jurisdiction for a justice at a preliminary inquiry to consider whether

---

[157] In this section, I relied on a comprehensive paper by David H. Doherty, "Charter Applications in Criminal Cases" (1988) (unpublished).

[158] An accused is not entitled to a remedy based on Charter breaches by police against a third party: *Edwards* (1996), 45 C.R. (4th) 307 (S.C.C.), discussed below Chapter 3.

[159] *Therens*, above note 22, decided that the remedy of exclusion of evidence is limited to that defined in s. 24(2).

[160] (1986), 52 C.R. (3d) 1 (S.C.C.). It is not necessary to review the full range of a complex series of divided opinion in the four judgments delivered. Subsequent decisions of the Supreme Court have now cleared up much but not all of the ambiguity.

[161] *Ibid.*, McIntyre J. at 19. See too Lamer J. at 53. A Provincial Court judge therefore has no Charter jurisdiction respecting an indictable offence before election: *Wilson* (1997), 121 C.C.C. (3d) 92 (N.S. C.A.).

[162] See McIntyre and Lamer JJ., *ibid.* See too La Forest J. at 93. See too *Carter* (1986), 52 C.R. (3d) 100 (S.C.C.).

evidence should be excluded under s. 24(2) as having been obtained in violation of the Charter.[163]

The Supreme Court has determined that judges at extradition hearings[164] and parole boards[165] are not courts of competent jurisdiction under s. 24. Although there is no clear authority it would seem that justices at show cause hearings have no Charter jurisdiction either and that Charter review would require application of an extraordinary remedy such as *habeas corpus*.[166]

(ii) *Supervisory jurisdiction of superior courts*

The Supreme Court in *Mills* unanimously determined that superior courts have a jurisdiction concurrent with that of trial courts to deal with Charter issues but that they should normally decline to exercise that jurisdiction in favour of trial courts. Mr. Justice Lamer for the majority further characterized this jurisdiction of superior courts as original.[167] For the minority, Mr. Justice McIntyre held that s. 24 had not given a new jurisdiction to the superior courts but that it had to be exercised under their traditional jurisdiction over prerogative remedies. On the latter view, not all Charter breaches could be remedied by the Superior Court since it would have to be shown that the error had been jurisdictional in nature.[168]

In *Mills*, Mr. Justice Lamer saw the danger of any unrestrained exercise of superior court jurisdiction as being that this would result in "unnecessary delay or disruption of proceedings."[169] Subsequently in *Rahey* (1987),[170] he restated his approach as follows:

> In *Mills*, it was also decided that the superior courts should have "constant, complete and concurrent jurisdiction" for s. 24(1) applications. But it was therein emphasized

---

[163] This was a ruling of four justices: McIntyre, Beetz, Chouinard and La Forest JJ. Lamer J. (Dickson C.J.C. and Wilson J. concurring) dissented on this point. For criticism of the majority view see annotation by Manson and Stuart, 52 C.R. (3d) 7-8. The notion of committing on inadmissible evidence is strange.

[164] *United States v. Kwok* (April 5, 2001) (S.C.C.). Arbour J. for the Court confirmed jurisdiction under the new Extradition Act over matters relevant to extradition hearings. These include s. 7 rights but not s. 6 mobility rights which arise under the Minister's surrender jurisdiction.

[165] *Mooring v. National Parole Board* (1996), 45 C.R. (4th) 265 (S.C.C.). Lamer C.J. suggests that on the *Mooring* rulings justices the preliminary inquiries have s. 24 jurisdiction. However the Chief Justice was alone on this point and La Forest J. expressly rejected it. In *Hynes* (1999), 26 C.R. (5th) 1 (Nfld. C.A.), the majority held that preliminary inquiry justices are not courts of competent jurisdiction to exclude evidence based on a Charter violation. However a differently composed majority expressed concern as to this being incongruous and unprincipled. A justice at a preliminary inquiry is not a court of competent jurisdiction to order disclosure: *Girimonte* (1997), 121 C.C.C. (3d) 33 (Ont. C.A.).

[166] *Pearson* (1992), 17 C.R. (4th) 1 (S.C.C.) at 50. See further Gary Trotter, *The Law of Bail in Canada* (2nd ed., 1999) pp. 184-191.

[167] Above note 160, at 44. Dickson C.J.C. and Wilson J. concurred. See similarly La Forest J. at 97-99.

[168] *Ibid.*, at 20. Beetz and Chouinard JJ. concurred.

[169] *Ibid.*, at 46.

[170] (1987), 57 C.R. (3d) 289 (S.C.C.).

that the superior courts should decline to exercise this discretionary jurisdiction unless, in the opinion of the superior court and given the nature of the violation or any other circumstance, it is more suited than the trial court to assess and grant the remedy that is just and appropriate. The clearest, though not necessarily the only, instances where there is a need for the exercise of such jurisdiction are those where there is as yet no trial court within reach and the timeliness of the remedy or the need to prevent a continuing violation of rights is shown, and those where it is the process below itself which is alleged to be in violation of the Charter's guarantees. The burden should be upon the claimant . . . to establish that the application is an appropriate one for the superior court's consideration.[171]

In *Rahey*, the Supreme Court had no difficulty in ruling that a superior court judge had rightly exercised jurisdiction as a court of competent jurisdiction where it was the very conduct of the trial judge that was alleged to be the cause of a violation of the accused's right to be tried within a reasonable time under s. 11(b).

In *Smith* (1989),[172] another s. 11(b) case, the Supreme Court also held that a superior court had properly exercised the supervisory jurisdiction. Where practicable s. 11(b) challenges should be dealt with by trial judges since the trial judge could "rely on *viva voce* evidence so as to more fully explore and consider the facts underlying [the] delay."[173] However, the superior court judge in *Smith* had properly exercised his jurisdiction four months before a preliminary inquiry, as by then 16 month's delay would have elapsed since the theft charge. The justice at the preliminary inquiry would have had no jurisdiction to consider the s. 11(b) violation and a committal for trial would have further delayed the accused's opportunity to assert his right.

Provincial Courts of Appeal appear to have been even less sympathetic than the Supreme Court to the possibility of superior court judges choosing to exercise a supervisory Charter jurisdiction. At an early stage of Charter jurisprudence, the British Columbia Court of Appeal declared that "each level of the judiciary should be free to perform its proper function" and that "counsel should not be encouraged to seek solutions to legal questions prematurely at the supervisory or appellate level."[174] Chief Justice Monnin of Manitoba warned that trials could not "proceed piecemeal or with frequent interruptions for supervisory or appellate rulings."[175]

Notwithstanding the Chief Justice's views, the Manitoba Court of Appeal in *Komadowski* (1986)[176] decided that a trial judge has no jurisdiction under s. 24(2) to exclude evidence obtained pursuant to a search warrant unless there has first been a successful motion to a superior court judge to quash the warrant. An inferior court order valid on its face could not, said the Manitoba Court, be subject

---

[171] *Ibid.*, at 298 (Dickson C.J. concurring). Wilson and Estey JJ. also concurred on this point (at 307).

[172] (1989), 73 C.R. (3d) 1 (S.C.C.). See discussion by Graeme G. Mitchell, "Smith: Old Doctrine for a New Decade" (1990), 74 C.R. (3d) 375.

[173] *Ibid.*, at 9. The Court reviews the above passage of Lamer J. in *Rahey* with apparent approval.

[174] *Anson* (1983), 4 C.C.C. (3d) 119 at 131 (B.C. C.A.) (prohibition not available to review trial judge's rejection of a Charter attack on a reverse onus clause). See too *McNabb* (1986), 33 C.C.C. (3d) 266 (B.C. C.A.).

[175] *Blackwood Beverages Ltd.* (1984), 43 C.R. (3d) 254 at 262 (Man. C.A.) (majority holding superior courts not to make interlocutory orders excluding evidence).

[176] (1986), 27 C.C.C. (3d) 319 (Man. C.A.).

to collateral attack. However, the Ontario Court of Appeal in *Zevallos* (1987)[177] refused to follow *Komadowski*. It held that a motion in the nature of *certiorari* to quash a search warrant should be rejected where the only real issue was the admissibility of evidence relating to search and seizure. This was normally[178] a matter for the trial judge.

In a series of rulings, the Ontario Court of Appeal has consistently held that any inherent or prerogative jurisdiction must be exercised only in exceptional circumstances.[179] Other courts[180] have pointed to the undesirability of exercising the discretion in the absence of evidence.

(iii) *Appellate review*

In *Mills* (1986),[181] Mr. Justice McIntyre for the majority on this point,[182] noting that there were only statutory rights of appeal in criminal matters[183] and that the Charter was silent on the question of appeals, concluded that the existing appeal structure had to be used for s. 24 claims.[184] His Lordship adopted the view of the Ontario Court of Appeal in *Morgentaler* (1984)[185] that:

> The weight of authority is that s. 24(1) does not create courts of competent jurisdiction, but merely vests additional powers in courts which are already found to be competent independently of the Charter.[186]

---

[177] (1987), 59 C.R. (3d) 153 (Ont. C.A.), since followed in *Williams* (1987), 38 C.C.C. (3d) 319 (Y.T. C.A.); *Tanner* (1989), 46 C.C.C. (3d) 513 (Alta. C.A.) and *Jamieson* (1989), 48 C.C.C. (3d) 287 (N.S. C.A.).

[178] The Court in *Zevallos, ibid.*, at 160 (per Morden J.A.) held that the reasoning did not relate to situations where the order was for other purposes such as preventing a search or having property returned.

[179] *Krakowski* (1983), 4 C.C.C. (3d) 189 (Ont. C.A.); *Kohler* (1984), 15 C.C.C. (3d) 327 (Ont. C.A.) and *Corbeil* (1986), 27 C.C.C. (3d) 245 (Ont. CA.) (each concerning s. 11(b) applications). See too *Multitech Warehouse Direct (Ontario) Inc.* (1989), 52 C.C.C. (3d) 175 (Ont. C.A.) (holding that the Competition Act was not contrary to Charter not to be subject to prohibition absent "palpable infringement" of constitutional right) and see now *Duvivier* (1991), 64 C.C.C. (3d) 20 (Ont. C.A.) (Charter attack on subpoena best left to trial judge).

[180] *Norton* (1988), 45 C.C.C. (3d) 574 (Alta. CA.) (Superior Court judge wrong to strike down legislation in chambers) and *Finta* (1989), 69 C.R. (3d) 223 (Ont. H.C.) (Superior Court judge not exercising jurisdiction to hear arguments that war crimes provisions unconstitutional in absence of "firm factual underpinning").

[181] Above note 160.

[182] Beetz and Chouinard JJ. concurred. La Forest J. concurred separately at 99 adding, however, that there might well be an appeal to the Supreme Court with leave from the superior court as the court of final resort. Lamer J. (Dickson C.J.C. and Wilson J. concurring) dissented (at 50-53), on the basis that, given there was an appeal of relief sought by prerogative writ, an appeal would have to be recognized from applications to superior courts based on s. 24. See discussion by Manson and Stuart, above note 163, p. 7.

[183] His Lordship pointed to what is now s. 674 in the Criminal Code:
> No proceedings other than those authorised by this Part [XXI. Appeals — Indictable Offences] and Part XXVI [Extraordinary Remedies] shall be taken by way of appeal in proceedings in respect of indictable offences.

[184] Above note 160, at 22.

[185] (1984), 41 C.R. (3d) 262 (Ont. C.A.).

[186] We have seen that this is no longer accurate in the case of the supervisory jurisdiction of superior courts.

. . . .

> Section 24(1) does not purport to create a right of appeal or bestow appellate powers on this or any other court. Rather it authorizes those courts which have statutory appellate jurisdiction independent of the Charter to exercise the remedial power in s. 24(1) in appropriate cases when disposing of appeals properly brought before the court.[187]

Mr. Justice McIntyre also rejected the claim that s. 52 could ground a right of appeal to an appellate court to hear an appeal from an interlocutory Charter motion. In justifying the reality that the accused would have to wait for the outcome of the trial to pursue an appeal, he refused to give priority to Charter issues. Not all claims would succeed and interlocutory appeals would not necessarily provide a quicker remedy than the ordinary processes.[188]

In *Meltzer v. Laison* (1989),[189] Mr. Justice McIntyre, on behalf of a panel of five judges,[190] held that there was no right to appeal a refusal of a review of a judicial authorization to electronically intercept a private communication. Following a preliminary hearing and committal to trial, the accused had applied to a Supreme Court judge to set aside a renewal of a judicial authorization. The judge dismissed the application and subsequent appeals were dismissed for lack of jurisdiction. In the Supreme Court, the application to review was characterized as an interlocutory motion in a criminal matter aimed at the exclusion of evidence at trial. There was no statutory basis for such an appeal and ordinary appellate procedure governed. The trial would have to proceed first. Thereafter, if the refusal of the application had been based on the Charter, there might well be a question of law which could be the basis of an appeal under the Criminal Code against conviction or acquittal.

This position is no longer clear following recent decisions of the Supreme Court to grant appellate relief on leave to third parties relying on Charter rights:[191] newspapers appealing publication bans[192] and complainants appealing orders to disclose medical records[193] and to accused or Crown wishing to challenge a Charter ruling but without a Criminal Code appeal right.[194]

---

[187] Above note 160, at 23.

[188] *Ibid.*, at 25-26. For strong criticism of *Morgentaler* see annotation by Allan Manson in 41 C.R. (3d) 263-265. Morgentaler challenged the constitutionality of the Criminal Code abortion provision under which he was charged. The pre-trial motion was dismissed on July 20, 1984. The Ontario Court of Appeal refused to hear the Charter issues before the trial. The accused was later acquitted following trial before judge and jury. On the Crown appeal, the Ontario Court of appeal dismissed a cross-appeal of the Charter challenges: (1986), 48 C.R. (3d) 1 (Ont. C.A.). On January 28, 1988 the majority of the Supreme Court declared the abortion provision unconstitutional: (1988), 62 C.R. (3d) 1 (S.C.C.), discussed below, Chapter 2.

[189] (1989), 70 C.R. (3d) 383 (S.C.C.).

[190] Lamer, Wilson, La Forest and L'Heureux-Dubé JJ. concurred. Beetz and Le Dain JJ. took no part in the judgment.

[191] In the context of s. 8, courts have repeatedly held that accused cannot rely on the breach of rights of third parties: see discussion in Chapter 3.

[192] *Dagenais v. C.B.C.* (1995), 34 C.R. (4th) 269 (S.C.C.).

[193] *L.L.A. v. A.B.* (1996), 44 C.R. (4th) 91 (S.C.C.).

[194] *Keegstra* (1995), 39 C.R. (4th) 205 (S.C.C.).

After trial it has not proved difficult to frame a Charter ruling as a question of law subject to appeal.[195] It is now also clear that there is a right of appeal from a judicial stay entered on the basis of a Charter violation. That decision is "tantamount to acquittal" grounding a Crown Appeal.[196]

Courts of Appeal have, however, proved reluctant to hear Charter arguments raised for the first time on appeal. Thus, the Ontario Court of Appeal in *Logan* (1988)[197] held that a Charter ground should not be raised for the first time before an appellate court if the issue is dependent upon findings of fact not made by a trial judge, particularly if such issues of fact are not even raised before him. Where the trial record *is* complete, the Supreme Court ruled in *Brown* (1993),[198] that the Charter issue should be considered even where raised for the first time on appeal. In *Brown*, the accused was allowed to take advantage of new Charter rights recognized after the trial.

(b) Section 52

Under the supremacy clause in s. 52, any law inconsistent with the Constitution, including the Charter, is of no force or effect to the extent of the inconsistency. In *Big M Drug Mart* (1985),[199] Chief Justice Dickson for a unanimous Supreme Court, established that s. 52 has a powerful remedial role in the context of criminal law quite independent of s. 24. An accused, whether corporate or individual, could defend a criminal charge by arguing that the law under which the charge had been brought was constitutionally invalid and inoperative under s. 52:[200]

> Section 24(1) sets out a remedy for individuals (whether real persons or artificial ones such as corporations) whose rights under the Charter have been infringed. It is not, however, the only recourse in the face of unconstitutional legislation. Where, as

---

[195] In *Collins* (1987), 56 C.R. (3d) 193 (S.C.C.), it was held that the decision to exclude evidence under s. 24(2) is a question of law. However, in *Duguay* (1989), 67 C.R. (3d) 252 (S.C.C.), the Court held that it ought not to intervene in such cases in the absence of an error of principle.

[196] *Jewitt* (1985), 47 C.R. (3d) 193 (S.C.C.).

[197] (1988), 68 C.R. (3d) 1 at 18 (Ont. C.A.). See too *Rabba* (1991), 6 C.R. (4th) 69 (Ont. C.A.) (s. 11(b)), *Byers Transport Ltd.* (1991), 63 C.C.C. (3d) 234 (Alta. CA.) (s. 11(d)), *Ryan* (1992), 12 C.R. (4th) 173 (Ont. C.A.), *Walker* (1992), 74 C.C.C. (3d) 97 (B.C. C.A.) and *Jamieson* (1998), 131 C.C.C. (3d) 347 (Ont. C.A.). In *Vickery v. Prothonotary of the Supreme Court of Nova Scotia* (1991), 64 C.C.C. (3d) 65 (S.C.C.), Stevenson J. for the majority similarly refused to hear a new Charter argument. He recognized, however, that the Supreme Court "undoubtedly has a discretion to entertain arguments not developed in the courts below" (at 90).

[198] (1993), 22 C.R. (4th) 145 (S.C.C.). *Brown* was followed in *Mayo* (1999), 133 C.C.C. (3d) 168 (Ont. C.A.) and *Weir* (1999), 27 C.R. (5th) 333 (Alta. C.A.) but distinguished in *Fertal* (1993), 85 C.C.C. (3d) 411 (Alta. C.A.) and *Trabulsey* (1995), 97 C.C.C. (3d) 147 (Ont. C.A.). See further David Tanovich, "Ensuring Justice For All: When Can a Change in Law be Raised on Appeal?" (1995), 38 C.R. (4th) 397.

[199] [1985] 1 S.C.R. 295.

[200] *Ibid.*, at 400. For a statistical review of successful s. 52 challenges to federal and provincial statutes see F.L. Morton *et al.*, "Judicial Nullification of Statutes Under the Charter of Rights and Freedoms, 1982-1988" (1990), 28 *Alta. L. Rev.* 396.

here, the challenge is based on the unconstitutionality of the legislation, recourse to s. 24 is unnecessary and the particular effect on the challenging party is irrelevant. Section 52 sets out the fundamental principle of constitutional law that the Constitution is supreme. The undoubted corollary to be drawn from this principle is that no one can be convicted of an offence under an unconstitutional law.[201]

The corporate accused charged with a violation of the Lord's Day Act[202] could defend itself on the basis that the legislation was an unconstitutional violation of the freedom of religion guaranteed in s. 2(a). The Court added that

it has always been open to provincial courts to declare legislation invalid in criminal cases. No one may be convicted of an offence under an invalid statute.[203]

Big M Drug Mart would appear to support the argument[204] that justices at preliminary inquiries, although not courts of competent jurisdiction for the purposes of s. 24(1) Charter remedies, have jurisdiction under s. 52 to hear and decide a Charter challenge to the constitutionality of the offence charged. However, in *Seaboyer* (1991)[205] the Supreme Court unanimously confirmed that a preliminary inquiry judge has no jurisdiction under s. 52 to determine whether a Charter right has been violated.

In the criminal law context most decisions respecting Charter jurisdiction have concerned s. 24. On the few occasions that s. 52 has been addressed directly,[206] it has been held that s. 52 does not confer original jurisdiction. A convicted accused can only claim the benefit of a ruling of unconstitutionality if still within the judicial system. That will not be so where time limits for appeal have expired and no extension can be obtained.[207]

It seems certain that courts of competent jurisdiction under s. 24 also have the jurisdiction to exercise the declaratory power under s. 52. Where the validity of legislation is being challenged, it would appear to be wise to bring the application under both ss. 24 and 52, given that the remedy under s. 52 is not at large in the sense that there must be a declaration that the unconstitutional law is inoperative.[208]

(c) Collateral Charter Attacks on Criminal Proceedings through Civil Action

Jurisdiction in criminal matters is normally governed by statutory provisions, particularly those under the Criminal Code. Civil proceedings are generally

---

[201] *Ibid.*

[202] R.S.C. 1970, c. L-13.

[203] Above note 120, at 402. The extent to which this allows corporations to rely on s. 7 challenges is a matter of conflicting authority: see below, Chapter 2.

[204] See Paul B. Schabas, "Charter Arguments at Preliminary Inquiries: Maybe You Can Make Them After All" (1990), 75 C.R. (3d) 86, but compare Hugh W. Silverman, "Constitutionality, Cuddy, Preliminary Inquiries and Mr. Bumble" (1990), 78 C.R. (3d) 48. See too Jack Watson, "Curial Incompetence in Criminal Trials: a Discussion of Section 24 of the Charter of Rights and Freedoms in the Criminal Trial Context" (1990), 32 *Crim. L.Q.* 162 at 182-198. See, however, Lamer C.J. in *Mooring*, above note 165.

[205] *Seaboyer*, above note 119, discussed below Chapters 2 and 11.

[206] See *Mills*, above note 160 (appellate jurisdiction) and *Seaboyer, ibid.* (preliminary inquiries).

[207] *Wigman* (1987), 33 C.C.C. (3d) 97 (S.C.C.); *Thomas* (1990), 75 C.R. (3d) 352 (S.C.C.).

[208] See further below, Chapter 11.

inapplicable and unavailable to challenge criminal legislation or behaviour of state officials in the course of a criminal proceeding.[209] Civil action may, however, be applicable in two contexts.

At the post-sentencing stage, civil actions may be the only available remedy in the case of Charter challenges concerning detention at, or release from, psychiatric hospitals[210] or prisons.[211] Although an extraordinary remedy such as *habeas corpus* may allow for Charter arguments,[212] it has now been held by the Ontario Court of Appeal that the guarantee of fundamental justice in s. 7 of the Charter does not provide access to the courts by way of an appeal.[213]

Second, a civil remedy may also be invoked by third parties, who are not parties to the criminal proceeding, who can establish that their rights have been adversely affected by a decision made in the course of that criminal proceeding. A common example is a newspaper publisher challenging a court-imposed "gag order".[214] In such cases, the exact nature of the procedure to be followed will depend on the relevant provincial rules relating to civil proceedings.

(d) Complainants (Principal Witnesses)

Since complainants only have statutory jurisdiction for limited purposes, such as to request a publication ban,[215] it follows under *Mills* that complainants have no legal standing at a criminal trial to make a Charter argument, or to appeal.

This position is no longer clear following the Supreme Court decision to grant appellate standing to complainants appealing orders to disclose medical and therapeutic records.[216] The Supreme Court has not directly pronounced on the issue of standing of complainants at trial. However the Court indirectly conferred complainants standing for a particular aspect of the trial in its holdings in *L.L.A. v. A.B.* (1996)[217] and *O'Connor* (1996)[218] that there must be a two-stage procedure before the trial judge to balance the accused's right of full answer and defence

---

[209] *Morgentaler* (1985), 19 C.C.C. (3d) 573 (Ont. C.A.); *Millar* (1989), 50 C.C.C. (3d) 574 (P.E.I. C.A.); *Robertson* (1988), 41 C.C.C. (3d) 478 (Alta. C.A.).

[210] *Abel v. Advisory Review Board* (1980), 56 C.C.C. (2d) 153 (Ont. C.A.).

[211] *Smith* (1987), 58 C.R. (3d) 193 (S.C.C.).

[212] *Gamble* (1988), 66 C.R. (3d) 193 (S.C.C.) but see *Steele v. Mountain Institution* (1990), 80 C.R. (3d) 257 (S.C.C.) criticized by Allan Manson, "The Effect of *Steele* on Habeas Corpus and Indeterminate Confinement" (1991), 80 C.R. (3d) 282. In *Sarson* (1996), 49 C.R. (4th) 75 (S.C.C.) the Court held *habeas corpus* was not available to an accused who had pleaded guilty to second degree murder and exhausted avenues of appeal before the constructive murder provision was declared unconstitutional.

[213] *Vaillancourt* (1989), 71 C.R. (3d) 43 (Ont. C.A.) (no appeal lying against unsuccessful application for reduction of period of parole in absence of statutory right to appeal).

[214] See, for example, *Canadian Newspapers Co. v. Canada (A.G.)* (1985), 17 C.C.C. (3d) 385 (Ont. C.A.). In *Therrien v. Quebec (A.G.)* (1987), 57 C.R. (3d) 392 (Que. C.A.), the majority held that third parties cited for contempt on application by an accused for a Charter remedy had a right of appeal under s. 24. There would be standing issues.

[215] Criminal Code, R.S.C. 1985, c. C-46, s. 486(4)(b).

[216] *L.L.A. v. A.B.* (1996), 44 C.R. (4th) 91 (S.C.C.).

[217] *Ibid.*

[218] (1996), 44 C.R. (4th) 1 (S.C.C.), fully discussed below Chapter 2.

against the complainant's privacy interests. The Court found those privacy interests protected in ss. 7 and 8 rights for complainants.

8. BALANCING RIGHTS

(a) No Hierarchy of Rights

In *Dagenais v. C.B.C.* (1994),[219] Chief Justice Lamer for the majority[220] determined that there is no hierarchy of Charter rights and that conflicting rights had to be balanced:

> A hierarchal approach to rights, which places some over others, must be avoided, both when interpreting the Charter and when fully developing the common law. When the protected rights of two individuals come into conflict. . . . Charter principles require a balance to be achieved that fully respects the importance of both sets of rights.[221]

In *Dagenais*, involving a publication ban, the right to make full answer and defence under s. 7 had to be balanced against the freedom of the press under s. 2(b).

The notion that there is no hierarchy of Charter rights is an uneasy one. As Professor Alan Young suggests:

> Given the inherently subjective nature of a balancing exercise, it is not surprising that the opposing parties will never be satisfied with a result which appears to be nothing more than a slight tilting of the balance in favour of one of the warring sides.[222]

In the context of criminal law both before and after *Dagenais* the Supreme Court has consistently recognized that some accused's rights, such as the right to make full answer and defence, the principle against self-incrimination and the presumption of innocence, should be given precedence. In its jurisprudence respecting exclusion of evidence under s. 24(2)[223] the Court has consistently excluded evidence where the Charter breach conscripted the accused to produce evidence as contrasted with real evidence which existed independently of the Charter breach. In that context, it is clear that some rights of accused are seen to be more worthy of protection than others. When there is a clash of Charter rights the Court's approach of seeking some balance seems appropriate but it is difficult to avoid the reality that in a criminal trial some accused's rights are and should be given greater respect. What of the rights of alleged victims?

---

[219] (1994), 34 C.R. (4th) 269 (S.C.C.).

[220] Sopinka, Cory, Iacobucci, and Major JJ. concurred.

[221] At 298. This approach was later adopted by Sopinka J. speaking for eight justices in *Crawford* (1995), 37 C.R. (4th) 197 (S.C.C.) at 216. In a joint trial, a co-accused's right to silence had to be balanced against the right to make full answer and defence.

[222] "When Titans Clash: The Limits of Constitutional Adjudication" (1996), 44 C.R. (4th) 152 at 153.

[223] Below Chapter 11.

In *Mills* (2000),[224] before delineating the accused's right to full answer and defence[225] the Court makes a point of quoting *Dagenais* for the proposition that no Charter right trumps any other and competing rights must be fully respected. This pronouncement of Lamer C.J. in *Dagenais* appears to have come back to haunt a justice who has done more than any other judge in the history of Canada to protect rights of accused.[226] Rights can surely only be balanced to a certain point. Where they conflict one right must prevail. The capitulation inherent in the "dialogue with Parliament" utterances seems to have considerably weakened Charter protection of minority rights, which should include rights of accused. In *Mills*, rights of accused were clearly weakened when they came to be balanced against privacy and equality rights of complainants in sexual assault cases. This raises the broader issue: what rights should be recognised for alleged victims?

(b) Victims' Rights

It is clear that victims have in the past been ignored and sometimes denigrated by the criminal justice system. Abuses have included unwarranted humiliation on cross-examination, especially in sexual assault trials, the trauma of endless Court appearances and delays often without proper explanation, and no consideration in sentencing of the impact of the offence on the victim. Clearly, victims have a right to be treated with respect. That they have not may in large part contribute to what Professor Alan Young has described as a "pronounced legitimacy crisis in the administration of justice".[227] Legislative changes to better protect interests of victims have included rape shield laws, greater restitution provisions, fine surcharge programs to support victim services, provisions for bans on publicity of the identity of victims, written victim impact statements on sentencing and victim input into parole decisions.

Madam Justice L'Heureux-Dubé for the Court in *L.(D.O.)* (1993)[228] (upholding the Criminal Code provision for videotaped statements of young complainants in sexual assault cases) and *Levogiannis* (1993)[229] (rejecting Charter challenges against the provision for young complainants in sexual abuse cases testifying behind a screen) balanced s. 7 rights of accused against the interests of victims. However in *L.D.O.*, seven justices through Chief Justice Lamer would only concur in the result. The reason for the separate judgment is ambiguous except that it is clear that the majority refused to accept L'Heureux-Dubé J.'s assessment that there was an issue of gender power imbalance that was an important part of the context. The Court has, however, on several occasions, considered Charter interests of victims when deciding whether a violation of an accused's Charter right can be demonstrably justified under s. 1, as it did in

---

[224] Above note 32.
[225] This is here more fully discussed in Chapter 2.
[226] See Stuart, "Chief Justice Tony Lamer: An Extraordinary Judicial Record of Reform of the Canadian Criminal Justice System", (2000) 5 *Can. Crim. L. Rev.* 51.
[227] "Two Scales of Justice: A Reply", (1993) 35 *Crim. L.Q.* 355.
[228] (1993), 25 C.R. (4th) 285 (S.C.C.).
[229] (1993), 25 C.R. (4th) 325 (S.C.C.).

rejecting Charter attacks on hate propaganda laws[231] and on obscenity provisions.[231]

Although there are often now calls to recognize new legal and constitutional rights for victims and complaints that accused have too many rights, there is room for considerable caution and concern. Thus far the court has avoided recognizing general Charter rights for victims. This is as it should be. A criminal trial is about determining guilt and just punishment of accused, not about personal redress for victims. What, for example, if the input of victims were to be determinative on the issue of sentence? It surely would be unjust to have the length of a prison sentence determined by whether the victim wants revenge or compassion? It seems clear that a general right of representation of victims at trial, even on the determination of guilt, would hopelessly burden and confuse an already overtaxed and under-resourced criminal justice system.

(c) Privacy and Equality Rights for Complainants in Sexual Assault Cases

An increasingly influential perspective on criminal law emanates from those who persuasively suggest that male values have predominated too long in the definition of criminal law at the legislative, judicial and enforcement stages.

In 1993, for example, a coalition of Women's Groups had a dominant influence over the passage of Bill C-49,[232] which changed the substantive law of consent and mistaken belief in the sexual assault context and further protected complainants against cross-examination as to prior sexual history. In 1995, the pattern repeated itself in the Minister of Justice, Allan Rock's Bill C-72 "in your face response" to a Charter ruling that extreme intoxication had to be recognized as a defence to specific intent crimes, including sexual assault[233] and his June 1996 Bill in response to *O'Connor*.

Strong support for taking feminist perspectives into account came in a Osgoode Hall law school speech by Madam Justice Wilson:

> In some . . . areas of the law . . . I think that a distinctly male perspective is clearly discernible and has resulted in legal principles that are not fundamentally sound and should be revisited as and when the opportunity presents itself. Canadian feminist scholarship has, in my view, done an excellent job of identifying those areas and making suggestions for reform. Some aspects of the criminal law in particular cry out for change since they are based on presuppositions about the nature of women and women's sexuality that in this day and age are little short of ludicrous.[234]

In both Bills C-49 and C-72 and in the 1996 *O'Connor* bill, Parliament invokes in aid in preambles equality rights of women and children. Feminist

---

[230] *Keegstra*, above note 194.
[231] *Butler* (1992), 11 C.R. (4th) 137 (S.C.C.).
[232] Discussed below Chapter 3.
[233] *Daviault*, discussed below Chapter 2.
[234] "Will Women Judges Really Make a Difference?" (1990), 28 *Osgoode Hall L.J.* 507.

commentators voiced increasing frustration at the courts for not recognizing equality rights for victims.[235]

Constitutional rights for complainants in sexual assault cases were recognized for the first time in *O'Connor* (1996)[236] in the form of privacy rights under ss. 7 and 8. The Court was unanimous on this point. However we have seen that a 5-4 majority would not even address the possibility of equality rights under s. 15, although the issue had been fully argued.

Recognition of equality rights for sexual assault complainants came with a revised composition of the Court in *Mills* (2000).[237] When it came to establish a s. 15 right to equality, the Court proceeded by mere assertion. Apart from an earlier reference to Parliament's preamble seeking to protect asserted s. 15 rights of women and children, the following is the Court's complete analysis of why such a right should be recognized:

> Equality concerns must also inform the contextual circumstances in which the rights of full answer and defence and privacy will come into play. In this respect, an appreciation of myths and stereotypes in the context of sexual violence is essential to delineate properly the boundaries of full answer and defence. . . .[The] right to make full answer and defence does not include the right to information that would only distort the truth-seeking goal of the trial process. In *R. v. Osolin*, [1993] 4 S.C.R. 595 (S.C.C.), Cory J., for the majority on this issue, stated, at pp. 669 and 670:
>
> > The provisions of ss. 15 and 28 of the *Charter* guaranteeing equality to men and women, although not determinative should be taken into account in determining the reasonable limitations that should be placed upon the cross-examination of a complainant. . . . A complainant should not be unduly harassed and pilloried to the extent of becoming a victim of an insensitive judicial system.
> >
> > . . .
> >
> > The reasons in *Seaboyer* make it clear that eliciting evidence from a complainant for the purpose of encouraging inferences pertaining to consent or the credibility of rape victims which are based on groundless myths and fantasized stereotypes is improper.[238]

Particularly stunning is the lack of any reference to the ten-part test for judging section 15 claims established in *Law* v. *Canada (Minister of Employment & Immigration)*[239] by Iacobucci J. for a unanimous Court, as recently as March, 1999. The Court in *Law* set out to describe basic principles under which courts are to analyze claims of discrimination under s. 15. The essence of the *Law* test

---

[235] One of the strongest criticisms of this aspect of *O'Connor* is Marilyn T. MacCrimmon, "Trial by Ordeal" (1996), 1 *Can.Crim.L.R.* 31. See generally, Christine Boyle, "The Role of Equality in Criminal Law" (1994), 58 *Sask. L. Rev.* 203 and John McInnes and Christine Boyle, "Judging Sexual Assault Law Against a Standard of Equality" (1995), 29 *U.B.C. L. Rev.* 341.

[236] Above note 31.

[237] Above note 32. See too *Darrach* (2000), 36 C.R. (5th) 223 (S.C.C.) (tape shield provisions), discussed below Chapter 2, under "Fair Rules of Evidence".

[238] Para. 48. There is also an enigmatic remark that "Parliament may also be understood to be recognizing "horizontal" equality concerns, where women's inequality results from the acts of other individuals and groups rather than the state, but which nonetheless may have many consequences for the criminal justice system" (para. 59).

[239] [1999] 1 S.C.R. 497.

is that there is in fact no Charter guarantee of equality *per se*. The guarantee is against discrimination within the meaning of s. 15. This is set out in part three of *Law* as follows:

> (3) Accordingly, a court that is called upon to determine a discrimination claim under s. 15(1) should make the following three broad inquiries:
>
> A. Does the impugned law (a) draw a formal distinctionbetween the claimant and others on the basis of one or more personal characteristics, or (b) fail to take into account the claimant's already disadvantaged position within Canadian society resulting in substantively differential treatment between the claimant and others on the basis of one or more personal characteristics?
>
> B. Is the claimant subject to differential treatment based on one or more enumerated and analogous grounds?
>
> and
>
> C. Does the differential treatment discriminate, by imposing a burden upon or withholding a benefit from the claimant in a manner which reflects the stereotypical application of presumed group or personal characteristics, or which otherwise has the effect of perpetuating or promoting the view that the individual is less capable or worthy of recognition or value as a human being or as a member of Canadian society, equally deserving of concern, respect, and consideration?[240]

The Court in *Law* also requires careful identification of "one or more relevant comparators", discrimination on an enumerated or analogous ground and a consideration of context.[241]

Why then did the Court in *Mills* not apply any of this careful analysis? In *Law*, Iacobucci J. did indicate that they were guidelines for analysis and not to be interpreted as a rigid test. He certainly didn't suggest they could be ignored. It would clearly be an error of law for lower courts to do so.

Is the comparator group in *Mills* all other victims of crime or is it male victims of sexual assault? It surely couldn't be the accused, given that the context is a criminal trial where the issue is punishment rather than compensation. Is the violation discrimination by gender or age or is it an analogous ground because complainants in sexual assault cases have been discriminated against through myths and stereotypical views?

It would appear that the Court just adopted the political equality polemic of the day, as do politicians of all stripes. The Supreme Court should proceed by orderly development of principle, rather than by rhetoric. Its sole reliance for authority on a line of Cory J.'s judgment in *Osolin* is ironic because that was a controversial case where the majority ordered a new trial to allow an intrusive cross-examination of a complainant based on a medical record.

The implications of an enforceable s. 15 claim for complainants in sexual assault cases is left unexplored. The policy issues are far wider than establishing rights for protection of therapeutic and other records of complainants. Can

---

[240] Para. 88.
[241] *Ibid.*, in points (2)B, 6 and 7.

complainants now seek status to be represented throughout a sexual assault trial? How about rights to cross-examine the accused, to challenge the similar fact evidence rule or to reverse the presumption of innocence?

The unfortunate reality is that all this uncertainty was quite unnecessary. Everyone, including the majority in *O'Connor*, accepts that complainants have privacy rights to be considered. The Court in *Mills* explores these at length and most persuasively. By the time it has completed that analysis, the Court has precious little to add by way of policy considerations under the head of equality.

That the judgment is reeking with politics is clear with the Court's remark that the accused is not permitted to "whack the complainant" through the use of stereotypes regarding victims of sexual assault. The Court does not provide the explanation for that controversial and denigrating phrase. It was used by an Ottawa defence counsel, Michael Edelson, at a meeting of defence counsel on strategies to prepare for preliminary inquiries. Since its publication[242] the comment has been referred to by Professor Elizabeth Sheehy[243] in a report recommending, in the best interests of women, the abolition of preliminary inquiries for sexual and wife assault cases. The same author, however, seeks the retention of preliminaries for women accused of serious crimes in the interests of justice!

It remains to be seen how these new s. 15 rights will be interpreted. While criminal law should be sensitive to issues of gender and race, this foray into the web of uncertain s. 15 jurisprudence seems unprincipled and unfortunate. It will likely bring a new range of complexity, subtlety and diminishment to the fundamental rights of accused the Court has been at such pains to develop since the Charter was proclaimed.

9. CONSTITUTIONAL NOTICE

Where a Charter challenge involves an attack on the constitutional validity or applicability of a law, the applicant must comply with statutory notices to be given to the Attorneys General of Canada and/or the Province.[244] The provincial notice requirements vary. For example, Ontario only requires notice for constitutional attacks on legislation, British Columbia whenever a constitutional issue is raised, while Manitoba excludes motions to exclude evidence under s. 24(2). There is also variation as to the prescribed consequences for non-

---

[242] *The Lawyers Weekly*, May 27, 1988, p.22. Mr. Edelson is quoted by the reporter, Cristin Schmitz, as having advised other defence counsel on how to "slice and dice" complainants:

"You have to go in there as defence counsel and whack the complainant hard at the preliminary.... and you've got to attack the complainant with all you've got so that he or she will say I'm not coming back in front of 12 good citizens to repeat this bullshit story that I have just told that judge".

[243] *Preliminary Inquiries: Gender Analysis* (1994), a report prepared for Status of Women Canada.

[244] See, for example, Rule 32 of the Supreme Court; Courts of Justice Act, S.O. 1984, c. 11 s. 22; British Columbia Constitutional Questions Act, R.S.B.C. 1979, c. 63, s. 8(2) and Constitutional Questions Act, S.M. 1986-87, c. 31 s. 7(2). See generally B.L. Strayer, *The Canadian Constitution and the Courts*, 3rd ed. (1988) pp. 73-86 and Dale Gibson, *The Law of the Charter: General Principles* (1986) pp. 275-278.

compliance. In some cases,[245] courts have refused to adjourn pending such notices and have simply refused to hear the Charter claim. Provincial notices have been held to be constitutionally within the provincial power over the administration of justice under s. 92(14) of the Constitution Act of 1867.[246]

10. ONUS AND STANDARD OF PROOF

It has always been clear that there is some onus on an accused applying for a Charter remedy. Some early authority saw the burden as merely evidentiary rather than a burden of proof. There were references to "the person who establishes that, *prima facie*, his freedom has been infringed or denied"[247] to the accused having to raise the Charter issue on cross-examination or call evidence,[248] or the "practical obligation to adduce sufficient evidence to put the complaint into issue: enough to invest it with an air of reality."[249]

However, Mr. Justice Lamer, for the Supreme Court of Canada in *Collins* (1987),[250] decided, by mere assertion, that the accused not only has the burden of presenting evidence but must also prove the violation on the civil standard of a balance of probability:

> The appellant, in my view, bears the burden of persuading the court that her Charter rights or freedoms have been infringed or denied. That appears from the wording of s. 24(1) and (2), and most courts which have considered the issue have come to that conclusion . . . The appellant also bears the initial burden of presenting evidence. The standard of persuasion required is only the civil standard of the balance of probabilities and, because of this, the allocation of the burden means only that, in a case where the evidence does not establish whether or not the appellant's rights were infringed, the court must conclude that they were not.[251]

In *Cobham* (1994),[252] Chief Justice Lamer observed that although the accused had the burden, this

> does not mean that the [accused] must formally prove every single fact upon which his or her claim of a violation is based, including one which is not in dispute between the parties and is (or should be) common knowledge amongst members of the criminal bar and those on the bench.[253]

In *Cobham*, judicial notice was taken of the broad parameters of duty counsel and legal aid services in the region.

---

[245] See, for example *M. (R.E.D.) v. Director of Child Welfare*, [1988] 6 W.W.R. 661 at 666 (Alta. C.A.).

[246] See, most recently, *McGillivary v. Manitoba* (1989), 51 C.C.C. (3d) 60 (Man. Q.B.).

[247] *Southam Inc.* (1983), 34 C.R. (3d) 27 (Ont. C.A.). See too Morris Manning, *Rights, Freedoms and The Courts* (1983) p. 487.

[248] *Cox* (1983), 37 C.R. (3d) 38 (Ont. Dist. Ct.).

[249] *Roach* (1985), 49 C.R. (3d) 237 at 240 (Alta. C.A.). The Court left the question open.

[250] Above note 195.

[251] *Ibid.*, at 205.

[252] (1994), 33 C.R. (4th) 73 (S.C.C.).

[253] At 81.

The Supreme Court now recognizes only two situations where the Crown must disprove an alleged Charter violation: where the issue is one of waiver,[254] and in the case of the presumption that a warrantless search is contrary to s. 8 of the Charter.[255] In the case of elements of delay under s. 11(*b*), the Court now only recognises that evidentiary burdens may shift to the Crown.[256]

We have seen[257] that where it has been established that a law violates the Charter, any party seeking to uphold the limitation as a demonstrably justified reasonable limit under s. 1 bears the burden of proof to a very high degree of probability.

Given that the accused has the burden of establishing a Charter violation, it follows that the accused also bears the burden of justifying a remedy under s. 24 or s. 52. This is indeed express in the case of s. 24(2), as confirmed by Mr. Justice Lamer in *Collins*:

> [T]he use of the phrase "if it is established that" places the burden of persuasion on the applicant, for it is the position which he maintains which must be established. Again, the standard of persuasion required can only be the civil standard of the balance of probabilities. Thus the applicant must make it more probable than not that the admission of the evidence would bring the administration of justice into disrepute.[258]

11. ESTABLISHING FACTS

The adversary process and rules of evidence followed on a daily basis in our criminal courts are primarily suited to finding what has become known as "adjudicative" facts concerning the immediate parties — "who did what, where, when, how, and with what motive or intent."[259] They are far less suited to the ascertainment of more general "legislative facts" which are "facts which inform . . . legislative judgment."[260] Some Charter inquiries, such as that into the purpose or effect of a law or the balancing of social policy necessitated when the issue is one of justification under s. 1 of the Charter, clearly call for new types of advocacy with wider social sources.

---

[254] See, for example, *Leclair* (1989), 67 C.R. (3d) 209 at 219 (S.C.C.).

[255] See below, Chapter 3. There were signs of second thoughts. In *Collins*, Lamer J. holds that, if there was no warrant for a search, the "burden of persuasion" shifts to the Crown to show that the search was, "on a balance of probabilities, reasonable" (at 206). In Lamer J.'s concurring judgment in *Dyment* (1988), 66 C.R. (3d) 348 (S.C.C.) [P.E.I.], this becomes "As it was a warrantless seizure, the *evidentiary burden* of establishing that it was nevertheless a lawful seizure rested upon the shoulders of the Crown" (at 353) (emphasis added). However, in *Mack* (1989), 67 C.R. (3d) 1 (S.C.C.), the Court through Lamer J. held that an accused had the burden of proving entrapment on a balance of probability, noting that it was not dependent on culpability and consistent with the onus in the case of the Charter. See below, Chapter 6.

[256] *Morin* (1992), 12 C.R. (4th) 1 (S.C.C.), discussed below Chapter 6.

[257] Above note 65.

[258] Above note 195, at 209. For discussion of the practical implications of these burdens for Crown and defence counsel see Gerard F. Mitchell, "Trial Counsel and the Facts on s. 24(2) Applications" (1990), 76 C.R. (3d) 304.

[259] K.C. Davis, "Judicial Notice" (1955), 55 *Col. L. Rev.* 945.

[260] *Ibid.*

In *Oakes* (1986),[261] Chief Justice Dickson saw the s. 1 inquiry as follows:

> Where evidence is required in order to prove the constituent elements of a s. 1 inquiry, and this will generally be the case, it should be cogent and persuasive and make clear to the court the consequences of imposing or not imposing the limit. . . . A Court will also need to know what alternative measures for implementing the objective were available to the legislators when they made their decisions. I should add, however, that there may be cases where certain elements of the s. 1 analysis are obvious or selfevident.[262]

Since that date the Supreme Court of Canada has routinely admitted and relied on a wide variety of extrinsic materials filed in a s. 1 determination.[263] These have included government and commission reports of various types, legislative history, accounts of foreign law, statistics, and all sorts of affidavits. The only resistance has been when there has been a lack of fair notice to the other side.[264]

There is a surprising lack of authority as to the proper procedure for establishing even the adjudicative facts of Charter issues, such as the determination of whether there has been a warrantless search, arbitrary detention or unreasonable delay.[265] At present,[266] the matter is left largely to the discretion of trial judges and practices differ.

The leading decision is that of the Ontario Court of Appeal. In *Kutynac* (1992),[267] Mr. Justice Finlayson for the Court refused to assert a rigid procedure for applications to exclude evidence under s. 24(2) of the Charter. He forcefully rejects the approach of General Division Judge Borins in the Court below, which had sought to mandate pre-trial motions with written notice and preliminary proof by way of affidavit. The Court of Appeal goes out of its way not to hamstring defence counsel and trial judges, pointing to a need for flexibility and discretion, especially in busy Provincial Division courts. The Borins procedure, holds the Court, would impose a "procedural straight-jacket". The Appeal Court's approach will ensure that Charter defences are not pre-empted by procedural technicalities. Procedural issues under the Charter should indeed also be approach purposively.[268]

The Ontario Court of Appeal in *Kutynec* does require "some element of discipline" in s. 24(2) applications. Objections are to be made before or when

---

[261] Above note 64.

[262] *Ibid.*, at 29-30.

[263] See, for example, *Edwards Books*, above note 72.

[264] See survey by Robert C. Maybank, "Proof of Facts Under Section 1 of the Charter" (1990), 77 C.R. (3d) 260. See too Brian G. Morgan, "Proof of Facts in Charter Litigation" in R.J. Sharpe (ed.), *Charter Litigation* (1987) p. 172.

[265] See especially *L. (W.K.)* (1989), 51 C.C.C. (3d) 297 (B.C. C.A.).

[266] J. Sandy Tse, "Charter Remedies. Procedural Issues" (1989), 69 C.R. (3d) 130.

[267] (1992), 12 C.R. (4th) 152 (Ont. C.A.), followed, for example, in *Dwernychuk* (1992), 77 C.C.C. (3d) 385 (Alta. C.A.), *Pelletier* (1995), 38 C.R. (4th) 242 (Sask. C.A.) and *Vukelich* (1996), 108 C.C.C. (3d) 193 (B.C. C.A.).

[268] See too Michael Code, "American Cadillacs or Canadian Compacts: What is the Correct Criminal Procedure for s. 24 Applications Under the Charter of Rights?" (1991), 33 *Crim. L.Q.* 298 but compare Wayne Gorman, "A Review and Analysis of Procedural Issues in Charter Applications Involving Criminal Cases or Matters: Pre-trial, Trial and Post-trial" (1995), 37 *Crim. L.Q.* 154.

evidence is tendered and notice of a Charter issue is normally to be expected plus a summary of proposed defence evidence to be called in support. However, the Court emphasizes throughout the need for flexibility and discretion. This aspect of *Kutynec* must be read subject to a companion decision in *Loveman* (1992),[269] that a trial judge had erred in refusing to hear a s. 8 challenge to breathalyzer evidence at the start of a trial on the basis of lack of notice to the Crown. The penalty for lack of notice was unwarranted and had resulted in a miscarriage of justice. The Court could have heard the entire case before, if necessary, granting a brief adjournment to allow the Crown to prepare a legal response to the Charter argument.

Some trial judges still require a separate *voir dire* for each Charter application. Given the *Collins* onuses on the accused, the accused is made to particularize the challenge and to call evidence to prove the case. Some have taken this as far as requiring defence counsel to call police witnesses and restrict themselves to examination-in-chief.[270] In most cases, the mere calling of the accused will satisfy the initial burden so that this confusion of roles can be avoided. It has been claimed[271] that such a procedure guarantees a full and separate consideration of Charter issues which do not concern guilt, focuses on relevant matters and is fair to the accused since the evidence led, which might prejudice the trial, will not be heard by the jury.

On the other hand, in many trials, Crown counsel are permitted and content to call police officers to describe as part of the narrative basic investigative procedures in issue, thereby allowing defence counsel to lay the evidentiary foundation for a Charter argument through cross-examination. This frequently occurs in the case of what has become known as a "blended" *voir dire* concerning the admissibility of a statement made to a police officer.[272] The same hearing will deal with a challenge based on the right to counsel where the accused bears the onus and also with the common law voluntary confession rule, where the Crown has to prove that the statement was voluntary beyond a reasonable doubt.[273] This practical and more flexible arrangement, which seems for more in keeping with *Kutynec*, clearly works better where there are proper relationships of openness and trust between counsel who respect their roles. This would not be so where the defence counsel acts as street fighter, indiscriminately impugning the integrity of police officers and prosecutors, and/or where the Crown Attorney performs as

---

[269] (1992), 12 C.R. (4th) 167 (Ont. C.A.), applied in *Loewen* (1997), 122 C.C.C. (3d) 198 (Man. C.A.), additional reasons at (1998), 122 C.C.C. (3d) 198 at 212 (Man. C.A.) (trial judge erring in refusing to hear s. 11 (b) motion on basis Crown only given notice 5 days before trial). See, however, Hill J. in *Kovac* (1998), 17 C.R. (5th) 203 (Ont. Gen. Div.) (Charter application not properly considered in an impaired driving trial where defence not giving notice of application to exclude evidence on an alleged s. 8 breach until the defence submission).

[270] This procedure was rejected by Kolenick J. in *Checkosis* (1999), 35 C.R. (5th) 44 (Sask. P.C.) on the basis that fairness of criminal proceedings, as well as public confidence in the administration of justice, are best served by the Crown first leading its evidence on the charge.

[271] Tse, above note 266, at 133.

[272] This procedure was approved in *Robertshaw* (1996), 49 C.R. (4th) 245 (Ont. Gen. Div.).

[273] See, for example, *Hobbins*, [1982] 1 S.C.R. 553.

partisan persecutor rather than a "Minister of Justice" in the best Anglo/Canadian tradition.[274]

---

[274] *Boucher*, [1955] S.C.R. 16.

2

Section 7: Right to Life, Liberty and Security of Person and Guarantee of Principles of Fundamental Justice

Under s. 7 of the Charter

Everyone has the right to life, liberty and security of the person and the right not to be deprived thereof except in accordance with the principles of fundamental justice.

The Supreme Court of Canada has interpreted s. 7 broadly such that it is now clear that it includes the review of the substance of legislation and guarantees far more than procedural fairness. Section 7 has become the most powerful vehicle for the establishment of new protections for the accused in the criminal law. The scope of s. 7 protection is still highly controversial and uncertain. Before assessing specific applications in a variety of contexts, general interpretations need to be addressed.

1. RESIDUAL RIGHT

Section 7 is the first of the "Legal Rights" to be found in ss. 7 to 14 of the Charter. Section 7 could be read to establish two separate sets of rights: (1) the right to life, liberty and security of the person and (2) the right not to be deprived thereof except in accordance with principles of fundamental justice. The Supreme Court, however, adopted the interpretation that the right to life, liberty and security is merely declaratory. It read s. 7 conjunctively to confer the right not to be deprived of life, liberty or security of the person except in accordance with principles of fundamental justice. The section was also held to be a residual right in the sense that the rights guaranteed in ss. 8 to 14 are specific examples of the broader principles of fundamental justice.

The leading judgment is that of Justice Lamer in the *Motor Vehicle Reference* (1985):[1]

> The term "principles of fundamental justice" is not a right, but a qualifier of the right not to be deprived of life, liberty and security of the person; its function is to set the parameters of that right.
>
> Sections 8 to 14 address specific deprivations of the "right" to life, liberty and security of the person in breach of the principles of fundamental justice, and as such, violations of s. 7. They are therefore illustrative of the meaning, in criminal or penal law, of "principles of fundamental justice"; they represent principles which have been recognized by the common law, the international conventions and by the very fact of entrenchment in the Charter, as essential elements of a system for the administration of justice which is founded upon a belief in the dignity and worth of the human person and the rule of law.
>
> Consequently, the principles of fundamental justice are to be found in the basic tenets and principles, not only of our judicial process, but also of the other components of our legal system.[2]

Even where the subject matter of the Charter challenge would appear to have been covered by one of the specific protections in ss. 8 to 14, it is now quite clear that an alternative argument can be tried under s. 7.

The strongest authority is the unanimous decision of the Supreme Court of Canada in *Hebert* (1990).[3] The Court ruled that a pre-trial right to silence is a principle of fundamental justice protected under s. 7 even though protection against self-crimination was expressly declared in s. 11(c) (protecting the accused against being compelled to testify) and s. 13 (protecting a witness from being incriminated by evidence used in another proceeding). *Hebert* is consistent with an earlier ruling in *Thomson Newspapers Ltd.* (1990),[4] which concerned a challenge to a power under the Combines Investigation Act[5] to compel testimony under oath. Although there was no majority as to whether s. 7 had been violated,[6] each of the five separate judgments recognized that s. 7 could provide wider protection against self-incrimination than afforded in ss. 11(c) and 13.[7]

Despite these dicta, it seems likely that, as in *Thomson* although not *Hebert*, courts will be reluctant to accept a submission that there has been a s. 7 violation when the matter appears to be covered by one of the other more specific sections.

---

[1] (1985), 48 C.R. (3d) 289 (S.C.C.).

[2] *Ibid.*, at 317. Dickson C.J.C., Beetz, Chouinard and Le Dain JJ. concurred. A different analysis of s. 7 in the concurring judgment of Wilson J. has not prevailed. See annotation by John D. Whyte, C.R. *ibid.*, p. 295. In *Rose* (1998), 20 C.R. (5th) 246 (S.C.C.) Cory J. confirmed for the majority that all the legal principles must be informed in their interpretation and application by the principles of fundamental justice (at 284).

[3] (1990), 77 C.R. (3d) 145 (S.C.C.).

[4] (1990), 76 C.R. (3d) 129 (S.C.C.). See too *Lyons* (1987), 61 C.R. (3d) 1 at 42 (S.C.C.) (respecting the right to a jury).

[5] R.S.C. 1970, c. C-23 [now the Competition Act, R.S.C. 1985, c. C-34].

[6] Wilson and Sopinka JJ. found that s. 7 had been violated. La Forest and L'Heureux-Dubé JJ. upheld s. 17. Lamer J. would not rule on the s. 7 issue. See below, Chapter 8.

[7] La Forest J. added, however, that "this court has indicated a preference for dealing with Charter issues in relation to specific provisions rather than under s. 7 where this is possible" (above note 4, at 220). See further *Dehghani v. Canada (Minister of Employment and Immigration)* (1993), 20 C.R. (4th) 34 (S.C.C.) at 52.

2. EVERYONE

In *Irwin Toy Ltd.* (1989),[8] a company brought a civil action for a declaration that provincial statutory provisions prohibiting advertising directed at children were unconstitutional. Chief Justice Dickson for a unanimous panel of five justices[9] held that a corporation could not avail itself of the protection of s. 7 since "everyone" in this context meant human beings.

> A plain, common sense reading of the phrase "Everyone has the right to life, liberty and security of the person" serves to underlie the human element involved; only human beings can enjoy those rights. "Everyone" then, must be read in light of the rest of the section and defined to exclude corporations and other artificial entities incapable of enjoying life, liberty or security of the person, and include only human beings.[10]

The Court, however, distinguished the situation of *Big M Drug Mart Ltd.* on the basis that this was a civil action for declaratory relief and there were no penal proceedings pending.[11] It will be recalled[12] that in *Big M Drug Mart* the Supreme Court unanimously decided that an accused, whether corporate or individual, could defend a criminal charge by arguing that the law under which the charge had been brought was constitutionally invalid and inoperative under s. 52.

Both before[13] and after[14] *Irwin Toy*, the Ontario Court of Appeal has confirmed that a corporation charged with an offence can defend on the basis that the offence is an unconstitutional violation of s. 7. On the other hand, the British Columbia Court of Appeal[15] has applied *Irwin Toy* to deny a corporation charged with an offence the protection of s. 7. That Court unconvincingly distinguished *Big M Drug Mart* on the basis that the status of the accused was in issue and that a corporation could not be subject to imprisonment.

The Saskatchewan Court of Appeal has ruled that a foetus is not included within "everyone" in s. 7 for purposes of challenging the Criminal Code provisions respecting abortion.[16]

3. LIFE, LIBERTY AND SECURITY OF PERSON

To establish a violation of s. 7, it must be shown that the right to life, liberty or security of the person has been violated. Although these concepts are seen to

---

[8] [1989] 1 S.C.R. 927.

[9] Beetz, McIntyre. Lamer and Wilson JJ. agreed on this point.

[10] Above note 8, at 1004. In contrast, "everyone" under s. 8 includes a corporation: *Hunter v. Southam Inc.*, discussed below, Chapter 3.

[11] *Ibid.*

[12] Above, Chapter 1

[13] *Metro News Ltd.* (1986), 53 C.R. (3d) 289 (Ont. CA.).

[14] *Wholesale Travel Group Inc.* (1989), 73 C.R. (3d) 320 at 335 (Ont. C.A.). See too *Ellis-Don Ltd.* (1990), 2 C.R. (4th) 118 (Ont. C.A.).

[15] *Quest Vitamin Supplies Ltd.* (1989), 73 C.R. (3d) 347 (B.C. C.A.).

[16] *Borowski v. Canada (A.G.)* (1987), 59 C.R. (3d) 223 (Sask. C.A.). The Court also held that a foetus could not claim the equality protection of "every individual" in s. 15. The Supreme Court later refused to hear the appeal on the basis it was moot, as the Supreme Court had earlier declared the abortion laws in question to be unconstitutional. See too *Demers* (1999), 137 C.C.C. (3d) 297 (B.C. S.C.) (protestors outside abortion clinic not able to assert rights of unborn when charged with sidewalk interference).

be closely linked, it is clear that it is not necessary to show a violation of each right.[17]

In the context of the criminal law, there will usually be no difficulty in grounding a s. 7 challenge by pointing to a threat to the liberty interest.[18] This is particularly because of the majority ruling of Mr. Justice Lamer in the *Motor Vehicle Reference* (1985),[19] that the right to liberty will be violated by a mere potential of imprisonment:

> Obviously, imprisonment (including probation orders) deprives persons of their liberty. An offence has that potential as of the moment it is open to the judge to impose imprisonment. There is no need that imprisonment . . . be made mandatory.[20]

The issue was the constitutionality of a provincial offence of driving a vehicle while prohibited from driving which carried a mandatory penalty of seven days "imprisonment".[21] Although not necessary for the decision, the majority of the Court[22] clearly went out of its way, by its reference to probation orders and situations where there was no mandatory prison sentence, to extend the scope of liberty interest protected. The Court even left open the question whether the possibility of imprisonment as an alternative to the non-payment of a fine would also violate the liberty interest.[23]

Since the *Motor Vehicle Act Reference*, provincial Courts of Appeal have held that the possibility of imprisonment in default of payment of a fine, even in the case of provincial offences, threatens the liberty interest such that s. 7 can be relied on for protection. For example, Mr. Justice Wakeling, for the majority of the Saskatchewan Court of Appeal in *Burt* (1987),[24] reasoned persuasively as follows:

> With reference to the application of s. 7, is there a basis to distinguish a sentence which is restricted to payment of a fine, with imprisonment for non-payment, from one where the sentence is for imprisonment in the first instance? To the person in prison, it is of little consequence to have it said that the original sentence only required payment of a fine and he is in jail because of his failure to do so. The

---

[17] *Singh v. Minister of Employment and Immigration*, [1985] 1 S.C.R. 177; *Thomson Newspapers*, above note 4, per Wilson J. at 13-14.

[18] The Quebec Court of Appeal however rejected a broad s. 7 challenge to the prohibition of marihuana possession and cultivation on the basis that the liberty interest was not engaged, *Hamon* (1993), 85 C.C.C. (3d) 490 (Que. C.A.).

[19] Above note 1.

[20] *Ibid.*, at 319.

[21] The ruling is further discussed in the next two sections.

[22] In her minority concurring judgment, Wilson J. observed: "Indeed, all regulatory offences impose some restriction on liberty broadly construed. But I think it will trivialize the Charter to sweep all those offences into s. 7 as violations of the right to life. liberty and security of the person even if they can be sustained under s. 1." (Above note 1, at 326). It is extremely difficult to understand why the prosecution of any so-called regulatory offences should proceed without the guarantee of principles of fundamental justice. The view of the majority seems preferable: see too Lee Stuesser, "Convicting the Innocent Owner: Vicarious Liability under Highway Traffic Legislation" (1989), 67 C.R. (3d) 316 at 321-322 and see further, below, under Fault.

[23] *Ibid.*, at 319.

[24] (1987), 60 C.R. (3d) 372 (Sask. C.A.). Cameron J.A. concurred. See too *Pellerin* (1989), 67 C.R. (3d) 305 (Ont. C.A.).

prisoner will surely be convinced that he is in jail because he was found guilty of the original offence and will be inclined to accuse judges and lawyers who say otherwise of exercising their legal skills to distinguish where no real difference exists.[25]

In his concurring judgment, Chief Justice Bayda held that a ''potential'' for imprisonment meant ''nothing more than a possibility which could develop into an actuality''[26] and pointed to statistics showing that imprisonment in a provincial institution for default in payment of a fine is common.[27]

In *Gray* (1988),[28] the Manitoba Court of appeal determined that the prospect of an accused being jailed for non-payment of a fine in that province was remote, given the province's fine option program of community work. Nevertheless, the Court held that there was a potential for imprisonment such that s. 7 was engaged. The Court did later rule that whether the potential for imprisonment was strong or weak was crucial to the determination of whether the violation could be demonstrably justified under s. 1 as a reasonable limit.

In *Pontes* (1995),[29] the Supreme Court appears to take it as already decided that the possibility of imprisonment in default of payment of a fine also threatens the liberty interest such as to engage s. 7 protection.

The Supreme Court of Canada has not yet pronounced on the question of whether temporary intrusions by the state on the rights of motorists to use the highways violate the interests protected by s. 7. The B.C. Court of Appeal held in *Robson* (1985)[30] that a 24-hour roadside licence suspension on mere suspicion that the motorist had consumed alcohol, without notice of hearing, was a deprivation of liberty not in accordance with s. 7 nor demonstrably justified under s. 1 The Court relied on American authority and held that a licensed motorist had the right to use his ability to drive.[31] While not every interference with freedom of action and movement would be a deprivation of liberty, this deprivation was not insignificant.[32]

On the other hand, the Alberta Court of Appeal in *Neale* (1986)[33] held that a similar provincial provision for suspension of driving privileges on the suspicion of alcohol impairment did not violate s. 7 as it had no effect on liberty. Although s. 7 protected the right of free movement of persons, this did not apply to motorists:

---

[25] *Ibid.*, at 390-391.

[26] *Ibid.*, at 377.

[27] Cited was the data provided by Keith Jobson and Andrew Atkins, ''Imprisonment for Default and Fundamental Justice'' (1986), 28 *Crim. L.Q.* 251:

> Such imprisonment accounts for the largest group of prisoners admitted to local prisons, ranging from 14% in British Columbia in 1983 to 32% in Ontario and 48% in Quebec.

Chief Justice Bayda reported the 1986-87 Saskatchewan figure as 44% for females and 32% for males.

[28] (1988), 66 C.R. (3d) 378 (Man. C.A.).

[29] (1995), 41 C.R. (4th) 201 (S.C.C.), discussed below note 124.

[30] (1985), 45 C.R. (3d) 68 (B.C. C.A.). The provision was amended and later held to be demonstrably justified: *Sengara* (1988), 42 C.C.C. (3d) 234 (B.C. S.C.).

[31] *Ibid.*, at 71. per Nemetz C.J.B.C. (Taggart J.A. concurring).

[32] *Ibid.*, at 76, per Esson J.A. (Taggart J.A. concurring).

[33] (1986), 52 C.R. (3d) 376 (Alta. C.A.).

> While one can speak of the liberty to operate a motor vehicle, we agree with Le Dain J., speaking for the majority in *Dedman v. R.*, [1985] 2 S.C.R. 2 . . . that the right to circulate in a motor vehicle on a public highway "is not a fundamental liberty like the ordinary right of movement of the individual, but a licensed activity that is subject to regulation and control for the protection of life and property". The ordinary right of movement is protected, but circulation in a motor vehicle is not.[34]

The overwhelming trend at the Court of Appeal level now favours the *Neale* view in rejecting challenges to administrative driver's licence suspension programmes. The Ontario Court of Appeal is of the view that applying the Charter to such citizen inconvenience would trivialise it.[35]

The 5th and 14th amendments in the American Bill of Rights provide that no person shall be deprived "of life, liberty or property, without due process of law."[36] In *Irwin Toy Ltd.*,[37] the Supreme Court held that economic rights generally included in the term "property" were not included within s. 7. Although going on to hold that "corporate commercial economic rights" were not included, the Court did specifically leave open the question of whether some economic rights "fundamental to human life or survival" could nevertheless fall within "security of the person."[38]

The right to "security of the person" was fully considered by the Supreme Court in its complex decision in *Morgentaler* (1988).[39] The Court, by a majority of five to two,[40] struck down the Criminal Code abortion provisions. Each of the majority judges found a violation of a woman's right to security of the person which was not in accordance with principles of fundamental justice and could not be justified under s. 1.

Chief Justice Dickson[41] concluded that

> state interference with bodily integrity and serious state-imposed psychological stress, at least in the criminal law context, constitutes a breach of security of the person. It is not necessary in this case to determine whether the right extends further,

---

[34] *Ibid.*, at 387-388. See similarly *Werhun* (1991), 62 C.C.C. (3d) 440 (Man. C.A.). This view seems likely to be accepted by the Supreme Court given its ready justification of arbitrary vehicle stops. See below, Chapter 4. In *Ladouceur* (1990), 77 C.R. (3d) 110 (S.C.C.), the s. 7 issue was, however, expressly left open. Provincial legislation requiring motorcyclists to wear helmets and seatbelt have been held not to violate s. 7 interests: see, respectively, *Fisher* (1985), 49 C.R. (3d) 222 (Man. Q.B.) and *Maier* (1989), 52 C.C.C. (3d) 419 (Alta. C.A.).

[35] *Horsefield v. Ontario (Registrar of Motor Vehicles)* (1999), 134 C.C.C. (3d) 161 (Ont. C.A.) at 182. *Horsefield* provides a full review of the case law.

[36] The 5th amendment was passed in 1791 and applied to state laws by the 14th amendment in 1868.

[37] Above note 8.

[38] *Ibid.*, at 1003-1004. In the *Prostitution Reference* (1990), 77 C.R. (3d) 1 (S.C.C.), Mr. Justice Lamer, speaking only for himself, held that the "rights to liberty and security of the person included in s. 7 of the Charter do not encompass the right to exercise a chosen profession." The majority through Dickson C.J. held that this was not the appropriate case for deciding whether s. 7 interests "could *ever* apply to any interest with an economic commercial or property component" (at 17). Compare M. David Lepofsky, "Section 7 — A Problematic Foray into Legislative Policy-Making, Wilson v. B.C. Medical Services Commission" (1988), 68 *Can. Bar Rev.* 615.

[39] (1988), 62 C.R. (3d) 1 (S.C.C.).

[40] McIntyre and La Forest JJ. dissented.

[41] Lamer J. concurred.

to protect either interests central to personal autonomy, such as a right to privacy, or interests unrelated to criminal justice.[42]

Mr. Justice Beetz[43] saw "security of the person" as including a "right of access to medical treatment for a condition representing a danger to life or health without fear of criminal sanction."[44] Madam Justice Wilson[45] agreed that the Criminal Code deprived a pregnant woman of her right to security of the person since this right protected both the physical and psychological integrity of the individual. It was a direct interference with a woman's physical "person" to assert that a woman's capacity to reproduce would be subject, not to her own control, but to that of the State.[46]

In contrast to *Morgentaler*, the Supreme Court was far more cautious in recognizing the interests protected in s. 7 in *Beare* (1988).[47] The Saskatchewan Court of appeal had struck down the procedure under the Identification of Criminals Act[48] for compelling fingerprinting of persons charged but not convicted of indictable offences. The majority had identified the s. 7 interest protected as the dignity and self-respect of the individual. In the course of reversing that decision, Mr. Justice La Forest, for the Supreme Court, found this approach to be "broad and indefinite and to introduce an undesirable notion of differentiation among those subjected to the procedure." He adopted the more specific minority finding in the Court below, that of Mr. Justice Cameron, that the provisions infringed the rights protected by s. 7 because they required the person to "appear at a specific time and place and oblige that person to go through an identification process on pain of imprisonment for failure to comply."[49]

In *Rodriguez* (1993),[50] Sopinka J. for the majority of the Supreme Court[51] saw the judgments in *Morgentaler*

> to encompass a notion of personal autonomy involving, at the very least, control over one's bodily integrity free from state interference and freedom from state-psychological and emotional stress.[52]

The Criminal Code offence of assisting suicide impinged on the applicant's security interest. She was suffering from a terminal disease and wished to control the circumstances, timing and manner of her death. The majority later held the

---

[42] Above note 39, at 20.
[43] Estey J. concurred.
[44] Above note 39, at 46.
[45] Wilson J. also found a violation of the right to liberty in s. 7, which "granted the individual a degree of autonomy in making decisions of fundamental personal importance" (*Ibid.*, at 103).
[46] *Ibid.*, at 109.
[47] (1988), 66 C.R. (3d) 97 (S.C.C.).
[48] R.S.C. 1970, c. I-1 (now R.S.C. 1985, c. I-1).
[49] Above note 47, at 110.
[50] (1993), 24 C.R. (4th) 281 (S.C.C.).
[51] La Forest J., Gonthier J., Iacobucci J., and Major J. concurred. See similarly McLachlin J. (L'Heureux-Dubé J. concurring), dissenting on another issue: "Security of the person has an element of personal autonomy, protecting the dignity and privacy of individuals with respect to decisions concerning their own bodies" (at 318).
[52] At 296.

provision was constitutional since the deprivation was not contrary to principles of fundamental justice[53].

The Supreme Court has not yet fully addressed the extent to which those in custody in prisons or psychiatric institutions can bring themselves within the liberty and security of the person interest protected by s. 7.[54]

The leading pronouncement of the right to security is now that of Chief Justice Lamer for the Supreme Court in *New Brunswick (Minister of Health & Community Services)* v. *G.(J.)* (1999).[55] The Court decided a government application for child custody implicates the right to security of the person such that an indigent parent may be constitutionally entitled to state-funded counsel. Lamer C.J. adopted the following definition of security of the person:

> For a restriction of security of person to be made out... the impugned state action must have a serious and profound effect on a person's psychological integrity. The effects of the state interference must be assessed objectively, with a view to their impact on the psychological integrity of a person of reasonable sensibility. This need not rise to the level of nervous shock or psychiatric illness, but must be greater than ordinary stress or anxiety.[56]

The Ontario Court of Appeal in *Parker* (2000)[57] had no difficulty in applying this definition to hold that a deprivation by criminal sanction of access to medication reasonably required for treatment of a medical condition threatening life or health constituted a deprivation of security of the person. The accused needed marihuana to control epilepsy. The Court has held that s. 7 is applicable to a continuing violation of liberty by reason of parole ineligibility provisions[58] and, in a trilogy of pre-Charter *habeas corpus* cases, has confirmed that prisoners, while denied their absolute liberty, retain residual liberties.[59]

The Federal Court of Appeal has recognized that the liberty interest is threatened, and thus s. 7 applicable, in the case of prison disciplinary hearings, given their potential consequences including loss of remission[60] and also in the case of a forced transfer of a prisoner to a higher security institution as a disciplinary measure.[61] However, a s. 7 challenge to a penitentiary policy of double-bunking two inmates in a cell failed. Although a "residual right to privacy

---

[53] Below note 92.
[54] See generally David Cole and Allan Manson, *Release From Imprisonment* (1990).
[55] (1999), 26 C.R. (5th) 203 (S.C.C.).
[56] Para. 60.
[57] (2000), 146 C.C.C. (3d) 193 (Ont. C.A.). The Court struck down the prohibition of possession of marihuana under the Controlled Drugs and Substances Act: see further below notes 94-102 and Chapters 1 and 11.
[58] *Gamble* (1988), 66 C.R. (3d) 193 (S.C.C.); but compare *Steele v. Mountain Institution* (1990), 80 C.R. (3d) 257 (S.C.C.) — criticized by Allan Manson, "The Effect of Steele on Habeas Corpus and Indeterminate Confinement", C.R. *ibid.*, pp. 282-289.
[59] *Miller*, [1985] 2 S.C.R. 613; *Cardinal v. Director of Kent Institution*, [1985] 2 S.C.R. 643 and *Morin v. National Special Handling Unit Review Committee*, [1985] 2 S.C.R. 662.
[60] *Howard* (1985), 45 C.R. (3d) 242 (Fed. C.A.).
[61] *Gallant v. Canada (Dep. Commr., Pac. Region, Correctional Service Can.)* (1989), 68 C.R. (3d) 173 (Fed. C.A.).

and dignity'' was a ''theoretically tenable position,'' there had been no evidence presented of a ''one-person-one-room'' standard for those living outside prison.[62]

At the level of applications before single judges, it is well accepted that the liberty interest is threatened and s. 7 engaged in revocation and suspension cases of prisoners who have been released. Recognition that s. 7 is applicable to the release granting stage has been ''more problematic.''[63]

4. PRINCIPLES OF FUNDAMENTAL JUSTICE

(a) Substantive Review

In *Latham v. Canada (Solicitor General)* (1984),[64] Mr. Justice Strayer of the Federal Court Trial Division rejected the view that s. 7 required a substantive review of the justice or fairness of laws. It was clear from its legislative history that it was intended to guarantee only procedural justice or fairness and that the potentially broader language of ''due process'' of law was ''obviously deliberately avoided.''[65] This repeated in his judicial capacity views he had expressed as an Assistant Deputy Minister of the Department of Justice to the special joint committee of the Senate and the House of Commons on the Constitution of Canada in 1981:

> Mr. Chairman, it was our belief that the words ''fundamental justice'' would cover the same thing as what is called procedural due process, that is the meaning of due process in relation to requiring fair procedure. However, it in our view does not cover the concept of what is called substantive due process, which would impose substantive requirements as to the policy of the law in question . . . [In the United States] the term due process has been given the broader concept of meaning both the procedure and substance. Natural justice or fundamental justice in our view does not go beyond the procedural requirements of fairness.[66]

When the issue reached Provincial Courts of Appeal, most took the view that s. 7 was limited to procedural review. This was, for example,[67] the first position of the Ontario Court of Appeal in *Potma* (1983),[68] although the Court did recognize the potentiality for further procedural protections:

> This is not to suggest that ''the principles of fundamental justice'' now recognized by the Charter of Rights and Freedoms are immutable. ''Fundamental justice'', like ''natural justice'' or ''fair play'', is a compendious expression intended to guarantee the basic right of citizens in a free and democratic society to a fair procedure. The principles or standards of fairness essential to the attainment of fundamental justice

---

[62] *Piche v. Canada (Solicitor General)* (1989), 47 C.C.C. (3d) 495 (Fed. C.A.).

[63] Cole and Manson, above note 54, at 117. See their detailed analysis of the issue: *ibid.*, pp. 117-123.

[64] (1984), 39 C.R. (3d) 78 (Fed. T.D.).

[65] *Ibid.*, at 93.

[66] *Minutes of Proceedings and Evidence*, 32nd Parliament, 1st Session, January 27, 1981, p. 43:32.

[67] The British Columbia Court of Appeal was at first the only Court of Appeal to accept that s. 7 demanded a review of the substance of legislation: *Motor Vehicle Reference* (1983), 33 C.R. (3d) 22 (B.C. C.A.). *Sed contra Hayden* (1983), 36 C.R. (3d) 187 (Man. C.A.).

[68] (1983), 31 C.R. (3d) 231 (Ont. C.A.).

are in no sense static, and will continue as they have in the past to evolve and develop in response to society's changing perception of what is arbitrary, unfair or unjust.[69]

Later, however, the Ontario Court of Appeal accepted the view of commentators that the language of principles of fundamental justice could not be taken to have precluded substantive review.[70] However, it did seek to impose limits on such substantive review:

> While the limits of such review will evolve as the interpretation of the *Charter* unfolds, it is sufficient to say at this juncture that such substantive review should take place only in exceptional cases where there has been a marked departure from the norm of civil or criminal liability resulting in the infringement of liberty or in some other injustice. We reiterate that the policy and wisdom of legislation should remain first and foremost a matter for Parliament and the legislatures.[71]

The majority of the Supreme Court of Canada in the *Motor Vehicle Reference* (1985)[72] settled that s. 7 *does* include a review of the substance of legislation. The substantive/procedural dichotomy was seen to be too narrow, too bound up with the American distinction between substantive and procedural due process and a difficult distinction to be avoided.[73] The task of the Court was

> ... not to choose between substantive or procedural content per se but to secure for persons "the full benefit of the Charter's protection" ... under s. 7, while avoiding adjudication of the merits of public policy. This can only be accomplished by a purposive analysis and the articulation . . . of "objective and manageable standards" for the operation of the section within such a framework.[74]

The distinction that both the Supreme Court and the Ontario Court of Appeal attempted to draw between substantive review and matters of policy seems tenuous.[75] The Supreme Court's authoritative formula is that only "basic tenets of our legal system are protected under s. 7."

(b) Basic Tenets of Our Legal System

Mr. Justice Lamer describes these basic tenets as "not only of our judicial process, but also of the other components of our legal system."[76] An open-ended approach is asserted:

> Whether any given principle may be said to be a principle of fundamental justice within the meaning of s. 7 will rest upon an analysis of the nature, sources, rationale

---

[69] *Ibid.*, at 241.

[70] *Young* (1984), 40 C.R. (3d) 289 at 318 (Ont. C.A.).

[71] *Morgentaler* (1985). 48 C.R. (3d) 1 at 39-40 (Ont. C.A.).

[72] Above note 1.

[73] *Ibid.*, at 305-306.

[74] *Ibid.*, at 306.

[75] In *Morgentaler*, above note 71, at 18, Dickson C.J. (Lamer J. concurring) found it unnecessary "to tread the fine line between substantive review and the adjudication of public policy". See too Eric Colvin, "Section Seven of the Canadian Charter of Rights and Freedoms" (1989), 68 *Can. Bar Rev.* 560.

[76] Above note 1, at 317.

and essential role of that principle within the judicial process and in our legal system, as it evolves.

Consequently, those words cannot be given any exhaustive content or simple enumerative definition, but will take on concrete meaning as the courts address alleged violations of s. 7.[77]

In subsequent applications of the *Motor Vehicle Reference* approach to s. 7, Mr. Justice La Forest has found majorities in the Supreme Court in favour of the view that the law must be considered "in light of the basic principles of penal policy that [have] animated legislative and judicial practice in Canada and other common law jurisdictions."[78] Both in the case of s. 7 challenges against the Criminal Code scheme for indeterminate detention of dangerous offenders[79] and that against the fingerprinting identification procedures under the Identification of Criminals Act,[80] the finding of similar provisions in other countries was most instrumental in the challenges being rejected. For Mr. Justice La Forest, both the interests of the individual and the State play a part in the assessment of whether there has been a violation of the principles of fundamental justice.[81]

The La Forest approach to s. 7 was persuasively criticized by Morris Manning[82] on the basis that the Court has previously insisted on a clear two-stage approach, under which the content of the right or freedom is first defined in terms of the individual interest it was meant to protect. On this approach, the State objectives are only to be considered if there is a violation and the State is attempting to demonstrably justify a reasonable limit under s. 1. A balancing of interest at the first stage will considerably dilute the protection of the Charter since the State will not have to bear the heavy onus of justification under s. 1.

Disagreement as to the proper approach to interpretation is express in the approaches of Madam Justice Wilson and Mr. Justice La Forest in the inconclusive decision in *Thomson* (1990).[83] Wilson J. fully examines the historical origins of the rights against compellability and self-incrimination and the policy justifications advanced in England, Canada, the United States and Australia before concluding that ss. 11(c) and 13 do not adequately reflect the basic tenets of our justice system. On the other hand, La Forest J. refused to accept a broad right against self crimination on the American model. Sections 11(c) and 13 were central to the s. 7 inquiry and the assessment had to be made in accordance with

---

[77] *Ibid.*, at 318.

[78] *Beare*, above note 47, at 110, adopted by the majority in *Seaboyer* (1991), 7 C.R. (4th) 117 (S.C.C.), discussed below, note 924.

[79] *Lyons*, above note 4. Dickson C.J.C., Estey, Mcintyre and LeDain JJ. concurred. Lamer and Wilson JJ. dissented in part.

[80] *Beare*, above note 47. The Court was unanimous. See too the majority judgment in *Hebert*, above note 3.

[81] For decisions under s. 7 balancing interests of victims, see *O'Connor* and *Mills*, discussed below at notes 734 and 752, and above Chapter 1.

[82] "Lyons: A One-Stage Approach to the Charter and Undue 'Constitutional Notice' " (1987), 61 C.R. (3d) 72. See too Thomas Singleton, "The Principles of Fundamental Justice, Societal Interests and Section 1 of the Charter", (1995) 74 *Can. Bar Rev.* 407.

[83] Discussed above note 4.

the spirit of those provisions, which built upon Canadian not American experience.

A Canadian focus is even more apparent in the majority judgment of Madam Justice McLachlin in *Hebert* (1990),[84] in which the Court unanimously held that a right to silence was a basic tenet under s. 7. Her Ladyship's judgment is also important for several general rulings on the relevance of the common law to the s. 7 inquiry. Reference to the "legal rules relating to the right which our legal system has adopted" was required but existing common law rules might not be conclusive.

> It would be wrong to assume that the fundamental rights guaranteed by the Charter are cast forever in the straight-jacket of the law as it stood in 1982.[85]

Furthermore, the scope of a fundamental principle of justice might be broader than a particular rule as this would also depend

> on the general philosophy and purpose of the Charter, the purpose of the right in question and the need to reconcile that right with others guaranteed by the Charter.[86]

In *Lyons*,[87] in which dangerous offender provisions were held to survive Charter review, Mr. Justice La Forest, on behalf of the majority, warned against generalizations:

> It is also clear that the requirements of fundamental justice are not immutable: rather, they vary according to the context in which they are invoked. Thus, certain procedural protections might be constitutionally mandated in one context but not in another.[88]

He added, in holding that an accused was not entitled to have dangerousness determined by a jury, that under s. 7 the accused had a right to a fair hearing but not "the most favourable procedures that could possibly be imagined."[89]

The views of La Forest J. in *Lyons* that s. 7 protections turn on the context and that accused cannot expect the most favourable procedures have been most influential. They are frequently cited, as in *Mills* (2000),[90] where the Court was defining the accused's right to full answer and defence for purpose of access to therapeutic records of complainants in sexual assault cases. Justices Iacobucci and McLachlin indicate that the

---

[84] Above note 3. Dickson C.J.C., Lamer, La Forest, L'Heureux-Dubé, Gonthier and Cory JJ. concurred.

[85] *Ibid.*, at 172.

[86] *Ibid.*, at 173.

[87] Above note 4.

[88] *Ibid.*, at 46.

[89] *Ibid.*, at 47.

[90] (1999), 28 C.R. (5th) 207 (S.C.C.). This aspect of *Mills* was in turn relied on by Gonthier J. for the Court in *Darrach*, below note 947, where the Court upheld the validity of rape shield provisions. The *Mills* rulings on therapeutic records are further discussed below, notes 752 *et seq.* See Chapter 1 for discussion of the controversial pronouncements in *Mills* on the need for dialogue with Parliament and its assertion of s. 15 equality rights for complainants in sexual assault cases.

ability to make full answer and defence, as a principle of fundamental justice, must...be understood in light of principles of fundamental justice which may embrace interests and perspectives beyond those of the accused.[91]

When the majority decided in *Rodriguez* (1993)[92] that the Criminal Code prohibition on assisting suicide was constitutional, the basis was that the deprivation of the security of interest of a terminally ill patient contemplating suicide was in accordance with principles of fundamental justice. Sopinka J. asserted a cautious approach:

> A mere common law rule does not suffice to constitute a principle of fundamental justice; rather, as the term implies, principles upon which there is some consensus that they are vital or fundamental to our societal notion of justice are required. Principles of fundamental justice must not, however, be so broad as to be no more than vague generalizations about what our society considers to be ethical or moral. They must be capable of being identified with some precision and applied to situations in a manner that yields an understandable result. They must also, in my view, be legal principles.[93]

A powerful new constitutional standard may have emerged in recent unsuccessful general challenges to marihuana possession laws before the B.C. Court of Appeal in *Malmo-Levine* (1999)[94] and the Ontario Court of Appeal in *Clay* (2000).[95] In *Malmo-Levine* Justice Braidwood for the majority[96] accepted, after a detailed analysis of the common law, Law Reform Commission recommendations, and federalism and Charter cases, that principles of fundamental justice under s. 7 include a harm principle:

> It is a legal principle and it is concise. Moreover, there is a consensus among reasonable people that it is vital to our system of justice. Indeed, I think that it is common sense that you don't go to jail unless there is a potential that your activities will cause harm to others.[97]

The test should be

> whether the prohibited activities hold a "reasonable apprehension of harm" to other individuals or society.... The degree of harm must be neither insignificant nor trivial.[98]

The majority found that the prohibition against marihuana did not offend this harm test as there was some harm involved. Any change in the law should be left for Parliament.

---

[91] Para 73.
[92] Above note 50.
[93] At 298.
[94] (2000), 34 C.R. (5th) 91 (B.C. C.A.).
[95] (2000), 146 C.C.C. (3d) 276 (Ont. C.A.). In the companion case of *Parker*, above note 57, the same Court declared the law inoperative in not providing a medical exemption.
[96] Rowles J.A. concurred.
[97] Para. 134.
[98] Para. 38.

In dissent Prowse J.A. preferred a higher threshold test of reasonable apprehension of harm that was of a "serious, substantial or significant nature".[99] Marihuana possession laws did not meet this standard.

In *Clay*, Justice Rosenberg for the Ontario Court of Appeal, reached the same conclusion as the majority in *Malmo-Levine*. For the purposes of the decision, the Court accepted the majority view as to the harm principle. It dismissed the Prowse approach as one that could lead to an unjustifiable intrusion into the legislative sphere.[100] Referring to Sopinka J.'s opinion in *Rodriguez*, Rosenberg J.A. expressed doubts about the harm principle as a constitutional standard:

> While it is a good basis for legislative policy, a helpful guide for the exercise of discretion by prosecutions and an important principle for judges in exercising discretion in sentencing, it is a difficult principle to translate into a means of measuring the constitutionality of legislation. For example, how much harm is sufficient to warrant legislative action? And, can the harm principle be applied outside the *mens rea* area in a manner that yields an understandable result?[101]

The harm principle awaits the imprimatur of the Supreme Court. If accepted, it would introduce a welcome new vehicle for restraint and give teeth to years of rhetoric about the need to use the criminal sanction with caution. The Braidwood test appears as workable as presently accepted Charter grounds of challenge under principles of vagueness and overbreadth.[102] Indeed it may be easier to apply. The resolution of the harm principle issue will provide a good barometer of how activist the present Supreme Court chooses to be.

The remainder of this chapter attempts to categorize and describe s. 7 challenges to date in the context of criminal and penal law.

5. CONSTITUTIONAL REQUIREMENT OF FAULT[103]

The monumental ruling is that of the Supreme Court of Canada in the *Motor Vehicle Act Reference* (1985).[104] A majority of five judges, through Mr. Justice Lamer, held that a penal law that imposes absolute liability will violate s. 7 of the

[99] Para. 171, relying on *Butler* (1992), 11 C.R. (4th) 137 (S.C.C.).
[100] Para. 26-8.
[101] Para. 25.
[102] See above note 98.
[103] See further Bruce Archibald, "The Constitutionalization of the General Part of the Criminal Law" (1988), 67 *Can. Bar Rev.* 403, David H. Doherty, "The Fault Element in Canadian Criminal Law", an unpublished paper presented to the Annual Convention of Criminal Lawyers Association in November, 1989. Bruce Archibald, "The Constitutionalization of the General Part of the Criminal Law" (1988), 67 *Can. Bar Rev.* 403, James Stribopoulos, "The Constitutionalization of Fault in Canada: A Normative Critique" (1999), 42 *Crim. L.Q.* 227, Simon France, "Gains and Lost Opportunities in Canadian Constitutional *Mens Rea* (1995), 20 *Queen's L.J.* 533, and Alan Brudner, "Guilt Under the Charter: The Lure of Parliamentary Supremacy" (1998), 3&4 *Crim. L.Q.* 287. The substantive law dimensions of the Charter fault requirement are fully explored, together with comparisons to other jurisdictions and reform options, in Stuart, *Canadian Criminal Law. A Treatise* (4th ed., 2001) c. 3.
[104] Above note 1.

Charter and be of no force or effect where there is a potential deprivation of the liberty interest. Absolute liability occurs where a conviction can be based on mere proof of the act without any necessity to prove any form of fault on the part of the accused. Thus it is quite clear in Canada, in marked contrast to the United States,[105] that there is a constitutional requirement of fault applicable to any type of penal responsibility and irrespective of legislative intent. The only question is what that constitutional standard amounts to.

Prior to the Charter our courts and legislatures have recognized three forms of fault. The first is the subjective approach, normally insisted upon by Canadian courts as the fault requirement for most crimes.[106] Often the only issue is whether the subjective approach is to be limited to intent or actual knowledge or, as is normally the case, to include subjectively determined recklessness or wilful blindness. Recklessness requires actual knowledge of a risk and wilful blindness a deliberate failure to enquire when that person knows there is a reason for enquiry. The second form of fault recognized, far less frequently in the case of Criminal Code offences, is that of simple negligence (carelessness). Here the test is not what the accused thought but whether there was a departure from the standard of care expected of a reasonably prudent person in the circumstances. The third form of fault sometimes recognized is that of gross negligence. Here the test is also the objective standard of care expected of a reasonably prudent person in the circumstances but there is a further requirement of a marked and substantial departure from that standard.

It will be convenient to begin the analysis of the constitutional standard of fault with ''public welfare'' offences as distinct from ''true crimes.''

(a) Public Welfare (Regulatory) Offences

(i) *Pre-Charter*

The notion that there is a distinction between crimes and what is variously described as ''regulatory'', ''public welfare'' or ''quasi-criminal'' offences was asserted by English Judges in the second half of the nineteenth century. The distinction was crucial. Once it had been determined that the acts were ''not criminal in any real sense'' but ''which in the public interest are prohibited under penalty,''[107] the courts no longer asserted a *mens rea* requirement but were content

---

[105] W.R. LaFave and A.W. Scott, *Substantive Criminal Law* (1986), Vol. 1, describe the United States position as follows:

> [The] Supreme Court has recognized that as a general matter it is constitutionally permissible to enact strict-liability criminal statutes. ''There is wide latitude in the lawmakers to declare an offense and to exclude elements of knowledge and diligence from its definition.'' The Court has on only one occasion struck down a strict-liability crime, and this was in rather unusual circumstances. Though it has been argued that the ruling in that case should be extended to proscribe strict-liability offenses more generally, this has not occurred. Rather, this decision has had very little impact.

[106] See, for example, *Pappajohn* (1980), 14 C.R. (3d) 243 (S.C.C.); *Lucas* (1998), 123 C.C.C. (3d) 97 (S.C.C.).

[107] *Sherras v. DeRutzen*, [1895] 1 Q.B. 918.

to convict on a basis of mere proof of the act. In this way they invented absolute liability with little rationalization.

In Canada the question of possible absolute responsibility has usually but not always arisen in the case of non-Criminal Code federal offences or provincial offences where *mens rea* is not expressly indicated by the wording of the prohibition. Until the pivotal decision of the Supreme Court of Canada in the *City of Sault Ste. Marie* (1978),[108] the stark choice lay between the polar positions of full subjective awareness and absolute responsibility. The courts overwhelmingly opted for absolute responsibility.

The issue in *Sault Ste. Marie* was whether the offence under the Ontario Water Resources Act[109] of permitting pollution required proof of fault. For the full Court, Mr. Justice Dickson engages in a comprehensive and principled review of "public welfare" offences, which were described as "in substance of a civil nature" which included such "everyday matters as traffic infractions, sales of impure food, violations of liquor laws, and the like."[110]

The judgment first examines the competing social policy considerations involved in any decision to impose absolute liability. The major arguments in favour of absolute responsibility were that it was more likely to exact a higher standard of care from those who knew mistakes and accidents would nevertheless incur liability and that such offences would promote administrative efficiency: "Proof of fault is just too great a burden in time and money to place on the prosecution." The courts would be unnecessarily burdened, especially considering the number of public welfare offences. Because they usually carried light penalties and less stigma, the individual would not be seriously prejudiced. However Dickson J. found "greater force" in the opposing arguments. Absolute liability violated "fundamental principles of penal liability." He continued:

> It also rests upon assumptions which have not been and cannot be, empirically established. There is no evidence that a higher standard of care results from absolute liability. If a person is already taking every reasonable precautionary measure, is he likely to take additional measures, knowing that however much are he takes, it will not serve as a defence in the event of breach? If he has exercised care and skill, will conviction have a deterrent effect upon him or others? Will the injustice of conviction lead to cynicism and disrespect for the law, on his part and on the part of others? These are among the questions asked.[111]

The Court concluded that there was indeed "opprobrium" attached to a public welfare conviction and that the administrative argument was likewise of "little force." Serious crimes also involve the public interest and their *mens rea* had still to be proven. While penalties for "health and safety" offences were often minor, many others carried heavy fines and the possibility of imprisonment.

---

[108] (1978), 40 C.C.C. (2d) 353 (S.C.C.).

[109] R.S.O. 1970, c. 332, s. 32(1) (now R.S.O. 1980, c. 361, s. 16(1)).

[110] Above note 108, at 357. For arguments that the real/regulatory distinction is not valid see Stuart, *Treatise*, above note 103, c. 3, and below Chapter 6, in reviewing the Supreme Court's attempted distinction in *Wholesale Travel Group Inc.*

[111] *Ibid.*, at 363-364.

The Court therefore decided to assert a fault requirement even in the case of public welfare offences, into which category this pollution offence was held to fall. The Court asserted a canon of interpretation whereby public welfare offences which did not have an express *mens rea* requirement were *prima facie* (strict) rather than absolute responsibility. For such offences, there was to be a fault requirement but not of the subjective *mens rea* type. The Court compromised and asserted the "half-way house" first adopted in Australia in a different context.[112] The fault is determined on the objective standard of simple negligence and, furthermore, the accused, to be acquitted, must prove on a balance of probability that reasonable care was taken. At this time of parliamentary supremacy the Court had to recognize that legislatures could on occasion insist on absolute liability. However, the Court went out of its way to make such liability exceptional. Negligence was clearly to be the usual yardstick for public welfare offences.

In 24 years of litigation since *Sault Ste. Marie*, it has become clear[113] that the Supreme Court was indeed successful in halting the previous overwhelming trend towards absolute responsibility for public welfare offences. In the vast majority of such offences, the unmistakable pattern has been one of reclassification to offences of strict liability allowing the due care defence. There is only a small minority of reported cases, conspicuously those involving speeding, where courts have still opted for absolute liability.

(ii) *Motor Vehicle Act Reference*

In the *Motor Vehicle Act Reference* (1985),[114] the issue was the constitutionality of s. 94(2) of the Motor Vehicle Act of British Columbia.[115] That provision declares it an offence to drive a motor vehicle while prohibited or under suspended licence and expressly makes it an absolute liability offence carrying a mandatory penalty of seven days' imprisonment. For the majority, Mr. Justice Lamer heavily relied on the judgment in *Sault Ste. Marie* for propositions that "there is a generally held revulsion against punishment of the morally innocent" and that absolute liability violates fundamental principles of penal liability. Absolute liability was not *per se* offensive to s. 7 but did violate the section "only if and to the extent that it has the potential of the depriving of life, liberty, or security of the person."[116] We have seen that the Court went out of its way to widely define the liberty interest to include the possibility of imprisonment or even probation.[117] The Court also made it quite clear that arguments of law

---

[112] *Proudman v. Dayman* (1941), 67 C.L.R. 536 (Austl. H.C.).

[113] See further Stuart, above note 103.

[114] Above note 1.

[115] R.S.B.C. 1979, c. 288, s. 94 (re-en. 1982, c. 36, c. 63).

[116] Above note 1, at 319. No mention is made of the fact that, in the case of public welfare offences, this basic tenet had only been asserted by the Court for seven years.

[117] The Court added (*ibid.*, at 320):
> I would not want us to be taken . . . as having inferentially decided that absolute liability may not offend s. 7 as long as imprisonment or probation orders are not available as a sentence. The answer to that question is dependent upon the content given to the words "security of

enforcement expediency will very rarely demonstrably justify an absolute liability offence as a reasonable limit under s. 1 of the Charter.

> Administrative expediency, absolute liability's main supportive argument, will undoubtedly under s. 1 be invoked and occasionally succeed. Indeed, administrative expediency certainly has its place in administrative law. But when administrative law chooses to call in aid imprisonment through penal law, indeed sometimes criminal law and the added stigma attached to a conviction, exceptional, in my view, will be the case where the liberty or even the security of the person guaranteed under s. 7 should be sacrificed to administrative expediency. Section 1 may, for reasons of administrative expediency, successfully come to the rescue of an otherwise violation of s. 7, but only in cases arising out of exceptional conditions, such as natural disasters, the outbreak of war, epidemics, and the like.[118]

The Court resolved that s. 94(2) violated s. 7 since the Government of British Columbia had not demonstrably justified the risk of imprisonment of a few innocents given the desirability of ridding the roads of bad drivers. That result had to be measured against the offence being one of strict liability open to a defence of due diligence. The Court did suggest that different considerations might apply in the case of corporations under both s. 7 and s. 1.[119] We have seen that the Supreme Court has subsequently held that, although s. 7 cannot be applied directly to corporations, corporations cannot be convicted on an unconstitutional law.[120] A corporation thus cannot be convicted of an absolute liability offence given that an individual person charged with the offence could rely on s. 7.[121]

The *Motor Vehicle Act Reference* decision made the *Sault Ste. Marie* standard of negligence the minimum constitutional standard whatever a legislature might have intended. Since *Sault Ste. Marie* there has been a legislative trend, especially in federal legislation, to incorporate the due diligence defence into some existing or new offences. Some courts[122] had held by contextual construction that this would preclude the possibility of such a common law of due diligence defence to be read into another offence in the same enactment which did not expressly have the defence. It has already been confirmed by several courts that the Charter, as interpreted in the *Motor Vehicle Act Reference*, has slammed the door shut on this form of statutory interpretation. The Charter fault standard is to be asserted whatever the legislature intended.[123]

In *Pontes* (1995),[124] the Supreme Court finally determined that the possibility of imprisonment in default of payment of a fine also threatens the liberty interest such as to engage s. 7 protection. It also confirmed that, where a conviction carries

---

the person''.
That issue was and is a live one. The Court may, however, have foreclosed it by not addressing it in *Pontes*, below note 124.

[118] *Ibid.*, at 321.

[119] Above note 1, at 332.

[120] Above note 8.

[121] *Wholesale Travel Group Inc.*, above note 110.

[122] See, for example, *Grottoli* (1979), 43 C.C.C. (2d) 158 (Ont. C.A.).

[123] *Cancoil Thermal Corp.* (1986), 52 C.R. (3d) 188 (Ont. C.A.) and *Martin* (1991), 63 C.C.C. (3d) 71 (Ont. C.A.).

[124] (1995), 41 C.R. (4th) 201 (S.C.C.).

no possibility of gaol, absolute liability *can* be constitutional. For this reason the Court now upheld the constitutionality of the B.C. provincial offence of driving while prohibited which the 5-4 majority interpreted to be one of absolute liability.[125]

In *Motor Vehicle Act Reference* the Supreme Court took direct aim at absolute liability offences. Now that imprisonment in default also triggers that protection, absolute liability should be rare unless the legislature has a scheme of punishment not dependent on imprisonment. Absolute liability where there is any possibility of imprisonment would have to be demonstrably justified under s. 1 or the legislature would have to resort to a notwithstanding clause under s. 33.

(iii) *Vicarious liability*

One of the most significant applications of the *Motor Vehicle Act Reference* has been the striking down of vicarious liability provisions. A doctrine of vicarious responsibility makes A automatically responsible for the wrongdoing of B solely on the basis of a prior relationship and irrespective of A's act or fault. This principle, which has proved useful in the law of torts where the issue is one of adjusting losses, cuts across normal principles of criminal liability. Even prior to the Charter our courts struggled to avoid its application in criminal law.[126] However, they could not avoid express provisions in most Highway Traffic Acts.[127] The owner of a motor vehicle is, for example, often made liable for any violation respecting that vehicle unless the court was satisfied that the vehicle was in the possession of a person without the owner's consent. In Ontario and the Northwest Territories the owner is, however, exempt from liability for specified "moving violations."

The Saskatchewan,[128] Ontario[129] and British Columbia[130] Courts of Appeal have declared that such provisions are inoperative. The provisions are viewed as contrary to principles of fundamental justice under s. 7 in imposing absolute responsibility in situations where the liberty interest is at stake. The Manitoba Court of Appeal[131] ruled similarly but, in the briefest of reasons and without hearing evidence, determined that the violation was demonstrably justified under s. 1:

> In the present case, no evidence was presented, but I do not think there was any necessity to do so. In the *Oakes* decision . . . the court recognized that "there may

---

[125] See critical reviews by Anne-Marie Boisvert, "Innocence Morale, Diligence Raisonnable et Erreur de Droit" (1995), 41 C.R. (4th) 243 and Jill Presser, "Absolute Liability and Mistakes of Law in the Regulatory Context: *Pontes* Disappoints and Confuses" (1995), 41 C.R. (4th) 249.

[126] See especially *Stevanovich* (1983), 36 C.R. (3d) 174 (Ont. C.A.) and authorities discussed by Stuart, above note 103, c. 10.

[127] See the comprehensive survey of legislation by Stuesser, above note 22.

[128] *Burt*, above note 24 (operating vehicle with unnecessary noise).

[129] *Pellerin*, above note 24 (failing to remain at scene of accident).

[130] *Geraghty* (1990), 55 C.C.C. (3d) 460 (B.C. C.A.) (owner liable for any vehicle violation).

[131] *Gray*, above note 28 (careless driving, speeding and failing to stop). Compare *Sutherland* (1990), 55 C.C.C. (3d) 265 (N.S. C.A.) (majority interpreting vicarious liability provision as allowing for due diligence defence and hence not violating s. 7).

be cases where certain elements of the s. 1 analysis are obvious or self-evident'' and I think that is so in this case. Indeed, there are some cases, and I think this is one of them, where it is undesirable to proceed on the basis of evidence . . . I do not think that the legislation is to be saved by a mountain of statistics and reports, but rather on the basis of a common sense analysis of what the legislation is intended to achieve and whether the objective is attained in a balanced and reasonable fashion.[132]

A minority view in the Saskatchewan Court of Appeal,[133] and in the trial court,[134] was that the vicarious provision in question was unconstitutional because it is a matter of fundamental principle that penal responsibility be based on a meaningful individual act. There is much to be said for this view.[135] The vicarious doctrine imputing responsibility to another is logically distinct from the notion of absolute responsibility.

(iv) *Due diligence standard not to be qualified*

In *Wholesale Travel Group Inc.* (1991),[136] the Court determined that all that could be constitutionally required in the case of the offence of false advertising under the Competition Act was a defence of due diligence. However the Court also decided that this defence could not be watered down by a more rigorous requirement than that of reasonable care. The Competition Act's requirement of prompt retraction was accordingly struck down. *Wholesale Travel* is a powerful and welcome new authority for the proposition that restrictive formulations of the due diligence defence may well amount to unconstitutional attempts to bypass the minimum Charter standard of objective negligence.

(v) *Reverse onus for regulatory offences*

The Supreme Court in *Wholesale Travel* determined by a narrow 5-4 majority that in the case of regulatory offences there is nothing unconstitutional about placing a persuasive burden of proving the due diligence defence on the accused. It will be submitted later[137] that this decision is flawed and, based on later Supreme Court decisions, ought to be reconsidered.

(b) True Crimes

Once the Supreme Court decided in *Motor Vehicle Act Reference* that a due diligence defence was the minimum standard of fault required by the Charter for

---

[132] *Ibid.*, at 387-388. See Stuesser, above note 22, pp. 325-328, for an argument that this reasoning "cannot withstand faithful application of the *Oakes* test." In *Holizki* (1990), 79 C.R. (3d) 80 (Sask. Q.B.), a provision imposing absolute liability for a parking violation vicariously on the owner was held to offend s. 7 but only to the extent it allowed imprisonment in default of payment. The provision for imprisonment was declared inoperative.

[133] Chief Justice Bayda.

[134] *Burt* (1985), 47 C.R. (3d) 49 (Sask. Q.B.).

[135] See too Stuesser, above note 22.

[136] (1991), 8 C.R. (4th) 145 (S.C.C.). See case comments by Patrick Healy in (1990) 69 *Can. Bar Rev.* 761 and Chris Tollefson in (1992) 71 *Can. Bar Rev.* 369.

[137] Below Chapter 6.

any type of offence threatening the liberty interest, it was only a matter of time before the Supreme Court would have to decide whether that standard was sufficient for Criminal Code offences. The first challenge came to the law of murder.

(i) *Constructive murder unconstitutional*

By the time of the entrenchment of the Charter in 1982, Canada had the widest definition of murder in the British Commonwealth and, indeed, one of the widest in North America.[138] Under what is now s. 229(a)(i) and (ii) of the Criminal Code, a culpable homicide is murder where there is an intent to kill or cause bodily harm knowing of a likelihood of death.

> 229. Culpable homicide is murder
> (a) where the person who causes the death of a human being
> > (i) means to cause his death, or
> > (ii) means to cause him bodily harm that he knows is likely to cause his death, and is reckless whether death ensues or not.

What made the Canadian definition of murder conspicuously wide was the additional provisions respecting unlawful object murder under s. 229(c) and a complex constructive murder provision under s. 230:

> 229. Culpable homicide is murder . . .
>
> (c) where a person, for an unlawful object, does anything that he knows or ought to know is likely to cause death, and thereby causes death to a human being, notwithstanding that he desires to effect his object without causing death or bodily harm to any human being.

> 230. Culpable homicide is murder where a person causes the death of a human being while committing or attempting to commit high treason or treason or an offence mentioned in section 52 (sabotage), 75 (piratical acts), 76 (hijacking an aircraft), 144 or subsection 145(1) or sections 146 to 148 (escape or rescue from prison or lawful custody), section 270 (assaulting a peace officer), section 271 (sexual assault), 272 (sexual assault with a weapon, threats to a third party or causing bodily harm), 273 (aggravated sexual assault), 279 (kidnapping and forcible confinement), 279.1 (hostage taking), 343 (robbery), 348 (breaking and entering) or 433 or 434 (arson), whether or not the person means to cause death to any human being and whether or not he knows that death is likely to be caused to any human being, if
>
> (a) he means to cause bodily harm for the purpose of
> > (i) facilitating the commission of the offence, or
> > (ii) facilitating his flight after committing or attempting to commit the offence, and the death ensues from the bodily harm;
> (b) he administers a stupefying or overpowering thing for a purpose mentioned in paragraph (a), and the death ensues therefrom;
> (c) he wilfully stops, by any means, the breath of a human being for a purpose mentioned in paragraph (a), and the death ensues therefrom; or

---

[138] For a detailed review of the history and jurisprudence of the Canadian law of murder and a comparison with other jurisdictions see the second edition of Stuart, *Canadian Criminal Law. A Treatise* (2nd ed., 1987), pp. 207-239. See too Grant, Chunn and Boyle, *The Law of Homicide* (1994).

(d) he uses a weapon or has it upon his person
      (i)   during or at the time he commits or attempts to commit the offence,
      (ii) during or at the time of his flight after committing or attempting to commit the offence,
and the death ensues as a consequence.

Under s. 229(c), it was murder if anyone did anything for an unlawful object that person ought to have known was likely to cause death. No other Anglo/American jurisdiction has a specific objective foresight requirement for murder. Canada's constructive murder rule appeared in our first Criminal Code of 1892. Under s. 230, a killing in the course of committing or escaping from listed offences in certain circumstances would be murder if death resulted, however unexpectedly or, indeed, accidentally. The widest constructive murder rule in s. 230 was that under subs. (d), added in 1947.[139] The only fault requirement was[140] that of a minimal intent to use or have a weapon which in some way caused the death of a person.

In his landmark judgment in *Vaillancourt* (1987),[141] Lamer J., speaking for seven judges[142] of the Supreme Court, over the sole dissent of Mr. Justice McIntyre, held that s. 230(d) violated s. 7 of the Charter as there was not even a requirement of objective foresight of death. The violation could not be justified under s. 1. Six justices,[143] again over the dissent of McIntyre J., found that s. 230(d) also infringed the presumption of innocence in s. 11(d) of the Charter in allowing a murder conviction in the absence of proof beyond a reasonable doubt of objective foreseeability of death. This violation could not be demonstrably justified as a reasonable limit under s. 1.

In *Martineau* (1990),[144] Chief Justice Lamer, for a majority of five justices,[145] held that it is a principle of fundamental justice under ss. 7 and 11(d) of the Charter that a conviction for murder "cannot rest on anything less than proof beyond a reasonable doubt of subjective foresight of death".[146] The stigma and punishment

---

[139] See J. Willis, "Comment", (1951) 29 *Can. Bar Rev.* 784 at 791-793.
[140] *Swietlinski* (1980), 55 C.C.C. (2d) 481 (S.C.C.) at 490.
[141] (1987), 60 C.R. (3d) 289 (S.C.C.). See discussion in "Vaillancourt: A Criminal Reports Forum", (1988) 60 C.R. (3d) 322; A. Gold, "Fundamental Justice - Constructive Murder", (1988) 13 *Queen's L.J.* 207; I. Grant and A.W. Mackay, "Constructive Murder and the Charter: In Search of a Principle", (1987) 25 *Alta. L. Rev.* 129; Peter MacKinnon, "Vaillancourt v. The Queen", (1988) 67 *Can Bar Rev.* 350; I. Grant, "R. v. Vaillancourt: The Constitutionalization of Mens Rea", (1988) 22 *U.B.C.L. Rev.* 369; Ross Macnab, "Case Comment: R. v. Vaillancourt", (1988) 13 *Queen's L. J.* 207; P. Lindsay, "The Implications of R. v. Vaillancourt: Much Ado About Nothing?", (1989) 47 *U. of T. Fac. of Law Rev.* 465; I. Grant, "The Impact of Vaillancourt v. The Queen on Canadian Criminal Law", (1990) 28 *Alta. L. Rev.* 443. There was a companion case: *Laviolette* (1987), 38 C.C.C. (3d) 476 (S.C.C.).
[142] Lamer J.'s judgment was concurred in by Dickson C.J., Estey and Wilson JJ. Separate concurring judgments were delivered by Beetz J. (Le Dain concurring) and La Forest J.
[143] La Forest J. only considered s. 7.
[144] (1990), 79 C.R. (3d) 129 (S.C.C.).
[145] Dickson C.J., Wilson, Gonthier and Cory JJ. concurred. Sopinka J. gave a concurring judgment. L'Heureux-Dubé J. dissented.
[146] At 139.

attaching to the most serious crime was to be "reserved for those who either intend to cause death or who intend to cause bodily harm that they know will likely cause death".[147] These are the forms of fault to be found in ss. 229(a)(i) and (ii) of the Criminal Code.

The majority further held that the inroads of subjective foresight in the expanded murder definitions in ss. 230 and 229(c) of the Criminal Code could not be demonstrably justified as reasonable limits under s. 1. The objective of deterring persons causing bodily harm could be met by very stiff sentences for other crimes such as manslaughter. The Court swept away the other three forms of constructive murder to be found in ss. 230(a), (b) and (c)[148] on the basis that the only *mens rea* requirement specified was that of an intent to cause bodily harm. Although the constitutionality of s. 229(c) had not been argued, the majority in *Martineau* also ruled[149] that s. 229(c) violated ss. 7 and 11(d) to the extent that it allowed conviction merely on proof that the accused ought to have known that death was likely to result. This objective component of s. 229(c) could not be saved by s. 1.

Despite *Martineau*, it is arguable[150] that a form of s. 229(c) has survived Charter challenge. If only the objective foresight complainant is excised there remains a murder category in s. 229(c) differing from that in s. 229(a)(ii) in that it requires an act in pursuit of an unlawful object and recklessness as to death, rather than an intent to cause bodily harm and recklessness as to death.

For over ten years after *Vaillancourt*, prosecutors appeared reluctant to test this possible interpretation and risk a murder conviction later being declared unconstitutional. However in *Meiler* (1999)[151] the Ontario Court of Appeal confirmed a murder conviction where a trial judge had instructed the jury it could convict on the basis of s. 229(c) if it found that the accused, for an unlawful object, did anything knowing that it was likely to cause someone's death. The decision has been rightly criticized[152] for not adopting a narrower interpretation limiting s. 229(c) to a person who had a subjective awareness of the likelihood of the actual victim's death. On the accused's evidence he was carrying a loaded and cocked gun with intent to kill a particular person and the gun discharged during a struggle and accidentally killed another. The particular application of s. 229(c) in *Meiler* appears to resurrect a type of constructive murder the Supreme Court declared unconstitutional. Any resort to s. 229(c) trials will also unfortunately return the law of murder to the former common law complexities

---

[147] *Ibid.*

[148] A Crown attempt to distinguish s. 230(c) was rejected in *Sit* (1991), 9 C.R. (4th) 126 (S.C.C.). It was ruled unconstitutional.

[149] At 138.

[150] See too Grant, Chunn and Boyle, pp. 4.51-4.52.

[151] (1999), 25 C.R. (5th) 161 (Ont. C.A.).

[152] R.J. Delisle, "Unlawful Object Murder Is Alive and Well" (1995), 25 C.R. (5th) 179. The author also criticizes the Ontario Court of Appeal on the issue of causation: see above Chapter 2, "The Actus Reus Requirement".

of trying to identify an unlawful object distinct from the immediate object accompanying the act of killing.[153]

The existence of these constitutional requirements for murder probably preclude any possibility of a radical reform of homicide laws in Canada along the lines of the proposal in the 1989 New Zealand Crimes Bill to combine murder and manslaughter into one crime of homicide with a flexible penalty. Such a reform appears, in any event, unwise. There seems to be an intuitive and well-established public consensus that the law should distinguish the intentional killer and subject such person to the stigma of a murder conviction subject to the most severe penalty. The legacy of the New Zealand proposal was such resistance by the public and legal profession that the whole New Zealand Crimes Bill was shelved.[154]

In declaring the minimum standard for murder to be subjective foresight of death, the Court clearly specified that there has to be knowledge of the *likelihood of death*. There has been little discussion of ''likelihood'' in this context.[155] The Supreme Court has spoken of a requirement that the accused will probably die.[156] Presumably knowledge of a possibility of death is not enough. The accused has to actually foresee death and that it was a likelihood.[157] To this extent, Madam Justice L'Heureux-Dubé J. is right in suggesting that it is a very high standard that finds no parallel in other Anglo-American jurisdictions.

The Supreme Court is to be commended for ridding Canada of our much criticised constructive murder provisions.[158] Mandatory life imprisonment should never have been based on inflexible rules under which the jury did not have to decide whether the accused anticipated death. The impact of *Vaillancourt* and *Martineau* on the law of murder should not, however, be exaggerated. Only 16% of all homicides in 1989 occurred during the course of committing other offences.[159] Furthermore, in the case of most murder charges such as those stemming from shootings, stabbings or beatings, the Crown will rarely have difficulty in proving *mens rea* under s. 229(a)(i) or (ii). Since *Vaillancourt* the ''no substantial wrong or miscarriage of justice'' proviso in s. 686(1)(b)(iii) has on several occasions been applied to avoid new trials. There is also the possibility of convictions for manslaughter or robbery which both carry a maximum sentence

---

[153] See especially *Tennant and Naccarato* (1975), 31 C.R.N.S. 1 Ont. C.A.) and *DeWolfe* (1976), 31 C.C.C. (2d) 23 (Ont. C.A.).

[154] See Simon France, ''Reforming Criminal Law — New Zealand's 1989 Code'', [1990] *Crim. L. Rev.* 827 and Report of the Crimes Consultative Committee, *Crimes Bill 1989* (1991).

[155] See discussion by Grant, Chunn and Boyle, pp. 4.42 - 4.43. The authors approve of a decision of the New Zealand Court of Appeal in *Piri*, [1987] 1 N.Z.L.R. 66 (C.A.) that the test should not be one of more likely than not but rather that of ''a real risk, a substantial risk, something that might reasonably happen'' (at 79).

[156] *Nygaard* (1989), 72 C.R. (3d) 257 (S.C.C.) at 278.

[157] In *Tutton* (1989), 69 C.R. (3d) 289 (S.C.C.), Lamer J., in a concurring opinion, speaks of conduct likely to cause death as ''high risk conduct'' (at 304).

[158] In the United States, felony murder rules have only sometimes been declared unconstitutional where combined with a death penalty: see Lafave and Scott, above note 105.

[159] Statistics Canada, *Juristat*, Vol. 10, No. 14: *Homicide in Canada, 1989*, p. 9.

of life imprisonment. There is indeed no reported decision of a killer walking free as a result of *Vaillancourt* or *Martineau*.

It is now clear that many murderers are serving life sentences on the basis of the jury having being directed to apply laws since declared unconstitutional. It is also clear that Courts are unlikely to review cases long through the judicial system.[160] It is a sign of law and order times that the Department of Justice and/or Parliament has not put into place an effective special review mechanism. On the evidence few convicted murderers may be entitled to relief. But what of those who are?[161]

(ii) *Constructive first degree murder not unconstitutional*

In 1976, Parliament, as a political compromise on the occasion of the formal abolition of the death penalty, drew a distinction between first and second degree murder. Under what is now s. 231, although both first and second degree murder carry a mandatory sentence of life imprisonment, a person convicted of first degree murder normally cannot be considered for release under parole until 25 years have elapsed, whereas a second degree murderer's parole eligibility date may be set at the discretion of the trial judge at anywhere between 10 and 25 years. Section 231(5) creates a unique automatic first degree murder category in which a murder in the course of a few listed offences must result in a verdict of first degree murder. Those offences are hijacking, various forms of sexual assault, kidnapping and forcible confinement and hostage-taking. The list is very much shorter than the list of offences included in the constructive murder rule in s. 230. The constructive first degree murder rule has thus always appeared anomalous and a product of its *ad hoc* legislative history.

The Supreme Court, in two unanimous and brief judgments in *Luxton* (1990)[162] and *Arkell* (1990),[163] however had no difficulty in holding that the provision was neither arbitrary nor irrational. The provision was not contrary to s. 7 or 9 and the mandatory penalty did not amount to cruel and unusual punishment under s. 12.[164] The sentencing scheme in s. 231(5) classified murders as more serious where committed while the offender was exploiting a position of power through illegal domination of a victim, as had been explained in its pre-Charter judgment in *Paré* (1987).[165] According to the Court the relationship between the sentence classification and the moral blameworthiness of the offender clearly existed. The section only came into play where murder had been proven beyond a reasonable doubt. In view of *Martineau* the offender would have to have had subjective foresight of death.

---

[160] See, most recently, *Sarson* (1996), 107 C.C.C. (3d) 21 (S.C.C.).

[161] See too Allan Manson, ''Vaillancourt: Implications for Persons Convicted of Murder'', (1987) 60 C.R. (3d) 339 and Grant, Chunn and Boyle, pp. 4-74–4-77.

[162] (1990), 79 C.R. (3d) 193 (S.C.C.).

[163] (1990), 79 C.R. (3d) 207 (S.C.C.).

[164] See critique by Allan Manson, ''The Easy Acceptance of Long Term Confinement in Canada'', C.R. *ibid.*, pp. 265-272. The s. 12 issue is discussed below, Chapter 7.

[165] (1987), 60 C.R. (3d) 346 at 370 (S.C.C.).

Given the Supreme Court's unanimity, it is quite clear that s. 231(5) has withstood Charter scrutiny. This does not, of course, make it defensible. Indeed, the reasoning of the Supreme Court in *Paré* is not persuasive. How can it possibly be said that the list of murders under s. 231 includes all murders involving unlawful domination over the person? Doesn't any murder involve such domination? What of the fact that murders committed in the course of break and entry or in the course of armed robbery are *not* included?[166] The classification was and is irrational and should have been declared unconstitutional.

In *Collins* (1989),[167] the Ontario Court of Appeal held that s. 231(4)(a) of the *Criminal Code*, providing that the murder of a police officer is first degree murder, is not contrary to the provisions of s. 7. The object of the categorization was to provide a heavier deterrent to protect against the murder of those obliged to maintain law and order. Section 231(4)(a), however only survived the constitutional challenge because the Ontario Court of Appeal, reversing a previous *obiter*,[168] read into the section a knowledge requirement. The Crown had to prove that the murderer knew the identity of the victim as one of the persons designated in the subsection and that such person was acting in the course of duty or was reckless as to such identity and acts of the victim. For the Court, Mr. Justice Goodman added:

> Where a statutory provision is open to two interpretations, one of which will contravene the Charter and the other of which will not, the provision should be interpreted in such a manner as will not contravene the Charter.[169]

(iii) *Subjective awareness required for few crimes to reflect stigma and proportional punishment*

When the Supreme Court struck down the constructive murder rule then in s. 230(d) of the Criminal Code in *Vaillancourt* (1987),[170] Lamer J. for the majority left the impression that the Court might one day decide that subjective *mens rea* was constitutionally required for all crimes. It is now clear that the Supreme Court is only likely to declare such a requirement for a very few offences. Chief Justice Lamer has later recognized that the Charter does not necessarily guarantee the ideal[171] and that the list of constitutionally required subjective offences is short[172]. At present, the Supreme Court has required subjective fault for murder,[173] attempted murder[174] accessory liability to an offence constitutionally requiring a

---

[166] See too *Strong* (1990), 2 CR. (4th) 239 at 251 (Alta. CA.).

[167] (1989), 69 C.R. (3d) 235 (Ont. C.A.). See too *Lefebvre* (1989), 71 C.R. (3d) 213 (Que. C.A.) and *Bowen* (1990), 59 C.C.C. (3d) 515 (Alta. C.A.).

[168] *Munro* (1983), 36 C.R. (3d) 193 at 296-297 (Ont. C.A.), criticized by this author in an annotation, C.R. *ibid.*, pp. 195-196.

[169] Above note 167, at 265.

[170] (1987), 60 C.R. (3d) 289 (S.C.C.).

[171] *Wholesale Travel*, at 205.

[172] (1993), 23 C.R. (4th) 189 (S.C.C.).

[173] *Martineau*, above note 144.

[174] *Logan* (1990), 79 C.R. (3d) 169 (S.C.C.).

subjective test,[175] and war crimes and crimes against humanity[176]. There is also *obiter* recognition that theft requires subjective awareness.[177]

The leading decision is that in *Creighton* (1993),[178] which is a highly complex and controversial decision.[179] Madam Justice McLachlin re-asserts three principles relied on by Lamer C.J. in *Martineau* (1990),[180] as follows:

1. The stigma attached to the offence, and the available penalties require a mens rea reflecting the particular nature of the crime;
2. The punishment must be proportionate to the moral blameworthiness of the offence; and
3. Those causing harm intentionally must be punished more severely than those causing harm unintentionally.[181]

The Court achieved welcome clarity in returning to principles it had ignored in other pronouncements.[182] However, as a practical matter, it would appear that these principles are highly unlikely to lead to further declarations of unconstitutionality of objective crimes.

The analysis is still turning on the unruly criterion of stigma criticized by most commentators as unreliable and potentially circular.[183] The focus on "stigma" can be traced to the pivotal decision of the Supreme Court in *Sault Ste. Marie*.[184] To resist the argument that there could be absolute liability for public welfare offences since they carried less stigma, Dickson J. concluded that there was indeed "opprobrium" attached to public welfare offences, even though penalties were often minor. Although the Court did recognize a distinction between true crimes and regulatory offences, it clearly decided that the distinction was not sharp enough to justify a departure from fault principles in the case of regulatory offences. Just as stigma did not work as a true discriminating factor in *Sault Ste. Marie*, stigma is a most inadequate criterion upon which to determine for which crimes there is to be a constitutional requirement of subjective foresight. Chief Justice Lamer seems to have in mind a list of offences: thus far murderers,

---

[175] *Ibid.*
[176] *Finta* (1994), 28 C.R. (4th) 265 (S.C.C.).
[177] See Lamer C.J. in *Vaillancourt*, above note 141, and *Martineau*, above note 144.
[178] (1993), 23 C.R. (4th) 189 (S.C.C.).
[179] See the Criminal Reports Forum, C.R. *ibid.*, pp. 240-279 for comments by Christine Boyle, Alan Gold, Isabel Grant, Patrick Healy and this writer.
[180] *Ibid.*
[181] At 8 (*Creighton*). A fourth *Martineau* principle, that fault be related to the consequence, was not accepted as a constitutional requirement: see below pp. 19-20.
[182] In *Nova Scotia Pharmaceutical Society* (1992), 15 C.R. (4th) 1 (S.C.C.) (conspiracy to lessen competition under the federal Competition Act, R.S.C. 1985, c. C-34) and *DeSousa*, below note 202 (Criminal Code offence of unlawfully causing bodily harm), the Court had simply asserted the position that, absent special stigma, the fault element for any type of offence, whether federal or provincial, could be either subjective or objective. The objective fault requirements of these offences were held, with surprisingly little scrutiny, to survive the Charter.
[183] See, for example, Isabel Grant and Christine Boyle, "Equality, Harm and Vulnerability: Homicide and Sexual Assault Post-Creighton", (1993) 23 C.R. (4th) 252 at 258-259 and Rosemary Cairns Way, "Constitutionalizing Subjectivism: Another View", (1990) 79 C.R. (3d) 260 and "Bill C-49 and the Politics of Constitutionalized Fault", (1993) 42 *U.N.B.L.J.* 325 at 332-333.
[184] (1978), 3 C.R. (3d) 30 (S.C.C.).

thieves and those who attempt murder. In *Logan*, he seems to suggest that a person charged with dangerous driving does not evoke such a stigma, but that someone charged with dangerous driving causing death would. Surely the stigma for any offence of dangerous driving is as least as much as that for a shoplifter? The question of whether there is a constitutional requirement of subjective foresight in the case of child abusers, rapists or polluters should not be made to depend on some uncertain notion of how certain offenders are branded in street discourse. L'Heureux-Dubé J., dissenting in *Martineau*, is persuasive in suggesting that social stigma has been "overemphasised".[185]

Defence counsel will be hard-pressed to win an argument that an objective crime carries such stigma as to require subjective *mens rea* given that the Supreme Court has already decided that such stigma does not follow a conviction of the Criminal Code offences of unlawful act causing bodily harm (*DeSousa*) (1992),[186] dangerous driving (*Hundal*),[187] manslaughter (*Creighton*), failing to provide neccessaries of life (*Naglik*) (1993),[188] and careless use of a firearm (*Finlay*[189] and *Gosset*).[190] Clearly, as La Forest J. points out in *Creighton*, it is not necessary that the objective offence be characterized as "regulatory". Nor does it seem necessary since *Creighton* for the court to engage in an analysis of context, as it did in *Hundal* in justifying an objective standard for dangerous driving.[191]

Provincial Courts of Appeal have also been unreceptive to Charter arguments to entrench subjective tests. Challenges have been rejected for offences of causing bodily harm in committing assault,[192] criminal negligence[193] and arson.[194]

(iv) *Intentional conduct to be punished more than negligence*

As for the overlapping second and third *Martineau* principles relating to proportional punishment, the reasons of McLachlin J. in *Creighton* and Lamer C.J. in *Gosset* are express that the principle is satisfied where there is no minimum penalty. The Court seems to require that the difference between deliberate and negligent conduct be addressed in sentencing.

This would appear to be consistent with the assertion by the Supreme Court[195] and Parliament[196] that proportionality is the pre-eminent principle in sentencing.[197]

---

[185] At 163. She proceeds to overstatement: "The concern that these offenders not endure the Mark of Cain is, in my view, an egregious example of misplaced compassion" (*ibid.*).
[186] (1992), 15 C.R. (4th) 66 (S.C.C.).
[187] (1993), 19 C.R. (4th) 169 (S.C.C.).
[188] (1993), 23 C.R. (4th) 335 (S.C.C.).
[189] (1993), 23 C.R. (4th) 321 (S.C.C.).
[190] (1993), 23 C.R. (4th) 280 (S.C.C.).
[191] However in *Finta*, above note 176, Cory J. speaking for the majority of four justices, again focuses on context. Cory J. was the majority judge in *Hundal*.
[192] *Brooks* (1988), 64 C.R. (3d) 322 (B.C. C.A.).
[193] *Nelson* (1990), 75 C.R. (4th) 70 (Ont. C.A.) and *Gingrich* (1991), 6 C.R. (4th) 197 (Ont. C.A.).
[194] *Peters* (1991), 11 C.R. (4th) 48 (B.C. C.A.).
[195] *M. (C.A.)* (1996), 46 C.R. (4th) 269 (S.C.C.).
[196] Section 718.1 reads:
    Fundamental principle - A sentence must be proportionate to the gravity of the offence and

This suggests, for example, that Parliament's new scheme for sexual assault,[198] which penalizes in the same prohibition carrying a flexible penalty, one who is deliberately aware of a risk of non-consent and one who did not take reasonable steps to ascertain whether there was consent, will survive Charter scrutiny. If the Supreme Court is consistent, it will insist on the principle that upon conviction a deliberate accused must receive a higher sentence than one who acted without taking reasonable steps.

Even if this is the outcome of Charter challenges to the substantive sexual assault reforms, there will still be much to be said,[199] on the basis of fair labelling and justice and also for ease of administration, for separate offences with separate penalties. This is now the case with murder and manslaughter, and intentional and negligent arson.[200] In the United Kingdom Professor Andrew Ashworth has made a strong case for the "principle of fair labelling":

> Full adoption of this principle would not necessarily lead to a massive code of finely graded and differentiated offences, sometimes derided as "the law professor's dream", although there are places where it might lead to greater detail and more offences than modern orthodoxy contemplates. The strength of the principle is to ensure that arguments of proportionality, fairness to individuals, and the proper confinement of executive and judicial discretion are taken seriously when new offences with broad definitions and high maximum penalties are under consideration.[201]

(v) *No constitutional requirement of foresight of consequence*

In *DeSousa* (1992),[202] five justices of the Supreme Court held that there is no common law or constitutional principle that a fault requirement must be related to each element of the *actus reus*, including any prohibited consequence. The Court relied principally on Blackstone, an 18th century Oxford professor:

> As far back as Blackstone's Commentaries, it was recognized that criminal guilt did not always require foresight of the consequences of an unlawful act . . .

> Provided that there is a sufficiently blameworthy element in the *actus reus* to which a culpable mental state is attached, there is no additional requirement that any other

---

the degree of responsibility of the offender.
See interpretation in *Priest* (1996), 1 C.R. (5th) 275 (Ont. C.A.) and by Justice William Vancise, "To Change or Not to Change — That is the Issue", (1996) 1 *Can. Crim. L.R.* 263.

[197] See further Bruce Archibald, " Fault, Penalty and Proportionality: Connecting Sentencing to Subjective and Objective Standards of Criminal Liability (with Ruminations on Restorative Justice)", (1998) 3&4 *Crim. L.Q.* 263.

[198] The controversial mistaken belief defence to sexual assault is further discussed below note 271 *et. seq.*

[199] See Stuart, *Treatise*, above note 103, c. 3. See too Alan Brudner, "Proportionality, Stigma and Discretion", (1996) 38 *Crim. L.Q.* 302 but compare Hamish Stewart, "R. v. Darrach: A Step Forward in the Constitutionalization of Fault?", (1999) 4 *Can. Crim. L. Rev.* 9.

[200] Parliament added the separate offence of arson by criminal negligence in 1990 (s. 436). The penalty is reduced to five years imprisonment.

[201] *Principles of Criminal Law* (3rd ed., 1999) pp. 92-93.

[202] Above note 186.

element of the actus reus be linked to this mental state or a further culpable mental state . . .

To require fault in regard to each consequence of an action in order to establish liability for causing that consequence would substantially restructure current notions of criminal responsibility. Such a result cannot be founded on the constitutional aversion to punishing the morally innocent.[203]

Writing in 1883,[204] Sir James Stephen, the drafter of our 1892 Criminal Code, offered a less than flattering assessment of Blackstone's work:

Blackstone's *Commentaries* give us a complete view of the whole system as it stood at the beginning of the last quarter of the century. This celebrated work has been made the subject alternately of high praise and extreme depreciation. Of late years I think its defects have attracted more attention than its merits. These defects are sufficiently obvious. Blackstone was neither a profound nor an accurate thinker, and he carried respect for the system which he administered and described to a length which blinded him to its defects, and led him in many instances to write in a tone of courtly, overstrained praise which seems absurd to our generation.[205]

It was quite unnecessary for the Court in *DeSousa* to pronounce on the general proposition that fault need not be related to the circumstances or consequences penalized. Whether this is true of the controversial and historically anomalous unlawful act causing death definition of manslaughter, and whether that offence was constitutional, were not questions before this Court. The issue was what fault was required for unlawfully causing bodily harm. Whether the Court decided that the test should be subjective or objective, it could well have stopped at holding that in this offence it had to be foresight of a risk of bodily harm — as, ironically, they so hold.

The further *obiter* general proposition that in causing harm offences the fault does not have to relate to the consequence such as death is on terribly shaky ground. A test of foresight, whether subjective or objective, has little meaning if it doesn't fully relate to the event that occurred. Surely the issue should be what did the accused risk or what was he or she careless about? Even the modern test of negligence in civil cases requires objective foresight of the type of harm.[206] Fault is not an abstract concept. It must be related to the factual context.

The Court blithely rejects respected positions to the contrary of Chief Justice Dickson, Mr. Justice G. Arthur Martin and Madam Justice Wilson. There is a casual reference to "objective intention"[207] which overlooks that it was that sort of characterization by the House of Lords in *D.P.P. v. Smith* (1961)[208] that led to a Parliamentary reversal[209] and to the Australian High Court abandoning its practice of following the House of Lords. At the time, Australian Chief Justice Dixon said the following:

---

[203] At pp. 21-26.

[204] *A History of the Criminal Law of England* (1883).

[205] Volume 2, p. 214.

[206] *Stewart v. Pettie*, [1995] 1 S.C.R. 131.

[207] "There is, however, no constitutional requirement that intention, either on an objective or a subjective basis, extend to the consequences of unlawful acts in general."

[208] [1961] A.C. 290 (H.L.).

[209] Criminal Justice Act of 1987.

There are propositions laid down in the judgment which I believe to be misconceived and wrong. They are fundamental and they are propositions which I could never bring myself to accept.[210]

The Court invokes in aid the following comment of Professor Eric Colvin, the only Canadian commentator the Court relied upon, made in the course of a discussion of offences Colvin dubs as those of partial *mens rea*:

There appears to be no general principle in Canada and elsewhere that, in the absence of an express legislative direction, the mental element of an offence attaches only to the underlying offence and not to the aggravating circumstances.

The Court overlooks the author's further analysis[211] that not requiring fault as to the consequence constitutes absolute liability to that extent and conflicts with s. 7 of the Charter. Professor Colvin does not provide authority for his suggestion that other jurisdictions do not require fault respecting consequences.[212] There is no such trend in modern criminal codes, starting with those based on the Model Penal Code of 1961.[213] The Supreme Court did not refer to the contrary view expressed after lengthy study by the Law Reform Commission of Canada.[214] Instead of relying on the views of a controversial 18th century Oxford law professor for a constructive fault rule, the Court might have consulted modern textwriters in the United Kingdom, such as Glanville Williams, J.C. Smith and Andrew Ashworth,[215] who take the contrary position.

The recent conclusion of the United Kingdom Law Commission[216] is that offences relating to assault and causing injury in that jurisdiction should be restructured but should only extend to intention or recklessness in the subjective sense *and be related to the particular risk* undertaken. There is no talk of a constructive unlawful act category.

The authority of *DeSousa* on this point appears to have survived the full Court's consideration in *Creighton* but in a qualified form. According to the majority in *Creighton*, the general rule that there is ''perfect symmetry'' between *mens rea* and the consequence of the offence is the ideal[217] but not a principle of fundamental justice. There can be exceptions and manslaughter by unlawful act is one.

---

[210] *Parker* (1963), 111 C.L.R. 610 (Aus. H.C.) at 632.

[211] *Ibid.*, p. 62.

[212] In Colvin's later article, ''Justice and Criminal Liability'' (1993) 3 *Canterbury L.Rev.* 321 at 330-331, he suggests that the principle has an ''established lineage''. However he only points to authority concerning assault causing bodily harm in England, Australia and Canada, and conflicting authority concerning assault on a peace officer, noting that some jurisdictions, such as Canada, required awareness that the victim is a peace officer.

[213] The American Law Institute, *Model Penal Code* (1962).

[214] Report No. 31: *Recodifying Criminal Law* (1987).

[215] *Principles of Criminal Law* (3rd ed., 1999), pp. 203-207.

[216] *Legislating the Criminal Code. Offences Against the Person and General Principles*: Law Com. No. 218 (1993), reflecting an earlier Consultation Paper No. 122, June 28, 1992. The members of the Commission included judges and practitioners and a former Oxford professor — Richard Buxton.

[217] See also McLachlin J.'s majority judgment in the fraud case of *R. v. Théroux* (1993), 19 C.R. (4th) 194 (S.C.C.).

For the minority Chief Justice Lamer, with Sopinka J., the author of *DeSousa* concurring, first distinguishes crimes where consequences form the essence of the offence. In such crimes (examples given are manslaughter and unlawfully causing bodily harm) the fault must be demonstrated in relation to that consequence. The minority then distinguishes the "few" offences where the essence of the offence is inherently risky so that objective foresight of harm is presumed and foresight of the consequence not required to be proved. Examples given are the offences of impaired driving causing bodily harm and dangerous operation causing bodily harm.

Since *Creighton* it seems clear that the *DeSousa* ruling must now be confined to the minority of offences where there is what the Court calls a "predicate" offence included in the definition.

(vi) *Objective crimes require marked departure*

The Supreme Court in *Creighton* and its companion cases adopts a new approach to the interpretation of objective crimes. The Court is unanimous in accepting the authority of *Hundal* (1993)[218] that the "test for negligence is an objective one requiring a marked departure from the standard of care of a reasonable person".[219] McLachlin J., citing *City of Sault Ste. Marie* (1978)[220] and *Sansregret* (1985),[221] explains that "The law does not lightly brand a person as a criminal".[222] This partly reconciles the recently neglected dicta in *Sault Ste. Marie* that a negligent person is innocent in the eyes of the criminal law and the *Sansregret* ruling that civil negligence is not an appropriate standard.

In *Hundal*, the Supreme Court had applied the gross departure test to a Criminal Code offence against operating a vehicle in a dangerous manner. In *Finlay*, an offence directed at "careless" storage of firearms, which had previously been interpreted as requiring the lowest standard of civil negligence, survived Charter challenge only because the Supreme Court read in a requirement of a marked departure. In *Gosset*, Chief Justice Lamer explains that this extra requirement is because penal negligence is concerned with punishment of moral blameworthiness while negligence under civil law is concerned with apportionment of loss. Similarly in *Naglik*, the Criminal Code offence of failure to provide necessaries of life to one's child under s. 215 of the Criminal Code, seen to involve the breach of an objective duty of care, was interpreted to require a marked departure from the norm.

At first impression, the Court seems to have held that whenever the reasonableness standard is encountered in a Criminal Code offence courts must require proof of a marked or gross departure from the norm. This would impose a welcomed new minimum constitutional standard. The gross departure test is a

---

[218] (1993), 19 C.R. (4th) 169 (S.C.C.).
[219] At 177.
[220] (1978), 3 C.R. (3d) 30 (S.C.C.).
[221] (1985), 45 C.R. (3d) 193 (S.C.C.).
[222] At 24 (*Creighton*).

normative one which clearly satisfies the need to use the criminal sanction with restraint. Triers of fact should be trusted with the discretion of deciding whether in all the circumstances the accused's conduct was so unreasonable that the accused deserves the criminal sanction. In the context of dangerous driving, Carthy J.A. for the Ontario Court of Appeal, welcomed the new standard as follows:

> My own view is that this is a very sensible resolution of the tension between conflicting concerns. Careless driving represents a major threat to other persons and property and the objective test facilities prosecution of offenders. On the other hand, most accidents on the highway involve at least one party who has driven imprudently, and if simple negligence is the test, it is only the discretion exercised by prosecuting authorities that keeps all of them from being tried in criminal courts. The higher standard of a marked departure from prudent conduct assuages that concern and supports the justification for an objective test for mens rea.[223]

The picture in the Supreme Court is, however, not quite so clear. In *Creighton*, unlawful act manslaughter was interpreted as an objective offence yet the marked departure test was *not* applied.[224] It would seem that the gross departure test is not to be applied to what the Supreme Court describes as offences with a "predicate offence", except where the predicate offence is one of criminal negligence. The Supreme Court has also refused to apply a marked departure test limit to the offence of impaired driving.[225]

Although the Supreme Court uses loose language such as "penal" negligence, the Court presumably cannot be taken to have been addressing their previous position in *Wholesale Travel Group Inc.*[226] that for so-called regulatory offences, all that is constitutionally required is that the accused be allowed to prove a defence of due diligence. In *Creighton*, the Supreme Court were considering Criminal Code offences. It seems clear that at the moment, the gross departure requirement only applies to Criminal Code offences.

(vii) *Objective crimes cannot consider individual factors short of incapacity*

This is the position of McLachlin J. for the 5-4 majority of the Supreme Court in *Creighton*. It was applied most dramatically in *Naglik* to exclude consideration of the inexperience, lack of education or youth of a mother charged with failing to provide necessaries to her child and, in *Gosset*, of the fact that the accused was a police officer who had experience and training in the use of

---

[223] At 214.

[224] *Sed contra* Grant, Chunn and Boyle, pp. 4-14-4-15, who somehow read *Creighton* as requiring a marked departure for unlawful act manslaughter.

[225] This had been asserted by the Alberta Court of Appeal in *Smith* (1992), 13 C.R. (4th) 125, adopting *McKenzie* (1955), 20 C.R. 412 (Alta. Dist. Ct.). However, the interpretation had been rejected by other Courts of Appeal: see, for example, *Bruhjell*, B.C. C.A., September 18, 1986, *Campbell* (1991), 26 M.V.R. (2d) 319 (P.E.I. C.A.), *Stellato* (1993), 18 C.R. (4th) 127 (Ont. C.A.) and *Aube* (1993), 85 C.C.C.(3d) 158 (Que. C.A.). When *Stellato* reached the Supreme Court, it simply adopted the position of the Ontario Court of Appeal that the Criminal Code had not adopted any special test for determining impairment: (1994), 31 C.R. (4th) 60 (S.C.C.).

[226] Above note 110.

firearms. McLachlin J.'s recognition of incapacity as an exception is grudging and she sees it arising only exceptionally. The only example she concedes is illiteracy in the case of a person handling a marked bottle of nitroglycerine.

Pity Chief Justice Lamer. He sets out to build on the academic consensus in Canada and elsewhere[227] that the objective standard is only morally appropriate for the criminal sanction where generous allowance is made for individual factors: the reasonable standard is only appropriate where the accused had capacity to take care. He carefully describes and develops such an approach, emphasizing that the test remains objective and that some factors such as intoxication are excluded from consideration, and that the traits must be those that the accused could not control or manage in the circumstances.

The Chief Justice's judgment appears to have been written on the assumption he had a majority. It looks very much like someone deserted the ship at the last moment! The suspects are Justices Cory and La Forest.

In delivering the majority judgment in *Hundal*, Cory J. had observed that:

> The potential harshness of the objective standard may be lessened by the consideration of certain personal factors as well as the consideration of a defence of mistake of fact.[228]

In concluding that a ''modified objective test'' should be adopted Mr. Justice Cory further wrote that:

> The test must be applied with some measure of flexibility. That is to say the objective test should not be applied in a vacuum but rather in the context of the events surrounding the incident.[229]

In *Creighton*, without explanation, Cory J. changes camps to join McLachlin J. *Hundal* is totally at odds with *Creighton* on this point.[230]

Given Cory J.'s defection, the swing judge in *Creighton* was La Forest J. His short concurring judgment explaining why he joined McLachlin J. on this point to form the majority opinion can be fairly described as perverse. As His Lordship documents, he has consistently opted for the subjective approach to fault. Given that he was expressly dissatisfied with both the approach of McLachlin J. and that of the Chief Justice, one would have confidently predicted that he would have opted for the objective approach nearest to the subjective standard. Clearly that was the approach of the Chief Justice. However, La Forest J. does not. He sees the qualified objective approach as not fully meeting the ''psychological and educative'' advantages of the subjective approach, introducing a differentiation between individuals that would be foreign to our law

---

[227] See Stuart, *Treatise*, above note 103, c. 3.

[228] At 177. Cory J. did later decide that personal factors need not normally be taken into account in dangerous driving cases given the licensing requirement for driving (at 181).

[229] At 179-180.

[230] Despite this inconsistency with *Creighton*, *Hundal*, including its modified objective standard, is still universally regarded as the controlling authority for dangerous driving offences: see, for example, *Reed* (1998), 15 C.R. (5th) 28 (S.C.C.), *Markovic* (1998), 17 C.R. (5th) 371 (Que. C.A.), *Bartlett* (1998), 15 C.R. (5th) 35 (Ont. C.A.) and *Brannan* (1999), 29 C.R. (5th) 380 (B.C. C.A.).

and difficult to explain to juries. Given that La Forest J. prefers a subjective approach that depends entirely on individual differences and has itself sometimes been difficult to explain, his reasons for concurring are utterly unconvincing. Surely a half a loaf is better than none!

What of the reasons advanced by McLachlin J. for so rigid an approach to the objective standard? Her major justifications are that there must be a single, uniform standard applying equally to all, and that this tough standard will deter others. Factors like experience, education, age, financial situation or cultural factors can be addressed at the time of sentencing. Her tough position here clearly contradicts her justification of a marked limit on the test of penal negligence. It seems strange that one category of subjective offences, including murder, can fully account for individual differences but the objective standard cannot consider any.

McLachlin J.'s sources are also odd. She frequently relies on tort law. Surely it is elementary that principles developed to respond to the needs of a wronged victim cannot simply be applied to the quite different task of deciding whether punishment can be justly imposed. This reversal to a rigid objective standard cuts across a well-recognized need to ensure that the criminal justice system is sufficiently sensitive to issues of gender, race and disadvantage.

A further objection to this aspect of the *Creighton* ruling is that it is so impractical. Take the case of a teenager who has been driving only a week and is involved in an accident. He is charged with dangerous driving or criminal negligence. Is the majority really serious that a jury must be instructed to ignore the age of the accused and to apply the standard of the average, experienced driver? This would defy common sense and the jury would likely ignore it. The law cannot say one thing and do another. In a case like *Gosset*, where a police officer is charged with an offence, are we really to ignore the fact that the accused was an officer trained in the use of firearms who knew about how the gun cocked? In *Prentice* (1993),[231] the House of Lords found it to be obvious that experience *should* be considered in applying the objective standard. The case involve several appeals in manslaughter cases heard together. Some accused were doctors:

> But in expert fields where duty is undertaken, be it by a doctor or an electrician, the criteria of what the ordinary prudent individual would appreciate can hardly be applied in the same way.[232]

The majority in *Creighton* is applying the objective test in an abstract vacuum such that the law is unworldly. Judging everyone by a inflexible standard of a monolithic reasonable person, where an accused could not have measured up, amounts to absolute liability. McLachlin J. anticipated such criticism and denies that the majority approach is applied in a vacuum. The standard is to be

> particularized in application by the nature of the activity and the circumstances surrounding the accused's failure to take the requisite care''.[233]

---

[231] [1993] 42 W.L.R. 927 (H.L.).
[232] At 936.
[233] At 217. In *Dixon* (1993), 26 C.R. (4th) 173 (N.B. C.A.), a case involving the reasonable standard

She accepts that a welder who lights a torch causing an explosion may be acquitted if he made an inquiry and was given advice, upon which he was reasonably entitled to rely, that there was no explosive gas in the area. Yes, but what if that mistake derived from his personal experience as a welder? According to McLachlin J. that experience cannot be considered.

This aspect of the definition of the objective standard in *Creighton* is, then, based on a shaky majority, far too insensitive and is likely to be sidestepped by trial judges and juries. The grave potential for injustice calls for Parliamentary intervention, but in law and order times, Parliament has not responded. Thankfully early signs indicate reluctance of lower courts to fall in line. The rigour of this aspect of *Creighton* may well disappear by generous interpretations seizing on McLachlin J.'s dicta that individual factors can be considered when the issue is capacity[234] and/or that the "de facto or applied standard of care . . . may vary with the activity in question and the circumstances in the particular case".[235]

The Supreme Court has already not followed its approach in the case of the reasonable belief requirement for self-defence. In *Pétel* (1994),[236] the full Court confirmed its *Lavallee* (1990)[237] that where self-defence is relied on by an accused in an abusive relationship the situation and experience of the accused *may* be considered. Later the Supreme Court in *Hibbert* (1995)[238] also adopted an individualised objective standard in assessing the defence of duress. Recognizing that he was bound by *Creighton*, Lamer C.J., speaking for the Court, nevertheless attempted to distinguish excuse-based defences on the basis that the policy and principle considerations were quite different as excuses were predicated on the fact that the accused's acts were involuntary.[239] This logic is not persuasive. Individual factors which the accused could not control are equally relevant to a just application of a reasonable standard of fault. The *Creighton* majority should change course on this key point.

---

for the defence of property under s. 41(1) of the Criminal Code, the Court relied on this passage in *Creighton* to enable it to consider the full context of a single parent arriving home to be confronted with his 15-year-old daughter drinking and partying with strange men. This approach is certainly understandable, but takes into account individual factors in a way not permitted by *Creighton*.

[234] See *Ubhi* (1994), 27 C.R. (4th) 332 (B.C. C.A.) (severe mental retardation to be considered) but compare *Canhoto* (1999), 29 C.R. (5th) 170 (Ont. C.A.) (not accepting incapacity due to religious belief in exorcism case resulting in death of infant).

[235] At 17. This dictum was relied upon in *Dixon*, above note 233, and *Blackwell* (1994), 29 C.R. (4th) 376 (Ont. C.A.) (police officer answering emergency call held to a higher standard on basis undertaking hazardous activity; lack of special training in high-speed driving not to be considered). See too *Brocklebank* (1996), 106 C.C.C. (3d) 234 (Can. Ct. Martial App. Ct.) (standard for negligent performance of military duty to take into account accused's rank, degree of responsibility and exigencies of operation).

[236] (1994), 26 C.R. (4th) 145 (S.C.C.).

[237] (1990), 76 C.R. (3d) 329 (S.C.C.).

[238] (1995), 40 C.R. (4th) 141 (S.C.C.). See too *Latimer* (2001), 39 C.R. (5th) 1 (S.C.C.) (modified objective approach required for two of three requirements for a necessity defence) and *Ruzic*, S.C.C., below note 325 (duress).

[239] At 176. See too Doherty J.A. in *Canhoto*, above note 234, distinguishing *Hibbert* on the issue of criminal negligence in a manslaughter case on the basis that "It is not concerned with personal exemptions from compliance with the standards of the criminal law" (at 180).

(viii) *Limited fault required for crimes based on predicate offences*

On the authority of *Creighton* and *DeSousa*, there are some offences based on predicate offences where the fault requirement is much reduced but constitutional. The problem will be how to identify them. Thus far there are three: *DeSousa* concerns the offence of unlawful act causing harm, *Creighton* the manslaughter category of unlawful act causing death and *Godin* (1994)[240] aggravated assault. In both cases, the unlawful act is interpreted to require objective foresight of harm. *DeSousa* also holds that the unlawful act must be a provincial or federal offence, that the fault for the predicate offence must be proved and that this cannot be absolute liability (applying the *Motor Vehicle Reference* ruling). There is no requirement of a marked departure from the objective norm. However where the predicate offence is one of negligence the gross departure limit must be applied.[241] On the majority approach to any objective standard no personal factors short of incapacity can be considered.

(ix) *Why have constructive liability?*

There is little convincing explanation of why a Court which struck down the constructive murder offences has battled so hard to save other types of constructive crimes. The result of all this analysis is that such constructive crimes have immensely complicated yet limited fault requirements. Modern Criminal Codes and suggested new Codes[242] appear to do without. In criminalizing the causing of bodily harm do we really need more than offences of *mens rea* and those of criminal negligence requiring a marked departure from the objective norm? In *DeSousa*, Sopinka J. emphasized the importance of punishment based on the consequence caused. This surely seems fair only where the accused anticipated that consequence or, in an objective crime, ought to have.

(x) *Special case for constructive manslaughter?*

According to the majority ruling in *Creighton* in the case of manslaughter by unlawful act the reasonable foresight need merely be of the risk of bodily harm which is neither trivial nor transitory. The majority rejected the view of Chief Justice Lamer that a requirement of objective foresight of the risk of death should be read in. McLachlin J.'s most persuasive policy justification is that the manslaughter sanction must reflect the fact that a death occurred to show societal concern for the victim's fate. She also argues her position promises the greatest

---

[240] (1994), 31 C.R. (4th) 33 (S.C.C.), a brief oral judgment, subjected to strong criticism in Stuart, *Treatise*, above note 103, c. 3.

[241] In *Curragh Inc.* (1993), 25 C.R. (4th) 377 (N.S. Prov. Ct.), it was held that a mining company could be convicted of manslaughter on the basis of breaches of provincial safety laws but that the Crown would have to prove a marked departure beyond a reasonable doubt.

[242] The U.K. Law Commission wishes to abolish all forms of crimes whose definition is based on the commission of an unlawful act: see discussion by Patrick Healy, "The Creighton Quartet: Enigma Variations in a Lower Key", (1993) 23 C.R. (4th) 265 at 276-277.

measure of deterrence and avoids troubling a trier of fact with drawing the "fine distinction" between foreseeability of the risk of bodily harm and foreseeability of the risk of death.

The result of *Creighton* is a very severe law of manslaughter. The Supreme Court has not pronounced on manslaughter by criminal negligence but will likely require a marked departure from the objective norm. It seems unlikely to require foresight of the risk of danger to life. Reasonable foresight of the risk to safety will undoubtedly be held to be enough. In any event, the Crown has the option of proceeding with the unlawful act charge which in essence requires proof of a dangerous act and that death resulted. There is no need to consider whether the departure was marked. In both cases personal factors short of incapacity are irrelevant. Is such a tough law really desirable or just?[243] Given the category of criminal negligence causing death the unlawful act category seems unnecessary. The Supreme Court has relied on authority in England for unlawful act manslaughter at a time when the Law Commission of the United Kingdom has recommended its abolition.[244] The High Court of Australia has interpreted an unlawful act manslaughter provision to require an appreciable risk of serious injury.[245]

The unfairness of the limited fault requirement of constructive manslaughter is exacerbated by the current causation test that the unlawful act need merely have been a contributing cause of the death.[246]

A severe category of unlawful act manslaughter contrasts strangely with authority recognizing various partial defences to murder,[247] some allowing intentional killings to result in verdicts of manslaughter.

(xi) *Doctrine of common intent*

Most common law jurisdictions rely on the doctrine of common intent to hold an offender responsible for the *actus reus* of a person involved in a joint enterprise. The Canadian rule in s. 21(2) is an anomaly because it also makes the accessory criminally responsible on an objective test for any offence he or she ought to have known the perpetrator was likely to commit. Courts of Appeal came to accept that the irrationality of imposing liability under s. 21(2) on the party on an objective standard while judging the perpetrator on a subjective one was contrary to the principles of fundamental justice of s. 7.[248]

In *Logan* (1990),[249] every Supreme Court Justice rejects this reasoning. There is held to be no principle of fundamental justice under which Parliament can

---

[243] Grant, Chunn and Boyle, p. 4-69, favour the result in *Creighton* and suggest that the majority decision represents an important shift from a culpability to a harms approach.
[244] Draft Report, *Unlawful Act Manslaughter* (1994).
[245] *Wilson* (1982), 174 C.L.R. 313 at 334.
[246] See Stuart, *Treatise*, above note 103, c. 2.
[247] See *ibid.*, Chapter 7.
[248] *Logan* (1988), 46 C.C.C. (3d) 354 (Ont. C.A.); *Couvrette* (1989), 72 C.R. (3d) 249 (Que. C.A.); *Harris* (1989), 70 C.R. (3d) 59 (Ont. C.A.) and *Sit*, above note 136.
[249] (1990), 79 C.R. (3d) 169 (S.C.C.).

never enact provisions requiring different levels of guilt for principal offenders and parties. However, the Court unanimously rules that s. 21(2) of the Criminal Code contravenes s. 7 and/or s. 11(d) on charges where subjective foresight is constitutionally required to the extent that the party may be convicted if that party objectively ought to have known that that offence was a probable consequence of carrying out the common purpose.

The significance of the Supreme Court's different approach is not evident. Like the lower courts, the approach stems from the irrationality of a lower fault standard for the party. It achieves the same result: the words "or ought to have known" are to be deleted from s. 21(2) when it is sought to make a party responsible for the perpetrator's offence where there is a constitutional requirement of subjective foresight, as is the case for murder or attempted murder.

(xii) *Attempted murder*

In *Logan*, Lamer J. for the majority[250] asserts that for a "few" offences, the principles of fundamental justice require proof beyond a reasonable doubt of a "minimum degree of *mens rea*."[251] The Court decides that attempted murder is one of those offences. Since the stigma associated with attempted murder is seen to be the same as for murder, and since the usual punishment for attempted murder is very severe, the Court holds that the constitutional *mens rea* requirement for attempted murder is that required for murder — subjective foresight of death. Under its pre-Charter decision in *Ancio* (1984),[252] the mental element required for attempted murder is that of the intent to kill required of a murderer under s. 229(a)(i). The Court observes that Parliament could constitutionally extend the definition of attempted murder to include murders with the intent required under s. 229(a)(ii), although it has chosen not to do so.[253]

It would appear that the majority in *Logan* settled the constitutional requirement for attempted murder partly on the logic of having the same *mens rea* for attempt as that required for the completed offence. With Madam Justice L'Heureux-Dubé, it is suggested that the *mens rea* standard for attempted murder could better have been developed from the general nature of the crime of attempt rather than the crime's relationship to the full offence. Quite apart from any constitutional dimension, many writers and judges have sought to restrict responsibility for attempting a crime to persons actually intending to commit an offence. The law of attempts substantially extends the net of criminal responsibility to include cases where the act is only partially completed. It therefore makes sense to restrict responsibility by asserting the most stringent test of *mens rea*, that of an intention.[254]

---

[250] *Rodney* (1990), 79 C.R. (3d) 187 (S.C.C.).
[251] *Logan*, above note 249.
[252] (1984), 39 C.R. (3d) 1 (S.C.C.). Dickson C.J.C., Wilson, Gonthier and Cory JJ. concurred. Sopinka and L'Heureux-Dubé JJ. gave separate concurring judgments.
[253] Above note 249, at 177.
[254] Above note 249, at 179.

(xiii) *Mistake of fact*

The majority of the Supreme Court of Canada in *Pappajohn* (1980),[255] held that an honest and not necessarily reasonable mistake as to consent would absolve the offence of rape. The Court viewed the defence of mistake of fact as simply a denial that the Crown had proved the fault requirement. It follows that a legislative exclusion of a mistake of fact defence constitutes absolute responsibility respecting that element and may well be a denial of the constitutional requirement of fault.[256]

There are two rulings to this effect by the Ontario Court of Appeal. In *Roche* (1985),[257] the Court interpreted the offence under what is now s. 271 of the Criminal Code — sexual assault on a person under 14 where there are more than three years between the age of the complainant and the age of the accused — to allow a defence of mistake of fact as to age. In *Metro News Ltd.* (1986),[258] the charge was distributing obscene material under what is now s. 163(1)(a) of the Criminal Code. The Court held that s. 163(6), which excluded the defence of the nature or presence of the obscene matter, was unconstitutional. Unfortunately, in both decisions the Ontario Court insisted that the mistake would have to be both honest *and reasonable*.[259] This flies in the face of *Pappajohn*, where the Court expressly held that any requirement that an excusing mistake be both honest and reasonable would connote liability based on objective negligence and, therefore, not be applicable to a *mens rea* offence.

The Supreme Court addressed the constitutionality of denying a mistake of fact defence in the statutory rape case of *Hess* (1990).[260] Until its replacement by a different range of sexual offences the crime of statutory rape under what was then s. 146(1) of the Criminal Code was an indictable offence punishable by a maximum of life imprisonment for a male to have sexual intercourse with a female under the age of 14 who was not his wife. Furthermore, the section expressly declared that it was an offence "whether or not he believes that she is fourteen years of age or more." The Supreme Court agreed that the denial of a mistake of fact defence violated s. 7 but disagreed as to whether the violation was a demonstrably justified reasonable limit under s. 1.

Madam Justice Wilson for the majority[261] emphasized that, since the Charter, a provision making it unnecessary for the Crown to prove *mens rea* and not providing an accused at a minimum with a due diligence defence would have to be justified under s. 1.[262] According to Wilson J. the doctrine of *mens rea*

---

[255] (1980), 14 C.R. (3d) 243 (S.C.C.).
[256] Any argument that the strict rule that ignorance of the law is no excuse is contrary to s. 7 may already have been pre-empted by the Supreme Court in *Pontes*, above note 124. See discussion on this point by Boisvert and Presser, above note 125.
[257] (1985), 46 C.R. (3d) 160 (Ont. C.A.).
[258] Above note 13, applied in *Regina News Ltd.* (1988), 39 C.C.C. (3d) 170 (Sask. C.A.).
[259] For further criticism see Stuart, "Metro News: Misplaced Objectivity" (1986), 53 C.R. 333.
[260] (1990), 79 C.R. (3d) 332 (S.C.C.).
[261] Lamer C.J.C., La Forest, L'Heureux-Dubé and Sopinka JJ. concurred.
[262] Above note 259, at 342.

reflects the conviction that a person should not be punished unless that person knew that he was committing the prohibited act or would have known that he was committing the prohibited act if . . . he had given to his conduct, and to the circumstances, that degree of attention which the law requires, and which he is capable of giving.[263]

Wilson J. further held that the violation of s. 7 by s. 146(1) could *not* be saved by s. 1. While the legislative objective of protecting female children from the harm that may result from premature sexual intercourse and pregnancy addressed a pressing and substantial concern, and the creation of an absolute liability offence was rationally connected to this concern, s. 146(1) did not impair the s. 7 right as little as possible.[264] Whatever deterrent value the fear of making a mistake might have would protect only that group of females close enough to the age of 14 that a mistake as to whether they were under or over 14 was a realistic possibility. The Crown had submitted no evidence to support the deterrence argument. Questions of mental innocence could not be left to the sentencing process and reliance on prosecutorial or judicial discretion could not justify a fundamentally unsound provision. Furthermore the fact that s. 146(1) had since been replaced by a series of measures that allowed the defence of due diligence,[265] showed that Parliament had concluded that its objective could be affected in a less restrictive manner. Section 146(1) therefore did not satisfy the proportionality test. At the minimum there had to be a provision for a defence of due diligence.

The minority through McLachlin J.[266] held that absolute liability was a demonstrably justified reasonable limit under s. 1 The objective was to protect female children from the harm which might result from premature sexual intercourse and pregnancy and to protect society from the impact of the social problems which sexual intercourse with children might produce, including protection from exploitation by those who might seek to use the children for prostitution and related nefarious purposes.[267] The infringement did not extend beyond what was reasonably necessary to achieve this purpose. Neither of the alternatives of defences of due diligence or reasonable belief provided as effective a deterrent[268] as removal of all defences based on the accused's lack of knowledge of the victim's age. Absolute liability put men who were contemplating

---

[263] *Ibid*. This passage is troubling. Wilson J. appears to be justifying the traditional *mens rea* requirement. The Supreme Court has previously been at pains to assert that this requires actual awareness: see, for example, *Pappajohn*, above note 106. Inattention even though an accused was capable is liability based on objective negligence and not on *mens rea*. The subjective/objective distinction was maintained and crucial in *Martineau*, above note 144.

[264] Above note 259, at 343-349.

[265] Under s. 150.1(4) of the Criminal Code, it is no defence to a number of sexual offences covering sexual conduct with a person under 14 that the accused believed the complainant was 14 years of age or more "unless the accused took reasonable steps to ascertain the age of the complainant."

[266] Gonthier J. concurred.

[267] Above note 259, at 363.

[268] *Ibid.*, at 370. Her Ladyship thus relies on an effectiveness test later repeated in *Chaulk* (1991), 2 C.R. (4th) 1 (S.C.C.), criticized in Chapter 1.

intercourse with a girl who might be under 14 on guard and many would conclude that they should not take the chance of a conviction if the girl was under the age.[269]

The majority ruling in *Hess* provides powerful authority for the constitutional requirement of fault, especially given the strong countervailing social interest in this context. While it noted the new formulation of a due diligence defence which constituted a less intrusive alternative the majority were clearly not yet pronouncing on the constitutionality of that option.

When Parliament responded to the Supreme Court's striking down of the rape shield provision[270] with Bill C-49,[271] it accomplished much more than a statutory rape shield law. The Minister of Justice and the women's groups behind the bill[272] seized the opportunity to enact Criminal Code provisions respecting the issue of what constitutes consent and on the long controversial mistake of fact defence. As to the latter, Parliament passed a new s. 273.2:

> Where belief in consent not a defence
>
> 273.2 It is not a defence to a charge under section 271, 272 or 273 that the accused believed that the complainant consented to the activity that forms the subject-matter of the charge, where
>
> (a) the accused's belief arose from the accused's
>
> > (i)   self-induced intoxication, or
> > (ii) recklessness or wilful blindness; or
>
> (b) the accused did not take reasonable steps, in the circumstances known to the accused at the time, to ascertain that the complainant was consenting.

The section creates special limits on the mistake of fact defence which apply to all sexual assault cases but not to assault offences. In the case of sexual assault, Parliament has reversed the substantive ruling in *Pappajohn*.[273] The accused cannot have that defence open where his mistaken belief arose from self-induced intoxication, recklessness or wilful blindness, or, most importantly, where he did not take reasonable steps in the circumstances known to him to ascertain that the complainant was consenting. Since *Creighton*, challenges based on the Supreme Court of Canada's assertion of a constitutional requirement of fault to safeguard

---

[269] *Ibid.*, at 369.

[270] *Seaboyer*, discussed below, note 924.

[271] For an interesting array of very different views on Bill C-49 see the Forum issue published in (1993) 42 *U.N.B.L.J.* 319-385. See Rosemary Cairns Way, "Bill C-49 and the Politics of Constitutionalized Fault", p. 325, R.J. Delisle, "The New Rape Shield Law and the Charter", p. 335, Patricia Hughes, "From a Woman's Point of View", p. 335, Stuart, "The Pendulum Has Been Pushed Too Far", p. 341, Martin, "Bill C-49: A Victory for Interest Group Politics", p. 357, Gayle MacDonald and Karen Gallagher, "The Myth of Consenting Adults: The New Sexual Assault Provisions", p. 373, and Alan D. Gold, "Flawed, Fallacious but Feminist: When One Out of Three is Enough", p. 381. See too Irit Weiser, " Sexual Assault Legislation: The Balancing Act", *ibid.* p. 213 and for a number of essays on Bill C-49 and the 1983 change from Rape to Sexual Assault see J.V. Roberts and R. Mohr (eds.), *Confronting Sexual Assault: A Decade of Legal and Social Change* (1994).

[272] For discussion of the politics of the reform, below notes 933-941.

[273] See below Chapter 6 for decision of its evidentiary ruling requiring an "air of reality" for the defence to go to the jury.

the guarantee of principles of fundamental justice under s. 7 now seem far less likely to succeed.[274]

In *Darrach* (1998),[275] Associate Chief Justice Morden held for the Ontario Court of Appeal that s. 273.2(b) does not violate principles of fundamental justice under s. 7 of the Charter. The Court was content to say it was far from satisfied that sexual assault is one of those "very few" offences which carries such a stigma that its *mens rea* component must be one of subjectivity. The stigma characterization had been fairly criticized as being a most unstable one for making important constitutional decisions. The issue could in any event be decided on that basis because, notwithstanding s. 273.2(b), the offence is still largely one based on subjective fault — at least to a level that would satisfy constitutional requirements. No doubt, the provision could be regarded as introducing an objective component into the mental element of the offence but it is one which, in itself, was a modified one. It was personalized according to the subjective awareness of the accused at the time. The accused is to "take reasonable steps, in the circumstances known to the accused at the time, to ascertain that the complainant was consenting". In other words, the accused is not under an obligation to determine all the relevant circumstances — the issue is what he actually knew, not what he ought to have known. In addition, while the provision requires reasonable steps, it does not require that all reasonable steps be taken, as it did in the first version of the Bill that resulted in s. 273.2. The subjective *mens rea* component of the offence remained largely intact. The provision did not require that a mistaken belief in consent be reasonable in order to exculpate.[276] Finally, having regard to the basic rationale underlying constitutionally mandated fault requirements that it is wrong to punish a person who is "morally innocent", it was difficult to contemplate that a man who has sexual intercourse with a woman who has not consented is morally innocent if he has not taken reasonable steps to ascertain that she was consenting.

This somewhat pragmatic dismissal[277] of the Charter arguments based on fault were unfortunately not placed in issue on the further appeal to the Supreme Court, where the issues were confined by the defence counsel to Charter arguments against the rape shield provisions. On general principles there are at least four arguments:[278]

> 1. Section 273.2's exclusion of any intoxication defence imposes absolute liability which threatens the liberty interest.[279]

---

[274] Above notes 186-191.

[275] (1998), 13 C.R. (5th) 283 (Ont. C.A.).

[276] The Court adds:
> Were a person to take reasonable steps, and nonetheless make an unreasonable mistake about the presence of consent, he or she would be entitled to ask the trier of fact to acquit on this basis (at 309-310, para. 90).

This proposition is startling and difficult to comprehend.

[277] Hamish Stewart, "R. v. Darrach: A Step Forward in the Constitutionalization of Fault?", (1999) 4 *Can. Crim. L.R.* 9 is supportive.

[278] See further *Treatise*, c. 4.

[279] Based on *Daviault*, below note 282.

2. Sexual assault is one of those few offences requiring a minimum degree of mens rea in the form of subjective foresight

3. The duty to take reasonable steps in s.273.2 is an objective standard which is unconstitutional because it does not require a marked departure from the objective norm.

4. Section 273.2 is unconstitutional because it violates the constitutional principle that those causing harm intentionally must be punished more severely than those causing harm unintentionally.

Of course, given the seriousness of the problem of sexual violence, if any of these challenges were accepted the Court might well wish to consider saving Parliament's recently enacted scheme as a demonstrably justified reasonable limit under s. 1.

(xiv) *Intoxication*

Prior to the Charter in *Leary* (1977),[280] and in *Bernard* (1988)[281] and *Daviault* (1994)[282] since the Charter, various majorities of the Supreme Court have rejected fundamental challenges to the common law *Beard* rule that voluntary intoxication is only a defence to crimes of specific intent and cannot be used to crimes of general intent. Chief Justice Dickson, in both *Leary* and *Bernard*, called for their rejection as unprincipled and unconstitutional but this was a minority position.

However, in a controversial ruling in *Daviault* (1994),[283] Mr. Justice Cory, for the majority,[284] determined that the strict application of the rule established in *Leary* that intoxication is not a defence to crimes of general intent, here sexual assault, offended both principles of fundamental justice under s. 7 of the Canadian Charter of Rights and Freedoms and the presumption of innocence under s. 11(d). A defence of extreme intoxication would have to be allowed in rare cases.[285]

According to the majority, the mental aspect of an offence, or this *mens rea*, had long been recognized as an integral part of crime. The concept was

---

[280] (1977), 33 C.C.C.(2d) 473 (S.C.C.).

[281] (1988), 67 C.R. (3d) 113 (S.C.C.).

[282] (1994), 33 C.R. (4th) 473 (S.C.C.).

[283] *Ibid.* See the Criminal Reports Forum, *ibid.*, for a variety of different comments by Professors Patrick Healy, Isabel Grant, Tim Quigley, and this author. See Stuart *Treatise*, above note 103, c. 6, for an expanded discussion of the decision itself and of reform options for intoxication defences.

[284] L'Heureux-Dubé, McLachlin and Iacobucci JJ. concurred. In separate concurring opinions, Lamer C.J. and La Forest J. expressed a continuing preference for the position of Dickson C.J. that the *Leary* rule should be abandoned, but they accepted that there had been no majority on the Court for this position. Both justices were of the view that the preferable analysis was that defect in excluding evidence of intoxication related to the voluntary component of the *actus reus* rather that *mens rea*.

[285] The Supreme Court in *Robinson* (1996), 46 C.R. (4th) 1 (S.C.C.) further overruled as violations of ss. 7 and 11(d) the further *Beard* rules that the defence of voluntary intoxication to specific intent crimes focuses on capacity and rebuts the presumption that a person intends the natural consequences. The enquiry in future is to be on proof of intent in fact and drawing common sense inferences. See discussion by Patrick Healy, "Beard Still Not Cut Off", C.R. (4th) *ibid.*

fundamental to our criminal law. That element might be minimal in general intent offences, but nonetheless existed. In this case, it was simply an intention to commit the sexual assault or recklessness as to whether the actions will constitute an assault. The necessary mental element could ordinarily be inferred from proof that the assault was committed by the accused. However, the substituted *mens rea* of an intention to become drunk could not establish the *mens rea* to commit the assault. It had the effect of eliminating the mental element such as to deprive an accused of fundamental justice. Furthermore, the presumption of innocence required that the Crown had the burden of establishing all elements of the crime. The mental element of voluntariness could not be eliminated without violating s. 11(d). It could not be automatically inferred that there would be objective foresight that the consequence of voluntary intoxication would lead to the commission of the offence. Assuming that voluntary intoxication was reprehensible, it did not follow that its consequences in any given situation were either voluntary or predictable. Further self-induced intoxication could not supply the necessary link between the minimal *mens rea* required for the offence and the *actus reus*.

According to Cory J., to deny that even a very minimal mental element was required for sexual assault offended the Charter in a manner that was so drastic and so contrary to principles of fundamental justice that it could not be demonstrably justified under s. 1. Experience of Australia and New Zealand,[286] where the *Leary* rule had been completely abandoned, coupled with the fact that the defence would be available only in the rarest of cases demonstrated no urgent policy or pressing objective which needed to be addressed. Studies on the relationship between intoxication and crime did not establish any causal link.[287] As the *Leary* rule applied to all crimes of general intent, it could not be said to be well tailored to address a particular objective and would not meet either the proportionality or the minimum intrusion requirements.

A new common law rule should be devised which would not be contrary to principles of fundamental justice. The solution was to adopt the flexible approach of Wilson J. in *R. v. Bernard*. Evidence of intoxication could properly be put to the jury only if the accused demonstrates such extreme intoxication akin to insanity or automatism. The accused should be called upon to establish this state on the balance of probabilities. This violation of the presumption of innocence under s. 11(d) could be justified under s. 1.[288] Only the accused could give evidence

---

[286] Cory J. refers to an Australian survey by Judge Smith and to similar findings by the New Zealand Criminal Law Reform Committee, *Report on Intoxication* (1984), as discussed by the United Kingdom Law Commission, *Consultation Paper No. 127: Intoxication and Criminal Liability* (1993) pp. 60-63.

[287] Citing a number of studies on the relationship between alcohol and crime (none of which had been referred to by counsel) Cory J. concluded that:

> It has not been established that there is such a connection between the consumption of alcohol and the crime of assault that it can be said that drinking leads inevitably to the assault. Experience may suggest that alcohol makes it easier for violence to occur by diminishing the sense of what is acceptable behaviour. However, studies indicate that it is not in itself a cause of violence (at 188).

[288] For criticism of this aspect of the judgment see Stuart, *Treatise*, above note 103, c. 6.

as to the amount of alcohol consumed and its effect on him. Expert evidence was required to confirm that the accused was probably in a state akin to automatism or insanity. It was obvious, noted Cory J., that the defence would only be advanced on rare occasions and would likely be successful on still rarer occasions. In light of the experience in Australia and New Zealand, to permit such a defence would not open the floodgates to allow every accused who had a drink before committing the prohibited act to raise the defence of drunkenness. It was always open for Parliament to fashion a remedy which would make it a crime to commit a prohibited act while drunk.

According to Cory J., should it be thought that the mental element involved related to the *actus reus*[289] rather than the *mens rea*, the result had to be the same. The *actus reus* required that the prohibited criminal act be performed voluntarily as a willed act. A person in a state of automatism could not perform voluntarily and so too someone in an extreme state of intoxication akin to automatism.[290] It would equally violate s. 7 of the Charter if someone not acting voluntarily could be convicted of a crime. Here again the voluntary act of becoming intoxication could not be substituted for the voluntary action involved in sexual assault. Such a fundamental denial of natural justice could not be justified under s. 1.

It is disappointing that the *Daviault* majority which was so strongly asserting fault and presumption of innocence principles would so casually reverse the onus of proof of this extreme intoxication defence and would, furthermore, insist on expert evidence. There was in fact uncontradicted expert evidence in *Daviault*. The suspicion is that the onus was pragmatically reversed to justify the order of a new trial in the hope that there would be a conviction. Like Wilson J. in *Bernard*, the majority seems determined to have it both ways: to assert fundamental Charter standards and yet make it virtually impossible for anyone charged with sexual assault to have a drunkenness defence.

A fundamental flaw of the majority judgment is that it does not adequately explain why the normal *Leary* rule that intoxication is not to be considered in the case of general intent crimes is not equally contrary to the important Charter principles of fault and voluntariness the Court relies on. The majority does not even try. It rests content with the fact that the *Leary* approach is established and that the majority in *Bernard* accepted it.

For the dissenting minority Sopinka J.[291] defended the strict *Leary* rule much along the lines of McIntyre J. in *Bernard*. Even though the distinction between general and specific intent had lead to some illogical results, this had been exaggerated. The rule that intoxication was no defence to a general intent crime was justified by sound policy considerations and did not offend the Charter. The fact that an accused had voluntarily consumed intoxicating amounts of drugs or

---

[289] This was the view of the concurring justices Lamer C.J. and La Forest J.

[290] Cory J. appears to reject the ruling in *R. v. Revelle* (1979), 48 C.C.C. 267 (Ont. C.A.). In *Revelle*, Martin J.A. held that if automatism was caused solely by drunkenness only the defence of drunkenness could be put to the jury, provided the offence was one of specific intent. According to Cory J. this ruling that self-induced automatism cannot be a defence predated the Charter and raised the same constitutional concerns as in *Daviault*.

[291] Gonthier and Major JJ. concurred.

alcohol could not excuse the commission of a criminal offence unless it gave rise to a mental disorder under s. 16 of the Criminal Code. The *Leary* rule did not violate ss. 7 and 11(d) of the Charter since it did not relieve the Crown of the responsibility of proving the existence of the *mens rea* or of any of the other elements of the offence of sexual assault required by principles of fundamental justice. On the finding of the trial judge, this was one of the rare cases where the accused was sufficiently intoxicated to raise a reasonable doubt as to whether he intended to commit the offence of sexual assault. However, none of the relevant principles of fundamental justice required that the intent to perform the *actus reus* of an offence of general intent be an element of the offence. The requirements of the principles of fundamental justice were satisfied by proof that the accused became voluntarily intoxicated. The majority of the Court had determined that the general rule that the mental fault element of a crime must extend to the *actus reus*, including consequence forming part thereof, was subject to exceptions. Individuals who rendered themselves incapable of knowing what they are doing through the voluntary consumption of alcohol or drugs were not morally innocent. To generally allow an accused who is not afflicted by a disease of the mind to plead absence of *mens rea* would be to undermine, indeed negate, that very principle of moral responsibility which the requirement of *mens rea* was intended to give effect to. Sexual assault did not fall into the category of a few offences for which either the stigma or the available penalties demanded the subjective standard as a constitutional requirement. The moral blameworthiness of an intoxicated offender was similar to that of any other person committing sexual assault and, to the extent that intoxication related to moral blameworthiness, could be taken into account in sentencing where the penalty was not fixed.[292]

According to the minority, the *Leary* rule did not violate the presumption of innocence because it permits an individual to be convicted despite the existence of reasonable doubt as to whether that individual performed the *actus reus* by his or her own volition. There was a general rule that the act of an accused must be voluntary but when elevated to a principle of fundamental justice it was, exceptionally, not absolute. One well-recognized exception was that automatism did not excuse if the accused's state was brought on by his or her own fault. An accused who voluntarily drinks alcohol or ingests a drug to the extent that he or she becomes an automaton is in the same position.

Although the minority opinion appears unresponsive to the detailed positions of Chief Justice Dickson, Sopinka J. does point to some strange weaknesses in the approach of Cory J. It is surprising that a Court in *Creighton* who so readily decided that subjective awareness of risk would seldom be constitutionally required for Criminal Code offences and that objective crimes were justified and constitutional, would here speak so much of the Charter standard of intent.

---

[292] According to Judge Patrick H. Curran, of the Nova Scotia Provincial Court, "Intoxication and the Criminal Law", a paper presented to the National Judicial Institute's 1994 Criminal Law Intensive Study Program, it is not easy to predict how intoxication will affect a sentence in any particular case. He suggests, "No doubt that is because the courts attempt to sentence whole persons and not isolated characteristics" (at 9).

Furthermore, Sopinka J. expresses a well-founded concern as to the majority's implicit rejection of the established common law position that an accused cannot rely on a state of involuntariness where he was at fault or negligent in getting into that state. In the case of *mens rea* crimes, Cory J. understandably found the exception so unprincipled that it had to be reconsidered. However, he went too far in abandoning it. The Court did not consider negligence offences. The notion that the act and fault must be simultaneous cannot be applied to fault in the form of negligence where the essence of liability is often to punish for conduct, often an omission, at a point in time much earlier than that at which the harm is caused. Hopefully the Court would reconsider in the context of a crime based on the objective standard and declare that negligence in getting into an involuntary state cannot excuse.

Although *Daviault* is a highly controversial ruling, the Supreme Court's concern with modern notion of fault and voluntariness compares most favourably with the most recent decision of the United States Supreme Court in *Montana v. Engelhoff*[293] on the issue of drunkenness. In *Engelhoff* the United States justices are constricted by a frozen rights theory. The due process enquiry is limited to determining whether, at the time the 14th amendment was adopted, an emerging 18th century English common law approach to allowing intoxication to be considered on the issue of intent had become "deeply rooted". Since that was not established, the Court concluded that in the state of Montana in 1996 a drunken killer can be constitutionally convicted of murder. It was not necessary to consider 20th century thinking on the drunkenness defence.

Public reaction to *Daviault* was swift. The Minister of Justice, Allan Rock, was reported to be "deeply troubled" by the ruling because of its "tremendous ramifications in sexual assault cases".[294] It was widely condemned as giving the wrong message to those who drink and harm. Commentators used extravagant hypotheticals of rapists getting off on the basis of having had a few drinks.[295] That such views were misreadings of the majority opinion is quite clear. That the Court ordered a new trial, rather than confirm Daviault's acquittal, despite the evidence as to extreme intoxication,[296] is a convincing indication that this new defence was intended to succeed only in very rare cases.

Some politicians even accused the Supreme Court of abolishing impaired driving laws! This rhetoric overlooked an earlier ruling of the Supreme Court in

---

[293] 116 S. Crt. 2013 (1996). See the unique open debate conducted on the U.S. *Crim. Prof. List Server* and published in (1997) 87 *J. of Crim. Law and Criminology* 633.

[294] *Lawyer's Weekly*, October, 1994.

[295] See, for example, "Drunkenness can't be excuse for rape", *The Toronto Star*, October 11, 1994, "A Licence to rape? Women fear that a Supreme Court ruling tells men sexual assault is okay as long as they're drunk", *The Toronto Star*, October 27, 1994, and "Drunk defence offensive", *The Vancouver Sun*, November 22, 1994.

[296] The new trial ordered in *Daviault* resulted in a judicial stay of proceedings: (1995), 39 C.R. (4th) 269 (C. Q.). The complainant by then was deceased and disclosure of statements made originally to the police revealed inconsistencies such that the cross-examination would have been quite different. It was held that to proceed would be a denial of natural justice. See comment by Patrick Healy in (1995) 39 C.R. (4th) 272.

Penno (1990)[297] that the offence of having care or control of a vehicle while impaired did not violate the Charter in not providing a defence of intoxication. The Court also gave an oral ruling in *Stellato* (1994)[298] that intoxication to even the slightest degree is sufficient for impaired driving defences.

The number of acquittals that followed *Daviault* was wildly exaggerated. There was alarm expressed by the Minister at more than 20 acquittals across the country. A later exhaustive survey[299] of reported and unreported judgments in the nine months following the Supreme Court's ruling could only document 11 *Daviault* cases. Only five resulted in acquittals. Two of these verdicts were later overturned on appeal. Given what must have been thousands of criminal cases involving intoxicated accused over that period, the survey provides some validation of Justice Cory's prediction that the defence would be rarely used and would rarely succeed.[300]

On February 24, 1995, the Minister of Justice, introduced Bill C-72 to abolish the *Daviault* defence. It was soon passed through Parliament with the result that s. 33.1 has been added to the Criminal Code:[301]

> 33.1(1) It is not a defence referred to in subsection (3) that the accused, by reason of self-induced intoxication, lacked the general intent or voluntariness required to commit the offence, where the accused departure markedly from the standard of care as described in subsection (2).
>
> (2) For the purposes of this section, a person departs markedly from the standard of reasonable care generally recognized in Canadian society and is thereby criminally at fault where the person, while in a state of self-induced intoxication that renders that person unaware of, or incapable of consciously controlling, their behaviour, voluntarily or involuntarily interferes or threatens to interfere with the bodily integrity of another person.
>
> (3) This section applies in respect of an offence under this Act or any other Act of Parliament that includes as and element an assault or any other interference or threat of interference by a person with the bodily integrity of another person.

The effect of this most complex provision is to use a deemed fault provision to remove the *Daviault* defence to most general intent offences. Most such

---

[297] (1990), 80 C.R. (3d) 97 (S.C.C.). See P. Healy, "Case Comment on R. v. Penno", (1992) 71 *Can. Bar Rev.* 143 and Stuart, "Annotation", (1990) 80 C.R. (3d) 99.

[298] (1994), 31 C.R. (4th) 60 (S.C.C.), discussed above Chapter 3. This is an ill-considered judgment which does not refer to the Criminal Code requirement that the intoxication must have impaired the ability to drive. There was a commendable attempt to distinguish *Stellato* in *Andrews* (1996), 46 C.R. (4th) 74 (Alta. C.A.). Although there was no requirement of a marked departure, the degree of deviation from the norm was an appropriate tool to assess the evidence of whether the ability to drive had been affected to some degree by alcohol or a drug. A similar instructive decision of Klebuc J. in *McCallum* (1994), 31 C.R. (4th) 62 (Sask. Q.B.) was, however, overturned on appeal on the basis of *Stellato* (1994), 35 C.R. (4th) 266 (Sask. C.A.).

[299] Martha Drassinower and Don Stuart, "Nine Months of Judicial Application of the Daviault Defence", (1995) 39 C.R. (4th) 280. Much of the inflation came from duplication in media reports.

[300] For appeal rulings denying airs of reality to *Daviault* defences see *Levy* (1996), 104 C.C.C. (3d) 423 (N.S. C.A.) (aggravated assault) and *Tom* (1998), 129 C.C.C. (3d) 540 (B.C.C.A.) (manslaughter).

[301] S.C. 1995, c. 32. s. 1.

offences involve at least threats to bodily integrity so as to come within the ambit of ss.(3). However s. 33.1 does not affect the common law defence of drunkenness available to specific intent crimes such as murder and robbery.

Whether s. 33.1 will survive Charter review remains to be seen. Lower courts have accepted that s. 33.1 flies in the face of the determination in *Daviault* that principles of fundamental justice require a defence of intoxication where this is akin to automatism. But they are equally divided on the further question of whether the s. 7 violation can be saved under s. 1 as a demonstrably justified reasonable limit.[302] The Supreme Court is not yet on record as justifying a s. 7 violation. On the other hand, in *Mills* the Court spoke of a need for dialogue with Parliament which should allow for deference to legislative schemes. Furthermore *Mills* also recognised that complainants in sexual assault cases have enforceable s. 15 rights which must be balanced not just as a matter of principles of fundamental justice.[303] The clear subtext to the negative reaction and Parliamentary response to *Daviault* was clearly grounded in that context. Another complication is that evidence was tendered at the Parliamentary committee hearings leading to Bill C-72 refuting the *Daviault* view that intoxication can lead to a state of automatism.[304] Even if s. 33.1 survives Charter review in the Supreme Court, fundamental questions will remain as to the wisdom of the current legal regime for intoxication, rooted as it still is on the untenable distinction between specific and general intent.

(c) Charter Challenges to Causation Requirements

For those crimes requiring as part of their substantive definition proof of the causing of a particular consequence the leading authority in Canada is *Smithers* (1977).[305] The accused kicked out at a rival ice hockey player after the game and the victim collapsed and died. The Supreme Court discounted any significance in the fact that the victim might have died as a result of a malfunctioning epiglottis. The thin skull rule applied in criminal law and it was sufficient that there was a contributing cause outside the *de minimis* range.

In *F.(D.L.)* (1989),[306] Mr. Justice McClung for the Alberta Court of Appeal suggested, *obiter*, that the *Smithers* "outside de minimis" test was one of such "sweeping accountability" that it might well conflict with principles of fundamental justice under s. 7 of the Charter. He referred to cases involving "parallel or competing causes" of an injury and was especially troubled by how

---

[302] Rulings of constitutionality were reached in *Vickberg* (1998), 16 C.R. (5th) 164 (B.C. S.C.) and *Decaire* (September 11, 1998) (Ont. Gen. Div.). Section 33.1 was ruled unconstitutional in *Dunn* (1999), 28 C.R. (5th) 295 (Ont. Gen.Div.) and *Brenton* (1999), 28 C.R. (5th) 308 (N.W.T. S.C.). These rulings are fully discussed by Kelly Smith, "Section 33.1: Denial of Daviault Defence Should Be Held Constitutional", (2000) 28 C.R. (5th) 350.

[303] Isabel Grant, "Second Chances: Bill C-72 and the Charter", (1995) 33 *Osgoode Hall L.J.* 381 argues sex equality considerations should determine that s. 33.1 does not offend s. 7.

[304] See review by Smith, above note 302, at 362-364. See too Joseph Wilkinson, "The Possibility of Alcoholic Automatism: Some Empirical Evidence", (1997) 2 *Can. Crim. L. Rev.* 217.

[305] (1978), 34 C.C.C. (2d) 427 (S.C.C.). See further Stuart, *Treatise*, above note 103, c. 2.

[306] (1989), 73 C.R. (3d) 391 (Alta. C.A.).

to justly resolve cases of multiple car collisions. For McClung J.A., the cause should be "real and truly contributing".

That there is much to be said for this point of view. The need to reconsider the *Smithers* test seems clear on consideration of the following hypothetical. Motorist A, travelling on a highway within the speed limit, miscalculates the distance between the car in front, driven by B and clips B's bumper. B's car skids off the road and comes to a halt, partly over the median step. Motorist A leaves his vehicle to check that motorist B is not injured. Motorist B is fine and A apologizes, admitting he was to blame. At that moment, truck driver, C, arrives at speed and collides with B's exposed vehicle. The second collision kills B. Quite apart from the issue of fault, surely motorist A should not be automatically criminally responsible for causing the death? This would fly in the face of common sense and would overreach the criminal law power.

A Charter challenge may well be needed to force a full review of *Smithers*. In *Pinske* (1989),[307] a trial judge had charged the jury that the accused's driving had to be the "substantial cause of the accident and not just a minimal or insignificant cause". The majority of the British Columbia Court of Appeal, relying on *Smithers*, held that this test placed too heavy a burden on the Crown. The Supreme Court dismissed the appeal without giving reasons. In view of *Pinske*, the Appeal Division of the Prince Edward Island Supreme Court[308] has considered itself bound to follow *Smithers*. However, the Alberta Court of Appeal still requires a cause to be a real cause.[309]

There are signs that the Supreme Court might be prepared to reconsider *Smithers*. In *DeSousa* (1992),[310] which concerned the fault requirement for the Criminal Code offence under s. 269 of unlawfully causing bodily harm, Sopinka J. for the five justice court remarked in passing that

> For liability to be imposed for unlawfully causing bodily harm, the harm caused must have sufficient causal connection to the underlying offence committed.[311]

The Court cited a 1940 Alberta Court of Appeal ruling.[312] In that decision, the accused was acquitted of manslaughter through an unlawful act causing death. Although the accused had been driving impaired there was evidence that the victim, a cyclist, had swerved into his path. It seems significant that the Supreme Court did not see this situation as having been resolved in favour of conviction by the *Smithers* contributing cause test.

The Supreme Court's decision in *Harbottle* (1993)[313] leaves a window of opportunity for a review of *Smithers*. Under s. 231(5) of the Criminal Code, it is first degree murder where "the death is caused by" the accused while committing

---

[307] [1989] 2 S.C.R. 979.
[308] *Arsenault* (1992), 16 C.R. (4th) 301 (P.E.I. C.A.).
[309] *Ewart* (1989), 53 C.C.C. (3d) 153 and *Colby* (1989), 52 C.C.C. (3d) 321 — criticized by Rick Libman in 18 M.V.R. (2d) 86.
[310] Above note 186.
[311] At 77.
[312] *Wilmot* (1940), 74 C.C.C. 1 (Alta. C.A.).
[313] (1993), 24 C.R. (4th) 137 (S.C.C.).

or attempting to commit a number of listed offences, including sexual assault and forcible confinement. Cory J., speaking for the full Court, held that under the causation test in s. 231(5)

> the actions of the accused must form an essential, substantial and integral part of the killing of the victim.[314]

Noting the various causation provisions concerning homicide, the Court held that

> In order to provide the appropriate distinctions pertaining to causation that must exist for the different homicide offences, it is necessary to examine the sections in their context while taking into account their aim and object.[315]

The Court noted that this test was a much higher test than the *Smithers* test of a contributing cause outside the *de minimis* range. That was a manslaughter case and here a strict test of substantial cause was required by the severe sentencing consequences of the section, its present wording, its history and its aim to protect society from the most heinous murders. The accused must have played a very active role in the killing. The accused's actions would usually but not always physically result in death. The provision included both perpetrators and those assisting in murder. Harbottle's act of holding a rape victim's legs while his co-accused strangled her met this stringent test for first degree murder. The Court further noted that

> there was no intervening act of another which resulted in the accused no longer being substantially connected to the death of the victim.[316]

Harbottle remains to be applied to contexts other than first degree murder. It appears to have decided[317] that the *Smithers* test of a contributing cause outside the *de minimis* range is not a test of general application, may well not apply in murder cases[318] or to offences defining the causal relationship in more direct language,[319] and that are cases where an intervening cause will break the chain of causation. Although *Smithers* has often been interpreted as a universal test of cause, this was clearly never the Court's intent. Dickson J. distinguished an "intervening" cause situation[320] and noted that:

---

[314] At 150.

[315] At 149.

[316] At 151. The Court were relying on the Australian decision in *Hallett*, [1969] S.A.S.R. 141 (S.C.), in which the accused was held guilty of murder where he had beaten the victim unconscious on a beach near the sea and the victim was later drowned by the incoming tide.

[317] See further Allan Manson, "Rethinking Causation: The Implications of Harbottle", (1994) 24 C.R. (4th) 153-165.

[318] The Australian case of *Hallett* clearly required more the *Smithers* test for a murder conviction: see Howard pp. 34-35. See too, more recently, *Royall* (1991), 172 C.L.R. 378 (Aus. H.C.), discussed by Manson, above note 317, at 159-160, and see the critical review by Stephen Shute, "Causation: Foreseeability v. Natural Causes", (1992) 55 *Mod. L. Rev.* 584-587.

[319] Manson, above note 317, points, for example, to the "thereby causes" language used in the case of the offences of dangerous driving causing bodily harm or death (s. 249 (3) and (4)) and impaired driving causing bodily harm or death (s. 255 (2) and (3)).

[320] At 435.

No question of remoteness or of incorrect treatment arises in this case.[321]

In *Cribbin* (1994),[322] the Ontario Court of Appeal however decided that the substantial cause test of *Harbottle* only applied to first degree murder. In a homicide case, the trial judge did not have to instruct the jury that the accused's act, here an assault, had to be the operative and substantial cause of the death. The proper test was that in *Smithers*. The Court acknowledged that an intervening cause question could arise but not on the particular facts. The accused had punched and kicked the victim first before a more vicious attack by the accused's companion. The injuries were not life-threatening, but when the accused and his companion abandoned the unconscious victim, the victim drowned in his own blood. The Court held that for an intervening cause question to arise the two assaulters would have to be truly independent, which was here a remote possibility.

Cribbin is most significant for its Charter rulings. Madam Justice Arbour determined on behalf of the Court that causation is embodied in the principles of fundamental justice that moral innocence not be punished. The law should refrain from holding a person criminally responsible for consequences that should not attributed to the accused. Criminal causation was a legal rule is based on concepts of moral responsibility rather than on demonstrable mechanical or scientific formulas. The morally innocent could be wrongly punished if criminal causation were reduced to a simple *sine qua non*. However, the Court then dismissed s. 7 challenges that the *Smithers de minimis* test was too vague and also too broad. The test was indistinguishable on a vagueness standard from the more stringent substantial cause test. As for being too broad, *Smithers* did not set the standard too low. Somewhat inconsistently with its first Charter ruling, the Court held that in practice there was no difference between the *Smithers* test and the substantial cause tests used in England and Australia. Any risk that the *de minimis* test of causation could engage the criminal responsibility of the morally innocent was removed by the additional fault requirement of objective foresight of bodily harm required for unlawful act manslaughter.

Cribbin is most welcome in its assertion of a minimum Charter standard for cause in criminal law. However, it is disappointing for its acceptance of the status quo. The constitutional standard was set far too low. Jill Presser[323] has rightly pointed out the Court overlooked that *Smithers* is a threshold test which attributes harm to the actor, even if the actual occurrence of the particular harm was fortuitous, and ignores any meaningful moral inquiry into whether the accused should be held responsible for the consequence. Under *Smithers*, the question of

---

[321] At 436.

[322] (1994), 28 C.R. (4th) 137 (Ont. C.A.). See too *Meiler* (1999), 25 C.R. (4th) 161 (Ont. C.A.), criticised by Ron Delisle "Unlawful Object Murder is Alive and Well", (1999) 25 C.R. (5th) 179 at 180-183 ("It is the context. Murder is murder"). See too *Nette* (1999), 29 C.R. (5th) 195 (B.C.C.A.) but there was a dissent by McEachern C.J.B.C. See comments by Stanley Yeo, "Giving Substance to Causation", (2000) 29 C.R. (5th) 215 and Michael Plaxton, "Imputable Cause as Mens Rea: A Reply to Professor Yeo", (2000) 33 C.R. (5th) 78.

[323] "All for a Good Cause: The Need for Overhaul of the Smithers Test of Causation", (1994) 28 C.R. (4th) 178.

imputability is never addressed. Arbour J.A.'s reliance on the fault requirement also overlooks that the fault requirement for manslaughter has been set very low at a reasonable foresight of *harm* rather than of death.[324] Furthermore a fault requirement is not available as a moral safeguard in a case of absolute liability where there is no fault requirement.

Hopefully, the minimum constitutional standard set in *Cribbin* will be revisited in a case where the causal link is more tenuous. Contrary to the opinion of Arbour J.A. it seems quite clear that the *Smithers* test *is* a lower threshold than approaches adopted in other jurisdictions. *Harbottle* certainly recognized a difference.

(d) "Moral Involuntariness" Becomes Charter Standard for Defences

In *Ruzic* (2001),[325] the Supreme Court for the first time recognized that principles of fundamental justice under s. 7 of the Charter require that defences have to meet a minimum constitutional standard in the form of the principle of moral involuntariness. Justice Lebel for a unanimous Court described this new standard in broad terms:

> Although moral involuntariness does not negate the *actus reus* or *mens rea* of an offence, it is a principle which, similarly to physical involuntariness, deserves protection under s. 7 of the Charter. It is a principle of fundamental justice that only voluntary conduct — behaviour that is the product of a free will and controlled body, unhindered by external constraints — should attract the penalty and stigma of criminal liability. Depriving a person of liberty and branding her with the stigma of criminal liability would infringe the principles of fundamental justice if the accused did not have any realistic choice. The ensuing deprivation of liberty and stigma would have been imposed in violation of the tenets of fundamental justice and would thus infringe s. 7 of the Charter.[326]

The Court used this principle to strike down the immediacy and presence requirement for the defence of duress in s. 17. Clearly this pronouncement has implications beyond the law of duress and could be the vehicle for constitutional review of any defence. The Court does not appear to seek to confine the notion of "moral involuntariness" to excuses, as did its original author, George Fletcher.

Lebel J. determines that for criminal responsibility this new Charter standard is distinct from the physical voluntariness requirement for *actus reus*. He also distinguishes it from the moral blameworthiness or moral innocence Charter standard the Court has required for fault. Here he invokes Fletcher for the view that excuses do not concern moral rightness:

> The State refrains from punishing him not because his actions were innocent, but because the circumstances did not leave him with any other realistic choice than to

---

[324] *Creighton*, above note 178.

[325] [2001] S.C.C. 24; April 20, 2001. See too the similar trailblazing judgments of Fish J.A. in *Langlois* (1993), 19 C.R. (4th) 87 (Que. C.A.) and Laskin J.A. in *Ruzic* in the Court below: (1998), 18 C.R. (5th) 58 (Ont. C.A.). The effect of *Ruzic* on the law of duress is further considered in Stuart, *Treatise*, above note 103, c. 7.

[326] Para. 47. The Court relied on Dennis Klimchuk, "Moral Innocence, Normative Involuntariness and Fundamental Justice", (1998) 18 C.R. (5th) 96.

commit the offence. As Fletcher, supra, puts it, at p. 798, excuses absolve the accused of personal accountability by focusing, not on the wrongful act, but on the circumstances of the act and the accused's personal capacity to avoid it. Necessity and duress are characterized as concessions to human frailty in this sense. The law is designed for the common man, not for a community of saints or heroes.[327]

This analysis is persuasive but there is a concern. Given that defences so often involve pragmatic determinations that someone in a situation of agonizing choice should not be punished, even if the act was morally blameworthy, it seems confusing to speak of a principle of *moral* involuntariness.

in *Ruzic*, Lebel J. rejects the view that special deference should be shown by courts in the case of Charter review of defences. Although there was a presumption in favour of constitutionality, there was no basis for limiting Charter review in this context to an "irrational and arbitrary" threshold.[328] There was no special case for a significantly more restrained approach:

> Determining when to absolve a person for otherwise criminal behaviour is a value-laden exercise. However, statutory defences do not warrant more deference simply because they are the product of difficult moral judgments. The entire body of criminal law expresses a myriad of policy choices. Statutory offences are every bit as concerned with social values as statutory defences.[329]

The Court did state that:

> Subject to constitutional review, Parliament retains the right to restrict access to a criminal defence or to remove it altogether.[330]

and that

> limitations on a criminal defence may very well be consistent with the Charter.[331]

This appears somewhat enigmatic given that the Court is also accepting that any defence may be subject to review under its announced Charter standard. Lebel J. refers to the possible removal of a defence of obedience to *de facto* law in the case of war crimes and crimes against humanity, and to the fact that drunkenness is no defence to impaired driving offences. In such cases, suggests Lebel J., the defence would be inconsistent with the very evil prohibited.[332]

The significance of the Court's above caveat will no doubt surface in the not too distant future as the Court in *Ruzic* left open the issue of whether it is constitutional for Parliament to remove the defence of duress from a number of offences listed in s. 17. The Court will then have to confront the argument, accepted in the alternative by Laskin J.A. for the Ontario Court of Appeal in the Court below, that an accepted ground for a s. 7 challenge is that of arbitrariness or irrationality. This point was not addressed in the Supreme Court where the Charter holding is confined to the principle of moral involuntariness.

---

[327] Para. 40.
[328] Para. 26.
[329] Para. 25.
[330] Para. 23.
[331] Para. 24.
[332] Para. 23, referring respectively to *Finta*, [1994] 1 S.C.R. 701 and *Penno*, [1990] 2 S.C.R. 865.

6. VOID FOR VAGUENESS AND OVERBREADTH[333]

It has been clear since the decision of the Supreme Court in the *Prostitution Reference* (1990)[334] that there is now a similar void for vagueness doctrine in Canada grounded in principles of fundamental justice guaranteed by s. 7 of the Charter. The Supreme Court was squarely faced with the argument that the provisions in s. 193 respecting the offence of keeping a common bawdy house and that in s. 195.1(1)(c) making it an offence for anyone in a public place to stop or attempt to stop any person or in any manner to communicate or attempt to communicate with any person for the purpose of prostitution, were unconstitutionally vague. In rejecting the challenges, each of the six participating justices on the panel accepted that an offence that was too vague would be contrary to the principles of fundamental justice under s. 7. The only full discussion is, however, to be found in the single judgment of Mr. Justice Lamer.[335]

According to Mr. Justice Lamer the genesis and development of the void for vagueness doctrine was largely to be found in American jurisprudence although the concept had been recognized in international law and was indeed not novel:

> The principles expressed in these two citations are not new to our law. In fact they are based on the ancient Latin maxim *nullum crimen sine lege, nulla poena sine lege* — that there can be no crime or punishment unless it is in accordance with law that is certain, unambiguous and not retroactive. The rationale underlying this principle is clear. It is essential in a free and democratic society that citizens are able, as far as is possible, to foresee the consequences of their conduct in order that persons be given fair notice of what to avoid, and that the discretion of those entrusted with law enforcement is limited by clear and explicit legislative standards.[336]

In applying the vagueness doctrine to the case at hand, Mr. Justice Lamer held that the doctrine did not "require that a law be absolutely certain: no law can meet that standard".[337] He expressly relied on a dictum of the Ontario Court of Appeal that

> the void for vagueness doctrine is not to be applied to the bare words of the statutory provision but, rather, to the provision as interpreted and applied in judicial decisions".[338]

According to Lamer J., the question was

> whether the impugned sections of the Criminal Code can be or have been given sensible meanings by the Courts. In other words, is the statute so pervasively vague that it permits a "standardless sweep" allowing law enforcement officials to pursue their personal predilections?[339]

---

[333] See especially Gary T. Trotter, "Le Beau: Toward a Canadian Vagueness Doctrine" (1988), 62 C.R. (3d) 157. See generally Stuart, *Treatise*, above note 103, c. 1, which includes a review of doctrine and commentary in the United States.

[334] (1990), 77 C.R. (3d) 1 (S.C.C.).

[335] Chief Justice Dickson with La Forest and Sopinka JJ. concurring, appears to have adopted Lamer's approach on this point (at 17-18).

[336] At 26.

[337] At 30.

[338] *LeBeau* (1988), 62 C.R. (3d) 157 (Ont. C.A.) at 167.

[339] At 30. For the latter proposition, Lamer J. relied on American authority, including *Kolender v. Lawson*, 103 S. Ct. 1855 (1983).

The most thorough consideration of the Canadian vagueness doctrine is that of Gonthier J. for a unanimous panel of seven justices in *Nova Scotia Pharmaceutical Society* (1992).[340] The Court held that a Combines Investigation Act offence of conspiracy to lessen competition "unduly" did not violate s. 7 of the Charter on grounds of vagueness. Gonthier J. took the opportunity to re-examine and refine the jurisprudence of the Supreme Court in the *Prostitution Reference* and other decisions.

The Court drew a clear distinction between vagueness and overbreadth.[341] A vagueness claim would usually be grounded under s. 7 as it was a principle of fundamental justice that a law could not be too vague. However, it might also be relevant to a section one inquiry as a vague law could not satisfy the requirement that a limitation on a Charter right be "prescribed by law". On the other hand, "overbreadth" had no autonomous value under the Charter and was always related only to a section one inquiry:

> [Overbreadth] is always related to some limitation under the Charter. Its is always established by comparing the ambit of the provision touching upon a protected right with such concepts as the objectives of the State, the principles of fundamental justice, the proportionality of punishment or the reasonableness of searches and seizures, to name a few. There is no such thing as overbreadth in the abstract. Overbroad has no autonomous value under the Charter.[342]

According to Gonthier J. for the Court, the "doctrine of vagueness" was founded on the rule of law, particularly on the principles of fair notice to citizens and limitation of enforcement discretion. Aside from the formal aspect, which the current system presumed by the maxim "ignorance of the law is no excuse",[343] fair notice also included a substantive aspect of "an understanding that some conduct comes under the law".[344] Gonthier J. then synthesized these rationales which were seen to point in the same direction:

> an unintelligible provision gives insufficient guidance for legal debate and is therefore unconstitutionally vague.[345]

This statement of the doctrine was seen to best conform to the dictates of the rule of law in the modern state and to reflect the prevailing argumentative, adversarial framework for the administration of justice. No higher requirement as to certainty could be imposed. It could not be argued that an enactment could and must provide enough guidance to predict the legal consequences of any given course of conduct in advance. All it could do was to enunciate some boundaries which created an area of risk. A vague provision did not provide an adequate basis for legal debate, that is, for reaching a conclusion as to its meaning by reasoned analysis applying

---

[340] (1992), 15 C.R. (4th) 1 (S.C.C.).

[341] At 18.

[342] At 20.

[343] Gonthier J. left open the question whether this rule embodied in s. 19 of the Criminal Code contradicted the rule of law and might have to be revised in light of the growing quantity and complexity of penal legislation (at 22-23).

[344] At 23.

[345] At 26.

legal criteria. The threshold for finding a law vague was relatively high. Factors to be considered included the need for flexibility and the interpretive role of the court, the impossibility of achieving absolute certainty, a standard of intelligibility being more appropriate and the possibility that many varying interpretations of a given disposition might exist and perhaps co-exist.[346]

A review of this complex analysis of Gonthier J. leaves the unmistakable impression that the Canadian doctrine of void for vagueness has arrived with no teeth. Such challenges seem very unlikely to succeed. Indeed, the Supreme Court itself has already rejected 11 out of 15 challenges,[347] including one against the notoriously vague obscenity laws.[348] Provincial courts applying the *Nova Scotia Pharmaceutical* test have universally rejected vagueness claims.[349] There are several reasons for suggesting that the approach is far too narrow.

There is, firstly, little indication that the Supreme Court accepts the persuasive view of the United States Supreme Court that the principal rationale for the doctrine should be that of a protection against arbitrary enforcement. Gonthier J.'s synthesis of the two rationales and his subsequent discussion clearly emphasizes fair notice to the virtual exclusion from consideration of the likelihood of vague laws leading to unacceptable arbitrariness in law enforcement. The vagueness doctrine becomes a much more powerful instrument where there is a specific focus on the dangers of unfettered discretion at the enforcement stage.

That this is so is evidenced by consideration of the later decision of the Supreme Court in *Morales* (1992),[350] the first decision in the highest Court accepting a vagueness challenge. The Court ruled 5-2 that the separate criterion of "public interest" under s. 515(10)(b) of the Criminal Code violated the right under s. 11(e) of the Charter not to be denied reasonable bail without just cause as the provision did not meet the *Nova Scotia Pharmaceutical* test for vagueness. For the majority, Chief Justice Lamer[351] emphasized both rationales of fair notice and limitation of law enforcement discretion. He reasserted his view in the *Prostitution Reference* that any provision authorizing imprisonment should not

---

[346] At 18, 26-30.

[347] Ten of the rejecting decisions are reviewed in *Nova Scotia Pharmaceutical*. See now *Lucas*, above note 106 (defamatory libel) and *Winko* (1999), 25 C.R. (5th) 1 (S.C.C.) (phrase "significant threat to safety of the public" respecting mental disorder provisions). The successful challenges occurred after *Nova Scotia Pharmaceutical* in *Morales* and *Heywood*, reviewed below at notes 350 and 356.

[348] *Butler* (1992), 11 C.R. (4th) 137 (S.C.C.). See too *Langer* (1995), 40 C.R. (4th) 204 (Ont. Gen. Div.) (child pornography laws not too vague) and *Mara* (1996), 46 C.R. (4th) 167 (Ont. C.A.) (term "indecent" in s. 167(1) of Criminal Code not too vague). The *Butler* ruling on this point was followed in *Little Sisters* (2000), 38 C.R. (5th) 209 (S.C.C.) (material respecting gay and lesbian sexuality).

[349] See, for example, *Fisher* (1994), 88 C.C.C. (3d) 103 (Ont. C.A.) (offence of government employee accepting benefits), *Ratelle* (1994), 92 C.C.C. (3d) 176 (Que. C.A.) (canvassing for assignment under Bankruptcy Act), *Sillipp* (1995), 99 C.C.C. (3d) 394 (Alta. Q.B.) (criminal harassment), *Berntt* (1997), 11 C.R. (5th) 131 (B.C. C.A.) and *Stromberg* (1999), 131 C.C.C. (3d) 546 (B.C. C.A.) (lottery offences).

[350] (1992), 17 C.R. (4th) 74 (S.C.C.).

[351] La Forest, Sopinka, McLachlin and Iacobucci JJ. concurred.

authorize a "standardless sweep". Having regard to current interpretations by the courts, the majority concluded that

> the term "public interest" is incapable of framing the legal debate in any meaningful manner or structuring discretion in any way.[352]

In contrast, the dissenting opinion of Gonthier J.[353] focused much more on the issue of whether the provision provided an adequate framework for legal debate. His brief discussion on the need to limit discretion favoured the value of flexibility.

The void for vagueness doctrine's protection of the principle of fair notice is also substantially weakened where courts, such as the Supreme Court and the Ontario Court of Appeal, place so much emphasis on clarification through prior judicial interpretation. As Gary Trotter points out,[354] the standard changes from "persons of common intelligence" to "jurists of unusual diligence". The focus is too much on specialist legal knowledge. It should not be open to the courts to *ex post facto* ascribe a "sensible meaning" to vague statutory provisions. If the language is vague, the legislature should be made to tighten it up.[355]

There may be an unintended weakening of the protection of the voidness doctrine in the recognition of vagueness as a constitutional vice *per se* in s. 7. In the United States, under what is known as the "chilling effect" doctrine, the void for vagueness doctrine is applied more strictly where a constitutional freedom such as the right of free speech is also infringed. It might be wise, then, where possible, to frame vagueness arguments by relying on both s. 7 and freedom of expression under s. 2(b).

New life may have been breathed into the vagueness doctrine by the Supreme Court's decision in *Heywood* (1994).[356] A 5-4 majority struck down the vagrancy offence under s. 179(1)(b) of the Criminal Code making it an offence for those convicted of certain listed sexual offences to be

> found loitering in or near a school ground, playground, public park or bathing area.

Cory J. for the majority[357] held that the section infringed liberty of the accused contrary to principles of fundamental justice guaranteed by s. 7 of the Charter because the offence suffered from overbreadth. The provision reached too many places no matter how remote or devoid of children they might be, applied for life without any process for review, caught persons who might not constitute a danger to children and imposed a prohibition without any notice to the accused. Cory J. noted that the provision had been replaced by a provision that had addressed these

---

[352] At 95, distinguished in *Farinacci* (1993), 25 C.R. (4th) 350 (Ont. C.A.) and *Branco* (1993), 25 C.R. (4th) 370 (B.C. C.A.) (bail pending appeal based on public interest) but applied in *Fosseneuve* (1995), 43 C.R. (4th) 260 (Man. Q.B.) (power of arrest in public interest).

[353] L'Heureux-Dubé J. concurring.

[354] "Lebeau Toward a Canadian Vagueness Doctrine", (1988) 62 C.R. (3d) 157.

[355] See too J.C. Jeffries Jr., "Legality Vagueness and the Construction of Penal Statutes", (1985) 71 *Va. L. Rev.* 189.

[356] (1994), 34 C.R. (4th) 133 (S.C.C.).

[357] Lamer C.J., Sopinka, Iacobucci and Major JJ. concurred.

concerns[358] but held that in any event overbroad legislation which infringed s. 7 was incapable of being demonstrably justified as a reasonable limit under s. 1.

The minority through Gonthier J.[359] were of the view that the offence was not too broad given a requirement of proof of a malevolent or ulterior purpose[360] relating to the predicate offence and that formal notice was not a principle of fundamental justice.

The most surprising aspect of *Heywood* is that, despite the apparent clear determination in the *Nova Scotia Pharmaceutical Society* case that overbreadth is only a matter for a section one inquiry, overbreadth is here held to ground the violation of s. 7. According to Cory J.:

> Overbreadth and vagueness are related in that both are the result of a lack of sufficient precision by a legislature in the means used to accomplish an objective. In the case of vagueness, the means are not clearly defined. In the case of overbreadth the means are too sweeping in relation to the objective.

> Overbreadth analysis looks at the means chosen by the state in relation to its purpose. In considering whether a legislative provision is over broad, a court must ask the question: are those means necessary to achieve the State objective? If the State, in pursuing a legitimate objective, uses means which are broader than is necessary to accomplish that objective, the principles of fundamental justice will be violated because the individual's rights will have been limited for no reason. The effect of overbreadth is that in some applications the law is arbitrary or disproportionate.[361]

Although Cory J. appears to rely on *Nova Scotia Pharmaceutical Society*, *Heywood* surely overrules it to the extent that it recognizes a s. 7 challenge grounded solely on overbreadth. In future courts can expect alternative challenges based on overbreadth according to *Heywood* and vagueness based on the "no room for legal debate test" of *Nova Scotia Pharmaceutical Society*. From the point of view of defence counsel, overbreadth would appear to be the much easier line of challenge.[362] However, Crown counsel will no doubt seek to distinguish

[358] Section 161, enacted by S.C. 1993, c. 45, s. 1.

[359] La Forest, L'Heureux-Dubé and McLachlin JJ. concurred.

[360] According to Cory J. for the majority such a requirement "could mean almost anything, and its definition would be dependent upon the subjective views of the particular judge trying the case" (at 152). Loiter had to be given its ordinary meaning of standing idly around.

[361] At 156.

[362] In *Budreo* (2000), 32 C.R. (5th) 127 (Ont. C.A.) the Court upheld the validity of s. 810.1 of the Criminal Code permitting a recognizance on a person likely to commit sexual offences against children under 14. However the legislation was read down to delete reference to community centres and the mandatory issuance of process. In *E.(B.)* (1999), 29 C.R. (5th) 57 (Ont. C.A.) the Court rejected a challenge against the Criminal Code offence in s. 172(1) of participating in sexual immorality endangering morals of children. The Court confined its ruling to the charge as particularised. In *Sharpe* (2001), 39 C.R. (5th) 72 (S.C.C.), the Supreme Court upheld the validity of the prohibition against child pornography in s. 163.1(4) of the Criminal Code. McLachlin C.J., writing for 6 justices, concluded that the prohibition was a demonstrably justified reasonable limit on freedom of expression guaranteed in s. 2(b) of the Charter. However the Court identified a problem of overbreadth and, apart from making careful clarification of many of the provisions, found it necessary to read in two exlclusions dealing with self-authored works of imagination and visual representation of sexual activity by teenagers for private use. The Court makes no mention of the doctrines of vagueness under *Nova Scotia Pharmaceutical Society* or overbreadth under *Heywood*.

Heywood as being a ruling on a particularly anomalous and special kind of crime prevention legislation.

The Supreme Court has already served notice that it may reconsider or at least qualify the *Heywood* doctrine of overbreadth. In *Canadian Pacific Ltd.* (1995),[363] the Court was unanimous in deciding that an offence under a provincial Environmental Protection Act prohibiting any use of the natural environment was not too vague or overbroad. Properly interpreted the provision provided a basis for legal debate and did not capture pollution with only a trivial or minimal impact. The Court saw the need to allow legislators considerable room to manoeuvre in the field of environmental regulation. Gonthier J. for the majority[364] added a caveat to his analysis that the provision was not overbroad. Since *Heywood* had not been argued, his reasons should not be taken to endorse the view that the independent principle of overbreadth recognized in *Heywood* was available in the circumstances of this case.[365]

The notion of courts striking down laws as too broad seems unruly. The principle may be defensible on the basis that a blunderbuss provision may provide too much scope for arbitrary discretion in enforcement.

7. RIGHT TO SILENCE[366]

The watershed ruling of the Supreme Court in *Hebert* (1990)[367] recognizes that s. 7 guarantees a pre-trial right to silence. It cannot be properly understood without an appreciation of the common law position.

(a) Pre-trial

(i) *Common law*

Although the scope and rationale of the common law right to remain silent are highly controversial, it is quite clear that our courts have consistently asserted that such a right exists and is fundamental. The predominant judicial explanation is that the right is a corollary to the absence of any legal right of the police to compel the accused to answer their questions. This is well expressed by Mr. Justice Martin for the Ontario Court of Appeal in *Esposito* (1985):[368]

> The right of a suspect or an accused to remain silent is deeply rooted in our legal tradition. The right operates both at the investigative stage of the criminal process

---

[363] (1995), 41 C.R. (4th) 147 (S.C.C.).

[364] La Forest, L'Heureux-Dubé, McLachlin, Iacobucci and Major JJ. concurred. Lamer C.J. and (Sopinka and Cory JJ. concurring) agreed but with no hesitation in applying *Heywood*.

[365] At 191.

[366] See generally E. Ratushny, *Self-Incrimination in the Canadian Criminal Process* (1979), but compare David M. Paciocco, ''Self-Incrimination: Removing the Coffin Nails'' (1989), 35 *McGill L.J.* 73. See too Marc Rosenberg, ''Right to Silence'', paper presented at C.B.A.O. conference on March 4,1989 and Patrick Healy, ''The Value of Silence'' (1990), 74 C.R. (3d) 176.

[367] (1990), 77 C.R. (3d) 145 (S.C.C.).

[368] (1985), 49 C.R. (3d) 193 (Ont. C.A.).

and at the trial stage. In Canada, save in certain circumstances, a suspect is free to answer or not to answer questions by the police. We say that he has a right to remain silent because there is no legal obligation upon him to speak: see *Rothman v. R.*, [1981] 1 S.C.R. 640, per Lamer J. at p. 64.

A police officer, when he is endeavouring to discover whether or by whom an offence has been committed, is entitled to question any person, whether suspected or not, from whom he thinks that useful information can be obtained. Although a police officer is entitled to question any person in order to obtain information with respect to a suspected offence, he as a general rule has no power to compel the person questioned to answer. Moreover, he has no power to detain a person for questioning, and if the person questioned declines to answer the police officer must allow him to proceed on his way unless he arrests him on reasonable and probable grounds.[369]

Common law rules relating to admissibility establish that respect for the right to silence at the pre-trial stage is "qualified".[370] Although courts have insisted that silence of the accused in the face of police questioning is generally inadmissible, there is uncertain jurisprudence that the failure to give an explanation may be admissible if it becomes relevant to an issue in the case.[371] Our courts have also, on occasion, allowed adverse comment to be made on the failure of an accused to comply with investigative tests.[372]

There is no recognized common law duty on the police to warn the accused of the right to silence, although this is customary.[373] If the accused does speak to a person in authority such as a police officer, the statement will be admissible provided that the Crown proves that it was voluntary. Until its recent reconsideration in *Oickle* (2000),[374] which we will here consider later, the Supreme Court has limited the determination of involuntariness to where it has been obtained "by fear of prejudice or hope of advantage exercised or held out by a person in authority"[375] *or* where the statement was not "the utterance of an operating mind,"[376] as is the case with one semi-conscious or under hypnosis.[377]

---

[369] *Ibid.*, at 200-201.

[370] Healy, above note 366, p. 177.

[371] The leading pronouncement is that by Martin J.A. in *Symonds* (1983), 38 C.R. (3d) 51 (Ont. C.A.) at 227:

> It is fundamental that a person charged with a criminal offence has the right to remain silent and a jury is not entitled to draw any inference against an accused because he chooses to exercise that right. We think that in the absence of some issue arising in the case which makes the statement of an accused, following the giving of a caution, that he has nothing to say relevant to that issue, such evidence is inadmissible.

See too *Machado* (1989), 71 C.R. (3d) 158 (B.C. C.A.) and the discussions by Paciocco, *Charter Principles and Proofing Criminal Cases* (1987) pp. 552-570 and in *McGill L.J.*, above note 366, pp. 84-85.

[372] *Sweeney (No. 2)* (1977), 35 C.C.C. (2d) 245 (Ont. C.A.) (psychiatric examination) and *Marcoux* (1975), 24 C.C.C. (2d) 1 (S.C.C.). See now *Leclair*, below, Chapter 5, respecting protection under s. 10(b).

[373] The usual caution used, for example, in *Manninen* is "You (are charged, will be charged) with . . . Do you wish to say anything in answer to the charge? You are not obliged to say anything unless you wish to do so, but whatever you say may be given in evidence."

[374] (2000), 36 C.R. (5th) 129 (S.C.C.), considered below note 461.

[375] This is the classic formula from *Ibrahim*, [1914] A.C. 599 (P.C.).

[376] *Rothman* (1981), 20 C.R. (3d) 97 (S.C.C.), discussed further below, Chapter 11.

[377] *Ward*, [1979] 2 S.C.R. 30 and *Horvath*, [1979] 2 S.C.R. 376.

In the determination of voluntariness it has long been clear that whether the accused was warned by the police as to the right to silence is merely an important but not determinative factor to be considered.[378] In *Rothman* (1981),[379] the majority of the Supreme Court further held that the test for whether the questioner is a person in authority depends on the subjective belief of the accused. Rothman had not realized that his cell-mate was an undercover police officer. His admission to the officer, despite the officer's deception and, of course, no warning as to the right to remain silent, was held to be admissible.

Mr. Justice Martland, speaking for five other justices,[380] bluntly held that a trial judge could not in any event reject a confession "solely because he disapproved of the method by which it was obtained".[381] The issue was one of reliability[382] to which the privilege against self-incrimination was irrelevant.[383]

In dissent, Mr. Justice Estey[384] would have applied an "exclusionary rule" under which confessions are not admissible

> where to admit them would bring the administration of justice into disrepute, or, to put it another way, would prejudice the public interest in the integrity of the judicial process.[385]

The ninth justice, Lamer J., would also have changed the law of confessions to focus on police methods but his approach was more cautious through a "community shock" test.[386] Applying this test he agreed with the majority on the facts. The use of the undercover agent in *Rothman* would not shock the community but would have, in Justice Lamer's opinion, had the officer posed as a priest or a defence counsel. He added that

> It must also be borne in mind that the investigation of crime and the detection of criminals is not a game to be governed by the Marquess of Queensbury rules. The authorities, in dealing with shrewd and often sophisticated criminals must sometimes of necessity resort to tricks or other forms of deceit and should not through the rule be hampered in their work.[387]

(ii) *Section 7 right: Hebert*

The issue in *Hebert* was the admissibility of a statement by an accused who had been arrested on a charge of robbery to an undercover police officer placed in his cell after he had indicated that he did not wish to speak to the police. The Supreme Court of Canada unanimously decided that the statement had been

---

[378] *Boudreau*, [1949] S.C.R. 262, discussed in *Esposito*, above note 368, at 202-203.
[379] Above note 376.
[380] Ritchie, Dickson, Beetz, McIntyre and Chouinard JJ.
[381] At 38.
[382] *Ibid.*
[383] At 37.
[384] Laskin C.J. concurred.
[385] At 52.
[386] At 74.
[387] *Ibid.*

obtained in violation of a breach of the right to silence under s. 7 and had been properly excluded under s. 24(2).

McLachlin J. (as she then was) delivered the majority judgment, with six justices concurring.[388] She found in the common law voluntary confession rule and in the privilege against self-incrimination, which granted the accused immunity from incriminating himself at trial, the essence of the right to silence:

> [T]he person whose freedom is placed in question by the judicial process must be given the choice of whether to speak to the authorities or not.[389]

Consideration of other Charter rights suggested that the right to silence of detained persons under s. 7 had to be broad enough to accord that person a free choice on the matter of whether to speak to the authorities. The most important function of the right to counsel was to ensure that the accused understood his rights, chief among which was his right to silence. The privilege against self-incrimination enshrined in ss. 11(c) and 13 of the Charter would be diminished if a person were to be compelled to make statements at the pre-trial stage. The right of a detained person to silence under s. 7 had to be viewed as broader in scope than the confessions rule existing in Canada at the time of the adoption of the Charter. The right had to reflect the Charter's concern for individual freedom and the integrity of the judicial process, and permit the exclusion of evidence offensive to those values. On a ''purposive approach'' to the right to silence, the scope of the right had to be extended to exclude police tricks which would effectively deprive the suspect of the choice of remaining silent:

> To permit the authorities to trick the suspect into making a confession to them after he or she has exercised the right of conferring with counsel and declined to make a statement, is to permit the authorities to do indirectly what the Charter does not permit them to do directly. This cannot be in accordance with the purpose of the Charter.[390]

McLachlin J. had earlier pointed out that *Rothman* had been decided after the majority ruling in *Wray* (1971)[391] that a court had no power to exclude admissible and relevant evidence on the basis that the administration of justice would be brought into disrepute. Distinguished scholars and judges had criticized this approach and it could no longer be maintained under the Charter.[392]

Having justified the right to silence at the pre-trial stage, the majority then turned to defining it and striking a proper balance between the interests of the State in law enforcement and the interest of the suspect.[393]

---

[388] Dickson C.J., Lamer, La Forest, L'Heureux-Dubé, Gonthier and Cory JJ. Wilson and Sopinka JJ. gave separate concurring reasons.

[389] Above note 367, at 182.

[390] *Ibid.*, at 186.

[391] [1971] S.C.R. 272.

[392] Above note 367, at 177-182.

[393] Wilson J. sees it as

> inappropriate to qualify [a right] by balancing the interests of the state against it or by applying to it the considerations relevant to the admissibility of evidence set out in s. 24(2) of the Charter (*ibid.*, at 153).

Consideration of whether the right to silence has been violated requires an "objective" approach:

> The Charter does not place on the authorities and the courts the impossible task of subjectively gauging whether the suspect appreciates the situation and the alternatives. Rather, it seeks to ensure that the suspect is in a position to make an informed choice by giving him the right to counsel.[394]
>
> . . . .
>
> The basic requirement that the suspect possess an operating mind has a subjective element. But this established, the focus under the Charter shifts to the conduct of the authorities vis-à-vis the suspect. Was the suspect accorded the right to consult counsel? Was there other police conduct which effectively and unfairly deprived the suspect of the right to choose whether to speak to the authorities or not?[395]

Madam Justice McLachlin further determines that her approach was not one of an "absolute right to silence in the accused, capable of being discharged only by waiver." On the subjective approach to waiver defined in *Clarkson* (1986),[396] all statements made by detainees not knowingly made to a police officer would be excluded because the Crown could not establish waiver. The majority decided that the scope of the right to silence should not be extended this far.[397]

Madam Justice McLachlin further identifies four limits to this newly recognized constitutional right to silence:

1. The police may question the accused in the absence of counsel after the accused has retained counsel:[398]

> Presumably, counsel will inform the accused of the right to remain silent. If the police are not posing as undercover officers and the accused chooses to volunteer information, there will be no violation of the Charter. Police persuasion, short of denying the suspect the right to choose or depriving him of an operating mind, does not breach the right to silence.[399]

2. The right to silence applies only after detention:

> In an undercover operation prior to detention, the individual from whom information is sought is not in the control of the state. There is no need to protect him from the greater power of the state. After detention, the situation is quite different; the state takes control and assumes the responsibility of ensuring that the detainee's rights are respected.[400]

---

[394] *Ibid.*, at 183.

[395] *Ibid.*, at 187.

[396] [1986] 1 S.C.R. 383.

[397] Both Sopinka and Wilson JJ. would have applied the accepted waiver standard.

[398] Above note 367, at 188.

[399] *Ibid.*

[400] *Ibid.*, at 189. Sopinka and Wilson JJ. dissented on this point. According to Sopinka J.:

> The right to remain silent, viewed purposively, must arise when the coercive power of the state is brought to bear against the individual — either formally (by arrest or charge) or informally (by detention or accusation) — on the basis that it is at this point that an adversary relationship comes to exist between the state and the individual (at 161).

According to Wilson J. there should be a right to silence whenever the coercive power of the state is brought to bear upon the citizen (at 153).

3. The right to silence does not affect voluntary statements to a cell-mate provided that person is not acting as a police informant or an undercover police officer.[401]

4. The right to silence is not violated where undercover agents observe the suspect and do not "actively elicit information in violation of the suspect's choice to remain silent."[402]

The majority provides little guidance as to how this key distinction between active and passive undercover work is to be drawn. The record in *Hebert* itself is not very helpful. There was an agreed statement of facts indicating that an undercover agent engaged Hebert in conversation in his cell after he had refused to talk to the police.[403] This trick was held to negate his choice not to speak in violation of his right to silence.[404] McLachlin J. seems to have adopted a United States Supreme Court holding in *Kuhlmann v. Wilson* (1986)[405] that the police cannot take "some action beyond merely listening, that was designed deliberately to elicit incriminating remarks."[406] The police must not, holds McLachlin J., "take active and intentional steps to elicit a confession."[407] She also appears to hold that the work of the undercover officers placed in protective custody in *Logan* (1988)[408] did not violate the right to silence. In that case, the officers testified that the accused had been bragging about his crime in the cell block and the officers had been instructed "not to initiate any conversation, if possible" and to avoid leading questions.[409]

The ambit of the *Hebert* right was clarified by Justice Iacobucci for a unanimous Court in *Broyles* (1991).[410] From *Hebert* it was clear that the purpose of the right to silence was to

> prevent the use of state power to subvert the right of an accused to choose whether or not to speak to the authorities.[411]

The right would only be infringed where (1) the evidence was obtained by an agent of the state and (2) the evidence was elicited. In determining whether an

---

[401] *Ibid.*, at 189. The Court is unanimous on this point.

[402] *Ibid.*

[403] *Ibid.*, at 168-169. According to the Court below this was not a case where the undercover officer repeated an earlier interrogation in the cells: (1988), 43 C.C.C. (3d) 56 at 60 (Y.T. C.A.). The transcript at the preliminary inquiry (1991), 3 C.R. (4th) 61, places the undercover officer, Corporal Miller, in the cell for two hours. After another officer questioned the accused about an armed robbery, the accused told Corp. Miller he could not be identified. At this point, Corp. Miller initiated a half-hour conversation about the robbery, in which he questioned the accused and obtained incriminating answers.

[404] *Ibid.*, at 191.

[405] 477 U.S. 436.

[406] *Ibid.*, at 459.

[407] Above note 367, at 190.

[408] (1988), 68 C.R. (3d) 1 (Ont. C.A.).

[409] At 190. The issue was not considered when *Logan* reached the Supreme Court, above note 228. Lamer C.J.C. described the undercover work in *Logan* as not encouraging the accused to talk but merely providing the opportunity to make statements (at 173).

[410] (1991), 9 C.R. (4th) 1 (S.C.C.).

[411] At 11.

informer is a state agent, the focus must be on the effect of the relationship between the informer and the authorities. The test is

> would the exchange between the accused and the informer have taken place, in the form and manner in which it did take place, but for the intervention of the state or its agents.[412]

Whether the state agent had elicited the statement required a broad enquiry:

> The first set of factors concerns the nature of the exchange between the accused and the state agent. Did the state agent actively seek out information such that the exchange could be characterized as akin to an interrogation, or did he or she conduct his or her part of the conversation as someone in the role the accused believed the informer to be playing would ordinarily have done? The focus should not be on the form of the conversation, but rather on whether the relevant parts of the conversation were the functional equivalent of an interrogation.
>
> The second set of factors concerns the nature of the relationship between the state agent and the accused. Did the state agent exploit any special characteristics of the relationship to extract the statement? Was there a relationship of trust between the state agent and the accused? Was the accused obligated or vulnerable to the state agent? Did the state agent manipulate the accused to bring about a mental state in which the accused was more likely to talk?[413]

Iacobucci J. repeated dicta in *Hebert* that instructions to the agent not to initiate the conversation nor ask leading questions would tend toward a finding of no violation. However, he added that instructing the agent not to elicit the information would not end the inquiry as the authorities could not take the benefit of actions of agents that had exceeded instructions.[414]

In *Broyles*, there had been a clear breach of s. 7 on these tests. The police arranged for a friend to visit the accused who was in custody on a fraud charge, providing him with a body-pack recording device and effectively instructed the friend to elicit information about a death for the purposes of a murder charge. The conversations had been functionally the equivalent of an interrogation and the agent had exploited the accused's trust in him as a friend to undermine the accused's confidence in his lawyer's advice to remain silent and to create a mental state in which the accused was more likely to talk.

Surprising, the Supreme Court in *Liew* (1999),[415] over the sole dissent of Lamer C.J., held that an undercover officer asking a cellmate, "What happened?" and stating, "Yeah. They got my fingerprints on the dope" was *not* the functional equivalent of an interrogation. The Ontario Court of Appeal has often distinguished *Hebert* in cases involving undercover agents and informants.

The Court decided in particular cases that there was no breach because the informant was not an agent of the state,[416] there was no detention,[417] no active

---

[412] At 12.

[413] At 14.

[414] *Ibid.*

[415] (1999), 27 C.R. (5th) 29 (S.C.C.).

[416] *Gray* (1991), 66 C.C.C. (3d) 6 (Ont. C.A.). The Court held the informant, an inmate with a long criminal record sharing the same range as the accused, had not been a police agent since he offered to obtained information from the accused and, although the police had put him in the

eliciting[418] and that *Hebert* had no application where the accused had not asserted his right to silence.[419] Not surprisingly, the Court held[420] that the s. 7 pre-trial right to silence had been violated where an undercover agent, posing as a student at a murder preliminary inquiry, had developed a relationship with the accused over six visits to a gaol, during which she had directed specific questions to obtain statements about the killing.

Provincial courts have proved reluctant to extend the *Hebert* pre-trial right to silence to situations where the officer is identified. It has been held that non-coercive questioning prior to detention is no violation.[421] The right does not protect against surreptitious videotaping of an accused who had refused to participate in a lineup,[422] the police taking a polaroid picture to preserve identity of an accused detained on a charge of communicating for the purpose of prostitution[423] or against police photographing in detention for identification purposes.[424] The taking of fingerprints from persons reasonably suspected to be involved with drugs but not charged and hence not under the Identification of Criminals Act does not violate s. 7.[425] However, a trial judge held that a common law rule that the accused's failure to provide identity to an officer constituted the Criminal Code offence of obstruction *did* violate s. 7 and was of no force or effect.[426] Another rare right to silence recognition[427] occurred in a trial judge's decision that police obtaining voice identification in a courtroom hallway on the pretext of obtaining disclosure violated the Charter right to choose not to speak.

In *Smith* (1996),[428] Mr. Justice Doherty for the Ontario Court of Appeal confirmed that a detained person has no absolute right to remain silent. The police are not absolutely prohibited from questioning a detained person and do not have to advise as to the right to remain silent. Where there is no s. 10(b) right to counsel, as in the case of a motorist asked to perform sobriety tests under the Highway Traffic Act, the s. 7 right to make an informed choice as to whether to speak to police required only that the police did not engage in conduct that effectively and

---

same cell, they had given him no special instructions as to how to proceed. Given *Broyles*, *Gray* now appears to be of doubtful authority. But see too *McInnis* (1999), 134 C.C.C. (3d) 515 (Ont. C.A.).

[417] *Miller* (1991), 9 C.R. (4th) 347 (Ont. C.A.).

[418] *Graham* (1991), 3 C.R. (4th) 44 (Ont. C.A.) and *Johnston* (1991), 64 C.C.C. (3d) 233 (Ont. C.A.). See too *Spanevello* (1988), 125 C.C.C. (3d) 97 (B.C. C.A.) (undercover officer telling accused that for a large sum of money friend would confess to his murder charge not amounting to active elicitation!)

[419] *Graham*, above note 418.

[420] *Jackson* (1991), 9 C.R. (4th) 57 (Ont. C.A.).

[421] *Hicks* (1988), 64 C.R. (3d) 68 (Ont. C.A.), affirmed (1990), 54 C.C.C. (3d) 574 (S.C.C.). See too *Imeson* (1992), 13 C.R. (4th) 322 (Ont. Gen. Div.).

[422] *Parsons* (1993), 24 C.R. (4th) 112 (Ont. C.A.), criticized by David Tanovich, "The Right to Counsel and Police Lineups", (1994) 24 C.R. (4th) 125.

[423] *Dilling* (1993), 24 C.R. (4th) 171 (B.C. C.A.).

[424] *Chung* (1997), 8 C.R. (5th) 189 (B.C. S.C.).

[425] *Bourque* (1995), 43 C.R. (4th) 327 (Que. C.A.).

[426] Pepler J. in *Leitch* (1992), 18 C.R. (4th) 224 (Alta. Prov. Ct.).

[427] *Gordon* (1999), 133 C.C.C. (3d) 349 (Ont. Gen. Div.).

[428] (1996), 46 C.R. (4th) 229 (Ont. C.A.).

unfairly deprives the detainee of the right to choose whether to speak. The Court held that s. 7 had not been violated by two simple questions as to whether the motorist had been drinking and as to the quantity.

Recent interpretations of the right to silence in the context of police questioning after the accused has been afforded an opportunity to consult counsel have turned on the following passage of McLachlin J. in *Hebert*:

> [The] Charter requires that the suspect be informed of his or her right to counsel and be permitted to consult counsel without delay. If the suspect chooses to make a statement, the suspect may do so. But if the suspect chooses not to, the state is not entitled to use its superior power to override the suspect's will and negate his or her choice.[429]

The B.C. Court of Appeal determined in *K. (H.W.)* (2000)[430] that the s. 7 right to silence was not breached by overriding the accused's choice not to speak where police asked the accused in a murder case whether he wished to take a breathalyser, after assuring the lawyer they would not be interviewing him. Because of the agreement with the lawyer, McEachern C.J.B.C., for the Court, found this case close to the line between "fair and unfair treatment" but noted that the accused had chosen freely and voluntarily to say far more than was necessary to answer the question.[431] So too the B.C. Court held there was no right to silence violation in *Ekman* (2000).[432] The accused had indicated that he was only willing to answer questions with his lawyer present, but did so without his lawyer when the police advised him he had no right to the presence of a lawyer and the choice was his. There had been no confusion in the accused's mind as to his rights.

However, in *Otis* (2000),[433] the Quebec Court of Appeal decided that the right to silence should be more meaningful. Although the Court decided that the accused had sufficient, though limited, cognitive capacity to make choices Justice Proulx for the Court decided that the continued police questioning, after he had asked them to stop four times, violated s. 7. The police were not entitled to use their superior power to totally disregard the accused's desires and undermine his choice to remain silent. Once an accused has clearly stated he wishes to remain silent, the police cannot act as if there has been a waiver.

In the end result, the majority in *Hebert*, while recognizing an important new constitutional right to silence at the pre-trial stage, clearly severely restricted it for pragmatic reasons. It is curious that, while the Supreme Court accepts that the voluntary confession rule operates on a subjective test for who is a person in authority and as to whether there is an operating mind, it asserts an otherwise objective approach to both the voluntary confession rule and to the new s. 7 right.

---

[429] Para. 80.

[430] (2000), 32 C.R. (5th) 359 (B.C. C.A.).

[431] Para. 18.

[432] (2000), 146 C.C.C. (3d) 346 (B.C. C.A.).

[433] (2000), 37 C.R. (5th) 320 (Que. C.A.). See Guy Cournoyer, "Otis: The Quebec Court of Appeal Asserts a Meaningful Right to Silence Where a Suspect Says No to Interrogation", (2000) 37 C.R. (5th) 342.

There is no requirement that the police advise of the right to silence,[434] as in the United States[435] and certainly no requirement that the accused understand the right to silence. The assertion of requirements of detention seem foreign to the s. 7 right which has no such express triggering mechanism, in contrast to s. 10 rights which only arise on arrest or detention. The apparent requirement that the accused must have asserted the right to silence is consistent with jurisprudence under s. 10(b)[436] requiring the accused to assert the right to counsel before implementational duties arise for the police but thereby only protects the knowledgeable and assertive. At risk are those ignorant or too timid.

Gordon Wall[437] has pointed out that some of the *Hebert* limits were clearly and understandably put in place so as not to outlaw all police undercover work and that policy considerations require different principles for the right to silence when applied to questioning by identified police officers. In that context, he persuasively suggests that there should be no detention limit,[438] a duty to advise of the right to silence[439] and the usual *Clarkson* standard for waiver should apply.[440] Such arguments for re-consideration can now invoke in aid the subsequently established "principle against self-incrimination".[441]

The notion that the police can persist in questioning an accused after there has been an opportunity to consult counsel is consistent with rulings on the right to counsel under s. 10(b).[442] However, it establishes a much weaker protection respecting the right to silence and the right to counsel than that existing in the United States.[443] Finally, the uneasy distinction between passive and active tricks by undercover agents should surely have been left to the determination under s. 24(2) of whether to exclude evidence.

(iii) *No adverse inference*

In *Chambers* (1990),[444] the Supreme Court of Canada declared that the exercise of the new pre-trial right to silence should normally not result in any adverse inference against the accused.

---

[434] See however *W. (W.R.)* (1992), 15 C.R. (4th) 383 (B.C. C.A.).

[435] *Miranda v. Arizona*, 384 U.S. 436 (1966).

[436] Below Chapter 5.

[437] "Doubts Cast on Hebert Limits on the Pre-trial Right to Silence", (1995) 36 C.R. (4th) 134. See too his unpublished LL.M. thesis "The Pre-trial Right to Silence in Canada and the United Kingdom" (Queen's University, September, 1995).

[438] Wall at 141-142 points to later dicta expressly leaving the issue open. In *Jones*, below note 544, Lamer C.J. specifically asks "Does the principle protect against self-incrimination evidence given by an individual who is not under detention by the state?" (at 47).

[439] *W.(W.R.)*, above note 434, appears to be the only authority to this effect.

[440] See too Hill J. in *Brunczlik* (1995), 103 C.C.C. (3d) 131 (Ont. Gen. Div.).

[441] Below at note 544 *et seq.*

[442] *Gormley* (1999), 140 C.C.C. (3d) 110 (P.E.I. C.A.).

[443] *Ibid.*, at 253.

[444] (1990), 80 C.R. (3d) 235 (S.C.C.), applied in *O.(G.A.)* (1997), 9 C.R. (5th) 16 (Alta. C.A.),*Cones* (2000), 32 C.R. (5th) 226 (Ont. C.A.), and *Poirier* (2000), 146 C.C.C. (3d) 436 (Ont. C.A.). See too *McNeill* (2000), 144 C.C.C. (3d) 551 (Ont. C.A.).

The accused, a lawyer, testified at his second trial on a charge of conspiring to import a narcotic that he had no intention of carrying out the agreement to import and that his real purpose was to recapture the affections of his former mistress and one of the conspirators. During the accused's cross-examination Crown counsel attempted to demonstrate that some of the accused's testimony was a recent concoction and suggested to the accused that when he told his story in Court it was the first time he had ever told it to anyone in authority. After lengthy argument, the Crown agreed with defence counsel that it had been made aware of the accused's position years before the trial. Both counsel requested that the judge direct the jury to ignore the questions and answers pertaining to the accused's silence not only on the issue of guilt or innocence but also with respect to the issue of the accused's credibility. The judge undertook to give these directions but did not do so. Neither counsel reminded him of his undertaking at the completion of the charge after some 50 days of trial. The jury returned a verdict of guilty.

When this issue was considered in the Supreme Court, Mr. Justice Cory for the Court confirmed that it had been recognized as a basic tenet of our legal system and thus protected by s. 7 that there was a right to remain silent at the investigative stage as well as at the trial. The Court then held that it would be a "snare and a delusion" to caution the accused that he need not say anything in response to the officer's question but then put in evidence that the accused had clearly exercised his right to remain silent in the face of a question which suggested guilt.[445] Here the questions had been improper and the evidence inadmissible. The failure of the trial judge to instruct the jury could not be cured by the no substantial wrong or miscarriage of justice proviso.[446] Madam Justice L'Heureux-Dubé[447] was the sole dissenter on the basis that the proviso should have been applied.

The application of the proviso by the majority seems, in all the circumstances, overly generous. In any event *Chambers* is a most powerful authority against adverse inferences being drawn from an accused exercising the right to remain silent. Given the importance the Court placed on the right to remain silent it seems strange that the Court has not declared a constitutional duty on the police to warn an accused of the right to remain silent.

In *Chambers*, Cory J. ruled that neither the questions by an investigating officer nor the evidence as to the accused's silence are admissible "unless the Crown can establish a real relevance and a proper basis for their admission".[448] This recognition of the uncertain common law exception[449] does not appear in the judgment of Justice Sopinka for the Court[450] in *Crawford* (1995),[451] which relied on *Chambers* for the following proposition:

---

[445] *Ibid.*, at 253.
[446] *Ibid.*, at 255.
[447] *Ibid.*, at 238-239.
[448] *Ibid.*
[449] The Court relied on *Symonds*, above note 371.
[450] McLachlin J. dissented on the application to the particular case, below note 457.
[451] (1995), 37 C.R. (4th) 197 (S.C.C.).

It is a corollary of the right to choose to remain silent during the pre-trial investigation that, if exercised, this fact is not to be used against the accused at a subsequent trial on a charge arising out of the interpretation and no inference is to be drawn against an accused because he or she exercised the right.[452]

Noting case law allowing for adverse inferences to the drawn against an accused for not testifying at trial,[453] Sopinka J. drew a clear distinction for the pre-trial right to silence:

> Prior to or on arrest, the accused is in a much more vulnerable position against the coercive power of the state. The environment in the police station is different from that of the courtroom where procedural rules protect the accused. In the police station, the accused may not be represented and he may be overwhelmed by the whole experience. The police possess considerably greater power than the accused and there are no disclosure obligations. The police can disclose some or misleading information or no information at all. Evidential use of silence forces the suspect to co-operate with his interrogators without a reciprocal exchange of information and without placing proper limits on the power of the police to demand cooperation. In contrast, in the courtroom, the accused is represented, he knows the case he has to meet (due to disclosure) and there are rules regarding admissibility of evidence.[454]

Notwithstanding this strong statement of policy for the pre-trial right to silence, Sopinka J. nevertheless holds that the right is not "absolute". The issue in *Crawford* concerned competing rights of co-accused. One accused asserted his right to pre-trial silence and that his exercise of the right could not be used against him. The other argued for the right to make full use of the co-accused's pre-trial silence in order to make full answer and defence. The proper approach was not to allow one right to trump the other, but to require a balance to fully respect the importance of both rights. Here the solution was to allow one accused to attack the credibility of the other by reference to the pre-trial silence, but not to allow that evidence to be considered as positive evidence of guilt.

Lower courts have recognized other exceptions to the principle that there can be no adverse inference from pre-trial silence. Such inferences have been held proper and not contrary to s. 7 respecting the ability of a trial judge to instruct a jury that late disclosure of an alibi defence may affect weight[455] and where an accused relying on a mental disorder defence refused to see a Crown psychiatrist.[456]

These exceptions appear *ad hoc* and unprincipled and should be reconsidered. It is not at all clear what the special justifications are in these cases for drawing adverse inferences. As a matter of common sense, adverse inferences will be drawn from pre-trial silence and for the policy reasons well expressed by Cory J. in *Chambers* and Sopinka J. in *Crawford*, the s. 7 right has been established

---

[452] At 211.

[453] See below Chapter 6, respecting s. 11(c).

[454] At 212.

[455] *Hill* (1995), 41 C.R. (4th) 299 (Ont. C.A.). The leading decision on the requirements of disclosure of an alibi defence is *Cleghorn* (1995), 41 C.R. (4th) 282 (S.C.C.), in which there was no consideration of s. 7.

[456] *Worth* (1995), 98 C.C.C. (3d) 133 (Ont. C.A.), followed in *Tanner* (1995), 104 C.C.C. (3d) 77 (Que. C.A.) and *Brunczlik*, above note 440.

in an attempt to avoid them. McLachlin J. put it well in sole dissent in *Crawford*, in explaining her view that the pre-trial silence of the co-accused should be inadmissible for any purpose. Pre-trial silence is ''either a right or it is not a right'' and it has to mean that a suspect has a right to refuse to talk to the police and not be penalized for it.[457]

(iv) *New common law voluntary confession rule: Oickle*

In the course of her lengthy judgment in *Hebert*,[458] McLachlin J. clearly expressed support for the minority approach to the voluntary confession rule expressed in *Rothman*. In particular, she suggests that the traditional voluntariness formula is too narrow and could include an inquiry into police tricks:

> The absence of violence, threats and promises by the authorities does not necessarily mean that the resulting statement is voluntary, if the necessary mental element of deciding between alternatives is absent. On this view, the fact that the accused may not have realized he had a right to silence (eg. where he has not been given the standard warning) or has been tricked into making a statement is relevant to the question of whether the statement is voluntary.[459]

She also makes it express that the better approach is that of a discretion to exclude a statement on the basis that it was improperly obtained:

> The logic upon which *Wray* . . . was based and which led the majority in *Rothman* . . . to conclude that a confession obtained by a police trick could not be excluded, finds no place in the Charter. To say there is no discretion to exclude a statement on grounds of unfairness to the suspect and the integrity of the judicial system, as did the majority in *Rothman*, runs counter to the fundamental philosophy of the Charter.[460]

After conflicting lower court rulings as to whether this meant a expanded common law confessions rule, the Supreme Court in *Oickle* (2000)[461] submitted the common law voluntary confession rule to full re-consideration.

The accused was charged with seven counts of arson, involving four buildings and a car (which belonged to his fiancée). Most of the fires appeared to be deliberately set. The accused was a member of a volunteer fire brigade and responded to each of the fires. The police asked the accused to take a polygraph test. He was properly cautioned, advised of the right to counsel, and told that he could leave at any time. He was also told that, while the results of the polygraph were inadmissible, anything that was said during the test was admissible.

---

[457] At 219-220. For a discussion of controversial recent modifications by the United Kingdom Parliament to the right to silence both at the pre-trial and trial stages see Ian Dennis, ''The Criminal Justice and Public Order Act, 1994 — The Evidence Provisions '', (1995) *Crim.L.Rev.* 4 and Gordon Wall, above note 437.

[458] Above note 367.

[459] At 174-175.

[460] *Ibid.* The Alberta Court in *Paternak* (1995), 42 C.R. (4th) 292 (Alta. C.A.) cannot be correct in suggesting that *Hebert* does not decide that confessions can be excluded on the basis of improper police conduct. A broader common law confession rule was recognized by Scolin J. in *Skinner* (1992), 17 C.R. (4th) 265 (Man. Q.B.), but the particular statement was admitted.

[461] (2000), 36 C.R. (5th) 129 (S.C.C.).

The accused arrived for his test at a local hotel at about 3:00 in the afternoon. Prior to the test, the accused was asked a number of control questions. These were designed to provide a basis for the polygraph itself, to establish control questions, and to establish a sense of intimacy between examiner and subject. After taking the test, which lasted a few minutes, the accused was told that he had failed. He was read his rights again and then questioned for an hour by the polygraph examiner. The accused asked whether, if he admitted to setting fire to the car, he could "walk out of here". He was told that he could leave at anytime. The interrogation was taken over by another officer. After about 30 minutes of questioning, the accused admitted to setting fire to his fiancée's car. He was emotionally distraught at the time. After giving a written statement confessing to the fire, he was arrested, given his right to counsel, as well as the secondary police caution. He was taken to the police station at about 8:15 p.m. Once at the police station, he was questioned about the other fires. He said he was tired and wanted to go home to bed. He was told he could not go home because he was under arrest, but that he could call his lawyer. The questioning continued until about 11:00 p.m., at which time the accused confessed to having set the rest of the fires. The accused provided a written statement, which was completed by about 1:00 a.m. The accused was lodged in a cell to sleep at about 2:45 a.m. At 6:00 a.m., the police noticed that the accused was awake. He was given another Charter warning and asked whether he would agree to a re-enactment of the fires. He agreed and the police drove him to the scene of several fires where he described how he set them.

The trial judge held a *voir dire* to determine the admissibility of the accused's statements, including the video re-enactment. The trial judge ruled that they were all admissible and convicted the accused. The Court of Appeal found that the statements were not voluntary because of psychologically oppressive police methods, excluded the confessions and entered acquittals on all counts. Justice Iacobucci, speaking for five other justices[462] over the sole dissent of Justice Arbour, reversed the decision of the Nova Scotia Court of Appeal and restored the convictions.

The Supreme Court is to be commended for trying to state the common law confessions rule in a compendious way that is accessible to lawyers and police. It is also salutary to see the Court's concern about the dangers of false confessions.[463] The judgment is, however, disturbing for at least four reasons:

1. It places the focus largely on reliability rather than police methods;

2. It provides the police with a manual for a wide range of excessively coercive interrogation techniques;

3. It is at odds with the Court's jurisprudence on the right to silence and the principle against incrimination; and

4. It requires a startling level of deference by Courts of Appeal to a trial judge's determination of voluntariness.

---

[462] McLachlin C.J. and L'Heureux-Dubé, Major, Bastarache and Binnie JJ.
[463] The Court relied heavily on the work of U.S. researchers, R.A. Leo and R.J. Ofshe: paras. 34-46.

Iacobucci J. states the Court's overall approach as follows:

> The common law confessions rule iswell-suited to protect against false confessions. While its overriding concern is with voluntariness, this concept overlaps with reliability. A confession that is not voluntary will often (though not always) be unreliable. The application of the rule will by necessity be contextual. Hard and fast rules simply cannot account for the variety of circumstances that vitiate the voluntariness of a confession, and would inevitably result in a rule that would be both over- and under-inclusive. A trial judge should therefore consider all the relevant factors when reviewing a confession.[464]

Iacobucci J. identifies four categories of the voluntary confessions rule: threats or promises, oppression, operating mind and "other police trickery". He emphasises that the first three categories require a factual determination as to whether there has actually been an impact on the suspect's will.[465] However, the fourth category is distinct:

> While it is still related to voluntariness, its more specific objective is maintaining the integrity of the criminal justice system.[466]

For that category the Court adopts the view of Lamer J. in *Rothman*[467] that at common law the Court should only be concerned with tricks that shock the community:

> [The] investigation of crime and the detection of criminals is not a game to be governed by the Marquess of Queensbury rules. The authorities, in dealing with shrewd and often sophisticated criminals, must sometimes of necessity resort to tricks or other forms of deceit and should not through the rule be hampered in their work. What should be repressed vigorously is conduct on their part that shocks the community.[468]

In the case of the first three categories the focus is on reliability, although the Court says that the enquiry into voluntariness is broader than reliability. Yet it does not say what that broader inquiry is about. Why is it that the integrity of the system is at stake in the fourth category, which prohibits tricks that would shock the community, but not, for example, in cases where statements are obtained in circumstances of oppression? That the Court has not thought through the key issue of rationale is clear when it asserts that:

> Obviously, any confession that is the product of outright violence is involuntary and unreliable, and therefore inadmissible.[469]

---

[464] Para. 47.

[465] The Court later muddles this analysis by the conclusion that:
> The doctrines of oppression and inducements are primarily concerned with reliability. However, as the operating mind doctrine and Lamer J.'s concurrence in *Rothman, supra*, both demonstrate, the confessions rule also extends to protect a broader conception of voluntariness "that focuses on the protection of the accused's rights and fairness in the criminal process" (para. 69).

[466] Para. 65.

[467] [1981] 1 S.C.R. 640.

[468] At 697, cited in *Oickle* at para. 66.

[469] Para. 53.

But surely another major reason why such statements should be excluded is because we do not wish to condone or encourage police to resort to any form of physical force or torture. No doubt torture does sometimes produce true confessions, but the statement has been obtained at too great a cost to larger values.

In contrast, the new United Kingdom statutory confession rule does not resort to *a priori* categorisation and states that statements must be excluded where they are unreliable *or* obtained by oppression.[470] This clearly recognises, as *Oickle* does not, that the modern confession rule must result in exclusion where police tactics can be described as oppressive.

Although the majority sees the issue as largely one of reliability, in the course of the judgment it characterises as "proper" or "improper" a number of interrogation techniques. The judgment reads like a Manual for Coercive Interrogation.

It is improper to obtain a confession by relying on

— physical abuse or outright violence;

— imminent threats of torture;

— offers of leniency in the form of reducing the charge or the sentence;

— telling a mother her daughter would not be charged;[471]

— phrases like "it would be better if you tell the truth" but only where they actually induce the suspect to confess;

— creating oppressive conditions[472] such as depriving the suspect of food, clothing, water, sleep, or medical attention, denying access to counsel, and excessively aggressive, intimidating questioning for a prolonged period of time; and/or

— using shocking tricks like pretending to be a chaplain, or a legal aid lawyer or injecting truth serum into a diabetic on the pretence it is insulin.[473]

On the other hand the Court in *Oickle* determines, mostly in its decision on the facts,[474] that it is proper in interrogation to

— lie, subject to few limits;

— offer psychiatric counselling or other counselling not conditional on confessing;[475]

---

[470] Police and Criminal Evidence Act 1984 (U.K.), ch. 60, s. 76(8), referred to by the majority at para. 62.

[471] Para. 52. The Court however adds that telling the suspect his former prison friend would be charged is not a sufficient inducement.

[472] Para. 60. The Court later changes this to a more cautious test of "utterly intolerable conditions". The Court approved of *Hoilett* (1999), 26 C.R. (5th) 332 (Ont. C.A.), where Feldman J.A. held such oppressive conditions had affected voluntariness.

[473] These were the examples provided by Lamer J. in *Rothman*.

[474] Paras. 72-103.

[475] "The distinction here is between the police suggesting the potential benefits of confession, and making offers that are conditional upon receiving a confession" (para. 78). This seems to be a distinction of little substance.

— make spiritual exhortations or appeals to conscience and morality;

— confront with inadmissible or even fabricated evidence (although this might be a factor, when combined with others, for exclusion);[476]

— use the polygraph test without necessarily having to advise as to the results being inadmissible;[477]

— suggest the polygraph is near infallible;

— exploit the trust developed with the suspect at the pre-test phase of the polygraph;

— use a "good cop, bad cop" routine;

— say the suspect, his fiancee and the community would feel better if he confessed;

— indicate it would be necessary to polygraph the suspect's fiancee if he did not confess; and/or

— discuss the possibility of a number of offences being "packaged" for sentencing purposes.[478]

The law and order impact of *Oickle* is apparent in the majority's determination that the trial judge had properly held the accused's confessions to having set other fires to have been voluntary. The majority discounts the context of a failed polygraph and decides that the police had only employed a number of minor inducements which did not impact on voluntariness. The majority appears to have strayed from its announced approach of considering the whole context. It assessed each contentious factor one at a time and never stood back to assess the cumulative effect.

In sole dissent, Madam Justice Arbour[479] was of the view that, given the context of a failed polygraph test, there was a series of improper threats and inducements which cumulatively overwhelmed the mind of the accused. She emphasises the police statement that the machine does not lie, the offer of psychiatric help, the talk of sparing the fiancee of being polygraphed and the police offer to bundle or package all the offences, as being improper.

Arbour J. also suggests[480] that an accused's fair trial rights are endangered by the admission of a confession, where there is an intimate and temporal connection with a failed polygraph. To effectively challenge the weight of the confession the accused will be forced to reveal the failed polygraph to the jury. What could be more prejudicial? The majority again reveals its law and order bias by retorting that a tactical disadvantage for the defence is not enough to constrain police discretion and the immense probative value of a voluntary

---

[476] The Court adds "of course the use of inadmissible evidence is inherently less problematic than fabricated evidence" (para. 91). It is not clear why that should be.

[477] The Court adopts the view of Hill J. in *Alexis* (1994), 35 C.R. (4th) 117 (Ont. Gen. Div.).

[478] Para. 77. The majority determines that it was the accused who was seeking a package deal. In dissent Arbour J. points to passages from the transcript which indeed seem to suggest that the police initiated the topic (paras. 128-131).

[479] Paras. 106-137.

[480] Paras. 13-149.

confession outweighs prejudicial effect.[481] It seems strange that the polygraph machine, which is too unreliable to be admitted into evidence, now has the status of a legitimate tool and is not too prejudicial to be referred to in a trial.

Although the majority expresses grave concern at the possible injustice of false confessions it also makes it clear that it does not want to hamstring police interrogations.

> In defining the confessions rule, it is important to keep in mind its twin goals of protecting the rights of the accused without unduly limiting society's need to investigate and solve crimes.[482]

> To hold that the police conduct in this interrogation was oppressive would leave little scope for police interrogation, and ignore Lamer J.'s reminder in *Rothman* ... that "[the] investigation of crime and the detection of criminals is not a game to be governed by the Marquess of Queensbury rules."[483]

According to my colleague, Professor Gary Trotter,[484] the *Oickle* ruling

> clarifies for the profession that the polygraph is a legitimate tool for investigation, if used properly. I think the complaint about the polygraph before was that it was actually *too* effective in bringing about confessions, and that argument didn't win the day in the Supreme Court.[485]

There is no doubt wisdom in the thought that police should be given some latitude in interrogation, just as lawyers are given in cross-examinations. Interrogations need not be benign and open-ended. But the balance struck in *Oickle* seems too pro-State. Was the polygraph really used properly in this case? The danger is that the Court's declaration of so many coercive techniques as proper will undoubtedly legitimate and encourage routine use of the polygraph and also a number of other manipulative techniques, including lying about the accuracy of the machine, not advising that the test need not be taken and deliberately ambiguous remarks about going after friends and relatives. As Clayton Ruby has said of *Oickle*, the Court has sent a message to all Canadian police:

> Lie, cheat, mislead if you must.[486] Ignore tears and repeated protestations of innocence. But get a confession from whoever you have in your hands....We're "playing with fire".[487]

Justice Cromwell for the Nova Scotia Court of Appeal[488] could surely be forgiven for his view that these methods created an atmosphere of psychological oppression

---

[481] Para. 102.

[482] Para. 32.

[483] Para. 86.

[484] He appeared in *Oickle* as intervenor for the Attorney General of Ontario. Fortunately we now have him safely cloistered at the Faculty of Law at Queen's!

[485] *The Lawyer's Weekly*, October 20, 2000.

[486] For a well reasoned argument that the law should not permit police deception, even at early investigative stages, see Andrew Ashworth, "Should the Police Be Allowed to Use Deceptive Practices", (1998) 114 *L.Q.R.* 109.

[487] *Globe and Mail*, October 17, 2000.

[488] So too in *Amyot* (1990), 58 C.C.C. (3d) 312 (Que.C.A.) Proulx J.A. said:

from which the courts should distance themselves. The issues were larger than the conviction of a serial arsonist.

Oickle expressly establishes that the voluntary confession rule is a matter of common law quite independent of, and not subsumed by, Charter rights such as the right to silence under s. 7 or the right to counsel under s. 10(b).

This position is the opposite of the position taken by the Court in *G.(B.)* (1999),[489] through Bastarache J., as recently as June 10, 1999:

> The principles which govern the admissibility of a statement made by an accused to a person in authority are essential to the integrity of the judicial process. As Sopinka J. stated in *Whittle*...at p. 931:
>
>> "While the confession rule and the right to silence originate in the common law, as principles of fundamental justice they have acquired constitutional status under s. 7 to the *Charter*."[490]

In *Oickle* Iacobucci J. decides to keep the common law separate as it is seen to give broader protection. It applies pre-detention, requires the State to prove voluntariness beyond a reasonable doubt and a violation always warrants exclusion.[491] These are undoubted advantages in keeping the common law separate.[492] The Charter is a vehicle for restraining rather than enhancing state power. Nevertheless it seems unfortunate that this restatement of the common law proceeded without any enrichment[493] from the Court's recognition in *Hebert* (1990)[494] of a pre-trial right to silence based on the fundamental right to choose not to speak. It also ignores the Court's later repeated assertion of an overarching principle against incrimination.[495] This was recently re-stated by Iacobucci for a 6-1 majority in *White* (1999):[496]

> It is now well-established that there exists, in Canadian law, a principle against self-incrimination that is a principle of fundamental justice under s. 7 of the *Charter*....[The] principle has at least two key purposes, namely to protect against

---

[A] polygraph test ...does not fall within the category of unacceptable techniques *per se*. However, and that is my conclusion in the present case, it is in its use that the police can abuse it and thereby raise questions as to recourse to this technique (at 324).

In *Oickle* the Court said "without expressing any opinion as to whether *Amyot* was correctly decided...the facts of this appeal are very different" (para. 97). Iacobucci J. noted that *Oickle* repeatedly rejected the accuracy of the polygraph test.

[489] (1999), 24 C.R. (5th) 266 (S.C.C.).

[490] At 284.

[491] Para. 30.

[492] See too David Tanovich, "The Unchartered Right to Silence and the Unchartered Waters of a New Voluntary Confession Rule", (1992) 9 C.R. (4th) 24.

[493] The Court states, "While obviously it may be appropriate, as in *Hebert*...to interpret one in light of the other" (para. 31).

[494] Above note 367.

[495] See below note 544 *et seq*.

[496] (1999), 24 C.R. (5th) 201 (S.C.C.). See criticism of Steven Penney, "The Continuing Evolution of the s. 7 Self-Incrimination Principle: R. v. White", (1999) 24 C.R. (5th) 247 and the reply by Michael Plaxton, "An Analysis and Defence of Free Choice Theory: A Response to Professor Penney", (1999) 27 C.R. (5th) 218.

unreliable confessions, and *to protect against abuses of power by the state*[497] (emphasis added).

Compare Justice Rosenberg for the Ontario Court of Appeal in *Sweeney* (2000),[498] handed down just four days before *Oickle*. The Ontario Court held that the *St. Lawrence* rule, that those parts of an involuntary confession confirmed by the finding of evidence could be admitted as reliable evidence to prove the truth, could not survive the Charter.[499] This was in no small measure due to the Court's analysis of recent Supreme Court jurisprudence[500] leading to the summary that

> [The] Supreme Court has affirmed that reliability is not the sole basis for the confessions rule. The court has identified the policy basis for the rule in broader concerns for the administration of justice, including deterrence of improper police conduct and fundamental principles of fairness such as the principle against self-incrimination.[501]

It may be that the Charter right to silence and the principle against self-incrimination cover much the same ground as the common law inquiry into whether a statement was in fact involuntarily made. In this case the accused was advised of a right to silence which is a factor going to voluntariness.[502] But what if he had not been? No inferences can be drawn from silence pre-trial[503] or at trial?[504] Wouldn't it be a "snare and delusion" not to hold that an accused must be advised of these rights? Given that Oickle's arrest after the first confession triggered his right to silence, wasn't there then an analogy to be drawn to the Court's rejection of a confession in *Hebert* because of the police trick of active elicitation by an undercover police office placed into a cell? In *White* an accident report to police was excluded at the criminal trial because the accused correctly believed he was compelled under a provincial statutory duty to give an account. Oickle appears to have been under greater compulsion than both Hebert and White. Hopefully the Court will return sooner rather than later to the scope of the Charter rights to pre-trial silence and the principle against self-incrimination in this important context of police questioning. If they do not apply here, they would be empty rhetoric.

A major disappointment of *Oickle* is that the Court has clearly de-emphasised the important emerging common law position that a confession should be excluded because a particular police interrogation practice is oppressive and

---

[497] At 219-220.

[498] (2000), 36 C.R. (5th) 198 (Ont. C.A.).

[499] See too Alan Mewett, "Illegally Obtained Evidence at Common Law After the Charter. Post Hoc Ergo Propter Hoc?", (1998) 3 *Can. Crim. L.R.* 285.

[500] The Court relies on *Hebert, G.(B.)* and *Hodgson* (1998), 127 C.C.C. (3d) 449 (S.C.C.) (where Cory J. holds that, "The confessions rule, including the burden on the Crown to prove voluntariness beyond a reasonable doubt, is carefully calibrated to ensure that the coercive power of the state is held in check and to preserve the principle against self-incrimination" (at 466)).

[501] Para. 57.

[502] *Hebert* at 174-175.

[503] *Chambers*, above note 444.

[504] *Noble*, below note 528.

should not be condoned.[505] Oppressiveness is recognised as a concern in *Oickle* but only when it results in involuntariness. A free standing inquiry into the legitimacy of police methods is only to occur under the Court's fourth category of "other police tricks". But the Court raises the bar to a test of whether the trick would shock the community.[506] Why should courts only seek to deter shocking tricks or shocking abuse when less demanding tests are in place for the Charter right to silence recognised in *Hebert*, the principle against self-incrimination or for exclusion of evidence obtained in violation of the Charter under s. 24(2) in *Collins*?[507]

The majority held[508] that it was not appropriate for the Nova Scotia Court of Appeal to have disputed the weight of various pieces of evidence on the issue of voluntariness. Justice Arbour is surely correct[509] that it is important for a Court of Appeal to determine whether the trier properly applied the confessions law and had a reasonable view of the facts. It is also odd to speak of deference in a case where the interrogations were videotaped. Now that deference has been decreed by the Supreme Court there should also be deference shown where trial judges decide that a statement was involuntary.

The Court in *Oickle* strongly supports[510] the growing practice of recording interrogations but hastens to say non-recorded confessions are still admissible. In Australia[511] a non-recorded interrogation requires an uncorroborated warning[512] and in some state jurisdictions there are statutory rules that an unrecorded confession or confirmation of a confession can only be admitted in exceptional cases.[513]

---

[505] See especially *S. (M.J.)* (2000), 32 C.R. (5th) 378 (Alta. Prov. Ct.). Fradsham J. excluded a confession in part because the videotape revealed the oppressive atmosphere and psychological brainwashing techniques developed using the Reid method pioneered in the United States.

[506] The Lamer test has found favour in lower courts: see, for example, *Miller* (1991), 9 C.R. (4th) 347 (Ont. C.A.) (s. 7 not protecting against police trick of getting accused's manager to obtain writing sample) and *Corak* (1994), 29 C.R. (4th) 388 (B.C. C.A.) (placing baseball cap found at crime scene in prominent position in police station so that accused would see it and pick it up being passive trick not in violation of s. 7).

[507] [1987] 1 S.C.R. 265, discussed below Chapter 11. Lamer J. in *Collins*, while rejecting the community shock for s. 24(2) purposes, did repeat the view he expressed in *Rothman*:

> "I still am of the view that the resort to tricks that are not in the least unlawful let alone in violation of the *Charter* to obtain a statement should not result in the exclusion of a free and voluntary statement unless the trick resorted to is a dirty trick, one that shocks the community" (at 286-297).

The Court in *Oickle* relies on this remark but makes no effort to reconcile it with subsequent Charter jurisprudence (para. 66). In its jurisprudence under s. 10(b) the Supreme Court has, of course, frequently excluded voluntary statements.

[508] Paras. 22-23.

[509] Para. 107.

[510] Para. 46.

[511] I am indebted for this comparison to Professor Lee Stuesser of the Faculty of Law at the University of Manitoba, who also provided me with the sources here relied on.

[512] *McKinney* (1991), 98 A.L.R. 577 (Australia H.C.), discussed by Graham Roberts, *Evidence. Proof and Practice* (1998) pp. 490-493.

[513] *Cross on Evidence* (5th, Australian ed.) (1996) paras. 33775-33785.

Justice Whealy of the Ontario Superior Court of Justice in *Nelson* (1999)[514] excluded a statement on the basis there was a conflict in testimony as to exchanges between the accused and the police in a police vehicle and there was no videotape. Noting that this was a "big city" matter where the police had adequate resources for videotaping, Whealy J. relied on the Ontario Court of Appeal's encouragement of such videotaping in *Barrett* (1993).[515] One of the Court of Appeal judgements was that of then Arbour J.A. *Barrett* was later reversed by the Supreme Court of Canada in short reasons by Iacobucci J.[516] The highest Court held that the decision that the statements were voluntary was a ruling on credibility and should not be reversed. This was despite the reality that the trial judge had given no reasons other than to say it was a matter of credibility,[517] there was an allegation of police brutality and it was undisputed the accused had suffered serious injuries while in police custody. *Barrett* was as disturbing then as *Oickle* is now.

(b) At Trial: No Adverse Inference from Accused Not Testifying

(i) *Pre-Noble*

We have seen[518] that the Supreme Court has determined that normally no adverse inference should be drawn from the accused remaining silent before trial. However, the Supreme Court[519] has suggested that different considerations apply to silence at trial given that the accused is represented, knows the case to meet due to disclosure and there are rules regarding the admissibility of evidence.

It appears to be clear[520] from various Supreme Court dicta that adverse inferences can be drawn against an accused for not testifying in some circumstances. What those circumstances are is far less clear. In *Francois* (1994),[521] McLachlin J. wrote for the majority that

> subject to the caveat that failure to testify cannot be used t oshoure up a Crown case which otherwise does not establish guilt beyond a reasonable doubt, a jury is permitted to draw an adverse inference from the failure of an accused person to testify.[522]

---

[514] November 15, 1999, not reported.

[515] (1993), 23 C.R. (4th) 49 (Ont. C.A.).

[516] (1995), 38 C.R. (4th) 1 (S.C.C.).

[517] On the issue of the duty to give reasons Justice Arbour appears to have later won the day in her judgement for the Supreme Court in *Biniaris* (2000), 32 C.R. (5th) 1 (S.C.C.).

[518] *Chambers*, above note 444.

[519] *Crawford*, above note 454.

[520] See too R.J. Delisle, *Evidence: Principles and Problems* (5th ed., 1999) pp. 772-778, where the jurisprudence is fully discussed, together with developments in other jurisdictions. For discussion of controversial recent modifications by the United Kingdom Parliament to the right to silence both at the pre-trial and trial stages see Ian Dennis, "The Criminal Justice and Public Order Act, 1994 — The Evidence Provisions" (1995) *Crim. L. Rev.* 4 and Gordon Wall, *The Pre-trial Right to Silence in the United Kingdom* (1995) (unpublished LL.M. thesis, Queen's University, Kingston, Ontario).

[521] (1994), 31 C.R. (4th) 201 (S.C.C.).

[522] At 210. La Forest J., Gonthier J. and Iacobucci J. concurred. Major J. (Sopinka J. and Cory J. concurring) dissented on the facts.

In *Lepage* (1995),[523] the Supreme Court divided 3-2 as to whether the trial judge had drawn an adverse inference from the accused's failure to offer an explanation for the presence of his fingerprints but was in agreement that such an inference could be drawn "once the Crown had proved a prima facie case".[524] Finally, Chief Justice Lamer in *P. (M.B.)* (1994),[525] in describing the "principle against self-incrimination" for the Court, stated the following:

> Once. . .the Crown discharges its obligation to present a prima facie case, such that it cannot be non-suited by a motion for a directed verdict of acquittal, the accused can be expected to respond. . .and failure to do so *may* serve as the basis for drawing adverse inferences. . .[Once] there is a "case to meet" which, if believed, would result in conviction, the accused can no longer remain a passive participant in the prosecutorial process and becomes — in a broad sense — compellable. That is, the accused must answer the case against him or her, or face the possibility of conviction.[526]

It would appear at this point that the Supreme Court had no objections to adverse inferences based on the accused's failure to testify provided that there is otherwise enough evidence to go to the jury. This appeared to be a wise compromise.[527]

(ii) *Noble*

The interpretation that the above dicta provide Supreme Court authority for drawing adverse inferences against accused who do not testify was strongly rejected by Chief Justice McEachern for the majority of the British Columbia Court of Appeal in *Noble* (1996).[528] The Chief Justice found the Supreme Court's pronouncements ambiguous and held that no proper inference could be drawn from an accused's failure to testify whether the Crown's case was overwhelming or just strong enough to withstand a directed verdict. Experience and logic informed that no inference should be permissible as one never knows why an accused does not testify. In dissent, Southin J.A. retorts that a judge must not tell a jury that it cannot draw an adverse inference from a failure of the accused to testfy and it would be strange if such an instruction were to be required for a judge sitting alone.

A 5-4 majority of the Supreme Court agreed with Chief Justice McEachern on the further appeal in *Noble* (1997).[529] Sopinka J.[530] determined for the majority that the trial judge erred in law in using the failure of the accused to testify, in a case of overwhelming evidence crying out for an explanation, as evidence going to identification to establish guilt beyond a reasonable doubt. If the case against

---

[523] (1995), 36 C.R. (4th) 145 (S.C.C.).
[524] Sopinka J. for the majority at 159, Major J. for the minority at 169. Both justices relied upon the decision of the Ontario Court of Appeal in *Johnson* (1993), 21 C.R. (4th) 336 (Ont. C.A.).
[525] (1994), 29 C.R. (4th) 209 (S.C.C.).
[526] At 227-228.
[527] See further Delisle, above note 520.
[528] (1996), 47 C.R. (4th) 258 (B.C. C.A.). Donald J.A. concurred in the result in a separate opinion.
[529] (1997), 6 C.R. (5th) 1 (S.C.C.).
[530] L'Heureux-Dubé, Cory, Iacobucci and Major JJ., concurred.

the accused does not otherwise prove guilt beyond a reasonable doubt, to permit the trier of fact to reach a guilty verdict on the basis of the failure to testify would, reasoned Sopinka J., significantly undermine the right not to testify. The right to silence, found in ss. 7 and 11(c) of the Charter, was based on society's distaste for compelling a person to incriminate him or herself with his or her own words. The use of silence to help establish guilt beyond a reasonable doubt was contrary to that rationale. Just as a person's words should not be conscripted and used against him or her by the state, it was equally inimical to the dignity of the accused to use his or her silence to assist in grounding a belief in guilt beyond a reasonable doubt.[531]

According to Sopinka J., while earlier cases on the appropriate use of silence by the trier of fact were admittedly ambiguous, recent decisions were clear: silence may not be used by the trier of fact as a piece of inculpatory evidence. The trier of fact, whether judge or jury, cannot treat the silence of the accused as a "make-weight". While the principles governing the judge and the jury as trier of fact were identical, it was clear that there are differences between the two in practice. Section 4(6) of the Canada Evidence Act, whose validity was not at issue in the present case, prevents a trial judge from commenting on the silence of the accused. The trial judge is therefore prevented from instructing the jury on the impermissibility of using silence to take the case against the accused to one that proves guilt beyond a reasonable doubt. The second practical difference was that, while judges give reasons which permit appellate review of the specific basis for a finding of guilt, juries do not give reasons and courts are prohibited from speculating about the reasoning process of a jury in reaching a verdict. While there were practical considerations which prevent appellate review of the use of the silence of the accused by a jury, it was an error of law for the jury to become convinced of guilt beyond a reasonable doubt as the result of the silence of the accused at trial.

Acknowledging that different principles might apply on appeal where there was no longer a presumption of innocence, Sopinka J. nevertheless seemed to be of the view that silence should not be treated as make-weight by an appeal court. However the point was left open for another day.[532]

Chief Justice Lamer lead the dissent.[533] According to the majority the silence of an accused can only be used by the trier of fact in two very limited senses: (1) to confirm prior findings of guilt beyond a reasonable doubt; and (2) to remind triers of fact that they need not speculate about unstated defences. This misinterpreted the existing case law relating to a "case to meet". When the Crown presents a case to meet that implicates the accused in a strong and cogent network of inculpatory facts, the trier of fact is entitled to consider the accused's failure

---

[531] Sopinka J. also considered that if silence could be used against the accused this would shift the burden of proof to the accused contrary to s. 11(d) of the Charter. This proposition has been persuasively criticised by R.J. Delisle "Annotation to *Noble*", (1997) 6 C.R. (5th) 5.

[532] Para. 109 at 55.

[533] La Forest J. (Gonthier J. concurring) agreed, but preferred that no comment be made on the constitutional validity of s. 4(6) of the Canada Evidence Act. McLachlin J. sided with the Chief Justice in a concurring opinion.

to testify in deciding whether it is in fact satisfied of his or her guilt beyond a reasonable doubt. This proposition was hardly novel. Silence could be very probative. Recognizing that silence can be probative, this Court had said in many cases that it is a factor that both juries and appellate courts may properly consider. As long as the Crown has first made out a case to meet, there are certain situations where the web of inculpation fashioned by the Crown requires the accused to account for unexplained circumstances or face the probative consequences of silence.

According to Lamer C.J., the act of drawing adverse inferences from the silence of an accused is not contrary to the accused's right of non-compellability or the presumption of innocence.[534] If the Crown establishes a case to meet, such that its case cannot be non-suited by a motion for a directed verdict of acquittal, it has put forth, by definition, sufficient evidence upon which a jury, properly instructed, could reasonably convict. There is nothing infirm in appropriate circumstances in drawing inferences from the silence of the accused. According to the Chief Justice, the accused's Charter protection lies, as it always has, in the case to meet. Silence cannot be used as part of the case to meet. But once the Crown has made out its case, such that a conviction would be reasonable and there is a logical expectation that the accused adduce evidence in response, all judicial decision-makers may draw inferences of guilt based on the silence of the accused.

Lamer C.J. addressed the rule against commenting on the accused's failure to testify, embodied in s. 4(6) of the Canada Evidence Act.[535] It was originally created to ensure that neither the court nor the prosecution would draw unfair attention to the silence of the accused. It was not, however, intended to preclude triers of fact from drawing natural and reasonable inferences from his silence. Once the trial judge has concluded that there is sufficient evidence such that a guilty verdict would be reasonable, s. 4(6) is invoked. At this point, s. 4(6) suggests that we do not want juries to be overwhelmed by the silence of the accused, but we also do not want juries to close their minds to the probative value of the failure to explain. The end result, reasons Lamer C.J., is that s. 4(6) permits what comes naturally. The intractable rule that emerges from the reasons of the majority, however, is that no trier of fact can use the accused's silence as inculpatory evidence adding to the weight of the Crown's case. If this Court is prepared to conclude that the fundamental Charter rights to silence and the presumption of innocence prohibit triers of fact from using the accused's silence as evidence, one would have thought, according to the Chief Justice, trial judges would be empowered, if not required, to say so. The majority's reasons therefore indirectly challenged the constitutionality of s. 4(6).

In *Noble* the bare majority of the Supreme Court therefore decided that no adverse inferences may be taken against the accused for remaining silent at trial.[536]

---

[534] Paras. 25-35 at 22-28.
[535] Paras. 36-38 at 28-29.
[536] A breach of *Noble* necessitated a new trial in *Daniels* (1999), 29 C.R. (5th) 184 (Nfld. C.A.).

Professor Ron Delisle[537]sides with the minority on the issue of precedent. He points to the strange fact that the majority were relying on cases of pre-trial silence and that Sopinka J. ignored his own views in *Creighton* that quite different considerations apply at trial where far more protections are in place. Delisle's conclusion is strong:

> The principal arguments for the Crown in *Noble* were that since a jury can take silence into account, and an appellate court commonly does, therefore it is just sensible for a judge sitting alone. The majority, in response, surprisingly, decides that neither a jury nor an appellate court is entitled to take silence into account. It is not too bold to describe this as classic revisionism.

Moving beyond the issue of manipulation of precedent, not drawing inferences from trial silence could be justified on McEachern C.J.'s more pragmatic basis or on a new development of the Court's commitment to the "principle against self-incrimination".[538] Regrettably the majority position is unsatisfactory for leaving several anomalies.

Section 4(6) of the Canada Evidence Act has been interpreted as prohibiting direct comments on the accused's silence by trial judges or Crown counsel in jury cases.[539] Given *Noble*, it appears inevitable that s. 4(6) should now be challenged and declared unconstitutional.[540] The decision upholding the section's validity in *Boss* (1988)[541] should be overruled. A major function of a trial judge in a jury trial is, of course, to instruct the jury as to the applicable law. In this case, s. 4(6) now stands in the way. We have a constitutional standard that no adverse inference can be drawn from the accused's silence but a statutory rule bars a trial judge from advising the jury not to do so. This appears to be so even if they were to ask "Is it true that the Supreme Court decided that a jury cannot draw an inference of guilt from the accused's silence"?

The majority recognise an exception for the defence of alibi.[542] Justice Sopinka advances two justifications — the expediency argument that alibi defences are so easy to fabricate and that the alibi defence is an "affirmative" defence which does not relate to proof of an element of an offence. The first argument shows little faith in the ability of triers of fact not to be duped and provides a weak justification for forcing the accused to testify in this one situation. The resort to the language of "affirmative" defences seems highly problematic. The classification of "affirmative" defence is usually applied to "yes but" defences

---

[537] "Annotation to *Noble*", (1997) 6 C.R. (5th) 5. Delisle also questions the wisdom on not allowing common sense to rule and suggest the majority wrongly speak of impacting the burden of proof. For criticism of the majority position see too I. Laing, "*R.* v. *Noble*: The Supreme Court and the Permissible Use of Silence", (1998) 43 *McGill L.J.*

[538] See further Hamish Stewart, "Nothing Can Come of Nothing: Three Implications of Noble", (1999) 42 *Crim. L.Q.* 286.

[539] *Vézeau* (1976), 34 C.R.N.S. 309 (S.C.C.). For recent interpretations of s. 4(6) see *Woodcock* (1996), 1 C.R. (5th) 306 (B.C. C.A.), *Smith* (1997) 11 C.R. (5th) 298 (Ont. C.A.), and *Miller* (1998), 21 C.R. (5th) 178 (Ont. C.A.).

[540] See too Stewart, above note 538.

[541] (1988), 68 C.R. (3d) 123 (Ont. C.A.).

[542] Paras. 110-113 at 56-57. See further *Cleghorn* (1995), 41 C.R. (4th) 282 (S.C.C.) and *Hill* (1995), 41 C.R. (4th) 299 (Ont. C.A.).

where the accused admits proof of the elements of the offence but argues that there is some reason, such as self-defence, for acquittal. It is formalistic to say alibi defences don't concern guilt. Even if this were so, how was it that the adverse inference drawn because of Noble's silence resulted in a new trial when the issue was one of identification? Was this not an "affirmative" defence not relating to guilt?

The Supreme Court should adopt a much crisper line prohibiting any inference from silence of accused at trial and requiring a mandatory direction to this effect in all jury cases where the accused does not testify. The alibi exception should be rejected as an historical anomaly and unconstitutional.[543] There should be no possibility of use of trial silence by courts of appeal, a final determination of which issue the Court left for another day. The majority declared an important new Charter standard, then blurred it.

8. PRINCIPLE AGAINST SELF-INCRIMINATION

(a) New Protections Under Section 7

Since *Hebert*, in a series of complex and split Supreme Court decisions, a majority position has emerged through the judgments of Chief Justice Lamer that within principles of fundamental justice guaranteed by s. 7 there is a "principle against self-incrimination" wider than the pre-trial right to silence, the protections against compellability in s. 11(c) and the privilege against self-incrimination in s. 13. The Chief Justice put it best for the majority of the Court in *P.(M.B.)*(1994):[544]

> Perhaps the single most important organizing principle in criminal law is the right of an accused not to be forced into assisting in his or her own prosecution... This means, in effect, that an accused is under no obligation to respond until the state has succeeded in making out a prima facie case against him or her. In other words, until the Crown establishes that there is a "case to meet", an accused is not compellable in a general sense (as opposed to the narrow, testimonial sense) and need not answer the allegations against him or her.[545]

The Chief Justice saw the presumption of innocence and the power imbalance between the state and the individual as being at the root of the principle.[546] In a later judgment, he describes the principle against self-incrimination in even broader terms:

---

[543] See too Stewart, above note 538, and John Craig, "The Alibi Exception to the Right to Silence", (1996) 39 *Crim. L.Q.* 227.

[544] (1994), 29 C.R. (4th) 209 (S.C.C.). In *S.(R.J.)* (1995), 36 C.R. (4th) 1 (S.C.C.) Iacobucci J., speaking for four justices not including Lamer C.J., expressly adopted the principle of self-incrimination outlined by the Chief Justice in *P.(M.B.)* and, dissenting, in *Jones* (1994), 30 C.R. (4th) 1 (S.C.C.). The dissent in *Jones* was seen to be limited to the Chief Justice's view that the principle should also be applied to dangerous offender proceedings where the accused had already been convicted.

[545] At 226.

[546] One month later in *Jones*, Lamer C.J. avoids this rationale in seeking to apply the principle to dangerous offender proceedings.

> Any state action that coerces an individual to furnish evidence against him or herself in a proceeding in which the individual and the state are adversaries violates the principle against self-incrimination. Coercion . . . means the denial of free and informed consent.[547]

This principle against self-incrimination or a "case to meet" is not merely an organizing principle of existing rules and principles but one that has the capacity to introduce new rules.[548] It is now seen to be the explanation of the recognition of a pre-trial right to silence in *Hebert*.

It also lead the Court in *B.C. Securities Commission v. Branch* (1995)[549] to create a doctrine of derivative use immunity and also a discretion to prevent the compellability of a co-accused. Two officers of a company were served with summonses from the Securities Commission under the provincial Securities Act compelling their attendance for examination and requiring them to produce all records in their possession. When the officers failed to appear, the Commission sought an order from the Court committing the officers for contempt. The officers applied for a declaration that the Act violated ss. 7 of the Charter. The Supreme Court decided that the principle against self-incrimination required that persons compelled to testify be provided with subsequent derivative-use immunity in addition to the use immunity guaranteed by s. 13 of the Charter. The accused would have the evidentiary burden of showing a plausible connection between the compelled testimony and the evidence later sought to be adduced. Once this was done, in order to have the evidence admitted, the Crown would have to satisfy the court on a balance of probabilities that the authorities would have discovered the impugned derivative evidence absent the compelled testimony. The Court also decided that, in addition, courts can, in certain circumstances, grant exemptions from compulsion to testify. The crucial question was whether the predominant purpose for seeking the evidence is to obtain incriminating evidence against the person compelled to testify or rather for some other legitimate public purpose. That test was seen to strike the appropriate balance between the interests of the state in obtaining the evidence for a valid public purpose on the one hand, and the right to silence of the person compelled to testify on the other.[550]

Branch was distinguished by La Forest J. for the Court in *Fitzpatrick* (1995),[551] in holding that s. 7 did not prevent the Crown from relying on statutorily required fishing logs on a charge of overfishing. The Court held that the principle against self-incrimination should not be applied as rigidly as it might in the context of a purely criminal offence. Fishing logs were required from all commercial

---

[547] *P.(M.B.)* at 41. This statement was adopted by La Forest J. for a unanimous Court in *Fitzpatrick* (1995) 43 C.R. (4th) 343 (S.C.C.), although distinguished on the facts.

[548] Iacobucci J. in *S.(R.J.)* at 49.

[549] (1995), 38 C.R. (4th) 133 (S.C.C.), where Sopinka J. and Iacobucci J. reached a consensus majority position not evident in the earlier 229-page inconclusively split decision in *S.(R.J.)* (1995), 36 C.R. (4th) 1 (S.C.C.). See further *Jobin* (1995), 38 C.R. (4th) 176 (S.C.C.) and *Primeau* (1995), 38 C.R. (4th) 189 (S.C.C.).

[550] This is further addressed by Cory J. (Iacobucci and Major JJ. concurring) in concurring reasons in *Phillips v. Nova Scotia (Commissioner, Public Inquiries Act)* (1995), 39 C.R. (4th) 141 (S.C.C.).

[551] Above note 547.

fishers as conditions of their license to assist in the routine administration of a regulated industry.[552]

In *G. (S.G.)* (1997),[553] the Supreme Court held 5-2[554] that the discretion to allow the Crown to reopen its case after the defence had begun to answer was extremely narrow and far less likely to be exercised, otherwise the s. 7 right of an accused not to be conscripted would be compromised. The minority pointed to the fact the late evidence had been unforeseen, had not arisen through fault of the Crown and should be left to a determination of whether there was prejudice to the defence case.[555]

In *White* (1999),[556] Iacobucci J. held for a 6-1 majority[557] of the Supreme Court that the s. 7 principle against self-incrimination barred the admission of motor vehicle accident reports made under the compulsion of a provincial Motor Vehicle Act at a trial for failing to stop at the scene of an accident under s. 252(1)(a) of the Criminal Code. To obtain this use immunity, the person who made the statement would have to prove compulsion on a balance of probabilities. The test was whether the declarant held an honest and reasonable belief that he or she was required by law to report the accident to the person to whom the report was given.[558]

Iacobucci J. restated the residual principle against self-incrimination in the following broad terms:

> It is now well-established that there exists, in Canadian law, a principle against self-incrimination that is a principle of fundamental justice under s. 7 of the *Charter*....[The] principle has at least two key purposes, namely to protect against unreliable confessions, and to protect against abuses of power by the state. There is both an individual and a societal interest in achieving both of these protections. Both protections are linked to the value placed by Canadian society upon individual privacy, personal autonomy and dignity....A state which arbitrarily intrudes upon its citizens' personal sphere will inevitably cause more injustice than it cures.

> The jurisprudence of this Court is clear that [it]...is an overarching principle within our criminal justice system, from which a number of specific common law and *Charter* rules emanate, such as the confessions rule, and the right to silence, among many others.[559]

---

[552] See above note 110 for references to criticism of the criminal/regulatory distinction. What is the distinction between the scheme for regulating securities and that for fishing?

[553] (1997), 8 C.R. (5th) 198 (S.C.C.).

[554] Per Cory J. (Lamer C.J., Sopinka J., Iacobucci J. and Major J. concurring). McLachlin J. (L'Heureux-Dubé J. concurring) dissented on this point.

[555] See comment by Delisle, "Annotation", (1997) 8 C.R. (5th) 204 in favour of the majority position.

[556] (1999), 24 C.R. (5th) 201 (S.C.C.). See criticism of Steven Penney, "The Continuing Evolution of the s. 7 Self-Incrimination Principle: R. v. White", (1999) 24 C.R. (5th) 247 and the reply by Michael Plaxton, "An Analysis and Defence of Free Choice Theory: A Response to Professor Penney", (1999) 27 C.R. (5th) 218. The *White* ruling on exclusion under s. 24(1) is discussed below Chapter 11, Charter Remedies.

[557] L'Heureux-Dubé J. dissented.

[558] At 230-232, applied in *Gibb* (1999), 30 C.R. (5th) 189 (Sask. Q.B.) (admitting statement made to parole officer after arrest).

[559] At 219-220.

However he also added an important general caveat.[560] The fact that the principle against self-incrimination had the status of an overarching principle did not imply that it provided absolute protection for an accused against all uses of information compelled by statute or otherwise. The residual protections were specific, contextually-sensitive and required a balancing process. In some contexts, the factors that favoured the importance of the search for truth would outweigh the factors that favour protecting the individual against undue compulsion by the state.

(b) Resistance in Lower Courts

The principle against self-incrimination has not caught fire in lower courts, but there are some signs of life. The Ontario Court of Appeal seized on Iacobucci J.'s above caveat in *White* to summarily dismiss an argument that the new DNA warrant powers in the Criminal Code violated the principle against self-incrimination.[561] Justice Finlayson went as far as to say that the principle against self-incrimination was not a right protected under s. 7 but was found in s. 7 only to the extent that it was a principle of fundamental justice.[562] The Ontario Court had no difficulty in holding that the principle did not bar the admission of a guilty plea at a subsequent criminal proceeding.[563]

So too the B.C. Court of Appeal determined that the principle against self-incrimination did not bar the admissibility of information provided to Revenue Canada in a fraud prosecution.[564] The principle has not availed in the context of compelled testimony under the Mutual Legal Assistance in Criminal Matters Act given the evidentiary immunity provided.[565] On the other hand, the Quebec Court of Appeal excluded the evidence of an accused and his wife compelled at a fire commissioner's inquiry from the subsequent arson trial.[566]

9. ABUSE OF PROCESS[567]

(a) Pre-Charter

Criminal courts have been most reluctant to review the exercise of discretion by a police officer or prosecutor. The reluctance has been based on a notion of

---

[560] At 220-221.
[561] *F.(S.)* v. *Canada (Attorney-General)* (2000), 32 C.R. (5th) 79 (Ont. C.A.).
[562] At 93. He also distinguished *Stillman* as grounded in the context of a bodily search without statutory authorization (at 94).
[563] *Ford* (2000), 33 C.R. (5th) 178 (Ont. C.A.). See too *Thompson* (2001), 151 C.C.C. (3d) 339 (Ont. C.A.) (upholding offence of failing to provide roadside test).
[564] *Wilder* (2000), 142 C.C.C. (3d) 418 (B.C. C.A.). See also *Graham* (1997), 121 C.C.C. (3d) 76 (B.C. S.C.).
[565] *États-Unis* v. *Ross* (1995), 41 C.R. (4th) 358 (Que. C.A.), *U.K.* v. *Hrnyk* (1996), 107 C.C.C. (3d) 104 (Ont. Gen. Div.).
[566] *Kabbabe* (1997), 6 C.R. (5th) 82 (Que. C.A.). See too *Sweeney*, above note 498.
[567] See the comprehensive and instructive analysis of Donna C. Morgan, "Controlling Prosecutorial Powers, Judicial Review, Abuse of Process and Section 7 of the Charter" (1986-87), 29 Crim. L.Q. 15. See too the general analysis by Boilard J. in *Faber* (1987), 38 C.C.C. (3d) 49 (Que. S.C.).

separation of powers and concerns that the administration of criminal justice would be jeopardized by endless applications for review and transfer too much discretion to judges.

In *Smythe* (1971),[568] the accused, charged with income tax evasion, relied on the equality before the law protection in the Canadian Bill of Rights to challenge a provision under the Income Tax Act under which the Crown had an absolute discretion to proceed by way of indictment rather than by summary conviction. This Crown option was particularly significant in that proceedings on indictment carried a minimum penalty of two months imprisonment. For the Court, Chief Justice Fauteux rejected the challenge. The manner in which the Attorney General exercised discretion could only be questioned in the Legislature. Enforcement of the criminal law would be "impossible" unless someone in authority was vested with discretionary power. Both before and after the Bill of Rights the Attorney-General's discretion "to elect the mode of prosecution as he saw fit was part of the British and Canadian conception of equality before the law."[569] The Court added that the success of the challenge would be

> potentially destructive of statutory ministerial discretion conferred upon a Minister of the Crown for the administration of the law in Canada and tantamount to a recognition that Parliament has used an oblique method to paralyze the administration of the law.[570]

Mr. Justice Pigeon for the majority of the Supreme Court in *Rourke* (1977)[571] flatly held that there was no "general discretionary power in courts of criminal jurisdictions to stay proceedings regularly instituted because the prosecution is considered oppressive."[572] The majority saw dangers in the exercise of an uncertain discretion by all courts and a threat to the independence of the judiciary. A trial judge had stayed a robbery trial on the basis that the two-year delay since the robbery was alleged to have occurred had resulted from a lack of reasonable diligence on behalf of the police. Even Chief Justice Laskin for the minority, while recognizing that there should be a general power to stay prosecutions on the basis of abuse of process, held that a stay could be not grounded on mere police delay in the absence of evidence of an "ulterior purpose."[573]

(b) Post-Charter Review of Police and Prosecutorial Discretion

Under the Charter, review of the exercise of discretion of police, prosecutors or an Attorney General should no longer be resisted on the basis of a separation of powers doctrine. In *Operation Dismantle* (1985),[574] the Supreme Court held

---

[568] [1971] S.C.R. 680.

[569] *Ibid.*, at 686.

[570] *Ibid.*, at 687.

[571] (1977), 38 C.R.N.S. 268 (S.C.C.).

[572] *Ibid.*, at 272. Martland, Ritchie, Beetz and De Grandpre JJ. concurred.

[573] Above note 571, at 289. Spence, Dickson and Judson JJ. concurred.

[574] [1985] 1 S.C.R. 441, applied in *Schmidt* (1987), 33 C.C.C. (3d) 193 at 214 (S.C.C.) (extradition). See however *Wilson* (1987), 35 C.C.C. (3d) 316 (Man. C.A.) (resisting review of the Minister of Justice's perogative power of mercy).

that decisions of the executive branch of government, including Cabinet decisions, are subject to Charter review by the courts.

However, in *Power* (1994),[575] L'Heureux-Dubé J. determined, for a 4-3 majority, that the courts should be extremely reluctant to interfere with prosecutorial discretion

> as a matter of principle based on the doctrine of separation of powers as well as a matter of policy founded on the efficiency of the system of criminal justice and the fact that prosecutorial discretion is especially ill-suited to judicial review.[576]

It seems odd that Her Ladyship is resting on a notion of separation of powers given the new division of powers inherent in entrenching the Charter and the Parliamentary declaration in s. 52 of the Constitution Act that the Charter is the supreme law.[577] The arguments of inefficiency and inappropriateness of judicial review conflict strangely with the reality that, since the Charter, police conduct is constantly under review in criminal trials. L'Heureux-Dubé J. relies on the view of Viscount Dilhorne that judicial review of prosecutorial conduct would jeopardize judicial impartiality:

> A judge must keep out of the arena. He should not have or appear to have any responsibility for the institution of a prosecution. The functions of prosecutors and of judges must not be blurred. If a judge has power to decline to hear a case because he does not think it should be brought, then it soon may be thought that the cases he allows to proceed are cases brought with his consent or approval.[578]

In the context of Charter review of police conduct, the Supreme Court has repeatedly indicated that it should *not* be seen to condone police misconduct.[579] There is also further inconsistency inherent in *Power* in that the separation of powers impediment does not prevent the Court from later acknowledging the power to stay a prosecutorial decision as an abuse of process in exceptional cases.

It would be very strange and unfortunate were the behaviour of a prosecutor to be immune or too sheltered from accountability. The Charter provides the best form of scrutiny of Crown conduct when consideration is given in a criminal trial to whether there has been a breach of the accused's Charter rights such as the right under s. 11(b) to be tried within a reasonable time[580] and right under s.7 to disclosure.[581] The soon-to-be discussed judicial power to stay as an abuse of process provides the widest form of accountability for Crown prosecutors.

---

[575] (1994), 29 C.R. (4th) 1 (S.C.C.).

[576] At 16. In *Leon* (1996), 105 C.C.C. (3d) 385 (S.C.C.), an extradition case, *Power* was relied upon by Cory J. for the full Court for the proposition that an appellate Court is empowered to enquire into the exercise of prosecutorial discretion only in the clearest cases of abuse of the court's process.

[577] See further the criticism of the "separation of powers bugaboo" by Lee Stuesser, "Abuse of process: The Need to Reconsider", (1994) 29 C.R. (4th) 92 at 93-94. See too Kent Roach, "Developments in Criminal Procedure: The 1993-1994 Term", (1995) 6 *Sup. Ct. L. Rev.* 281 at 337-340.

[578] *R. v. Humphrys*, [1977] A.C. 1 (H.L.).

[579] Below Chapter 11.

[580] Below Chapter 6.

[581] Below at note 701.

Other than the Charter, there is little effective legal, political or administrative accountability for prosecutors.[582] At the apex of the Canadian system, the Attorney-General is politically accountable in the legislature, but this is largely ineffective.[583] The office is not free from considerations of political expediency hidden from public scrutiny. Front-line prosecutors have wide powers and, especially given administrative realities and the tradition of a prosecutor as an independent ''Minister of Justice,'' largely unfettered discretion as to how and who to charge. Canadian prosecutors now risk civil suits for malicious prosecution but this has proved to be little risk. Since *Nelles* (1989),[584] an accused can hold the Attorney General and/or the prosecutors personally legally accountable by a civil suit if there is proof on a balance of probabilities of a malicious prosecution. There are considerable hurdles to such actions, including notoriously high costs. Experience throughout the common law world indicates that actions for malicious prosecution rarely succeed.[585] The cause of action provides no remedy against the incompetent or negligent Crown. There is thus still a contrast with the civil liability of police officers who, in addition to liability for malicious prosecution, face potential liability for breaches of the duty of care or statutory duty.

Courts have resisted frontal s. 7 attacks on discretionary powers of police or prosecutors but have accepted that the exercise of power in a exceptional case may require judicial intervention.

In *Beare* (1988),[586] the Saskatchewan Court of Appeal had struck down the Criminal Code fingerprinting powers in cases where police have reasonable and probable grounds to believe that the person has committed an indictable offence. The Saskatchewan Court held there was too much discretion for police officers and the provision should require an officer to show reasonable and probable grounds for believing fingerprinting was necessary. The Supreme Court, through La Forest J., disagreed and reversed:

> The existence of the discretion conferred by the statutory provisions does not, in my view, offend principles of fundamental justice. Discretion is an essential feature of the criminal justice system. A system that attempted to eliminate discretion would be unworkably complex and rigid. Police necessarily exercise discretion in deciding when to lay charges, to arrest and to conduct incidental searches, as prosecutors do in deciding whether or not to withdraw a charge, enter a stay, consent to an adjournment, proceed by way of indictment or summary conviction, launch an appeal and so on.

> The Criminal Code provides no guidelines for the exercise of discretion in any of these areas. The day-to-day operation of law enforcement and the criminal justice system nonetheless depends upon the exercise of that discretion.[587]

---

[582] See further, Stuart, ''Prosecutorial Accountability in Canada'' in Philip C. Stenning (ed.), *Accountability for Criminal Justice* (1995) pp. 330-354.

[583] See, for example, P. Stenning, *Appearing for the Crown* (1986).

[584] *Nelles v. Ontario* (1989), 71 C.R. (3d) 358 (S.C.C.).

[585] The Supreme Court itself noted that the province of Quebec has allowed suits against the Attorney General and Crown prosecutors since 1986 and there has been no evidence of a flood of claims.

[586] Above note 47. See too *Lyons* above note 4, at 37-38; *Jones*, [1986] 2 S.C.R. 284 at 303-304 and *Blackplume* (1990), 56 C.C.C. (3d) 363 (Alta. Q.B.).

[587] *Ibid.*, at 116.

The Court added, however, that there would be a remedy under s. 24 of the Charter where it was established in a particular case that police or prosecutorial discretion had been exercised "for improper or arbitrary motives".[588]

In *V.T.* (1992),[589] L'Heureux-Dubé J., for a unanimous Court, re-asserted the *Beare* ruling that discretionary powers of prosecutors do not *per se* violate principles of fundamental justice under s. 7. There was good reason for judicial deference to the prosecutor's decision. Here, the Youth Court judge had no power under the Young Offenders Act to dismiss a charge on the basis that it was so minor that it should not have been brought.[590]

Lower courts have consistently held that the power given the Attorney General by s. 577 of the Criminal Code to directly indict even where an accused has been discharged at a preliminary inquiry, is not *per se* contrary to the Charter but that a court may intervene in a particular case to avoid a Charter violation or an "abuse of process."[591] Similarly, it has been held that the court should not interfere with the exercise of a stay of prosecution by an Attorney General, absence evidence of "flagrant impropriety."[592] There are several instances where trial judges have overridden Crown refusals to consent to a murder trial by judge alone.[593]

The power to intervene in the case of particular conduct by a police officer or prosecutor is now generally litigated under an application to "stay as an abuse of process," and, far less often, as discriminatory law enforcement contrary to s. 15.[594] In both cases such challenges face an uphill battle.

(c) Common Law Power to Stay in Clearest of Cases

At face value, the majority decision in *Rourke* sounded the doctrine's death knell. However, some courts, particularly at the trial level, subsequently manoeuvred around *Rourke*, distinguishing it on the facts or regarding the ruling as *obiter*. Finally, in *Jewitt* (1985),[595] Chief Justice Dickson, speaking for a panel of seven judges, went out of his way to resolve the long-festering issue.

---

[588] *Ibid.*

[589] (1992), 12 C.R. (4th) 133 (S.C.C.).

[590] The Court did recognize the power to stay as an abuse of process in the clearest of cases.

[591] *Ertel* (1987), 35 C.C.C. (3d) 398 at 415 (Ont. C.A.), applying *Arviv* (1985), 45 C.R. (3d) 354 (Ont. C.A.) (discussed below note 691); *Moore* (1986), 50 C.R. (3d) 243 (Man. C.A.).

[592] *Chartrand v. Quebec (Min. of Justice)* (1987), 59 C.R. (3d) 388 (Que. CA.); *Campbell v. Ontario (A.G.)* (1987), 31 C.C.C. (3d) 289 (Ont. H.C.); *Osiowy* (1989), 50 C.C.C. (3d) 189 (Sask. C.A.); *Kowalski* (1990), 57 C.C.C. (3d) 168 (Alta. Prov. Ct.) and *Kostuch v. A.G. of Alberta* (1995), 43 C.R. (4th) 81 (Alta. C.A.) (private prosecutor not having right to continue stayed prosecution of those involved in construction of dam).

[593] *Cardinal* (1996), 105 C.C.C. (3d) 163 (Alta. Q.B.), *Bird* (1996), 107 C.C.C. (3d) 186 (Alta. Q.B) and *McGregor* (1999), 22 C.R. (5th) 233 (Ont. C.A.).

[594] Below Chapter 10. The uncertain defence recognised in the United States has yet to be recognized in Canada: see discussion by R.K. Allen, "Selective Prosecution: A Viable Defence in Canada?", (1992) 34 *Crim. L.Q.* 414 and R.W. Hubbard, P.M. Brauti and C. Welsch, "Selective Prosecutions and the Stinchcombe Model for Disclosure", (1999) 42 *Crim. L.Q.* 338.

[595] (1985), 47 C.R. (3d) 193 (S.C.C.).

The Supreme Court held that there should be such a power to control its own processes. The courts could not transfer to the executive the responsibility for seeing that the process of law is not abused. The Court in *Jewitt*, and again later in *Keyowski* (1988),[596] asserted the approach first formulated by the Ontario Court of Appeal in *Young* (1984).[597] A stay should be granted where "compelling an accused to stand trial would violate those fundamental principles of justice which underlie the community's sense of fair play and decency" or where the proceedings are "oppressive or vexatious."[598] The Supreme Court also asserted the caveat in *Young* that this is a power which should be exercised only in the "clearest of cases."[599]

The stay as an abuse power is available to all trial judges, although it is now clear that it is beyond the jurisdiction of justices at preliminary inquiries.[600] A stay is "tantamount to an acquittal" entitling the Crown to appeal.[601]

In its landmark decision in *Mack* (1988),[602] the Supreme Court determined that the common law doctrine of stay as abuse in the clearest of cases was also applicable to situations of police entrapment. Mr. Justice Lamer for a unanimous Court held that entrapment occurred when authorities provide the opportunity to commit a crime without having reasonable suspicion of criminal activity or having made *bona fide* inquiry and also where, despite such suspicion or *bona fides*, authorities go beyond providing the opportunity and induce the offence. A drug trafficking case was to be stayed where there had been persistent approaches by a police informer over six months, threats and inducement of large sums of money. The defence was not dependent on the culpability of the accused but required an objective assessment of the conduct of the police and their agents. The onus on the accused was a balance of probabilities. Requiring an accused merely to raise a reasonable doubt would be entirely inconsistent with permitting a stay only in the "clearest of cases." Making the accused bear the onus of proof was consistent with the rules governing s. 24(2) applications under the Charter.[603] The matter of entrapment was for the trial judge but only where the Crown had clearly first proved the essential elements of the offence beyond a reasonable doubt.[604]

The doctrine of stay as an abuse of process was broadened by the ruling of Madam Justice Wilson for a unanimous Supreme Court in *Keyowski* (1988)[605]

---

[596] (1988), 62 C.R. (3d) 349 (S.C.C.).

[597] (1984), 40 C.R. (3d) 289 (Ont. C.A.).

[598] *Ibid.*, at 329.

[599] *Ibid.*

[600] *Republic of Argentina v. Mellino* (1987), 33 C.C.C. (3d) 334 at 346 (S.C.C.).

[601] *Jewitt*, above note 595. See also *Hinse* (1995), 44 C.R. (4th) 209 (S.C.C.) respecting appeals to the Supreme Court.

[602] (1988), 67 C.R. (3d) 2 (S.C.C.), applied in *Barnes* (1991), 3 C.R. (4th) 1 (S.C.C.) (majority rejecting entrapment defence where buy-and-bust undercover action directed at six-block area where drugs activity reasonably suspected). Since *Barnes* stays for entrapment have been extremely rare : see generally Stuart, *Treatise*, above note 103, c. 8.

[603] For criticism of this view see Stuart, "Mack: Resolving Many But Not All Questions of Entrapment" (1988), 67 C.R. (3d) 68 at 72-73.

[604] Above note 602, at 55-58.

[605] Above note 596.

that prosecutorial conduct and improper motivation are "but two of many factors to be taken into account".[606] Many rulings on abuse have turned on this question and therefore earlier decisions should be considered with caution. In *Keyowski*, the Court held that a series of trials could *per se* constitute an abuse of process. However, on the facts, the accused's charge of criminal negligence causing death had been improperly stayed by the trial judge. He had been twice tried but in each case the jury had been unable to reach a verdict. The Supreme Court held that the accused had failed to demonstrate that this was one of the clearest cases which justified a stay. The charge was serious, the proceedings had not occupied an undue amount of time and the accused had not been held in custody.[607]

(d) Appeal Courts' Resistance to Common Law Stays

Although the Supreme Court had now so clearly accepted the common law power to stay as an abuse of process, decisions at the Supreme Court and provincial Courts of Appeal level continued to show great reluctance to actually granting a stay.

At the Supreme Court a particularly striking example of this attitude occurred in *Scott* (1990).[608] The Court ruled 6-3 that a Crown's conduct in entering a stay in a drugs case, and recommencing the same proceedings in another Court for the purpose of avoiding an unfavourable evidentiary ruling which would reveal an informer's identity, did not constitute an abuse of process which should result in a stay of proceedings. On the evidence, the minority view is compelling. This was the type of undue manipulation of the judicial process that the stay power is designed to control. The Crown had the option of calling no evidence and appealing the resulting acquittal.

Consider the recent record of the Ontario Court of Appeal. It did stay proceedings in *Young*[609] of criminal charges against a lawyer who could have been charged five years earlier under a provincial statute and who had been cleared by the Law Society Disciplinary Committee. On the other hand, that Court has not allowed stays against a direct indictment for first degree murder where the Supreme Court of Canada had ordered committal for trial on a charge of second degree murder.[610] Moreover, the Court has overturned stays by trial judges of an incest charge laid two days after an acquittal on a charge of sexual assault against her daughter,[611] of an indecent assault case where the Crown was seeking a trial following a mistrial in which there had been a delay of a year and a half since the original preliminary inquiry.[612] Stays were also held inappropriate when, prior to plea, the Crown re-elected to proceed on indictment in a case of sexual assault to

---

[606] *Ibid.*, at 351.

[607] *Keyowski* was distinguished in a decision staying the fourth impaired driving trial: *Mitchelson* (1992), 71 C.C.C. (3d) 471 (Man. C.A.).

[608] (1990), 2 C.R. (4th) 153 (S.C.C.).

[609] Above note 597.

[610] *Chabot* (1985), 44 C.R. (3d) 70 (Ont. C.A.).

[611] *B. (K.R.)* (1986), 53 C.R. (3d) 216 (Ont. C.A.).

[612] *D. (T.C.)* (1987), 61 C.R. (3d) 168 (Ont. C.A.).

avoid a six-month time bar[613] and, in the case of illicit sexual intercourse involving step-daughters, where the charge had been revived at the request of the complainants three years after the police had informed the accused that the charges would not be laid.[614]

Not surprisingly the Court reversed a stay of a sexual assault trial where the basis had been that the courtroom had become too hot during a heat wave.[615] It also refused to stay drug charges on the basis that payment of an undercover agent had been contingent on a successful investigation.[616]

A majority of the Ontario Court of Appeal in *Miles of Music Ltd.* (1989)[617] overturned a stay of breach of copyright charges laid against a disc jockey based on his preparation of a set of compilation cassette tapes, even though the Court accepted that a trade association and an individual had contrived to have the criminal prosecution brought for their own commercial ends of promoting an audio licensing scheme. For the majority, Mr. Justice Krever expressly held that a prosecution could not be stayed as an abuse unless

> [t]he cause of the apparent unfairness complained of can be laid at the doorstep of the executive, that is to say, can be attributed to either the police or the Crown or both.[618]

The other majority judge, Mr. Justice Tarnopolsky, accepted that the abuse of process doctrine was not directed solely at executive action but held that there had to be "some knowing participation by the police or the Crown."[619] With dissenting judge, Mr. Justice Blair, it is difficult to find other authority or logic to compel such a restriction of the doctrine of abuse of process.[620]

The Quebec Court of Appeal appears to have been more receptive to stays as an abuse of process. It quashed convictions and entered stays in a case of robbery where the prosecution had been in breach of a police agreement not to prosecute,[621] and in the case of a proceedings on indictment for possession of a

---

[613] *Belair* (1988), 64 C.R. (3d) 179 (Ont. C.A.), distinguishing its earlier decision in *Parkin* (1986), 28 C.C.C. (3d) 252 (Ont. C.A.) on the basis that there evidence had been led. See too *Maramba* (1995), 104 C.C.C.(3d) 85 (Ont. C.A.). Other Courts of Appeal have held that stays are appropriate in such cases. See the Quebec Court of Appeal, below notes 621-623 and *Boutilier* (1995), 104 C.C.C.(3d) 327 (N.S. C.A.).

[614] *D. (E.)* (1990), 78 C.R. (3d) 112 (Ont. C.A.). For the Court, Madam Justice Arbour provides a thorough review of recent Ontario Court of appeal rulings and holds that "A claim of abuse of process is necessarily fact specific as it expresses societys changing views about what is unfair or oppressive" (at 12). See similarly *G. (W.G.)* (1990), 58 C.C.C. (3d) 263 (Nfld. CA.) and compare *D. (A.)* (1990), 60 C.C.C. (3d) 407 (Ont. C.A.).

[615] *Gostick* (1991), 62 C.C.C. (3d) 276 (Ont. C.A.).

[616] *Dikah* (1994), 31 C.R. (4th) 105 (Ont. C.A.), appeal to Supreme Court dismissed on December 9, 1994, and *Zito* (1994), 94 C.C.C. (3d) 477 (Ont. C.A.).Compare the approach of the Quebec Court of Appeal in *Xenos*, below note 623.

[617] (1989), 69 C.R. (3d) 361 (Ont. C.A.).

[618] *Ibid.*, at 383.

[619] *Ibid.*, at 377.

[620] *Ibid.*, at 375.

[621] *Demers* (1989), 49 C.C.C. (3d) 52 (Que. C.A.). For a review of similar rulings in other jurisdictions see *D. (E.)*, above note 614.

small quantity of cocaine laid 14 months after the event and where a previous Crown Attorney had refused to indict because of the small quantity involved.[622] In an arson case,[623] the Court held that police involvement in a deal, under which the insurers would pay an informer $50,000 to testify if a conviction resulted, amounted to an abuse of process. However the proper remedy was to exclude the evidence of the informer rather than stay the proceedings.

(e) O'Connor: Common Law to be Subsumed under Section 7

Mr. Justice Dubin, in *Young*, expressly based his approach in part on the principles of fundamental justice guaranteed by s. 7 of the Charter. In dissent in the Saskatchewan Court of Appeal in *Keyowski*,[624] Chief Justice Bayda pointed out[625] that the "only in the clearest" language of *Young* inexplicably places a higher onus on the accused to prove abuse than is the case for a s. 7 challenge. As this point was not argued in the Supreme Court, Wilson J. left "the issue of the relationship between s. 7 and the common law doctrine of abuse of process to another day".[626]

That day dawned with the Supreme Court's decision in *O'Connor* (1996).[627] This is now the controlling decision on abuse of process. Madam Justice L'Heureux-Dubé spoke for a Court unanimous on the law, although the Court divided 6-3 on whether there should have been a stay because the Crown had not complied with an order to disclose medical and therapeutic records of rape complainants. L'Heureux-Dubé J. decided for the Court that the common law doctrine of abuse of process was subsumed under the principles of fundamental justice guaranteed by s. 7 of the Charter, except in rare cases where the Charter did not apply. The remedy was now discretionary with a variety of interests to weigh:

> It is important to recognize that the Charter has now put into judges's hands a scalpel instead of an axe — a tool that may fashion, more carefully than ever, solutions taking into account the sometimes complimentary and sometimes opposing concerns of fairness to the individual, societal interests, and the integrity of the judicial system.[628]

The remedy of a stay was to be reserved for the "clearest of cases". L'Heureux-Dubé J. further adopted the guidelines suggested by Professor David Paciocco that a stay would only be appropriate where

---

[622] *Quinn* (1989), 73 C.R. (3d) 77 (Que. C.A.). Proceeding by way of summary conviction was time barred. See too *Chaussé* (1986) 51 C.R. (3d) 332 (Que. C.A.). Compare *Bridges* (1989), 58 C.C.C. (3d) 1 (B.C. S.C.). Peter Rosenthal, "Crown Election Offences and the Charter", concludes that the entire procedure of Crown election should be held to violate s. 7 and/or s. 11(d) and s. 11(f) (right to jury).

[623] *Xenos* (1991), 70 C.C.C. (3d) 362 (Que. C.A.).

[624] (1986), 53 C.R. (3d) 1 (Sask. C.A.).

[625] At 11.

[626] At 352.

[627] (1996), 44 C.R. (4th) 1 (S.C.C.).

[628] At 39.

(1) the prejudice caused by the abuse in question will be manifested, perpetuated or aggravated through the conduct of the trial, or by its outcome; and

(2) no other remedy is reasonably capable of removing that prejudice.[629]

As to what may constitute an abuse, L'Heureux-Dubé J. indicated that there was no one particular "right against abuse of process". Depending on the circumstances, particular Charter guarantees might be engaged such as the right to trial within a reasonable time under s. 11(b) and the right to a fair trial under ss. 7 and 11(d). There was a "residual category" which

> does not relate to conduct affecting the fairness of the trial or impairing other procedural rights enumerated in the Charter, but instead addresses the panoply of diverse and sometimes unforeseeable circumstances in which a prosecution is conducted in such a manner as to connote unfairness or vexatiousness of such a degree that it contravenes fundamental notions of justice and thus undermines the integrity of the judicial process.[630]

On the issue of whether a stay should have been granted on the facts, a 6-3 majority decided the appeal should be dismissed. The assessment of this ruling requires a full consideration of the evidence. A Bishop was charged with four counts of sexual offences, two involving rape, alleged to have occurred over a three-year period some 25 years ago. Defence counsel obtained a pre-trial order requiring that the Crown disclose the complainants' entire medical, counselling and school records and that the complainants authorize production of such records.[631] The accused later applied for a judicial stay of proceedings based on non-disclosure of several items. Crown counsel asserted that the non-disclosure of some of the medical records was due to inadvertence on her part, and that she had "dreamt" the transcripts of certain interviews had been disclosed. She submitted that uninhibited disclosure of medical and therapeutic records would re-victimise the victims, and suggested that the disclosure order exhibited gender bias. The trial judge dismissed the application for a stay, finding that the failure to disclose certain medical records had been an oversight. He concluded that while the conduct of the Crown was "disturbing", he did not believe that there was a "grand design" to conceal evidence, nor any "deliberate plan to subvert justice". On the second day of the trial, counsel for the accused made another application for a judicial stay of proceedings based largely on the fact that the Crown was

---

[629] At 42.

[630] At 41.

[631] The stunningly wide order included the following:

> The Court orders that Crown counsel produce names, addresses, and telephone numbers of therapists, counsellors, psychologists or psychiatrists whom have treated any of the complainants with respect to allegations of sexual assault or sexual abuse.
>
> This Court further orders that the complainants authorize all therapists, counsellors, psychologists and psychiatrists whom have treated any of them with respect to allegations of sexual assault or sexual abuse to produce to the Crown copies of their complete file contents and any other related material including all documents, notes, records, reports, tape recordings and video tapes, and the Crown to provide copies of all of this material to counsel for the accused forthwith.

still unable to guarantee to the accused that full disclosure had been made. The trial judge stayed proceedings.

The British Columbia Court of Appeal and later a majority of the Supreme Court held that the proceedings should not have been stayed and ordered a new trial. L'Heureux-Dubé J., La Forest, Gonthier and McLachlin JJ. concurring, decided that while the Crown's conduct in the case was shoddy and inappropriate, the non-disclosure could not be said to have violated the accused's right to full answer and defence. The order had been issued without any form of inquiry into the relevance of the documents, let alone a balancing of the privacy rights of the complainants and the accused's right to a fair trial, and was thus wrong. Cory J., with Iacobucci J. concurring, decided that although the actions of Crown counsel were extremely high-handed and thoroughly reprehensible, the Crown's misdeeds were not such that, upon a consideration of all the circumstances, the drastic remedy of a stay was merited. Major J., Lamer C.J. and Sopinka J. concurring, dissented on the basis that in their view the Crown's conduct impaired the accused's ability to make full answer and defence and violated fundamental principles of justice underlying the community's sense of fair play and decency. In their view the impropriety of the disclosure order did not excuse the Crown's failure to comply.

L'Heureux-Dubé J.'s judgment on the principles of abuse of process and her decision on the facts make the chances of a defence counsel having a criminal charge stayed as an abuse of process even less likely than before.[632] It is arguable, however, that L'Heureux-Dubé J. has slightly softened her previous position for the majority of the Supreme Court in *Power* (1994),[633] that the remedy of abuse of process could only apply to cases which shocked the conscience of the community.[634] The recognition of the wide "residual category" makes it clear that trial judges may still enter stays for abuse where continuation would threaten the integrity of the process. The principle established by Chief Justice Dickson in *Jewitt* that trial judges cannot abdicate control of their process is still intact. It could not be that s. 7 has served to narrow a common law right. The Charter was intended to constrain not to extend governmental action. The decision not to allow a stay in *O'Connor* should be seen to be confined to the issue of a remedy for non-disclosure where alternative remedies such as adjournments for proper disclosure are possible and arguably sufficient. The majority decision not to stay notwithstanding their characterisation of the behaviour of the Crown may well be explicable by the high profile nature of the case and the seriousness of the charges.

---

[632] In *Gray* (1995), 43 C.R. (4th) 52 (B.C.S.C.), Oppal J. stayed drugs conspiracy charges delayed for over five years where the vast majority of the delay was clearly accountable to lack of Crown disclosure. The decision considers the *O'Connor* ruling of the British Columbia Court of Appeal but pre-dates that of the Supreme Court.

[633] Above note 575.

[634] At 11. See further the comment on this aspect of *O'Connor* by Graeme G. Mitchell, "Abuse of Process and the Crown's Disclosure Obligation", (1996) 44 C.R. (4th) 130. Stuesser, above note 577, suggests L'Heureux-Dubé J. in *Power* wrongly invoked the discredited community shock test.

A judicial stay as an abuse is a drastic remedy which avoids a trial on the merits. It seems wise that the remedy be used with restraint. But the remedy of stay should not become a dead letter particularly where a Crown Attorney has abused his or her position. After all, the remedy of exclusion of evidence obtained as a result of Charter violation often avoids trial on the merits, sometimes in serious cases. The Supreme Court has been too cautious.

(f) Emphasising Trial Fairness Over Integrity of the System[635]

Regrettably since *O'Connor* the Supreme Court, although it has not been consistent, has become even more resistant to the notion of judicial stays. In *Tobiass* (1997)[636] the Court in a *per curiam* judgment went out of its way to emphasise that the key issue was whether there could still be a fair trial held and that the residual category mentioned in *O'Connor* was to be very small one:

> [A] stay of proceedings does not redress a wrong that has already been done. It aims to prevent the perpetuation of a wrong that, if left alone, will continue to trouble the parties and the community as a whole.... For a stay of proceedings to be appropriate in a case falling into the residual category, it must appear that the state misconduct is likely to continue in the future or that the carrying forward of the prosecution will offend society's sense of justice. Ordinarily, the latter condition will not be met unless the former is as well — society will not take umbrage at the carrying forward of a prosecution unless it is likely that some form of misconduct will continue. There may be exceptional cases in which the past misconduct is so egregious that the mere fact of going forward in the light of it will be offensive. But such cases should be relatively very rare.[637]

This fundamental attack on the residual category proceeds by assertion. It is hard to fathom or accept[638] given that the emergence of a common law doctrine of stay as an abuse had everything to do with the need for a power for a Court to protect its own integrity from being implicated in a variety of police or prosecutorial abuses. There are some abuses the Court should not be seen to condone. As a practical matter an argument for a stay as an abuse of process will now be far more likely to succeed if it can be demonstrated that a fair trial is no longer possible. For example, the Supreme Court itself has confirmed stays where material evidence is missing and a fair trial is no longer possible.[639]

Where a fair trial is still possible, the Supreme Court is now usually resistant to arguments for a stay to protect the integrity of the court system. In *Tobiass* the Supreme Court held that a Federal judge had wrongly stayed a citizenship

---

[635] See generally Kent Roach, "The Evolving Test for Stays of Proceedings", (1998) 3&4 *Crim. L.Q.* 400 and David MacAlister, "Does the Residual Category for Abuse of Process Still Exist", (2000) 28 C.R. (5th) 72 and in his *Accountability of Crown Prosecutors under the Canadian Charter of Rights and Freedoms* (2000), as yet unpublished LL.M. thesis, Faculty of Law, Queen's University.

[636] *Canada (Minister of Citizenship & Immigration) v. Tobiass* (1997), 10 C.R. (5th) 169 (S.C.C.).

[637] Para 91.

[638] See too Roach and MacAlister, above note 635.

[639] *Carosella* (1997), 4 C.R. (5th) 139 (S.C.C.) and *MacDonnell* (1997), 114 C.C.C. (3d) 145, but see later *La* (1997), 8 C.R. (5th) 155 (S.C.C.), discussed below note 773.

revocation hearing for suspected war criminals even though it accepted that judicial independence had been damaged. At the insistence of the Assistant Deputy Attorney General, the Chief Justice had met with the hearing judge to urge the hearings be expedited. Opposing counsel had not been invited. Similarly the Supreme Court would not consider a stay in the mercy killing murder trial of *Latimer* (1997)[640] although it accepted that it was a "flagrant abuse" for a Crown Attorney to conduct a police-administered questionnaire to prospective jurors about their possible attitudes without disclosure to the defence counsel. So too in *Curragh Inc.* (1997),[641] a manslaughter trial of two managers at a mine where an explosion had killed 26 miners, the Supreme Court favoured a new trial, rather than a stay, where it was accepted that the trial judge's words and action had created a reasonable apprehension of bias through interference with the Crown's conduct of the prosecution.

However the Supreme Court has not been consistent in its treatment of integrity of the system cases. In *Simpson* (1995),[642] the Court upheld a stay of proceedings as a remedy for an illegal 48-hour detention without a bail hearing for the systemic reason that no justice of the peace was available in that location at the weekend. So too in *Shirose and Campbell* (1999)[643] Justice Binnie speaking for the Supreme Court, without even reference to *Tobiass*, ordered a new trial to consider whether a stay was appropriate given that an illegal reverse sting operation had been conducted in which an undercover officer had offered drugs for sale in a manner not authorised by the drug legislation then in force. It was important that police abide by the rule of law. The Court did emphasise that a stay would not be automatic and would depend on a determination of good faith and the legal advice received. In *Shirose* the Court recognises in passing that the defence of entrapment is "simply an application of the abuse of process doctrine",[644] while in *Brown* (1999)[645] the Court confirmed a stay of proceedings for entrapment in a drugs case involving a Canadian soldier without giving any consideration to the possibility of a fair trial.

Hopefully the Supreme Court will reconsider its virtual obliteration of the residual category evident in *Tobiass*. There should be a strong remedy to reserve the right to preserve the integrity of the criminal justice system from abuses by police, prosecutors and sometimes judges. Compare the attitude of Lord Lowry for the majority of the U.K. House of Lords in *Horseferry Road Magistrates' Court, ex parte Bennet* (1994):[646]

> [A] court has a discretion to stay any criminal proceedings on the ground that to try those proceedings will amount to an abuse of process either (1) because it will be impossible (usually by reason of delay) to give the accused a fair trial or (2) because

---

[640] (1997), 4 C.R. (5th) 1 (S.C.C.) at 18.

[641] (1997), 5 C.R. (5th) 291 (S.C.C.).

[642] (1995), 95 C.C.C. (3d) 96 (S.C.C.).

[643] (1999), 24 C.R. (5th) 365 (S.C.C.). See more generally Peter M. Brauti and Candice Welsch, "Illegal Police Conduct in the Course of a Bona Fide Investigation", (1999) 43 *Crim. L.Q.* 64.

[644] Para. 381.

[645] (1999), 139 C.C.C. (3d) 492 (S.C.C.).

[646] [1994] 1 A.C. 42 (H.L.). I am indebted to David McAlister for this comparative insight.

it offends the court's sense of justice and propriety to be asked to try the accused in the circumstances of the particular case.[647]

The House of Lords accepts the goal of deterring police from improper behaviour and has stated that

the categories of abuse of process like the categories of negligence are never closed.[648]

The Supreme Court may already have changed course. In two recent extradition cases,[649] the Court stayed extraditions on the basis of the common law doctrine of abuse of process. The abuse was improper threats by U.S. prosecutors to deal harshly with accused who fought extradition in Canada. For the Court, Arbour J. spoke of Canadian courts having

an inherent and residual discretion at common law to control their own process and prevent its abuse.[650]

If *Tobiass* is considered controlling, as it already has been,[651] stay as abuse of process will even less frequently be entered. Hopefully trial judges will continue to distance themselves from abuses in appropriate cases by entering stays, subject of course to appellate review. Judicial stays were recently entered, for example, in integrity cases where a Crown tried to transfer included offences where an attempted murder case was proceeding in Youth Court,[652] where a Crown stayed an aggravated assault case for 16 months to await appeals of co-accused,[653] in a case of deliberate non-disclosure by police and prosecutors[654] and of the third trial of mischief given prosecutorial misconduct, false publicity that the accused was a serial killer and an 8-year delay.[655]

On the other hand the Ontario Court of Appeal in *S.(F.)* (2000)[656] did not consider a stay when it ordered a new trial in a sexual abuse case where the Crown was held to have breached every aspect of the proper role of a Crown. He had injected his own credibility, stated a goal of obtaining a conviction and justice for the complainant, misstated evidence, been inflammatory, disrespectful, asked

---

[647] At 74.

[648] *Martin*, [1998] 2 W.L.R. 1 (H.L.).

[649] *United States v. Cobb* (April 5, 2001) (S.C.C.) and *United States v. Shulman* (April 5, 2001) (S.C.C.).

[650] *Cobb, ibid.*, para. 37. Arbour J. sees *Keyowski* as the controlling authority and does not mention *Tobiass* or the restrictive approach of *O'Connor*.

[651] *Regan* (1999), 28 C.R. (5th) 1 (N.S. C.A.) (trial judge wrong to stay 9 of 18 counts of sexual offences against a former premier given judge shopping, Crown's pre-charge interviewing and premature police press release). See critical review by McAlister, above note 635. See too *Kormos* (1997), 12 C.R. (5th) 348 (Ont. Prov. Ct.) and *B.(R.)* (1998), 133 C.C.C. (3d) 229 (Que. C.A.).

[652] *Alberta (Attorney General) v. M. (M.W.)* (1997), 11 C.R. (5th) 88 (Alta. C.A.).

[653] *Cole* (1998), 16 C.R. (5th) 110 (N.S. S.C.).

[654] *Greganti* (2000), 142 C.C.C. (3d) 31 (Ont. S.C.) but see *Gagne* (1998), 131 C.C.C. (3d) 444 (Que. C.A.).

[655] *Wise* (1996), 47 C.R. (4th) 6 (Ont. Gen. Div.). Compare *Pan* (1999), 26 C.R. (5th) 87 (Ont. C.A.), (third murder trial not to be stayed absent prosecutorial misconduct).

[656] (2000), 31 C.R. (5th) 159 (Ont. C.A.). See too Paul Calarco, "S.(F.): When Crowns Go Bad (Again!)", (2000) 31 C.R. (5th) 173.

the accused whether the complainant was a known liar and had referred to and misstated a case in his jury address.

(g) Pre-Charge Delay

The Supreme Court has determined that pre-charge delay cannot ground a Charter challenge on the basis that there has been a violation of the right to be tried within a reasonable time contrary to s. 11(b).[657] The accused only has a remedy if there has been a violation of the right to fair trial under ss. 7 and 11(d) or an abuse of process. It has indicated that this could be grounded on "deviousness or maliciousness" or "offensive or vexatious conduct on the part of the police."[658]

In *L. (W.K.)* (1991),[659] Mr. Justice Stevenson for a unanimous Court confirmed that delay between the commission of a crime and the laying of the charge cannot without more justify a stay as an abuse at common law or violate the Charter:

> Staying proceedings based on the mere passage of time would be the equivalent of imposing a judicially created limitation period for a criminal offence. In Canada, except in rare circumstances, there are no limitation periods in criminal law. The comments of Laskin C.J. in *Rourke* are equally applicable under the Charter.[660]

The Court further held that the right to a fair trial protected by ss. 7 and 11(d) of the Charter was not "automatically undermined by even a lengthy pre-charge delay."[661] Pre-charge delay was relevant under those provisions not because of the length of the delay but as to the effect of that delay upon the fairness of the trial. The fairness of a particular trial could not be assessed without considering the particular circumstances.

The accused had been charged in 1987 with 17 counts of sexual assault, gross indecency and assault relating to his step-daughter and two daughters. The first incident was alleged to have occurred in 1957 and the last one in 1985. The charges were laid after two of the alleged victims complained to the police in 1986, the first time that either had reported any incident to the police. The Supreme Court held that there had been no factual foundation for the trial judge's rulings that the explanation for the reporting was "ludicrous" and "specious" and that the delay in reporting the offences was unexplained and extraordinary.[662] The trial judge should have heard *viva voce* testimony and had wrongly stayed the charges.

---

[657] *Mills* (1986), 52 C.R. (3d) 1 (S.C.C.) and *Carter* (1986), 52 C.R. (3d) 100 (S.C.C.). See too *Morrison* (1984), 44 C.R. (3d) 85 (Ont. C.A.) (involving a 25-year delay); and *F. (G.A.)* (1989), 69 C.R. (3d) 92 (Ont. C.A.). The stay as abuse was considered in a post-charge delay case in *Conway* (1989), 70 C.R. (3d) 209 at 221-225 (S.C.C.), below Chapter 6.

[658] *Carter* at 105. In *Parker v. Canada (Solicitor General)* (1990), 78 C.R. (3d) 209 (Ont. H.C.), it was held that an arbitrary delay in executing an arrest warrant for murder, delaying commencement of a 15-year review of parole eligibility, violated s. 7.

[659] (1991), 64 C.C.C. (3d) 321 (S.C.C.).

[660] *Ibid.*, at 328.

[661] *Ibid.*

[662] *Ibid.*, at 329-330.

Stevenson J. added that the nature of the particular kind of offence in question provided additional support for his conclusion:

> For victims of sexual abuse to complain would take courage and emotional strength in revealing those personal secrets in opening old wounds. If proceedings were to be stayed based solely on the passage of time between the abuse and the charge, victims would be required to report incidents before they were psychologically prepared for the consequences of that report.[663]

Courts have proved difficult to convince that a fair trial is not still possible, as in cases where a witness had left the country[664] and where there was some evidence the accused had amnesia.[665]

10. RIGHT TO A FAIR TRIAL (RIGHT TO MAKE FULL ANSWER AND DEFENCE)

Section 11(d) guarantees one charged with an offence the right, *inter alia*, to a "fair and public hearing." In criminal courts, judges frequently speak more loosely of a constitutional right to a fair trial or a constitutional right to make full answer and defence. Sometimes the right is located in s. 11(d),[666] at other times in s. 7,[667] while sometimes ss. 7 and 11(d) are referred to in the same breath.[668] It seems preferable to consider what is included in the right to a fair trial in this context of s. 7. After all, whatever is included in a right to a fair hearing under s. 11(d) would "in any event be protected under s. 7 as an aspect of the principles of fundamental justice."[669] Section 7 must be relied on in cases where s. 11(d) is not available because an offence has not been charged.

(a) Right to Disclosure

(i) *Pre-Charter*

In Canada, there is no statutory scheme under which every accused can discover from the Crown the case to be met at trial. There are Criminal Code provisions[670] requiring that charges provide sufficient details of the alleged circumstances to give the accused reasonable information as to the precise charge. There are procedures for obtaining further particulars.[671] In the case of most but not all proceedings on indictment, the accused may elect to have a preliminary

---

[663] *Ibid.*, at 328.
[664] *Flamand* (1999), 141 C.C.C. (3d) 169 (Que. C.A.).
[665] *H.(L.J.)* (1997), 120 C.C.C. (3d) 88 (Man. C.A.).
[666] *Corbett* (1988), 64 C.R. (3d) 1 (S.C.C.); *Stoddart* (1987), 59 C.R. (3d) 134 at 147 (Ont. C.A.).
[667] *Stinchcombe* (1991), 8 C.R. (4th) 277 (S.C.C.), discussed below note 701, and *Williams* (1985), 44 C.R. (3d) 351 at 366-367 (Ont. C.A.).
[668] Beetz J. in *Corbett*, above note 666, at 23.
[669] La Forest J. in *Thomson*, above note 4, at 238. See also McLachlin J. for the majority in *Seaboye* below note 924.
[670] Sections 581 and 583.
[671] Section 587.

inquiry.[672] The Supreme Court of Canada once saw the purpose of a preliminary inquiry as being solely to determine whether there was sufficient evidence to put the accused on trial[673] but now recognize[674] that it also informs the important discovery function of providing defence counsel with an opportunity of ascertaining the nature and strength of the case. Although preliminary inquiries exist only in a very small minority of criminal cases and are sometimes waived by defence counsel, the preliminary inquiry is seen by the defence bar to be a vitally important discovery instrument for serious cases, primarily because they allow cross-examination of Crown witnesses on oath. There are a few other statutory rights to discovery,[675] such as a limited right to receive copies of evidence after a preliminary inquiry,[676] to obtain release of exhibits for testing[677] and the right at trial to obtain copies of prior statements of a witness for cross-examination.[678]

The common law position is that pre-trial discovery is in the discretion of the Crown while discovery at trial is in the discretion of the Court.[679] The recognition of the power of a trial judge to order discovery apart from a specific statutory power to do so is relatively recent. In *Savion* (1980),[680] Mr. Justice Zuber for the Ontario Court of Appeal confirmed that there was a wider power to compel Crown to produce a statement of the accused to the police and a tape recording of an intercepted conversation, that flowed from the "ability of the court to control its process so as to manifestly ensure fundamental fairness and see that the adversarial process is consistent with the interests of justice."[681] In *Doiron* (1985)[682] the Nova Scotia Court of Appeal further held that this power should be "exercised in favour of production in the absence of any cogent reason to the contrary."[683]

The Law Reform Commission of Canada long advocated that there should be formal legislative procedures for pre-trial disclosure. The Commission[684] saw the problem as follows:

> Apart from specific and limited requirements currently prescribed by law, pre-trial disclosure in Canada is characteristically an informal process, predicated upon the Crown's discretion in the management of its case. To the extent that it exists, pre-trial disclosure is subject to the vagaries of regional practice, plea-bargaining and

---

[672] Part XVIII.
[673] *Patterson*, [1970] S.C.R. 409.
[674] *Skogman*, [1984] 2 S.C.R. 93 at 95-111 (per Estey J.).
[675] Freedom of Information Acts invariably have law enforcement exemptions: for example, Access to Information Act, S.C. 1980-81-82-83, c. 111, s. 16(1) and (3).
[676] Section 603.
[677] Section 605.
[678] Canada Evidence Act, R.S.C. 1985, c. C-5, s. 10(1).
[679] For a full survey of Canadian law see J.J. Attrens, P.T. Burns and J.P. Taylor (eds.), *Criminal Procedure: Canadian Law and Practice* (1981) Vol. 2, chap. 13 (revised and updated in 1987).
[680] (1980), 13 C.R. (3d) 259 (Ont. C.A.).
[681] *Ibid.*, at 269.
[682] (1985), 19 C.C.C. (3d) 350 (N.S. C.A.).
[683] *Ibid.*, at 363.
[684] *Report 22: Disclosure by the Prosecution* (1984).

personal relations among members of the criminal bar; for these reasons alone it defines systematic analysis as an integral feature of Canadian criminal procedure.[685]

No political consensus emerged for a formal scheme. In the reality that in the vast number of cases disclosure was a matter for the discretion of the individual prosecutor, defence counsel turned to s. 7 of the Charter for a constitutional remedy.

(ii) *Charter pre-Stinchcombe*

The first signs were not encouraging. In *Potma* (1983),[686] the Ontario Court of Appeal held that, although the right to make full answer and defence was a principle of fundamental justice long recognized as an essential ingredient of a fair trial, and indeed enshrined in the Criminal Code,[687] it was ''in no sense a new right created or expanded by the Charter.''[688] It had not been infringed by police denial of requests for the test and reference ampoules used in a breathalyzer test where those ampoules had been routinely discarded in good faith. The Court pointed to a dictum of the Supreme Court of Canada under the Bill of Rights in *Duke* (1972)[689] that ''the failure of the Crown to produce evidence to an accused person does not deprive the accused of a fair trial unless, by law, it is required to do so.''[690]

In *Arviv* (1985),[691] Mr. Justice Martin for the Ontario Court of Appeal held that the preferment of a direct indictment by the Attorney General under what is now s. 577 of the Criminal Code does not *per se* contravene principles of fundamental justice under s. 7. Although the preliminary inquiry did serve an ancillary purpose of providing discovery, s. 7 had not elevated the preliminary inquiry to a constitutional right. The right to a preliminary inquiry could be bypassed by the Attorney General preferring an indictment. However, the Court did add that

> The preferring of a direct indictment under s. 507(3) of the Code *in combination with* the failure of the Crown to make adequate disclosure might, however, result in an accused being unable to make full answer and defence at his trial, thereby contravening s. 7 of the Charter and enabling the trial judge to fashion a remedy under s. 24(1).[692]

The strongest provincial authority in favour of a constitutional right to discovery was the decision of the Saskatchewan Court of Appeal in *Bourget*

---

[685] *Ibid.*, at 3.

[686] (1983), 31 C.R. (3d) 231 (Ont. C.A.).

[687] Now ss. 650(3) and 802(1).

[688] Above note 686, at 241.

[689] [1972] S.C.R. 917.

[690] Above note 686, at 240.

[691] (1985), 45 C.R. (3d) 354 (Ont. C.A.).

[692] *Ibid.*, at 366. See too *Plamondon* (1991), 4 C.R. (4th) 279 (Que. C.A.), but compare *Parades* (1994), 35 C.R. (4th) 387 (Que. C.A.) (direct indictment on same evidence previously resulting in discharge at preliminary inquiry violating s. 7).

(1987).[693] Prior to his trial on a charge of driving a motor vehicle with excess alcohol in his blood, the accused had asked the Crown to provide representative ampoules of the solution used to analyze the samples of the accused's breath in the breathalyzer. The defence counsel wished to test the ampoules for accuracy since they were not those specified to be used by the manufacturer of the breathalyzer system. Mr. Justice Tallis for the Court reasoned as follows:

> In my opinion s. 7 of the Charter gives the court broad power to promote the proper administration of criminal justice by ordering disclosure and discovery of material and objects for the purpose of independent testing. Section 7 is no longer limited to the notion of procedural fairness in court, and encompasses the whole process, including discovery and disclosure. If our system of criminal justice is to be marked by a search for truth, then disclosure and discovery of relevant materials, rather than suppression, should be the starting point. I appreciate that special circumstances may militate in favour of "protective" orders, but no such considerations apply in this case. We do not address the regulation of such discovery but deal with the general principle.[694]

Bourget has been distinguished by the Nova Scotia Court of Appeal in *Eagles* (1989).[695] That Court agreed that the Crown now had a duty "to make disclosure to the defence of all evidence, objects or materials supporting innocence or mitigating the offence'."[696] However the duty of disclosure related only to "relevant and material matters" and had to be reasonable in the sense that it was "founded on something more than mere speculation" and had an "air of reality." In *Eagles*, it was held that the Crown had been under no duty to produce the representative ampoule because, unlike *Bourget* where the accuracy of the breathalyzer using ampoules not provided by the manufacturers was a live issue, here the defence counsel had not established that examination of the ampoule would have meant that the test was defective. The request was nothing more than a "fishing expedition" which was to be discouraged rather than encouraged.[697] The mandatory automatic production of all evidence, material or objects in the Crown's possession was neither desirable nor necessary and could lead to abuses and delays in the trial process.

The Nova Scotia Court of Appeal subsequently held in *Delaney* (1989)[698] that a refusal of the police and the Crown to give an accused access to a breathalyzer machine, requested nearly five months after the test had been

---

[693] (1987), 56 C.R. (3d) 97 (Sask. C.A.).

[694] *Ibid.*, at 105.

[695] (1989), 68 C.R. (3d) 271 (N.S. C.A.). See comment by Rick Libman, "Eagles: Requests for Representative Ampoules" (1989), 68 C.R. (3d) 281, including documentation of the futility of such requests.

[696] *Ibid.*, at 278.

[697] *Ibid.*, at 278-279.

[698] (1989), 48 C.C.C. (3d) 276 (N.S. C.A.). See too *Hodgson* (1990), 78 C.R. (3d) 333 (B.C. C.A.), following *Eagles. Hodgson* has been confirmed since *Stinchcombe* in *Anutooshkin* (1994), 92 C.C.C. (3d) 59 (B.C. C.A.), but has also been distinguished in *Oakman* (1993), 81 C.C.C. (3d) 560 (Man. Q.B.). In *Selig* (1991), 4 C.R. (4th) 20 (N.S. C.A.), it was held that s. 7 had been violated where the accused was denied a polite and reasonable request to read the breathalyzer gauge as the tests were administered.

performed and without showing why and how the inspection would advance the accused's case, did not violate s. 7. The Provincial Court Judge who had made the order prior to trial had not been a court of competent jurisdiction under s. 24(1), given that he had no statutory jurisdiction to hear such application.

The leading decision in Ontario in a non-breathaylzer context, where disclosure is more likely to be of real assistance to the defence, became that of the Court of Appeal in *Wood* (1989).[699] For the Court, Mr. Justice Griffith noted that there was no common law or statutory right to full disclosure but added that, in general, the practice of Ontario Crown had been to furnish the accused more than that which was provided at the preliminary inquiry and to comply with wide disclosure guidelines of the Attorney-General. He concluded that s. 7

> guarantees the accused the right only to such disclosure from the Crown as is necessary to make full answer and defence. The disclosure given under the requirements of the Charter should be sufficient to fairly apprise the accused of the case to be met in sufficient time and substance to enable the accused to adequately prepare and defend that case.[700]

The accuseds' rights had not been violated. Disclosure had been extensive. Even though the trial judge had not ordered production by the Crown of police statements of certain witnesses, their full names and addresses and places of employment had been provided.

(iii) *Stinchcombe right to disclosure*

In its far-reaching decision in *Stinchcombe* (1991),[701] the Supreme Court recognised a broad constitutional duty on the Crown to disclose all relevant information subject only to a limited and reviewable discretion to withhold.

Mr. Justice Sopinka, on behalf of a unanimous Court, pointed to the role of the prosecutor outlined by Mr. Justice Rand in *Boucher* (1955)[702] under which prosecution is a matter of public duty which excludes any notion of winning or losing. It followed that the fruits of the investigation which are in the possession of counsel for the Crown are not its property for use in securing a conviction, but the property of the public to be used to ensure that justice is done. In contrast, the defence had no obligation to assist the prosecution and was entitled to assume a purely adversarial role. The absence of its duty to disclose could be justified as being consistent with that role. The Court saw no valid practical reason against a broad duty of disclosure. Discovery experiments across the country had shown that there was a significant increase in the number of cases settled and pleas of guilty entered or charges withdrawn. There was in any event an overriding concern

---

[699] (1989), 51 C.C.C. (3d) 201 (Ont. C.A.).

[700] *Ibid.*, at 236.

[701] (1991), 8 C.R. (4th) 277 (S.C.C.). See case comments by Gerry Ferguson, "Judicial Reform of Crown Disclosure", C.R. *ibid.* pp. 294-306 and Brian Gover, "Stinchcombe: Bad Case, Good Law?, C.R. *ibid.* pp. 307-315. See also reviews of later developments by Lee Stuesser, "General Principles Concerning Disclosure", (1996) 1 *Can. Crim. L.R.* 1.

[702] [1955] S.C.R. 16.

that failure to disclose could impede the ability of the accused to make full answer and defence. This was a right now protected under s. 7:

> This common law right has acquired new vigour by virtue of its inclusion in s. 7 of the [Charter] as one of the principles of fundamental justice . . . The right to make full answer and defence is one of the pillars of criminal justice on which we heavily depend to ensure that the innocent are not convicted.[703]

The Court referred to the *Marshall Commission Report* (1989),[704] in which the Commissioners had found that lack of disclosure of prior inconsistent statements to the defence counsel had been an important contributing factor in the miscarriage of justice which had occurred in the wrongful murder conviction of an aboriginal accused.

The Court makes it quite clear that the Crown is under a general legal duty to disclose all relevant information whether inculpatory or exculpatory and whether or not the Crown intends to introduce it as evidence. The Crown may exercise discretion as to what is relevant. While it need not produce what is "clearly irrelevant" it must "err on the side of inclusion".[705]

The obligation to disclose imposed by the Supreme Court is not absolute and is subject to some discretion of Crown counsel relating both to the timing of disclosure and the withholding of certain information:

> The obligation to disclose will be triggered by a request by or on behalf of the accused. Such a request may be made at any time after the charge. Provided the request for disclosure has been timely, it should be complied with so as to enable the accused sufficient time before election or plea to consider the information. In the rare cases in which the accused is unrepresented, Crown counsel should advise the accused of the right to disclosure and a plea should not be taken unless the trial judge is satisfied that this has been done. At this stage, the Crown's brief will often not be complete and disclosure will be limited by this fact. Nevertheless, the obligation to disclose is a continuing one and disclosure must be completed when additional information is received.[706]

Rules of privilege must be respected and the Crown has a duty to protect the identities of informers. In rare cases, disclosure can be delayed if it will impede an ongoing investigation. The Crown's exercise of discretion is reviewable by the trial judge at the initiation of defence counsel.

In *Chaplin* (1995),[707] Sopinka J., again speaking for a unanimous Court, set out the procedure for challenging non-disclosure by the Crown. In the situation where the material is in existence and has been identified, the Crown must justify non-disclosure by

---

[703] At 285.

[704] *Royal Commission on the Donald Marshall Jr. Prosecution* (1989) vol. 1, pp. 238-242, discussed by Theresa M. Brucker, "Disclosure and the Role of the Police in the Criminal Justice System", (1992) 35 *Crim.L.Q.* 57.

[705] At 288. See *Wilson* (1994), 87 C.C.C. (3d) 115 (Ont. C.A.) for a finding that a videotape was clearly irrelevant.

[706] At 290.

[707] (1994), 36 C.R. (4th) 201 (S.C.C.).

demonstrating either that the information sought is beyond its control or that it is clearly irrelevant or privileged.[708]

The trial judge must afford the Crown an opportunity to call evidence to justify non-disclosure. Justification of non-disclosure on the grounds of public interest privilege or other privilege may involve special procedures such as that referred to in s. 37(2) of the Canada Evidence Act to protect the confidentiality of the evidence.[709] In the situation, held the Court, where the existence of the material alleged to be relevant is disputed by the Crown, the Crown cannot be required to justify the non-disclosure. The defence must first establish a basis which could enable the judge to conclude that there is in existence further material which is potentially relevant. Relevance here means that there is a reasonable possibility of being useful to the accused in making full answer and defence.[710] The existence of the disputed material must be sufficiently identified not only to reveal its nature but also to enable the judge to determine that it may meet the test with respect to material which the Crown is obliged to produce. The matter could be resolved by oral submissions or by evidence at a *voir dire*. In cases involving confidential information it may be appropriate for the trial judge to order a hearing in camera or to inspect the material privately, applying procedures such as those set out in s. 37(2) of the Canada Evidence Act.

The remedy given in *Stinchcombe* was an order of a new trial. The accused, a practising lawyer, faced fraud and theft charges relating to securities deposited in trust. Crown counsel had refused to provide key statements of his former secretary to the defence counsel and the trial judge and Alberta Court of Appeal had refused to order that they be provided. At the new trial the Crown disclosed two transcripts of a taped interview and a photocopy of the handwritten statement in question. The Crown informed defence counsel that the police had been unable to find the original tape recording and statement. The trial judge thereupon stayed the proceedings. When the matter again reached the Supreme Court,[711] the Supreme Court this time agreed with the Alberta Court of Appeal that the trial judge had erred. The Crown must only produce what is in its possession or control. There was no absolute right to production of the originals and there had been no

---

[708] At 210.

[709] In *Durette* (1994), 28 C.R. (4th) 1 (S.C.C.), the Court had held that non-disclosure of affidavits in support of a wiretap application required justification by the Crown that the interests of informants, innocent persons and law enforcement authorities were more important than the accused's interests. A new trial was ordered because the trial judge had unduly edited affidavits where continuing confidentiality was not justified. Compare however *Leipert* (1997), 4 C.R. (5th) 259 (S.C.C.). A trial judge had erred in editing an anonymous Crime Stoppers tip sheet with a view to disclosure to defence respecting a challenge to a search warrant. This purpose did not meet the necessary to establish innocence exception to the informer privilege. See too *M.(A.) v. Ryan* (1997), 4 C.R. (5th) 220 (S.C.C.) (Wigmore's test for confidentiality of communications to be balanced against Charter values of privacy and equality).

[710] Sopinka J. quoted his earlier judgment for the Court in *Egger* (1993), 21 C.R. (4th) 186 (S.C.C.), and approved its application in *Hutter* (1993), 86 C.C.C. (3d) 81 (Ont. C.A.) at 89.

[711] *Stinchcombe* (1995), 38 C.R. (4th) 42 (S.C.C.).

misconduct by the Crown. The Supreme Court has also held that the right to disclosure does not extend to producing witnesses for oral discovery.[712]

Even where non-disclosure by the Crown in violation of the Charter has been established the Supreme Court has now made it very clear in its decision in *O'Connor* (1996)[713] that a stay of proceedings is only appropriate in exceptional cases.[714] A trial judge must fully explore other remedies which include adjournments, costs,[715] orders of full disclosure and declarations of a mistrial.[716] On appeal there is substantial provincial case law to the effect that any order of a new trial requires the accused to establish that the non-disclosure had a material effect on the right to make full answer and defence.[717]

In *Stinchcombe*, Sopinka J. expressly left two matters open: the issue of whether the disclosure principles applied to summary conviction proceedings and whether there should be reciprocal obligations to disclose imposed on the defence. As to the first issue, given that the procedural classification of Criminal Code offences as indictable, hybrid or summary is a most inaccurate measure of seriousness of offence, it would be most technical, cumbersome and unjust to make any distinction as to the type of disclosure to be made. Fortunately provincial courts have been content to apply *Stinchcombe* to any type of offence,[718] including provincial offences.

A duty of reciprocal disclosure would fundamentally change the nature of criminal trials. In *Stinchcombe*, although Sopinka J. explicitly states that whether the duty should be reciprocal "may deserve consideration by this court in the future",[719] he appears to decide against it *obiter* in the following remarks:

---

[712] *Khela* (1995), 43 C.R. (4th) 368 (S.C.C.). See too *Sterling* (1993), 84 C.C.C.(3d) 65 (Sask. C.A.) and *Olscamp* (1994), 30 C.R. (4th) 106 (Ont. Gen. Div.). Hard copy rather than electronic disclosure was ordered in *Hallstone Products Ltd.* (1999), 140 C.C.C. (3d) 145 (Ont. S.C.J.) and *Cheung* (2000), 35 C.R. (5th) 48 (Alta. Prov. Ct.). Videotapes were ordered disclosed at Crown cost in *Blencowe* (1997), 9 C.R. (5th) 320 (Ont. Gen. Div.).

[713] (1996), 44 C.R. (4th) 1 (S.C.C.), discussed above note 627 and below note 734.

[714] A stay was entered in *Khela* (1998), 126 C.C.C. (3d) 341 (Que. C.A.).

[715] *AGAT Laboratories Ltd.* (1998), 17 C.R. (5th) 147 (Alta. Prov. Ct.) and further in Chapter 11.

[716] See, for example, *Antinello* (1995), 39 C.R. (4th) 99 (Alta. C.A.) and *Fineline Circuits Ltd.* (1991), 10 C.R. (4th) 241 (Ont. Prov. Div.).

[717] See, for example, *Ford* (1993), 78 C.C.C. (3d) 481 (B.C. C.A.), *Malcolm* (1993), 81 C.C.C. (3d) 196 (Ont. C.A.), *Pearson* (1994), 89 C.C.C. (3d) 535 (Que. C.A.) (where the new trial ordered was limited to the issue of entrapment) and *Noble* (1996), 106 C.C.C. (3d) 161 (B.C. C.A.). In *Creamer* (1995), 97 C.C.C. (3d) 108 (B.C. C.A.), it was held that the normal rule for the admission of fresh evidence on appeal should be relaxed in such cases.

[718] *Petten* (1993), 81 C.C.C. (3d) 347 (Nfld. C.A.), *Fineline Circuits Ltd.*, above note 716. See too disclosure guidelines of the Department of Justice, "Federal Prosecutors Now Have Uniform Disclosure Policy", *The Lawyers Weekly*, July 17, 1992 and the recommendation of the Ontario Attorney General's Advisory Committee (the Martin Committee), *Charge Screening, Disclosure and Resolution Discussions* (1993) p. 184, that the nature and extent of disclosure should not vary based on whether the charge was prosecuted by way of indictment, summary conviction procedure or under the Ontario Provincial Offences Act. However a justice at a preliminary inquiry is not a court of competent jurisdiction to order disclosure: *Girimonte* (1997), 121 C.C.C. (3d) 33 (Ont. C.A.).

[719] At 283.

> In contrast [to the Crown], the defence has no obligation to assist the prosecution and is entitled to assume a purely adversarial role toward the prosecution. The absence of a duty to disclose can, therefore, be justified as being consistent with this role.[720]

This was the interpretation of the Quebec Court of Appeal in *Peruta, Brouillette* (1992).[721] Defence counsel in a murder trial were held to have been under no obligation to disclose written statements obtained from the defence witnesses by a private investigator. Tyndale J.A. added two further reasons to those considered by the Supreme Court:

> First, the fact that the power and resources for investigation and litigation available to the prosecution are out of all proportion to those normally available to the defence. Secondly, the long and flourishing tradition in the British system of justice, if not of making things difficult for the prosecution, at least of making things less difficult for the defence, on the excellent ground that it is better that a guilty man go unpunished than that an innocent man be convicted.[722]

A reciprocal defence obligation to disclose would jeopardize the presumption of innocence and the now strongly entrenched principle against self-incrimination.[723] An unrepresented accused would be particularly vulnerable.

Stinchcombe's impact on the administration of criminal justice has been immense and provides a powerful illustration of the power of judicial declarations of Charter standards. Crown disclosure is now a fundamental feature of a Canadian criminal justice. The Supreme Court forced a needed reform where political consensus and will was lacking. The gains of *Stinchcombe* should not, however, be exaggerated. It is curious that the accused has a right to full disclosure but that this is only triggered by a defence request. Surely the right is so fundamental that it should be automatic. Accused may well have less rights if they are not properly represented in this respect or are unrepresented.[724] *Stinchcombe* also assumes that defence counsel always have the time and resources for full defence preparation, which includes obtaining proper disclosure.

---

[720] *Ibid.* See too Lamer C.J. in *P. (M.B.)*, above note 544 at 227.

[721] (1992), 78 C.C.C. (3d) 350 (Que. C.A.).

[722] At 357. Proulx and Moison J. (*ad hoc*) concurred.

[723] See above note 544. For a detailed justification of a limited defence duty to disclose see David Tanovich and Lawrence Crocker , "A Modest Proposal for Reciprocal Defence Disclosure", (1994) 26 C.R. (4th) 333 but compare the rebuttal by Charles B. Davison, "Putting Ghosts to Rest", (1996) 43 C.R. (4th) 105. Gil D. McKinnon, "Accelerating Defence Disclosure : A Time for Change", (1996) 1 *Can. Crim. L.R.* 59 argues that mandatory pre-trial disclosure is desirable and would not undermine the principle against self-incrimination. Both positions are refuted by Suzanne Coston, "Disclosure by the Defence: Why Should I Tell You?", (1996) 1 *Can. Crim. L.R.* 73. See too Brian Maude, "Reciprocal Disclosure in Criminal Trials: Stacking the Deck Against the Accused or Calling Defence Counsel's Bluff", (1999) 37 *Alta. L. Rev.* 715 and Michael Tochor and Keith Kilback, "Defence Disclosure: Is It Written in Stone?", (2000) 43 *Crim. L.Q.* 393. In *Underwood* (1998), 121 C.C.C. (3d) 117 (S.C.C.) the proceeding the Court required for *Corbett* applications concerning cross-examination of the accused on a prior criminal record required a limited form of disclosure of the defence case.

[724] See below note 783.

From the defence point of view, the *Stinchcombe* disclosure obligation was substantially weakened in *Dixon* (1998)[725] where the Supreme Court emphasised that defence counsel must not remain passive and must diligently pursue disclosure.[726] Negligence or a tactical decision not to pursue full disclosure might well jeopardise the success of an appeal based on non-disclosure. According to Cory J., speaking for the five-justice Court:

> If defence counsel knew or ought to have known on the basis of other disclosures that the Crown through inadvertence had failed to disclose information yet remained passive as a result of a tactical decision or lack of due diligence it would be difficult to accept a submission that the failure to disclose affected the fairness of the trial[727].

This *Dixon* obligation on defence counsel clearly seeks to prevent defence ambush and other tactics resulting in new trials. However the defence obligation seems onerous[728] and seems to saddle accused with the sins of their lawyers. It certainly carries the message that defence counsel are well advised to pursue disclosure with rigour at every point.

Stinchcombe as interpreted in *Chaplin* confines the right to disclosure to material in the possession or control of the Crown.[729] Since evidence gathering in Canada is in the exclusive domain of the police what if the police choose to keep material from the Crown. Is such material not within the Crown's control and therefore not subject to the duty to disclose? If so the right to disclose might become hollow. Thus far provincial Courts of Appeal have been commendably demanding. According to the Ontario Court of Appeal

> There is a duty on the Crown to make full disclosure and, accordingly, the Crown has a duty to obtain from the police — and the police have a corresponding duty to provide for the Crown — all relevant information and material concerning the case.[730]

---

[725] (1998), 13 C.R. (5th) 217 (S.C.C.) and companion cases of *Skinner, Smith, McQuaid* and *Robart*, reported respectively C.R. *ibid.* at 241, 246, 251, and 256. In each case there was non-disclosure of witness statements. New trials were only ordered in *Smith* and *Skinner*. The other appeals were dismissed on the basis the right to make full answer and defence had not been sufficiently impaired. See reviews by Graeme Mitchell, "R. v. Dixon: The Right to Crown Disclosure — A Road Map for the Future?", (1998) 13 C.R. (5th) 260 and Charles Davison, "Disclosure, Due Diligence and Defence Counsel — Increasing the Burden and Raising the Standards", (1998) 13 C.R. (5th) 269.

[726] Para. 37.

[727] Para. 38.

[728] See further Davison, above note 725.

[729] Prior to *Chaplin* the Alberta Court of Appeal refused to extend the *Stinchcombe* obligation to material not within the Crown's control (here files held by a federal civil servant in another province): *Gingras* (1992), 11 C.R. (4th) 294 (Alta. C.A.).

[730] *L.A.T.* (1993), 84 C.C.C. (3d) 90 (Ont. C.A.) at 94, relying on *R. v. V. (W.J.)* (1992), 14 C.R. (4th) 311 (Nfld. C.A.). The Martin Committee, above note 718, pp. 264-265, recommends that the police be under a duty to report all relevant information to the Crown and that a failure to do so be made a disciplinary offence. In *Adams* (1995), 38 C.R. (4th) 257 (Nfld. Prov. Ct.), the Crown was ordered to disclose a police operations manual in an impaired driving trial where there was conflicting police testimony as to the procedure of the breathalyzer technician. Police misconduct findings were ordered to be disclosed in a case arising out of a fracas with police: *Tomlinson* (1998), 16 C.R. (5th) 333 (Ont. Prov. Div.).

In order that an accused may take advantage of the broad protection against unreasonable search and seizure under s. 8 it is now clear that the accused must be given access to the information behind a search warrant[731] or the contents of a sealed packet upon which a judicial authorization to electronically survey was made.[732] Courts have recognized that sometimes the identity of an informer might have to be disclosed, unless it can be judicially edited.

(iv) *Discovery of medical records of sexual assault complainants*

The constitutional right to full disclosure has proved particularly controversial where relied upon by defence counsel to gain access to medical records of sexual assault complainants.[733] The matter reached the Supreme Court in *O'Connor* (1996)[734] and *L.L.A. v. A.B.* (1996).[735] We have earlier examined the facts in *O'Connor* and the Supreme Court rulings respecting abuse of process. The Court also announced a special procedure respecting discovery of medical records in the possession of third parties.[736] The decision represents a fundamental broadening of the *Stinchcombe* right to disclosure of material in the Crown's possession or control to a right to discovery.

Through the judgment of Madam Justice L'Heureux-Dubé in *L.L.A. v. A.B.*, the Court unanimously decided that production should not be determined by class or case-by-case privilege.[737] According to L'Heureux-Dubé J. the creation of a class privilege in favour of private records in criminal law raised concerns relating to

(1) the truth-finding process of our adversarial trial procedure; (2) the possible relevance of some private records; (3) the accused's right to make full answer and

---

[731] *Hunter* (1987), 57 C.R. (3d) 1 (Ont. C.A.). This is, however, subject to the informer privilege: *Leipert*, above note 709.

[732] *Dersch* (1990), 80 C.R. (3d) 299 (S.C.C.). The Supreme Court has also settled several technical issues respecting the scope, jurisdiction and procedure for review; see *Garofoli* (1990), 80 C.R. (3d) 317 (S.C.C.), discussed by James O'Reilly, "Reviewing Wiretap Authorizations — The Supreme Court Goes Through the Motions", C.R. *ibid.*, pp. 386-395, and A.D. Gold, "Notes and Comments, Wiretaps" (1991), 33 *Crim. L.Q.* 274.

[733] Both Young and Bennett, below note 736, point out that the issue of access to medical records of witnesses also arises in cases other than sexual assault.

[734] (1996), 44 C.R. (4th) 1 (S.C.C.).

[735] (1995), 44 C.R. (4th) 91 (S.C.C.).

[736] This aspect of *O'Connor* produced a flurry of commentary. See Heather J. Holmes, "Access to Third Party Records: Does R. v. O'Connor Occupy the Field?", (1996) 44 C.R. (4th) 144, Alan N. Young, "When Titans Clash: The Limits of Constitutional Adjudication", C.R. *ibid.* 152, Jodie van Dieen, "L.L.A. v. A.B.; The Privilege Analysis", C.R. *ibid.* 166, Martin Peters, "Third Party Disclosure under O'Connor: Defence Concerns", C.R. *ibid.* 179, Stuesser, above note 701, Elizabeth Bennett, "Disclosure of Complainant's Medical and Therapeutic Records", (1966) 1 *Can. Crim. L.R.* 17, and Marilyn T. MacCrimmon, "Trial by Ordeal", *Can. Crim. L.R. ibid.* 31.

[737] The majority judgment of Lamer C.J. and Sopinka J. does not address the issue of privilege in the context of records in the possession of third parties. However the majority implicitly rejects any notion of privilege in adopting the two-stage balancing procedure. For an argument that a statutory privilege for therapeutic records of a sexual assault crisis centre is nevertheless desirable and constitutional see MacCrimmon, above note 736, at 53-57.

defence; (4) the categories of actors included in a class privilege; and (5) the experience of other countries.[738]

Carefully examining case law dealing with privilege and confidential information, including that relating to police informants, solicitor-client privilege and public interest immunity, she points out that the courts have consistently ordered production where necessary to establish innocence.[739] While there was ground to recognize a case-by-case privilege along Wigmore lines[740] for private records in some instances, such exceptions to the general evidentiary rule of admissibility and disclosure "should not be encouraged".[741] The better approach was one of balancing competing Charter rights. L'Heureux-Dubé J., with La Forest, Gonthier and McLachlin JJ. concurring, saw the need to balance the accused's right to a fair trial and full answer and defence with the complainant's rights to privacy and to equality without discrimination.[742] The majority through a joint judgment by Lamer C.J. and Sopinka J., with Cory, Iacobucci and Major JJ. concurring, determined that the accused's right to full answer and defence should be balanced against the complainant's rights to privacy under ss. 7 and 8. However the majority, in not referring to a s. 15 equality right for complainants, although it was fully argued, implicitly reject it.[743]

The Court agreed that there should be a two-stage procedure but divided 5-4 as to the precise tests. For the majority Lamer C.J. and Sopinka J. decided[744] that when the defence seeks information in the hands of a third party the onus should be on the accused to satisfy a judge that the information is likely to be relevant. In the context of disclosure, the meaning of relevance was whether the information might be useful to the defence. In the context of production, the test of relevance should be higher: the presiding judge must be satisfied that there is a reasonable possibility that the information is logically probative to an issue at trial or the competence of a witness to testify. While likely relevance was the appropriate threshold for the first stage of the two-step procedure, the majority determined that it should not be interpreted as an onerous burden upon the accused. A relevance threshold, at this stage, was simply a requirement to prevent the defence from engaging in speculative, fanciful, disruptive, unmeritorious, obstructive and time-consuming requests for production. The crux of the *O'Connor* regime is the determination by the majority that the first stage of establishing likely relevance had to be a low threshold as the accused might often be in a Catch-22 situation where he was disadvantaged by arguing relevance of a

---

[738] At 119. Van Dieen, above note 736, suggests that the Court may have been inaccurate and incomplete in its review of United States jurisprudence respecting class privilege for therapeutic records.

[739] At 108-114.

[740] As adopted in *Slavutych v. Baker* (1976), 38 C.R.N.S. 306 (S.C.C.).

[741] At 122.

[742] At 122.

[743] See above Chapter 1 for my view that, on a proper analysis of s. 15 jurisprudence, s. 15 rights for complainants should not be recognized.

[744] At 19-27. For careful consideration of practical difficulties with the *O'Connor* procedure see Holmes and Peters, above note 736.

document he had not seen. The majority in *O'Connor* disagreed with L'Heureux-Dubé J.'s position that such records would only be relevant in rare cases. They gave as examples[745] of possible relevance records which may contain information about the unfolding of the complaint, the use of therapy to influence memory and information bearing on credibility. L'Heureux-Dubé J. thought the Charter mandated less, but she did not carry the day. Upon their production to the court, the judge should examine the records to determine whether, and to what extent, they should be produced to the accused. In making that determination, the judge must examine and weigh the salutary and deleterious effects of a production order and determine whether a non-production order would constitute a reasonable limit on the ability of the accused to make full answer and defence.

For the minority, L'Heureux-Dubé J. saw[746] the first stage burden on an accused to demonstrate likely relevance as significant and, if it could not be met, the application for production should be dismissed as amounting to no more than a fishing expedition. The mere fact that the complainant had received treatment or counselling could not be presumed to be relevant to the trial as therapy generally focuses on emotional and psychological responses rather than being oriented to ascertaining historical truth.

There was a further difference of opinion as to the criteria at the production stage. Lamer C.J. and Sopinka J., for the majority, agreed with L'Heureux-Dubé J. that the following factors should be considered:

> (1) the extent to which the record is necessary for the accused to make full answer and defence; (2) the probative value of the record in question; (3) the nature and extent of the reasonable expectation of privacy vested in that record; (4) whether production of the record would be premised upon any discriminatory belief or bias and (5) the potential prejudice to the complainant's dignity, privacy or security of the person that would be occasioned by production of the record in question.[747]

However, the majority departed from L'Heureux-Dubé J. further view that it was also necessary to balance two other factors:

> the extent to which production of records of this nature would frustrate society's interest in encouraging the reporting of sexual offences and the acquisition of treatment by victims

[and]

> the effect on the integrity of the trial process of producing, or failing to produce, the record, having in mind the need to maintain consideration in the outcome.[748]

According to the majority the second factor was more appropriately dealt with at the admissibility stage and not in deciding whether the information should be produced. As for society's interest in the reporting of sexual crimes, the majority pointed to other avenues available to the judge to ensure that production does not frustrate the societal interests, such as publication bans and barring spectators.

---

[745] Para. 29.
[746] At 63-67.
[747] At 26.
[748] *Ibid.*

The majority decided[749] that quite different considerations should apply where records were in the possession of the Crown. In such cases the complainant's privacy interests in medical records would not have to be balanced. The Crown's disclosure obligations established in *Stinchcombe* were not be affected. Concerns relating to privacy or privilege disappeared when the documents were in the Crown's possession. If the records were in the possession of the Crown their relevance was to be presumed. It was unfair in the adversarial process for the Crown to have knowledge that was not shared with the accused. When the records had been shared with the Crown, an agent of the State, the records had become the property of the public to be used to ensure that justice was done. In deciding whether the complainant had waived any potential claim of privilege the waiver would have to be informed. There was to be an onus on the Crown to inform the complainant of the potential for disclosure. Any form of privilege would in any event have to yield where such a privilege precluded the accused's right to full answer and defence.

The majority opinion that privacy issues disappear where the medical records are in the possession of the Crown is utterly unconvincing and has been strongly criticized. Heather Holmes puts the problem well:

> This reasoning appears to assume a formal investigative dialogue by which relevant information is requested by the police or Crown and either provided or refused by the witness, with full opportunity for discussion of legal consequences. It cannot have been intended to apply to the hurly-burly of ordinary existence. A wide variety of material will make its way into the police or Crown files by accident, inadvertence, or because of an investigator's less than perfect appreciation of relevance.
>
> Complainants who muster the considerable courage required for the bringing of criminal charges usually do so without counsel. The Crown prosecutor, as the lawyer tasked with presenting the complainant's report to the court, may appear to the complainant to be "her" lawyer. It is not unusual or unreasonable for a complainant to tacitly consider her relationship with the prosecutor to have a special, albeit undefined, legal status, that at the very least provides some basic protection of confidentiality. Waiver is a strained concept in this situation.[750]

Even under *Stinchcombe* there is no absolute duty for the Crown to disclose. Disclosure is subject to determinations of relevance and privilege both issues here predetermined against the Crown. The notion that the complainant no longer has a privacy issue in the records simply because they are in the possession of the Crown is extraordinary. What if they were stolen, given to the Crown by a therapist without the knowledge of the complainant or handed over to the police by the complainant on the basis that there would otherwise be no prosecution. The minority through L'Heureux-Dubé J. point out that the majority opinion is *obiter* as the appeal did not concern the extent of the Crown's obligation to disclose private records in its possession.

Following *O'Connor* the Parliament of Canada passed the comprehensive Bill C-46 to restrict the production of records in sexual offence proceedings.[751]

---

[749] At 16-19.
[750] Above note 736, at 144.
[751] For a full review of the legislation see Heather Holmes, "An Analysis of Bill C-46, Production

In essence the legislation now contained in ss. 278.1 to 278.9 of the Criminal Code in large measure reflects word for word the minority position of L'Heureux-Dubé J. in *O'Connor*. In particular:

1. The preamble asserts a s. 15 equality right for women and children who are complainants in sexual cases.

2. Although the *O'Connor* likely relevance test is maintained, s. 278.3(4) specifies ten assertions which are declared not sufficient on their own to establish that a record is likely relevant to an issue at trial or to the competence of a witness to testify.

3. Under s. 278.5 a trial judge has to balance privacy and the interests of justice before deciding whether to order the production of a record for review by the Court.

4. Under s. 278.7 the trial judge may only order production to the accused on consideration of all seven factors listed by L'Heureux-Dubé J. rather than the five adopted by the *O'Connor* majority.

5. Under s. 278.2 the two-stage balancing process must be applied to records in the possession of the Crown.

In *Mills* (2000),[752] a joint judgment by Justices McLachlin and Iacobucci holds constitutional the more comprehensive Parliamentary scheme for access to complainants' records in sexual assault cases, which had enacted the minority approach in *O'Connor*. Of the *O'Connor* majority, only Lamer C.J. dissented in *Mills* and only on the issue of applying the balancing of complainants' rights approach to records in the possession of the Crown. Justice Cory chose not to participate before his retirement and Justices Iacobucci and Major no longer supported their positions. One suspects that Justice Sopinka may well not have capitulated so easily.

It has been suggested above[753] that the *Mills* decision is particularly disturbing for its broader pronouncements on the need for dialogue with Parliament and on its assertion of equality rights for complainants without reference to current s. 15 tests or the implications of its ruling. It is also disturbing for some of its pronouncements on the issue of access to third party records, to which we now turn.

The shift in approach to when the accused may have access is subtle but profound, especially at the first stage of production to the judge. When Justices Iacobucci and McLachlin define the accused's right to full answer and defence

---

of Records in Sexual Offence Proceedings", (1997) 2 *Can. Crim. L.R.* 71. For an argument prior to *Mills* that the Bill was unconstitutional see David Paciocco, "Bill C-46 Should Not Survive Constitutional Challenge", (1996) 3 *S.O.L.R.* 185. See too Douglas Alderson, "R. v. O'Connor and Bill C-46: Two Wrongs Do Not Make A Right", (1996) 39 *Crim.L.Q.* 181, but compare Jodie van Dieen, "O'Connor and Bill C-46: Differences in Approach", (1997) 23 *Queen's L.J.* 1.

[752] (1999), 28 C.R. (5th) 207 (S.C.C.).
[753] See Chapter 1.

they turn first to the views of La Forest J. in *Lyons*[754] that s. 7 protections turn on the context and that accused cannot expect the most favourable procedures.

> [T]he ability to make full answer and defence, as a principle of fundamental justice, must...be understood in light of principles of fundamental justice which may embrace interests and perspectives beyond those of the accused.[755]

The accused's right to full answer and defence would not automatically be breached where the accused was deprived of relevant or potentially relevant information[756] and did

> not include the right to evidence that would distort the search for truth inherent in the trial process.[757]

In *Mills* the Court meekly accepts Parliament's much tougher likely relevance hurdle for production to the judge in s. 278.5 where not even the judge may see the disputed document. According to the majority in *Mills*, this new standard was the result of lengthy consultations and years of Parliamentary study and debate. The record indicated that Parliament received many submissions[758] that, under the *O'Connor* regime, private records were routinely being produced to the court at the first stage, leading to the recurring violation of the privacy interests of complainants and witnesses. While it was true, acknowledged the Court, that little statistical data existed at the time of the drafting of Bill C-46 on the application of *O'Connor*, it was open to Parliament to give what weight it saw fit to the evidence presented at the consultations. This process was seen to be a notable example of the dialogue between the judicial and legislative branches. The final line the *Mills* Court drew is decidedly pro-Crown:

> Full answer and defence will be more centrally implicated where the information contained in a record is part of the case to meet or where its potential probative value is high. A complainant's privacy interest is very high where the confidential information contained in a record concerns the complainant's personal identity or where the confidentiality of the record is vital to protect a therapeutic relationship.[759]

While Parliament could construct a legislative scheme for disclosure and discovery it should not have been allowed to lower the bar of the minimum Charter standard the majority of the Court had declared in *O'Connor*. The Court was unduly favourable to the Crown on this crucial likely relevance test at the first stage of whether there should be an order of production to the judge, especially, as the trial judge Belzil J. rightly noted, as the inquiry is now to proceed in a vacuum without the judge seeing the document. Hopefully the Court will reconsider this in subsequent cases less politically charged than *Mills*.

---

[754] Above note 4.

[755] Para. 73.

[756] Paras. 74-75.

[757] Para. 76.

[758] The Court also referred to K. Busby, "Discriminatory Use of Personal Records in Sexual Violence Cases", (1997) 9 *Can.J. of Women and the Law* 89.

[759] Para. 94.

Professor Stephen Coughlan[760] has suggested that a close reading of *Mills* shows that, although the language is in deference to Parliament, the Court has read in discretion at every point such that its regime still conforms to its earlier majority judgment in *O'Connor*. Accepting that there is reading down in *Mills*, this appears to place far too little emphasis on the raising of the bar at the first stage of production to the judge. Several courts have already decided that *Mills* has indeed raised that threshold test.[761] In *Shearing* (2000)[762] the B.C Court of Appeal even applied *Mills* to deny the right to cross-examine on the diary of a complainant. The Court saw *Mills* as having shifted the balance away from the primary emphasis on the rights of accused to require consideration of equality rights of the complainant. *Shearing* did not involve rape shield laws or the issue of production. As Ron Delisle has put it:

> It concerns the fundamental right of an accused to cross-examination. The ruling is a significant curtailment of that right at the expense of a fair trial.[763]

The Court in *Mills* certainly reads down the "insufficient grounds" s. 278.3(4) which declares the long list of assertions[764] which would not meet the likely relevant test. Pointing to the words "on their own" the Court holds this merely requires an evidentiary foundation. The Court sees the purpose of the provision to be the prevention of speculative myths, stereotypes, and generalized assumptions about sexual assault victims and classes of records from forming the entire basis of an otherwise unsubstantiated order for production of private

---

[760] "Complainant's Records After Mills: Same As It Ever Was", (2000) 33 C.R. (5th) 300.

[761] See *Batte* (2000), 34 C.R. (5th) 197 (Ont. C.A.) (criticized by Joseph Wilkinson, "Batte: Raising the Defence Hurdle for Access to Third Party Records", (2000) 34 C.R. (5th) 257) and *M. (D.)* (2000), 37 C.R. (5th) 80 (Ont. S.C.J.) (denying access to a diary and counselling records because the evidentiary foundation was not laid at the preliminary inquiry).

[762] (2000), 31 C.R. (5th) 177 (B.C. C.A.).

[763] "Annotation to *Shearing*", (2000) 31 C.R. (5th) 179.

[764] Any one or more of the following assertions by the accused are not sufficient on their own to establish that the record is likely relevant to an issue at trial or to the competence of a witness to testify:
   (a) that the record exists;
   (b) that the record relates to medical or psychiatric treatment, therapy or counselling that the complainant or witness has received or is receiving;
   (c) that the record relates to the incident that is the subject-matter of the proceedings;
   (d) that the record may disclose a prior inconsistent statement of the complainant or witness;
   (e) that the record may relate to the credibility of the complainant or witness;
   (f) that the record may relate to the reliability of the testimony of the complainant or witness merely because the complainant or witness has received or is receiving psychiatric treatment, therapy or counselling;
   (g) that the record may reveal allegations of sexual abuse of the complainant by a person other than the accused;
   (h) that the record relates to the sexual activity of the complainant with any person, including the accused;
   (i) that the record relates to the presence or absence of a recent complaint;
   (j) that the record relates to the complainant's sexual reputation; or
   (k) that the record was made close in time to a complaint or to the activity that forms the subject-matter of the charge against the accused.

records. The problem, as Kent Roach points out,[765] is that only some of the prohibited assertions involve sexist rape myths. Those relating to credibility do not. The section requires only, holds the Court in reading the section down, that the accused be able to point to case specific evidence or information to show that the record in issue is likely relevant to an issue at trial or the competence of a witness to testify. The Court indicates one source of such an evidentiary base to be the preliminary inquiry. The difficulty here is that many sexual assault trials across Canada are now proceeded with, through Crown election, by way of summary proceedings where there is no preliminary (and no jury trial). In such cases is it a good idea to encourage free-ranging and intrusive inquiries into the existence and type of records presumably necessitating adjournments where production is ordered?

The various other rulings in *Mills* on the records issues are supportable.[766] This includes the acceptance by the majority of Parliament's view that the balancing of rights of complainants must also occur, in the absence of express waiver, where the records are in the possession of the Crown. We have seen[767] that the majority ruling to the contrary in *O'Connor* was *obiter* and not persuasive[768] in holding that privacy had necessarily been waived by complainants in such cases.[769]

(v) *Lost evidence cases*

In *Carosella* (1997)[770] the accused, a teacher, was charged with gross indecency against a former student in 1964. The complainant went to the Windsor Sexual Assault Centre in 1992 for advice as to how to lay charges. She was interviewed by a social worker for about an hour to two hours. The social worker took notes and advised the complainant that whatever she said could be subpoenaed to court. The complainant said that was all right. Shortly after, the complainant went to the police and the charge was laid. Following a preliminary inquiry the accused was committed to trial. At the trial the accused brought an application for production of the Sexual Assault Centre file. The Crown, complainant and Centre, consented to the order. However the trial did not contain the notes or anything of substance. The Centre had destroyed the documents. It had been unsuccessful in opposing applications for production of records in the past and, to protect the privacy interests of its clients, had instituted a policy of taking misleading notes or shredding files with police involvement.

---

[765] "Editorial on Mills", (2000) 432 *Crim. L.Q.* 145.

[766] The definition of the records subject to Bill C-46 was held not overly broad as the legislation only applies to records in which there is a reasonable expectation of privacy within meaning of s. 8 of the Charter.

[767] Above note 750.

[768] But see Peter Sankoff, "Crown Disclosure After Mills: Have the Ground Rules Suddenly Changed?", (2000) 28 C.R. (5th) 285.

[769] *Ibid.*

[770] (1997), 4 C.R. (5th) 139 (S.C.C.).

The trial judge stayed the charges. The notes were likely relevant and the accused's Charter right to full answer and defence had been breached. The Ontario Court of Appeal set aside the stay on the basis that there had to be evidence that disclosed something more than a mere risk to a Charter right.

The Supreme Court of Canada restored the stay in a very lengthy decision. Sopinka J. for the 5-4 majority[771] held that there had been a breach of the accused's s. 7 right to production from the Crown or third parties. Prejudice was relevant at the stage of remedy rather than breach. Here the relevance standard of *Stinchcombe* had been met and also the higher likely relevant test of *O'Connor* for production of third party records. Balancing of interests before production was not in issues as the complainant had consented to the disclosure of the notes. The stay was warranted as the prejudice to the accused's right to make full answer and defence could not be remedied or, alternatively, irreparable prejudice would be caused to the integrity of the judicial system if the prosecution were continued. The majority did not address abuse of process.

L'Heureux-Dubé J. for the minority[772] held that, where evidence is unavailable, the accused must demonstrate that a fair trial, not a perfect one, cannot be held as a result of the loss. The accused has to demonstrate a real likelihood of prejudice. It is not enough to speculate that there was a potential for harm. Materials can be easily lost and setting too low a standard for dismissal would bring the justice system to a halt. In any event, the notes would not meet the likely relevant test of *O'Connor* as there had merely been an assertion that the material would be useful in cross-examination. This was also no abuse of process.

Following *Carosella*, the Supreme Court considered a series of lost evidence cases culminating in *La* (1997).[773] It appears that the Court has adopted a different course where evidence has been lost rather than deliberately destroyed.

At around midnight police found a 13-year-old runaway girl they were looking for in a vehicle driven by the accused, known to be a pimp. The girl later became the complainant in a charge of sexual assault against the accused, La. At the police station an officer made a 45-minute tape recording of one of his conversations with her relating to her life on the run and her being forced into prostitution. The tape was referred to by the officer at Family Court in an application for a secure treatment order. When the matter was handed over to the vice unit to investigate various complaints of prostitution and sexual assault, the tape was not turned over. By the time of the accused's preliminary inquiry, the officer testified that he had searched for but lost the tape.

When the matter reached the Supreme Court, the Court was unanimous that the trial judge had wrongly stayed the charges. The 5-4 split was only as to the reasons. Sopinka J. for the majority[774] gave separate consideration to the s. 7

---

[771] Lamer C.J., Cory, Iacobucci and Major JJ. concurred.
[772] La Forest, Gonthier and McLachlin JJ. concurred.
[773] (1997), 8 C.R. (5th) 155 (S.C.C.).
[774] Lamer C.J., Cory, Iacobucci and Major JJ. concurred.

issues of disclosure, abuse of process and full answer and defence. Here none of these rights had been breached.

As for disclosure, according to the majority, the Crown's duty to disclose all relevant evidence in its possession gives rise to a duty on the Crown and the police to preserve evidence known to be relevant. Where evidence is lost the Crown has a duty to explain the loss. Where the Crown's explanation satisfies the trial judge that the evidence has not been destroyed or lost owing to unacceptable negligence, the duty to disclose has not been breached. Where the Crown is unable to satisfy the judge in this regard, it has failed to meet its disclosure obligations and there has accordingly been a breach of s. 7 of the Charter. One circumstance that must be considered is the relevance that the evidence was perceived to have at the time. The police cannot be expected to preserve everything that comes into their hands on the off-chance that it will be relevant in the future. Even the loss of relevant evidence will not result in a breach of the duty to disclose if the conduct of the police is reasonable. As the relevance of the evidence increases, so does the degree of care for its preservation that is expected of the police. Here the Crown explanation was satisfactory. There was no evidence of negligence. The conversation had not been taped for the purposes of a criminal investigation. The officer had not failed to take reasonable steps to preserve the tape.

Conduct that will amount to an abuse of process, held Sopinka J., includes conduct on the part of governmental authorities that violates those fundamental principles that underlie the community's sense of decency and fair play. The deliberate destruction of material by the police or other officers of the Crown for the purpose of defeating the Crown's obligation to disclose the material would, typically, fall into this category.[775] An abuse of process was not limited to conduct of officers of the Crown which proceeds from an improper motive. Accordingly, other serious departures from the Crown's duty to preserve material subject to production might also amount to an abuse of process, notwithstanding that a deliberate destruction for the purpose of evading disclosure was not established. In some cases an unacceptable degree of negligent conduct might suffice.[776] Here the loss did not amount to an abuse of process.

According to the majority, in extraordinary circumstances, the loss of a document may be so prejudicial to the right to make full answer and defence that it impairs the right of an accused to receive a fair trial. In such circumstances, a stay may be the appropriate remedy.[777] This was not so here. The interview

---

[775] A stay as an abuse of process may have been a better and more direct basis for the stay Sopinka J. entered in *Carosella*.

[776] In *Fournier* (2000) 145 C.C.C. (3d) 420 (Que. C.A.) a stay in a double first degree murder case was confirmed on this basis. Police had destroyed objects seized from both crime scenes after an informer pleaded guilty to both murders. Compare, however *Bero* (2000), 39 C.R. (5th) 291 (Ont. C.A.). A vehicle involved in an accident had been destroyed by police before forensic testing. Doherty J.A. for the Court found that this was a sufficiently serious departure from the Crown's duty to preserve evidence that it constituted an abuse of process. However, finding no systemic disregard or improper motive, the Court rejected a stay and ordered a new trial.

[777] Applying *La*, courts have been hard to convince in lost evidence cases that the remedy should be

recorded was not regarded by the officer as a detailed conversation and alternative information was available to attack the witness's credibility.

L'Heureux-Dubé J.[778] dissented, mainly on the basis that the duty to disclose resting upon the Crown does not constitute a separate and distinct right operating on its own as a principle of fundamental justice. Not every error or omission by the Crown in making disclosure should automatically lead to a violation of the Charter. The majority's lower threshold for establishing a violation of the "right to disclosure" than for demonstrating an abuse of process was an unacceptable development in the law.

The Court in *Dixon* (1998)[779] later confirmed that the right to disclosure is indeed a self-standing right recognised under s. 7. The threshold for disclosure is "set quite low".[780] A breach will be established where there was a "reasonable possibility"[781] that the undisclosed information would have affected the conduct of the case. However the Court in *Dixon* also held that on appeal the focus changes to whether the right to make full answer and defence has been impaired by the lack of disclosure by a realistic possibility that non-disclosure affected the outcome or the overall fairness of the trial process.[782]

(b) Right to Counsel at Trial[783]

The Special Joint Committee of the Senate and House of Commons on the Constitution of Canada rejected a proposed clause 10(d) which would have read

> if without sufficient means to pay for counsel and if the interests of justice so require, to be provided with counsel.[784]

This legislative history was key in the determination of the Supreme Court in *Prosper* (1994)[785] that s. 10(b) of the Charter does not impose a substantive constitutional obligation on governments to ensure that duty counsel is available on arrest or detention to provide free and immediate, preliminary advice on request. The Court left open the issue of whether the Charter guaranteed a right to state-funded counsel at trial and on appeal.[786]

According to Provincial Courts of Appeal, while s. 7 does not confer a general constitutional right for an accused to be provided counsel at trial at the

---

a stay rather than an order of a new trial; see *B. (F.C.)* (2000), 142 C.C.C. (3d) 540 (N.S. C.A.) and *Bero*, above note 776.

[778] La Forest, Gonthier and McLachlin JJ. concurred.

[779] Above note 725.

[780] Para. 21.

[781] Para. 22.

[782] See further Mitchell, above note 725.

[783] See Bruce A. MacFarlane, "The Right to Counsel at Trial and on Appeal," (1990) 32 *Crim. L.Q.* 440.

[784] See discussion in *Deutsch v. Law Society of Upper Canada Legal Aid Fund* (1985), 48 C.R. (3d) 166 (Ont. Div. Ct.) at 172-173.

[785] (1994), 33 C.R. (4th) 85 (S.C.C.).

[786] See Chapter 5 for discussion of the Court's division over the issue of whether police should as a result have to "hold off".

expense of the State, it may be the source of relief for some accused who cannot afford counsel.

The leading decision is that of the Ontario Court of Appeal in *Rowbotham* (1988).[787] The Charter did not in terms constitutionalize the right of an indigent accused to be provided with funded counsel. The framers of the Charter had not expressly provided that right because they considered that Provincial Legal Aid schemes were generally adequate to provide counsel for accused charged with serious crimes who could not afford counsel. However, the Court held that there might be exceptional cases where the right to a fair trial would necessitate counsel being provided:

> However, *in cases not falling within provincial legal aid plans*, ss. 7 and 11(d) of the Charter, which guarantee an accused a fair trial in accordance with the principles of fundamental justice, require funded counsel to be provided if the accused wishes counsel but cannot pay a lawyer, and representative of the accused by counsel is essential to a fair trial.[788]

In *Rowbotham*, it was only necessary to apply this right to an accused charged with a serious offence.[789] The appropriate remedy under s. 24(1) was a judicial stay of proceedings until funded counsel had been provided.[790] The Court did not decide whether the trial judge would have the power to direct that legal aid or the appropriate Attorney-General pay the fees. In *Rowbotham* the trial judge had erred in confirming the opinion of the Area Director of Legal Aid that an accused had the means to pay counsel where the income was $1,432 per month and the trial had lasted one year. It would not, however, given the evidence against her, be necessary for counsel to be present in court every day during a very long trial. At the new trial, it would be necessary to work out which parts of the trial would be crucial for the accused and also to consider the possibility of her accepting legal aid on a contributory basis.[791]

Mr. Justice Griffiths for the Ontario Court of Appeal in *McGibbon* (1988)[792] has subsequently clearly spelled out what a trial judge should do where an accused is not represented:

[787] (1988), 63 C.R. (3d) 113 (Ont. C.A.).
[788] Above note 787, at 172-173. See too *Rain* (1998), 130 C.C.C. (3d) 167 (Alta. C.A.) (but not for impaired driving) and *Chan* (2000), 146 C.C.C. (3d) 494 (Alta. C.A.) (per Berger J.A. for a bail hearing).
[789] This was also all that was necessary to decide *Panacui v. Legal Aid Society of Alberta* (1987), 40 C.C.C. (3d) 459 (Alta. Q.B.), where the charges were kidnapping and attempted murder. In the pre-Charter ruling in *Ewing v. Kearney* (1974), 18 C.C.C. (2d) 356 (B.C. C.A.), the majority refused to accept the argument that a drug possession charge is highly complex. Rather than the murky test of seriousness of offence, our courts might be better off at following the view of the United States Supreme Court in *Argersinger v. Hamlin*, 407 U.S. 25 (1970) that the right is engaged whenever imprisonment is anticipated.
[790] Above note 787, at 176. See too *Zylstra* (1996), 47 C.R. (4th) 314 (Ont. Gen. Div.) and *Anderson* (2000), 33 C.R. (5th) 364 (N.S. Prov. Ct.).
[791] *Ibid.*, at 174-179.
[792] (1988), 45 C.C.C. (3d) 334 (Ont. C.A.). See too similarly *Hardy* (1990), 62 C.C.C. (3d) 28 (Alta. Q.B.).

The trial judge, of course, has a duty to the accused to see that he or she has a fair hearing and that duty will generally cast upon the judge an obligation to point out to the accused that he or she would be at a distinct disadvantage in proceeding without the assistance of competent counsel and that the accused is entitled to have such counsel. Where the accused expressly desires counsel, it is clear that unless the accused has deliberately failed to retain counsel, or has discharged counsel, with the intent of delaying the process of the court, the trial judge should afford the accused an opportunity to retain counsel either at his expense or through the services of Legal Aid. If Legal Aid will not fund counsel it may be necessary at least in long complicated trials to stay the proceedings until counsel is funded.[793]

. . . .

Consistent with the duty to ensure that the accused has a fair trial, the trial judge is required within reason to provide assistance to the unrepresented accused, to aid him in the proper conduct of his defence, and to guide him throughout the trial in such a way that his defence is brought out with its full force and effect. How far the trial judge should go in assisting the accused in such matters as the examination and cross-examination of witnesses must of necessity be a matter of discretion.[794]

How far the trial judge should go in a particular case calls for a delicate balance. The trial judge must avoid getting into the

impossible position of being both advocate and impartial arbiter at one and the same time.[795]

This is clearly a very difficult line to draw.[796]

In *Shupe* (1987),[797] sexual assault charges against a deaf mute who had not learned sign language were stayed. Treating a deaf mute person as an insane person subject to indefinite confinement violated the accused's rights under ss. 7, 14 and 15 (1) of the Charter and the infringements could not be demonstrably justified under s. 1. In contrast, in *Roy* (1994)[798] sexual assault charges against a deaf accused were also stayed but on a quite different basis. The fitness provisions had no application because deafness was not a mental disorder. Since the accused had never been taught to communicate and did not read or write, a prosecution would violate s. 7 of the Charter. The accused could not properly instruct counsel, could not understand the proceedings and would not be able to make full answer and defence. If the authority of *Roy* is accepted, the Charter will provide the remedy for genuine cases of unfitness not associated with mental disorder. For

---

[793] *Ibid.*, at 346. In *Smith* (1989), 52 C.C.C. (3d) 90 (Ont. C.A.), the Court ordered a new trial where the trial judge had refused the accused's request for an adjournment to find a new lawyer. See too *Sechon* (1995), 45 C.R. (4th) 231 (Que. C.A.).

[794] *Ibid.*, at 347.

[795] *Taubler* (1987), 20 O.A.C. 64 (Ont. C.A.) at 71 (*per* Thorsen J.A.). See too *Fabrikant* (1995), 39 C.R. (4th) 1 (Que. C.A.) (unrepresented accused in multiple murder trial not denied full answer and defence where not allowed to testify after accused being disruptive and stubbornly defiant).

[796] As to appointment of an *amicus curiae* see *Samra* (1998), 129 C.C.C. (3d) 144 (Ont. C.A.) and *Lee* (1998), 125 C.C.C. (3d) 363 (N.W.T. S.C.).

[797] (1987), 59 C.R. (3d) 329 (Alta. Q.B.).

[798] (1994), 31 C.R. (4th) 388 (N.S. Prov. Ct.).

reasons of fair notice it would be preferable for Parliament to remove the "mental disorder" limit from the fitness to stand trial provisions.[799]

The Nova Scotia Court of Appeal in *Rockwood* (1989)[800] adopted and extended *Rowbotham*. When an indigent faces a complex and serious charge there is a right to funded counsel and, furthermore, a right to competent counsel and to counsel of choice. Counsel provided had to be sufficiently qualified to deal with the case with a reasonable degree of skill. The evidence had not established that Rockwood could not be defended in a competent manner by counsel willing to accept the terms of a legal aid certificate.[801]

In a series of decisions culminating in *Joanisse* (1995),[802] the Ontario Court of Appeal has decided that an accused who is represented by counsel at trial is entitled under ss. 7 and 11(d) to effective legal assistance. For the Court, Mr. Justice Doherty established a "cautious" approach to considering such claims on appeal. The accused must establish (1) the facts on which the claim is based,[803] (2) that the representation was incompetent as determined by a reasonableness standard and (3) that the incompetent representation resulted in a reasonable probability of a miscarriage of justice. This approach relies heavily on that of the United States Supreme Court in *Strickland v. Washington* (1984).[804] Doherty J.A. declared the standard of competence to be one of reasonableness measured by reference to counsel's performance at the particular time and without the wisdom of hindsight. Furthermore:

> Appellate courts must give deference to the choices made by counsel and the competence assessment must be informed by a presumption in favour of competence.[805]

This is indeed a cautious approach and has been criticized for being insufficiently demanding and for wrongly requiring proof of prejudice.[806] In *Joanisse* itself, Doherty J.A. was in the minority on the facts. The majority[807] ruled that the defence counsel at a second degree murder trial had not fallen below the reasonableness standard in not seeking an adjournment where the client had suddenly advised that he did not wish to testify. However the Ontario Court of Appeal has ordered new trials in a case where joint representation produced a

---

[799] See too *Hajian* (1995), 104 C.C.C. (3d) 352 (Que. S.C.) (right to fair trial requiring linguistic ability to communicate with counsel) and *Savard* (1996), 47 C.R. (4th) 281 (Y.T. C.A.).

[800] (1989), 49 C.C.C. (3d) 129 (N.S. C.A.).

[801] *Ibid.*, at 134-135.

[802] (1995), 44 C.R. (4th) 364 (Ont. C.A.).

[803] In *W. (W.)* (1995), 43 C.R. (4th) 26 (Ont. C.A.), the Court admitted fresh evidence in the form of affidavits of trial counsel and cross-examination on those affidavits.

[804] 104 S. Ct. 2052 (1984).

[805] At 389.

[806] See David Tanovich, "Charting the Constitutional Right to Effective Assistance of Counsel in Canada" (1994), 36 *Crim. L.Q.* 404 and "Further Developments on Claims of Ineffectiveness of Counsel" (1995), 34 C.R. (4th) 32.

[807] *Per* Austin J.A. (Robins J.A. concurring).

conflict of interest[808] and where a defence counsel was held to have failed to take the rudimentary step of investigating witnesses who would support an alibi defence.[809] On the other hand, the Court held[810] that the right had not been violated where a defence counsel in a sexual assault trial had not met the accused face to face until the morning of the trial. The defence counsel had stated "I don't do jails". The claim was rejected on the basis that assuming that there was a violation, it had not been established that the result would have been different.[811]

When the issue of the right to competent counsel reached the Supreme Court in *B. (G.D.)* (2000),[812] the Court was uncharacteristically terse. For the Court Major J. adopted the *Strickland* approach as justified by Doherty J.A. in *Joanisse*.[813] The right to effective assistance of counsel extended to all accused as a principle of fundamental justice. It is derived from the evolution of the common law, s. 650(3) of the Criminal Code of Canada and ss. 7 and 11(d) of the Charter. An appellant had to establish incompetence and prove that a miscarriage of justice resulted.

> Incompetence is determined by a reasonableness standard. The analysis proceeds upon a strong presumption that counsel's conduct fell within the wide range of reasonable professional assistance. The onus is on the appellant to establish the acts or omissions of counsel that are alleged not to have been the result of reasonable professional judgment. The wisdom of hindsight has no place in this assessment.[814]

Major J. added that miscarriages of justice could take many forms, but could include procedural unfairness or[815] a compromise of the trial's result. Where no prejudice had occurred, appellate courts should refrain from grading counsel's performance or professionalism which was a matter best left to the profession's self-governing body. In *B. (G.D.)* the defence counsel's failure to introduce an audio-taped conversation between the complainant and her mother had been tactical and had not resulted in a miscarriage of justice.

It is unfortunate[816] that the Court did not justify its resort to the low level *Strickland* test or its focus on prejudice. In *Strickland* there is a strong dissent by Justice Marshall who points to disparities in representation and asks whether the test is

> a reasonably competent adequately paid retained lawyer or a reasonably competent appointed attorney.[817]

---

[808] *Silvini* (1991), 9 C.R. (4th) 233 (Ont. C.A.), distinguished, however, in *W. (W.)* (1995), 43 C.R. (4th) 26 (Ont. C.A.).
[809] *McKellar* (1994), 34 C.R. (4th) 28 (Ont. C.A.) and *Delisle* (1999), 25 C.R. (5th) 198 (Que. C.A.).
[810] *B. (L.C.)* (1996), 46 C.R. (4th) 368 (Ont. C.A.).
[811] See too *R. (P.)* (1998), 23 C.R. (5th) 313 (Que. C.A.) (no right to representation by most brilliant lawyer and examination and cross-examination is a difficult art, their result often uncertain and sometimes unpredictable).
[812] (2000), 32 C.R. (5th) 207 (S.C.C.).
[813] Paras. 23-29.
[814] Para. 27.
[815] This "or" seems to allow for remedies where there was no prejudice.
[816] See further criticism by Charles Davison, "Importing Strickland: Some Concerns in Light of the Supreme Court's Adoption of the American Test for Ineffective Counsel", (2000) 32 C.R. (5th) 220.
[817] Para. 116 in *Strickland*, as quoted by Davison at 816.

With legal aid budgets slashed across the country, this was a matter the Court ought to have addressed.

In *Romanowicz* (1999)[818] the Ontario Court of Appeal held that an accused who chooses to be represented by an agent in a summary conviction matter is nevertheless guaranteed a fair trial but has no constitutional right to competent representation at a level expected from counsel.

Justice Mercer of the Newfoundland Supreme Court in *Lawlor* (1999)[819] decided the right to effective assistance of counsel requires that the accused be able to communicate with counsel during the trial except where the accused is being cross-examined.

The Alberta Court of Appeal in *Robinson* (1989)[820] ruled that, as there was no general right to the provision of funded counsel at trial, there would be no unqualified constitutional right to counsel for an appeal. The accused wished to appeal their robbery and murder convictions. They had been refused legal aid and had no resources to fund the appeal. The Court of Appeal refused to order the provision of counsel in the preparation of appeal books at public expense.

In the landmark decision in the Federal Court of Appeal in *Howard v. Presiding Officer of Inmate Disciplinary Court of Stony Mountain Institution* (1985),[821] it was held that penitentiary disciplinary proceedings implicated the prisoner's liberty interest and that fundamental justice under s. 7 normally entitled the prisoner to be represented by counsel.[822]

In *Dehghani v. Canada (Minister of Employment and Immigration* (1993)[823] the Supreme Court confirmed that s. 7 may possibly ensure the right to counsel in situations not covered by s. 10(b). However, the Court decided that secondary examination of a refugee claimant at the port of entry was a routine information-gathering situation to which the right to counsel did not extend.

In *New Brunswick (Minister of Health & Community Services) v. G. (J.)* (1999)[824] the Supreme Court determined that a government application for custody of children implicates the right to security of the person and the right to a fair hearing such that an indigent parent may have a s. 7 right to a state-funded counsel. The judge would have to consider the seriousness of the issue, the complexity of the proceeding and the capacity of the parent. Speaking for the majority Lamer C.J. expressly distinguished his judgment for the Court in *Prosper*[825] where he had held there was no positive right to statefunding under s. 10. This did not

---

[818] (1999), 26 C.R. (5th) 246 (Ont. C.A.).

[819] (1999), 135 C.C.C. (3d) 249 (Nfld. T.D.).

[820] (1989), 73 C.R. (3d) 81 (Alta. C.A.). For contrary views see Max H. Epstein, "The Guiding Hand of Counsel: The Charter and the Right to Counsel on Appeal" (1987), 30 *Crim. L.Q.* 35 and R. Moon, "The Constitutional Right to State Funded Counsel on Appeal" (1989), 14 *Queen's L.J.* 171.

[821] (1985), 45 C.R. (3d) 242 (Fed. C.A.).

[822] For an argument that the potential loss of remission was not the only trigger for s. 7 see Manson, "Annotation" in C.R. *ibid.*, pp. 244-247.

[823] (1993), 20 C.R. (4th) 34 (S.C.C.).

[824] (1999), 26 C.R. (5th) 203 (S.C.C.).

[825] (1994), 33 C.R. (4th) 85 (S.C.C.), discussed below Chapter 5.

preclude a limited right to state-funded counsel under s. 7. How this will be determined in the criminal context remains to be seen.

(c) Procedural Fairness

(i) *General tests*

In the context of a criminal trial the most general pronouncement as to what is meant by procedural fairness is to be found in the judgment of the Ontario Court of appeal in *Cohn* (1984).[826] Mr. Justice Goodman for the Court held that, when trying a contempt offence by way of summary proceedings, a Court was under an obligation to ensure that the accused had a fair trial in accordance with the principles of fundamental justice under s. 7. Those principles included

> the right to be presumed innocent until proven guilty beyond a reasonable doubt, to be informed without unreasonable delay of the specific offence with which he is charged, to have counsel, to have a reasonable time to prepare a defence, to call witnesses and not to be compelled to give evidence. He has the right to be tried by an independent and impartial tribunal. In that regard, where the contempt alleged consists of insolent or contemptuous behaviour or other disorderly conduct or behaviour which reflects adversely upon the character, integrity or reputation of the initiating judge, the charge should be tried by another judge.[827]

The Court added that there might be very exceptional cases where the circumstances were so compelling and the need to preserve order and authority of the Court so urgent that some limitation, particularly with respect to time, might be demonstrably justified as a reasonable limit under s. 1.[828]

There had been no violation in *Cohn*, which concerned contempt proceedings against a prisoner who had refused to be sworn or give evidence in proceedings involving a charge of robbery against another. However, in another prisoner contempt proceeding in *Ayres* (1984),[829] the Ontario Court of Appeal held that the principles outlined in *Cohn had* been breached. Although the trial judge had given the accused several opportunities to reconsider his refusal to testify, the show cause hearing had been proceeded with soon after the citation for contempt and the accused had not been given a reasonable opportunity to consult his lawyer, consider his possible defence of duress and to procure his witnesses.

In *Morgentaler* (1988),[830] the Supreme Court of Canada struck down the Criminal Code abortion provisions on the basis of violation of s. 7 of the Charter. Each of the majority judgments found that the provisions violated the procedural fairness protection in s. 7. Each puts it differently.

---

[826] (1984), 42 C.R. (3d) 1 (Ont. C.A.).
[827] *Ibid.*, at 31-32. The Court also held that the contempt procedure did not violate the presumption of innocence in s. 11(d) or trigger the right to a jury under s. 11(f).
[828] *Ibid.*, at 32.
[829] (1984), 42 C.R. (3d) 33 (Ont. C.A.).
[830] Above note 39. See earlier review of judgments concerning the interests the majority held to have been violated.

According to Chief Justice Dickson,[831] one of the basic tenets of our criminal justice system is that "when parliament creates a defence to a criminal charge, the defence should not be illusory or so difficult to obtain as to be practically illusory."[832] The administrative structures and procedures established by what was then s. 251 concerning therapeutic abortion committees, the accreditation or approval of hospitals and the restrictive criteria of certain committees would in many circumstances make the defence under s. 251(4) practically unavailable to women who would *prima facie* qualify or would at least force such women to travel great distances at substantial expense and inconvenience.

In the opinion of Beetz J.,[833] while Parliament had been justified in requiring a reliable, independent and medically sound opinion as to the life or health of the pregnant woman in order to protect the State interest in the foetus, and while any such statutory mechanism would inevitably result in some delay, certain criminal procedure requirements such as the rule that therapeutic abortions must take place in an eligible hospital, were nevertheless manifestly unfair. They were unnecessary given Parliament's objectives in establishing the administrative structure and resulted in additional risks to the health of pregnant women.[834]

Wilson J. agreed with both the Chief Justice and Beetz J. that the deprivation of the s. 7 right was not in accordance with procedural fairness for the reasons that they had given,[835] but considered that this was not the central issue to be addressed.[836]

Justice Rosenberg in *Parker* (2000)[837] relied heavily on *Morgentaler* in his determination for the Ontario Court of Appeal that the prohibition on possession of marihuana violated the accused's s. 7 rights in that it did not allow a medical exception. Parker needed marihuana to control his epilepsy. The Court concluded that

> the common-law treatment of informed consent, the sanctity of life and commonly held societal beliefs about medical treatment suggest that a broad criminal prohibition that prevents access to necessary medicine is not consistent with fundamental justice.[838]

In *Swain* (1991),[839] Lamer J. for the Supreme Court confirmed that the principles of fundamental justice contemplated "an accusatorial and adversarial system of criminal justice which is founded on respect for the autonomy and

---

[831] Lamer J. concurred.

[832] Above note 39, at 31. This enigmatic principle has not been considered or applied in any subsequent reported case.

[833] Estey J. concurred.

[834] Above note 39, at 64-70.

[835] *Ibid.*, at 110.

[836] *Ibid.*, at 100.

[837] Above note 57.

[838] Para. 139. The Court held that a declaration of invalidity suspended for one year was the appropriate remedy, with the accused entitled to a constitutional exception during the period of suspended invalidity. See discussion in Chapter 11.

[839] (1991), 63 C.C.C. (3d) 481 (S.C.C.).

dignity of human beings.''[840] For the majority[841] it followed that the accused had the right to control his or her defence and that the common law rule allowing the Crown to raise the defence of insanity contravened s. 7.[842]

We have already examined important recent pronouncements of the Supreme Court on procedural fairness in its jurisprudence on the principle against self-incrimination and the case to meet[843] and in establishing the right of an accused to full disclosure.[844]

In *Rose* (1998)[845] Justice Cory saw these and other rights as interrelated:

> The right to make full answer and defence manifests itself in several more specific rights and principles, such as the right to full and timely disclosure,the right to know the case to be met before opening one's defence, the principles governing the re-opening of the Crown's case, as well as various rights of cross-examination, among others. The right is integrally linked to other principles of fundamental justice, such as the presumption of innocence, the right to a fair trial, and the principle against self-incrimination.[846]

On the other hand, La Forest J. for the Court in *Lyons* (1987)[847] held that

> the requirements of fundamental justice are not immutable; rather, they vary according to the context in which they are invoked[848]

and that

> s. 7 of the Charter entitles the [accused] to a fair hearing; it does not entitle him to the most favourable procedures that could possibly be imagined.[849]

We have seen[850] that the Supreme Court in *Mills* (2000)[851] relied on La Forest J.'s views in *Lyons* when balancing privacy and equality rights of complainants in sexual assault cases to allow very limited access to therapeutic records. So too in *Darrach* (2000),[852] where the Court upheld Parliament's rape shield provisions. Gonthier J. starts by citing *Lyons* before confirming that the accused is not entitled to have

> procedures crafted that take only his interests into account. Still less is he entitled to procedures that would distort the truth-seeking function of a trial by permitting irrelevant and prejudicial material at trial.[853]

---

[840] *Ibid.*, at 505.
[841] L'Heureux-Dubé J. dissented.
[842] Above note 57, at 523. The s. 1 ruling is discussed above, Chapter 1.
[843] Above note 548.
[844] Above note 701.
[845] (1998), 20 C.R. (5th) 246 (S.C.C.), discussed below note 868.
[846] Para 98.
[847] (1987), 61 C.R. (3d) 1 (S.C.C.).
[848] At 46. The context in *Lyons* was constitutional challenges to dangerous offender application, see below note 900 for the Court's rulings.
[849] At 47.
[850] Above Chapter 1.
[851] Above note 752.
[852] (2000), 36 C.R. (5th) 223 (S.C.C.), discussed further below note 947.
[853] Para. 24.

(ii) *Attacks on established trial procedures*

Provincial courts have been generally timid when considering arguments that well established trial procedures are unfair.

In *Czuczman* (1986),[854] Brooke J.A. for the Ontario Court of appeal had little difficulty in rejecting a challenge against what is now s. 475(1)(a) of the Criminal Code, which deems that an accused who absconds from his trial has waived his right to be present at the trial. The Court accepted that the accused's right to be present was constitutionally protected under s. 7:

> In our system, the right of an accused to be present to face his accuser and cross-examine him, to give evidence, to make full answer and defence and generally to participate in the trial is fundamental. Fairness demands no less than this, s. [650(1)] of the Code requires this and the Charter guarantees this.[855]

However, the Court held that constitutional rights are not absolute and that their scope had to be measured against the corresponding rights of others and of society in the due administration of justice. A constitutional right could be waived. An accused should not be able to thwart the rights of others in society by deliberately absenting himself from his trial. It was fair that the trial proceed and the section had not offended any right guaranteed by s. 7.

This reasoning has been persuasively criticized by Gary Trotter[856] on the basis that there was a *prima facie* violation of the right to be present at trial and the focus should have been on s. 1 However, the Ontario Court of Appeal, in applying *Czuczman* in *Tzimopoulos* (1986),[857] added that, even if the proper focus for the analysis was to be located in s. 1, the limitation was patently reasonable and demonstrably justified.[858]

In *Tzimopoulos* the Court also rejected a challenge against the rule in what is now s. 651(3) of the Criminal Code[859] that the defence counsel loses the right to address the jury last if any defence evidence has been laid. An historical and comparative survey of other jurisdictions[860] revealed that all had abandoned the rule. The Court agreed that reform recommended by the Law Reform Commission of Canada[861] would be a significant improvement. But the issue was whether there had been a violation of s. 7. Accepting the challenge would imply that all trials

---

[854] (1986), 49 C.R. (3d) 385 (Ont. C.A.).

[855] *Ibid.*, at 388.

[856] "The Absconding Accused and the Charter: 'The Show Must Go On!' ", C.R. *ibid.*, pp. 391-400. Trotter also argues the standard of waiver was too low.

[857] (1986), 54 C.R. (3d) 1 (Ont. C.A.).

[858] *Ibid.*, at 23.

[859] Under s. 651(3)

> Where no witnesses are examined for an accused, he or his counsel is entitled to address the jury last, but otherwise counsel for the prosecution is entitled to address the jury last.

> In *Chambers*, above note 444, Cory J. for the Supreme Court held, without reference to the Charter, that an accused does not have an absolute right to be present at a hearing considering the dismissal of a juror for health reasons (at 246).

[860] At 28-38.

[861] *Report. The Jury* (1982), p. 68.

in Canada in which a defence had been called had been unfair.[862] This comment seems beside the point. Surely under the Charter concepts of fairness and justice are changing?

Although it is fundamental that a Charter challenge can be made against the purpose or effect of the law in the abstract or against its application in an individual case, provincial courts are often reluctant to declare unconstitutional a procedure which may be unfair in the abstract but not in the case in point. The concern may well be associated with the question of remedy. The effect has been to substantially weaken the force of the right to a fair trial.

Until 1992, Crown counsel had an undoubted advantage in the empanelling of jurors in that, although the Crown only had four peremptory challenges and the accused sometimes 12 or 20 depending on the nature of the case, the Crown in practice always held the advantage as in any case it could exercise a power under the Criminal Code to stand aside up to 48 jurors. Provincial Courts of Appeal nevertheless rejected Charter challenges. The Ontario Court of Appeal[863] recognized that the process appeared unfair and could possibly lead to unfairness and the Saskatchewan Court of Appeal[864] called for legislation to equalize the number of challenges along the lines suggested by the Law Reform Commission in 1982.[865] A 4-3 majority of the Supreme Court in *Bain* (1992)[866] were not wedded to the *status quo*. The Criminal Code provisions would lead a reasonable person to conclude that there was an apprehension of Crown bias. Whenever the Crown is granted statutory power that can be used abusively then on occasion it would, suggested Justice Cory for the majority,[867] be used abusively. The Court deemed the provisions invalid, an order it suspended for 6 months. Parliament duly enacted a scheme equalising peremptory challenges and abolishing Crown stand asides. *Bain* provides another example of Charter-inspired pro accused reform which appears unlikely without a push from the courts.

Supreme Court decisions such as those in *Bain* suggested that the Supreme Court would overrule *Tzimopoulos*. In *Rose* (1998)[868] the Ontario Court of Appeal had convened a five justice panel to reconsider but a 3-2 majority decided to maintain the Court's early position that there was no Charter violation in the rule that defence counsel must address the jury first, where defence has led evidence. On the further appeal the Supreme Court agreed, but only by a 5-4 majority. Given *Bain*, it is surprising that it was Justice Cory who co-authored the majority judgment with Justices Iacobucci and Bastarache. [869] Referring to the statement of La Forest in *Lyons* that the accused's entitlement to procedural fairness did not

---

[862] Above note 857, at 38-39.
[863] *Stoddart* (1985), 44 C.R. (3d) 377 (Ont. C.A.).
[864] *Favel* (1987), 39 C.C.C.(3d) 378 (Sask. C.A.).
[865] Above note 857, p. 46.
[866] (1992), 10 C.R. (4th) 257 (S.C.C.).
[867] Lamer C.J. and La Forest J. concurred. Stevenson J. delivered a separate concurring opinion. Gonthier J. dissented (McLachlin and Iacobucci JJ. concurring).
[868] Above note 845.
[869] Gonthier J. concurred. L'Heureux-Dubé J. concurring in part.

require "the most favourable procedures that could possibly be imagined",[870] the majority saw the issue as whether the order of jury addresses in s. 651(3) and (4) of the Criminal Code created an unfairness.[871] The majority found no procedural unfairness especially as there was little evidence that there was a tactical disadvantage in addressing the jury last, some suggesting it was advantageous.[872] The existing rule was fair, although not necessarily the most desirable. The majority accepted it would be preferable to adopt the Law Reform Commission's recommendation to change the law to give defence counsel a choice of addressing first or last. However Cory J. added that s. 651 did not impair the Court's inherent jurisdiction to achieve fairness by granting a right of reply to defence counsel when required.[873]

Justice Binnie for the dissenters was not convinced that the problem could be solved by creating a limited right of reply.[874] In the realities of a courtroom it was often vital for a party to address the "spin" the other party had given. The accused might be prejudiced where the Crown, having heard the accused's address, could re-orient the final address. There was no logic in placing the ultimate burden on the Crown while requiring the accused to answer the Crown's arguments before they were made. In having to anticipate the Crown theory, the accused might risk reinforcing it. Sections 651(3) and (4) should be declared inoperative.

In *Rose* every justice expressed the opinion that the present jury order rule should be improved. That Parliament shows no signs of making an amendment is another sign that politicians are reluctant to make pro-accused reforms and re-inforces the view that the caution shown by the majority was unnecessary and unfortunate.

Given the majority approach and ruling in *Rose*, it was no surprise that the Ontario Court of Appeal rejected a challenge to s. 635(2) respecting the order of peremptory challenges where there are co-accused.[875] In *Pan* (1999)[876] the Court divided 4-1 on the issue of whether the common law rule of exclusion of evidence of jury deliberations and the jury secrecy rule in s. 649 could survive Charter review. McMurtry C.J.O. for the majority decided that there was no violation given the overriding need to ensure the proper and effective operation of the jury system. Finlayson J.A. in dissent viewed the current law as overkill and difficult to justify if evidence of jury matters was relevant to whether there had been a fair trial.

---

[870] Para. 99.

[871] Para. 100.

[872] Para. 120.

[873] L'Heureux-Dubé J. did not agree. Such a right of reply could not be found in inherent power given s. 651(3) but relief could be found in s. 24(1) of the Charter. Finding a similar line in Binnie J.'s judgment Allan Manson argues that there is a hidden majority for a constitutional exemption: "The Claim of the Rose Case: Jury Addresses and Humble Echoes of Reply", (1999) 20 C.R. (5th) 300. For criticism of the solution of a reply see Peter Sankoff, "Creating a Right of Reply: Rose is Not Without a Few Thorns", (1999) 20 C.R. (5th) 305.

[874] Paras. 28-38.

[875] *Suzack* (2000), 30 C.R. (5th) 346 (Ont. C.A.) at 369, paras. 68-70.

[876] (1999), 26 C.R. (5th) 87 (Ont. C.A.).

Similarly, Courts of appeal have rejected general challenges to wide *ex parte* trial procedures to be found in the case of summary conviction proceedings under the Criminal Code[877] or under provincial laws.[878]

Provincial courts *have* intervened when there has been procedural unfairness in a particular case. In *Babcock* (1989),[879] a second trial on the charge of leaving the scene of an accident commenced more than two years after the original information had been sworn. On the conclusion of the first day of the hearing the Crown advised the trial judge that the matter would probably not finish within the two days that had been scheduled. The trial judge, on his own motion and over the objections of both counsel, acted under what is now s. 555 of the Criminal Code, and declared that he would no longer adjudicate over the proceedings as a trial judge and was continuing the matter as a preliminary inquiry. The reasons given were that, since the trial could not be concluded within another nine months because of his busy docket, it would be more expeditious to hold a preliminary inquiry and have the trial conducted by a District Court Judge. The Ontario Court of Appeal held that the power in question was very broad but there was nothing in the record to justify the trial judge's decision. Section 7 of the Charter contemplated "procedural irregularities." Here, having regard to the nature of the charge and the history of delay, the accused had been denied the right to a timely trial at his election under the Criminal Code. The appropriate remedy was a stay under s. 24(1).[880]

In *Zurlo* (1990),[881] the Quebec Court of Appeal held that a joint manslaughter indictment against a husband and wife, where separate preliminaries had indicated antagonistic defences, violated the accused's right to a fair trial and should be stayed. By joining the trials, the Crown had ensured that neither accused could cross-examine the other on contradictory statements made previously because of s. 13 of the Charter.

In *McGregor* (1999),[882] the Ontario Court of Appeal accepted that the trial judge had properly overriden the Crown's refusal to consent to a non-jury murder trial. The case had attracted considerable notoriety and the Crown exercise of discretion would result in an infringement of the accused's right to trial by an independent and impartial tribunal.

---

[877] *Tarrant* (1984), 13 C.C.C. (3d) 219 (B.C. CA.). However, in *McLeod* (1983), 36 CR. (3d) 378 (N.W.T. S.C.), a new trial was ordered on the basis that proceeding with a summary conviction trial where weather had prevented the accused from attending violated s. 7 and in *Favreau v. Quebec (Cour of Kahnawake)* (1993), 22 C.R. (4th) 257 (Que. S.C.) (*ex parte* convictions of motorists by Court on Indian reserve quashed where police advising security not assured on reserve).

[878] *Felipa* (1986), 27 C.C.C. (3d) 26 (Ont. C.A.). In *Richards* (1997), 3 C.R. (5th) 1 (S.C.C.), the Court based its ruling on the issue of waiver.

[879] (1989), 68 C.R. (3d) 285 (Ont. C.A.).

[880] *Ibid.*, at 288. See too *N. (A.)* (1983), 32 C.R. (3d) 176 (Y.T. Terr. Ct.) (information bypassing procedural safeguards for laying charge being a nullity) and *Lachance* (1985), 22 C.C.C. (3d) 119 (Que. S.C.) (accused to be released from prison where incompetence or inefficiency of authorities concerning warrant of committal lengthening time in custody).

[881] (1990), 78 C.R. (3d) 167 (Que. C.A.). See too *Praisoody* (1990), 3 C.R. (4th) 91 (Ont. Gen. Div.).

[882] (1999), 22 C.R. (5th) 233 (Ont. C.A.).

(iii) *Duty to give reasons*

Prior to the Charter Chief Justice Laskin in *MacDonald* (1977)[883] refused to declare a common law rule that trial judges in criminal cases should be required to give reasons:

> The desirability of giving reasons is unquestionable. As was said in a Note in (1970), 48 Can. Bar Rev. 584 by Professor Hooper,
>
> > The arguments in favour of reasoned judgments are obvious. The process of publicly formulating his reasons may lead the judge to a conclusion other than that reached upon the basis of "intuition". The parties to the case, both the Crown and defence, will want to assure themselves that the judge properly understood the issues before him and will want to know whether he reached any conclusions of law or fact that could be challenged at the appellate level. The general public, or at least the victim if there was one, may have an interest in knowing why a certain verdict was reached.
>
> These considerations and others that could be mustered go to show what is the preferable practice, but the volume of criminal work makes an indiscriminate requirement of reasons impractical, especially in provincial criminal courts, and the risk of ending up with a ritual formula makes it undesirable to fetter the discretion of trial judges.[884]

The pragmatism of *MacDonald* is also evident in the refusal of the Supreme Court in *Burns* (1994)[885] to declare a duty to give reasons under the Charter. A unanimous Court held that a failure of a trial judge to indicate expressly all relevant considerations was not a basis for allowing an appeal. According to McLachlin J. for the Court:

> This accords with the general rule that a trial judge does not err merely because he or she does not give reasons for deciding one way or the other on problematic points. . . . The judge is not required to demonstrate that he or she knows the law and has considered all aspects of the evidence. Nor is the judge required to explain why he or she does not entertain a reasonable doubt as to the accused's guilt. Failure to do any of these things does not, in itself, permit a court of appeal to set aside the verdict.
> This rule makes good sense. To require trial judges charged with heavy caseloads of criminal cases to deal in their reasons with every aspect of every case would slow the system of justice immeasurably. Trial judge are presumed to know the law with which they work day in and day out. If they state their conclusions in brief compass, and these conclusions are supported by the evidence, the verdict should not be overturned merely because they fail to discuss collateral aspects of the case.[886]

The message given by the Supreme Court in *Burns* to trial judges was that they could rest content with no reasons or the most minimal of reasons. Allowing a trial judge to avoid giving reasons for reasons of expediency makes them far less accountable and appears grossly unjust to accused. More should be expected of judges. Section 7 should be interpreted to ensure that a person convicted of a

---

[883] [1977] 2 S.C.R. 665.
[884] *Ibid.*, at 672.
[885] (1994), 29 C.R. (4th) 113 (S.C.C.).
[886] At 121.

criminal offence has a right to know the basis upon which the conviction is entered.[887] *Burns* has been repeatedly criticized.

A most disturbing application of *Burns* occurred in the Supreme Court's decision in *Barrett* (1995).[888] At the accused's trial on 10 counts of robbery, a *voir dire* was held to determine the admissibility of the accused's statements to the hold-up squad one hour after his arrest. The *voir dire* concerned both Charter and common law voluntariness grounds. The *voir dire* lasted four days. The trial judge reserved judgment. After approximately six weeks defence counsel was advised by the trial judge's secretary that he had ruled the statements admissible on the basis of credibility. No other reasons were delivered. The accused was convicted and appealed. The Ontario Court of Appeal[889] allowed the appeal and ordered a new trial. Madam Justice Arbour held for the Court that, although a failure of a trial judge to give reasons did not constitute an error of law, the absence of reasons could have a bearing on the appellate determination of the correctness of the ruling and also on whether there had been a miscarriage of justice. Here the trial judge must have be taken to have been satisfied beyond a reasonable doubt that the statements were freely and voluntarily made. This was a proper case for the Court of Appeal to intervene because the conclusion of the trial judge could not, in the absence of reasons, be supported given the disputed and contradicted Crown evidence. There would have to have been a finding that injuries suffered by the accused in police custody were attributable to a fight with other inmates. Yet there was no evidence.

The Supreme Court allowed the Crown's appeal in a brief oral judgment from the bench and substituted convictions. According to Iacobucci J. for the Court the answer lay in *Burns*:

> While it is clearly preferable to give reasons and although there may be some cases where reasons may be necessary, by itself, the absence of reasons of a trial judge cannot be a ground for appellate review when the finding is otherwise supportable on the evidence or where the basis of the finding is apparent from the circumstances.

The issue was the reasonableness of the finding not an absence or insufficiency of reasons. Here, the basis for the trial judge's ruling was clear and the only issue was credibility.

This ruling is stunning. At the time, Justice Arbour was a highly respected justice of the Ontario Court of Appeal. In a meticulous judgment she found that a ruling that the statement was voluntary was unreasonable given disturbing implausibilities and contradictions in the Crown evidence at the *voir dire*. In the circumstances, the mere statement of the trial judge that the statements were admissible on the basis of credibility could not permit the Ontario Court of Appeal

---

[887] See further Judge Ian MacDonnell, "Reasons for Judgment and Fundamental Justice", in Cameron (ed.), *The Charter's Impact on the Criminal Justice System* (1996) pp. 151-159 and critical comments by Guy Cournoyer, David Schermbrucker and Egya Sangmuah in (1994) 29 C.R. (4th) 113, M. Naeem Rauf in (1994) 31 C.R. (4th) 74 and Kent Roach, above note 577, pp. 336-337.

[888] (1995), 38 C.R. (4th) 1 (S.C.C.).

[889] (1993), 23 C.R. (4th) 49 (Ont. C.A.).

to determine that the finding was reasonable. The trial judge was asked to determine a serious issue concerning an allegation of police brutality where there was undisputed evidence that the accused had suffered injuries while in police custody. Surely the case was serious enough for proper reasons to be provided? The Supreme Court in *Burns* recognizes that in some cases reasons may be necessary. Arbour J.A. makes a most compelling case why this was just such a case. It is curious that a Supreme Court which has so often been scrupulous in its considerations of allegations of police misconduct would here be so disinterested. The Supreme Court should have taken the opportunity in *Barrett* to review and refine *Burns* rather than mechanically apply it.

In *McMaster* (1996),[890] Chief Justice Lamer takes the Court in a welcome new direction. Guarded dicta now provide some authority for appeal courts to intervene where no reasons were given. According to the Chief Justice, *Burns* and *Barrett* do not decide that there is no obligation on trial judges to provide reasons. The Chief Justice draws a new distinction in holding that appeal courts may intervene where the law was uncertain and no adequate reasons were given:

> I am of the view that in cases where the law is settled and the disposition turns on an application of the law to particular facts of the case, it will be difficult for an appellant to argue that the failure to provide reasons requires appellate intervention. ... However, in a case where it appears that the law is unsettled, it would be wise for a trial judge to write reasons setting out the legal principles upon which the conviction is based so that an error may be more easily identified, if error there be.[891]

Although, as L'Heureux-Dubé J. in her concurring opinion is at pains to point out, this passage does not amount to a legal obligation to give reasons in every case, it is most certainly a reinterpretation of *Burns*. There is express jurisdiction for intervention by appeal courts where the law was unsettled and the trial judge did not enunciate an acceptable basis for the decision.

An even more significant reconsideration of *Burns* came in the majority judgment of Mr. Justice Major in *D. (R.)* (1996).[892] In a case involving allegations of sexual and physical abuse against children, the Supreme Court held that the trial judge had erred in law in failing to address confusing evidence and to separate fact from fiction. *Burns* had clearly set out the law relating to the requirement of trial judges to give reasons but had dealt with a case where the Court of Appeal had agreed that the trial judge had evidence to support the conclusion reached but had overturned the verdict due to lack of reasons. According to Major J.

> [*Burns*] does not stand for the proposition that trial judges are never required to give reasons. Nor does it mean that they are always required to give reasons. Depending on the circumstances of a particular case, it may be desirable that trial judges explain

---

[890] (1996), 46 C.R. (4th) 41 (S.C.C.).

[891] At 51.

[892] (1996), 48 C.R. (4th) 368 (S.C.C.). Lamer C.J. and Sopinka J. concurred. Cory and Iacobucci JJ. express agreement with Major J.'s reasons but dissent on the issue of whether an acquittal should be substituted. The concurring opinion of McLachlin J. expresses no disagreement with the Major J. opinion on inadequacy of the reasons. L'Heureux-Dubé J. in a strong dissent suggests that the Court has "never strayed from the proposition that the absence of reasons or an omission from the reasons are not in themselves an error of law" (at 401).

their conclusions. Where the reasons demonstrate that the trial judge has considered the important issues in a case, or where the record clearly reveals the trial judge's reasons, or where the evidence is such that no reasons are necessary, appellate courts will not interfere. Equally, in cases such as this, where there is confused and contradictory evidence, the trial judge should give reasons for his or her conclusions. The trial judge in this case did not do so. She failed to address the troublesome evidence or failed to identify the basis on which she convicted. . . . This is an error of law necessitating a new trial.[893]

Given the dicta in *McMaster* and *D.R.* trial judges who do not give reasons whether this relates to disputed law or the evidence risk being reversed by courts of appeal.[894] With L'Heureux-Dubé J. in dissent it is difficult not to see this statement as a reversal of *Burns*. Unlike L'Heureux-Dubé J. there is good reason to applaud the Court for reaching a much better compromise.

After all this complex backtracking from *Burns*, it is time for the Supreme Court to be more forthright. In *Biniaris* (2000)[895] Justice Arbour speaking for the full Court on the issue of the standard for review of the reasonable of a verdict, said:

I wish to stress the importance of explicitness in the articulation of the reasons that support a finding that a verdict is unreasonable or cannot be supported by the evidence. Particularly since this amounts to a question of law that may give rise to an appeal, either as of right or by leave, the judicial process requires clarity and transparency as well as accessibility to the legal reasoning of the court of appeal.[896]

Given that such "clarity and transparency" is needed for appellate review, so too with trial judgments for purposes of review by Courts of Appeal. The accused and complainants are entitled to know why there was a conviction or an acquittal. There is already a duty under s. 726.2 of the Criminal Code to give reasons for sentence. Recently L'Heureux-Dubé J. in *Baker* v. *Canada* (1999)[897] asserted a requirement of *written* reasons in immigration cases given the important significance for the individual. So too, in the context of a criminal trial, it is time for the Supreme Court to reverse *Burns* as a decision that "does not enhance justice"[898] and require a simple rule that reasons always be provided.[899]

(iv) *Post-trial challenges*

Section 7 challenges based on a lack of procedural fairness have rarely succeeded in the context of post-trial proceedings. The Supreme Court in *Lyons* (1987)[900] unanimously rejected such a challenge to the dangerous offender

---

[893] At 388.
[894] See, for example, *Sheppard* (1999), 138 C.C.C. (3d) 254 (Nfld. C.A.), *Hache* (1999), 25 C.R. (5th) 127 (N.S. C.A.) and *N. (P.L.F.)* (1999), 27 C.R. (5th) 105 (Man. C.A.).
[895] (2000), 32 C.R. (5th) 1 (S.C.C.).
[896] Para. 42.
[897] [1999] 2 S.C.R. 817.
[898] Justice Gerard Mitchell, "Do Judges Have A Duty to Give Reasons for Convicting?", (1999) 25 C.R. (5th) 150 at 153.
[899] See Guy Cornoyer, "Annotation to *Biniaris*", (2000) 32 C.R. (5th) 4.
[900] Above note 4.

provisions in Part XXIV of the Criminal Code. It dismissed arguments that the provisions offended s. 7 in their penalogical objectives, their imposition of indeterminate attention, in the standard of proof and use of psychiatric evidence in predicting dangerousness, in the lack of a requirement of a jury trial and in the Crown's failure to provide notice of the intention to make the application prior to election and plea.

The Supreme Court determined that detention provisions of the Parole Act authorizing detention of an inmate until warrant expiry implicate the liberty interest, but in accordance with principles of fundamental justice given the need to protect the public.[901] The Court has also ruled[902] that s. 7 requires the National Parole Board to comply with rules of fairness and natural justice. This meant it had to consider the source of information and whether the source was unreliable or unfair.[903] The Board could not exclude evidence because of a Charter violation as its was not a court of competent jurisdiction.

In *Winko* v. *Forensic Psychiatric Institute* (1999)[904] the Supreme Court decided[905] that the new Part XX.1 of the Criminal Code providing a comprehensive administrative and adjudicatory structure for those found not criminally responsibility on account of mental disorder conformed to principles of fundamental justice under s. 7. The context was one in which public safety interests had to be balanced. The provisions did not violate principles of fundamental justice through vagueness, an improper onus and overbreadth. The majority interpreted the regime as requiring the absolute discharge of an NCR accused, unless there was a foreseeable and substantial risk that a serious criminal offence would be committed. There were also rights of review and appeal.

The British Columbia Court of Appeal has held[906] that a probation order which compels the accused to take psychiatric treatment or medication is an unreasonable restraint on liberty and security of the person contrary to principles of fundamental justice under s. 7. Save in exceptional circumstances, such an order could not be saved under s. 1.

In a case of an involuntary transfer of a prisoner to a maximum security institution, the Federal Court of Appeal has held that the inmate is entitled to the principles of fundamental justice under s. 7 to an extent that will depend on the circumstances. The majority held that the danger to informants had justified the authorities not disclosing the detailed basis for the transfer decision.[907]

---

[901] *Cunningham* (1993), 20 C.R. (4th) 57 (S.C.C.).
[902] *Mooring v. National Parole Board* (1996), 45 C.R. (4th) 262 (S.C.C.), criticized by Allan Manson in an annotation, C.R. *ibid.* 268.
[903] According to the Federal Court of Appeal this does not include the right of an inmate serving an indeterminate sentence to require the author of a clinical report to appear for cross-examination at a parole hearing: *MacInnis* (1996), 1 C.R. (5th) 144 (Fed. C.A.).
[904] (1999), 25 C.R. (5th) 1 (S.C.C.). See further Chapter 10 for the ruling that s. 15 rights had also not been violated.
[905] Paras. 64-73.
[906] *Rogers* (1990), 2 C.R. (4th) 192 (B.C. C.A.).
[907] *Gallant v. Canada (Dep. Commr., Pac. Region, Correctional Service Can.)*, above note 61. Compare *Cardinal v. Canada (National Parole Board)* (1990), 61 C.C.C. (3d) 185 (Fed. T.D.). *Habeas corpus* will be refused where other remedies have not been exhausted: (2000), 147 C.C.C.

(d) Fair Rules of Evidence

Professor David Paciocco[908] in his thorough, comparative study of the potential impact of the Charter on the laws of evidence, suggests that the Charter should be "used wisely to improve the law of evidence in criminal cases without challenging or undermining our system of justice."[909] Following full analysis of complex American constitutional law the author makes ambitious claims for s. 7. For example, he suggests that s.7 can be the basis for a constitutional right to adduce exculpatory evidence, for a right of an accused to cross-examine witnesses (which would have a considerable impact on existing hearsay exceptions) and that s. 7 should prevent the Crown from adducing some unduly prejudicial information.

(i) *Challenges to rules excluding evidence*

It is already clear that our Courts have accepted that the right to a fair trial under s. 7 may give rise to successful constitutional challenge to the existence or application of established rules of evidence. According to Mr. Justice Lamer for a unanimous Supreme Court in *Albright* (1987):[910]

> The conduct of a trial in general, including the application of the rules of evidence in a given case, must not result in the trial being unfair because the accused has been denied a full opportunity to prepare his case and challenge and answer the Crown's case. If a rule of law, statutory or common law, were framed in such a way that it would be per se a violation of the right to a fair trial, then the statute would be declared inoperative or the common law declared to be otherwise.[911]

The Court held that s. 7 had not been violated by the failure of the Crown to give notice of its intention to use a certificate of a prior impaired driver conviction at the sentence hearing following conviction for failure to provide a breath sample. In itself the common law rule of admissibility of the certificate did not violate the Charter. Lack of such notice and the unavailability of the officer who would otherwise have testified to prove the convictions could result, in a particular case, in a violation of the accused's right to a fair trial. In such a case there would have to be a challenge under s. 24 of the Charter.[912]

(3d) 48 (Que. C.A.). For a review and discussion of the difficult jurisprudence on the common law and s. 7 protections in prison settings, see Cole and Manson, above note 54.

[908] *Charter Principles and Proof in Criminal Cases* (1987). See too Marc Rosenberg, "The Impact of the Charter on the Law of Evidence in Criminal Cases", in Cameron (ed.), *The Charter's Impact on the Criminal Justice System* (1996) pp. 181-199.

[909] David Doherty, now a member of the Ontario Court of Appeal, in "The Charter and Reforming the Law of Evidence" (1987), 58 C.R. (3d) 314, voices concern at the judiciary becoming the "ultimate maker of the laws of evidence" since it has an "inherent bias for well-worn legal formulae" and a "limited prospective imposed by the adversary system" (at 319).

[910] (1987), 60 C.R. (3d) 97 (S.C.C.).

[911] *Ibid.*, at 106.

[912] *Albright* was applied in *Triumbari* (1988), 42 C.C.C. (3d) 481 (Ont. C.A.) (provincial legislation permitting use of certified copy of licence suspension without notice not offending s. 7). See too *Boufford* (1988), 46 C.C.C. (3d) 116 (Ont. Dist. Ct.).

Similar principles were asserted by the Ontario Court of Appeal in *Rowbotham* (1988):[913]

> The accused had the right to make full answer and defence, a right encompassed in the term "fundamental justice" now enshrined in s. 7 of the Charter. As stated in *R. v. Williams* (1985), 44 C.R. (3d) 351 "an accused in exercising his right to make full answer and defence must comply with the established rules of procedure and the rules respecting the admissibility of evidence", but the rule is not absolute. It was apparent in *Williams* that the court will recognize exceptions when the rigid adherence will prevent or hinder a fair trial.[914]

In *Williams*, the Ontario Court recognized a constitutional right to full answer and defence could be violated by a refusal to hear technically inadmissible hearsay evidence or by a refusal to allow cross-examination of a non-adverse witness.[915] However, this was inapplicable to Williams, who was seeking to introduce the confession of a third party and to cross-examine the third party about his prior confessions. The Court was skeptical about the reliability of the out-of-court confession. Paciocco[916] finds the assertion of "assurances of trustworthiness" too extreme a test and not being required by the American authority upon which it rested. He also views the confessions in question as, in any event, sufficiently trustworthy.

The *Rowbotham* principle that s. 7 may require different evidentiary rules for accused was relied upon by Cory J. *obiter* speaking for four justices in *Finta* (1994).[917] However, this remark and that in *Albright* stand in marked contrast to the following comment of Sopinka J. for the Court in *Crawford* (1995):[918]

> The right to full answer and defence does not imply that an accused can have, under the rubric of the Charter, an overhawl of the whole law of evidence such that a statement inadmissible under, for instance, the hearsay exclusion, would be admissible if it tended to prove his or her innocence.[919]

This remark is also *obiter* and appears totally at odds with Justice Sopinka's later positions.[920]

The leading pronouncement on the right to cross-examine is that of Justice Cory for the majority of the Supreme Court in *Osolin* (1993).[921] This was a controversial case where the majority ordered a new trial to allow cross-

---

[913] Above note 787. See too *Cruikshanks* (1990), 58 C.C.C. (3d) 26 (B.C. C.A.).

[914] *Ibid.*, at 164.

[915] In *Rowbotham*, the Court held that the trial judge might have allowed an accused to answer based on hearsay but that this did not amount to an error.

[916] Above note 908, pp. 234-236.

[917] (1994), 28 C.R. (4th) 265 (S.C.C.) at 329. Lamer C.J., Gonthier and Major JJ. concurred. The point was not considered in the dissenting judgment of La Forest J. (L'Heureux-Dubé and McLachlin JJ. concurring).

[918] Above note 451.

[919] At 214, repeated a view Sopinka J. had asserted in *Dersch* (1991), 80 C.R. (3d) 299 (S.C.C.) at 308.

[920] See especially concurrence in the majority positions in *O'Connor*, above note 734, and *Harrer*, below note 990.

[921] (1993), 26 C.R. (4th) 1 (S.C.C.).

examination on mental health records of a complainant in a sexual assault. According to Cory J.:

> Cross-examination must be permitted so that an accused can make full answer and defence. The opportunity to cross-examine witnesses is fundamental to providing a fair trial to an accused. This is an old and well established principle that is closely linked to the presumption of innocence. . . That right is now protected by ss. 7 and 11(d) of the *Charter*. As a result it should be interpreted in the "broad and generous manner befitting its constitutional status". . . .[922]

The right was not, however, absolute:

> Despite its importance the right to cross-examine has never been unlimited. It must conform to the basic principle that all evidence must be relevant in order to be admissible. In addition the probative value of evidence must be weighed against its prejudicial effect.[923]

Recently, in *Parrott* (2001),[924] in a ruling on hearsay, Binnie J. held for the majority:

> While in this country an accused does not have an absolute right to confront his or her accuser in a trial, the right to full answer and defence generally produces this result.[925]

The most controversial Charter attack on rules excluding evidence has been against Criminal Code "rape shield" provisions, enacted as recently as 1985 after an extensive legislative history[926] to protect victims of sexual offences from unwarranted cross-examination at trial. In the case of a number of listed sexual offences, including sexual assault, what is now s. 277 excludes evidence of sexual reputation for the purpose of challenging or supported the credibility of the complainant while at the time s. 276 prohibits evidence concerning the complainant's sexual activity with persons other than the accused, subject to three statutory exceptions. Under s. 276(1)

> . . . no evidence shall be adduced by or on behalf of the accused concerning the sexual activity of the complainant with any person other than the accused unless
>
> (a) it is evidence that rebuts evidence of the complainant's sexual activity or absence thereof that was previously adduced by the prosecution;
> (b) it is evidence of specific instances of the complainant's sexual activity tending to establish the identity of the person who had sexual contact with the complainant on the occasion set out in the charge; or
> (c) it is evidence of sexual activity that took place on the same occasion as the sexual activity that forms the subject-matter of the charge, where that evidence relates to the consent that the accused alleges he believed was given by the complainant.

Courts of Appeals upheld the validity of s. 277 but, with the exception of

---

[922] Paras. 25 and 28.
[923] Para. 30.
[924] (2001), 39 C.R. (5th) 255 (S.C.C.).
[925] Para. 52.
[926] R.S.C. 1985, c. 19 (3rd Supp.), s. 13. For a review of the legislative history see Grange J.A. in *Seaboyer* (1987), 58 C.R. (3d) 289 at 302-304 (Ont. C.A.).

the British Columbia Court of Appeal,[927] ruled[928] that s. 276 was not in accordance with principles of fundamental justice under s. 7 and could not be saved by s. 1 That was also the seven to two majority position of the Supreme Court in *Seaboyer* (1991).[929]

Madam Justice McLachlin, for the majority,[930] declared it to be a principle of fundamental justice that relevant defence evidence could only be excluded where the potential prejudice to the trial process clearly outweighed its value:

> Canadian courts, like courts in most common law jurisdictions, have been extremely cautious in restricting the power of the accused to call evidence in his or her defence, a reluctance founded in the fundamental tenet of our judicial system that an innocent person must not be convicted. It follows from this that the prejudice must substantially outweigh the value of the evidence before a judge can exclude evidence relevant to a defence allowed by law.[931]

The Court held that s. 277 did not infringe the right to a fair trial. The provision excluded evidence of sexual reputation on the issue of the credibility of the complainant. However, such evidence served no legitimate purpose. The idea that a complainant's credibility might be affected by whether she had had other sexual experience was "today universally discredited."[932]

However, according to the majority, the blanket exclusion by s. 276 of evidence of prior sexual history of the complainant, subject to three exceptions, violated s. 7. It could not be said *a priori* that any and all evidence excluded by s. 276 would necessarily be of such trifling weight in relation to prejudicial effect that it might be fairly excluded.[933] The legislation could not be saved by s. 1 as it did not restrict as little as possible and struck the wrong balance between the rights of complainants and those of accused.[934]

The majority further held that the striking down of s. 276 should not revive old common law rules permitting liberal and often inappropriate reception of evidence of the complainant's sexual conduct. Common law rules had to be adopted to conform to current reality. McLachlin J. then declared suggested guidelines for the reception and use of sexual conduct evidence. These guidelines were expressed to be "not judicial legislation cast in stone":

---

[927] (1986), 54 C.R. (3d) 46 (B.C. C.A.). See criticism by Anne Stalker, "LeGallant: Law Reform and the Charter", C.R. *ibid.*, pp. 64-66.

[928] *Seaboyer* (1987), 58 C.R. (3d) 289 (Ont. C.A.); *Wald* (1989), 68 C.R. (3d) 289 (Alta. C.A.); and *Gervais* (1990), 78 C.R. (3d) 53 (Que. C.A.).

[929] (1991), 7 C.R. (4th) 117 (S.C.C.). For a critical review and assessment of the majority position, see Marilyn MacCrimmon and Christine Boyle, "Seaboyer: A Lost Cause?", (1991) 7 C.R. (4th) 225. For earlier contrasting views on this controversial issue, see David Paciocco, "The Charter and the Rape Shield Provisions of the Criminal Code: More about Relevance and the Constitutional Exemption Doctrine", (1989) 21 *Ottawa L. Rev.* 119 and Elizabeth Sheehy, "Canadian Judges and the Law of Rape: Should the Charter Insulate Bias", (1989) 21 *Ottawa L. Rev.* 151. See too David Doherty, "Sparing the Complainant 'Spoils' the Trial", (1984) 40 C.R. (3d) 55.

[930] Lamer C.J.C., La Forest, Sopinka, Cory, Stevenson and Iacobucci JJ. concurred.

[931] Above note 929, at 139.

[932] *Ibid.*, at 140.

[933] *Ibid.*, at 141.

[934] *Ibid.*, at 152.

1. On a trial for a sexual offence, evidence that the complainant has engaged in consensual sexual conduct on other occasions (including past sexual conduct with the accused) is not admissible solely to support the inference that the complainant is by reason of such conduct:

(a) more likely to have consented to the sexual conduct at issue in the trial;

(b) less worthy of belief as a witness.

2. Evidence of consensual sexual conduct on the part of the complainant may be admissible for purposes other than an inference relating to the consent or credibility of the complainant where it possesses probative value on an issue in the trial and where that probative value is not substantially outweighed by the danger of unfair prejudice flowing from the evidence.

. . . .

3. Before evidence of consensual sexual conduct on the part of a victim is received, it must be established on a voir dire (which may be held in camera) by affidavit or the testimony of the accused or third parties, that the proposed use of the evidence of other sexual conduct is legitimate.

4. Where evidence that the complainant has engaged in sexual conduct on other occasions is admitted on a jury trial, the judge should warn the jury against inferring from the evidence of the conduct itself either that the complainant might have consented to the act alleged, or that the complainant is less worthy of credit.[935]

In a strongly worded dissent, Madam Justice L'Heureux-Dubé[936] was of the opinion that s. 276 did *not* infringe ss. 7 and 11(d) and, if it did, would be saved by s. 1. Of paramount importance was a consideration of the prevalence and impact of discriminatory beliefs on trials of sexual offences. Unlike other violent crimes, sexual assaults were for the most part unreported. Evidence excluded by s. 276 was, in a myth- and stereotype-free decision-making context, irrelevant. The accused did not have a constitutional right to adduce irrelevant evidence nor evidence prejudicing and distorting the fact-finding process at trials.[937]

Seaboyer immediately produced an outcry in the media. Headlines blared that the Supreme Court had struck down the rape shield provision and that women and children would be even less likely to pursue charges of sexual assault given that there would be unrestricted cross-examination of their prior sexual history. Such comments were an over-reaction and unfair to the majority of the Supreme Court. For the majority, Madam Justice McLachlin had indeed struck down s. 276. However, expressing grave concern at leaving the matter to unfettered judicial discretion, she set out[938] what she considered to be rigid guidelines as to the admissibility of evidence of prior sexual history of the complainant with the accused. She also extended the protection to such conduct *with the accused.*

It is fair to say, however, that the majority of the Supreme Court took but a line to hold that although victims might have equality rights, these had to give

---

935 *Ibid.*, at 158-159.
936 Gonthier J. concurred.
937 *Ibid.*, at 210.
938 Above note 935.

way to the accused's right to make full answer and defence.[939] It may well have been this weighing of rights that led usually moderate feminist writers to strong statement:

> It may not be the case that the majority betrayed women, or even necessarily made a wrong decision by neglecting the constitutional value of sex equality. They may have illustrated, in the clearest, most 'rational' terms, the fact that law will inevitably value the interests of men and require women to pay the price.[940]

The response from the Minister of Justice, the Honourable Kim Campbell, was swift. She announced that Parliament would respond to better protect women and children.[941] She called a meeting of national and regional women's groups. The record[942] seems clear that the Minister thereafter worked very closely in drafting and revising the Bill with the coalition of some 60 groups that emerged. The coalition reached unanimity at each point and agreed to oppose any attempt to water down the Bill. In this sense, the process was a partisan with voices of men, no doubt for the first time in the history of the development of Canadian criminal law, largely excluded.[943] By the time Bill C-49 reached the Senate, Professor Sheila McIntyre, the spokesperson for L.E.A.F. (Women's Legal Education and Action Fund), the sponsor of the Bill, stated that the aim had been to reflect women's constitutional rights under s. 7 and women's equality rights under s. 15[944] and also to achieve formal education:

> We also wanted comprehensive judicial education not through weekend seminars but in the body of the law, and we got it. We are very happy with the codified guidelines to judges that framed Seaboyer's broad principles and very specific factors to keep in mind, many of which are mindful of equality. No prejudicial, discriminatory stereotype language made its way in there and we are very pleased with that.[945]

---

[939] At 152.

[940] Christine Boyle and Marilyn MacCrimmon, "R. v. Seaboyer: A Lost Cause?", (1991) 7 C.R. (4th) 225.

[941] The need to change the criminal law to better respond to violence against "women and children" is now frequently the way the issue of violence is presented. This is mere political rhetoric. Women and children are disproportionately the victims of violence and men are overwhelmingly the perpetrators of violence. However violence by men against other male adults and abuse of children by women are also serious problems and defy explanation by gender analysis or reliance on equality rights under s.15 of the Charter. For careful documentation of how Canadian estimates of violence against women and children have been exaggerated see John Fekete, *Moral Panic: Biopolitics Rising* (1994).

[942] *Proceedings of the Standing Senate Committee on Legal and Constitutional Affairs*, 3rd Sess., 34 Parl., 1991-1992, (June 22, 1992): 29-31, Sheila McIntyre, "Redefining Reformism: The Consultations that Shaped Bill C-49" in J. Roberts and R. Mohr (eds.), *Confronting Sexual Assault: A Decade of Legal and Social Change* (1994) 293-326 and Robert Martin, "Bill C-49: A Victory for Interest Group Politics", (1993) 42 *U.N.B.L.J.* 356.

[943] This writer prepared a brief to the *Parliamentary Sub-Committee* but was not given permission to appear until one hour after a reporter from *The Lawyers' Weekly* started to seek an explanation as to why I had been excluded.

[944] *Proceedings of the Standing Senate Committee on Legal and Constitutional Affairs*, Third Session, Thirty-Fourth Parliament, 1991-92, June 22, 1992: 29-31.

[945] *Ibid.*, 29-32.

The Bill received Royal Assent on June 23, 1992 and was proclaimed in force on August 15, 1992. The whole process had taken just less than a year since the *Seaboyer* decision.

Bill C-49 was enthusiastically welcomed by politicians of every stripe for having replaced *Seaboyer* with a new rape shield that would protect women and children. This is ironic, given that the new rape shield laws so closely mirror the guidelines suggested by the majority in *Seaboyer*. It is certainly true, however, that the new statutory scheme does at one point,[946] in declaring the factors for trial judges to consider, include concerns for interests of the victim on the same level as the accused's right to make full answer and defence.

The crucial substantive sections of the "new" rape shield protection are in ss. 276(1) and (2):

> 276. (1) In proceedings in respect of [...sexual offences] evidence that the complainant has engaged in sexual activity, whether with the accused or with any other person, is not admissible to support an inference that, by reason of the sexual nature of that activity, the complainant
>
> > (a) is more likely to have consented to the sexual activity that forms the subject-matter of the charge; or,
> > (b) is less worthy of belief.
>
> (2) In proceedings in respect of an offence referred to in subsection (1), no evidence shall be adduced by or on behalf of the accused that the complainant has engaged in sexual activity other than the sexual activity that forms the subject-matter of the charge, whether with the accused or with any other person, unless the judge, provincial court judge or justice determines, in accordance with the procedures set out in sections 276.1 and 276.2, that the evidence
>
> > (a) is of specific instances of sexual activity;
> > (b) is relevant to an issue at trial; and
> > (c) has significant probative value that is not substantially outweighed by the danger of prejudice to the proper administration of justice.

Professor Ron Delisle[947] read what is commonly referred to as the "twin myths" prohibition in s. 276(1) as an express and blanket prohibition of the use of prior sexual history of the complainant on the issue of consent or to show that the complainant was less worthy of belief. As such, he argued that the section was unconstitutional as *Seaboyer* had called for discretion. He also pointed out that the Supreme Court (followed by Parliament) had extended the protection to prior sexual history *with the accused*, contrary to views expressed by Professors Harriet Galvin and Vivian Berger in the very works McLachlin J. had heavily relied on in *Seaboyer*. According to these writers, the issue of prior sexual history with the accused should be treated differently as such evidence would likely be more probative and not based on myths and stereotypes. Professor Galvin had written that:

> Even the most ardent reformers acknowledged the high probative value of past sexual conduct in at least two instances. The first is when the defendant claims consent and

---

946 Section 276(3).
947 "Potential Charter Challenges to the New Rape Shield Law", (1992) 13 C.R. (4th) 309.

establishes prior consensual relations between himself and the complainant. Although the evidence is offered to prove consent, its probative value rests on the nature of the complainant's specific mindset toward the accused rather than on her general unchaste character. ... All twenty-five statutes adopting the Michigan approach (to rape shield laws) allow the accused to introduce evidence of prior sexual conduct between himself and the complainant. The high probative value and minimal prejudicial effect of this evidence have been discussed.[948]

Professor Berger had justified the reception of evidence of sexual conduct with the accused in this way:

> The inference from past to present behaviour does not, as in cases of third party acts, rest on highly dubious beliefs about women who do and women who don't but rather relies on common sense and practical psychology. Admission of the proof supplies the accused with a circumstance making it probable that he did not obtain by violence what he might have secured by persuasion.[949]

However Professor David Paciocco[950] suggested that the legislation could be read down. Section 276(1) only prohibited general stereotypical inferences. Evidence of prior sexual history with the accused could be admitted under s. 276(2) where the defence could establish that a specific inference can be drawn from such evidence to an issue relevant in the trial. In Charter challenges in lower courts the Paciocco position carried the day and was increasingly relied on as the proper interpretation.[951]

When the Supreme Court finally considered the constitutionality of the "new" statutory scheme in *Darrach* (2000),[952] Justice Gonthier for a unanimous Court had little difficulty in declaring constitutional both the substantive and procedural.[953] The current version in s. 276 was in essence a codified version of the *Seaboyer* guidelines. The accused was not entitled to

> the most favourable procedures that could possibly be imagined (*Lyons*...cited in *Mills*...). Nor is the accused entitled to have procedures crafted that take only his

---

[948] "Shielding Rape Victims in the State and Federal Courts: A Proposal for the Second Decade", (1996) 70 *Minn. L. Rev.* 763 at 807-808.

[949] "Man's Trial. Woman's Tribulation: Rape Cases in the Courtroom", (1977) 77 *Columb. L. Rev.* 1 at 58-59.

[950] "The New Rape Shield Provision Should Survive Charter Challenge", (1993) 21 C.R. (4th) 223. Both the Delisle and Paciocco positions were strongly attacked by Hart Schwartz, "Sex with the Accused on Other Occasions, The Evisceration of Rape Shield Protection", (1994) 31 C.R. (4th) 232. This resulted in a reply by Paciocco, "Techniques for Eviscerating the Concept of Relevance", (1995) 33 C.R. (4th) 365. For further criticism of Paciocco's views see Christine Boyle and Marilyn MacCrimmon, "The Constitutionality of Bill C-49: Analysing Sexual Assault As If Equality Really Mattered", (1998) 41 *Crim. L. Q.* 198 at 222-230 and for further support see Daniel Stein, "Admissibility of Sexual Conduct Evidence After D. (A.S.)", (1998) 13 C.R. (5th) 312. For a comprehensive analysis of jurisprudence see Susan M. Chapman, "Section 276 of the Criminal Code and the Admissibility of 'Sexual Activity' ", (1999), 25 *Queen's L.J.* 121.

[951] See, for example, *Ecker* (1995), 37 C.R. (4th) 51 (Ont. C.A.) and *Darrach* (1998), 13 C.R. (5th) 283 (Ont. C.A.).

[952] (2000), 36 C.R. (5th) 223 (S.C.C.).

[953] The Court rejected arguments that the affidavit, *voir dire* and cross-examination requirements violated the accused's pre-trial right to silence under s. 7, his right not to be compelled to testify under s. 11(c) (see Chapter 6) or his presumption of innocence under s. 11(d). Section 13 was however held to protect the accused against self-incrimination: see Chapter 8.

interests into account. Still less is he entitled to procedures that would distort the truth-seeking function of a trial by permitting irrelevant and prejudicial material at trial.[954]

The Court also invoked in aid its recognition in *Mills*[955] that the scope of the right to make full answer and defence must be determined in light of the privacy and equality rights of complainants and witnesses.[956]

The accused was mistaken in characterising s. 276(1) as a blanket exclusion:

> Far from being a "blanket exclusion", s. 276(1) only prohibits the use of evidence of past sexual activity when it is offered to support two specific, illegitimate inferences. These are known as the "twin myths", namely that a complainant is more likely to have consented or that she is less worthy of belief "by reason of the sexual nature of the activity" she once engaged in.

> This section gives effect to McLachlin J.'s finding in *Seaboyer* that the "twin myths" are simply not relevant at trial. They are not probative of consent or credibility and can severely distort the trial process.[957]

The Court also found that s. 276(1) had clarified *Seaboyer*. The protection now applied to all sexual activity, whether with the accused or with someone else, to non-consensual as well as consensual sexual activity, and the "twin myths" are not limited to inferences about "unchaste" women.[958]

Without referring to Professor Paciocco's writing, the Court then appears to adopt[959] his general/specific inference distinction:

> The Criminal Code excludes all discriminatory generalizations about a complainant's disposition to consent or about her credibility based on the sexual nature of her past sexual activity on the grounds that these are improper lines of reasoning.

> The phrase "by reason of the sexual nature of the activity" in s. 276 is a clarification by Parliament that it is inferences from the sexual nature of the activity, as opposed to inferences from other potentially relevant features of the activity, that are prohibited. If evidence of sexual activity is proffered for its non-sexual features, such as to show a pattern of conduct or a prior inconsistent statement,[960] it may be permitted. The phrase "by reason of the sexual nature of the activity" has the same effect as the qualification "solely to support the inference" in *Seaboyer* in that it limits the exclusion of evidence to that used to invoke the "twin myths".[961]

When referring to s. 276(2) Gonthier J. writes

---

[954] Para. 24.

[955] Above note 657.

[956] Para 28. For further discussion of *Mills* see Chapter 1.

[957] Paras. 32-33.

[958] Para. 33.

[959] See too R.J. Delisle, "Adoption, *Sub-silentio*, of the Paciocco Solution to Rape Shield Laws", (2000) 36 C.R. (5th) 254.

[960] The Court noted that in *Crosby*, [1995] 2 S.C.R. 912 it had admitted such evidence under s. 276 because it was inextricably linked to a prior statement that was relevant to the complainant's credibility (para. 36).

[961] Paras. 34-35.

If evidence is not barred by s. 276(1) because it is tendered to support a permitted inference, the judge must still weigh its probative value against its prejudicial effect to determine its admissibility.[962]

Although the Supreme Court has determined the issue of constitutionality, it seems very likely that *Darrach* has not resolved the question of the proper application of ss. 276(1) and (2), especially in the context of prior sexual history with the accused where the issue is consent. We have seen that the Court in *Darrach* at one point says that such evidence is not relevant, then in the next breath says it may be admitted. Towards the end of the judgment this is put in yet another way:

> Evidence of prior sexual activity will rarely be relevant to support a denial that sexual activity took place or to establish consent .... As the Court affirmed in *R. v. Ewanchuk*...the determination of consent is "only concerned with the complainant's perspective. The approach is purely subjective." Actual consent must be given for each instance of sexual activity.

Here the Court admits that the evidence of prior sexual history will sometimes be relevant to establish consent, but this will be rare. The Court determined in *Ewanchuk* (1999)[963] that consent is a matter of the subjective perspective of the complainant and that consent must be given for each sexual activity. This is a troubling passage. *Ewanchuk* surely could not have decided that the complainant's evidence is determinative in every case on the issue of consent.

That judges have different views on the issue of the relevance and probative value of evidence of prior sexual history with the accused on the issue of consent is reflected in the views of the Ontario Court of Appeal in *Darrach*, which were not addressed in the Supreme Court. According to Morden A.C.J.O. for the Court:[964]

> It will likely be that evidence of previous sexual activity with the accused will satisfy the requirements of admissibility in s. 276(2) more often than that relating to sexual activity with others. This does not mean that this evidence should always be admitted.[965]

Trial judges appear to regularly admit evidence of a prior or ongoing relationship where there is a viable issue of consent. Otherwise the trial would be devoid of context and potentially unfair to accused. Where evidence of prior sexual history is tendered under s. 276(2) on the issue of mistaken belief in consent the relevancy hurdle will now have to be weighed in the light of the several new substantive limits on that defence imposed by the Supreme Court in *Ewanchuk*.[966]

---

[962] Para. 38. The Court also determined, *ibid.*, that the word "significant" added by Parliament to "probative value" did not raise the threshold such that it was unfair to accused.

[963] (1999), 22 C.R. (5th) 1 (S.C.C.).

[964] (1998), 13 C.R. (5th) 283 (Ont. C.A.). Osborne and Doherty JJ.A. concurred.

[965] At 299.

[966] Above note 963. See Stuart, *Canadian Criminal Law. A Treatise* (4th ed., 2001) c. 4 and "Ewanchuk: Asserting No Means No at the Expense of Fault and Proportionality Principles", (1999) 22 C.R. (5th) 393.

(ii) *Excluding to ensure fair trial*

It also now seems clear that a defence counsel can rely on the right to a fair trial to challenge an established rule of evidence, under which Crown evidence has previously been admissible. In two important decisions in the Supreme Court of Canada this has resulted in a much wider discretion to exclude evidence than had hitherto been recognized. Mr. Justice La Forest has suggested[967] that

> this does not, any more than does the common law, prevent the admission in evidence of matters that are damaging to the accused as opposed to unfair. What it may do is to encourage the flexibility which some judges were (wrongly in my view) reluctant to exercise at common law; see in this context R.J. Delisle, "Evidence — Judicial Discretion and Rules of Evidence — Canada Evidence Act, s. 12: *Corbett v. The Queen*" (1988), 67 Can. Bar Rev. 706.[968]

In *Corbett* (1988)[969] the issue was whether the long-standing rule in s. 12 of the Canada Evidence Act[970] under which the Crown may adduce evidence of prior convictions as they relate to credibility violated the accused's right to a fair trial. Under s. 12(1) any witness

> may be questioned as to whether he has been convicted of any offence and upon being so questioned, if he either denies the fact or refuses to answer, the opposite party may prove such conviction.

Prior to *Corbett*, the generally accepted interpretation[971] was that the trial judge had no discretion to exclude evidence of an accused's previous convictions on the basis of undue prejudice to the accused. In *Corbett* the unanimous opinion of the six justices who heard the appeal was that s. 12 did not offend the accused's right to a fair trial under s. 7 or 11(d). It seems likely that the section would not have survived the s. 7 challenge had not four justices construed the section as allowing the trial judge discretion to disallow cross-examination of an accused as to prior convictions.[972]

The lead judgment in *Corbett* was delivered by Chief Justice Dickson.[973] Section 7 did not deprive the accused of a fair trial in the sense that the introduction of such evidence would divert the jury from the task of deciding the case on the basis of admissible evidence legally relevant to the proof of the charge faced by the accused. There was perhaps a risk that, if told of the fact that the accused had a criminal record, the jury would make more than it should of that fact. But concealing the prior criminal record of an accused who testified would deprive the jury of information relevant to credibility and create a much more serious risk that the jury would be presented with a misleading picture. It was preferable to trust the good sense of the jury and give them all the information, but at the same time a clear direction regarding the extent of its probative value. In "unusual

---

[967] *Thomson Newspapers*, above note 4.
[968] At 51-52.
[969] (1988), 64 C.R. (3d) 1 (S.C.C.).
[970] R.S.C. 1985, c. C-5.
[971] See, for example, *Stratton* (1978), 42 C.C.C. (2d) 449 (Ont. C.A.).
[972] This is express in a brief concurring judgment of Beetz J., above note 969, at 23.
[973] Beetz and Lamer JJ. concurred.

circumstances where a mechanical application of s. 12 would undermine the right to a fair trial''[974] a trial judge had discretion to exclude evidence of prior convictions on the basis set out by Mr. Justice La Forest.

La Forest J., who dissented on the facts,[975] held that statute rules of evidence had to be interpreted in light of the organizing principle of the law of evidence that all relevant evidence is admissible:

> subject to a discretion to exclude matters that may unduly prejudice, mislead or confuse the trier effect, take up too much time, or should otherwise be excluded on clear grounds of law or policy.[976]

The language of s. 12 did not require the trial judge to omit all convictions, but left room for an exercise of a sound judicial discretion that was independent of the statute. Among the most important factors to be taken into account in assessing probative value and potential prejudice were the nature of the previous conviction and its remoteness from or nearness to the present charge.[977]

In *Potvin* (1989),[978] the accused and two others, D and T had been convicted of first degree murder. The Crown had proceeded against the accused first, and called D as a witness. Although D had testified at the preliminary inquiry he refused to testify at the trial. The transcript of D's testimony at the preliminary had been received into evidence at trial under what is now s. 715 of the Criminal Code which specifically provided that in such circumstances:

> Where it is proved that his evidence was taken in the presence of the accused, it may be read as evidence in the proceedings without further proof.

In the Supreme Court, the Charter challenge to s. 715 failed. Wilson J.[979] held that the admission of previous testimony would not be contrary to s. 7 provided there had been an opportunity to cross-examine when the evidence had been originally given:

> It is, in my view, basic to our system of justice, that the accused have had a full opportunity to cross-examine the witness when the previous testimony was taken if a transcript of such testimony is to be introduced as evidence in a criminal trial for the purpose of convicting the accused. This is in accord with the traditional view that it is the opportunity to cross-examine and not the fact of cross-examination which is crucial if the accused is to be treated fairly. As Professor Delisle has noted:

---

[974] Above note 969, at 118.

[975] At a first degree murder trial his previous criminal record had been admitted including a previous conviction of murder. La Forest J. would have excluded the murder conviction. The majority through Dickson C.J. held that the discretion should not be exercised, given that the accused had deliberately attacked the credibility of Crown witnesses, largely on the basis of their prior records. See comment by R.J. Delisle in (1988), 67 *Can. Bar Rev.* 706 at 709-710.

[976] Above note 969, at 33-34 — a much wider discretion than that recognized by the majority in *Wray*, above note 359.

[977] *Ibid.*, at 52. In the case of the offences of theft and stolen property there are anomalous rules in ss. 359 and 360 of the Criminal Code allowing evidence of bad character and prior criminal record. Courts seem prepared to hold these provisions to be contrary to s. 7 or to read them down: *Hewitt* (1986), 55 C.R. (3d) 42 (Man. C.A.); *Guyett* (1989), 72 C.R. (3d) 383 (Ont. C.A.) and *Hudyma* (1988), 46 C.C.C. (3d) 88 (Ont. Dist. Ct.).

[978] (1989), 68 C.R. (3d) 193 (S.C.C.), criticized by R.J. Delisle, C.R. *ibid.*, pp. 194-195.

[979] Lamer and Sopinka JJ. concurred.

> If the opposing party has had an opportunity to fully cross-examine he ought not to be justified in any later complaint if he did not fully exercise that right.[980]

However, Wilson J. further held that the trial judge has under s. 715 discretion to exclude previous testimony even though the statutory conditions have been met. This was a discretion not confined to circumstances where the prohibitive worth of the evidence is minimal. A new trial was ordered so that the trial judge could properly exercise his discretion. La Forest J.[981] gave a concurring judgment preferring to find the discretion under the ordinary principles under the law of evidence which allow a trial judge to exclude admissible evidence if "its prejudicial effect substantially outweighs its probative value."[982]

Section 715.1 of the Criminal Code, enacted in 1987,[983] provides for the admission in child abuse cases of a videotaped statement where the complainant is under 18, provided that the videotape was made "within a reasonable time after the alleged offence" and that the complainant "while testifying, adopts the contents of the videotape." Some early s. 7 attacks succeeded at the trial level.[984] However, the Supreme Court had no difficulty upholding the provision's validity in *D.O.L.* (1993).[985] It neither offended the principles of fundamental justice under s. 7 law nor the right to a fair trial under s. 11(d). It was consistent with rules against the admission of hearsay evidence and prior consistent statements. There was no constitutionally protected requirement that cross-examination be contemporaneous with the giving of evidence and the judicial discretion in the section allowed a trial judge to edit or refuse admission where its prejudicial effect outweighed the probative value.[986]

The new power in s. 486(2.1) of the Criminal Code enacted to enable a young complainant in a sexual case to testify behind a screen also survived Charter scrutiny by the Supreme Court in *Levogiannis* (1993).[987] The fact that the complainant's giving of evidence might be facilitated in no way restricted or impaired an accused's ability to cross-examine. The provision provided a very limited exception and specifically for judicial discretion.

The Supreme Court in *Harrer* (1995)[988] is now the leading authority on an overriding discretion to exclude evidence to ensure trial fairness. The majority ruling of Mr. Justice LaForest in *Harrer* is that even where there was no Charter breach, a trial judge has a discretion to exclude evidence as an adjunct to the right to a fair trial under s. 11(d) or as a principle of fundamental justice under s. 7

---

[980] Above note 978, at 230.
[981] Dickson C.J. concurred.
[982] Above note 978, at 244.
[983] S.C. 1987, c. 24 [now R.S.C. 1985, c. 19 (3rd Supp.)].
[984] See, for example, *Thompson* (1989), 68 C.R. (3d) 328 (Alta. Q.B.).
[985] (1993), 25 C.R. (4th) 285 (S.C.C.).
[986] See generally, Nicholas Bala and Hilary McCormack, "Accommodating the Criminal Process to Child Witnesses . . .", (1993) 25 C.R. (4th) 341. See earlier Chapter 1 for consideration of the majority's rejection of the gender disparity issue recognized by L'Heureux-Dubé J. (Gonthier J. concurring).
[987] (1993), 25 C.R. (4th) 325 (S.C.C.).
[988] (1995), 42 C.R. (4th) 269 (S.C.C.). See too *White*, above note 556.

rather than under s. 24(1) or s. 24(2). The minority through McLachlin J. recognized the same discretion but found it under the common law or s. 24(1). The ruling is *obiter*. Both justices found that admission would not render the trial unfair in the circumstances.[989]

---

[989] The decision is fully reviewed in Chapter 11. What is startling is that the discretion in *Harrer* was recognized respecting evidence obtained by unfair police methods in disregard of previous rulings respecting ss. 24(1) and (2).

3

Section 8: Right to be Secure Against Unreasonable Search or Seizure[1]

In October 1980, the draft s. 8 of the proposed Charter read:

> Everyone has the right not to be subjected to search or seizure except on grounds and in accordance with procedures established by law.

In response[2] to complaints by civil libertarians that this would enshrine the status quo, and would not curb governmental power to enact unreasonable search and seizure laws, s. 8 was re-drafted in February 1981 to its present wording:

> Everyone has the right to be secure against unreasonable search or seizure.

The French version focuses on "abusive" rather than merely "unreasonable" search and seizure:

> Chacun a droit à la protection contre les fouilles les perquisitions ou les saisies abusives.

Section 8 differs from the more elaborate Fourth Amendment to the United States Constitution:

> The right of the people to be secure in their persons, houses, papers and effects, against unreasonable searches and seizures, shall not be violated, and no warrants shall issue, but upon probable cause, supported by oath or affirmation, and particularly describing the place to be searched, and the persons or things to be seized.

---

[1] In this chapter I am indebted to an unpublished Queen's University LL.M. thesis by Glen Luther, *Warrantless Search and Seizure in Canada* (1986). Some of the material in this chapter first appeared in Stuart, "The Unfortunate Dilution of Section 8 Protection: Some Teeth Remain", (1999) 25 *Queen's L.J.* 65.

[2] See E.G. Ewaschuk, "Search and Seizure: Charter Implications" (1982), 28 C.R. (3d) 153.

Before examining judicial interpretation of the constitutional requirement of reasonableness, it will be helpful to sketch the picture of existing powers to search and seize.

1. LEGAL POWERS TO SEARCH AND SEIZE

(a) Statutory

Most powers to search or seize in Canada are statutory. There are literally hundreds of search powers under various provincial statutes. Noticeably wide powers of stop, inspection and seizure are, for example, to be found under various provincial Highways, Traffic and Liquor Acts.

Powers to search and seize under the Criminal Code are comparatively limited and appear haphazard. The major power is a general search warrant provision.[3] Under s. 487(1):

> A justice who is satisfied by information on oath in Form 1 that there are reasonable grounds to believe that there is in a building, receptacle or place
>
> (a) anything on or in respect of which any offence against this Act or any other Act of Parliament has been or is suspected to have been committed,
> (b) anything that there are reasonable grounds to believe will afford evidence with respect to the commission of an offence, or will reveal the whereabouts of a person who is believed to have committed an offence, against this Act or any other Act of Parliament,
> (c) anything that there are reasonable grounds to believe is intended to be used for the purpose of committing any offence against the person for which a person may be arrested without warrant, or
> (c.1) any offence-related property,
>
> may at any time issue a warrant under his hand authorizing a person named therein or a peace officer
>
> (d) to search the building, receptacle or place for any such thing and to seize it, and
> (e) subject to any other Act of Parliament, to, as soon as practicable, bring the thing seized before, or make a report in respect thereof to, the justice or some other justice for the same territorial division in accordance with section 489.1.

Under the scheme of s. 487(1), as judicially interpreted,[4] there are three broad requirements of a valid search warrant:

1. The informant must present the justice with an information upon oath which provides sufficient factual details to confer jurisdiction under s. 487(1)(a), (b), (c) or (c.1);
2. The justice must act judicially in her independent assessment of the facts and in exercising her discretion as to whether to issue a search warrant; and
3. The warrant to search must contain sufficient description of the objects of the search.

---

[3] Sections 487-489.

[4] See, for example, *Gillis* (1982), 1 C.C.C. (3d) 545 (Que. S.C.); *Church of Scientology* (1987), 31 C.C.C. (3d) 449 (Ont. C.A.), *Harris* (1987), 57 C.R. (3d) 356 (Ont. C.A.); *Conrad* (1989), 72 C.R. (3d) 364 (Alta. C.A.) and *Sanchez* (1994), 32 C.R. (4th) 269 (Ont. Gen. Div.).

Whether an information or search warrant contains sufficient details will necessarily be a matter of judgment for the reviewing justice or for a judge on a motion to quash. Rulings have often turned on their context. Courts have, for example, not required much specificity for a complex fraud investigation[5] or for raids for obscene books.[6] However more detail has been required respecting requests to seize videotapes and photographs from news media following street riots.[7] In reviewing sufficiency[8] an appeal court may amplify the record by considering issues of fraud, non-disclosure, misleading evidence and new evidence[9] to determine whether there was a proper basis for issuing the warrant. Deception as to the reasonable grounds relied on, especially respecting the reliability of confidential informants, has been a frequent basis for declarations of invalidity.[10]

Since an amendment in 1985,[11] there has been a procedure for authorization over the telephone or other means of telecommunication where a peace officer believes that an indictable offence has been committed and that it would be impracticable to appear personally before a justice. As our courts[12] have consistently interpreted "a building, receptacle or place" not to include a person, Criminal Code search warrants are generally not available in respect of searches of the person. However, there are now two special warrant powers to search the person. A carefully limited s. 256 allows for a search warrant for a blood sample where a person is reasonably believed to have caused bodily harm through impaired driving and is unable to consent to the taking of a sample. In 1995, following all party consent, Parliament enacted in just one day a power for provincial court judges to issue warrants to obtain bodily substances for forensic

---

[5] See, for example, the *Scientology* ruling, above note 4.

[6] In *Harris*, the Court authorized the seizure of "any films in the adult section which appeared from the circumstances in which they were discovered to be similar in content to the named films and which were found to be such after viewing them on the premises" (at 370).

[7] *C.B.C. v. B.C.* (1994), 32 C.R. (4th) 256 (B.C. S.C.) but compare *C.B.C. et al.* (1992), 17 C.R. (4th) 198 (Ont. Gen. Div.).

[8] A recent study of 100 search warrants issued over a two to three week period at the Old City Hall Courts in Toronto reaches the disturbing conclusion that 69% were invalid due to defects in the information and/or warrant : Casey Hill, Scott Hutchinson and Leslie Pringle, "Search Warrants: Protection or Illusion?", (2000) 28 C.R. (5th) 89.

[9] *Garofoli* (1990), 60 C.C.C. (3d) 161 (S.C.C.), applied by Rosenberg J.A. in *Hosie* (1996), 49 C.R. (4th) 1 (Ont. C.A.). See too full discussion of amplification of the record by Cromwell J.A. in *Morris* (1998), 23 C.R. (5th) 354 (N.S. C.A.). See now *Araujo* (2000), 38 C.R. (5th) 307 (S.C.C.).

[10] *Hosie*, above note 9, *Donaldson* (1990), 58 C.C.C. (3d) 294 (B.C. C.A.) and *Monroe* (1998), 8 C.R. (5th) 324 (B.C. C.A.). See, however, decisions that there was a sufficient basis for the warrant despite evidence of deception: *Morris*, above note 9, and *Gordon* (1999), 28 C.R. (5th) 168 (Man. C.A.).

[11] Section 487.1, enacted by R.S.C. 1985 (1st Supp.), c. 27, s. 69.

[12] *Laporte v. Laganière* (1972), 18 C.R.N.S. 357 (Que. Q.B.); *Miller* (1987), 38 C.C.C. (3d) 252 (Ont. C.A.); *Tomaso* (1988), 70 C.R. (3d) 152 (Ont. C.A.) and *Legere* (1988), 43 C.C.C. (3d) 502 (N.B. C.A.).

DNA analysis in the investigation of certain listed offences such as murder, assault, sexual assault, robbery, kidnapping and arson.[13]

The only express Code powers to search and seize without warrant are in respect of a strange assortment of specific offences: weapons,[14] common gaming house,[15] impaired driving,[16] suspected stolen timber,[17] cockpits'[18] and counterfeit money.[19] There are no general Criminal Code powers to stop and search persons on streets or in vehicles. Under the Federal Drugs Acts[20] there are, however, wide powers to search without warrant which include powers to search persons.

(b) Common Law

There are three important powers to search at common law:

(i) *Incident to arrest*

The Ontario Court of Appeal has for many years relied on the following summary of the power by Mr. Justice Martin:

> At common law there is no power to search premises[21] without a warrant (or with a warrant except for stolen goods) save as incident to a lawful arrest. After making a lawful arrest, an officer has the right to search the person arrested and take from his person any property which he reasonably believes is connected with the offence charged, or which may be used as evidence against the person arrested on the charge, or any weapon or instrument that might enable the arrested person to commit an act of violence or effect his escape . . .[22]

This common law power is undoubtedly the most important and frequently exercised police power to search the person.[23] Prior to the Charter the Ontario

---

[13] Sections 487.04-487.09, discussed by Renee Pomerance, ''Bill C-104. A Practical Guide to the New DNA Warrants'', (1995) 39 C.R. (4th) 224.

[14] Sections 101(1) and 103(2).

[15] Section 199(2).

[16] Section 254(2)-(4).

[17] Section 339(3).

[18] Section 447(2).

[19] Section 462.

[20] Narcotic Control Act, R.S.C. 1985, c. N-1, ss. 10-14; Food and Drugs Act, R.S.C. 1985, c. F-27, ss. 22-27. See now Controlled Drugs and Substances Act, S.C. 1996, c-19, s. 11-17.

[21] The *Report of the Canadian Committee on Corrections (Ouimet Report)* (1969) p. 63 asserts, with little authority provided, that

> Where a person has been arrested, either with or without a warrant, the right of search extends not only to the person of the accused, but to premises under his control. In modern times, the right to search premises, no doubt, also extends to a vehicle or other means of conveyance under the control of the accused.

[22] *Rao* (1984), 40 C.R. (3d) 1 (Ont. C.A.) as adopted in *Morrison* (1987), 58 C.R. (3d) 63 at 68 (Ont. C.A.) and *Miller*, above note 12.

[23] An empirical study in the United States found that searches incident to arrest occurred at least 40 times more often than searches under warrant: American Law Institute, *Model Code of Pre-Arraignment Procedure* (1975) pp. 493-494.

Court of Appeal ruled that the search may actually precede the arrest [24] and that, although there must be reasonable grounds for the arrest, the power to search is automatic in that there need not be reasonable grounds for the search itself. [25] Few judges sought to limit the power. It was held to include the power to search for drugs by throat holds[26] and other more intrusive procedures.[27] However, in *Laporte v. Laganière* (1972),[28] Hugessen J. (as he then was) held that the power could not authorize a surgical intrusion into the accused's shoulder where the arrest had been 18 months later on another offence. The judge did, however, leave open the question of minor medical procedures such as blood tests or X-rays.[29]

Since the Charter, three decisions of the Supreme Court have asserted new contours to the power. Unfortunately the Court has been divided and the law is still in a state of flux and uncertainty.[30]

A quick reading of *Cloutier v. Langlois* (1990)[31] is that Madam Justice L'Heureux-Dubé decided for a unanimous Supreme Court that there is an automatic right for police officers to search incident to a lawful arrest which arises at common law and has survived the Canadian Charter. The Court expressly adopted the view of the Ontario Court of Appeal in *Morrison*. There are, however, several reasons for rejecting such a wide interpretation. The Supreme Court speaks with a forked tongue. Although it holds that the police need not have reasonable grounds, it determines that the power is not unlimited and can be exercised only where the police have acted with discretion, have a valid objective in pursuit of the ends of criminal justice, and have not been abusive.[32] The Charter was not specifically raised in argument. Finally, the Courts were at pains to point out that the search in question was a mere "frisk" or "pat-down" search in which the invasion of privacy was relatively minor. A lawyer was being arrested for outstanding fines and was abusive.

In its controversial decision in *Stillman* (1997)[33] Justice Cory for a 7-2 majority[34] ruled that evidence of hair samples, buccal swabs and dental impressions could not be authorised as a search incident to arrest and had therefore been obtained in violation of s. 8 of the Charter.[35] A group of teenagers consumed drugs and alcohol at a camp in the woods. The accused, aged 17, left the group

---

[24] *Debot* (1986), 54 C.R. (3d) 120 (Ont. C.A.), provided that there were reasonable grounds for the arrest and that arrest followed quickly after the search. In *Tomaso*, above note 12, the Court balked at two weeks!
[25] *Morrison*, above note 22.
[26] *Brezack* (1949), 9 C.R. 73 (Ont. C.A.).
[27] *Reynen v. Antonenko* (1975), 30 C.R.N.S. 135 (Alta. T.D.) (rectal examination by finger and sigmoidoscope).
[28] Above note 12.
[29] *Ibid.*, at 365.
[30] See further Dwight Newman, "Stripping Matters to Their Core: Intrusive Searches of the Person in Canadian Law", (1999) 4 *Can. Crim. L.R.* 85.
[31] (1990), 74 C.R. (3d) 316 (S.C.C.).
[32] *Cloutier, ibid.*, at 364-365.
[33] (1997), 5 C.R. (5th) 1 (S.C.C.).
[34] L'Heureux-Dubé J. (Gonthier J. concurring) dissented.
[35] The majority also found a violation of s. 7.

with a 14-year-old girl. When the accused arrived home that night he was obviously cold, shaken and wet from the upper thighs down. He was cut above one eye, and had mud and grass on his pants. The explanation for his condition, that he had been in a fight with five others, and his account of where he had last seen the victim, varied over time. The girl's body was found near where she had last been seen by the group. The cause of death was a wound or wounds to the head. Semen was found in her vagina and a human bite mark had been left on her abdomen.

A week later the accused was arrested for the murder. At the police station police advised his lawyers that they wished to take hair samples and teeth impressions and to question the accused. The lawyers informed the police in writing that their client had been advised not to consent to providing any bodily samples or to speak to the police without a lawyer being present. Once the lawyers left, the police took bodily samples from the accused under threat of force. A sergeant took scalp hair samples by passing a gloved hand through the accused's hair, as well as by combing, clipping and plucking hairs. The accused was made to pull some of his own pubic hair. Plasticine teeth impressions were then taken. In the absence of the accused's parents or lawyers, a police officer interviewed the accused for an hour in an attempt to obtain a statement. The accused did not say anything but sobbed throughout the interview. When he asked to see a lawyer, the interview stopped and he was permitted to call his lawyer. While waiting for his lawyer the accused was allowed to use the washroom, escorted by an officer. He blew his nose with a tissue and threw it into a waste bin. The tissue containing mucous was seized by the officer and later used for DNA testing.

The accused was released from custody but was arrested again several months later after the police had received the DNA and ondontology results. Without the accused's consent, impressions of his teeth were taken by a dentist in a procedure which took two hours. More hair was taken, as well as a saliva sample and buccal swabs.

On the issue of search incident to arrest all justices accept the authority of *Cloutier v. Langlois*. However the majority held that the common law power to search incident to arrest cannot authorise non-consensual taking of the bodily samples in question — hair, buccal swabs and dental impressions. These were searches far beyond the usual "frisk search" in issue in *Cloutier* and more intrusive than fingerprinting. Cory J. pointed out that Parliament found it necessary to enact an express Criminal Code power to obtain bodily samples under its new DNA warrant power under s. 487.05.[36] Cory J. appears to go further in adopting the view that

---

[36] Para. 43. Cory J. later remarks that the new provisions "might well meet all constitutional requirements" (at para. 92).The provisions survived a Charter challenge: *F. (S.)* (2000), 32 C.R. (5th) 79 (Ont. C.A.). See now Carol-Ann Bauman, "The DNA Data Bank: Privacy Concerns and Safeguards", (2000) 34 C.R. (5th) 39.

Searches made incidentally to an arrest are justified so that the arresting officer can be assured that the person arrested is not armed or dangerous and seizures are justified to preserve evidence that may go out of existence or be otherwise lost.[37]

Cory J. noted that *Cloutier* has been extended by lower courts to authorize the search of vehicles in the immediate vicinity of the arrest[38] and to searches not limited by necessity.[39] Observing that those searches were less intrusive, he expressly left the validity of such decisions open.[40] Cory J. expressed agreement with the reasoning and conclusion of Justice Doherty for the Ontario Court of Appeal in *Belnavis* (1996).[41] It was there held that an arrest for outstanding traffic fines did not authorise the search of the trunk of the vehicle.

In *Caslake* (1998)[42] Chief Lamer for a 4-3 majority[43] confirmed two further limits: the search incident to arrest[44] has to be truly incidental to the arrest and police must have an objectively reasonable reason relating to arrest. The majority held that here a police search of vehicle six hours after a highway arrest for marihuana possession solely because of police inventory policy was not lawful.[45]

According to Lamer C.J.[46] the most important of these limits is that the search must be truly incidental to the arrest. The police must be able to explain, within the purposes recognized in the jurisprudence (protecting the police, protecting the evidence, discovering evidence) or by reference to some other valid purpose, why they conducted a search. They do not need reasonable and probable grounds. However, they must have subjectively had some reason related to the arrest for conducting the search at the time the search was carried out, and that reason must be objectively reasonable. Delay and distance do not automatically preclude a search from being incidental to arrest, but they may cause the court to draw a negative inference that the search is not sufficiently connected. That inference may be rebutted by a proper explanation.

Here a police search of the car, even hours after the arrest, for the purpose of finding evidence which could be used at the accused's trial on the charge of possessing marihjuana for purposes of trafficking would have been well within the scope of the search incident to arrest power, as there was clearly sufficient circumstantial evidence to justify a search. However, the sole reason for the search had been the inventory policy and this was not within the legitimate purposes of search incident to arrest. The police could not rely on the fact that, objectively, a

---

[37] Per Hoyt C.J.N.B. in *Paul* (1994), 155 N.B.R. (2d) 195 (N.B. C.A.) at 203, adopted by Cory J. in para. 41.

[38] *Speid* (1991), 8 C.R.R. (2d) 383 (Ont. C.A.), considered by Cory J. at para. 35.

[39] *Smellie* (1994), 95 C.C.C. (3d) 9 (B.C. C.A.), considered by Cory J. at para.37.

[40] Para. 39.

[41] (1996), 48 C.R. (4th) 320 (Ont. C.A.).

[42] (1998), 13 C.R. (5th) 1 (S.C.C.).

[43] Cory J., McLachlin J. and Major J. concurred. Bastarache J. (L'Heureux-Dubé and Gonthier JJ. concurring) dissented.

[44] Some courts have recognized a common law power to such to incident to detention: see, for example, *Lake* (1996), 113 C.C.C. (3d) 208 (Sask. C.A.).

[45] *Caslake* was applied in *Bedard* (1998), 125 C.C.C. (3d) 348 (Ont. C.A.) to authorize a warrantless search of a residence for a second suspect believed to be armed.

[46] Para. 25.

legitimate purpose for the search existed when that was not the purpose for which they searched. Agents of the state must act in accordance with the rule of law. They must not only objectively search within the permissible scope but also turn their mind to this scope before searching, and satisfy themselves that there is a valid purpose for the search. The six-hour delay in searching the vehicle was not in and of itself problematic, as there were only two officers on duty.[47]

The dissenting opinion of Bastarache J.[48] would have found that the inventory search was authorised by the common law power of search incident to arrest and thus no violation of s. 8. The arrest was lawful and the search incidental to the arrest because it was related, subordinated, to the arrest. The trial judge had been correct in finding that, regardless of the police officer's subjective belief in the purpose and justification for his inventory search, the officer had the right to search the vehicle pursuant to the common law power of search incident to an arrest. There was no onus on the Crown to establish at trial that the police officer subjectively turned his mind to whether he was properly exercising his power to search incidentally to the arrest. A search conducted for the purpose of taking an inventory can be considered as a search for a valid objective under proper circumstances. Since the test was not a subjective one, the intention of the officer was irrelevant and without any consequence, unless it was evidence of bad faith. There was no need to require the purpose of the search to be related to the purpose of the arrest or to require a subjective test.

There may have been an argument that an inventory search was lawful under *Cloutier v. Langlois*.[49] But the minority is surely wrong in suggesting the belief of the officer was irrelevant. That would run roughshod over a mountain of jurisprudence saying that in assessing the legality of police action it is crucial to take into account the actual assessment of the situation by the officer in question. Otherwise there would be few meaningful controls on the exercise of state power.

(ii) *On consent*

Police regularly purport to exercise search power on the basis of consent to the search. This principle, which has the potential to drive a cart and horses through the effort to define and control police power has been barely touched upon at common law.[50] The Law Reform Commission of Canada[51] see the issues as including the notions of true, limited and informed consent, the problem of proving consent and the question of consent by a party other than the suspect.

---

[47] The majority decided the evidence of the cocaine should not be excluded under s. 24(2) of the Charter: see below Chapter 11.

[48] Paras. 46-50.

[49] In *Nicolosi* (1998), 17 C.R. (5th) 134 (Ont. C.A.) Doherty J.A. found such a power to be authorised under s. 222(1) of the Highway Traffic Act, R.S.O. 1990, c. H.8.

[50] In *Reynen*, above note 27, the accused's positioning himself for the sigmoidoscope examination was held, most unpersuasively on the facts, to amount to consent.

[51] *Working Paper No. 30: Police Powers, Search and Seizure in Criminal Law Enforcement* (1983) p. 8.

In its pre-Charter ruling in *Dedman* (1985),[52] the Supreme Court agreed that the notion of consent should be approached carefully in the policing context. The Court rejected the ruling of the Ontario Court of Appeal in the Court below that the accused's compliance with the police signal to stop at a roadblock could be regarded as voluntary such that there had been a legal search on consent. Both judgments rest on the coercive character of police action. According to Le Dain J.:

> Because of the intimidating nature of police action and uncertainty as to the extent of police powers, compliance in such circumstances cannot be regarded as voluntary in any meaningful sense.[53]

Chief Justice Dickson agreed, noting that submission to the apparent exercise of police authority could not be characterized as consensual unless it was "clear to the person at the time that he was free to refuse to comply."[54]

Since any issue of consent is personal to the person consenting, it would appear obvious that a consent search could only be properly authorized by the person whom or whose property is searched. There is a holding from the Ontario Court of Appeal to this effect,[55] but otherwise surprisingly little authority.[56]

(iii) *Within the general scope of police duties under statute or common law and the interference with liberty is reasonably necessary, having regard to the nature of the liberty interest interfered with and the importance of the public purpose (Ancillary powers doctrine)*

This broad common law power, developed in the English *Waterfield* decision,[57] was adopted by the Supreme Court in *Dedman* (1985).[58] Le Dain J. for the majority[59] held that it authorized a random vehicle stop program to detect impaired drivers even though there was at the time no statutory authority for the program.[60] In a strong dissent, Chief Justice Dickson[61] was of the view that general duties of police officers could not provide the foundation for common law authority:

> It has always been a fundamental tenet of the rule of law in this country that the police, in carrying out their general duties as law enforcement officers of the state, have limited powers and are entitled to interfere with the liberty or property of the citizen only to the extent authorized by law.[62]

---

[52] (1985), 46 C.R. (3d) 193 (S.C.C.).
[53] *Ibid.*, at 215.
[54] *Ibid.*, at 200.
[55] See *Kenny*, below note 136.
[56] See P.G. Barton, "Consent by Others to Search Your Place", (1993) 35 *Crim. L.J.* 441.
[57] [1964] 1 Q.B. 164.
[58] Above note 52. But see now *Kokesch*, below note 158.
[59] McIntyre, Lamer and Wilson JJ. concurred.
[60] See discussion below, Chapter 4.
[61] Beetz and Chouinard JJ. concurred.
[62] Above note 52, at 200-201.

. . .

> A police officer is not empowered to execute his or her duty by unlawful means. The public interest in law enforcement cannot be allowed to override the fundamental principle that all public officials, including the police, are subject to the rule of law. To find that arbitrary police action is justified simply because it is directed at the fulfilment of police duties would be to sanction a dangerous exception to the supremacy of law. It is the function of the legislature, not the courts, to authorize arbitrary police action that would otherwise be unlawful as a violation of rights traditionally protected at common law.[63]

The Law Reform Commission of Canada,[64] following by far the most thorough review of the law and practice relating to search and seizure in Canada, has recommended the adoption of a comprehensive new legislative scheme. Its call should be heeded. As the minority in *Dedman* put it, uncertain common law power threatens civil liberties. Greater certainty is also in the police interest. Police officers are often called upon to act on the spur of the moment in many varied and often dangerous situations. Despite the huge array of statutory powers to search in Canada, there are still large areas very important to police enforcement, where the scope of power is still hotly disputed by courts. It is not satisfactory, for example, that the power of entry into a dwelling house in cases of domestic violence, so fraught with danger to the police, is still unclear.[65]

Few would not applaud Chief Justice Lamer for the Supreme Court in *Godoy* (1998)[66] for recognizing a police power to enter a dwelling house to investigate a disconnected 911 call. However the Supreme Court raises wider issues in relying not on a narrow common law power to intervene to protect life and limb[67] but rather on a broad "ancillary powers" doctrine. According to Chief Justice Lamer for the full Court

> The accepted test for evaluating the common law powers and duties of the police was set out in *Waterfield,* supra (followed by this Court in *R. v. Stenning*, [1970] S.C.R. 631 (S.C.C.); *R. v. Knowlton*, [1974] S.C.R. 443 (1973), (S.C.C.); and *R. v. Dedman*, [1985] 2 S.C.R. 2 (S.C.C.)). If police conduct constitutes a *prima facie* interference with a person's liberty or property, the court must consider two questions: first, does the conduct fall within the general scope of any duty imposed by statute or recognized at common law; and second, does the conduct, albeit within the general scope of such a duty, involve an unjustifiable use of powers associated with the duty.[68]

The Court has in fact been anything but consistent in relying on the ancillary powers doctrine. The Court did not even refer to such a possibility when it refused

---

[63] *Ibid.*, at 204-205.

[64] *Report 33: Recodifying Criminal Procedure* (1991) Vol. 1. This first title deals comprehensively with "Search and Related Matters".

[65] See, for example, *Custer* (1984), 12 C.C.C. (3d) 372 (Sask. C.A.) and *Miller* (1986), 25 C.C.C. (3d) 554 (Sask. C.A.).

[66] (1998) 21 C.R. (5th) 205 (S.C.C.).

[67] Such a power was used to authorise forcible entry into an apartment in response to a call not emanating from the accused's apartment: *Nicholls* (1999), 28 C.R. (5th) 180 (Ont. C.A.).

[68] Para. 12.

to authorise search powers for a weapons seizure warrant (*Colet*),[69] a warrantless perimeter search for drugs (*Kokesch*),[70] seizure of bodily samples for DNA samples (*Stillman*)[71] or warrantless entry into a trailer to investigate a murder (*Feeney*).[72]

If the Court is consistent in the future in resorting to the ancillary powers doctrine it will always be open to the Crown to argue that, although there was no specific common law or statutory authority for the search, it was lawful as reasonably necessary to police duty. Since illegal searches are automatically violations of s. 8[73] the ancillary powers doctrine may therefore markedly weaken s. 8 protection. Unless courts are cautious in applying the ancillary powers doctrine, s. 8 challenges will become the occasion to authorise state action after the event which cuts across many of the principles Chief Justice Dickson held so dearly in *Hunter*.

Such a fact-specific *ex post facto* inquiry seems far too vague and speculative and a matter best left to Parliament after full debate. Both citizens and the police officer need to know in advance what the powers of the state are. Such criticism seems equally applicable to the carefully crafted approach to the justification portion of the ancillary powers doctrine by Justice Doherty for the Ontario Court of Appeal in *Simpson* (1993).[74] The Court decided that the ancillary powers doctrine will allow for detention for brief questioning on articulable cause but not in all circumstances. The distinctions are subtle:

> I should not be taken as holding that the presence of an articulable cause renders any detention for investigative purposes a justifiable exercise of a police officer's common law powers. The inquiry into the existence of an articulable cause is only the first step in the determination of whether the detention was justified in the totality of the circumstances and consequently a lawful exercise of the officer's common law powers as described in *Waterfield*, supra, and approved in *Dedman*, supra. Without articulable cause, no detention to investigate the detainee for possible criminal activity could be viewed as a proper exercise of the common law power. If articulable cause exists, the detention may or may not be justified. For example, a reasonably based suspicion that a person committed some property-related offence at a distant point in the past, while an articulable cause, would not, standing alone, justify the detention of that person on a public street to question him or her about that offence. On the other hand, a reasonable suspicion that a person had just committed a violent crime and was in flight from the scene of that crime could well justify some detention of that individual in an effort to quickly confirm or refute the suspicion. Similarly, the existence of an articulable cause that justified a brief detention, perhaps to ask the person detained for identification, would not necessarily justify a more intrusive detention complete with physical restraint and a more extensive interrogation.

Doherty J.A. has since held for the Ontario Court of Appeal that the ancillary powers doctrine can justify a warrantless entry and search of a residence as

---

[69] (1981), 19 C.R. (3d) 84 (S.C.C.).

[70] (1990), 1 C.R. (4th) 62 (S.C.C.).

[71] Above note 33.

[72] (1997), 7 C.R. (5th) 101 (S.C.C.).

[73] See below notes 156-158.

[74] (1993), 20 C.R. (4th) 1 (Ont. C.A.), discussed further in Chapter 4.

incident to an arrest to preserve safety,[75] but not large scale police checkpoint stops of motorcycle gangs given the liberty interference and the nature of the detention.[76]

2. MINIMUM CONSTITUTIONAL STANDARDS: HUNTER V. SOUTHAM INC. (1984)[77]

In *Hunter v. Southam*, Mr. Justice Dickson, for a unanimous Supreme Court, asserted a "purposive" approach to the interpretation of the Charter.[78] When the Court turned to an examination of s. 8, it first determined the nature of the interest the section was meant to protect. Adopting the reasoning of Justice Stewart of the United States Supreme Court in *Katz v. U.S.* (1967),[79] the interests protected were found to be wider than the right to enjoy property free of trespass at common law and to extend at least so far as to protect a right of privacy, described as "the right to be left alone by other people."[80] The guarantee of security from unreasonable search and seizure only protected against a reasonable expectation of privacy. An assessment would have to be made whether in a particular case the public's interest in being left alone by government had to give way to the government's interest in advancing its goals, notably those of law enforcement.[81]

Later in *Dyment* (1988),[82] the Court further expanded the privacy interest as follows:

> Society has come to realize that privacy is at the heart of liberty in a modern state . . . Grounded in man's physical and moral autonomy, privacy is essential for the well-being of the individual. For this reason alone, it is worthy of constitutional protection, but it also has profound significance for the public order. The restraints imposed on government from prying into the lives of the citizen go to the essence of a democratic state.
>
> . . . .
>
> Those who have reflected on the matter have spoken of zones or realms of privacy . . . involving territorial or spatial aspects, those related to the person, and those that arise in the information context. All three, it seems to me, are directly implicated in the present case.[83]

---

[75] *Golub* (1997), 9 C.R. (5th) 98 (Ont. C.A.).

[76] *Brown* v. *Durham* (1998), 21 C.R. (5th) 1 (Ont. C.A.). The Quebec Court of Appeal relied on the ancillary powers doctrine to hold legal a police roadblock to try to apprehend escaping bank robbers: *Murray* (1999), 32 C.R. (5th) 253 (Que. C.A.) (per Fish J.A.). However it has been held that the doctrine cannot authorise a perimeter court security programme: *Lindsay* (1999), 29 C.R. (5th) 386 (Man. C.A.).

[77] (1984), 41 C.R. (3d) 97 (S.C.C.).

[78] Above, Chapter 1.

[79] 389 U.S. 347 (1967).

[80] Above note 77, at 113.

[81] *Ibid.*, at 114.

[82] (1988), 66 C.R. (3d) 348 (S.C.C.).

[83] *Ibid.*, at 359-360. Dickson C.J. concurred. Lamer J. (Beetz and Wilson JJ. concurring) concurred on this point (at 353). See too *Mills* (1999), 28 C.R. (5th) 207 (S.C.C.) at paras. 77-95.

In *Hunter*, the Supreme Court decided that the purpose of s. 8 required that unjustified searches be prevented. It was not enough that a determination be made after the fact. The Court asserted three constitutional standards. It first established a basic requirement of a warrant and then declared Charter standards for such warrants:

1. Where "feasible" prior authorization is a "precondition for a valid search and seizure."[84]

As Stewart J. had held in *Katz*, a warrantless search was *prima facie* "unreasonable" under s. 8. The party seeking to justify a warrantless search would have to rebut "this presumption of unreasonableness."[85]

2. The person authorizing the breach of privacy must make the assessment "in an entirely neutral and impartial manner."

The person need not be a judge but "must at a minimum be capable of acting judicially."[86]

3. There has to be reasonable and probable grounds established upon oath to believe that an offence has been committed or that evidence will be found at the place of the search.

> The state's interest in detecting and preventing crime begins to prevail over the individual's interest in being left alone at the point where credibly-based probability replaces suspicion. History has confirmed the appropriateness of this requirement as the threshold for subordinating the expectation of privacy to the needs of law enforcement. Where the state's interest is not simply law enforcement, as, for instance, where state security is involved, or where the individual's interest is not simply his expectation of privacy, as, for instance, when the search threatens his bodily integrity, the relevant standard might well be a different one.[87]

In *Collins* (1987),[88] the Supreme Court held[89] that an accused has the burden of persuading the Court on a balance of probabilities of any Charter violation, including an infringement of s. 8. However, applying *Hunter*, the Court also held that, once the accused had demonstrated that the search was warrantless, the Crown had the "burden of showing that the search was, on a balance of probabilities, reasonable."[90] The Court then added, in a now frequently quoted dictum,

---

[84] *Ibid.*, at 115.

[85] *Ibid.*

[86] *Ibid.*, at 116.

[87] *Ibid.*, at 120. A minimum standards approach had also been asserted by the Court below: (1983), 32 C.R. (3d) 141 (Alta. C.A.). It had held that, unless there are exceptional circumstances, the requirements under the Criminal Code and at common law should be treated as minimal standards to be met before a search warrant was issued in connection with the investigation of an indictable offence. See also the trail-blazing but rarely acknowledged judgment of Belanger P.J. in *Carriere* (1983), 32 C.R. (3d) 117 (Ont. Prov. Ct.) (striking down writs of assistance).

[88] (1987), 56 C.R. (3d) 193 (S.C.C.).

[89] Above, Chapter 1.

[90] Above note 88, at 206. In Lamer J.'s concurring judgment in *Dyment*, above note 82, this persuasive burden on the Crown was reduced to being an "evidentiary burden" (at 353).

A search will be reasonable if it is authorized by law, if the law itself is reasonable and if the manner in which the search was carried out is reasonable.[91]

(a) "Search or Seizure"

The Supreme Court of Canada has confirmed that s. 8 protects an individual from unreasonable search *or seizure*.[92] Although often, as in *Hunter*, there is a search *and* seizure, s. 8 is available where there is a search without a seizure or where there has been a seizure without a search.[93]

In earlier Charter jurisprudence, judges were sometimes resistant to a wide definition of search. For example, in the course of a ruling that the taking of a sample of breath did not constitute a search (or seizure) a trial judge was content with the observation "if you are not breathing, you are not living, and there can be no search."[94] Courts now readily accept that a demand for a breath sample *is* a search, or at least a seizure.[95]

A rare definition of search was provided in this context by Judge Ayotte in *Enns* (1987):[96]

> It appears to me that the key concepts which should be applied in any given situation to determine whether what has occurred is a "search", where that issue may be in doubt, are "intrusion", "examination" and "consent". These concepts are in accord with the Supreme Court of Canada's characterization of the right protected by s. 8 of the *Charter* as the right of the individual to the reasonable expectation that his privacy will not be intruded upon by government in order to advance its goals, ". . . notably those of law enforcement" . . . The word *intrusion* implies by its very definition a lack of consent and the word *search* connotes by its very definition an examination.[97]

Lower courts have held that a police officer looking into a vehicle stopped at an intersection does not constitute a search.[98] On the other hand, it has been held that a police officer observing the accused in a cubicle in a public washroom does amount to a search,[99] as does police entry into an open residence to investigate a noise complaint.[100] It is now well accepted that audio[101] or video[102] electronic

---

[91] *Ibid.*

[92] *Dyment*, above note 82, at 362 (per La Forest J. for the Court on this point over the dissent of McIntyre J.). See also each of the judges in *Thomson Newspapers Ltd. v. Can. (Dir. of Investigation & Research)* (1990), 76 C.R. (3d) 129 (S.C.C.).

[93] *Holman* (1982), 28 C.R. (3d) 378 (B.C. Prov. Ct.). See too *Broadhurst* (1985), 24 C.C.C. (3d) 27 (per Kreever J., as he then was).

[94] *Holman*, at 382.

[95] See the extensive case law reviewed by Rick Libman, "The Admissibility of Breath Certificates. Has Rilling Survived the Charter?" (1989), 67 C.R. (3d) 372.

[96] (1987), 85 A.R. 7 (Alta. Prov. Ct.).

[97] *Ibid.*, at 362, relied on in *Hutton* (1988), 67 C.R. (3d) 356 at 362 (Alta. Prov. Ct.).

[98] *Hebb* (1985), 17 C.C.C. (3d) 545 (N.S. C.A.).

[99] *O'Flaherty* (1987), 35 C.C.C. (3d) 33 (Nfld. C.A.). Morgan J.A. dissented on this point.

[100] *Martin* (1995), 97 C.C.C. (3d) 241 (B.C. C.A.).

[101] See, for example, *Duarte (Sanelli)* (1990), 74 C.R. (3d) 281 (S.C.C.) and *Finlay* (1985), 48 C.R. (3d) 341 (Ont. C.A.).

[102] *Wong* (1990), 1 C.R. (4th) 1 (S.C.C.). See the critical comment by Marc Rosenberg, "Controlling Intrusive Police Investigation Techniques Under Section 8", C.R. *ibid.*, pp. 32-44. See generally Elliott Goldstein, "Surreptitious Video Surveillance and the Protection of Privacy" (1986), 56 C.R. (3d) 368.

interceptions of private communications by the police amount to searches subject to s. 8 standards. Whether fingerprinting following arrest can amount to a search has been left open by the Supreme Court.[103]

The definition of a "seizure" was authoritatively settled by Mr. Justice La Forest in *Dyment* (1988),[104] for a majority of five Supreme Court justices. A seizure under s. 8 is the "taking of a thing from a person by a public authority without that person's consent."[105]

A doctor, called to the scene of a highway accident, found Dyment in a bloody condition, sitting in the driver's seat of his vehicle. A police officer drove him to hospital, but did not arrest or detain him. Neither the doctor nor the officer noted any signs that the accused had been drinking. At the hospital, the doctor, when preparing to suture the accused's head, collected a sample of free-flowing blood for medical purposes. The accused did not consent to the test and was not even aware of the sample being taken, as he was concussed. The doctor handed the sample to the officer. At that time there was no Criminal Code provision requiring a person to give a sample of blood. The officer had not requested one and did not have a search warrant. The Supreme Court held that the taking of the blood sample without consent constituted a seizure under s. 8.

According to La Forest J., the use of a person's body without consent to obtain information about that person invades an area of personal privacy essential to the maintenance of human dignity. The doctor had a right to take a blood sample for medical purposes. He had no right to take it for other purposes and no right to give it to a stranger for non-medical purposes unless otherwise required by law. Any such law would be subject to Charter review. The Charter protected against a police officer taking a substance "as intimately personal as a person's blood from a person who holds it subject to a duty to respect the dignity and privacy of that person."[106] In rejecting the Crown submission that the officer had merely been given the evidence by the doctor rather than demanding or seizing it, La Forest J. said

> If I were to draw the line between a seizure and a mere finding of evidence, I would draw it logically and purposefully at the point at which it can reasonably be said that the individual had ceased to have a privacy interest in the subject matter allegedly seized.[107]

According to La Forest J. an example of a case where the individual had ceased to have a reasonable expectation of privacy was a situation where the police, after

---

[103] *Beare* (1988), 66 C.R. (3d) 97 (S.C.C.), which turned on the question of reasonable expectation of privacy. Lower court authority holds that fingerprinting is neither a search nor a seizure: *McGregor* (1983), 3 C.C.C. (3d) 200 (Ont. H.C.) and *M.H. v. R. (No. 2)* (1984), 17 C.C.C. (3d) 443 (Alta. Q.B.).

[104] Above note 82.

[105] *Ibid.*, at 362.

[106] *Ibid.*, at 363.

[107] *Ibid.*, at 364-365. The Court noted that in *Pohoretsky* (1987), 58 C.R. (3d) 113 (S.C.C.), s. 8 had been "immediately triggered" when a police officer had a blood sample taken by the doctor. The sample was not required for medical purposes and no consent was obtained.

taking the accused to hospital, obtained a sample of his blood found on the front seat of the vehicle.[108]

In Thomson Newspapers (1990)[109] and *McKinlay Transport* (1990),[110] the Supreme Court held that powers to compel the production of documents under, respectively, s. 17 of the Combines Investigation Act and s. 231(3) of the Income Tax Act, constituted seizures for the purposes of s. 8.

(b) No Reasonable Expectation of Privacy: No Section 8 Rights

(i) *Property interests crucial: Gomez test in Edwards*

The rot really set in with the Supreme Court's decision in *Edwards* (1996).[111] The accused had been arrested on a drugs charge. The drugs were later found in his girlfriend's apartment in clear violation of her s. 8 rights. The Court held that s. 8 is a personal right and that the accused could not rely on the breach of a third party's rights.[112] Furthermore the majority held that the accused had no s. 8 rights because he had no reasonable expectation of privacy in his girlfriend's apartment. Although this depended on the "totality of the circumstances" the Court nevertheless placed great weight on factors identified in the U.S. case of *Gomez* as follows:

> The factors to be considered in assessing the totality of the circumstances may include, but are not restricted to, the following:
>
>   (i)   presence at the time of the search;
>   (ii) possession or control of the property or place searched;
>   (iii) ownership of the property or place;
>   (iv) historical use of the property or item;
>   (v) the ability to regulate access, including the right to admit or exclude others from the place;
>   (vi) the existence of a subjective expectation of privacy; and
>   (vii) the objective reasonableness of the expectation.[113]

There are a number of problems with the Court's reliance on *Gomez*. The *Gomez* principles are, first and foremost, quite contrary to the *Hunter* choice to protect people rather than places. The emphasis is on protecting those with property interests rather than focusing on personal privacy. Such an emphasis is better suited to the United States, whose Constitution expressly protects property rights.[114] The two-page judgment of the U.S. Court of Appeals, Eighth Circuit, in

---

[108] The Court referred to *LeBlanc* (1981), 64 C.C.C. (2d) 31 (N.B. C.A.). In *Tomaso*, above note 12, the Ontario Court of Appeal followed *Dyment* and *Pohoretsky* in holding that there had been a seizure where police had collected blood flowing from the accused's ear at a hospital at a time when he was unconscious. In *Lunn* (1990), 61 C.C.C. (3d) 193 (B.C. C.A.), *Dyment* was distinguished where the police learnt about a blood sample taken for medicinal purposes and had seized it pursuant to a search warrant.

[109] (1990), 76 C.R. (3d) 129 (S.C.C.).

[110] (1990), 76 C.R. (3d) 283 (S.C.C.), discussed below note 336.

[111] (1996), 45 C.R. (4th) 307 (S.C.C.).

[112] See below note 145.

[113] See *United States v. Gomez*, 16 F. 3d 254 (U.S. 8th Cir., 1994), at p. 256.

[114] U.S. Constitution, amendments IV, V and XIV.

Gomez is distinguishable on its facts — the search of a vehicle suspected to be stolen. In any event, U.S. jurisprudence on search and seizure should be followed with caution in Canada. It is notoriously complex and coloured by the backdrop of an automatic exclusionary rule such that U.S. courts are cautious about not unduly hamstringing police. In Canada balancing of law enforcement interests can also be done in exercising the discretion to exclude under s. 24(2).

Edwards was held by the majority, over the vehement dissent of La Forest J., to have had no reasonable expectation of privacy. Although he was an occasional visitor, stayed over occasionally and had keys, he did not contribute to rent or household expenses and his girlfriend had authority to regulate access. He was no more than a "privileged guest". The Court attached particular significance to the fact that the accused had denied that the drugs found were his.

The majority ruling on the facts belies the majority's approval of a previous dictum[115] that a possessory interest was *not* required to establish s. 8 protection and ignores "case to meet" and right to silence issues.[116] With Justice Abella, dissenting in the Ontario Court of Appeal, the ruling also ignores the social realities of the relationship.

(ii) *Passengers in vehicles*

The full significance of the adoption of the *Gomez* focus on property interests became even clearer in the startling ruling in *Lawrence and Belnavis* (1998)[117] that a passenger in a vehicle normally has no reasonable expectation of privacy in the vehicle to even advance a s. 8 claim.

At about 8:30 p.m., a police officer stopped a speeding car with New York licence plates for speeding on the Highway 401 near Kitchener. In the car were three young women, the accused, B and L, and a teenager. When the driver of the vehicle, B, admitted she had no documentation for the vehicle the officer asked her to go to his cruiser, where he ran a computer check, suspecting that the vehicle had been stolen. B indicated that the vehicle belonged to a friend. While waiting for the information on the vehicle the officer returned to the vehicle to look for any vehicle documents in the glove compartment. This was so messy that the officer gave up. He opened the back door of the vehicle to speak to L and poked his head inside due to the highway noise. He noticed three garbage bags on the driver's side of the back seat. He could see garments with price tags on them. He asked L who owned the bags and she replied they each owned one bag. The officer looked into the trunk and discovered five more garbage bags with clothing. The officer returned to the cruiser and asked B who owned the bags. She told him the bags were in the car when she got it. At this point the computer search showed that the car was not stolen, but there was an outstanding warrant for B for unpaid traffic fines. The officer arrested B and the vehicle was towed to the police station.

---

[115] *Plant*, [1993] 3 S.C.R. 281 at 291.
[116] See Chapter 3.
[117] (1998), 10 C.R. (5th) 65 (S.C.C.).

L told the officer that the car had been given to B by her boyfriend. L and B were later charged with possession of stolen property.

The experienced trial judge, Judge Salhany, found clear s. 8 violations of the rights of both L and B. When the matter reached the Supreme Court Cory J. decided for the majority[118] that as a passenger in the vehicle L had no reasonable expectation of privacy to advance her s. 8 claim. Although L was present at the time of the search, there were few other factors which would suggest she had an expectation of privacy in the vehicle. Her connection to the vehicle was extremely tenuous. She did not own the vehicle and was merely a passenger in a car driven by a friend of the owner of the vehicle. There was no evidence that she had any control over the vehicle, nor that she had used it in the past or had any relationship with the owner or driver which would establish some special access to the vehicle or any privilege in regard it. She did not demonstrate any ability to regulate access to the vehicle. There was no evidence that she had a subjective expectation of privacy in the vehicle. There might well be other situations in which a passenger could establish a reasonable expectation of privacy in a vehicle, such as the owner-operator of a car and his or her spouse, or two people travelling together on an extended journey and sharing driving responsibilities and expenses. L could also not demonstrate a reasonable expectation of privacy in relation to the garbage bags. She did not identify one of the bags as hers, or make any gesture which suggested that she claimed one bag in particular as her own.

As driver of the vehicle with apparent permission of the owner, B had reasonable expectation of privacy in the vehicle. Her s. 8 rights under the Charter had been violated. The trial judge's finding that the officer had no reasonable and probable grounds for the search had been unreasonable, but the vehicle search without warrant violated s. 8.

What is particularly disturbing about the majority position is that it was in the face of another strong dissent, by La Forest J. According to the dissent both L and B had a reasonable expectation of privacy and s. 8 had been violated in both cases by a search on suspicion rather than reasonable and probable grounds.

Justice La Forest is particularly compelling in arguing that passengers in vehicles have a reasonable expectation of privacy. According to La Forest J., taking a drive with one's spouse, friend or anyone else permitted to do so by the owner or driver, is a common and perfectly legitimate activity in a free society and one which the citizen should generally be left free to pursue in the reasonable expectation that he or she will be left alone by the police. Drivers and passengers have an equally reasonable expectation of privacy, not only as to their person, but also with regard to any goods they may be carrying in a motor vehicle. The majority standard was vague, offered almost no protection to the citizen from interference by the police and also had grave implications for equality in the application of the law. The majority's approach drew distinctions based on the personal relationships and undermined the fact that s. 8 of the Charter applies to everyone. Since police power to search passengers depended on the relationship with the driver, the police will be forced to asked motorists irrelevant and

---

[118] Lamer C.J., L'Heureux-Dubé, Gonthier, McLachlin, and Major JJ. concurring.

unreasonable questions.[119] Justice La Forest understandably considered that it should not be the business of the police to know whether a woman sitting beside a male driver is his wife, his mistress or a friend of long standing.[120]

There is an empirical basis for concerns about discrimination in the case of vehicle stops and searches. According to research for the *Report of the Commission on Systematic Racism in the Ontario Criminal Justice System* (1995) black male residents in Metro Toronto are particularly vulnerable to police stops. About 43% of black male residents, but only 25% of white and 19% of Chinese male residents, reported being stopped in the previous two years. Significantly more black men (29%) than white (12%) or Chinese (7%) reported two or more stops.

Surely all passengers in vehicles reasonably expect some degree of privacy from police intrusion? The focus in *Lawrence and Belnavis* on who controlled the vehicle and whether L sufficiently laid claim to a particular bag seems quite beside the point. On a straight reading of *Lawrence and Belnavis* only the owner of a vehicle or those persons able to exercise control over the vehicle are likely to have s. 8 rights to protect against searches of the vehicle or its contents. Mere passengers have no such protection. This is the antithesis of a purposeful interpretation.[121]

Hopefully *Lawrence and Belnavis* will be distinguished or not applied respecting searches of the person but the language of the majority is wide. It should also be distinguished where a passenger more clearly asserts a right of ownership or possession of particular property in the vehicle such as of a purse[122] or a suitcase.

(iii) *Other contexts*

The implications of *Edwards* and *Lawrence and Belnavis* are troubling in other contexts. Like mere passengers in vehicles, do guests in houses,[123] tenants respecting apartment hallways,[124] children in their homes,[125] homeless people in shelters,[126] or indeed anyone not having rights of ownership or control, have no reasonable expectation of privacy and thus no s. 8 rights? There is much to commend the recent approach of Justice Sparrow of the Ontario Court of Justice

---

[119] Para. 67.

[120] *Ibid.*

[121] See too David Schwartz, "Front and Rear Door Exceptions to the Right to be Secure from Unreasonable Search and Seizure", (1998) 10 C.R. (5th) 100.

[122] This was an alternative basis for the grounding of s. 8 protection in *Sauve*, below note 127.

[123] In *Khuc* (2000), 142 C.C.C. (3d) 276 (B.C. C.A.) persons found in premises subject to a drugs raid sought s. 8 protection on the basis they had been babysitters. Considering the absence of *Edwards* factors, the Court held that the trial judge had been correct in refusing a *voir dire*. It might have been different, said McEachern C.J.B.C., had the accused offered to verify their babysitting position.

[124] *Laurin* (1997), 6 C.R. (5th) 201 (Ont. C.A.) (no reasonable expectation of privacy from smelling of marijuana in hallway outside apartment).

[125] *Ibid.*

[126] *Ibid.*

in *Sauvé* (1998).[127] She held that patrons of an after-hours illegal drinking establishment had a reasonable expectation of privacy. To rule otherwise, said Justice Sparrow,

> would be to permit unreasonable searches of all sorts simply by virtue of a choice to enter a non-private establishment.[128]

The Supreme Court has now held that there can be no reasonable expectation of privacy respecting Crown land in plain sight of a road,[129] a taxi office open to the public,[130] and a trespasser on unused farmland.[131] In contrast to this trend to cut off s. 8 scrutiny, Courts of Appeal have recently rejected the application of a U.S. "open fields" doctrine as inimical to the proper approach under s. 8.[132]

A majority of the Nova Scotia Court of Appeal[133] subsequently applied *Boersma* to hold that an accused cultivating marihuana in a secluded plot of his land surrounded by woods in a rural area had no reasonable expectation of privacy and thus no s. 8 protection. With the dissenting judge,[134] this situation was surely distinguishable. The police only reached the property by leaving the paved highway and travelling a few miles on a road through woods, then walking a short distance on a secondary road through woods to a clearing. The marihuana was growing within 500 feet of a residence. The narrow majority ruling pre-empted any inquiry into whether the police had reasonable belief or should have obtained a warrant. It is easier to accept rulings that there can be no reasonable expectation in discarded garbage left on the street for collection.[135] The Ontario Court of Appeal also appears sensibly realistic in holding[136] that an occupant of a hotel

---

[127] (1998), 22 C.R. (5th) 152 (Ont. Prov. Div.).

[128] At 158.

[129] *Boersma* (1994), 31 C.R. (4th) 386 (S.C.C.).

[130] *Fitt* (1996), 46 C.R. (4th) 267 (S.C.C.). See too *Joyal* (1995), 43 C.R. (4th) 317 (Que. C.A.) (persons living in 50-unit apartment building having no reasonable expectation of privacy in common entrance hall).

[131] *Lauda* (1998), 20 C.R. (5th) 316 (S.C.C.).

[132] *Kelly* (1999), 22 C.R. (5th) 248 (N.B. C.A.) and *Lauda* (1999), 25 C.R. (5th) 320 (Ont. C.A.). See supportive analysis of James Stribopoulos, "Reasonable Expectation of Privacy and "Open Fields" - Taking the American Risk Analysis Head On", (1999) 25 C.R. (5th) 351.

[133] *Patriquen* (1994), 36 C.R. (4th) 363 (N.S. C.A.). The appeal to the Supreme Court was rejected on the s. 24(2) determination: (1996), 43 C.R. (4th) 134 (S.C.C.). The Court avoided ruling on the issue of reasonable expectation of privacy for "open-space" searches.

[134] Pugsley J.A. Roscoe J.A. (Chipman J.A. concurring) wrote the majority opinion.

[135] *Krist* (1995), 42 C.R. (4th) 159 (B.C. C.A.) and *Kennedy* (1996), 3 C.R. (5th) 170 (Ont. C.A.). *Sed contra* Alan Gold who criticises *Krist* on the basis that "a citizen does *and should* have a reasonable expectation that material left for the municipal disposers will be disposed of as anticipated and not...rifled through first by the police for evidence of crime without a search warrant", (1995) 38 *Crim.L.Q.* 155 at 156-157.

[136] *Kenny* (1992), 11 C.R. (4th) 325 (Ont. C.A.). The initial finding by the hotel housekeeper would not have triggered the Charter as there was no State action until the police were called. In contrast in *Fitch* (1994), 93 C.C.C. (3d) 185 (B.C. C.A.), it was held that a check by university police to determine whether a student who had not paid his rent had abandoned his room did not involve state action which would trigger s. 8, nor did a subsequent police warrantless entry to investigate the report of stolen property in the room. The later ruling seems highly problematic. See too *Caucci* (1995), 43 C.R. (4th) 403 (Que. C.A.) (Charter not applying to vehicle stop by private security agents hired by employer to conduct surveillance of employees suspected of theft).

suite despite placing a "Do Not Disturb" sign only has a reasonable expectation of privacy respecting property not left in plain view or stored in areas not requiring daily maintenance by hotel staff.

The Supreme Court in *Plant* (1993),[137] with only McLachlin J. dissenting, held that there was no reasonable expectation of privacy in computer-retrieved records of electricity consumption kept by the City utilities commission. They did not reveal intimate details of the accused's life nor were they confidential. The majority appears inconsistent in holding that they could, however, help to provide reasonable grounds for believing that premises were being used to cultivate marihuana.

A controversial aspect of *Stillman* was the decision of a 5-4 majority that the police had violated s. 8 in seizing a tissue which the accused had used to blow his nose and had discarded. Cory J. reasoned for that majority that an abandonment by the accused of such an item would normally relinquish any privacy interest. However, contrary to the views of lower courts and the four dissenting justices,[138] Justice Cory held that different considerations arose where an accused was in custody. A person in custody had no ability to exercise the right not to consent to the taking of bodily samples which would be released through normal bodily functions.[139] There was a lower expectation of privacy after an arrest but not so low as to permit such seizures.[140]

Cory J. acknowledged that after conviction there would be a lesser expectation of privacy in custody as there would be no longer a presumption of innocence.[141] This obiter provides a window of opportunity for Charter challenges in prison settings.[142]

(c) Third Party Privacy Interests

An accused cannot rely on s. 8 guarantees based on police intrusion into the reasonable expectation of privacy of a third party. It has been held, for example, that an accused has no standing to seek exclusion of evidence on the basis of violation of the rights of a co-accused[143] nor where the premises searched were not owned or leased by the accused.[144]

The leading authority is now the Supreme Court decision in *Edwards* (1996).[145] Although the appeal as of right was limited to the issue of reasonable

---

[137] (1993), 24 C.R. (4th) 47 (S.C.C.).
[138] Major J. joined the dissenters on this point.
[139] paras. 58-59.
[140] para. 61.
[141] *Ibid.*
[142] This is in marked contrast to the quick ruling in *Conway (Weatherall)* (1993), 23 C.R. (4th) 1 (S.C.C.) that male prisoners challenging cross-gender searches had no reasonable expectation of privacy such as to trigger s. 8 consideration. See below note 350.
[143] *Sandhu* (1993), 22 C.R. (4th) 300 (B.C. C.A.).
[144] *R. v. Arason* (1992), 78 C.C.C. (3d) 1 (B.C. C.A.) and *Spinelli* (1995), 101 C.C.C. (3d) 385 (B.C. C.A.).
[145] Above note 111.

expectation of privacy, Mr. Justice Cory, speaking for five justices,[146] pronounced on the issue of third party interests.

According to the majority, a claim for relief under s. 24(2) can only be made by the person whose Charter rights have been infringed. Like all Charter rights, s. 8 is a personal right. It protects people not places. The right to challenge the legality of a search depends upon the accused establishing that his personal rights to privacy have been violated. As a general rule, two distinct inquiries must be made in relation to s. 8. First, has the accused a reasonable expectation of privacy? Second, if he has such an expectation, was the search by the police conducted reasonably? Usually the conduct of the police will only be relevant to the second inquiry. The degree of intrusion on privacy rights of third parties may be relevant to the second stage inquiry of whether the search was conducted in a reasonable manner. In the opinion of the majority, the reasonable expectation of privacy concept has worked well in Canada. It has proved to be reasonable, flexible and viable. There was no reason to abandon it in favour of the discredited rule of automatic standing for a search of a third party's premises where the Crown alleges that the accused is in possession of property which was discovered and seized.

The Supreme Court in *Edwards* has clearly determined that an accused cannot rely on a s. 8 violation of a third party to establish a breach of s. 8. La Forest J.'s persuasive reasoning has no support. However, the Court appears to have left open the possibility of a s. 7 abuse of process argument based on police abuse directed at a third party.[147] It has also been long accepted[148] that, in determining whether evidence obtained in violation of the Charter should be excluded under s. 24(2) as bringing the administration of justice into disrepute, a factor to be considered is whether there has been a larger pattern of disregard for Charter rights. A purposeful interpretation would consider the total picture of police misconduct whether this concerned the accused or others. The Supreme Court has not confronted the third party issue directly in this context but there are no Supreme Court dicta preventing such consideration.[149]

---

[146] Lamer C.J., Sopinka, McLachlin , Iacobucci and Major JJ. L'Heureux-Dubé J. and Gonthier J., in separate concurring opinions, agreed with the ruling that that there was no reasonable expectation of privacy but considered that the third party issue was not properly before the Court. La Forest J. was also of the opinion that the third party issue was not before the Court.

[147] See further the analysis of Ursela Hendel and Peter Sankoff, "*Edwards*: When Two Wrongs Might Just Make A Right", (1996) 45 C.R. (4th) 330. The authors invoke in aid *Harrer* (1995), 42 C.R. (4th) 269 (S.C.C.), here discussed in Chapters 3 and 11.

[148] See Hendall and Sankoff, above note 147, relying on *Strachan* (1989), 67 C.R. (3d) 87 (S.C.C.) at 108 and *Genest* (1989), 67 C.R. (3d) 224 (S.C.C.) at 250. Section 24(2) jurisprudence is here discussed later in Chapter 11.

[149] In *Silveira* (1995), 38 C.R. (4th) 330 (S.C.C.) at 379, La Forest J., in dissent, in determining that the breach in question was serious rejected the opinion of the Ontario Court of Appeal in the Court below that police disregard of the rights and interests of the accused's family was irrelevant. The majority in the Supreme Court admitted the evidence but did not pronounce on this third party aspect.

(d) Proper Approach to Section 8 Challenges

A s. 8 challenge can be made against the exercise or potential exercise of a search or seizure with or without warrant. As *Hunter v. Southam* made clear, the challenge can be to the law itself as in *Hunter* or, as has proved much more common, to the manner of exercise in the particular case.

Collins was of the latter type. The challenge was to a warrantless search for drugs. The police had purported to act under a power given to them under the Narcotic Control Act but there had been no challenge to the power itself. This was the context for the Lamer formula that a search will be reasonable if authorized by law, if the law is reasonable and if the manner in which the search was conducted is reasonable.[150] This dictum purports to state a general approach but does not adequately cover s. 8 principles. The shorthand reference to "reasonable" may be confusing. It must be remembered that *Collins* confirmed that warrantless searches are presumed to be unreasonable. It is thus clear that unreasonable includes a breach of *any* of the *Hunter v. Southam* standards.

Given present jurisprudence on s. 8, it can be stated in summary that a s. 8 challenge to a search or seizure law or its execution will succeed if the search or seizure is illegal, or if there is a breach of the constitutional warrant requirement, the constitutional minimum standards for warrants, or the constitutional minimum standards for warrantless searches or is conducted in an otherwise unreasonable manner. Each of these dimensions will be reviewed in turn.

(e) Illegal Search or Seizure Necessarily Unreasonable Under Section 8

When the Supreme Court in *Hunter* asserted a purposive approach to the Charter, it saw the Charter as an instrument intended to "constrain governmental action" inconsistent with Charter rights and freedoms but not in itself an "authorization for governmental action."[151] It would seem to be a necessary corollary that a search or seizure that is not legal under a statute or common law can never be constitutional.

Provincial Courts of Appeal were long resistant. In an often-quoted dictum in *Heisler* (1984),[152] the Alberta Court of Appeal held that "it does not follow that because a search is illegal it must therefore be unreasonable."[153] In *Heisler*, an illegal search of the accused's purse prior to her entering a rock concert where there were no reasonable grounds to suspect was not necessarily unreasonable. In a leading decision on search warrants, Mr. Justice Martin for the Ontario Court of Appeal, in *Harris* (1987),[154] accepted that a search or seizure under a search warrant "invalid in substance" would be unreasonable under s. 8 but added:

---

[150] Above note 88.
[151] Above note 77, at 111, and Chapter 1.
[152] (1984), 11 C.C.C. (3d) 475 (Alta. C.A.).
[153] *Ibid.*, at 477. In contrast, in *Dyment* (1986), 49 C.R. (3d) 338 (P.E.I. C.A.), MacDonald J.A. suggests that it "would appear to be much more logical to hold that all illegal searches are also unreasonable than to hold some illegal searches as being reasonable" (at 346).
[154] Above note 4.

> I find it difficult to think, however, that minor or technical defects in the warrant automatically make an ensuing search or seizure unreasonable under s. 8 of the Charter.[155]

At face value, the ruling in *Collins*[156] that a search that is not authorized by law will be unreasonable under s. 8 determined the matter against the more flexible view preferred by Provincial Courts of Appeal. For a Court unanimous on this point, Mr. Justice Lamer, in ordering a new trial to determine the facts, makes it express that a basis for the drug search in question being held unreasonable would be that the Crown had not discharged its burden of establishing that the search came within the power under s. 10(1) of the Narcotic Control Act (requiring belief on reasonable grounds that there was a narcotic in the place where the person search was found).[157]

In *Kokesch* (1990),[158] the Supreme Court reasserted *Collins* in a ruling making it quite clear[159] that an illegal search will necessarily violate s. 8. Police officers had conducted a perimeter search of a dwelling house. They admitted acting on suspicion that drugs were being cultivated in the house but without the reasonable grounds necessary for a warrant. Chief Justice Dickson for a Court unanimous on this point held, as in *Collins*, that s. 10(1) of the Narcotic Control Act could not provide the authority where there was no reasonable belief. Since no common law power was available, the perimeter search had been in the absence of lawful authority and ''must be found unreasonable.''[160] On this view of the Supreme Court the question of whether the illegality of the search was trivial or serious should only arise on the consideration of whether evidence should be excluded under s. 24(2).

In *Wong* (1991),[161] La Forest J. for the majority, in holding that video surveillance was not authorized under the Criminal Code, added:

> It is for Parliament, and Parliament alone, to set out the conditions under which law enforcement agencies may employ video surveillance technology in their fight against crime. Moreover, the same holds true for any other technology which the progress of science places at the disposal of the state in the years to come. Until such time as Parliament, in its wisdom, specifically provides for a code of conduct for a particular invasive technology, the courts should forebear from crafting procedures authorizing the deployment of the technology in question. The role of the courts should be limited to assessing the constitutionality of any legislation passed by Parliament which bears on the matter.[162]

---

[155] *Ibid.*, at 23.

[156] Above note 88.

[157] *Ibid.*, at 206.

[158] (1990), 1 C.R. (4th) 62 (S.C.C.).

[159] In *Dyment*, above note 82, La Forest J. (Dickson C.J. concurring) appeared to leave the point open.

[160] Above note 158, at 84. Dickson C.J.'s further ruling (L'Heureux-Dubé and Cory JJ. concurring) that the evidence should not be excluded under s. 24(2) was in the minority, discussed below, Chapter 11.

[161] Above note 102.

[162] *Ibid.*, at 17-18. See too Glen Luther ''Police Power and the Charter of Rights and Freedoms: Creation or Control?'' (1986-87), 51 *Sask. L. Rev.* 217.

In *Caslake* (1998)[163] the majority indicated there are three ways in which a search can fail to meet the requirements of being authorised by law. First, the state authority conducting the search must be able to point to a specific statute or common law rule that authorizes the search. Second, the search must be carried out in accordance with the procedural and substantive requirements the law provides. Third, a search must not exceed its scope as to area and as to the items for which the law has granted the authority to search.

Given this approach courts should continue to assert that the so-called "plain view" doctrine can only extend the search powers of one already conducting a lawful search.[164]

(f) Constitutional Requirement of Warrant

The most basic ruling in *Hunter* is that s. 8 requires prior authorization in the form of a warrant. The Court recognizes that this will not be a requirement where a warrant is not "feasible".

Prior to *Hunter*, Mr. Justice Martin had, for the Ontario Court of Appeal in *Rao* (1984),[165] decided that there was no constitutional requirement of a warrant under s. 8. While the refined distinctions of American jurisprudence under the Fourth Amendment were to be avoided in developing principles under s. 8, the American experience could be valuable in developing "common sense" exceptions to their warrant requirement. Martin J.A. refers to a summary by Justice Rehnquist (as he then was) in *Texas v. Brown* (1983):[166]

> Our cases hold that procedure by way of a warrant is preferred, although in a wide range of diverse situations we have recognized flexible, common-sense exceptions to this requirement. See, *e.g.*, *Warden of Maryland Penitentiary v. Hayden* (1967), 387 U.S. 294, 18 L. Ed. (2d) 782, 87 S. Ct. 1642 (hot pursuit); *U.S. v. Jeffers* (1951), 342 U.S. 48 at 51-52, 96 L. Ed. 59, 72 S. Ct. 93 at 95-96 (exigent circumstances); *U.S. v. Ross* (1982), 72 L. Ed. (2d) 572, 102 S. Ct. 2157 (automobile search); *Chimel v. California* [above]; *U.S. v. Robinson* (1973), 414 U.S. 218, 38 L. Ed. (2d) 427, 94 S. Ct. 467; and *New York v. Belton* (1982), 453 U.S. 454, 69 L. Ed. (2d) 768, 101 S. Ct. 2860 (search of person and surrounding area incident to arrest); *Almeida-Sanchez v. U.S.* (1973), 413 U.S. 266, 37 L. Ed. (2d) 596, 93 S. Ct. 2535 (search at border or "functional equivalent"); *Zap v. U.S.* (1946), 328 U.S. 624, 630, 90 L. Ed. 1477, 66 S. Ct. 1277 at 1280 (consent). We have also held to be permissible intrusions less severe than full-scale searches or seizures without the necessity of a warrant. See, *e.g.*, *Terry v. Ohio* (1968), 392 U.S. 1, 20 L. Ed. (2d) 889, 88 S. Ct. 1868 (stop and frisk); *U.S. v. Brignoni-Ponce* (1975), 422 U.S. 873, 45 L. Ed. (2d) 607, 95 S. Ci. 2574 (seizure for questioning); *Delaware v. Prouse* (1979), 440 U.S. 648, 59 L. Ed. (2d) 660, 99 S. Ct. 1391 (roadblock). One frequently mentioned "exception to the warrant requirement," *Coolidge v. New Hampshire* (1971), 403 U.S. 443, 29 L. Ed. (2d) 564, 91 S. Ct. 2022, is the so-called "plain view" doctrine, relied upon by the state in this case.[167]

---

[163] Above note 42.
[164] This doctrine is considered below notes 304 *et seq.*
[165] (1984), 40 C.R. (3d) 1 (Ont. C.A.).
[166] 103 S. Ct. 1535 (1983).
[167] *Ibid.*, at 1539.

At issue in *Rao* was the constitutionality of a power under s. 10(1)(a) of the Narcotic Control Act to search a business premise without a warrant. The Court held that a warrantless search of a person's office required justification in order to meet the constitutional standard of reasonableness under s. 8. Where there were no circumstances making the obtaining of a warrant "impracticable" and where the obtaining of a warrant would not impede effective law enforcement, a warrantless search of an office of fixed location, except as an incident of lawful arrest, could not be justified. To that extent, s. 10(1)(a) was of no force or effect.[168]

The *Rao* decision that there can be no constitutional search of a business premise without a warrant unless it is impracticable to obtain one, was an important decision in favour of privacy interests in respect of business premises. Since *Hunter* recognizes an exception to the warrant requirement where it was not "feasible" to get one, and since feasibility can be equated with practicality, the basic ruling in *Rao* has survived and is consistent with *Hunter*. Indeed, Martin J.A. re-asserted his general approach in *Rao* in the post-*Hunter* decision of *Noble* (1984).[169] The power of a writ of assistance[170] which had allowed writ holders to conduct warrantless searches, even of dwelling houses was struck down. Leave to appeal to the Supreme Court was later refused.

There is, however, an important difference of emphasis between *Hunter* and *Rao* which should not be overlooked.[171] Under *Hunter*, for any type of search — of premises, the person or a vehicle — the question is whether a warrant was feasible. Under *Rao*, the focus is on reasonableness and a warrant is only a critical factor in respect of searches of premises. In the case of searches of persons or vehicles, the courts are far less likely to assert a warrant requirement. For example, in *Rao*, Martin J.A. readily accepted the rationale of the "automobile" exception in the United States that the warrant requirement in the case of searches of vehicles is not practical because the vehicle "can be quickly put out of reach of the jurisdiction of a police officer."[172]

There is still no decision of the Ontario Court of Appeal[173] accepting the possibility of a warrant requirement in the context of a vehicle search. Other

---

[168] Above note 22, at 33. See too *Crane* (1985), 45 C.R. (3d) 368 (Nfld. Dist. Ct.) (warrantless search of private mailbox being contrary to s. 8 where no urgency).

[169] (1984), 42 C.R. (3d) 209 (Ont. C.A.), rejecting the contrary view in *Hamill* (1984), 41 C.R. (3d) 123 (B.C. C.A.).

[170] That writ powers have since been repealed is strong evidence of the power of the Charter to force needed reform. *Noble* is also important for holding it was not for the courts to read an exigent circumstance exception into the express statutory authorization.

[171] For a similar argument that the *Rao* approach is inconsistent with *Hunter* see D. Fletcher Dawson, "Unreasonable Search and Seizure: A Comment on the Supreme Court of Canada Judgment in *Hunter v. Southam Inc.*" (1985), 27 *Crim. L.Q.* 450.

[172] Above note 165, at 28.

[173] The warrant would appear to have been feasible in *Annett* (1983), 43 C.R. (3d) 350 (Ont. C.A.), criticized by Glen Luther in an annotation, C.R. *ibid.*, pp. 350-352, and see generally the same author in "The Search and Seizure of Motor Vehicles: Learning From an American Mistake" (1987), 12 *Queen's L.J.* 239. In *Debot*, above note 24, at 132, Martin J.A. says, "Even if it could be said that these may be circumstances in which a warrantless search of an automobile where it is feasible to obtain a warrant is unreasonable," the point did not arise on the evidence. Compare,

Courts of Appeal have been quite content to apply the *per se* warrant requirement of *Hunter* to vehicle searches.[174] In most cases of vehicle searches, such as those during a highway stop, a warrant will not be feasible. However, in some cases a warrant *is* feasible and should be required. It is on this basis that a proper distinction can be drawn between two recent decisions of the New Brunswick Court of Appeal. Both involved police stopping vehicles close to the United States border reasonably believing that the vehicles were being used to smuggle goods. Such a stop and search is authorized under the Customs Act. In one of these cases, the search was held to became unreasonable when the vehicles were only searched four hours later at the police station. It was feasible to obtain a warrant.[175]

The most carefully considered application of the *Hunter* standards to a vehicle search occurred in the Saskatchewan Court of Appeal decision in *D. (I.D.)* (1987).[176] For the Court, Sherstobitoff J.A. declared that a provincial power to search a vehicle without warrant on suspicion of open liquor[177] was contrary to s. 8 of the Charter and of no force or effect. There was a lesser expectation of the right to privacy in a vehicle, as opposed to a dwelling house or place of business. However, although the exigent circumstance exception to the warrant requirement under s. 7 would often apply, there was no basis for a blanket exception for vehicle searches. Four minimum constitutional requirements for a warrantless vehicle search were asserted:

> (1) that the vehicle be stopped or the occupants be detained lawfully;
> (2) that the officer conducting the search have reasonable and probable grounds to believe that an offence has been, is being or is about to be committed and that a search will disclose evidence relevant to that offence;
> (3) that exigent circumstances, such as imminent loss, removal, or destruction of the evidence, make it not feasible to obtain a warrant; and
> (4) that the scope of the search itself bear a reasonable relationship to the offence suspected and the evidence sought.[178]

In *Grant* (1993),[179] although the Supreme Court did not pronounce on the minimum standards approach adopted in *I.D.D.*, it did expressly adopt its holding that there is no blanket exception to the warrant requirement for motor vehicles.

In the case of physical searches of the person, the *Hunter* warrant requirement has been, to say the least,[180] inconsistently asserted by the Supreme Court. It was not mentioned in *Collins* nor in *Beare*, where the Supreme Court held that the

---

however, *McDonough* (1988), 65 C.R. (3d) 245 (Ont. Dist. Ct.) (Criminal Code power under what is now s. 101 for warrantless search for weapons held unconstitutional in context of search of trunk of car).

[174] *Belliveau* (1986), 54 C.R. (3d) 144 (N.B. C.A.); *MacDonald* (1988), 66 C.R. (3d) 189 (P.E.I. C.A.); and *Klimchuk* (1991), 67 C.C.C. (3d) 385 (B.C. C.A.).

[175] *Gillis* (1995), 37 C.R. (4th) 125 (N.B. C.A.). The other decision was reached eight days earlier in *Jacques* (1995), 37 C.R. (4th) 117 (N.B. C.A.).

[176] (1987), 61 C.R. (3d) 292 (Sask. C.A.).

[177] Liquor Act, R.S.S. 1978, C. L-18, s. 31.

[178] Above note 176, at 301.

[179] (1993), 24 C.R. (4th) 1 (S.C.C.).

[180] See criticism of Stanley A. Cohen, "Searching for Answers under Section 8," (1988) 66 C.R. (3d) 369.

fingerprinting procedure under the Identification of Criminals Act was constitutional.[181] We have seen that the *Hunter* warrant requirement was stressed in *Simmons* although it was departed from in the context of customs searches. In *Dyment*,[182] La Forest J., in a concurring minority judgment,[183] rules that one of the reasons why the blood sample taken by the hospital and handed over to the police had been obtained contrary to s. 8 was that a search warrant should have been sought for the seizure of the medical sample.[184] This *Dyment* dictum requiring a warrant for blood samples has since been adopted by the majority of the Court where, as in *Dyment*, police had seized a medical sample,[185] and also in a case[186] where the police commandeered blood and urine samples taken by the Coroner in investigating a fatal accident. In both *Pohoretsky*[187] and *Dyment*[188] at the stage of determining whether the evidence should be excluded under s. 24(2), it was observed that "a violation of the sanctity of a person's body is much more serious than that of his office or even of his home."

It may be implicit in the majority ruling in *Stillman*[189] not to extend the common law power to search incident to arrest to authorise non-consensual body samples, that a warrant was to be required. The Court notes that there was no warrant and points with approval to the new DNA warrant powers. It remains to be seen whether Parliament and the courts will rest content with the DNA warrant power in s. 487.05, which is limited to certain designated offences.

The judicial reticence may lie in the fact that the general search warrant power under the Criminal Code does not to extend to the power to search the person.[190] This should surely not stop the courts from applying the constitutional standard? Stanley Cohen suggests[191] that the courts could assert a constitutional warrant process. If the courts were not prepared to go this far, they could simply declare a particular search unconstitutional and await an appropriate legislative scheme.[192] In the case of the important power to search the person following an arrest, it would surely be preferable, both from the point of view of civil liberties and the interests of the police in knowing what they are empowered to do, to have

---

[181] R.S.C. 1985, c. I-1. See too *Connors* (1998), 14 C.R. (5th) 200 (B.C. C.A.).

[182] Above note 104.

[183] Dickson C.J. concurred.

[184] Above note 104, at 364. La Forest J. referred to *Carter* (1982), 31 C.R. (3d) 76 (Ont. C.A.). See too *Katsigiorgis* (1987), 39 C.C.C. (3d) 256 (Ont. C.A.) (distinguishing the seizure of a urine sample) but compare *Tomaso*, above note 12.

[185] *Dersch* (1993), 25 C.R. (4th) 88 (S.C.C.).

[186] *Colarusso* (1994), 26 C.R. (4th) 289 (S.C.C.). In both *Dersch* and *Colarusso*, the Court did *not* exclude the evidence under s. 24(2).

[187] Above note 107, at 949.

[188] Above note 104, at 367.

[189] Above note 33.

[190] Above note 12.

[191] Above note 180, p. 191.

[192] In *Racette* (1988), 39 C.C.C. (3d) 289 (Sask. C.A.), it was held the provincial powers to obtain blood samples in impaired driving cases did not meet the full *Hunter* requirements including that of prior authorization. The more carefully designed new powers under the Criminal Code have thus far survived Charter attacks: *Pelletier* (1989), 50 C.C.C. (3d) 22 (Sask. Q.B.).

at least more intrusive search powers controlled by a warrant procedure, as the Law Reform Commission of Canada has recommended.[193]

The *Hunter* warrant requirement was vigorously asserted by the Supreme Court in *Duarte (Sanelli)* (1990).[194] The exercise of the Criminal Code power under what is now s. 184(2)(a) of the Criminal Code to electronically intercept a communication on consent of one party to the communication violated s. 8 of the Charter when exercised by an instrument of state. Mr. Justice La Forest, for an overwhelming majority,[195] held that s. 8 imposed on the police the obligation to seek prior judicial authorization before engaging in participant surveillance, as the Criminal Code already provided in the case of third party electronic surveillance. The police should not be allowed absolute discretion to resort to participant surveillance "against whom they wish and for whatever reasons they wish, without any limit as to place or duration."[196]

In *Silveira* (1995),[197] the Supreme Court, through Justice Cory and over the sole dissent of L'Heureux-Dubé J., held that police entry into a dwelling house to preserve evidence of drugs before a search warrant arrived was a serious violation of s. 8. Cory J. implicitly rejects a remedy of reading down the warrant requirement in the Narcotic Control Act to allow for an exigent circumstances exception.[198] Reliance could have been placed upon the view of Martin J.A. for the Ontario Court of Appeal in *Noble* (1984),[199] in striking down writs of assistance:

> Where a statute in affirmative language directs a thing to be done in a certain way, that thing shall not, even if there be no negative words, be done in any other way . . . I do not think, having held that the provisions of s. 10(1)(a) are unconstitutional in so far as they authorize the search of a dwelling under a writ of assistance that we are entitled to truncate or whittle down the statutory requirement of a warrant by writing into the statute an exception to the requirement of a warrant where exigent circumstances existed.[200]

Cory J. could also have relied on the key *Hunter v. Southam* position that the Charter was intended to constrain rather than authorise government action.

---

[193] Above note 51.
[194] Above note 101.
[195] The sole dissenter was Lamer J.
[196] Above note 101, at 293. See the discussion by Stanley A. Cohen, "Not As Easy As It Seems: Closing the Consent Loophole," (1990) 74 C.R. (3d) 304.
[197] (1995), 38 C.R. (4th) 330 (S.C.C.).
[198] Compare *Grenkow* (1994), 95 C.C.C. (3d) 255 (N.S. C.A.), where the Court held that provincial legislation allowing firemen to break into an apartment to extinguish a fire or to prevent its spread was reasonable. The Court observed that five firemen have no time to wait for a search warrant. On the other hand, Mayrand J. in *St-Yves* (1994), 34 C.R. (4th) 39 (Que. S.C.) declared that provisions for emergency electronic surveillance under s. 188(2) of the Criminal Code violated s. 8 in not requiring an affidavit or any other document.
[199] (1984), 42 C.R. (3d) 209 (Ont. C.A.).
[200] At 239-240. In *Martin* (1995), 40 C.R. (4th) 382 (B.C. C.A.), the majority of the Court relied on the Martin analysis to hold that a police entry into a residence to investigate a complain of a loud stereo and subsequent walk through the house had violated s. 8 in the absence of common law or clear statutory authority.

The *Silveira* ruling that exigent circumstances was only a matter to be considered under s. 24(2)[201] is difficult to reconcile with the unanimous decision of the Supreme Court in *Grant* (1993).[202] For the Court, Mr. Justice Sopinka held that the power under the Narcotic Control Act to search the perimeter of a dwelling house without a warrant violated the warrant requirement of s. 8, but it could be read down. Searches would not breach s. 8 where there were exigent circumstances such as

> an imminent danger of the loss, removal, destruction or disappearance of the evidence sought in a narcotics investigation if the search or seizure is delayed.[203]

Grant rests on a shaky footing as Sopinka J. relies on a remark of Martin J.A. in *Rao* (1984)[204] hinting at reading down. *Rao* preceded *Hunter v. Southam*, and Mr. Justice Martin clearly modified his approach in his later judgment in *Noble*.[205]

In *Silveira*, L'Heureux-Dubé J. would have had the majority apply *Grant*. This would have established a wide precedent for courts to declare exigent circumstances exceptions to any search power. It seems vastly preferable to wait for Parliament to clarify search powers in emergency situations.

In its controversial ruling in *Feeney* (1997)[206] Sopinka J. makes a compelling case for the majority that since prior judicial authorization is the fundamental Charter requirement for searches under *Hunter v. Southam Inc.*[207] so too should there be a general constitutional requirement of warrant before entry into a dwelling house to arrest.

An 85-year-old man was found bludgeoned to death in his home in an isolated community. Blood was splattered everywhere. The police learned that the victim's truck had been found abandoned in a ditch a half kilometer west of the murder scene. A resident of the area had seen the accused walking away from the truck accident carrying something in his hand. Another resident told the police the accused had earlier that day stolen another vehicle or had crashed at the same location. Police officers went to the house where the accused was staying and confirmed with the owner that the accused had gone into his trailer at the back. An officer knocked on the door and yelled "Police". Receiving no answer the officers entered, roused the accused from his bed, touched his leg, ordered him to get up and took him to the front of the trailer for better lighting. On seeing blood on his shirt, the officers placed him under arrest and read him his rights. They asked him whether he understood his rights and he responded, "Of course, do you think I am illiterate?" or words to that effect. The officer-in-charge asked him a couple of questions about how the blood had gotten onto him and as to who

---

[201] See too *Martin*, *ibid*.

[202] (1993), 24 C.R. (4th) 1 (S.C.C.). In *Silveira*, the majority does not refer to the *Grant* remedy. In his dissent, La Forest J. assert simply that *Grant* only applies to searches of dwellings. L'Heureux-Dubé J.'s view is that *Grant* is not distinguishable and should be applied.

[203] At 19. See discussion of this reading down by Kent Roach, "Developments in Criminal Procedure: The 1993-1994 Term", (1995), 6 *Sup. Ct. Rev.* 281 at 290-291.

[204] (1984), 40 C.R. (3d) 1 (Ont. C.A.).

[205] Above note 169.

[206] (1997), 7 C.R. (5th) 101 (S.C.C.).

[207] (1984), 41 C.R. (3d) 97 (S.C.C.).

owned a pair of shoes. The accused's shirt was seized and he was taken to the police detachment where, before the accused had consulted with counsel, further statements were obtained. After many hours he met with a lawyer, after which his fingerprints were taken. The police obtained a search warrant pursuant to which they seized shoes, cigarettes and money from the trailer.

The accused was convicted of second degree murder. A 5-4 majority of the Supreme Court quashed the conviction and ordered a new trial. For the majority Sopinka J.[208] held that the entry into the trailer and the search and seizure of the accused's clothing violated s. 8 of the Charter.[209] The arrest was unlawful because the requirements for a warrantless arrest under s. 495 of the Code were not met as the officer had not had a belief he had reasonable grounds for an arrest prior to entry. Futhermore the majority were of the view that police cannot make warrantless arrests in private dwellings unless there were exceptional circumstances, which the majority held were not present in this case. The Court added that the protection of privacy does not end with a warrant. Before forcibly entering a dwelling house to make an arrest with a warrant for an indictable offence, proper announcement must be made.

The problem with the majority judgment lies in its refusal to recognize a general exigent circumstances exception. Sopinka J.[210] explains that that issue was not argued and there were no exigent circumstances on the evidence. The majority accept, however, that hot pursuit would be an exception. With L'Heureux-Dubé J.[211] it is difficult to understand the majority's reluctance to recognize a general exigent circumstances exception. *Hunter v. Southam Inc.* only requires a warrant where it is feasible to obtain one. In the context of drugs searches, Sopinka J. lead the Court[212] in reading an exigent circumstances exception into the Narcotic Control Act. Surely L'Heureux-Dubé J. is correct in pointing out that the traditional hot pursuit exception is one based on exigency. Sopinka J. is persuasive in asserting that no exigent circumstances existed in *Feeney* given that the police had no grounds to believe that evidence would be destroyed prior to the entry into the trailer. In his view[213] if exigent circumstances were recognized simply on the basis that a serious offence had been committed and evidence might be destroyed, there would be little left of the warrant requirement.

In the absence of the recognition of a general exigent circumstances exception, *Feeney* placed the police in an unenviable position. Even in the presence of clear exigent circumstances, they might well be reluctant to move

---

[208] La Forest, Cory, Iacobucci and Major JJ. concurred. L'Heureux-Dubé J. (Gonthier and McLachlin JJ. concurring) and Lamer C.J. (separately) dissented.
[209] The Court also held that the accused's rights to counsel under s. 10(b) had been violated: see discussion in Chapter 5. The majority also decided that all the evidence should be excluded under s. 24(2): see Chapter 11.
[210] Para. 166.
[211] Para. 71.
[212] *Grant* (1993), 24 C.R. (4th) 1 (S.C.C.). See however a contrary view in *Silveira* (1995), 38 C.R. (4th) 330 (S.C.C.).
[213] Para. 194.

least the case be jeopardised. The Supreme Court was insufficiently attentive to the practical consequences of their judgment. What of the reality that police often have to act decisively in entering homes in the interest of protecting themselves and others from harm?

The Supreme Court was later unanimous in granting a British Columbia request, supported by the Federal, Alberta, Ontario and Quebec governments, for a six-month transition period.[214] Parliament soon enacted entry warrant powers to reflect the *Feeney* requirements. However it included an exigent circumstances exception which is defined in s. 529.3(2) to include

> circumstances in which the police officer
> (a) has reasonable grounds to suspect that entry into the dwelling-house is necessary to prevent imminent bodily harm or death to any person; or
>
> (b) has reasonable grounds to believe that evidence relating to the commission of an indictable offence is present in the dwelling-house and that entry into the dwelling-house is necessary to prevent the imminent loss or imminent destruction of the evidence.

The second definition of exigent circumstances may well run afoul of the Sopinka J. position in *Feeney*. It remains to be seen whether it will survive a further challenge.[215]

(g) Minimum Constitutional Standards for Warrant

The authority of *Hunter*[216] that the prior authorization procedure must be meaningful is direct and powerful. Acting under what was then s. 10(1) of the Combines Investigation Act, the Director of Investigation and Research of the Combines Investigation Branch authorized several representatives to enter the premises of a newspaper publishing company to examine and take away any

---

[214] *Feeney* was declared to operate prospectively, except for Feeney. For analysis of transitional problems see Anne-Marie Boisvert, "Feeney, ou comment generer l'incertitude", (1997) 7 C.R. (5th) 182 and "Editorial" in (1997) 2 *Can. Crim. L.R.* 1. On the new trial Feeney was convicted on the basis of DNA evidence obtained and admitted under the new DNA power: *Feeney* (1999), 23 C.R. (5th) 74 (B.C. S.C.).

[215] For arguments that the scheme is constitutional see Renee Pomerance, "Parliament's Response to R. v. Feeney: A New Regime for Entry and Arrest in Dwelling Houses", (1998) 13 C.R. (5th) 84. But see Heather Pringle "Kicking in the Castle Doors: The Evolution of Exigent Circumstances", (1999) 43 *Crim. L.Q.* 86. She points to the post *Feeney* decision in *Damianakos* (1997), 13 C.R. (5th) 64 (Man. C.A.) rejecting necessity to prevent the destruction of evidence as capable of constituting exigent circumstances to avoid the warrant requirement. See however *Golub*, above note 75 (exigent circumstances in necessity to protect persons at scene) and *McCormack* (2000), 143 C.C.C. (3d) 260 (B.C. C.A.) (risk of destruction of evidence constituting exigent circumstance for warrantless search under undefined exigent circumstances exception in Controlled Drugs and Substances Act, S.C. 1996, c. 19, s. 11(7)).

[216] At 117-118. The Supreme Court has rejected general attacks against provincial judges and part-time municipal judges on the basis that they are not independent and impartial tribunals under s. 11(d), see below, Chapter 6. The Supreme Court has not yet heard such a challenge against justices of the peace.

book, paper, record or other document that might afford evidence in connection with an inquiry into whether there should be charges laid of the offence of being a party to a monopoly or that of lessening competition. The authorization was certified by a member of the Restricted Trade Practices Commission under s. 10(3) of the Act. The Supreme Court determined that the prior authorization procedure violated s. 8 because there was no neutral and impartial review by one capable of acting judicially and because there was no requirement for reasonable and probable grounds established upon oath to believe that an offence had been committed and that there was evidence to be found at the place of the search.

In *Hunter*, the significant investigatory functions given to the Commission and its members by the Act vitiated its ability to act in a judicial capacity and did not accord with the neutrality and detachment necessary to balance the interests involved. In *Baylis* (1988),[217] the Saskatchewan Court of Appeal applied this aspect of *Hunter* to hold[218] that a drug search warrant was both illegal and unreasonable contrary to s. 8 because of a lack of neutrality and impartiality by the issuing Justice of the Peace. She was also a member of the Corps of Commissionaires for Southern Saskatchewan, with specific duties to enforce traffic regulations at an airport. In that capacity, although she did not work directly for the police, she was subject to the direct control of the special constable in charge of the airport, who assigned her work and supervision on a day-to-day basis. The Court held there was a reasonable apprehension of bias. A reasonable person would believe that there was a real danger of partiality. So too, according to the Manitoba Court of Appeal in *Gray* (1993),[219] a serious violation of the obligation to act as a neutral and detached assessor occurred where a justice gave advice on a still unexecuted and draft information.

The *Hunter* reasonable grounds requirement has been much more frequently litigated.[220] A provincial power to issue a search warrant to search for liquor based on mere suspicion was struck down,[221] as was a power in a Customs Act that authorizes a Justice of the Peace to issue a search warrant where satisfied that there were reasonable grounds to believe the goods ''may'' be found in premises rather than that they would be found there.[222] On the other hand, a majority of the Federal Court of Appeal[223] surprisingly rejected a challenge to the very wide search warrant power under the Canadian Security Intelligence Service Act.[224] The requirement that the judge be satisfied on reasonable and probable grounds that a threat to the security of Canada existed was held constitutional in light of the Act's purposes.

---

[217] (1988), 65 C.R. (3d) 62 (Sask. C.A.).
[218] *Ibid.*, at 67, 83-84.
[219] (1993), 22 C.R. (4th) 114 (Man. C.A.).
[220] Case law on whether reasonable grounds can be based on information supplied by an informer is considered in the next section on ''Minimum Standards for Warrantless Searches''.
[221] *MacAusland* (1985), 19 C.C.C. (3d) 365 (P.E.I. C.A.).
[222] *Goguen v. Shannon* (1989), 50 C.C.C. (3d) 45 (N.B. C.A.).
[223] *Atwal* (1987), 59 C.R. (3d) 339 (Fed. C.A.). Hugessen J.A. dissented.
[224] S.C. 1984, c. 21, s. 21.

In *Baron* (1993),[225] Justice Sopinka, speaking for a unanimous panel of six justices of the Supreme Court, held that s. 231.3 of the Income Tax Act violated s. 8. Under s. 231.3, the judge hearing the application "shall issue the warrant" where satisfied that there are reasonable grounds to believe that an offence under the Income Tax Act has been committed, a document or thing that may afford evidence of the commission of the offence is likely to be found and the building, receptacle or place specified is likely to contain such a document or thing. The Court found the violation in the words "shall issue" which were incompatible with the discretion recognized in *Hunter* to balance the interests of the taxpayer to be free of state intrusion on privacy and the state interest in law enforcement.[226] Although the Income Tax was regulatory, what was important was not a label, but the intrusiveness of the search and the purpose of gathering evidence for a tax evasion prosecution. The appropriate remedy was to strike out s. 231.3. Issuing the warrant was the linchpin of the whole scheme. The Court rejected the argument that the use of "reasonable grounds" in s. 231.3, rather than "reasonable and probable grounds", did not meet the requirements of s. 8 of the Charter. The *Hunter* standard was one of credibly based probability. The standard to be met in order to establish reasonable grounds for a search was "reasonable probability". The Court might have relied on the following analysis of Mr. Justice Martin for the Ontario Court of Appeal in *Debot* (1986):[227]

> The standard of "reasonable ground to believe" and that of "probable cause", which is contained in the Fourth Amendment to the American Constitution, are identical: *Hunter v. Southam*, . . .

> The standard of "reasonable ground to believe" or "probable cause" is not to be equated with proof beyond a reasonable doubt or a prima facie probability.[228]

The Court in *Baron* further rejected the argument that section's requirement that the authorizing judge be satisfied that a document or thing which "may afford evidence" is "likely to be found" violated s. 8. This formulation did not make the standard the possibility of finding evidence and met the "credibly based probability" standard required by s. 8. The use of the word "may" regarding the use of the thing found as evidence in a prosecution simply reflected one of the realities of the investigation of offences. It was impossible to know with certainty at an early stage in any investigation what particular items will provide evidence in a trial. Although the Court purports not to be weakening the *Hunter* standard, it may well have done so.

We have seen that in *Harris*,[229] Mr. Justice Martin for the Ontario Court of Appeal distinguished between "mere minor and technical defects" which would

---

[225] (1993), 18 C.R. (4th) 374 (S.C.C.).

[226] For jurisdictional rulings on interlocutory orders and appeals, see *Kourtessis* (1993), 20 C.R. (4th) 104 (S.C.C.) and, on impounding orders, see *143471 Canada Inc.* (1994), 31 C.R. (4th) 120 (S.C.C.).This ruling was applied by McCombs J. in *Langer* (1995), 40 C.R. (4th) 204 (Ont. Gen. Div.). The removal of discretion in the issuance of a warrant of forfeiture of obscene material under s. 164 of the Criminal Code violated s. 8. The remedy was to read down "shall" to "may".

[227] Above note 24.

[228] At 132.

[229] Above note 154.

not automatically lead to a s. 8 violation and invalidity "in substance" which would. There would be a defect of substance where the information did not set out facts upon which the justice acting judicially could be satisfied that there were the requisite reasonable grounds or where a search warrant failed to meet the minimum requirements of particularity respecting things to be searched for and seized. Such defects have now been repeatedly held[230] to have been searches conducted in violation of s. 8. We have seen that, since *Collins*, it has been clear that any illegality in the search necessarily violates s. 8. It follows that, contrary to *Harris*, the proper view is that *any* legal defect in obtaining a search warrant should be held to violate s. 8 and shift the inquiry to the possibility of excluding evidence under s. 24(2). An example would be executing a search warrant realizing that it inadvertently contained the wrong address.[231] However, there is one caveat. The Supreme Court has held that a search warrant will be lawful and constitutional, even though it was partly based on a prior warrantless search violating s. 8 if there was otherwise sufficient information to obtain a valid warrant.[232] In the case of the wider search warrant to search dwelling houses for drugs under the Narcotic Control Act, the Supreme Court has held that the requirement that a peace officer who will execute the warrant be named is not merely a technical defect but an important safeguard which will lead to a s. 8 violation.[233]

In *Société Radio Canada v. Nouveau-Brunswick* (1991),[234] the Supreme Court held that there were to be no special constitutional requirements for issues of search warrants to search media offices. However, the justice was to take into account the vital role the media played in the functioning of a democratic society. Although it was not a constitutional requirement,

> the affidavit should ordinarily disclose whether there are alternative sources from which the information may reasonably be obtained and, if there is an alternative source, that it has been investigated and all reasonable efforts to obtain the information have been exhausted.[235]

Given this specific perspective, it is not clear why the Supreme Court balked at declaring a new Charter standard for media searches.

---

[230] See, for example, *Times Square Book Store* (1985), 21 C.C.C. (3d) 503 (Ont. C.A.) (containing careful judicial direction as to how search warrants to search for obscene books could be constitutional: at 513-514); *Turcotte* (1987), 39 C.C.C. (3d) 193 (Sask. C.A.); *Moran* (1987), 36 C.C.C. (3d) 225 (Ont. C.A.); *Pastro* (1988), 42 C.C.C. (3d) 485 (Sask. C.A.); *Donaldson* (1990) 58 C.C.C. (3d) 294 (B.C. C.A.); and *Jones* (1991), 64 C.C.C. (3d) 181 (Sask. C.A.). See too *Vella* (1984), 14 C.C.C. (3d) 513 (Ont. H.C.) (power in what is now s. 199 of the Criminal Code respecting disorderly houses).

[231] See *Silvestrone* (1991), 66 C.C.C. (3d) 125 (B.C. C.A.).

[232] *Grant* (1993), 24 C.R. (4th) 1 (S.C.C.), *Wiley* (1993), 24 C.R. (4th) 34 (S.C.C.) and *Plant* (1993), 24 C.R. (4th) 47 (S.C.C.).

[233] *Genest* (1989), 67 C.R. (3d) 224 (S.C.C.); *Strachan* (1988), 67 C.R. (3d) 87 at 100-101 (S.C.C.). *Strachan* holds that the warrant must make it clear who is in charge of the search. Listing an entire drug squad would not suffice.

[234] (1991), 9 C.R. (4th) 192 (S.C.C.).

[235] At 211.

The elaborate Criminal Code procedure for the obtaining of judicial authorizations for electronic surveillance have thus far withstood Charter challenge,[236] including attacks on wide "basket" clauses extending the authorization far beyond named persons.[237]

(h) Minimum Standards for Warrantless Searches

The focus in *Hunter* was on asserting the warrant requirement and meaningful standards for such warrants. In those exceptional cases where a warrant is not required, it is consistent with *Hunter* to assert "the minimal constitutional requirement that there be reasonable and probable grounds to believe that the search would yield evidence."[238] Indeed, from an early date our courts have asserted a requirement that a warrantless search without reasonable belief is necessarily contrary to s. 8.[239] The reasonable belief requirement is exactly that asserted in the context of warrants, with the exception that there is, of course, no possibility of insisting upon this belief being on oath.[240]

In its often-relied upon pronouncement in *Stevens* (1983),[241] a majority[242] of the Nova Scotia Court of Appeal made it clear that mere suspicion is not enough:

> In my opinion no police officer has the right to search any person based upon suspicion alone. He must have reasonable and probable grounds for believing that the suspect is committing or has committed an offence and must seek his justification under the Criminal Code provisions relating to lawful arrest or some other special statutory authorization. If the police officer searches on suspicion alone he has committed an illegal act, and one that, in my view, would be within the meaning of "unreasonable" in s. 8 of the Charter.[243]

A police officer had approached the accused on the street and asked him to empty his pockets. He did so, but the officer searched another pocket and found a packet of drugs. The officer testified that he had been acting on suspicion based on information that the accused was involved in the drug trade and also on having been personally involved only a month earlier in a successful drugs charge against the accused. The police action was found to have been unlawful and unreasonable and contrary to s. 8.

---

[236] See especially *Thompson* (1990), 80 C.R. (3d) 129 (S.C.C.). See earlier *Finlay* (1986), 48 C.R. (3d) 341 (Ont. C.A.) and *Galbraith* (1989), 49 C.C.C. (3d) 178 (Alta. C.A.).

[237] In *Thompson* the Supreme Court did hold that interceptions at pay phones in the absence of reasonable and probable grounds for believing a target was using the telephone violated s. 8. The Court further ruled that interceptions by surreptitious entry into residences not mentioned in the authorizations would also violate s. 8.

[238] La Forest J. in *Dyment*, above note 104, at 366.

[239] See, for example, *Rao*, above note 22.

[240] *D. (I.D.)*, above note 176, at 297.

[241] (1983), 35 C.R. (3d) 1 (N.S. C.A.). See too *Nielsen* (1988), 43 C.C.C. (3d) 548 (Sask. C.A.) discussed below, note 308. See also *Vaughan* (1987), 33 C.C.C. (3d) 426 (Que. C.A.); *Ironeagle* (1989), 70 C.R. (3d) 164 (Sask. C.A.) and *Ferguson* (1990), 1 C.R. (4th) 53 (Ont. C.A.). See earlier *Phillips* (1983), 35 C.R. (3d) 330 (B.C. Co. Ct.) and *Theriault* (1983), 35 C.R. (3d) 344 (Que. C.S.P.).

[242] Per Hart J.A. Jones and Pace JJ.A. concurred but dissented on a different point.

[243] *Stevens*, above note 241, at 11.

In *Mellenthin* (1992),[244] Cory J., for a unanimous five justices of the Supreme Court, held that police conducting a random roadside stop cannot, in the absence of reasonable grounds for doing so, question a driver about matters other than those related to the vehicle and its operation nor can they search the driver and the vehicle. The Court had previously determined[245] that random vehicle stops constituted arbitrary detention or imprisonment contrary to s. 9, but that this violation could be demonstrably justified under s. 1. However, in *Mellenthin*, the Court made it clear that the stop programs were limited to checks for sobriety, licences, ownership, insurance and mechanical fitness of vehicles:

> The police use of check stops should not be extended beyond these aims. Random stop programs must not be turned into a means of conducting either an unfounded general inquisition or an unreasonable search.[246]

Mellenthin was directed into an R.C.M.P. check stop. The accused was asked for his driver's licence, vehicle registration and insurance papers. He complied. The officer then shone his flashlight to check for drugs and "for the safety of the officers conducting the checkpoint". He saw neither liquor nor drugs, but did see an open gym bag on the front seat beside the accused. The officer asked what was in the bag and the accused pulled the bag open, indicating that there was food inside. The officer saw a reflection from a plastic sandwich bag which he thought was glass. He became suspicious that the bag contained narcotics. The officer also saw a brown baggie in the bag and asked the accused what was in it. Mellenthin pulled it out and it was found to contain an empty glass vial commonly used to store cannabis resin. The officer thereupon arrested the accused and searched the bag and vehicle and found hash oil and cannabis. The Supreme Court held that the search for drugs was not grounded on suspicion let alone reasonable and probable grounds. There had been a serious violation of s. 8 and the real evidence of the drugs should be excluded as the admission of the evidence would render the trial unfair.[247] The only part of the search that the Supreme Court found lawful and constitutional was the visual inspection which was essential for the protection of those on duty in the check stop. There could be no basis for a consent search since there was no evidence the accused had been aware of his right to refuse to consent.[248]

Debot (1986)[249] is also the leading authority on the question of whether reasonable grounds can be based on information supplied by an informer. The test was set out by Mr. Justice Martin in the Ontario Court of Appeal:

---

[244] (1992), 16 C.R. (4th) 273 (S.C.C.).

[245] *Hufsky* (1988), 63 C.R. (3d) 14 (S.C.C.) and *Ladouceur* (1990), 77 C.R. (3d) 110 (S.C.C.), discussed below Chapter 9.

[246] At 280. *Mellenthin* was relied upon in *Denys* (1995), 41 C.R. (4th) 369 (Sask. C.A.). The powers under the Saskatchewan Wildlife Act to stop vehicles to check for hunting licences, whether the weapon was loaded and whether it was of small calibre did not allow the wildlife officer to note the precise calibre of the firearm and the name of the manufacturer.

[247] See Chapter 11 for a consideration of the s. 24(2) ruling.

[248] The consent ruling is further considered below note 295.

[249] Above note 24. See now also *Hosie* (1996), 107 C.C.C. (3d) 385 (Ont. C.A.).

I am of the view that such a mere conclusory statement made by an informer to a police officer would not constitute reasonable grounds for conducting a warrantless search. . . . Highly relevant . . . are whether the informer's "tip" contains sufficient detail to ensure it is based on more than mere rumour or gossip, whether the informer discloses his or her source or means of knowledge and whether there are any *indicia* of his or her reliability, such as the supplying of reliable information in the past or confirmation of part of his or her story by police surveillance.[250]

This approach was adopted on the further appeal to the Supreme Court.[251] Madam Justice Wilson, for a Court unanimous on this point, confirmed that it is the police officer who decides that the suspect should be searched who must have reasonable and probable grounds. That officer may or may not perform the actual search. If another officer conducts the search, he or she is entitled to assume that the officer who ordered the search had reasonable and probable grounds for doing so. In respect of relying on an informer, there were held to be at least three concerns. First, was the information predicting the commission of a criminal offence compelling? Second, where that information was based on a "tip" from a source outside the police, was the source credible? Finally, was the information corroborated by police investigation prior to the making of the decision to conduct the search? These factors were not separate tests. The "totality of the circumstances" had to meet the standard of reasonableness. The reputation of the suspect alone could not provide reasonable grounds for a search, but was germane, provided it was reputation related to the ostensible reasons for the search. If the reputation was based on hearsay rather than police familiarity with the suspect, its veracity could not be assumed.[252]

On the facts,[253] the Supreme Court held that these standards had been met where a police officer had been told by an informer that three people were meeting at the home of one of them to complete a drug transaction. This informer had proved reliable in the past. Two individuals were known to have been involved with drugs before. Members of another police force were asked to keep the suspects under surveillance. They did so, and saw a car, which they ascertained to be the accused's, with four occupants, stop briefly at the house. Another officer on patrol was instructed by radio to stop this car and to search it and its occupants for drugs. The actual search was conducted by an officer who had earlier been informed about the information leading to the surveillance.

The Ontario Court of Appeal has held[254] that a warrantless search of a vehicle was based on reasonable grounds where the police were relying on detailed information from another police department for their belief that the vehicle contained contraband. On the other hand, the Saskatchewan Court of Appeal ruled that there were no reasonable grounds where the police were relying on

---

[250] *Ibid.*
[251] *Debot* (1989), 73 C.R. (3d) 129 (S.C.C.). See too *Greffe*, below note 279, at 286.
[252] *Debot, ibid.*, at 150-153.
[253] See similar rulings in *Jones* (1991), 64 C.C.C. (3d) 181 (Sask. C.A.); *MacFarlane* (1992), 76 C.C.C. (3d) 54 (P.E.I. C.A.); *Breton* (1994), 93 C.C.C. (3d) 171 (Ont. C.A.); *Beauregard* (1999) 136 C.C.C. (3d) 80 (Que. C.A.) and *Kesselring* (2000), 145 C.C.C. (3d) 119 (Ont. C.A.).
[254] *McComber* (1988), 66 C.R. (3d) 142 (Ont. C.A.).

information from another police officer that the accused had drugs at a particular location but there was no indication of the source of the information or its reliability.[255]

Similarly, the Manitoba Court of Appeal[256] held that a vehicle search for drugs based on a tip from an informant had not been based on reasonable grounds as the officer had not within the seven-hour period since the tip taken steps to satisfy himself that the tip was reliable. It seems clear that a higher level of verification will be required where the credibility of the informant cannot be assessed and few details are supplied.[257] On the other hand the Supreme Court in *Leipert* (1997)[258] held that police informer privilege prevented an accused from gaining access to a document describing a Crime Stopper's tip. A challenge to a search did not fall within the narrow "necessary to establish innocence" exception.

The Supreme Court of Canada held in *Evans* (1996)[259] that the police cannot satisfy this requirement to confirm the reliability of a tip by a "knock on" procedure of going to the premises, knocking on the door and detecting the smell of marihuana when the door is opened.

It is vital that the evidence establishing the reasonable belief be led at trial, particularly in cases of warrantless searches where the Crown bears the onus of establishing reasonableness.[260] The majority of the British Columbia Court of Appeal has gone as far as holding that there is no Crown onus to establish the existence of a warrant as part of its case.[261]

In *Hunter* Chief Justice Dickson decided for the Supreme Court that the standard for securing the right to be free from unreasonable search and seizure should be where "credibly-based probability replaces suspicion". A standard of reasonable belief in the possibility of finding evidence was rejected as a very low standard which would authorise fishing expeditions on suspicion. The *Hunter* standard was seen to be the same as the United States constitutional standard of probable cause.

Subsequently the Court has on occasion found the *Hunter* standard too demanding. The result is confusion and inconsistency. In *Baron* (1993)[262] the Court rejected the argument that the use of "reasonable grounds" in an Income Tax search power rather than "reasonable and probable grounds" did not meet the *Hunter* standard. The standard of reasonable grounds was held to be one and the same as it required "reasonable probability". However in *Caslake* (1998)[263]

---

[255] *Cheecham* (1989), 51 C.C.C. (3d) 498 (Sask. C.A.). Compare, however, *Jones*, above note 253.
[256] *Lamy* (1993), 22 C.R. (4th) 89 (Man. C.A.). Compare *Leipert* (1996), 47 C.R. (4th) 31 (B.C. C.A.) (no requirement for police to disclose identity of Crime Stoppers tip).
[257] *Hosie*, above note 249, *Bennett* (1996), 49 C.R. (4th) 206 (Que. C.A.).
[258] (1997), 4 C.R. (5th) 259 (S.C.C.).
[259] (1996), 45 C.R. (4th) 210 (S.C.C.).
[260] See *Collins*, above note 88, at 207; *Greffe*, below note 279, at 286-288 and *Brown* (1996), 47 C.R. (4th) 134 (Ont. C.A.). See Gerard E. Mitchell, "Trial Counsel and the Facts on S. 24(2) Applications" (1990), 76 C.R. (3d) 304.
[261] *Feldman* (1994), 91 C.C.C. (3d) 256 (B.C. C.A.).
[262] Above note 225.
[263] Above note 42.

the Court held that, although there need not be reasonable and probable grounds for search incident to an arrest, there had to be reasonable grounds in the form of a reasonable prospect of securing evidence. Similarly in *M. (M.R.)* (1998)[264] the Court decided that school authorities could search on the standard of reasonable grounds as compared with what was seen to be the higher standard of reasonable and probable grounds required for searches in schools by police and agents of the police. In the context of arrests the Supreme Court in *Storrey* (1990)[265] asserted a reasonable and probable standard, even though s. 495 of the Criminal Code now only speaks of reasonable grounds. There has to be a subjective belief in reasonable and probable grounds and one that was objectively reasonable. However the Court decided that the police did not need to establish a *prima facie* case. On the other hand we saw in *Monney* (1999)[266] that the Court reduced the standard to reasonable suspicion in the case of customs officers submitting travellers to detention in drug loo facilities.

Justice Doherty of the Ontario Court of Appeal has persuasively suggested in *Golub* (1997)[267] that the assessment of reasonable grounds must take into account the context. According to Doherty J., less should be demanded of the officer making a decision to arrest, as often the decision must be made quickly in volatile and rapidly changing situations, as compared to a justice reflecting on an application for a search warrant.

Justice Doherty is also instructive in *Simpson* (1993).[268] He resorts to the ancillary powers doctrine to authorise detention for brief questioning on articulable cause. Articulable cause is defined as a reasonable suspicion. The belief must be based on "a constellation of objectively discernible facts" to distinguish subjective hunches which could too easily lead to discriminatory conduct based "on such irrelevant factors as the detainee's sex, colour, age, ethnic origin or sexual orientation".[269] Even though Justice Doherty relied on the low level test of reasonable suspicion, he nevertheless held that this test had not been met in the police stop of a vehicle where a police officer was relying on information of unknown age and reliability that a particular house was a being used to sell crack and several people, including the person stopped, had been observed entering and leaving the house after short visits.

There does not seem to be a meaningful distinction to be made between reasonable grounds and reasonable and probable grounds. If this is so, the Supreme Court has gone down the wrong path in *Caslake* and *M. (M.R.)*. However the distinction between reasonable suspicion and reasonable and probable grounds,

---

[264] Below note 317.

[265] (1990), 75 C.R. (3d) 1 (S.C.C.).

[266] (1999), 24 C.R. (5th) 97 (S.C.C.).

[267] Above note 75. See too Doherty J. in *Nicolosi* (1998), 127 C.C.C. (3d) 176 (Ont. C.A.) at 185.

[268] (1993), 20 C.R. (4th) 1 (Ont. C.A.).

[269] The Ontario Court of Appeal appears poised to rule that a stop where there is evidence that it was only based on race is illegal and unconstitutional: see *Brown v. Durham*, above note 76, and *Richards* (1999), 26 C.R. (5th) 286 (Ont. C.A.). An alternative basis would be discrimination contrary to s. 15. This has been recognized by the Nova Scotia Court of Appeal, also in *obiter* rulings, in *Smith* (1993), 23 C.R. (4th) 164 (N.S. C.A.) and *White* (1994), 35 C.R. (4th) 88 (N.S. C.A.).

while it will always remain a somewhat speculative and subjective inquiry for the trier of fact,[270] is one, for the reasons indicated by Chief Justice Dickson in *Hunter*, that should be required and not lightly discarded.[271] There is an important distinction between searches on mere suspicion and those where there is a probability of success. Sometimes, as in the case of brief detention for questioning, the *Hunter* standard may be too restrictive on police. In most other contexts, it should be seen as an important part of s. 8's protection of privacy.[272]

(i) Reasonable Manner of Search

In *Hunter*, the Supreme Court distinguished "the reasonableness or otherwise of the manner" of a search.[273] Many of the decisions already reviewed have dealt with a challenge to a particular search on the basis that, on the evidence, it breached one of the *Hunter* criteria, including that of reasonable belief. It is also now quite clear that a s. 8 attack on the manner of the search can also relate to other factors such as a breach of another right such as the right to counsel,[274] police subterfuge[275] or excessive force.[276]

In *Collins*,[277] Mr. Justice Lamer for the majority held that the nature of the reasonable belief which would justify a drug search would also determine whether a throat hold would be reasonable.[278] Furthermore, in *Greffe* (1990),[279] Lamer J.

---

[270] For example, in *Polashek* (1999), 25 C.R. (5th) 183 (Ont. C.A.) Rosenberg J.A. for the Court held that the smell of marihuana alone may not suffice for reasonable and probable grounds for arrest, but it did given the circumstances of its presence in a high drug use area and the time of 1 a.m. It is difficult to reconcile this factual ruling with that in *Simpson*, where the Court was applying the lower test of reasonable suspicion. The issue of police profiling based on a perception of a high crime risk can give rise to legitimate concerns about systemic discrimination and has been the subject of much wider debate in the United States: see, for example, David Harris, "Factors for Reasonable Suspicion: When Black and Poor Means Stopped and Frisked", (1994) 69 *Indiana L.J.* 659. For a comprehensive judgment on the issue of whether a mere smell of marihuana can constitute reasonable grounds see *Huebschwerlen* (1997), 10 C.R. (5th) 121 (Y.T. Ct.). In *Leipert* (1996), 47 C.R. (4th) 31 (B.C. C.A.) a sniffer dog's indication of the presence of marihuana in following a tip was held to provide reasonable grounds for a warrant. The matter was not addressed on the further appeal to the Supreme Court, (1997), 4 C.R. (5th) 259 (S.C.C.).

[271] See too Peter Sankoff and Stéphane Perrault, "Suspicious Searches: What's So Reasonable About Them?", (1999) 24 C.R. (5th) 123.

[272] For recent application of the *Hunter* standard that suspicion is not enough see *Hosie*, above note 249, and *Fry* (1999), 29 C.R. (5th) 337 (Nfld. C.A.).

[273] *Ibid.*, at 110. These further remarks were ignored by the British Columbia Court of Appeal in *Smellie* (1994), 95 C.C.C. (3d) 9 (B.C. C.A.), where *Cloutier v. Langlois* was applied to authorize as incident to a lawful drugs arrest an interior vehicle search which included the removal of a loose door panel.

[274] *Greffe*, below note 279 at 288; *Gogol* (1994), 27 C.R. (4th) 357 (Ont. Prov. Div.).

[275] *Bamford* (1986), 32 C.C.C. (3d) 221 (Sask. Q.B.).

[276] *Genest* (1989), 67 C.R. (3d) 224 (S.C.C.). See too *Gogol*, above note 274 (unnecessary force in executing search warrant violating s. 8)

[277] Above note 88, at 206.

[278] In *Truchanek* (1984), 39 C.R. (3d) 137 (B.C. Co. Ct.), Hogarth C.C.J. held that the "violent and dangerous techniques of a 'choke hold' would only be reasonable if there was reason to believe the drug was in the accused's mouth" (at 158).

[279] (1990), 75 C.R. (3d) 257 (S.C.C.). See Allan Young, "Greffe: A Section 8 Triumph or a Thorn in the Side of Drug Law Enforcement", C.R. *ibid.*, pp. 293-306.

for the majority[280] held that a rectal examination by a doctor using a sigmoidoscope was an extremely serious violation of the accused's Charter rights where the accused had been ostensibly arrested for outstanding traffic warrants absence any evidence on the record of reasonable and probable grounds for believing that the accused was in possession of heroin. Such an intrusive rectal search and considerations of human and bodily integrity were held to demand the highest standard of justification before such a search could be reasonable.[281] The Supreme Court in *Conway (Weatherall)* (1993)[282] has already held that in the context of a prison, cross-gender searches of male inmates by female guards are reasonable. However, the reasoning depended very much on the Court's determination that the inmates had a much reduced expectation of privacy and was also confined to limited types of search.

A powerful authority is the determination of Cory J. in *M. (M.R.),*[283] in the context of school searches, that a search should be conducted in a "sensitive manner and be minimally intrusive" having regard to all factors including age and gender.

The majority position in *Stillman*[284] that the taking of hair samples violated s. 8 had not been the view of the Ontario Court of Appeal[285] but was that of the New Brunswick Court of Appeal.[286]

The issue of the constitutionality of strip searches is presently before the Supreme Court. Ontario Court of Appeal decisions conflict. In *Morrison* (1987)[287] the Court reversed the decision of a trial judge that a strip search of a female arrested for theft violated s. 8 because it had been conducted as a matter of routine.

---

[280] La Forest, Wilson and Gonthier JJ. concurred. Dickson C.J. (L'Heureux-Dubé and Cory JJ. concurring) dissented.

[281] Above note 279, at 289. The dissenting justices viewed the violations as technical and an example of "minor police stupidity" (at 269). See too *Truchanek*, above note 278, for a ruling that rectal searches in drug cases through methods other than digital searches were contrary to s. 8. In *Garcia-Guitterez* (1991), 5 C.R. (4th) 1 (B.C. C.A.), Wood J.A. would have declared that a choke hold to prevent a drug suspect from breathing, distinguishable from the normal throat search, was a life-threatening procedure that was unreasonable. However, the majority opinions of Macdonald and Hollinrake JJ.A. would make no such pronouncement, given the accused's resistance and the urgency of the situation.

[282] (1993), 23 C.R. (4th) 1 (S.C.C.), discussed below note 350.

[283] Below note 317.

[284] Above note 33.

[285] *Alderton* (1985), 44 C.R. (3d) 254 (Ont. C.A.). The accused had submitted to the police running a comb through his hair.

[286] *Legere* (1988), 43 C.C.C. (3d) 502 (N.B. C.A.), *Hodge* (1993), 80 C.C.C. (3d) 189 (N.B. C.A.), *Legere* (1994), 95 C.C.C. (3d) 139 (N.B. C.A.) and *Stillman*, in the court below: (1995), 97 C.C.C. (3d) 164 (N.B. C.A.). In the second *Legere* case a prosecutor had instructed the police to follow the Ontario Court in *Alderton* rather than his own Court's ruling in the earlier *Legere* case involving the very same accused. The New Brunswick Court decided not to exclude. The justices somehow found good faith, no doubt pragmatically determined not to set free a serial killer.

[287] (1987), 58 C.R. (3d) 63 (Ont. C.A.) at 68.

The Court of Appeal held that the search had been reasonable as it had been conducted in the privacy of a police office, in the presence of a female officer and the suspect had not objected to the removal of her clothing. In *Ferguson* (1990),[288] in a brief endorsement by a panel including Arbour J.A. (as she then was), a warrantless vehicle search conducted on mere suspicion was held to be a serious violation. The Court noted that the strip search at the side of the highway was "highly intrusive". Finally in *Flintoff* (1998)[289] Finlayson J.A. for the Court excluded breathalyzer evidence because the police had subjected the driver to a strip search as part of a general policy applicable to all arrested persons. The strip search was held to be outrageous and a flagrant violation of the Charter and an abuse of police power. Although the common law allows the police to search a person as incident to arrest, the degree of intrusion must be reasonable and in pursuit of a valid objective such as safety.

There is wide agreement among lower courts[290] that the special procedures enacted in s. 488.1 for the execution of search warrants in lawyer's offices violate s. 8 because they do not provide adequate protection of solicitor/client privilege. Special concern has been expressed at the provision for automatic waiver without notice having to be given to clients.

(j) Demonstrably Justified Unreasonable Searches or Seizures

In *Hunter* the Supreme Court of Canada specifically left open "the difficult question" of the relationship between s. 8 and s. 1 and in particular, "What further balancing of interest, *if any*, may be contemplated by s. 1, beyond that envisaged by s. 8".[291] In *Noble*, Martin J.A. indicated[292] that he would have "great difficulty" in concluding that an unreasonable search power was justifiable under s. 1 as a reasonable limit. Subsequently, the Supreme Court seems to have accepted that justification under s. 1 is possible in this context although thus far s. 1 arguments have been rejected.[293]

(k) Consent and Waiver

We earlier noted the warning of the Supreme Court in the pre-Charter decision in *Dedman*[294] that the notion of consenting to a search or seizure must

---

[288] (1990), 1 C.R. (4th) 53 (Ont. C.A.).

[289] (1998), 16 C.R. (5th) 248 (Ont. C.A.). See discussion by Peter Sankoff, "Routine Strip Searches and the Charter: Addressing Conceptual Problems of Right and Remedy", (1998) 16 C.R. (5th) 266 at 266-269. See too *Mattis* (1998), 20 C.R. (5th) 93 (Ont. Prov. Div.) (involvement of male officer in strip search of arrested accused at police station violating s. 8 where no threat to safety of female officers or concerns as to loss of evidence).

[290] *Claus* (1999), 139 C.C.C. (3d) 47 (Ont. S.C.J.), *Lavallee* (2000), 143 C.C.C. (3d) 187 (Alta. C.A.), *Festing* (2000), 31 C.R. (5th) 203 (B.C. S.C.), and *White* (2000), 35 C.R. (5th) 222 (Nfld. C.A.). *Sed contra Fink* (2000), 143 C.C.C. (3d) 566 (Ont. S.C.J.).

[291] Above note 77, at 122 (emphasis added).

[292] Above note 169, at 237.

[293] *Simmons* (1988), 66 C.R. (3d) 297 at 324 (S.C.C.); *Duarte (Sanelli)*, above note 194, at 301, and *Baron*, above note 225.

[294] Above note 52.

be viewed in the light of the coercive realities of police/citizen contact. This consideration was evident in the Supreme Court's quick determination in *Mellenthin*[295] that when the accused opened his bag in the vehicle in response to the police inquiry as to its contents, he could not have been taken to have consented to the search.

Our courts have now gone further in linking the issue of consent searches to that of waiver of a constitutional right. Before a search, purportedly on consent, can be held to be a reasonable search under s. 8, there must be proof of a waiver of that right. This, the Supreme Court held in *Borden* (1994),[296] requires a full knowledge of the right:

> In order for a waiver of a right to be secure against an unreasonable seizure to be effective, the person purporting to consent must be possessed of the requisite informational foundation for a true relinquishment of the right. A right to choose requires not only the volition to prefer one option over another, but also sufficient available information to make the preference meaningful. This is equally true whether the individual is choosing to forgo consultation with counsel or choosing to relinquish to the police something which they otherwise have no right to take.[297]

The dramatic ruling on the facts in *Borden* is the best illustration of how seriously the courts now take this requirement. The accused was under arrest for sexual assault. The police obtained his written consent to the taking of a blood sample ''for the purposes relating to their investigations''. The police use of the plural ''investigations'' was deliberate as they wished to use the sample to incriminate the accused in an earlier sexual assault. They later matched his blood by DNA analysis to semen found at the earlier crime scene. The Supreme Court held[298] the oblique indication of the true intentions of the police was wholly insufficient. At a minimum, the police would have had to make it clear to the accused that they were treating his consent as a blanket consent to the use of the sample in relation to other offences they were investigating. The failure of the police to impart to the accused any real sense of the extent of the jeopardy or about their willingness to proceed in the face of knowledge of his lack of understanding furthermore lead the Court to a determination that admission of the evidence would render the trial unfair. Despite the DNA identification, the accused was acquitted on the earlier sexual assault charge.

Borden erects a powerful Charter barrier against too easy justification of police power through reliance on consent.[299] The Court later held that *Borden* was

---

[295] Above note 244.

[296] (1994), 33 C.R. (4th) 147 (S.C.C.). The Court expressly relied on the judgment of Doherty J.A. for the Ontario Court of Appeal in *Wills* (1992), 12 C.R. (4th) 58 (Ont. C.A.). See too, earlier, Chief Justice Bayda in *Nielson* (1988), 43 C.C.C. (3d) 548 (Sask. C.A.) at 564.

[297] At 158.

[298] Only McLachlin J. dissented on the s. 8 issue, although she agreed with the majority that ss. 10(a) and 10(b) had been breached.

[299] *Borden* was, however, distinguished where an accused consented to a blood sample after the proper Criminal Code demand and after he had consulted his lawyer: *Deprez* (1994), 95 C.C.C. (3d) 29 (Man. C.A.) and, by a majority, where an accused had permitted officers to have a ''quick look in your car'': *Clement* (1995), 42 C.R. (4th) 40 (Ont. C.A.); affirmed in a brief oral judgment: (1996), 1 C.R. (5th) 393 (S.C.C.).

distinguishable in a case[300] where the accused had provided a hair sample with full consent on a particular occasion and police now wanted to use that sample in an unrelated case years later. The Court found no breach and admitted the evidence. The Ontario Court of Appeal has also held[301] that the police are not under a duty to advise persons of the right to refuse to consent to a search in the sense that a failure to do so would amount to a violation of s. 8. Section 8, unlike s. 10(b), has no informational component. However a failure to so advise might lead to the conclusion that the person was unaware of the right to consent and therefore could not give an informed consent.

In *Evans* (1996),[302] the Supreme Court accepted that the common law has long recognized an implied licence for all members of the public, including police, to approach the door of a residence and knock. However, a 4-3 majority[303] ruled that this did not authorise the police to employ a "knock on" method of confirming a tip that marihuana was being grown in a dwelling house by knocking on the door and smelling for marihuana when the door was opened. According to the majority the implied invitation to knock extends no further than is required to permit convenient communication with the occupant of the building. Where members of the public (including police) exceed the terms of this waiver and approach the door for some unauthorized purpose, they exceed the implied invitation and approach the door as intruders. The police had violated s. 8 by the "knock on" tactic and the violation tainted the subsequently obtained warrant. According to the majority, where agents of the state approach a dwelling with the intention of gathering evidence against the occupant, the police have exceeded any authority that is implied by the invitation to knock.

(l) "Plain View" Doctrine

Under the jurisprudence of the United States Supreme Court, the "plain view" doctrine is often viewed as an exception to the warrant requirement. According to Justice Stewart in *Coolidge v. New Hampshire* (1971),[304] police officers the Fourth Amendment to the United States Constitution permitted warrantless seizure of items observed in plain view provided:

1. The officers were lawfully in a position to observe the items,
2. The discovery of the items was "inadvertent"[305] and

---

[300] *Arp* (1998), 20 C.R. (5th) 1 (S.C.C.).

[301] *Lewis* (1998), 13 C.R. (5th) 34 (Ont. C.A.). See similarly respecting the right to refuse a police request for a blood or saliva sample: *Blackstock* (1997), 10 C.R. (5th) 385 (Ont. C.A.). The Court left open the issue of one detained or under arrest. Vaso Maric, "Annotation", (1998) 13 C.R. (5th) 385 supports the Court's approach and suggests the same should hold true in cases of detention or arrest.

[302] (1996), 45 C.R. (4th) 210 (S.C.C.). *Evans* was distinguished in *Laurin*, above note 124, on the basis that there is no reasonable expectation of privacy from smelling of marihjuana in a hallway outside the accused's apartment.

[303] *Per* Sopinka J. (Cory and Iacobucci JJ. concurring). La Forest J. concurred in a separate opinion. Major J. (Gonthier and L'Heureux-Dubé JJ. concurring) dissented.

[304] 403 U.S. 443 (1971).

[305] In *Texas v. Brown*, 460 U.S. 730 (1983), Renquist J., with four justices concurring, interpreted

    3.   It was immediately apparent to the officers that the items were evidence of a crime.[306]

The United States Supreme Court in *Horton* v. *California* (1990),[307] held by a 7-2 plurality that the second requirement that the discovery be "inadvertent" did not find a majority in *Coolidge* and should no longer be asserted as a requirement. According to the majority decision of Justice Stevens, the inadvertent requirement was wrongly based on a subjective rather than objective requirement and the requirement was not necessary to prevent the police from conducting general searches or converting a specific into a general search.

The "plain view" doctrine has not been directly considered by the Supreme Court although there is mention in *Mellenthin* of a constitutional seizure of evidence in plain view following a random vehicle stop.

Lower courts have consistently required that the officers have a legal power to search before the "plain view" doctrine can be resorted to.[308] This is consistent with the *Hunter* view that the Charter is intended to constrain rather authorize State power. Assuming that officers were lawfully searching our courts have been content to assert the three *Coolidge* requirements.[309] The abandonment of the inadvertent finding requirement in *Horton* has not yet been considered. Especially in the case of a search pursuant to a warrant, the *Horton* approach would appear to carry the considerable danger that police officers can bypass the need to particularise in advance. We have seen that our courts have often held that deliberate non-disclosure when obtaining a search warrant may make the search warrant illegal and thus contrary to s. 8. This should be the approach especially given that, unlike the automatic exclusionary rule in the United States, in Canada the remedy of exclusion under s. 24(2) is discretionary.

When officers are searching pursuant to a Criminal Code warrant they may well invoke in aid s. 488 of the Criminal Code under which a person executing a search warrant issued under the Criminal Code

> may seize, in addition to the things mentioned in the warrant, anything that the person believes on reasonable grounds has been obtained by or has been used in the commission of the offence.

Section 488 is in essence a statutory version of a "plain view" search power respecting executions of search warrants. However, it is much wider than the "plain view" doctrine established in the United States, even under *Horton*, and appears ripe for Charter review. The omens may not be encouraging. In a pre-

---

    this requirement to mean that the officer must not know about the location of the evidence in advance, relying only on the plain view doctrine as a pretext.

[306] In *Coolidge*, the vehicles searched were in plain view but their evidentiary value was uncertain until their interiors were swept and microscopically examined.

[307] February 21, 1990.

[308] *Askov* (1987), 60 C.R. (3d) 261 (Ont. Dist. Ct.), *Nielsen*, above note 241, *Donaldson* (1990), 58 C.C.C. (3d) 294 (B.C. C.A.), *Ruiz* (1991), 10 C.R. (4th) 34 (N.B. C.A.), *Grenier* (1991), 65 C.C.C. (3d) 76 (Que. C.A.). and *Smith* (1998), 16 C.R. (5th) 397 (Alta. C.A.).

[309] The exception is *Mousseau* (1994), 94 C.C.C. (3d) 84 (Ont. Gen. Div.), where Brockenshire J. held that the inadvertent finding requirement was not part of Canadian common law. However, no authority, not even *Horton*, was cited.

Charter ruling in *Commisso* (1983),[310] Lamer J., for a 5-4 majority, held that an authorization for electronic surveillance respecting a designated offence would allow the admission of "windfall" evidence found respecting an offence for which an authorization could not be obtained. The majority reasoned that an invasion of privacy had been authorized and there would be no point in exclusion. Dickson J., in dissent, was of the view that specification in advance of what the police were targeting would be the only viable way of controlling "subterfuge searches".

(m) Reduced Standards Based on Context

(i) *Customs*

In *Simmons* (1988),[311] involving a s. 8 challenge to the powers of customs officers to search at the border under ss. 143 and 144 of the Customs Act,[312] Chief Justice Dickson for the majority[313] strongly urged that the *Hunter* standards should not be "lightly rejected" and departures should be "exceedingly rare".[314] Ironically, Chief Justice Dickson for the majority in *Simmons* decided to relax the *Hunter v. Southam Inc.* standards for customs searches. The degree of personal privacy to be reasonably expected at customs was lower than in most other situations. Sovereign states have the right to control both who and what enters their boundaries. The Court distinguished three types of border searches. The first, least intrusive type, of routine questioning by customs officers, searches of luggage, frisk or pat searches, and the second type, strip or skin searches permitted under the Customs Act on "reasonable cause to suppose", were held to be reasonable within the meaning of s. 8.[315] The Court left open the constitutionality of the third and most intrusive type, body cavity searches, in which customs officers might resort to medical doctors, x-rays, emetics or other highly invasive procedures.

In *Monney* (1999)[316] the issue was the constitutionality of a drugs loo facility used by customs officers at Pearson International Airport. A majority of the Ontario Court of Appeal had narrowly interpreted the Customs Act to not authorize such searches and violate ss. 8 and 9 of the Charter. The Supreme Court would have none of this. Parliament must have envisaged such searches on reasonable suspicion. Furthermore, the compelled production of a urine sample or a bowel movement were searches conducted in a reasonable manner and not contrary to s. 8 of the Charter. While the passive "bedpan vigil" was an

[310] (1983), 36 C.R. (3d) 105 (S.C.C.).

[311] (1988), 66 C.R. (3d) 297 (S.C.C.).

[312] R.S.C. 1970, c. C-40, repealed by S.C. 1986, c. 1, s. 212(3).

[313] Beetz, Lamer and La Forest JJ. concurred. L'Heureux-Dubé J. (McIntyre J. concurring) concurred on the s. 8 issue. Wilson J. dissented in part.

[314] At 320-321.

[315] At 321-322. The majority did hold that the particular search had been conducted in an unreasonable manner (at 322-323). For application of the test of suspicion based on reasonable grounds for border searches see *Granston* (2000), 146 C.C.C. (3d) 411 (Ont. C.A.).

[316] (1999), 24 C.R. (5th) 97 (S.C.C.).

embarrassing process, it did not interfere with a person's bodily integrity, either in terms of an interference with the "outward manifestation" of an individual's identity, or in relation to the intentional application of force. As is the case with other investigation techniques in the second category of customs searches previously recognized as constitutional in *Simmons*, such as a strip search, subjecting travellers crossing the Canadian border to potential embarrassment was the price to be paid in order to achieve the necessary balance between an individual's privacy interest and the compelling countervailing state interest in protecting the integrity of Canada's borders from the flow of dangerous contraband materials. The constitutionality of more invasive forms of collection, such as surgery or inducing a bowel movement, was left for another day.

(ii) *School children*

In *M. (M.R.)* (1998)[317] the Supreme Court decided that students in schools have a diminished expectation of privacy such that the full *Hunter* standards could not be applied to searches by school authorities. In such cases there is to be no warrant requirement and the standard is reasonable belief rather than reasonable and probable grounds. However the full *Hunter* standards were held to apply where the school authority is acting as an agent of the police.

C, the vice-principal of a high school, was in charge of enforcing school policies mandated by the school and county school board. According to these policies, a student in possession of drugs on school property was to be suspended and the police called. Prior to a school dance, C received information from a number of students that M, a 13-year-old junior high school student, was selling drugs on school property and that it was believed that he would be carrying drugs to the dance. When C saw M arrive at the dance he called a police officer to come to the school. Before the officer arrived, C asked M to come to his office. He closed the office door and asked the student whether he had drugs. He said he would search him. At that point the plainclothes officer arrived and spoke briefly with C outside the office. He entered the office with C and identified himself. M stood up and turned out the inside lining of his pants pocket. C noticed a bulge in M's sock. He removed a cellophane bag and gave it to the officer who identified the contents as marihuana. The officer then arrested him for possession of a narcotic and advised him of his rights.

According to Justice Cory, speaking for the Court,[318] the accused had a reasonable expectation of privacy with respect to his person although he would have reasonably expected a lesser degree of privacy in a school environment in which searches by school authorities were to be expected.[319] A reduced expectation of privacy coupled with the need to protect students and provide a

---

[317] (1998), 20 C.R. (5th) 197 (S.C.C.).

[318] Major J.'s dissent was limited to the ruling that the search was not conducted by an agent of the police.

[319] The Court noted that in some cases, such as locker searches, a court might have to determine with greater precision whether and to what extent a student had a reasonable expectation of privacy (para. 34). In *Z. (S.M.)* (1998), 21 C.R. (5th) 170 (Man. C.A.) the Court held that the expectation of a student with respect to a locker was at the lower end of the scale.

positive atmosphere for learning clearly indicated that a more lenient and flexible approach should be taken to searches conducted by teachers and principals than would apply to searches conducted by the police. The Court indicated three departures from the *Hunter* standards:

1. A warrant is not essential in order to conduct a search of a student by a school authority;

2. The school authority must have reasonable grounds to believe that there has been a breach of school regulations or discipline and that a search of a student would reveal evidence of that breach but this is lower than reasonable and probable grounds; and

3. School authorities will be in the best position to assess information given to them and relate it to the situation existing in their school.[320]

The Court did stress that the search had to be conducted reasonably and must be authorized by a statutory provision which is itself reasonable. In particular:

1. The relevant *Education Act* has to authorise or imply the right of teachers and principals to conduct searches of their students in appropriate circumstances.

2. The search itself must be carried out in a reasonable manner. It should be conducted in a sensitive manner and be minimally intrusive.

3. In order to determine whether a search was reasonable, all the surrounding circumstances will have to be considered, including the age and gender of the student.[321]

These modified standards would not apply to searches beyond the scope of authority and normal standards applied to searches by the police or their agents. In this case the modified standards applied, as the vice-principal was not the agent of the police nor had the police conducted the search. The reduced standards had been met.

Once again the single dissenting opinion, here of Justice Major, is more compelling, especially his view that the finding of the trial judge that the vice-principal was acting as an agent of the police should not be reversed. C and the officer conferred outside the office prior to the search and the trial judge could and reasonably did conclude that the vice-principal received instructions from the police officer on how to conduct the search. The warrantless search was *prima facie* unreasonable. Section 8 had been violated, held Major J., here far less convincingly, because the search had not met the standard for reasonable grounds. The vice-principal had not investigated to corroborate the information he had received.

It is not self-evident why school children should be more vulnerable to searches than adults and why the school authorities should have more powers than the police. At an early point of his judgment, Cory J. relies on the political rhetoric of the day:

---

[320] Para. 50.
[321] Para. 54.

> Schools today are faced with extremely difficult problems which were unimaginable a generation ago. Dangerous weapons are appearing in schools with increasing frequency. There is as well the all too frequent presence at schools of illicit drugs.[322]

No data of any kind was provided for this assessment which was to justify wide search powers in every school across the land.

Justice Cory relies on a decision of the U.S. Supreme Court,[323] noting in passing that it had been the subject of criticism in that country. The Court did not address significant criticism expressed in the Canadian context by Professor Wayne MacKay.[324]

Even if *Hunter* standards are to be reduced in the context of maintaining school discipline, surely school authorities must be considered as police agents when they search for something like drugs knowing that the police will be called, and criminal charges laid, if something is found. The majority determined that the vice-principal was here not an agent of the police. The test was whether the search would have taken place in the same form and manner had the police not been present. Here the school principal would not have behaved differently without the police present. This is a most inapt test. The less respectful school authorities are of police or Charter standards, the better their legal position and the wider their search powers. The Court applied out of context part of the test developed in *Broyles*[325] to distinguish between active and passive listening by undercover officers in police cells for the purposes of the s. 7 pre-trial right to silence. Other key *Broyles* criteria such as whether the conversation was "functionally the equivalent of an interrogation" were ignored.

As dramatically demonstrated in Windsor soon after *M. (M.R.)* was handed down, in a situation where two teachers strip-searched 20 grade nine boys to find stolen money,[326] teachers may abuse their powers once told that they are extensive.

In fairness, the majority decision in *M. (M.R.)* does establish significant s. 8 protection for school children. The Supreme Court could have decided that there is no reasonable expectation of privacy at school so that s. 8 does not apply at all.[327] The Court requires a reasonable belief. Although this is held to be a lesser test than the *Hunter* standard of "credibly-based probability replacing suspicion", it still requires a belief and that the belief be reasonable.

The Supreme Court also carefully requires school searches to be conducted in a reasonable and sensitive manner. It is therefore likely that the Windsor strip searches were unconstitutional although they were apparently carried out as a last

---

[322] Para. 3.

[323] *New Jersey* v. *T.L.O.*, 105 S. Ct. 733 (U.S. Sup. Ct., 1985).

[324] See in Gregory Dickinson and A. Wayne MacKay, *Rights, Freedoms and the Educational System in Canada* (1989) p. 370, and his comments "Students as Second Class Citizens under the Charter", (1986) 54 C.R. (3d) 390 and "Don't Mind Me, I'm From the R.C.M.P.: R. v. M.(M.R.) -Another Brick in the Wall Between Students and Their Rights", (1997) 7 C.R. (5th) 24.

[325] (1991), 9 C.R. (4th) 1 (S.C.C.).

[326] *Globe and Mail*, December 9, 1998.

[327] The majority formally left open the question whether there was governmental action to engage the Charter as the Crown had conceded the point.

resort after other measures failed.[328] Strip searches should never be conducted as a matter of routine, as recently held by the Ontario Court of Appeal.[329]

(iii) *"Administrative" or "regulatory"*

It is now clearly established by the Supreme Court[330] that the *Hunter* criteria are best reserved for criminal or "quasi-criminal" matters and can be departed from in some "administrative" or "regulatory" matters. When and how that is to occur is distressingly uncertain.

The Supreme Court first attempted to distinguish between crimes and regulatory offences for the purposes of fault requirements.[331] The principles relied upon have been criticized as incoherent[332] and have certainly produced inconsistent results. In the context of section 8 the Supreme Court's determination[333] that a search under the Income Tax Act requires the full *Hunter* standards is hard to reconcile with its decisions in *Monney* and *M.(M.R.)*. Would the search under the Combines Investigation Act in *Hunter* now itself be classified as regulatory rather than criminal?

The leading pronouncement is that of Sopinka and Iacobucci JJ. in *B.C. (Securities Commission) v. Branch* (1995),[334] where they determined that

> it is clear that the standard of reasonableness which prevails in the case of a search and seizure made in the course of enforcement in the criminal context will not usually be the appropriate standard for a determination made in an administrative or regulatory context. . . . The greater the departure from the realm of criminal law, the more flexible will be the approach to the standard of reasonableness.[335]

The majority also adopted a previous comment of Wilson J. in *McKinlay Transport Ltd* (1990):[336]

> Since individuals have different expectations of privacy in different contexts and with regard to different kinds of information and documents, it follows that the standard of review of what is "reasonable" in a given context must be flexible if it is to be realistic and meaningful.[337]

---

[328] Above note 326.
[329] *Flintoff*, above note 289.
[330] See especially *British Columbia (Securities Commission)* v. *Branch* (1995), 38 C.R. (4th) 133 (S.C.C.), *Comité paritaire de l'industrie de la chemise* v. *Potash* (1994), 91 C.C.C. (3d) 315 (S.C.C.) and *Nicolosi* (1998), 127 C.C.C. (3d) 176 (Ont. C.A.).
[331] *Wholesale Travel Group Inc.* (1991), 8 C.R. (4th) 145 (S.C.C.).
[332] See Stuart, *Canadian Criminal Law: A Treatise* (4th ed., 2001) c. 3. Compare Robert Hubbard and Peter DeFreitas, "Administrative Revenue Searches: Can They Be Utilised in Aid of Criminal Investigations and Prosecutions?", (1999) 42 *Crim. L. Q.* 412 discussing the interplay between administrative and criminal searches.
[333] *Baron*, above note 225. But see *Del Zotto*, S.C.C., January 21, 1999 (inquiry powers under s. 231.4 of Income Tax Act not violating s. 8 (or s. 7)).
[334] (1995), 38 C.R. (4th) 133 (S.C.C.).
[335] At 158.
[336] (1990), 76 C.R. (3d) 283 (S.C.C.).
[337] At 298 , cited in *Branch* at 158.

Under this approach, the Supreme Court in *Branch* determined that a power under the Securities Act of British Columbia[338] to order the production of documents did not violate s. 8. Persons involved in the business of trading securities did not have a high expectation of privacy and the demand for production of business records was one of the least intrusive methods respecting documents which had a lesser privacy right attaching to them than personal documents. The Supreme Court had previously determined in *Potash* (1994)[339] that the power under Quebec labour legislation[340] to permit inspectors to examine employment records constituted a seizure power under s. 8, but was reasonable despite no requirements of reasonable grounds or of a warrant.

We have seen[341] that the Supreme Court has now determined that search powers under Income Tax Acts are regulatory, but nevertheless subject to the *Hunter* standards because of their degree of obtrusiveness.

Prior to *McKinlay*, lower courts had also declined to apply *Hunter* to a variety of so-called "administrative" contexts. The *Hunter* criteria were held inapplicable in the contexts of a drugs search of a student by a school principal,[342] an inspection by an employment standards officer,[343] or a chicken marketing inspector,[344] a seizure of fishing gear by fishing inspectors,[345] and entry by a municipal by-law building inspector.[346] The trend is not uniform. *Hunter* was applied in the case of a search by a wildlife officer[347] and in the case of seizure of videotapes by a film inspector.[348] In *McKinlay*, Wilson J. reviews such decisions as evidence of the need to take a flexible and purposive approach but leaves open the question of whether the results achieved were correct.[349]

A particularly troubling ruling is that of a unanimous Supreme Court in *Conway (Weatherall)* (1993).[350] The Supreme Court took but a few lines to dismiss a s. 8 claim by a male penitentiary inmate against cross-gender touching that might occur during a frisk search by a female guard and against the possibility that a female guard could see the inmates undressing or using the toilet during

---

[338] B.C. S.C. 1985, c. C-5, s. 128.

[339] (1994), 91 C.C.C. (3d) 315 (S.C.C.).

[340] Act respecting Collective Agreement Decrees, R.S.Q. 1977, c. D-2, ss. 22-23.

[341] See *Baron*, above note 225.

[342] *G. (J.M.)* (1986), 54 C.R. (3d) 380 (Ont. C.A.). See criticism by A. Wayne MacKay, "J.M.G.: Students as Second Class Citizens under the Charter", C.R. *ibid.*, pp. 390-400.

[343] *Re Belgoma Transportation Ltd.* (1985), 51 O.R. (2d) 509 (C.A.).

[344] *Quesnel* (1985), 24 C.C.C. (3d) 78 (Ont. C.A.).

[345] *Milton* (1986), 32 C.C.C. (3d) 159 (B.C. C.A.).

[346] *Bichel* (1986), 29 C.C.C. (3d) 438 (B.C. C.A.).

[347] *Sheppard* (1984), 11 C.C.C. (3d) 276 (Nfld. C.A.).

[348] *Nightingale Galleries Ltd. v. Ontario (Director of Theatres Branch)* (1984), 15 C.C.C. (3d) 398 (Ont. Co. Ct.).

[349] Above note 336, at 299-300. Wilson J. does not refer to the ruling in *Print Three Inc.* (1985), 47 C.R. (3d) 91 (Ont. C.A.), that an Income Tax power to enter any building to search for any documents offended s. 8. That particular power was replaced by what is now s. 231.3. In *Kourtessis v. M.N.R.* (1989), 72 C.R. (3d) 196 (B.C. C.A.), a s. 8 challenge on the basis that the section referred to "reasonable grounds" rather than "reasonable and probable grounds" was rejected. *Kourtessis* was reversed on jurisdictional grounds: (1993), 20 C.R. (4th) 104 (S.C.C.).

[350] (1993), 23 C.R. (4th) 1 (S.C.C.).

scheduled and unscheduled counts. According to La Forest J. for the Court, such practices

> are all practices necessary in a penitentiary for the security of the institution, the public and indeed the prisoners themselves. A substantially reduced level of privacy is present in this setting and a prisoner thus cannot hold a reasonable expectation of privacy with respect to these practices. This conclusion is unaffected by the fact that the practices at times may be conducted by female guards.[351]

This ruling appears to be limited to the particular searches in question. As such, there is room for difference of opinion.[352] The discounting of privacy interests of inmates respecting such searches seems strange coming from Justice La Forest, the author of purposeful interpretations in *Duarte* and *Wong*. The ruling is another in which the Supreme Court appears disinterested is establishing any meaningful Charter rights for inmates.

After making this ruling, which is expressly limited to "these practices", La Forest J. concluded with the remark that

> There being no reasonable expectation of privacy, s. 8 or the Charter is not called into play.[353]

Despite Professor Allan Manson's warning[354] that this remark should not be taken out of context, the British Columbia Court of Appeal[355] has already relied on it to reject a section 8 challenge to random urinalysis tests conducted in prisons. Hopefully, the Supreme Court will return to the issue of the reasonable expectation of prisoners respecting more intrusive practices such as urinalysis, electronic monitoring[356] and skin and body cavity searches. Prisoners and indeed those who work in or visit prisons have a reduced expectation of privacy but surely there is some personal privacy expectations which should engage s. 8 protection?

In the case of search or seizure powers other than those respecting Criminal Code prosecutions, whether the *Hunter* standards will be applied will now often depend on the uncertain vagaries of classification as regulatory or administrative or a contextual analysis of the particular power and the particular form of regulation. At least in the prosecution of Criminal Code and drugs offences, other

---

[351] At 8. The Court also rejected a s. 15 challenge based on the fact that at that time cross-gender searches of female inmates by male guards was prohibited. This aspect of the ruling is considered later, Chapter 15.

[352] Compare the comments of Elizabeth Thomas in an annotation on the judgment of the Court below, the Federal Court of Appeal in (1990), 78 C.R. (3d) 258 with those of Allan Manson on the Supreme Court ruling in (1993), 23 C.R. (4th) 2 ("it was not surprising that the claims of the prisoner did not succeed").

[353] *Ibid.*

[354] See Manson, above note 352.

[355] *Fieldhouse* (1995), 40 C.R. (4th) 263 (B.C.C.A.), despite strong criticism of the lower Court ruling by Allan Manson, "Fieldhouse and the Diminution of Charter Scrutiny", (1994) 33 C.R. (4th) 358. See too *Dorfer* (1996), 104 C.C.C. (3d) 528 (B.C. C.A.) (prisoner having no reasonable expectation of privacy respecting dental treatment from which police obtained blood and saliva samples).

[356] In *Re Williamson and Gladue and R* (1998), 123 C.C.C. (3d) 540 (Alta. Q.B.) universal taping of inmate's telephone conversations in violation of the Corrections and Conditional Release Act and Commissioner's directives was held to be contrary to s. 8 as illegal and unreasonable.

than those in prisons, the *Hunter* and *Collins* approach has been universally asserted.

4

Section 9: Arbitrary Detention or Imprisonment

Under s. 9 of the Charter:

Everyone has the right not to be arbitrarily detained or imprisoned.

1. DETENTION

In the context of s. 10,[1] the Supreme Court has asserted a wide definition of detention which includes physical but also psychological compulsion by a state official. In that context, the Court has held that a motorist subjected to a breathalyzer demand[2] or required to provide a roadside breath sample[3] is "detained" for the purposes of s. 10.

The Court has now determined that these principles apply equally in the case of detention for the purposes of s. 9. In *Hufsky* (1988),[4] it was held that a motorist who had been stopped at a random police check point had been detained. In checking the driver's licence and proof of insurance and observing his sobriety, the police had assumed control over his movements by a demand or direction that might have significant legal consequence.[5] In *Ladouceur* (1990),[6] it was further held that a motorist who had been stopped at random, not at a fixed check point, and merely to ensure that his driving papers were in order, had also been detained. The officers had assumed control over his movements by a demand or direction. Although the detention only involved traffic offences, the maximum penalties of

---

[1] Below, Chapter 5.
[2] *Therens* (1985), 45 C.R. (3d) 97 (S.C.C.).
[3] *Thomsen* (1988), 63 C.R. (3d) 1 (S.C.C.).
[4] (1988), 63 C.R. (3d) 14 (S.C.C.).
[5] *Ibid.*, at 22.
[6] (1990), 77 C.R. (3d) 110 (S.C.C.).

a $2,000 fine or six months imprisonment demonstrated that the legal consequences of the detention were significant.[7]

2. ARBITRARY

As is the case with any Charter challenge, a challenge under s. 9 can allege that the law itself is arbitrary and therefore of no force or effect or that a constitutional law has been applied in an arbitrary fashion.[8] In the latter instance, there can be no question of the State resorting to an argument based on a demonstrably justified reasonable limit under s. 1.

(a) Unfettered Discretion

In *Hufsky* and *Ladouceur*, the Supreme Court held that a detention in the unfettered discretion of a police officer is necessarily "arbitrary" contrary to s. 9. The issue in both cases was the constitutionality of the spot check procedure in s. 189a of the Ontario Highway Traffic Act[9] which reads as follows:

> (1) A police officer, in the lawful execution of his duties and responsibilities, may require the driver of a motor vehicle to stop and the driver of a motor vehicle, when signalled or requested to stop by a police officer who is readily identifiable as such, shall immediately come to a safe stop.
> (2) Every person who contravenes subsection (1) is guilty of an offence and on conviction is liable to a fine of not less than $100 and not more than $2,000 or to imprisonment for a term of not more than six months, or to both.

For a unanimous Court in *Hufsky*, Mr. Justice Le Dain had little difficulty in finding a contravention of s. 9:

> Although authorized by statute and carried out for lawful purposes, the random stop for the purposes of the spot check procedure nevertheless resulted, in my opinion, in an arbitrary detention, because there were no criteria for the selection of the drivers to be stopped and subjected to the spot check procedure. The selection was in the absolute discretion of the police officer. A discretion is arbitrary if there are no criteria, express or implied, which govern its exercise.[10]

Similarly in *Swain* (1991),[11] the Supreme Court held that the automatic detention of persons found not guilty by reason of insanity required at that time by the Criminal Code, was arbitrary detention contrary to s. 9. Under s. 614(2), the trial judge "shall order" that the person acquitted be kept "in strict custody . . . until the pleasure of the lieutenant governor of the province is known." For

---

[7] *Ibid.*, 127.
[8] See, for example, *Sieben* (1989), 73 C.R. (3d) 33 at 55 (Alta. C.A.):
> The right guaranteed by s. 9 may be infringed by the fact of detention as well as by the manner in which a constitutionally permitted detention is carried out.
[9] R.S.O. 1980, c. 198, enacted by the Highway Traffic Amendment Act, S.O. 1981, c. 72. See now Highway Traffic Act, R.S.O. 1990, c. H.8.
[10] Above note 4, at 23, followed in *Ladouceur*, below note 14.
[11] (1991), 63 C.C.C. (3d) 481 (S.C.C.).

the majority,[12] Chief Justice Lamer held that the provision violated s. 9 because the trial judge's duty to detain was "unqualified by any standards whatsoever."[13]

(b) Capricious

Lower courts have distinguished from this notion of unfettered discretion being arbitrary the "more odious meaning" of "capriciousness", which is "based on a notion of whim" or "despotic".[14]

The Supreme Court has yet to confront this meaning. The Court has quickly dismissed s. 9 attacks on procedures for preventive detention of dangerous offenders: *Lyons* (1987);[15] and fingerprinting in the case of indictable offences: *Beare* (1988);[16] and against 25 year minimum periods of parole ineligibility for first degree murderers: *Luxton* (1990)[17] and *Arkell* (1990).[18]

In *Cayer* (1988),[19] the Ontario Court of Appeal turned to the definition to be found in Black's Law Dictionary:

> *Arbitrary.* Means in an "arbitrary" manner, as fixed or done capriciously or at pleasure. Without adequate determining principle; not founded in the nature of things; nonrational; not done or acting according to reason or judgment; depending on the will alone; absolutely in power; capriciously; tyrannical; despotic . . . Without fair, solid, and substantial cause; that is, without cause based upon the law . . . not governed by any fixed rules or standard. Ordinarily, "arbitrary" is synonymous with bad faith or failure to exercise honest judgment and an arbitrary act would be one performed without adequate determination of principle and not one founded in nature of things . . .[20]

In the light of this definition, the Court accepted that "arbitrary", for the purpose of the appeals before them, meant "capricious, despotic or unjustifiable."[21] The issue in *Cayer* was whether an arrest in a situation where the Criminal Code requires proceedings to be commenced by an appearance notice or a summons is necessarily contrary to s. 9 of the Charter. The issue cannot be understood without a review of complex Criminal Code provisions.

One of the aims of the Bail Reform Act[22] amendments to the Criminal Code was to reduce the number of accused detained before trial. One strategy was to

---

[12] Only L'Heureux-Dubé J. dissented on this point.

[13] Above note 11, at 535.

[14] *Ladouceur* (1987), 57 C.R. (3d) 45 at 64 (Ont. C.A.) (per Tarnopolsky J.A., Houlden J.A. concurring).

[15] (1987), 61 C.R. (3d) 1 at 36-38 (S.C.C.) ("anything but arbitrary" and "clearly designed to segregate a small group of highly dangerous criminals"). The Court through La Forest J. saw an overlap with s. 7 arguments based on arbitrariness and recognized that "if and when it is alleged that a prosecutor in a particular case was motivated by improper or arbitrary reasons . . . a s. 24 remedy would lie" (at 38).

[16] (1988), 66 C.R. (3d) 97 at 119 (S.C.C.).

[17] (1990), 79 C.R. (3d) 193 at 202 (S.C.C.).

[18] (1990), 79 C.R. (3d) 207 at 214 (S.C.C.). The rulings on s. 9 in *Luxton* and *Arkell* overlap with the further rejection of s. 7 challenges and have been discussed, above, Chapter 2.

[19] (1988), 66 C.R. (3d) 30 (Ont. C.A.).

[20] 5th ed. (1979) p. 96, quoted *ibid.*, at 43.

[21] Above note 19, at 43.

[22] S.C. 1970-71-72, C. 37.

declare, in what is now s. 495(2), that a power of arrest available to a peace officer under s. 495(1) for stipulated types of less serious offences — offences in the absolute jurisdiction of provincial judges, those hybrid and those punishable on summary conviction — shall not be exercised (an appearance notice or summons being possible) if certain conditions are met. An appearance notice is very much like a summons except that it is issued by a peace officer and not a justice. Unfortunately, s. 495(2) is characterized by bewildering complexity.[23] The correct interpretation is that a police officer may still arrest for "an appearance notice offence" when he or she has reasonable grounds for believing that an arrest is in the public interest, having regard to all the circumstances and the needs identified (s. 495(2)(d)) *or* where the police officer has reasonable grounds for believing that the accused will fail to attend court (s. 495(2)(e)). Police officers and courts have often had difficulty in interpreting the section. The Bail Reform Act, having limited the power of arrest in s. 495(2), however, enacted a wide justification clause in s. 495(3) in which a peace officer arresting contrary to subsection (2) is "deemed to be acting lawfully and in the execution of his duty for the purposes of (a) any proceedings under this or any other Act of Parliament." Appeal courts have construed this provision literally to conclusively deem an arrest contrary to s. 495(2) as legal for all purposes connected with criminal proceedings.[24]

In *Cayer*, the Ontario Court of Appeal was faced with rulings in lower courts that an arrest of impaired drivers pursuant to a blanket police policy to arrest all impaired drivers, regardless of the circumstances and regardless of the criteria in s. 495(2), was arbitrary detention.[25] The Ontario Court of Appeal disagreed and held that

> the arrest by a police officer of an impaired driver in the act, or virtually in the act, of driving, pursuant to a police policy or a policy adopted by the individual police officer, does not make the arrest or detention arbitrary where, in the circumstances of the particular case, the arrest is in fact reasonable in the public interest in order to prevent the continuation or repetition of the offence.[26]

---

[23] Under s. 495(2)

    A peace officer shall not arrest a person without warrant . . . in any case where
    (d) he believes on reasonable grounds that the public interest, having regard to all the circumstances including the need to
        (i) establish the identity of the person,
        (ii) secure or preserve evidence of or relating to the offence, or
        (iii) prevent the continuation or repetition of the offence or the commission of another offence,
    may be satisfied without so arresting the person, and
    (e) he has no reasonable grounds to believe that, if he does not so arrest the person, the person will fail to attend court in order to be dealt with according to law.

[24] *Adams* (1973), 21 C.R.N.S. 257 (Sask. C.A.) (obstructing peace officer), *McKibbon* (1973), 12 C.C.C. (2d) 66 (B.C. C.A.) (assault with intent to restrict arrest) and *Tully* (1984), 41 C.R. (3d) 182 (Ont. Co. Ct.) (assaulting peace officer).

[25] *Ware* (1987), 49 M.V.R. 97 (B.C. Co. Ct.) and *Christiensen* (1987), 3 M.V.R. (2d) 116 (B.C. Co. Ct.).

[26] Above note 19, at 44. This was adopted by the majority in *Sieben*, above note 8. In dissent, Harradence J.A. sought to distinguish Cayer on the basis that this was not a situation where the arrest was reasonable in the public interest in order to prevent the continuation or repetition of the

The Court accepted that the deeming provision in s. 495(3) could not be conclusive of the constitutional issue[27] but held, relying on its previous decision in *Duguay* (1985),[28] that a "detention may not be arbitrary even though it was in fact unlawful."[29]

In *Rudko* (1999)[30] Judge Johnstone of the Alberta Court of Queen's Bench determined that the detention of a person cited for *in facie* contempt without consideration of bail within 24 hours violated s. 9. Although there was no statutory bail procedure specified for such cases, not addressing bail within the normal maximum period was arbitrary. The appropriate remedy was a stay of proceedings and a motion for prohibition.

(c) Is Unlawful Action Necessarily Arbitrary?

In *Duguay*, experienced police officers had arrested three youths on suspicion that they were involved in a residential burglary. The victims of the theft had noticed three young men in their neighbour's backyard the evening of the break-in. One had asked the owners as they left whether it was their custom to put the dog in the garage. The victims gave the police descriptions of these young men. The neighbour was able to identify one of the young men as M. The neighbour telephoned M. and asked him to come over with his friends of the night before. When they arrived, the victims recognized M. and S. At this point the police placed them under arrest. The trial judge found that the police officers had neither reasonable and probable grounds for an arrest nor an honest belief that they had the necessary grounds.

Associate Chief Justice MacKinnon for the majority of the Court of Appeal[31] held that, on the facts found by the trial judge, the arrest had been arbitrary since it was for the improper purpose of assisting in the investigation. A "hunch" of an experienced detective had to have some reasonable basis and could not be an excuse for "irrational and high-handed actions."[32] The majority did, however, make it quite clear that in its view, the mere fact that an arrest was unlawful did not necessarily make it contrary to s. 9:

> It cannot be that every unlawful arrest necessarily falls within the words "arbitrarily detained". The grounds upon which an arrest was made may fall "just short" of constituting reasonable and probable cause.[33]

---

offence (at 42). In *Pithart* (1987), 57 C.R. (3d) 144 (B.C. Co. Ct.), it was held that arrest and overnight detention on a charge of communicating for the purpose of prostitution pursuant to a blanket police policy without consideration of Criminal Code provisions including s. 495(2), was arbitrary detention contrary to s. 9. See too *Lewis* (1989), 73 C.R. (3d) 246 (Man. Prov. Ct.) (arbitrary arrest of apartment occupant in drugs raid). See the full review of s. 9 rulings in arrest cases by Vittorio C. Toselli, "Arbitrary Detention and Judicial Stay of Proceedings" (1990), 80 C.R. (3d) 86.

[27] *Ibid.*, at 43.

[28] (1985), 45 C.R. (3d) 140 (Ont. C.A.).

[29] Above note 19, at 43.

[30] (1999), 28 C.R. (5th) 375 (Alta. Q.B.).

[31] Martin J.A. concurring.

[32] Above note 28, at 148.

[33] *Ibid.*, at 147. In dissent, Zuber J.A. held that "detention that follows an arrest based on something

The Supreme Court of Canada did not consider this ruling when it dismissed the further appeal in *Duguay*.[34]

In a subsequent ruling in *Storrey* (1990),[35] Mr. Justice Cory for the Supreme Court did review the s. 9 ruling in *Duguay* with apparent approval but held that *Duguay* could not be taken to establish a principle that,

> Whenever a lawful arrest is made in circumstances where the police intend to do further investigation, the arrest should then be considered to have been made for an improper purpose.[36]

In *Storrey*, the Supreme Court ruled that an 18 hour delay before a charge after a lawful arrest for aggravated assault was not unreasonable and contrary to s. 9. In the circumstances, a line-up was the fairest and sole practical means of identification and it took time to arrange as the victims were not in the jurisdiction.

Brown v. Durham (1998)[37] involved a civil suit by biker gangs against the police for a large scale stop alleged to violate s. 9. In the course of confirming the dismissal of the action Justice Doherty, for the Ontario Court of Appeal, suggested that although not all unlawful detentions are necessarily arbitrary the absence of lawful authority was "at least strongly suggestive of arbitrariness" and "crucial" if s. 1 was reached.[38] Here the stops were lawful under the Highway Traffic Act but too intrusive to be authorised by the common law ancillary powers doctrine.[39]

A quite different, and arguably more purposeful interpretation of s. 9 was provided by Mr. Justice Sherstobitoff for the majority of the Saskatchewan Court of Appeal in *Iron* (1987).[40] In the course of a ruling that a routine random stop by the police on a rural highway for the purpose of checking documents had been contrary to s. 9, he held as follows:

> For any detention to be constitutional under s. 9 it must be provided for by either statute or common law, and the law providing for the power to detain must not permit detention to be effected on the basis of unfettered police discretion or in the absence of reasonable and probable grounds to believe that an offence has been or is being committed . . . Whether or not a particular detention is justified does not speak to whether it is arbitrary.
>
> The essence of arbitrariness is capriciousness in, and the lack of a reasoned foundation for, the interference with the right that is at the center of both s. 8 and s. 9: the right to be left alone. Justification, on the other hand, is an element of policy, and the only proper forum within the Charter for the balancing of rights and policy is s. 1.[41]

---

less than reasonable grounds is not necessarily arbitrary. The arrest in this case was neither capricious nor random'' (at 154). See too *Moore* (1988), 67 C.R. (3d) 369 (N.S. C.A.) and *Simpson* (1993), 20 C.R. (4th) 1 (Ont. C.A.), discussed below note 77.

[34] (1989), 67 C.R. (3d) 252 (S.C.C.). The Crown could not appeal this ruling: see the annotation in C.R., *ibid.*, p. 253.

[35] (1990), 75 C.R. (3d) 1 (S.C.C.).

[36] *Ibid.*, at 11.

[37] (1998), 21 C.R. (5th) 1 (Ont. C.A.).

[38] Para. 19.

[39] See further below note 89.

[40] (1987), 55 C.R. (3d) 289 (Sask. C.A.). Bayda C.J.S. concurred. Wakeling J.A. dissented. See too, for a more purposeful approach to s. 9: *Konechny* (1983), 10 C.C.C. (3d) 233 (B.C. C.A.).

[41] *Ibid.*, at 311.

We shall soon see that the *Iron* ruling on random vehicle stops must now be taken to have been overruled. However, two aspects of its analysis seem to be important and still authoritative. The ruling that an illegal detention is necessarily arbitrary seems to be consistent with the ruling of the Supreme Court of Canada in *Hunter v. Southam Inc.*, in the context of s. 8,[42] that the Charter should be used to constrain and not to authorize governmental action. Surely, the Charter should not become the indirect means of legitimating the by-passing of legal procedures.[43] Insisting that illegal procedures are necessarily contrary to s. 9 would clearly make it a far more powerful protection.[44] The other ruling in *Iron* which still seems wise and authoritative is the consideration that balancing of interests under the Charter should be left to the stage of a s. 1 inquiry.

3. RANDOM VEHICLE STOPS: DEMONSTRABLY JUSTIFIED ARBITRARY DETENTION

In a series of decisions, the Supreme Court of Canada has established that the police have wide but not unlimited powers to stop motor vehicles.

The dye was cast in the pre-Charter decision in *Dedman* (1985).[45] Dedman had been charged with failing to provide a breath sample without reasonable excuse. His defence was that he had been apprehended under an illegal random vehicle stop to detect impaired drivers in Ontario, under what is known as the R.I.D.E. program. At the time the program had no statutory authority. Mr. Justice Le Dain, for the majority of four justices,[46] held that police power at common law, according to the English *Waterfield* decision,[47] arose where the action was within the general scope of police duties under statute or common law and the interference with liberty was reasonably necessary, having regard to the nature of the liberty interfered with and the importance of the public purpose.[48] The majority further concluded that the R.I.D.E. program fell within such common law power:

> Because of the seriousness of the problem of impaired driving, there can be no doubt about the importance and necessity of a program to improve the deterrence of it. The right to circulate on the highway free from unreasonable interference is an important one, but it is, as I have said, a licensed activity subject to regulation and control in the interest of safety. The objectionable nature of a random stop is chiefly that it is made on a purely arbitrary basis, without any grounds for suspicion or belief that the particular driver has committed or is committing an offence. It is this aspect of the random stop that makes it capable of producing unpleasant psychological effects

---

[42] Above, Chapter 3.

[43] *N. (A.)* (1983), 32 C.R. (3d) 176 (Y.T. Terr. Ct.) (ignoring procedure for swearing information) and *M.* (1982), 70 C.C.C. (2d) 123 (Ont. Fam. Ct.) (juvenile not brought before the Court within 24 hours).

[44] Compare *Pomfret* (1990), 53 C.C.C. (3d) 56 (Man. C.A.) (no violation of s. 9 despite no 90-day bail review mandated by Criminal Code).

[45] (1985), 46 C.R. (3d) 193 (S.C.C.).

[46] McIntyre, Lamer and Wilson JJ.

[47] [1964] 1 Q.B. 164.

[48] Above note 45, at 220-221.

for the innocent driver. These effects, however, would tend to be minimized by the well-publicized nature of the program, which is a necessary feature of its deterrent purpose. Moreover, the stop would be of relatively short duration . . .[49]

In vehement dissent, Chief Justice Dickson[50] held that the police had no common law authority to execute their general duties by means of random stops of motorists whom they had no reason to believe had committed, were committing or would commit a criminal offence.[51] The arbitrary stops under the R.I.D.E. program were indistinguishable from detention for questioning and, without validly-enacted legislation to support them, were unlawful. To find that arbitrary police action was justified simply because it was directed at the fulfillment of police duties would be to sanction a dangerous exception to the supremacy of law.[52]

In the context of random police stops of vehicles under the Charter, several courts of appeal sought to restrict the impact of *Dedman*. For example, the Manitoba Court of Appeal held such stops to be unconstitutional only where there had been prior publicity.[53] The Saskatchewan Court of Appeal insisted upon reasonable ground to believe that an offence has been or is being committed.[54] In *Ladouceur*,[55] Mr. Justice Tarnopolsky, for the majority of the Ontario Court of Appeal, held that the wide power to stop motorists in s. 189(a)(1) of the Highway Traffic Act, by then the purported authority for the R.I.D.E. program, was indeed arbitrary and contrary to s. 9 and had to be read down as

> limited to an organized program of stopping, like the R.I.D.E. program, or roadblocks where all vehicles are required to halt, or to stopping for some articulable cause.[56]

These attempts to restrict random vehicle stop powers were swept away by the Supreme Court. In *Hufsky* (1988),[57] Mr. Justice Le Dain for a unanimous Court, including Chief Justice Dickson, determined that the power in s. 189(a)(1) of the Ontario Provincial Highway Traffic Act authorizing random vehicle stops constituted an implied limit on the right not to be arbitrarily detained and was reasonable and demonstrably justified under s. 1. The Court stressed the importance of highway safety and the role to be played by random stops in detecting motor vehicle offences, many of which could not be detected by mere

---

[49] *Ibid.*, at 221.

[50] Beetz and Chouinard JJ. concurred.

[51] Above note 45, at 202.

[52] *Ibid.*, at 205-207. In *Kokesch* (1990), 1 C.R. (4th) 62 at 73 (S.C.C.), Sopinka J., for a majority in a search case, see above, Chapter 3 and below Chapter 11, held, however:
> Where . . . police powers are already constrained by statute or judicial decisions, it is not open to a police officer to test the limits by ignoring the constraint and claiming later to have been "in execution of my duties".

[53] *Neufeld* (1986), 48 C.R. (3d) 176 (Man. C.A.).

[54] *Iron*, above note 40, *Pashovitz* (1987), 59 C.R. (3d) 396 (Sask. C.A.).

[55] Above note 14.

[56] *Ibid.*, at 76.

[57] Above note 4. For highly critical comments on *Hufsky*, see Thomas E.K. Fitzgerald (1988), 63 C.R. (3d) 28; M. Naeem Rauf (1988), 63 C.R. (3d) 34; and Eric Colvin and Tim Quigley, "Developments in Criminal Law and Procedure: The 1987-88 Term" (1989), 11 *Sup. Ct. L. Rev.* 165 at 194-197.

observation of driving. The stop in question had the dual purpose of checking for driving papers and also the sobriety of drivers. The only guideline had been that at least one marked police vehicle had to be present. There were no criteria to determine which vehicle should be stopped. This was in the sole discretion of the officer. The officer who stopped the accused was in uniform but in an unmarked car. There had been nothing unusual about the accused's driving. The Court concluded its brief reasons as follows:

> The nature and degree of the intrusion of a random stop for the purposes of the spot check procedure in the present case, remembering that the driving of a motor vehicle is a licensed activity subject to regulation and control in the interests of safety, is proportionate to the purpose to be served. If the stopping of motor vehicles for such purposes is not to be seriously inhibited, it should not, in my respectful opinion, be subjected to the kinds of conditions or restrictions reflected in the American jurisprudence,[58] which would appear seriously to undermine its effectiveness while not significantly reducing its intrusiveness. As for publicity, which was referred to in *Dedman*, supra, in connection with common law authority for a random stop for the purposes contemplated by the R.I.D.E. program, I think it may be taken now that the public is well aware of random stop authority because of both its frequent and widespread exercise and its recognition by legislatures.[59]

Some commentators[60] and even the Saskatchewan Court of Appeal[61] attempted to distinguish *Hufsky* in the case of random roving stops, which were seen to be more arbitrary and more intrusive than a check-point stop. However, a five to four majority of the Supreme Court in *Ladouceur* (1990)[62] held that there was to be no such distinction and such random stops were also to be demonstrably justified under s. 1 as reasonable limits on arbitrary detention. For the majority, Mr. Justice Cory[63] noted that stopping vehicles was the only way of checking a driver's licence and insurance, the mechanical fitness of a vehicle, and the sobriety of the driver. Random stops supplied the only effective deterrent. Furthermore, effective organized programs were an impossibility in rural areas and generally difficult to establish due to physical constraints and shortages of personnel. The stops were of relatively short duration, requiring the production of only a few documents and caused minimal inconvenience to the driver.[64]

Mr. Justice Sopinka for the minority[65] would have read the power down, as had the Ontario Court of Appeal:[66]

> This case may be viewed as the last straw. If sanctioned, we will be agreeing that a police officer can stop any vehicle at any time, in any place, without having any

---

[58] Under U.S. jurisprudence, permanent check points are more likely to be constitutional than temporary, roving patrols: see Thomas Fitzgerald, comment in C.R. *ibid.*, at 31-32.

[59] Above note 4, at 25-26.

[60] Fitzgerald, above note 58.

[61] *Emke* (1989), 70 C.R. (3d) 347 (Sask. C.A.).

[62] Above note 6.

[63] Lamer, L'Heureux-Dubé, Gonthier and McLachlin JJ. concurred.

[64] Above note 6, at 132-135.

[65] Dickson C.J., Wilson and La Forest JJ. concurred. The minority concurred in the result as it would not have excluded the evidence in the circumstances.

[66] Compare the view of Julian Falconer, "Hufsky v. The Queen and Leave in Ladouceur: What's Left?" (1988), 30 *Crim. L.Q.* 467 at 474-475, that it was not the Court's role to redraft legislation.

reason to do so. For the motorist, this means a total negation of the freedom from arbitrary detention guaranteed by s. 9 of the Charter. This is something that would not be tolerated with respect to pedestrians in their use of the public streets and walkways.[67]

This random, roving stop infringed the right far more than the organized random stops at predetermined locations authorized by *Hufsky* and had the potential for abuse.[68]

In *Hufsky* and *Ladouceur*, the Supreme Court clearly recognized a wide constitutional power for police to stop motorists at random. There is a clear risk of arbitrariness and discriminatory treatment in the decision to stop against which there is no Charter protection.[69] We have seen, however, that in *Mellenthin* (1992),[70] Cory J. for a unanimous 5-judge Court, imposed Charter limits on police questioning and searches following a random vehicle stop.[71] Stop programs are limited to checks for sobriety, licences, ownership, insurance and mechanical fitness. Visual inspection for officer safety and more intrusive searches require reasonable grounds.

Hufsky and *Ladouceur* confirm that before a random vehicle check can be held to be demonstrably justified under s. 1, it must be prescribed by law in the form of a statute or at common law, as in the case of *Dedman*. In a companion case to *Ladouceur*, that in *Wilson* (1990),[72] the Supreme Court held that a random vehicle stop power could be implied from s. 119 of the Highway Traffic Act of Alberta. That provision requires a driver not merely to surrender his licence on demand but, when ''signalled or requested to stop,'' to bring his vehicle to a stop and furnish any information respecting the driver or the vehicle requested by the peace officer. A holding of the Saskatchewan Court of Appeal on similar legislation that a random stop power should *not* be implied from police duties has thus been implicitly overruled.[73]

---

67 Above note 6, at 118.

68 *Ibid.*, at 119. See too *Emke*, above note 61, and comment by M. Naeem Rauf, C.R., above note 57, pp. 34-36.

69 The *Report of the Commission on Systemic Racism in the Ontario Criminal Justice System* (December, 1995) has recently documented that members of visible minorities are far more likely to be stopped by police in Toronto. Courts have thus far been unreceptive to Charter challenges against allegedly discriminatory law enforcement in particular cases under s. 7, above Chapter 2, or under s. 15, below Chapter 11.

70 (1992), 16 C.R. (4th) 273 (S.C.C.), discussed above Chapter 3 and below Chapter 11.

71 See generally David Tanovich, ''The Constitutionality of Searches Incident to Vehicle Stops'', (1993) 35 *Crim.L.Q.* 323.

72 (1990), 77 C.R. (3d) 137 (S.C.C.). *Wilson* was applied in *MacLennan* (1995), 97 C.C.C. (3d) 69 (N.S. C.A.).

73 *Emke*, above note 61. In *Caissie* (1999) 138 C.C.C. (3d) 205 (N.B. C.A.) the implied power was held not to extend to a stop on private property. Compare, however, *Mulligan* (2000), 31 C.R. (5th) 281 (Ont. C.A.) which disturbingly finds such a power on the basis of an implied licence to enter to protect interests of the property owner or occupant from reasonably suspected crime. A better inquiry would have been under the ancillary powers doctrine identified by Doherty J.A. in *Simpson,* below note 75.

What of vehicle stops for a reason other than to check for a driving offence? The Saskatchewan Court of Appeal[74] relied on Sopinka J.'s dissenting judgment in *Ladouceur* for the view that the stop could be for any reason not just related to traffic offences.

Since *Mellenthin*, however, it has been widely accepted[75] that a random vehicle stop relying on a Highway Traffic power must have a purpose related to the operation of motor vehicles. It cannot be for other reasons. The danger here, as Sopinka J. identified in his dissent in *Ladouceur*, is that it will be difficult to review a vehicle stop to determine whether a reason said to have been "routine vehicle inspection" was not really a pretext for something quite different. Furthermore the Ontario Court of Appeal has recently confirmed in *Brown v. Durham* that the random vehicle stop will not become illegal and will be constitutional if the police have another purpose for the stop provided that it is not improper. Large scale checkpoint stops of motorcycle gang members on the way to their club property was held to be authorised by s. 216(1) of the Highway Traffic Act where the trial judge had found that highway safety was one of the reasons for the stops. Additional purposes such as intelligence gathering did not make the stop unlawful.

The Newfoundland Court of Appeal[76] is alone in resolutely continuing, despite *Hufsky* and *Ladouceur,* to require an articulable cause for any vehicle stop.

4. DETENTION FOR QUESTIONING ON ARTICULABLE CAUSE

In his influential judgment for the Ontario Court of Appeal in *Simpson* (1993),[77] Mr. Justice Doherty held that, where an individual is detained by the police in the course of efforts to determine whether that individual is involved in criminal activity, detention can be justified under the common law ancillary powers doctrine if the detaining officer has some "articulable cause" for the detention. The Court reviewed American jurisprudence on "articulate cause"[78] to arrive at a test of

> a constellation of objectively discernible facts which give the detaining officer reasonable cause to suspect that the detainee is criminally implicated in the activity under investigation.[79]

---

[74] *Duncanson* (1991), 12 C.R. (4th) 86 (Sask. C.A.), an issue expressly avoided by the Supreme Court in dismissing the further appeal: (1992), 12 C.R. (4th) 98 (S.C.C.).

[75] *Simpson* (1993), 20 C.R. (4th) 1 (Ont. C.A.), *Wilson* (1993), 86 C.C.C. (3d) 145 (B.C. C.A.), *Soucisse* (1994), 5 M.V.R. (3d) 207 (Que. C.A.), *MacLennan* (1995), 97 C.C.C. (3d) 69 (N.S. C.A.) and *Guénette* (1999), 136 C.C.C. (3d) 311 (Que. C.A.).

[76] *Griffin* (1996), 111 C.C.C. (3d) 490 (Nfld. C.A.), *Burke* (1997), 118 C.C.C. (3d) 59 (Nfld. C.A.) and *Pearce* (1997), 120 C.C.C. (3d) 467 (Nfld. C.A.). Wayne Gorman, "Arbitrary Detentions and Random Stops", (1998) 41 *Crim. L.Q.* 41 rightly sees this requirement as inconsistent with the position of the Supreme Court on random vehicle stops.

[77] *Ibid.*

[78] *Terry v. Ohio*, 392 U.S. 1 (1968) and *U.S. v. Cortez*, 449 U.S. 411.

[79] At 22. For applications see *S. (C.)* (1997), 13 C.R. (5th) 375 (Ont. Prov. Div.) (observation accused

A "hunch" based entirely on intuition gained by experience would not be enough even if it proved accurate. Such subjectively based assessments could

> too easily mask discriminatory conduct based on such irrelevant factors as the detainee's sex, colour, age, ethnic origin or sexual orientation.[80]

Doherty J.A. further held that, even if there was an articulable cause under this test, this would not end a broader inquiry. Justifiability under the ancillary powers doctrine required an assessment of the totality of the circumstances which depended upon a number of factors including the nature of the duty, the extent of interference with individual liberty necessitated, the importance of the duty to the public good, the liberty interfered with and the nature and extent of the interference.[81] Even if there was articulate cause, detention might not be justified. He provided several examples:

> [A] reasonably based suspicion that a person committed some property-related offence at a distant point in the past without an articulate cause, would not, standing alone, justify the detention of that person on a public street to question him or her about the offence. On the other hand, a reasonable suspicion that a person had just committed a violent crime and was in flight from the scene of that crime could well justify some detention of that individual in an effort to quickly conform or refute the suspicion. Similarly, the existence of an articulable cause that justified a brief detention, perhaps to ask the person detained for identification, would not necessarily justify a more intrusive detention complete with physical restraint and a more extensive interrogation.[82]

The recognition in *Simpson* of a power to detain for questioning can be criticized on a number of fronts. The Court, in the guise of regulating police action, was undoubtedly creating new police powers, yet the Charter was intended to constrain rather than authorise governmental action.[83] The Court relies heavily on the ancillary powers doctrine adopted by the Supreme Court in *Dedman*, but makes no mention of subsequent Supreme Court decisions where that doctrine was not employed in rulings that police power must be explicitly authorised by statute.[84] Wasn't it for Parliament to define a "stop and frisk" power? This criticism has now been blunted. We have seen in the previous chapter that the Supreme Court in *Godoy* (1998)[85] later embraced the ancillary powers doctrine in the context of police investigation of a disconnected 911 call and expressly gave its *imprimatur* to Justice Doherty's approach.

---

black and having cell phone not enough for articulable cause that he was drug dealer) and *Cox* (1999), 132 C.C.C. (3d) 256 (N.B. C.A.) (profile of tobacco smugglers as driving older model large car with big trunk not constituting articulable cause for vehicle stop). The issue of racial profiling has been the subject of much wider debate in the United States: see, for example, David Harris, "Factors for Reasonable Suspicion: When Black and Poor Means Stopped and Frisked", (1994) 69 *Indiana L.J.* 659.

[80] *Ibid.*

[81] At 20.

[82] At 24.

[83] See R.J. Delisle, "Judicial Creation of Police Powers", (1993) 20 C.R. (4th) 29.

[84] See, for example, *Colet* (1981), 57 C.C.C. (2d) 105 (S.C.C.) and *Kokesch* (1990), 1 C.R. (4th) 62 (S.C.C.), discussed above Chapter 3.

[85] (1998), 21 C.R. (5th) 205 (S.C.C.).

On the positive side, the Court in *Simpson* has adopted a carefully crafted compromise that by no means gives a free hand to the police. *Simpson* provides authority to make preliminary investigations in situations where citizens might well expect the police to have power to act.

That the *Simpson* power is limited is well illustrated by the Court's ruling on the facts. A police officer read an internal police memorandum describing a particular residence as a suspected "crack house". He decided to patrol the area and saw a vehicle in the driveway of the residence. The sole occupant, a woman, left the car running, entered the residence briefly, and then, accompanied by the accused, returned to the vehicle and drove off. The officer followed them, pulled the vehicle over and, observing a bulge in the accused's front pants pocket, asked him to remove the object. It was a baggie containing cocaine. For the Court, Doherty J.A. held that the stop could not be authorized under the Highway Traffic Act as it was not related to the operation of motor vehicles. The Court further held that there was no articulate cause that could justify its newly recognized common law power to detain for questioning. The officer had no information as to the source or reliability of the information that the residence was a "crack house" and no knowledge about either person in the vehicle. This, held the Court, did not amount to reasonable suspicion. Both ss. 8 and 9 had been breached and the evidence of the drugs should be excluded.

The distinction between reasonable suspicion for detention and reasonable grounds for arrest seems hard to draw. It is at least clear that the Ontario Court of Appeal requires more for a legal arrest and hence for search incident to that arrest. The Court has held[86] that the arrest of a black person in a mall near the scene of a recent robbery as he answered the general description of the suspect as "male, black, 5' 8" to 5' 11", with a short afro, wearing a dark jacket, armed with a knife and a gun" could not amount to reasonable and probable grounds for arrest. The physical description matched any number of persons in downtown Toronto. An articulable cause for detention was not enough. The Court has also held[87] that the drugs arrest of a person an officer recognized from previous dealings because he put something in his mouth, turned his head and walked away very quickly, could not provide the subjective or objective basis required to provide reasonable and probable grounds for an arrest without warrant.[88]

There is important case law on the interpretation of the *Simpson* stop power. In *Brown v. Durham* (1998)[89] Doherty J.A. decided for the Ontario Court of Appeal that the police could not rely on the ancillary powers doctrine in the case of their wholesale checkpoint stop of members of a biker gang. Any apprehended harm was not imminent. There was no specific identifiable harm which the

---

[86] *Charley* (1993), 22 C.R. (4th) 297 (Ont. C.A.).

[87] *Johnson* (1995), 39 C.R. (4th) 78 (Ont. C.A.).

[88] *Hall* (1995), 39 C.R. (4th) 66 (Ont. C.A.) is authority that the "constellation of objectively discernible facts" test for investigation is also part of the test for a lawful arrest. An arrest of a hitchhiker and search incident to arrest were based on reasonable grounds as the officer believed that the accused matched the description of the suspect in a break and enter and observed that the accused was wearing an expensive watch and jewellery.

[89] Above note 37.

detentions sought to prevent. The police concern that some harm could occur rested not on what those detained had done, but rather on what others who shared a similar lifestyle with those who were detained had done at other places and at other times. The liberty interfered with was not a qualified liberty like the right to drive, but rather the fundamental right to move about in the community. The interference with individual liberty resulting from the police conduct was substantial in terms of the number of persons detained, the number of times individuals were detained and the length of the detentions. Finally the detentions could not be said to be necessary to the maintenance of the public peace. A large police presence without detention would have served that purpose. In fact, it was arguable that the confrontational nature of the detentions served to put the public peace at risk.

In *Powell* (2000)[90] Judge Lane of the Ontario Court of Justice determined that police stopping a pedestrian for identification and subsequent C.P.I.C. check amounted to arbitrary detention contrary to s. 9 of the Charter. There had been a movement away from a strict application of the *Moran* test in the determination of whether or not a detention has occurred. Recent cases appeared to indicate:

(1) that there can be a range of detentions including a "brief detention" for the purpose of identification;
(2) that compulsion to respond to questions posed by a police officer can be presumed, unless there is evidence indicating informed consent; and,
(3) that consideration of whether the police had "articulable cause" or other authority to stop someone in the first place is fundamental to the legality of the entire encounter.

Where there is no "articulable cause," the court could find that there was a detention and an illegal search without the need for any testimony by the accused as to his subjective perception of a sense of compulsion, and without considering the specific factors set out in the *Moran* test. In this case, although the encounter occurred at mid-day and was initially relatively innocuous, the entire sequence of events smacked somewhat of a "fishing expedition," if not an even more pernicious "bait and switch" operation. In all the circumstances, detention began with stopping the accused's freedom of movement on the street, it continued with a "brief detention for the purpose of identification," and extended to the wait for the results of the C.P.I.C. search. The detention had been arbitrary as the officers had no articulable cause to stop the accused and his cousin. They were not suspects in any matter, nor did they match the description of anyone banned under the Trespass to Property Act. The officers were not investigating any particular offense, but were engaged in proactive policing to deal with a variety of problems in a high-crime neighbourhood. There was no "constellation of objectively-discernible facts" which gave the police team any justification to interfere with the accused. The common law ancillary power doctrine could not justify the detention which had occurred.

On the authorisation side, the Quebec Court of Appeal turned to the ancillary powers doctrine to hold legal a police roadblock to try to apprehend escaping

---

[90] (2000), 35 C.R. (5th) 89 (Ont. C.J.).

bank robbers,[91] and there appears to be recognition of a power to search incident to detention for articulable cause.[92]

5. REMEDY

Where the violation of s. 9 results in evidence, the normal remedy will be to consider the possibility of exclusion of evidence under s. 24(2). When the arbitrary detention follows the obtaining of sufficient evidence for guilt, the question of remedy is uncertain and controversial and is separately discussed later in Chapter 11. Some courts grant stays or reduce the sentence. Other courts refuse to give any remedy.

---

[91] *Murray* (1999), 32 C.R. (5th) 253 (Que. C.A.).

[92] *Ferris* (1998), 16 C.R. (5th) 287 (B.C. C.A.) and *Johnson* (2000), 32 C.R. (5th) 236 (B.C. C.A.) (power to search for weapons being automatic; power to search for evidence requiring reasonable and probable grounds). See too *Lake* (1996), 113 C.C.C. (3d) 208 (Sask. C.A.) and *McAuley* (1998), 124 C.C.C. (3d) 117 (Man. C.A.).

5

Section 10: Rights on Arrest or Detention

Under s. 10 of the Charter

Everyone has the right on arrest or detention

(a) to be informed promptly of the reasons therefor;
(b) to retain and instruct counsel without delay and to be informed of that right; and
(c) to have the validity of the detention determined by way of *habeas corpus* and to he released if the detention is not lawful.

Section 2 of the Canadian Bill of Rights provides that

no law of Canada shall be construed or applied so as to . . .

(c) deprive a person who has been arrested or detained
   (i) of the right to be informed promptly of the reason for his arrest or detention,
   (ii) of the right to retain and instruct counsel without delay, or
   (iii) of the remedy by way of habeas corpus for the determination of the validity of his detention and for his release if the detention is not lawful.

1. TRIGGERING MECHANISM: ARREST OR DETENTION

The rights conferred in s. 10 are not absolute and are available only to one under arrest or detention. The judicial interpretation of ''arrest'' or ''detention'' determines the very existence of the rights.

(a) Arrest

For the purpose of engaging s. 10 rights, the key question is whether an arrest occurred rather than whether the arrest was legal. In the pre-Charter decision in *Whitfield* (1970)[1] the majority of the Supreme Court adopted the following definition from *Halsbury's Laws of England*:[2]

---

[1] (1970), 9 C.R.N.S. 59 (S.C.C.).
[2] 10 *Hals.*, 3rd ed., p. 342.

Arrest consists of the actual seizure or touching of a person's body with a view to his detention. The mere pronouncing of words of arrest is not an arrest unless the person sought to be arrested submits to the process and goes with the arresting officer. An arrest may be made either with or without a warrant.[3]

In the view of the majority, the police officer had arrested the accused when he grabbed Whitfield's shirt through his car window saying, "You're under arrest", although the accused had broken the officer's hold and accelerated away.[4] Arrest by touching where there is no submission seems to assert a fiction. The attempt to arrest failed.

In *Latimer* (1997)[5] the father of a severely disabled daughter advised the police that she had passed away in her sleep. When an autopsy found signs of poisoning the police visited the father and advised him: "You are being detained for investigation into the death of your daughter". The Supreme Court, in the course of dismissing an argument that there had been arbitrary detention contrary to s. 9 of the Charter, held that there had been a *de facto* arrest. It would be unduly formalistic to require the police to use the word "arrest".

(b) Detention

(i) *Including psychological compulsion*

The Supreme Court of Canada unanimously decided in *Therens* (1985)[6] that one under demand to accompany a police officer to a police station to submit to a breathalyzer test is detained within the meaning of s. 10(b) and therefore entitled to be informed of the right to retain and instruct counsel without delay.

The only fully reasoned judgment, and still the leading judgment on the meaning of detention, is that of Mr. Justice Le Dain speaking for half the Court.[7] Pre-Charter judicial decisions were "not a reliable guide"[8] to the interpretation of the Charter. The Court could reject its narrow interpretation of detention in *Chromiak* (1980),[9] in which it had held that a person subjected to a roadside test was *not* detained under s. 2(c) of the Bill of Rights. Le Dain J. adopted the views of Mr. Justice Tallis in the Saskatchewan Court of Appeal, the Court below, that the Charter had to be interpreted "in a meaningful way from the standpoint of an average citizen" and not "blunted . . . or thwarted by technical or legalistic interpretations of ordinary words."[10] Detention within s. 10 of the Charter extended beyond "deprivation of liberty by physical constraint"[11] to include two other situations:

---

[3] *Ibid.*

[4] In dissent, Hall J. (Spence J. concurring) rejected the technical notion of arrest by touching but held there would have to be a submission.

[5] (1997), 4 C.R. (5th) 1 (S.C.C.).

[6] (1985), 45 C.R. (3d) 97 (S.C.C.).

[7] Dickson C.J.C., McIntyre and Lamer JJ. concurred on this point.

[8] Above note 6, at 120.

[9] (1980), 12 C.R. (3d) 300 (S.C.C.).

[10] (1983), 33 C.R. (3d) 204 at 221 (Sask. C.A.). Prior to *Therens* all other Courts of Appeal had applied *Chromiak* to the Charter context.

[11] Above note 6, at 124.

[W]hen a police officer or other agent of the state assumes control over the movement of a person by a demand or direction which may have significant legal consequence and which prevents or impedes access to counsel;[12] [and] [E]ven where there is in fact a lack of statutory or common law authority for the demand or direction and therefore an absence of criminal liability for failure to comply with it" but "the person concerned submits or acquiesces in the deprivation of liberty and reasonably believes that the choice to do otherwise does not exist.[13]

This third and wider meaning of what was referred to as "psychological compulsion, in the form of a reasonable perception of suspension of freedom of choice''[14] was expressly *obiter* and justified on the basis that it is generally not realistic to regard compliance with a demand or direction by a police officer as truly voluntary.[15]

Later, for a unanimous seven judge panel in *Thomsen* (1988),[16] Mr. Justice Le Dain reasserted his approach to detention in ruling that a person subjected to a demand to provide a roadside breath sample was also "detained" for the purposes of s. 10. The Court went on to hold that there was no right to counsel since the particular demand provision constituted a demonstrably justified reasonable limit on s. 10(b).[17] The following is its authoritative summary of the present approach to detention under s. 10 of the Charter:

1. In its use of the word detention', s. 10 of the Charter is directed to a restraint of liberty other than arrest in which a person may reasonably require the assistance of counsel but might be prevented or impeded from retaining and instructing counsel without delay but for the constitutional guarantee.
2. In addition to the case of deprivation of liberty by physical constraint, there is a detention within s. 10 of the Charter when a police officer or other agent of the state assumes control over the movement of a person by a demand or direction which may have significant legal consequence and which prevents or impedes access to counsel.
3. The necessary element of compulsion or coercion to constitute a detention may arise from criminal liability for refusal to comply with a demand or direction, or from a reasonable belief that one does not have a choice as to whether or not to comply.

---

[12] *Ibid.*

[13] *Ibid.*, at 125-126.

[14] *Ibid.*

[15] *Ibid.*, at 125. This is consistent with the unanimous holding in *Dedman* (1985), 46 C.R. (3d) 193 (S.C.C.) that an accused's compliance with a police signal to stop at a roadblock is not voluntary so as to confer a legal power to search on consent.

[16] (1988), 63 C.R. (3d) 1 (S.C.C.). Courts of Appeal are now unanimously of the view that a motorist required to perform physical co-ordination tests for sobriety is detained: *Bonogofski* (1987), 39 C.C.C. (3d) 457 (B.C. C.A.); *Saunders* (1988), 63 C.R. (3d) 37 (Ont. C.A.); *Baroni* (1989), 49 C.C.C. (3d) 553 (N.S. C.A.); *Gallant* (1989), 70 C.R. (3d) 139 (Alta. C.A.); *Oldham* (1996), 49 C.R. (4th) 251 (N.B. C.A.) and *Roy* (1997), 117 C.C.C. (3d) 243 (Que. C.A.).

[17] See above, Chapter 1. In *Grant* (1991), 7 C.R. (4th) 388 (S.C.C.), Lamer C.J., for the Court, expressed an inclination to agree with the view that *Thomsen* was still authoritative despite a 1985 amendment that had deleted the word "roadside" from the approved screening demanded in s. 254(2) of the Criminal Code. In *Bernshaw* (1995), 35 C.R. (4th) 201 (S.C.C.), the majority held that a delay in the order of 15 minutes in order to obtain a proper reading was not inconsistent with *Thomsen.*

4. Section 10 of the Charter applies to a great variety of detentions of varying duration and is not confined to those of such duration as to make the effective use of habeas corpus possible.[18]

In *Simmons* (1988),[19] the Supreme Court confirmed that on the Le Dain approach to detention "not all communications with police officers and other state authorities will amount to 'detention' within the meaning of s. 10(b) of the Charter."[20] Clearly, the Supreme Court envisages distinctions of degree. This is evident in the decision in *Simmons* itself. Routine questioning by customs officials or random luggage searches by such officials does not constitute detention for the purposes of s. 10, but there is a detention and entitlement to s. 10 rights where a person has been "taken out of the normal course and forced to submit to a strip search."[21]

In *Dehghani v. Minister of Employment and Immigration* (1993),[22] the Supreme Court confirmed that a secondary examination by an immigration officer at point of entry into Canada did not constitute a detention such as to engage s. 10(b) rights. The questioning remained a routine part of the general screening process of entry of those who were not citizens. The British Columbia Court of Appeal subsequently held[23] there was equally no detention where the secondary inspection at an airport was on suspicion that the person entering was carrying drugs.

(ii) *Police questioning*

Courts have had difficulty with the *Therens* notion of psychological detention in situations where police are questioning an accused short of an arrest or physical detention. Decisions, including those of the Supreme Court, have been inconsistent.

The issue has received the most comprehensive consideration by the Ontario Court of Appeal. The approach of that Court was first established in *Esposito* (1985).[24] Police officers, investigating the fraudulent use of a lost bank credit card, obtained 18 invoices of gas purchases with the missing card at a gas station at which the accused was an attendant. Twelve different licence plate numbers appeared on the invoices. Some invoices were initialled, and of those some bore the accused's initials. Late one evening the police questioned the accused at his

---

[18] Above note 16, at 8-9.

[19] (1988), 66 C.R. (3d) 297 (S.C.C.). In *Debot* (1989), 73 C.R. (3d) 129 (S.C.C.), the Court confirmed that the occupant of a vehicle suspected of a drug offence was detained when stopped and frisked.

[20] *Ibid.*, at 316-317. In *Grafe* (1987) 60 C.R. (3d) 242 (Ont. C.A.), it was held that a pedestrian asked for identification by an officer had not been detained.

[21] *Ibid.*, at 319. See too the companion decision in *Jacoy* (1988), 66 C.R. (3d) 336 (S.C.C.). For criticism of this distinction see Eric Colvin and Tim Quigley, "Developments in Criminal Law and Procedure: The 1988-89 Term" (1990), 1 *Sup. Ct. L. Rev.* 187 at 224-225.

[22] (1993), 20 C.R. (4th) 34 (S.C.C.).

[23] *Hardy* (1995), 103 C.C.C. (3d) 289 (B.C. C.A.).

[24] (1985), 49 C.R. (3d) 193 (Ont. C.A.), followed in *Maclean* (1987), 36 C.C.C. (3d) 127 (N.S. C.A.) and *Boutin* (1989), 49 C.C.C. (3d) 46 (Que. C.A.). See too *Arnold* (1991), 65 C.C.C. (3d) 171 (N.S. C.A.).

home, confronting him with the invoices. The Court held that he had not been detained at this point and was not entitled to be advised of his right to counsel. Mr. Justice Martin for the Court referred to the "deeply rooted"[25] right to remain silent, noting that the police have the common law power to question but not to compel answers nor to detain for questioning. The Court carefully assessed the Le Dain approach to psychological detention and expressed concern that the approach might lead to the result that, in any case of police questioning, the subject should be regarded as detained and entitled to his s. 10 rights. The Court found a limit in jurisprudence of the United States Supreme Court that their Miranda warning[26] of the right to remain silent is not required for every type of police questioning and applies only in a coercive environment. Here, the questions did not have intimidating or inducing over-tones. There was no evidence that the accused actually believed that his freedom was restrained, and the circumstances would not have lead him to reasonably believe that his freedom had been restrained.[27]

The Ontario Court further developed its cautious approach in the context of questioning at a police station. In the leading decision in *Moran* (1987),[28] Mr. Justice Martin, for the Court, summarized an approach of considering all the circumstances in which the following factors might be relevant, although none was determinative:

1. The precise language used by the police officer in requesting the person who subsequently becomes an accused to come to the police station, and whether the accused was given a choice or expressed a preference that the interview be conducted at the police station, rather than at his or her home;
2. whether the accused was escorted to the police station by a police officer or came himself or herself in response to a police request;
3. whether the accused left at the conclusion of the interview or whether he or she was arrested;
4. the stage of the investigation, that is, whether the questioning was part of the general investigation of a crime or possible crime or whether the police had already decided that a crime had been committed and that the accused was the perpetrator or involved in its commission and the questioning was conducted for the purpose of obtaining incriminating statements from the accused;
5. whether the police had reasonable and probable grounds to believe that the accused had committed the crime being investigated;
6. the nature of the questions: whether they were questions of a general nature designed to obtain information or whether the accused was confronted with evidence pointing to his or her guilt;
7. the subjective belief by an accused that he or she is detained, although relevant, is not decisive, because the issue is whether he or she *reasonably* believed that he or she was detained. Personal circumstances relating to the accused, such as low intelligence, emotional disturbance, youth and lack of sophistication are circumstances to be considered in determining whether he had a subjective belief that he was detained.[29]

---

[25] *Ibid.*, at 200.
[26] *Miranda v. Arizona*, 384 U.S. 436 (1966).
[27] See too *Smith* (1986), 49 C.R. (3d) 210 (Man. C.A.).
[28] (1987), 36 C.C.C. (3d) 225 (Ont. C.A.).
[29] *Ibid.*, at 258-259.

Moran, the friend of a victim in a murder case, had not been detained when he had been interviewed for a second time by the police at the police station at a time in which he was suspect and subjected to pressing questioning. He had been allowed to leave and had only been arrested for the offence some two months later.

The advantage of this multi-factor approach is to make it clear beyond *Dedman* that the knowledge and tactics of the police must also be considered. In applying *Moran*, the Ontario Court of Appeal may well have been too protective of law enforcement interests. At the heart of the purposive Le Dain approach is the notion that voluntary cooperation with police is often not truly voluntary. The Ontario Court has often been curiously impervious to the coercive realities behind "requests" by police to answer questions at home, at the office or at a police station, especially when it is clear to the person to be questioned that he or she is a suspect.[30] This may encourage police to defer arrests until after interrogation without the need to advise of the right to counsel.The right to silence is effectively bypassed.

A decision of the Ontario Court of Appeal in *Johns* (1998)[31] appears to establish a welcome change in approach in applying *Moran*. The accused was convicted on five counts of break and enter. The trial judge based the conviction in part on an oral statement made by the accused to police officers during a lengthy interview at a police station. The trial judge admitted the statement even though the accused had not been advised as to his right to counsel under s. 10(b) of the Canadian Charter of Rights and Freedoms. The right had not been denied as he was not in detention. The Ontario Court of Appeal reversed this ruling. Justice Laskin for the Court held that there were a number of considerations leading to the conclusion that he had been detained when he made the inculpatory statement and should have been advised of his rights under s. 10(b) of the Charter. Despite the accused's express preference to be interviewed at home, the police wanted to question him at the police station. He was taken to the police station in a police cruiser escorted by two officers, one of whom had come along solely to pick him up. After the interview he was arrested. The police's interview was not part of a general investigation of a crime or possible crime. When the officers questioned

---

[30] See, for example, *Lawrence* (1990), 59 C.C.C. (3d) 55 (Ont. C.A.) (cyclist stopped on street by police cruiser and questioned for 25 minutes concerning break and entry in area not detained) and *Pabani* (1994), 29 C.R. (4th) 364 (Ont. C.A.) (police not violating s. 10(b) by photographing accused's right hand at police station during investigation on night his wife was killed).

[31] (1998), 14 C.R. (5th) 302 (Ont. C.A.). See too *Voss* (1989), 71 C.R. (3d) 178 (Ont. C.A.) (accused being questioned in death of wife detained from moment his implication in her death became evident from the forensic evidence and the investigation changed from one of trying to determine the cause of death to getting information from a man who had admitted having assaulted his wife), *Calder* (1994), 32 C.R. (4th) 197 (Ont. C.A.) (police officer suspected of sexual assault detained where ordered by superiors to speak to investigators) and *Young* (1997), 8 C.R. (5th) 343 (Ont. C.A.) (accused detained when stopped in street on suspicion of burglary, expressly overruling *Lawrence*, above note 30). But see *Caputo* (1997), 114 C.C.C. (3d) 1 (Ont. C.A.) (accused not detained when police interviewed him in windowless and probably locked room at station as to suspicious death after police learned deceased had recently broken off relationship with the accused).

him they already knew that a crime had been committed and that he was a suspect. The police admitted that they had reasonable and probable grounds to arrest him for possession of stolen property, the same stolen property taken in the break and enters that they were investigating. He was asked pointed questions about his participation in the break and enters. His denials were not accepted; instead he was confronted with his inconsistent answers and with other evidence pointing to his guilt and repeatedly told that he was not telling the truth. He believed that he was detained while he was being questioned and this belief was reasonable. He knew that his cousin was in custody for the same offences as those he was being questioned about. The questioning took place in a coercive environment: he was interviewed in a small room which was closed most of the time, the questioning was prolonged and at least one officer was in the room during the entire interview. The interview was not recorded and though both police officers were experienced, neither took proper notes of their questioning. Moreover, although one officer claimed to have told him that he could leave if he wished, the police still continued to question him, continued to confront him with his inconsistent answers and continued to suggest that he was lying. Understandably, he grew more nervous and confused during questioning, and he broke down and began to cry before giving an inculpatory statement. The remark, "you may leave if you wish", by a police officer during more than two hours of questioning was not determinative. To give effect to this utterance and thus to allow the police to avoid their constitutional obligations under the Charter would ignore the coercive realities of police questioning.

Other Courts of Appeal[32] have adopted a simpler and more pro-accused approach under which detention occurs at the moment the accused becomes a suspect. In *Hawkins* (1992),[33] Mr. Justice Marshall for the majority of the Newfoundland Court of Appeal,[34] however, rejected this view as too broad and instead drew the line of detention at

> when ... suspicions become crystallised and the investigator's approach to the encounter is changed from a questioning of the individual to an examination with intent to charge him or her with the offence.[35]

According to the majority, this was the moment that the individual was subject to the coercive power of the state and was most in need of being advised of the right to silence and the right to counsel. It was immaterial that the person being interviewed did not feel that the only choice was to respond. The accused had been detained when he was interviewed at a police station with a view to charging him although he was at no time given the impression that the complaint of sexual assault against him was serious or would amount to anything.[36]

---

[32] See especially *Mickey* (1988), 46 C.C.C. (3d) 278 (B.C. C.A.). See too *Keats* (1987), 60 C.R. (3d) 250 (Nfld. C.A.); *Belliveau* (1986), 54 C.R. (3d) 144 (N.B. C.A.) and *Amyot* (1990), 78 C.R. (3d) 129 (Que. C.A.) (from the time the accused failed a polygraph test at the police station). See too *Siemens* (1994), 30 C.R. (4th) 208 (Man. C.A.).

[33] (1992), 14 C.R. (4th) 286 (Nfld. C.A.).

[34] O'Neill J.A. concurred. Goodridge C.J.N. dissented.

[35] At 298.

[36] At 299.

When *Hawkins* reached the Supreme Court as of right, the highest Court was disappointingly cryptic in allowing the appeal on the basis that accused had not been detained on the facts. The Newfoundland approach may have been an extension of the Le Dain definition of psychological detention, but it was a carefully crafted judgment on an important issue. It also seems to be a balanced and wise compromise.[37] The issue, which was fully argued before the Supreme Court, should have been carefully addressed. The highest Court clearly rejected the conclusion of the Newfoundland Court of Appeal. At face value on this ruling there can never be psychological detention unless the accused actually and reasonably believed that there was no choice but to comply.[38] However the Supreme Court's one line pronouncement does not declare principles upon which to decide future cases. It is also inconsistent with its earlier, equally unreasoned, pronouncement in *Grant* (1991),[39] a vehicle chase case, which found detention based solely on police suspicion.[40] Despite *Hawkins,* the Ontario Court of Appeal has continued to apply its multi-factor approach declared in *Moran.*[41]

The Supreme Court needs to return to the issue. It should decide that the focus should not be exclusively on the state of mind of the accused. As Courts of Appeal have persuasively suggested, detention should also take into account the perceptions of the police. If the accused's perception is the only criterion naive, ignorant and/or scared accused, who give no thought to whether they can leave, will not have been detained and will have no Charter right to be advised of the right to counsel. Those perhaps most in need of Charter protection against coercive police practices will have none.[42] On the other hand, it would be unfortunate if preliminary police questioning of any suspect would have to be peppered with

---

[37] See too David M. Tanovich in his annotation in (1992), 14 C.R. (4th) 287. Anthony Allman in (1993) 18 C.R. (4th) 17, criticises the Court for being too pro-accused and declaring a standard too hard to prove. The test is no less challenging than the usual police standard of reasonable belief.

[38] This appears to be the interpretation applied in *F. (D.M.)* (1999), 139 C.C.C. (3d) 144 (Alta. C.A.).

[39] (1991), 7 C.R. (4th) 388 (S.C.C.).

[40] Lamer C.J. for the Court in *Grant,* above note 17, held that "both the initial detention in (based on the suspicion of driving while disqualified) and the subsequent detention in the police car (based on the suspicion of driving under the influence of alcohol) satisfy the [*Therens*] test . . . [for] detention" (at 398). Earlier, in rejecting an appeal in *Hicks* (1990), 73 C.R. (3d) 204 (S.C.C.), the Court adopted the view of the Ontario Court of Appeal, that the owner of a van involved in an accident had not been detained when asked at a police station whether anyone else had been driving. See similarly *Schmautz* (1990), 75 C.R. (3d) 129 (S.C.C.). The issue of psychological detention was not considered by the majority in *Elshaw* (1991), 7 C.R. (4th) 333 (S.C.C.), but was rejected by L'Heureux-Dubé J. in dissent. She would have had the Court adopt a U.S. doctrine of "preliminary investigatory detention short of arrest". This suggestion has been criticized by David Tanovich, "Elshaw — Rethinking the Meaning of Detention . . .", (1992) 7 C.R. (4th) 374.

[41] See *Johns,* above note 31.

[42] See too Alan D. Gold, "Perspectives on Section 10(b) — The Right to Counsel under the Charter", (1993) 22 C.R. (4th) 370, who suggests that police should be under a duty to advise of any right to leave without which there should be a finding of detention. In reply, Anthony Allman, in (1994) 25 C.R. (4th) 280, notes that Gold is proceeding by assertion rather than authority and that the framers of the Charter did not envisage an expanded meaning of detention.

Charter warnings. The Newfoundland Court of Appeal's compromise position appears to achieve a better balance.

According to some Courts of Appeal, actions that would amount to detention in the case of police officers or other government agents are not detention within the meaning of s. 10 when performed by private[43] or non-governmental persons, as in the case of a school principal[44] or a private investigator acting for an employer.[45]

In *M. (M.R.)* (1998),[46] the leading s. 8 decision on searches in the school context, the Supreme Court gave short shrift to the argument that a school child searched for drugs by the principal in his office was detained such as to trigger s. 10 protection. The Court was brutally pragmatic. Even if there had been psychological detention within the meaning of *Dedman*, this concept did not apply in the case of investigations by school authorities otherwise there would be "absurd results".[47] What these results would be and why s. 10(b) should only be engaged in the case of arrests and physical detention by school authorities was not made clear.

2. SECTION 10(a): RIGHT "TO BE INFORMED PROMPTLY OF THE REASONS" FOR THE ARREST OR DETENTION

(a) Pre-Charter

General principles respecting the common law duty to provide the reason for an arrest were laid down in the classic decision of the House of Lords in *Christie v. Leachinsky* (1947):[48]

1. If a policeman arrests without warrant on reasonable suspicion of felony, or of other crime of a sort which does not require a warrant, he must in ordinary circumstances inform the person arrested of the true ground of arrest. He is not entitled to keep the reason to himself or to give a reason which is not the true reason. In other words, a citizen is entitled to know on what charge or on suspicion of what crime he is seized.
2. If the citizen is not so informed, but is nevertheless seized, the policeman, apart from certain exceptions, is liable for false imprisonment.[49]
3. The requirement that the person arrested should be informed of the reason why he is seized naturally does not exist if the circumstances are such that he must know the general nature of the alleged offence for which he is detained.

---

[43] *J. (A.M.)* (1999), 137 C.C.C. (3d) 213 (B.C. C.A.) (person making citizen arrest not required to give Charter warning).

[44] *G. (J.M.)* (1986), 54 C.R. (3d) 380 (Ont. C.A.), criticized by A. Wayne MacKay, "Students as Second Class Citizens under the Charter", C.R. *ibid.*, p. 390.

[45] *Shafie* (1989), 68 C.R. (3d) 239 (Ont. C.A.). *Sed contra Lerke* (1986), 49 C.R. (3d) 324 (Alta. C.A.). *Lerke* was followed in *Dean* (1991), 5 C.R. (4th) 176 (Ont. Gen. Div.) (Charter applicable to arrest by store security guard on basis that guard was exercising a governmental function).

[46] (1998), 20 C.R. (5th) 197 (S.C.C.).

[47] At 224.

[48] [1947] 1 All E.R. 567 (H.L.).

[49] In Canada see, for example, *Koechlin v. Waugh* (1956), 118 CCC. 24 (Ont. C.A.) and *Cheese v. Hardy*, [1975] 1 W.W.R. 249 (B.C. S.C.).

4. The requirement that he should be so informed does not mean that technical or precise language need be used. The matter is a matter of substance, and turns on the elementary proposition that in this country a person is, *prima facie*, entitled to his freedom and is only required to submit to restraint on his freedom if he knows in substance the reason why it is claimed that this restraint should be imposed.
5. The person arrested cannot complain that he has not been supplied with the above information as and when he should be, if he himself produces the situation which makes it practically impossible to inform him, e.g., by immediate counter-attack or by running away.[50]

The principles are expressly geared to protect the important personal liberty of not being taken into custody by an agent of the State without being told the reason why. They are held to be equally applicable to a citizen arrest.[51] The House of Lords clearly crafted a flexible set of principles designed to be fair as well to persons having to make arrests in situations that are often volatile and dangerous. A practical corollary of the duty to give reasons for an arrest is that a citizen is entitled to resist an arrest if no such reasons were given.[52] The policy considerations seem to be that an accused to be taken into custody should be given fair notice of the reason and that any confrontation resulting from the attempt to arrest might be lessened if it is clear to everybody what is happening and why.

Christie was widely followed by Canadian courts until Mr. Justice Ritchie for the majority of the Supreme Court in *Gamracy* (1974)[53] held that the duty had been exhaustively codified in s. 29(2) of the Criminal Code. That section reads as follows:

> It is the duty of every one who arrests a person, whether with or without a warrant, to give notice to that person, where it is feasible to do so, of
>
> (a) the process or warrant under which he makes the arrest; or
> (b) the reason for the arrest.

Gamracy had injured a police officer when he had forcibly ejected him from his home. The officer had been trying to arrest him on the basis of information that there was an outstanding warrant. The majority held that the accused could be convicted of assault on a police officer. The arrest had been lawful and in compliance with s. 29(2)(a). The officer had fully discharged his duty by advising Gamracy that the reason for the arrest was the existence of an outstanding warrant. The minority agreed that the duties in subsections (2)(a) and (2)(b) were disjunctive but were prepared to rely on *Christie* to hold that the officer could and should have gone further in the circumstances to find out and advise Gamracy of the reason for the warrant. The minority held that it had been feasible for the officer to do so when he had called the police station for reinforcements.

It is certainly possible that the minority approach in *Gamracy* could now be reasserted as the proper and more purposeful interpretation of the right enshrined in s. 10(a) of the Charter.

---

[50] Above note 48, at 572-573.
[51] *Ibid.*
[52] *Kelly* (1985), 17 C.C.C. (3d) 419 at 424 (Ont. C.A.).
[53] (1974), 22 C.R.N.S. 224 (S.C.C.). Judson and Pigeon JJ. concurred. Spence J. (Laskin J. concurring) dissented.

(b) Charter

Section 10(a) was briefly considered by the Supreme Court of Canada in *Greffe* (1990).[54] The Crown conceded there had been a violation of s. 10(a) where customs inspectors had detained and searched a drug suspect at the airport on the spurious reason of outstanding traffic warrants, although unexecuted warrants for arrest on minor matters did exist. The majority excluded the real evidence considering the cumulative effect of violations of ss. 8, 10(a) and 10(b).[55]

In *Evans* (1991),[56] Madam Justice McLachlin for the majority of the Supreme Court[57] interprets s. 10(a) conservatively. When arresting the accused the officer informed him that ''I am arresting you for trafficking in narcotics''. The police had obtained wiretapping evidence indicating that the accused might have been involved in the sale of a small amount of marijuana but the real reason for the arrest was that they wanted to question him as to two brutal killings they suspected had been committed by his elder brother. The officers read him his right to counsel, cautioned him, and asked him whether he understood. He replied ''no''. Although the officers had been advised of the accused's mental deficiency — his I.Q. placed him in a borderline retardation level and he functioned at the emotional level of a 14-year-old — the officers made no further attempts to explain the Charter or the police warning to him. During subsequent interrogations the accused became the principal suspect in the two murders. However the police did not formally advise the accused that he was then being detained for murder nor did they reiterate his right to counsel. Eventually, incriminating statements were obtained from the accused.

Although the Court held that there had been a violation of the right to counsel under s. 10(b) and excluded the evidence under s. 24(2),[58] the majority through McLachlin J. held that s. 10(a) had *not* been violated. The right to be promptly advised of the reason for arrest or detention in s. 10(a) was seen to be founded ''most fundamentally'' on the notion that one was not obliged to submit to an arrest if one did not know the reason for it and also as an adjunct to the right to counsel under s. 10(b):

> [An accused could not exercise that] right in a meaningful way if he [did not know] the extent of his jeopardy.[59]

However, the majority held that the question of breach turned on the substance of what the accused could reasonably be supposed to have understood, rather than the formalism of the precise words used.

> The question is whether what the accused was told, viewed reasonably in all the circumstances of the case, was sufficient to permit him to make a reasonable decision

---

[54] (1990), 75 C.R. (3d) 257 (S.C.C.).

[55] See below, Chapter 11.

[56] (1991), 4 C.R. (4th) 144 (S.C.C.).

[57] Gonthier and Cory JJ. concurred on this point. Stevenson J. would not comment and Sopinka J. dissented.

[58] For the ruling on s. 10(b) see below, notes 88 and 102 and for that on exclusion under s. 24(2), see Chapter 11.

[59] Above note 56, at 159, quoting *Black*, discussed below note 100.

to decline to submit to arrest, or alternatively, to undermine his right to counsel under s. 10(b).[60]

Shortly after the accused had become a prime suspect the officer had said to him that, although he had been arrested on the marijuana charges, things had now taken ''quite a change.'' The accused, in denying that he had killed anybody, indicated that he was aware that the focus of the question had changed and that he was then being questioned with respect to the killings.

In *Evans* only Sopinka J. was of the opinion that s. 10(a) had been violated. Section 10(a) contained relatively simple instructions to the authorities. The right to be informed of the true grounds for the arrest or detention was firmly rooted in the common law. The reasons for an arrest are set out in a warrant and an arrest without warrant is only lawful if the type of information which would have been contained in the warrant is conveyed orally. Here, given that the arresting officers knew they were dealing with a person of subnormal intelligence, they had to be scrupulous in ensuring that his rights were respected. They were obliged to disabuse him of the false reason for the arrest that they had given him before seeking to elicit incriminating evidence from him. They should have explicitly told him the true grounds for his arrest and not left him to deduce this from the content of their questions.[61]

There is much to be said for the minority opinion.[62] It seems strange to convert a duty to inform to a duty on an accused to draw reasonable inferences as to the reason for the arrest. The majority ruling seems inconsistent with its own later ruling on the duty to inform on the right to counsel.[63] Surely the obligations respecting the duties to inform under s. 10(a) and 10(b) should be consistent?

In *Latimer* (1997)[64] the Supreme Court applied *Evans* to hold that s. 10(a) had not been violated where a father had been informed by the police that he was being detained for investigation into the death of his disabled daughter. Although he had not been specifically advised he would be charged with murder, he had been advised this was a very serious matter. The trial judge was correct in finding that the accused knew the basis for his apprehension and hence the extent of his jeopardy.

3. SECTION 10(b): RIGHT TO RETAIN AND INSTRUCT COUNSEL ON ARREST OR DETENTION

(a) Purpose of Right

The Supreme Court's interpretation of the content of the s. 10(b) guarantee has been dominated by the majority judgments of Chief Justice Lamer. In *Bartle*

---

[60] *Ibid.*, at 160.
[61] *Ibid.*, at 163.
[62] See too David Michael Tanovich, ''Annotation to Evans'', C.R. *ibid.*, pp. 146-148.
[63] See below note 88.
[64] Above note 5.

(1994),[65] speaking for 7 justices,[66] he found that the purpose of s. 10(b) is to protect the disadvantaged against the risk of self-incrimination:

> The purpose of the right to counsel guaranteed by s. 10(b) of the Charter is to provide detainees with an opportunity to be informed of their rights and obligations under the law and, most importantly, to obtain advice on how to exercise those rights and fulfil those obligations. This opportunity is made available because, when an individual is detained by state authorities, he or she is put in a position of disadvantage relative to the state. Not only has this person suffered a deprivation of liberty, but also this person may be at risk of incriminating him- or herself. Accordingly, a person who is "detained" within the meaning of s. 10 of the Charter is in immediate need of legal advice in order to protect his or her right against self-incrimination and to assist him or her in regaining his or her liberty. Under s. 10(b), a detainee is entitled as of right to seek such legal advice "without delay" and upon request.[67]

In *Bartle*, the Chief Justice drew a distinction between what he called "informational" and "implementation" duties under s. 10(b) to reflect important differences in jurisprudence.

(b) Informational Duties

(i) *Content of duty*

Unlike the Bill of Rights, s. 10(b) of the Charter expressly confers the right to be informed of the right to retain and instruct counsel. It is clearly mandatory on arrest or detention. A failure to so inform will by itself constitute a violation of s. 10(b).

From an early point in the history of the Charter, judges have expressed concern lest this right become "a mere ritual without significance or meaning."[68] Judge Scollin of the Manitoba Queen's Bench expressed this view most forcefully in *Nelson* (1982):[69]

> Real opportunity is what is meant by the provision of the Charter, not the incantation of a potted version of the right followed immediately by conduct which presumed a waiver. Understanding and real opportunity are best evidenced by a considered and recorded election. The elegant and measured exchange of the drawing-room is unlikely to prevail in the investigation of violent crime, but the form of words in the Charter is not complicated and should be followed unless the exigencies of the situation render that course impractical; if another form of words is used to convey the substance of the right, it is all the more vital that there be a responsive reply to demonstrate that the essence of the right is understood.[70]

Concern has been expressed that this duty to give legal advice is being performed by the police.[71] Critics point to the investigatory role of the police

---

[65] (1994), 33 C.R. (4th) 1 (S.C.C.).

[66] Only L'Heureux-Dubé J. dissented.

[67] At 18-19 (authorities omitted).

[68] *Manninen* (1983), 37 C.R. (3d) 162 (Ont. C.A.) at 171.

[69] (1982), 32 C.R. (3d) 256 (Man. Q.B.).

[70] *Ibid.*, at 261.

[71] See especially Peter B. Michalyshyn, "Brydges: Should The Police Be Advising of the Right to Counsel?" (1990), 74 C.R. (3d) 151.

which is seen to be antithetical to the interests of protecting civil liberties. As Professor Ratushny put it:

> A police officer who is anxious to obtain a statement, with frequently effective means at his disposal and with the noblest of motivations related to the "protection of society", is likely to go a long way towards ensuring that any warning given will *not* be effective![72]

However persuasive these views, there seems to be little realistic alternative to requiring those making arrests or detentions to provide at least the initial information as to the right to counsel.

How far the police must go in informing as to the right to counsel was set out by Lamer C.J. for the majority of the Supreme Court in *Bartle* (1994).[73] Noting that the implementation duties were only triggered by an assertion by the detainee,[74] the Court held that it is critical that the informational component of the right to counsel be comprehensive in scope and presented by police in a timely and comprehensive manner. Unless they are clearly and fully informed of their rights at the outset, detainees cannot be expected to make informed choices about whether to contact counsel and whether to exercise other rights, such as their right to silence. Absent special circumstances indicating that a detainee may not understand the s. 10(b) caution, such as language difficulties[75] or a known or obvious mental disability, police are not required to assure themselves that a detainee fully understands the s. 10(b) caution. In light of this rule, the Court held it is important that the standard caution given to detainees be as instructive and clear as possible.

The Supreme Court in *Bartle* also confirmed its previous ruling in *R. v. Brydges* (1990),[76] that police authorities are required to inform detainees about Legal Aid and duty counsel services in existence and available in the jurisdiction at the time of detention. In *Brydges*, the majority ruling that this advice must be given in all cases and not just where the detainee has expressed a concern about being able to afford a lawyer was *obiter*. The *Bartle* ruling makes it clear that basic information about how to access available services which provide free, preliminary legal advice must be included in the standard s. 10(b) caution. The detainee must be told in plain language that he or she will be provided with a phone number should he or she wish to contact a lawyer right away. Failure to provide such information is a violation of s. 10(b).[77] The breach of s. 10(b) is

---

[72] "The Role of the Accused in the Criminal Process" in Tarnopolsky and Beaudoin (eds.), *The Canadian Charter of Rights and Freedoms; Commentary* (1982) p. 347 — quoted by Michalyshyn, *ibid.*, p. 153.

[73] Above note 65, at 19-30.

[74] See below notes 189 *et seq.*

[75] See, for example, *Vanstaceghem* (1987), 58 C.R. (3d) 121 (Ont. C.A.), *Sabourin* (1984), 13 C.C.C. (3d) 68 (Man. C.A.) and *Tam* (1995), 100 C.C.C. (3d) 196 (B.C. C.A.).

[76] (1990), 74 C.R. (3d) 129 (S.C.C.).

[77] In *Latimer*, above note 5, the accused was detained for investigation of the death of his daughter during normal hours. He was advised of the option of legal aid but not provided with the telephone number. The Court held there had been no breach of s. 10(b) as the toll-free number was only available after normal hours. This weakens the obligation declared in *Bartle*.

complete, except in cases of waiver or urgency, upon a failure to properly inform a detainee of his or her right to counsel until such time as that failure is corrected. Unlike the implementation duties, the informational duty is not triggered by assertion by the detainee.

Bartle's s. 10(b) rights had been violated. At about 1 a.m., he had failed a roadside A.L.E.R.T. test and was arrested for impaired driving. Cautions at the roadside and at the police station had mentioned the right to free advice from a Legal Aid lawyer, but not the availability of immediate, preliminary legal advice by duty counsel or the existence of the 24-hour, toll-free legal aid number printed on the card. The accused testified that he thought he could only contact a lawyer during normal working hours and that he had indicated to the officer that he did not know who to call. The Supreme Court reversed the ruling of the Ontario Court of Appeal[78] in the Court below, that such information need only be provided when there is something in the circumstances indicating that the accused did not fully appreciate his rights.

Bartle imposes clear and meaningful obligations on the police respecting what has to be communicated to the detainee as to the right to counsel. The Supreme Court was commendably more concerned than the Ontario Court of Appeal that the detainee be properly informed as to the feasibility of obtaining immediate legal advice. The Supreme Court should have gone further. In accepting the rule that, absent special circumstances, the police need not take steps to ensure that the detainee truly understands, the Court implicitly accepts a position first adopted in the Ontario Court of Appeal in *Anderson* (1984)[79] that that would put too onerous an obligation on the police. The reasoning of the Court in *Bartle* respecting the necessity of properly advising as to the existence of legal aid and duty counsel systems could equally have been used to reject *Anderson* altogether. *Anderson* has been judicially challenged as inconsistent with the later decision on waiver in *Clarkson*[80] and criticized as unduly diluting the right to counsel.[81] *Anderson* certainly does little to protect those who are ignorant of, or do not fully understand, their rights.[82] As Alan Gold has suggested, a full right to

---

[78] *Sub nom. Baldwin* (1993), 22 C.R. (4th) 1 (Ont. C.A.) at 14.

[79] (1984), 39 C.R. (3d) 193 (Ont. C.A.).

[80] *Menzies* (1986), 51 C.R. (3d) 387 (Ont. Div. Ct.) (*per* Misener D.C.J.) — an argument rejected on appeal: (1987), 56 C.R. (3d) 284 (Ont. C.A.). See too the minority judgment of Hetherington J.A. in *Williams* (1986), 54 C.R. (3d) 336 (Alta. C.A.). *Clarkson* is considered below note 170.

[81] See Stanley A. Cohen, "The Impact of Charter Decisions on Police Behaviour", (1984) 39 C.R. (3d) 264 at 275-277.

[82] Compare too s. 56(2)(b) of the Young Offenders Act, R.S.C. 1985, c. Y-1, applying to statements by accused under 18:

No oral or written statement given by a young person to a peace officer or other person who is, in law, a person in authority is admissible against the young person unless . . .

(b) the person to whom the statement was given has, before the statement was made, clearly explained to the young person, in language appropriate to his age and understanding, that

(i) the young person is under no obligation to give a statement,

(ii) any statement given by him may be used as evidence in proceedings against him,

(iii) the young person has the right to consult another person in accordance with paragraph (c), and

counsel announcement

> achieves the following in both fact and perception in the police-citizen encounter: equality and fairness, by equalizing the knowledge of citizens of this basic right; fairness, by eliminating timidity in its exercise; and respect for the administration of justice, by showing that rights are not just to be paid lip service, but that practical steps (such as this announcement) will be taken to make the rights a reality in the everyday world.[83]

The Supreme Court should follow the approach of the New Zealand Court of Appeal in interpreting that jurisdiction's Bill of Rights requirement that those arrested or detained be informed of the right to counsel:

> The crucial question is whether it was brought home to the arrested person that he or she had those rights. That is not the same question as whether the police were justified in assuming that he or she did understand them. To look at it simply from the perspective of the police officer would mean that the person arrested who did not in fact understand the position would not be able to make an informed choice with respect to the exercise or waiver of the guaranteed right.[84]

The advantages from the point of view of accused of such a subjective approach becomes clear when considering reluctance of Canadian Courts of Appeal to require that police always advise detainees that the right to counsel may be exercised in private. In *Jackson* (1993),[85] Goodman J.A. for the Ontario Court of Appeal decided that this advice would be desirable but not constitutionally required. However, there would be a duty to advise about privacy and breach if there was no advice given in cases where the accused reasonably believed that the consultation would not take place in private or where the accused showed he did not understand the privacy right or raised a privacy concern.[86] This is especially surprising given that most Courts of Appeal agree[87] that there is a right to consult in private whether or not the detainee requests privacy. Hopefully, when the matter reaches the Supreme Court, the Court's advice as to the right to privacy will become part of the mandatory warning requirements.

> (iv) any statement made by the young person is required to be made in the presence of the person consulted, unless the young person desires otherwise.

Section 56 and the requirements of s. 10(b) respecting young persons is considered by the Supreme Court in *I (L.R.)* (1993), 26 C.R. (3d) 119 (S.C.C.).

[83] Above note 42, at 372.

[84] *Mallinson*, [1993] 1 N.Z.L.R. 528 (C.A.) at 530-531, fully discussed by Andre S. Butler, " An Objective or Subjective Approach to the Right to be Informed of the Right to Counsel? A New Zealand Perspective", (1994) 36 *Crim. L.Q.* 317.

[85] (1993), 25 C.R. (4th) 265 (Ont. C.A.).

[86] At 273-274. In *Butler* (1995), 104 C.C.C. (3d) 198 (B.C. C.A.) Prowse J.A. (Southin J.A. concurring) even expressed doubts about *Jackson* on the basis of the onus on the police to divine whether an accused knew that he had the right to consult counsel in private. The majority however agreed that information about the right to consult in privacy was wise and that the law should clearly state whether there was such an obligation. Williams J.A. was of the view that the police should not be burdened with "yet another add-on to an already lengthy standard warning" (at 212).

[87] See below note 136.

The leading decision on the police duty to go further where there are special circumstances indicating that the accused may not understand is *Evans* (1991).[88] The police knew that they were dealing with a mentally challenged subject when they arrested him on a drugs charge. Madam Justice McLachlin, for a Court unanimous on this point, held that although the accused had been read his rights, the police had violated s. 10(b) by not explaining to him that right when he indicated he did not understand. She stated that a ''person who does not understand his or her right cannot be expected to assert it''.[89] The purpose of s. 10(b) was to require the police to ''communicate'' the right to counsel to the person in detention. In most cases, one could infer from the circumstances that the accused understood and the police would not be required to go further. But where, as here, there was a positive indication that the accused did not understand

> the police cannot rely on their mechanical recitation of the right to the accused; they must take steps to facilitate that understanding.[90]

(ii) *Waiver*

According to the Supreme Court in *Bartle*,[91] although detainees can waive s. 10(b) Charter rights, a waiver of the informational component will be rare. The detainee would have to have been already fully apprised of the information he or she had the right to receive. The fact that a detainee indicated that he or she did not wish to hear the information conveyed by the standard police caution would not by itself be enough to constitute a valid waiver. There would have to be an explicit waiver and a reasonable basis for believing that the detainee in fact knew and adverted to his rights and was aware of the means by which those rights could be exercised.

(iii) *Timing: When must accused be informed?*

In *Kelly* (1985),[92] the Ontario Court of Appeal, noting that the phrase ''without delay'' was only used with respect to the right to retain and instruct counsel, nevertheless held that it had to be implied in the case of the right to be informed of that right. However, the Court found that the right to be informed does not arise immediately after the accused has been given his rights under s. 10(a) to be informed of the reason for the arrest or detention. Section 10(a) used the word ''promptly'' and also performed a different function. The delay in advising Kelly of his s. 10(b) rights had been insignificant in the circumstances and explained by the fact that he had been drunk and screaming. It would have made no sense to inform him of his right at that point.

---

[88] (1991), 4 C.R. (4th) 144 (S.C.C.), referred to with approval in *Bartle* at 20.
[89] At 162.
[90] *Ibid.*
[91] Above note 73, at 27-29.
[92] Above note 52.

These pragmatic arguments have not carried the day in the Supreme Court of Canada since the judgment of Madam Justice Wilson in *Debot* (1989).[93] In holding that a motorist stopped and subjected to a frisk search for drugs is detained and entitled to be advised of the right to counsel under s. 10(b), she held that the police must inform a detainee of his or her rights to counsel "without delay" and that this does not permit of "internal qualifications" such as "at the earliest possible convenience", or after police "get matters under control", or "without reasonable delay" or "after police have had a chance to search the suspect."[94] She did acknowledge that there might be "situations in which the police for their own safety have to act in the heat of the moment to subdue the suspect and may be excused for not pausing to advise the suspect of his rights and permit him to exercise them."[95] Three other justices concurred to form a majority,[96] subject to the caveat that the police were not obliged to suspend a search incident to arrest until a detainee had the opportunity to retain counsel.

In *Feeney* (1997)[97] the Supreme Court through Sopinka J. held that a murder suspect should have been read his rights immediately after the police entered his darkened trailer, roused him from his sleep, touched his leg and ordered him to get out of bed. The dissenting opinion of Justice L'Heureux-Dubé[98] is persuasive in suggesting that the police should have been allowed latitude to assess and gain control of a potentially dangerous situation such as this and that the delay of a few minutes was reasonable in the circumstances.

In *Polashek* (1999)[99] Justice Rosenberg for the Ontario Court of Appeal partially bowed to this Supreme Court authority, requiring the informing of the right to counsel to be immediate. A delay of 13 minutes after a drug arrest was held to be a violation of s. 10(b). However, while determining that there was a systemic problem in that police were not being trained to give the advice immediately on arrest or detention, the Court nevertheless decided not to exclude the real evidence found in the trunk after the violation as the breach was not too serious. This appears to pay only lip service to the current overly rigid Supreme Court standard.

(iv) *Where reasons change*

Where the reason for the arrest or detention changes, it is now clear that the police are under a duty to re-inform the person arrested or detained of the right to counsel. A new s. 10(b) right is triggered. The leading decision is the unanimous

---

[93] Above note 19.
[94] *Ibid.*, at 147.
[95] *Ibid.*
[96] Lamer J. (Dickson C.J. and Cory J. concurring), *ibid.* at 133. Sopinka J. found no violation of s. 10(b), *ibid.* at 158.
[97] (1997), 7 C.R. (5th) 101 (S.C.C.).
[98] Gonthier and McLachlin J. concurred.
[99] (1999), 25 C.R. (5th) 183 (Ont. C.A.).

judgment of the Supreme Court of Canada in *Black* (1989).[100] The accused had been arrested on a charge of attempted murder but the victim died and the charge became first degree murder. For the Court, Madam Justice Wilson held that

> s. 10(b) should not be read in isolation. Its ambit must be considered in light of s. 10(a). S. 10(a) requires the police to advise an individual who is arrested or detained of the reasons for such arrest or detention. The rights accruing to a person under s. 10(b) arise because he or she has been arrested or detained for a particular reason. An individual can exercise his s. 10(b) right in a meaningful way only if he knows the extent of his jeopardy.[101]

Given that the charge of first degree murder was significantly different, it could not be concluded that the advice that the accused had previously received from a lawyer on the first charge would inevitably have been the same. This would be sheer conjecture and improper speculation.

In *Evans* (1991),[102] McLachlin J. for the Court on this point[103] applied *Black* to a case where an accused had been arrested on a charge of drugs and later became the prime suspect in murder cases. She added the slight qualification that the police would not have to reiterate the right to counsel every time an investigation touched on a different offence. However, they would have to restate the right to counsel

> when there is a fundamental and discrete change in the purpose of the investigation, one involving a different and unrelated offence or a significantly more serious offence than that contemplated at the time of the warning.[104]

Evans was the basis for the later decision of the Supreme Court in *Borden* (1994).[105] The accused was in custody on a sexual assault charge. The police were held to have breached s. 10(b) by not reading him his rights again when their investigation changed to another sexual assault.

In a brief and enigmatic judgment in *Paternak* (1996)[106] Sopinka J. for the Court[107] found a s. 10(b) violation where the detainee under police questioning

---

[100] (1989), 70 C.R. (3d) 97 (S.C.C.). See too *Jacobs* (1987), 54 C.R. (3d) 352 (Alta. C.A.) (prisoner at remand centre subject to new detention when questioned about robberies).

[101] *Ibid.*, at 108.

[102] Above note 56.

[103] Stevenson J.

[104] Above note 56, at 163. In *Mastin* (1991), 65 C.C.C. (3d) 204 (B.C. C.A.), the Court considers whether *Black* would apply to where an accused mistakenly believes there has been a substantial change of circumstances but leaves the issue open. *Evans* was applied in *Chartrand* (1992), 15 C.R. (4th) 231 (Man. C.A.), *Kharsekin* (1994), 30 C.R. (4th) 252 (Nfld. C.A.), *McIntosh* (1999), 30 C.R. (5th) 161 (B.C. C.A.), *Sawatsky* (1997), 9 C.R. (5th) 23 (Ont. C.A.), and *Witts* (1998), 124 C.C.C. (3d) 410 (Man. C.A.). See too *Williams v. Canada (Regional Transfer Board, Prairie Region)* (1993), 19 C.R. (4th) 151 (Fed. C.A.) (penitentiary segregation pending transfer being new detention and requiring new information as to right to counsel). However, *Evans* has been distinguished in cases where the more serious charge related to a death of which the detainee was aware: *Young* (1992), 73 C.C.C. (3d) 289 (Ont. C.A.), *Power* (1993), 81 C.C.C. (3d) 1 (Nfld. C.A.) and *Baptiste* (1994), 88 C.C.C. (3d) 211 (B.C. C.A.).

[105] (1994), 33 C.R. (4th) 147 (S.C.C.), fully discussed above Chapter 3, respecting its ruling on s. 8.

[106] (1996), 2 C.R. (5th) 119 (S.C.C.)

[107] Cory, McLachlin , Iacobucci and Major JJ. concurred.

had not been rewarned when the police concluded he had committed manslaughter. The Court characterised this as a substantial change in jeopardy.

Provided that there is no significant change in the reason for the arrest or detention, it is now clear since *Hebert* (1990),[108] that the right to counsel arises only on the initial arrest or detention and that there is no continuing right as the investigation proceeds and the police have further contact with the accused. The ruling was *obiter*, *Hebert* turning on the recognition of a pre-trial right to silence under s. 7. However, lower courts' decisions[109] confronting the counsel issue directly have in the main rejected the view that s. 10(b) also protects a continuing solicitor-and-client relationship such that the police should continue to provide counsel with reasonable notice of their intent to interrogate an accused who has retained counsel.[110] Thus in *Pavel* (1989),[111] the Ontario Court of Appeal held that the police, having informed a person subjected to a breathalyzer demand of his right to retain and instruct counsel, had no further obligation when, one hour later, they demanded a blood sample. Mr. Justice Goodman, for the Court, held that

> absent some extenuating circumstance, such as the laying of some additional serious charge, there is no obligation on the police to re-instruct an accused of his rights on every occasion when they seek to obtain a statement or breath or blood sample in moving on to a different stage of their investigation.[112]

(c) Implementation Duties

(i) *Not absolute*

In *Bartle*,[113] Lamer C.J. confirmed that the effect of extensive jurisprudence in the Supreme Court is that the right to counsel under s. 10(b) is not absolute.[114] This is so because the correlative implementation duties on the police do not arise or will be suspended unless a detainee asserts the right and is reasonably diligent in exercising it. Furthermore, s. 10(b) rights may be waived although the standard for waiver is high.

The correlative duties thus far established will here first be examined before consideration is given to conflicting case law on assertion, reasonable diligence and waiver.

---

[108] (1990), 77 C.R. (3d) 145 (S.C.C.), discussed above, Chapter 2.

[109] *Hebert* (1988), 43 C.C.C. (3d) 56 (Y.T. C.A.); *Emile* (1988), 65 C.R. (3d) 135 (N.W.T. C.A.); *Logan* (1988), 68 C.R. (3d) 1 (Ont. C.A.); *Bain* (1989), 68 C.R. (3d) 50 (Ont. C.A.); *Cuff* (1989), 49 C.C.C. (3d) 65 (Nfld. C.A.); *McLean* (1989), 71 C.R. (3d) 167 (Ont. C.A.); *Pavel* (1989), 74 C.R. (3d) 195 (Ont. C.A.), *Wood* (1994), 94 C.C.C. (3d) 193 (N.S. C.A.) at 225 and *Plata* (1999), 136 C.C.C. (3d) 436 (Que. C.A.). But see *Nugent* (1988), 63 C.R. (3d) 351 (N.S. C.A.) and *R. (P.L.)* (1988), 44 C.C.C. (3d) 174 (N.S. C.A.).

[110] *Greig* (1987), 56 C.R. (3d) 229 (Ont. H.C.). See too T. Breen, "Annotation to *Playford*" (1987), 61 C.R. (3d) 101.

[111] Above note 109.

[112] *Ibid.*, at 210.

[113] Above note 65.

[114] At 19.

(ii) *Police duty to afford reasonable opportunity to exercise right*

The notion that the right to counsel must impose correlative duties on the police was established by the Supreme Court in *Manninen* (1987).[115] The accused was arrested for theft and possession of a stolen car and armed robbery. The arresting officer twice read the accused his rights from a card because of a flippant remark the accused made following the first reading. At this point, the accused said:

> Prove it. I ain't saying anything until I see my lawyer. I want to see my lawyer.

The officer then questioned the accused as follows:

> Q. What is your full name? A. Ronald Charles Manninen.
> Q. Where is your address? A. Ain't got one.
> Q. Where is the knife that you had along with this [showing the respondent the CO2 gun found in the car] when you ripped off the Mac's Milk on Wilson Avenue?
> A. He's lying. When I was in the store I only had the gun. The knife was in the tool box in the car.[116]

There was a telephone in the small office where the accused was arrested. The accused did not directly ask to use the telephone and the officers did not volunteer it.

Mr. Justice Lamer, for a unanimous Supreme Court, held that s. 10(b) had been clearly violated. It was not necessary to decide whether the person arrested or detained had to positively assert the right to counsel before a duty was imposed on the police.[117] Manninen had clearly asserted his right to remain silent and his wish to consult with a lawyer. In the circumstances, he had been denied a reasonable opportunity to exercise his right;

> There was a telephone immediately at hand in the office, which the officers used for their own purposes. It was not necessary for the respondent to make an express request to use the telephone. The duty to facilitate contact with counsel included the duty to offer the respondent the use of the telephone. Of course, there may be circumstances in which it is particularly urgent that the police continue with an investigation before it is possible to facilitate a detainee's communication with counsel. There was no urgency in the circumstances surrounding the offences in this case.[118]

The other major Supreme Court of Canada ruling on the duty to afford a reasonable opportunity to exercise the right to counsel is *Leclair and Ross*

---

[115] (1987), 58 C.R. (3d) 97 (S.C.C.), adopting the minority approach of Laskin J. (as he then was) in the case of s. 2(c)(ii) of the Canadian Bill of Rights: *Brownridge* (1972), 18 C.R.N.S. 308 at 328 (S.C.C.).

[116] *Ibid.*, at 100.

[117] *Ibid.*, at 103.

[118] *Ibid.*, at 104. The Court appears to have approved (1985), 44 C.R. (3d) 1 (Sask. C.A.) the decision in *Dombrowski*, that the police should not have delayed the accused's opportunity to contact counsel until arrival at the police station given that a telephone was available at the place of arrest.

(1989).[119] Three youths were arrested in the middle of the night and charged with break, enter and theft. They were advised of their right to counsel and tried unsuccessfully to contact their counsel by telephone at about 2:00 a.m. Leclair was asked if he wished to call another lawyer and he indicated that he did not. The police conducted a line-up an hour later. The boys were not advised that they were under no obligation to participate.

The Supreme Court were in agreement that there had been no reasonable opportunity provided to exercise the right to counsel. Given the time of the call, it was highly unlikely that they would have been able to contact their counsel before normal office hours. There was "no urgency or other reason justifying that the police proceed forthwith" and it could not be said that the boys had had a "real opportunity" to exercise their right to counsel.[120] The Court also confirmed that there is normally a right to counsel of one's choice, provided that this is reasonable in the circumstances:

> [a]ccused or detained persons have a right to choose their counsel and it is only if the lawyer chosen cannot be available within a reasonable time that the detainee or the accused should be expected to exercise the right to counsel by calling another lawyer.[121]

Courts have consistently held that whether a reasonable opportunity has been provided depends on all the circumstances,[122] including the conduct of the accused who is under a duty, to be discussed below, to exercise his right with reasonable diligence. They have sought to avoid "blanket rules".[123] Even in the case of the right to counsel following a breathalyzer demand, where the Criminal Code provides that the first breath sample must be taken within two hours to be admissible,[124] the courts have held that the police cannot establish "arbitrary time limits" although the detainee is "not automatically entitled to two full hours" for the consultation.[125]

It seems clear that a reasonable opportunity to instruct counsel does not require the presence of counsel.[126]

---

[119] (1989), 67 C.R. (3d) 209 (S.C.C.). L'Heureux-Dubé J. (McIntyre J. concurring) dissented on the question of whether the evidence should be excluded.

[120] *Ibid.*, at 216-217.

[121] *Ibid.*, at 217. See earlier *Speid* (1983), 37 C.R. (3d) 220 (Ont. C.A.) and M. Brown, "Annotation" (1989), 67 C.R. (3d) 210-211.

[122] *Dubois* (1990), 74 C.R. (3d) 216 (Que. C.A.).

[123] *Top* (1989), 48 C.C.C. (3d) 493 at 499 (Alta. C.A.).

[124] Section 258(1)(c)(ii).

[125] *McLean* (1988), 67 C.R. (3d) 377 at 391 (B.C. Co. Ct.) (providing a full review of the possibilities in breathalyzer cases); *Dunnett* (1990), 62 C.C.C. (3d) 14 (N.B. C.A.). See too M.F. Brown, "Providing an Accused with a Reasonable Opportunity to Exercise the Right to Retain and Instruct Counsel Without Delay" (1989), 1 *J. of Motor Vehicle Law* 13 at 18-23 and Ulrich Gautier, "The Right to Counsel and the Breathalyzer" (1990), 50 *Rev. du Barreau* 163. See too similarly *Greene* (1991), 62 C.C.C. (3d) 344 (Nfld. C.A.) (no reasonable opportunity before blood sample).

[126] *Kavanagh* (1981), 25 C.R. (3d) 171 (B.C. S.C.); *Stark* (1984), 27 M.V.R. 161 (N.S. C.A.) and *Naugler* (1986), 27 C.C.C. (3d)257 (N.S. C.A.). See too Laskin J.A. (as he then was) in *Brownridge* (1972), 18 C.R.N.S. 308 (S.C.C.) at 328 (accused under Bill of Rights not entitled

In *Pavel* (1989),[127] the Ontario Court of Appeal flatly ruled that an abortive telephone call to a lawyer following erroneous police advice that he could only make one telephone call necessarily violated s. 10(b). Mr. Justice Goodman adopted a pre-Charter decision of the Manitoba Court of Appeal in *Louttit* (1974):[128]

> The "one phone call" rule is a fiction propagated by Hollywood. Reasonable conduct by a police is always required, and that may, in appropriate circumstances, require that a plurality of telephone calls be permitted.[129]

In *Prosper* (1994),[130] the Supreme Court was unanimous in holding that there is no constitutional obligation on governments to provide a free duty counsel system on arrest or detention. Chief Justice Lamer pointed out that s. 10(b) of the Charter does not expressly constitutionalize such a right. The legislative history of s. 10 revealed that the framers of the Charter decided not to incorporate even a relatively limited substantive right to legal assistance in the form of a clause (d) reading,

> "if without sufficient means to pay for counsel and if the interests of justice so require, to be provided with counsel".

The fact that such an obligation would almost certainly interfere with governmental allocation of limited resources was a further consideration weighing against this interpretation. Devising a remedy in provinces and territories where no duty counsel existed would be very difficult.[131]

For a 6-3 majority, Lamer C.J. asserted an alternative solution of enforcing the obligation on police to "hold off" eliciting information until a detainee has been given a reasonable opportunity to contact counsel, an obligation which the Chief Justice understandably saw as fully consistent with existing jurisprudence. The unavailability of duty counsel in a particular jurisdiction was a factor to be considered in the determination of reasonableness. Chief Justice Lamer warned that in jurisdictions without a duty counsel system the delay may have to be longer even if this means in impaired driving cases that the breathalyzer test cannot be taken within the two-hour limit. This ruling produced a strong dissent by L'Heureux-Dubé J.,[132] for whom the "holding off" proposal was neither warranted nor appropriate.

---

to insist on personal attendance of counsel if counsel could be reached by telephone). But see now *Burlingham*, below note 154.

[127] Above note 109, at 210.

[128] (1974), 21 C.C.C. (2d) 84 (Man. C.A.).

[129] *Ibid.*, at 86 (per Freedman C.J.M.). See too *Whitford* (1997), 115 C.C.C. (3d) 52 (Alta. C.A.)(Charter right not exhausted by contact with law office and immediate refusal to speak with police until he had contacted legal aid).

[130] (1994), 33 C.R. (4th) 85 (S.C.C.). See further below note 160.

[131] Limited rights to funded counsel have, however, been recognized under s. 7: see Chapter 2 under Right to Counsel.

[132] La Forest and Gonthier JJ. concurred.

(iii) *Right to communicate in private*

The Supreme Court of Canada has only considered the issue of whether there is a right to communicate with a lawyer in private in interpreting the right to counsel under s. 2(c)(ii) of the Bill of Rights. In *Jumaga* (1977),[133] a bare majority[134] held that there had been no violation of the right to counsel, such as to grant a reasonable excuse for failing to provide a breath sample, where the accused had accepted the police facilities without objection and had not asked for privacy. Mr. Justice Pigeon for the majority noted that the Bill of Rights was phrased in terms of no one being deprived of a right to counsel and he had difficulty seeing how an accused could say he was "deprived" of something he did not ask for. The majority was furthermore seriously troubled by the whole notion of privacy:

> I should point out that there would be serious difficulties involved in allowing persons in the situation of the accused to have the free use, unsupervised for any length of time, of a private room such as a sergeant's office. It would also be a serious matter to require the provision of safe and adequate facilities for private communication with legal counsel wherever breathalyzer test is to be performed, failing which everyone would have a reasonable excuse for refusing it.[135]

At the level of provincial courts of appeal there is now overwhelming authority that privacy is inherent in the right to retain and instruct counsel, whether or not privacy is requested.[136] *Jumaga* has been distinguished on the basis that the right in s. 10(b) is a positively-phrased right and must receive a purposive interpretation.

In *Playford* (1987),[137] Mr. Justice Goodman for the Ontario Court of Appeal described the privacy right as follows:

> In my opinion the right to retain and instruct counsel without delay carries with it the right to do so in privacy. It would defy common sense to expect an accused person to instruct counsel properly when his instructions can be overheard by other persons, and in particular by police officers. Such lack of privacy might even seriously prejudice his ability to retain counsel. Retention of counsel usually requires some explanation by the accused of the circumstances which have led to his arrest.[138]

> . . . .

> Privacy is a matter which is inherent in that right. In my opinion, proof that an accused could instruct and consult counsel in private only by whispering or by some

---

[133] [1977] 1 S.C.R. 486.
[134] Per Pigeon J. (Martland, Judson, Ritchie and De Grandpre JJ. concurring). Laskin C.J.C. (Spence, Dickson and Beetz JJ. concurring) dissented.
[135] Above note 133, at 497-498.
[136] *Playford* (1987), 61 C.R. (3d) 101 (Ont. C.A.); *Gilbert* (1988), 61 C.R. (3d) 149 (Ont. C.A.); *LePage* (1986), 54 C.R. (3d) 371 (N.S. C.A.); *Young* (1987), 38 C.C.C. (3d) 452 (N.B. C.A.), *Kennedy* (1995), 103 C.C.C. (3d) 161 (Nfld. C.A.); *Jackson* (1993), 25 C.R. (4th) 265 (Ont. C.A.) and *Jones* (1999), 133 C.C.C. (3d) 1 (Ont. C.A.). In both *Jackson* and *Jones* the evidence was not excluded under s. 24(2). See too *Skwark* (1983), 3 C.C.C. (3d) 300 (Sask. C.A.) and *Butler* (1995), 104 C.C.C. (3d) 198 (B.C. C.A.).
[137] *Ibid.*
[138] *Ibid.*, at 114.

other unusual device does not meet the test of privacy. . . . Where the circumstances are such that an accused would reasonably believe that his conversation to retain or instruct counsel could be overheard by police, it cannot he said that his right to privacy has not been infringed unless it can be shown that he was in fact able to retain and instruct counsel privately.[139]

In marked contrast to Pigeon J.'s concern for practical difficulties in busy police stations, Goodman J.A. bluntly asserts[140] that if the physical layout makes a private telephone conversation impossible given the need to preserve police security, no questioning of the accused should take place before such privacy can be achieved. *Playford* is also important for holding that there must be privacy not only for actual calls to lawyers but respecting calls attempting to contact lawyers. Playford had been afforded an opportunity to contact a lawyer and phoned a friend and the lawyer's secretary.[141] Lack of privacy for these calls was held to violate s. 10(b). The Supreme Court should adopt this purposeful interpretation when the occasion arises.

(iv) *Police duty to refrain from questioning or attempting to elicit evidence until there has been a reasonable opportunity to instruct counsel*[142]

This duty on the police to stop their investigation of the accused was first imposed in *Manninen*[143] where Mr. Justice Lamer provided the following rationale:

> The purpose of the right to counsel is to allow the detainee not only to be informed of his rights and obligations under the law but, equally if not more important, to obtain advice as to how to exercise those rights. In this case, the police officers correctly informed the respondent of his right to remain silent and the main function of counsel would be to confirm the existence of that right and then to advise him as to how to exercise it. For the right to counsel to be effective, the detainee must have access to this advice before he is questioned or otherwise required to provide evidence.[144]

Manninen's right to counsel had been violated when the officer started to question him even though he had asserted his right to remain silent and his interest in consulting a lawyer. The Court did recognize, again, that there might be circumstances of urgency which would allow the police to proceed with their questioning before providing the reasonable opportunity to consult counsel.[145] However, no such circumstances existed in *Manninen*.

---

[139] *Ibid.*, at 117.

[140] *Ibid.*, at 119.

[141] *Sed contra Standish* (1988), 41 C.C.C. (3d) 340 (B.C. C.A.) (the right to privacy only starts when a lawyer is reached).

[142] *Brydges*, above note 76, at 140.

[143] Above note 115.

[144] *Ibid.*, at 104. There is, however, no obligation on the police to leave the accused and there may be no violation if the accused chooses to speak while the police and the accused are waiting for the lawyer to arrive: *Sims* (1991), 64 C.C.C. (3d) 403 (B.C. C.A.) and *MacKenzie* (1991), 64 C.C.C. (3d) 336 (N.S. C.A.).

[145] *Ibid.*, at 110.

In *Leclair* (1989),[146] the Supreme Court established that the second duty also means that, once the right to counsel has been asserted by the accused, the police "cannot in any way compel the detainee or accused person to make a decision or participate in a process which could ultimately have an adverse effect in the conduct of an eventual trial" until a reasonable opportunity to exercise the right has been provided.[147] Section 10(b) had been violated because there had been no real opportunity to retain and instruct counsel before the accused was made to participate in a line-up in the middle of the night. In deciding that the police had not been justified in proceeding, the Court examined whether there was "any urgency or other compelling reason"[148] for their action. The Court rejected the Crown contention that the line-up had been necessary immediately while the witnesses' memories were still fresh. Although there was no right to have counsel present at a line-up, there was still a need to advise the accused that, while there was no legal obligation to participate in a line-up, failure to do so could have legal consequences respecting evidence admissible at trial.[149]

Further *dicta* give some relief to the police from this rigorous duty to stop investigating the accused. The opportunity to consult counsel need not be provided before physical evidence has been secured,[150] before the police have gained control of the premises while conducting an arrest[151] and before they have searched a person for drugs.[152] It has also now been settled that the approach of the two-hour limit for the obtaining of breathalyzer evidence can be considered as a circumstance of urgency.[153]

(v) *Police cannot denigrate reputation of defence counsel*

In *Burlingham* (1995),[154] Iacobucci J. for a unanimous Supreme Court[155] declared this to be a new substantive right under s. 10(b):

> s. 10(b) specifically prohibits the police . . . from belittling an accused's lawyer with the express goal or effect of undermining the accused's confidence in and relationship with defence counsel.[156]

---

[146] Above note 119.

[147] *Ibid.*, at 218.

[148] *Ibid.*

[149] See discussion by Brown, above note 125, pp. 211-212.

[150] *Gilbert*, above note 136, at 155.

[151] *Strachan* (1986), 49 C.R. (3d) 289 (S.C.C.). See, however, *Feeney*, above note 97.

[152] *Debot*, above note 19.

[153] *Tremblay* (1987), 60 C.R. (3d) 59 (S.C.C.); *Gilbert*, above note 136; *Top*, above note 123; and *Dubois*, above note 122.

[154] (1995), 38 C.R. (4th) 265 (S.C.C.).

[155] L'Heureux-Dubé J. dissents only on the s. 24(2) issue, agreeing that the accused's rights to counsel had been "clearly violated" (at p. 1).

[156] At 280.

"Specifically" is clearly hyperbole as there is no such express guarantee in the words of s. 10(b). The police had breached s.10(b) by constantly denigrating counsel in a murder case, suggesting that the police were more trustworthy.[157]

(vi) *Police or Crown cannot enter into a plea bargain without the participation of defence counsel unless the accused expressly waives that right*

This was a further new substantive right declared by Iacobucci J. for the Supreme Court in *Burlingham*.[158]

Burlingham establishes important and welcome new constitutional standards against clear police manipulation to bypass the right to counsel requirement. *Burlingham* provides a good example. The accused was arrested on a charge of murder of B.H. He confessed. The police suspected him of an earlier murder of D.W., committed in the same time in a similar manner. Over a three-day period, the police subjected the accused to an intensive and often manipulative interrogation about the D.W. murder. He was systematically questioned although he repeatedly stated that he would not speak unless he could consult a lawyer. The police urged him to reveal what he knew about the crime, suggesting that any delay would hurt his parents who would be doubly hurt by a second murder charge just as they were getting over the shock of the first murder. The police also constantly denigrated the integrity of defence counsel, suggesting that the police were more trustworthy. On the fourth day, the police offered the accused a "deal". They indicated their "boss" and Crown counsel had instructed them to tell him that he would only be charged with second degree murder in the D.W. case in exchange for providing the police with the location of the gun and other information. When the accused refused to accept the deal without consulting his lawyer, the officers continued to express doubts about the usefulness of the lawyer, emphasizing that he was taking the weekend off. They then made it clear that the deal was a "one-time chance" only open during that weekend when the lawyer was not available. The accused eventually acquiesced despite advice from another lawyer not to talk to the police. He fulfilled his part of the bargain: he confessed, brought the police to the murder site and told them where the murder weapon had been thrown.

Plea negotiations usually include defence counsel but a Canadian study has documented that accused sometimes enter deals with the police alone with no lawyer in sight.[159] The Court in *Burlingham* does not confront the situation where the accused cannot obtain counsel, for example where he or she has no funds and legal aid is not available. Presumably, on analogy with the Supreme Court's earlier majority ruling in *Prosper* (1994)[160] respecting breathalyzer tests in

---

[157] *Burlingham* was applied in *Singer* (1999), 25 C.R. (5th) 374 (Sask. Q.B.) (police officer denigrating advice of lawyer in impaired driving case and intervening to change it).

[158] Above note 154, at 282.

[159] J. Klein, *Let's Make a Deal* (1976). This careful empirical study of inmate perceptions concluded that deals with police, such as exchanging information for leniency, often did not materialise.

[160] (1994), 33 C.R. (4th) 85 (S.C.C.).

jurisdictions with no duty counsel systems, the police would be at least expected to "hold off" until it was clear that no lawyer would be available.

Iacobucci J., while recognizing that s. 10(b) does not guarantee an accused the right to counsel of choice at all times, held that in the circumstances the failure to allow the accused to contact his lawyer about the deal violated s. 10(b):

> Allowing the [accused] to call a random lawyer is, given the seriousness of the situation he faced and the circumstances of the case, insufficient for the officers to discharge their responsibilities under s. 10(b).[161]

He found it unnecessary to deal with the submission that the Crown breach of the deal also triggered constitutional violations,[162] but he did suggest that

> to the extent that the plea bargain is an integral element of the Canadian criminal process, the Crown and its officers engaged in the plea bargaining process must act honourably and forthrightly.[163]

(vii) *No continuing obligation*

The overwhelming trend amongst provincial decisions is to hold that, once a reasonable opportunity to consult counsel has been afforded, there is no continuing obligation for counsel to re-inform the accused of his right to counsel and to provide further opportunities to consult when police continue their investigation with the accused.[164] This was also the Supreme Court's position, *obiter*, in *Hebert*.[165] There is one dramatic decision of the Nova Scotia Court of Appeal in *Nugent* (1988),[166] where the majority of the Court refused to admit the evidence of a video-enactment of a murder conducted after the accused had been allowed to consult counsel and without that counsel's knowledge.

The principle that police can investigate and interrogate at will after the accused has been given a reasonable opportunity to consult counsel results in detainees in Canada having considerably less protection than those in the United States where custodial interrogation without the presence of counsel is unconstitutional.[167] Since the principle was established with little justification by *obiter* pronouncement in *Hebert*, there is room for reconsideration by the Supreme Court. The recent new implementation duties set out in *Burlingham* may provide some avenue for review.[168]

---

[161] At 280. See further on issue of counsel of choice *McCallen* (1999), 22 C.R. (5th) 103 (Ont. C.A.).

[162] At p. 16.

[163] *Ibid.*

[164] Above note 109.

[165] Above note 108.

[166] Above note 109.

[167] See Breen, above note 110.

[168] The Alberta Court of Appeal has held in *Friesen* (1995), 101 C.C.C. (3d) 167 (Alta. C.A.), that this cannot sustain a proposition that "police would violate the Charter if they ever did anything under any circumstances which by any means or to any degree dissuaded a detained accused from again speaking to a lawyer or from answering questions without a lawyer present" (at 179).

(viii) *Waiver*

The Supreme Court developed its demanding approach[169] to waiver of Charter rights in the context of the right to counsel. In *Clarkson* (1986),[170] Wilson J. for the Court insisted that an effective waiver would require "full knowledge of the rights the procedure was enacted to protect and of the effect of waiver"[171] and "a true appreciation of the consequences of giving up the right."[172] In *Manninen*, the Supreme Court held that waiver of the right to counsel under s. 10(b) of the Charter can be implicit although it asserted that "the standard will be very high."[173] The Court held that where the detainee has asserted his right to counsel, there is a right not to be asked questions by the police and the detainee must not be held to have implicitly waived that right simply because he answered their questions.[174]

When the Supreme Court has characterized the issue as one of waiver, it has already repeatedly demonstrated its reluctance to find that there has been a waiver of the right to counsel. The Court held that Clarkson[175] had not waived her right to counsel as she was so intoxicated that she had not been aware of the consequences of speaking to the police. This was so even though she had rejected a suggestion by an aunt that she should not be interrogated before a lawyer was present on the basis that there was "no point" and that she did not need a lawyer.[176] Manninen[177] had not intended to waive his right as he had asserted it at the beginning and the end of the police questioning. The police had ignored his request to consult counsel and had resorted to questions designed to elicit involuntary answers. The fact that Leclair and Ross[178] had not refused to participate in the line-up could not amount to an implied waiver. The purpose of the right to counsel was to ensure that those detained were advised of their legal rights and how to exercise them. The youths had been ignorant of their legal position. Black[179] had been concerned throughout about her legal rights, both upon her arrival at the police station and upon being advised of the change of

---

[169] Above, Chapter 1.

[170] (1986), 50 C.R. (3d) 289 (S.C.C.).

[171] Quoting *Korponay v. Canada (A.G.)* (1982), 26 C.R. (3d) 343 (S.C.C.).

[172] About note 170, at 302-303.The ruling in *Bartle*, above note 65, and that in *Tran* (1994), 32 C.R. (4th) 34 (S.C.C.) (respecting waiver of the s. 14 right to an interpreter) appear to supercede the unanimous judgment of the Supreme Court in *Whittle* (1994), 32 C.R. (4th) 1 (S.C.C.), handed down only one month earlier. In *Whittle* the Court determined that the trial judge had erred in holding that any waiver of the right to counsel required an "awareness of consequences" test. *Whittle* has been criticized as drawing a false analogy to tests for fitness to stand trial and for ignoring the authority of *Clarkson* (1986), 50 C.R. (3d) 303 (S.C.C.): see R.J. Delisle, "Whittle or Tran: Conflicting Messages on How Much an Accused Must Understand", (1994) 32 C.R. (4th) (S.C.C.). The authority of *Clarkson* appears to be fully restored in *Bartle* and *Tran*.

[173] Above note 115, at 105.

[174] *Ibid.*

[175] Above note 170.

[176] *Ibid.*, at 296.

[177] Above note 115.

[178] Above note 119, at 219.

[179] Above note 100.

charge from attempted murder to murder. She was a person of limited intelligence, had been under the influence of alcohol at the time, was emotionally distraught and was suffering from injuries which required medical attention. She had initiated the conversation with the officer, after she had spoken to her grandmother, but that conversation related to the safety of her children and it had been the officer who had turned the conversation back to the circumstances of the stabbing. He had not been as coercive as the officers in *Manninen* but his purpose had been to extract a confession. Since Brydges[180] had been left with the mistaken impression by the police that his inability to afford a lawyer prevented him from exercising his right to counsel, he clearly did not understand the full meaning of the right to counsel and had not been in a position to carefully consider the consequences of waiving. When Evans[181] had finally been given the choice of contacting a lawyer but had continued to complete a written statement he could not have been taken to waive his rights given his subnormal mental capacity and the day of aggressive and at times deceptive interrogation, which had left him feeling that he had "no choice" but to confess.[182]

The Supreme Court decision in *Smith* (1991)[183] seems to be at odds with this very clear and long line of authority applying the doctrine of waiver very strictly. The morning after the accused had shot his friend during a fight he surrendered to the police. In the police vehicle he was advised that he was under arrest "for a shooting incident" at the victim's residence, advised of the right to counsel and given the standard police warning. At the police station the police became aware that the accused did not know that the victim had died but they did not inform him of this fact in the initial interrogation. The accused did not avail himself of the opportunity to speak to counsel and made a statement in which he admitted the shooting but sought to explain it on the grounds of drunkenness and provocation. Although it was conceded that there had been a violation of s. 10(a),[184] Madam Justice McLachlin for a unanimous Court held that the initial s. 10(b) advice had been sufficient and in the circumstances the accused had waived his right to counsel. In so doing the Court held that

> to establish a valid waiver of the right to counsel, the trial Judge must be satisfied that in all the circumstances revealed by the evidence the accused generally understood the sort of jeopardy he faced when he or she made the decision to dispense with counsel. The accused need not be aware of the precise charge faced. Nor need

---

[180] Above note 76, at 142.

[181] Above note 56, at 125.

[182] Similarly provincial Courts of Appeal have been reluctant to find a valid waiver: see *Meunier* (1997), 120 C.C.C. (3d) 473 (Que. C.A.), *Small* (1998), 15 C.R. (5th) 345 (Alta. C.A.), and *A. (S.)*(1998), 129 C.C.C. (3d) 548 (Que. C.A.). Waiver has only been accepted in those cases where the statement was a spontaneous voluntary statement, not the result of police questioning and where the accused understood his jeopardy: see *Legere* (1994), 35 C.R. (4th) 1 (N.B. C.A.) at 26, *Haynes* (1997), 121 C.C.C. (3d) 1 (B.C. C.A.) and *Smith* (1999), 134 C.C.C. (3d) 453 (Ont. C.A.).

[183] (1991), 4 C.R. (4th) 125 (S.C.C.). See the criticism of David Michael Tanovich, "To Be or Not To Be: Doctrinal Schizophrenia and the Right to Counsel" (1991), 34 *Crim. L.Q.* 205.

[184] The decision *not* to exclude evidence because of the s. 10(a) violation is discussed below, Chapter 11.

the accused be made aware of all the factual details of the case. What is required is that he or she be possessed of sufficient information to allow making an informed and appropriate decision as to whether to speak to a lawyer or not. The emphasis should be on the reality of the total situation as it impacts on the understanding of the accused, rather than on technical detail of what the accused may or may not have been told.[185]

Unfortunately, even without *Smith*, this picture of waiver was not nearly as clear as it might seem given the Supreme Court's parallel development of a duty on the accused to exercise the right to counsel with reasonable diligence.

(ix) *Accused's duty to assert right with reasonable diligence*

In *Manninen*,[186] the Supreme Court held that the right to counsel leads to correlative obligations on the police. The Court left open the question of whether the police duties were dependent upon the accused asserting the right as Manninen had done. The Ontario Court of Appeal in *Anderson*[187] had earlier held that the police duties only arose where the accused had in any manner chosen to invoke or exercise his right to retain and instruct counsel. *Anderson* has been strongly criticized[188] as unduly weakening the right to counsel by only protecting those accused who are knowledgeable, thoroughly understanding and assertive. The language of obligation throughout *Manninen* and its strong ruling on the facts suggested that the Supreme Court might well reverse *Anderson*. In *Baig* (1987),[189] the Supreme Court did exactly the opposite in adopting the *Anderson* proposition that the duties depend on the accused asserting his right.

Following Baig's arrest for murder, he was advised that he need not say anything and that he had a right to retain and instruct counsel without delay. He was then asked whether he understood. He replied: "How can you prove this thing?" Later, at the police station, just before he confessed, he was reminded that the caution given on arrest still applied. The written confession was obtained immediately after the taking of the oral statement, and included affirmative answers to questions as to whether he understood the charge and the caution and the fact that he had the right to retain and instruct counsel without delay. In a short *per curiam* judgment, which makes no reference to *Manninen*, the Supreme Court held that Baig had not been denied the right to counsel, since there was nothing on the record to indicate that once he had been advised of his right to counsel and said that he understood it, he had chosen to exercise it. Therefore, no correlative duties had been triggered. The Court indicated that there was no need to determine the issue of waiver and adopted the conclusion in *Anderson* that

> absent proof of circumstances indicating the accused did not understand his right to retain counsel when he was informed of it, the onus has to be on him to prove that

---

[185] Above note 183, at 139.
[186] Above note 115.
[187] Above note 79, discussing its impact and authority on the issue of the right to be informed.
[188] Above note 81.
[189] (1987), 61 C.R. (3d) 97 (S.C.C.).

he asked for the right but it was denied or he was denied any opportunity to even ask for it.[190]

It is quite clear that the protection of the right to counsel is substantially eroded by this view that the accused must assert the right before any duties arise for the police when one considers subsequent applications by provincial courts. It has been held[191] that a person subjected to a breathalyzer demand and advised of the right to counsel at the roadside need not be re-advised nor given the opportunity to use the telephone before the test is administered at the police station, absent a request for counsel. The courts have also been most ungenerous in their interpretation of what constitutes asserting the right to counsel: there were no assertions where an accused on several occasions shouted out to his wife in the next room to call a lawyer;[192] where the accused left it to his father to call a lawyer, the lawyer called but the accused only asked whether his father had called;[193] and where the accused indicated that he wished to call his mother without indicating that he wanted her to secure counsel.[194]

There is, however, an important ruling of the Ontario Court of Appeal in *Woods* (1989)[195] that there would be a violation of s. 10(b) where a detainee, advised of his right to counsel and indicating that he understands, is immediately questioned before any opportunity to assert his right. For the Court, Mr. Justice Griffiths held:

> It is fundamental that once the detainee has been informed of his right to counsel, some reasonable time should he allowed to permit him to consider his rights before any further questioning begins, if for no other reason than to be satisfied that the detainee fully understands his rights.[196]

Subsequent to *Baig*, the Supreme Court has not only continued to insist that police duties only arise where the accused asserts the right to counsel but have further insisted that the detainee is under a duty to exercise the right with reasonable diligence. According to the Court, if the detainee is not reasonably diligent, then the correlative duties on the police are "suspended". What constitutes reasonable diligence was considered in *LeClair and Ross* (1989):[197]

> Reasonable diligence in the exercise of the right to choose one's counsel depends upon the context facing the accused or detained person. On being arrested, for example, the detained person is faced with an immediate need for legal advice and must exercise reasonable diligence accordingly. By contrast, when seeking the best lawyer to conduct a trial, the accused person faces no such immediacy. Nevertheless, accused or detained persons have a right to choose their counsel and it is only if the

---

[190] *Anderson*, above note 79, at 209, cited in *Baig, ibid.*, at 100.
[191] *Elgie* (1987), 35 C.C.C. (3d) 332 (B.C. C.A.) and *Shannon* (1987), 58 C.R. (3d) 117 (N.W.T. C.A.).
[192] *Van Den Meerseche* (1989), 74 C.R. (3d) 161 (B.C. C.A.).
[193] *Bain*, above note 108.
[194] *Adams* (1989), 49 C.C.C. (3d) 100 (Ont. C.A.).
[195] (1989), 70 C.R. (3d) 45 (Ont. C.A.). Wood J.A. adopted *Woods* in *Hollis* (1992), 17 C.R. (4th) 211 (B.C. C.A.). However, Gibbs and Carrothers JJ.A. left the issue open.
[196] *Ibid.*, at 55.
[197] Above note 118.

lawyer chosen cannot be available within a reasonable time that the detainee or the accused should be expected to exercise the right to counsel by calling another lawyer.[198]

In the circumstances of that case, both the accused had exercised reasonable diligence and had not waived their right to counsel. The police should have afforded them a reasonable opportunity and there was no urgency in holding the line-up in the middle of the night.[199]

In subsequent decisions, the Supreme Court would appear to have been inconsistent in the application of this requirement of reasonable diligence in the exercise of the accused's right. Consistent with *LeClair and Ross*, it was held in *Black*[200] that the accused had been reasonably diligent in asserting her rights when, in a distraught and drunkened state, she had requested to speak again with the lawyer of her choice when she was advised that the charge was being changed from attempted murder to first degree murder. It was the middle of the night and a delay of approximately eight hours until normal office hours of lawyers would be not unreasonable given that the charge was first degree murder and that there was no urgency for the interrogation. There had, furthermore, been no waiver.[201]

Only a month after it had handed down its unanimous decision in *Black*, a majority of the Supreme Court in *Smith* (1989)[202] held that an accused arrested on a charge of robbery had *not* been reasonably diligent in the exercise of his rights when at the police station he had advised the police that he would not call his lawyer at 9:00 p.m. but would contact him in the morning. An hour later, the police questioned the accused in his cell. Smith agreed to answer questions about himself but would make no comment about the robbery until he had spoken to his lawyer. The questioning continued and the accused indicated on two other occasions that he wanted to speak to his lawyer. Finally, he made an incriminating statement, specifying that it was made "off the record."

Three separate judgments were given for the majority. For Mr. Justice Lamer (Gonthier J. concurring)[203] it was significant that the police had suggested that the accused phone his lawyer, even though it was 9:00 p.m., as it was always possible that there would be somebody at the office or an answering machine could indicate where the lawyer could be reached. The right to counsel was not absolute or unlimited and had to be exercised in a way "reconcilable with the needs of society." Madam Justice L'Heureux-Dubé agreed[204] that the accused had been given a reasonable opportunity and had not availed himself of that opportunity. Effective police investigation may include as one of its aim the

---

[198] *Ibid.*, at 216-217.
[199] See too *Charron* (1990), 57 C.C.C. (3d) 248 (Que. C.A.).
[200] Above note 100.
[201] *Ibid.*, at 216-217.
[202] (1989), 71 C.R. (3d) 129 (S.C.C.). See too *Top*, above note 123 and *Ferron* (1989), 49 C.C.C. (3d) 432 (B.C. C.A.) (no reasonable excuse for failing to provide breath sample where accused not advising police that lawyer not able to be contacted).
[203] *Ibid.*, at 136.
[204] *Ibid.*, at 145-147.

obtaining of a confession from a suspect. According to Mr. Justice Sopinka,[205] the accused had been "most casual in asserting his right" in that in the previous two hours he had been concerned with comparative trivialities at a time when a lawyer might well have been available.

In dissent, Mr. Justice La Forest (Chief Justice Dickson and Madame Justice Wilson concurring) held[206] that there had been no waiver and that the accused had in the circumstances exercised reasonable diligence in asserting his right. The case was governed by *Ross* and the attempt to distinguish it on the basis that the call in *Smith* had been at 9:00 p.m. rather than 2:00 a.m., as in *Ross*, was to "interpret the Charter in a grudging way and to give the police, who must administer the law, very unclear guidelines."

The majority ruling in *Smith* has been soundly criticized by commentators[207] both respecting its inroads on the right to remain silent and also the right to counsel. In respect of the latter, Stanley Cohen observes

> In the interrogation setting this means that, although the police must desist from questioning a suspect who requests counsel until contact is made, they may nevertheless persist in their endeavours if any indecisiveness is shown. Also it appears that in the period prior to his receiving counsel's assistance the police may apply considerable pressure on a suspect to waive the s. 10(b) right.[208]

The justifications offered by the majority in *Smith* seem inconsistent with a purposive approach to the Charter right to counsel. It is difficult to reconcile the Supreme Court's notion of the duty to exercise due diligence and the very high standard of implicit waiver insisted upon in *Manninen*. Although the majority in *Smith* do not mention waiver, their holding seems to be that Smith's failure to resist the persistent efforts of the police to get him to talk amounted to an implicit waiver. What else can the Supreme Court mean by a "suspension of rights"? What happened to the notion that waiver must be unequivocal? The subsequent return to the language of duty by the majority in *Brydges*,[209] irrespective of the accused conduct, may occasion some rethinking of the accused's duty to assert with reasonable diligence. Apart from the issue of knowing waiver, surely the accused's conduct should go to the question of remedy not the breach?

---

[205] *Ibid.*, at 147.

[206] *Ibid.*, at 153. The minority supported the views of McLachlin J. (as she then was) dissenting in the Court below.

[207] Stanley A. Cohen, "Police Interrogation of the Wavering Suspect" (1989), 71 C.R. (3d) 148; Patrick Healy, "The Value of Silence", (1990) 74 C.R. (3d) 176 and Stephen Coughlan, "When Silence Isn't Golden: Waiver and the Right to Counsel", (1990) 33 *Crim.L.Q.* 43 and in "Annotation to *Hollis*", (1992) 17 C.R. (4th) 211.

[208] *Ibid.*, at 155.

[209] Above note 76.

4. SECTION 10(c): RIGHT "TO HAVE THE VALIDITY OF THE DETENTION DETERMINED BY WAY OF HABEAS CORPUS AND TO BE RELEASED IF THE DETENTION IS NOT LAWFUL"

Section 459.1 of the Criminal Code expressly denying *habeas corpus* to review or vary any order made under bail provision was held[210] to have yield to s. 10(c). It has been repealed.

---

[210] *Jack* (1982), 1 C.C.C. (2d) 193 (Nfld. S.C.).

6

Section 11: Rights of Persons Charged with an Offence

1. TRIGGER: CHARGE OF OFFENCE

The various rights set out in s. 11(a) to (i) only arise when a person has been "charged with an offence." As such they have been held to be limited to pre-trial and trial rights.[1] Of course that does not preclude appeal courts assessing whether such rights were properly afforded.

(a) Wigglesworth Tests

Since *Wigglesworth* (1987),[2] it has been clear that s. 11 protections are available in the case of charges of all federal and provincial offences to be tried by courts irrespective of penalty. For a Court unanimous on this point,[3] Wilson J. held as follows:

> The rights guaranteed by s. 11 of the Charter are available to persons prosecuted by the state for public offences involving punitive sanctions, i.e., criminal, quasi-criminal and regulatory offences, either federally or provincially enacted.[4]

---

[1] See *Potvin* (1993), 23 C.R. (4th) 10 (S.C.C.), below s. 11 (b), and *Farinacci* (1993), 25 C.R. (4th) 350 (Ont. C.A.), below s. 11(e). In *Whitty* (1999), 24 C.R. (5th) 131 (Nfld. C.A.) and *Casey* (2000), 30 C.R. (5th) 126 (Ont. C.A.) it was held s. 11(d) did not protect against a reverse onus applying at a conditional sentence breach hearing. In all these decisions, the courts recognised residual s. 7 protection but found it did not avail.

[2] (1987), 60 C.R. (3d) 193 (S.C.C.).

[3] Dickson C.J., Beetz, McIntyre, Lamer and La Forest JJ. concurred. Estey J. dissented on the s. 11(h) issue in question.

[4] Above note 2, at 206, applied in *Thibault v. Corp. professionnelle des médecins du Québec* (1988), 63 C.R. (3d) 273 at 289 (S.C.C.). See, however, *Quebec (Procureur general) v. Robitaille* (1991), 3 C.R. (4th) 267 (Que. C.A.) (s. 11 not applying to traffic ticket). This ruling appears to be wrongly decided given *Wigglesworth*, to which the Court did not refer. In *Manitoba (A.G.) v. Groupe Quebecor Inc.* (1987), 37 C.C.C. (3d) 421 at 428 (Man. C.A.) it was held that "charge" did not bear a technical meaning and included a citation for contempt of court. The Court, however, held that s. 11(f) (right to jury trial) had no application.

. . . .

> It cannot be seriously contended that just because a minor traffic offence leads to a very slight consequence, perhaps only a small fine, that offence does not fall within s. 11.[5]

. . . .

> But all prosecutions for criminal offences under the Criminal Code and for quasi-criminal offences under provincial legislation are automatically subject to s. 11. They are the very kind of offences to which s. 11 was intended to apply.[6]

Wilson J. noted that the text of s. 11 contained terms classically associated with criminal proceedings, and that some of the rights guaranteed by s. 7 would seem to have no meaning outside the criminal or quasi-criminal context. The history of s. 11 indicated that it was not intended to be restricted solely to the criminal law but extended also to penal proceedings. This view was supported by the marginal note, which reads "Proceedings in criminal and penal matters."[7]

The Supreme Court has also held that s. 11 rights are not applicable at extradition hearings[8] or post-conviction applications to have an accused declared a dangerous offender.[9] The Court through Mr. Justice La Forest held that the phrase "any person charged with an offence" had to be given "a constant meaning that harmonizes" with the various protections under s. 11.[10] Some rights such as the presumption of innocence (s. 11(d)), right to bail (s. 11(e)) and the right to a jury trial (s. 11(f)) might not apply in these contexts. It would be inappropriate to have the question of applicability vary from paragraph to paragraph.[11]

Ambiguity arises in the further ruling in *Wigglesworth* that certain types of disciplinary and administrative proceedings are not protected under s. 11. A matter could fall under s. 11 because of its "very nature" or because a conviction of the offence would lead to a "true penal consequence."[12]

Explaining its "by nature" test, the Court held that s. 11 applied to offences which were of a "public nature, intended to promote public order and welfare within a public sphere of activity" but not to "private, domestic or disciplinary matters which are regulatory, protective or corrective and which are primarily intended to maintain discipline, professional integrity and professional standards

---

[5] Above note 2, at 210.

[6] *Ibid.*, at 208.

[7] *Ibid.*, at 207-209.

[8] *Schmidt* (1987), 58 C.R. (3d) 1 (S.C.C.). However in *U.S. v. Kwok* (April 5, 2001) (S.C.C.) the Court held that s. 7 rights are engaged at extradition hearings under the new Extradition Act. The issue of the applicability of s. 11 was not addressed.

[9] *Lyons* (1987), 61 C.R. (3d) 1 (S.C.C.). Lamer J. dissented on this point.

[10] *Lyons, ibid.*, at 41. The Court also rejected a s. 7 challenge: see above, Chapter 2.

[11] In *741290 Ontario Inc.* (1991), 2 O.R. (3d) 336 (Ont. Prov. Div.), Macdonnell J. held that these dicta did not preclude a ruling that a corporation can rely on the right to be tried within a reasonable time (s. 11(b)) even though the Supreme Court had already held that a corporation could not rely on the s. 11(c) right not to be compelled to be a witness: See below, *Amway Corp.*, note 163.

[12] Above note 2, at 209-210.

or to regulate conduct within a limited private sphere of activity.''[13] Also excluded were proceedings to determine fitness to obtain or maintain a licence and administrative proceedings to protect the public in accordance with the policy of a statute.[14]

Proceedings excluded by the ''nature'' test from s. 11 could still fall within the scope of s. 11 if they involved ''true penal consequences.'' The Court adopted the view that

> other *punitive* forms of disciplinary measures, such as fines or imprisonment, are indistinguishable from criminal punishment and should surely fall within the protection of s. 11(*h*).[15]

The Court entered two ''caveats''. A fine imposed for the purpose of redressing the wrong done to society at large would be a true penal consequence but s. 11 would not be triggered by a fine to maintain discipline and order within a limited private sphere of activity. One indicium of the purpose of a particular fine was held to be whether it was paid into the Consolidated Revenue Fund or kept within a private sphere.[16] The second caveat was that it would be difficult to conceive of the possibility of a proceeding failing the ''by nature'' test but passing the ''true penal consequence'' test. The second caveat appears to have been quite empty in that *Wigglesworth* itself was later seen to be such a case. The Court determines that, although police disciplinary proceedings were concerned with the maintenance of internal discipline and did not pass the ''by the nature'' test, s. 11 applied to proceedings in respect of a major service offence before the police service court because the officer faced a true penal consequence in that he or she might face possible imprisonment of one year if convicted.[17] Wilson J. had indicated that an individual subject to imprisonment ''should be entitled to the highest procedural protection known to our law.''[18]

In companion decisions[19] to *Wigglesworth*, the Supreme Court held that s. 11 protections did *not* apply to police disciplinary proceedings not involving the risk of imprisonment. A charge under a Police Act where the penalties ranged from a reprimand to dismissal was not criminal in nature and did not involve penal consequences. Presumably the same would be true, as held by lower courts, of professional misconduct proceedings against lawyers[20] or doctors.[21]

---

[13] *Ibid.*, at 219.

[14] *Ibid.*, at 210-211.

[15] This was a view on the meaning of punishment in s. 11(h) expressed by this author in ''Annotation to R. v. Wigglesworth'' (1984), 38 C.R. (3d) 388 at 389. See further below under s. 11(h).

[16] Above note 2, at 211.

[17] *Ibid.*, at 213.

[18] *Ibid.*, at 212.

[19] *Trimm v. Durham Regional Police Force* (1987), 37 C.C.C. (3d) 120 (S.C.C.); *Burnham v. Ackroyd* (1987), 37 C.C.C. (3d) 118 (S.C.C.) and *Trumbley v. Metropolitan Police Force* (1987), 37 C.C.C. (3d) 120 (S.C.C.).

[20] *Belhumeur v. Discipline Committee of Quebec Bar Association* (1983), 34 C.R. (3d) 279 (Que S.C.) and *Law Society of Manitoba v. Savino* (1983), 6 W.W.R. 538 (Man. C.A.).

[21] *Fang v. College of Physicians and Surgeons of Alberta*, [1986] 2 W.W.R. 380 (Alta. C.A.).

(b) Prison Disciplinary Proceedings

What of disciplinary proceedings within a prison? In *Shubley* (1990),[22] the accused, a prisoner in a provincial institution, was found to have assaulted another prisoner, and as a consequence was placed in solitary confinement for five days on a restricted diet. The accused was subsequently charged with assault causing bodily harm relating to the same event and argued that s. 11(h) protected him against being tried and punished twice. A narrow three to two majority of the Supreme Court held that the original prison disciplinary proceedings had not constituted a trial for the offence such as to trigger the protection of s. 11. Madam Justice McLachlin J. for the majority[23] held that neither *Wigglesworth* test had been met. The prison disciplinary proceedings were not by their nature criminal proceedings. The accused was answerable to the prison officials for his breach of discipline but was not being called to account to society for a crime. The purpose of the proceedings was to maintain order and the proceedings were conducted informally, swiftly and in private.[24] Furthermore, the punishment involved in the disciplinary proceedings did not involve true penal consequences. They were generally confined to privileges and conditions under which a prisoner lives. The sanctions of solitary confinement or forfeiture of remission did not involve a punitive fine or imprisonment.[25]

In dissent, Mr. Justice Cory, with the notable concurrence of Madam Justice Wilson, the author of *Wigglesworth*, held that the prison disciplinary process in question came within the protection of s. 11 because it imposed true penal consequences. Solitary confinement was a quite different and severe form of punishment. It was an additional violation of whatever residual liberty an inmate retained in the prison context and should be used only where it was justified. Likewise, the loss of earned remission or the ability to earn remission was a penal consequence. While the opportunity to earn remission might be a privilege, once earned it should be viewed as an acquired right. The effect of remission was to reduce the time spent in prison and had the same effect as a reduction in sentence.[26]

Shubley has been strongly criticized[27] and, given the narrow majority and the dissent of Wilson J., the issue of whether s. 11 applies to prison discipline cannot be taken to have been finally settled.

(c) Meaning of Charge

In *Kalanj* (1989),[28] a case involving the right to be tried within a reasonable time under s. 11(b) of the Charter, another brittle three to two majority of the

---

[22] (1990), 74 C.R. (3d) 1 (S.C.C.).

[23] Sopinka and Gonthier JJ. concurred.

[24] Above note 22, at 13-14.

[25] *Ibid.*, at 15-16.

[26] *Ibid.*, at 6-8.

[27] Allan Manson, "Solitary Confinement, Remission and Prison Discipline" (1990), 75 C.R. (3d) 356.

[28] (1989), 70 C.R. (3d) 260 (S.C.C.).

Supreme Court[29] determined that a person is charged with an offence within the meaning of s. 11 from the moment an information is sworn to a justice alleging an offence or, where a direct indictment is laid, when no information is sworn. The minority position is that the section's protection should apply not upon an *ex parte* formal laying of an information before a justice but rather when the impact of the criminal justice is felt by the accused through the service of process in the form of a summons, notice of appearance or an arrest with or without warrant.[30]

The minority position seems far more consistent with a "purposive" approach to the Charter. It much better furthers the interests protected by the various s. 11 rights. Despite the appeal of the minority position, the brittle *Kalanj* position on this point was later adopted as the position of the full Court.[31]

2. SECTION 11(a): RIGHT "TO BE INFORMED WITHOUT UNREASONABLE DELAY OF THE SPECIFIC OFFENCE"

Provincial Courts have on several occasions[32] adopted the following analysis of Professor Ed Ratushny as to the interests protected by s. 11(a):

> It is easy to see why the requirement of a proper accusation is an important protection to an accused. A specific accusation presupposes a specific offence in law. It, therefore, provides an opportunity at the outset for the accused to challenge the authority of the officials of the state to subject him to the criminal process. If no offence exists in law, the accusation can be attacked and quashed, thereby terminating the proceeding.
>
> It is also important in specifying the exact conduct which is said to constitute the offence. The accused must be aware of such details as the specific time and place, when and where the offence occurred, the manner in which it is alleged to have been committed and the identity of the victim, if any, so that he may prepare his defence. It could be argued that s. 11(a) requires only that the "offence" be specified (for example, rape, robbery, etc.) since it makes no reference to identifying the details of the act or transaction. However, once again, to take such a narrow interpretation would render the protection a sham.
>
> The accused should also know his accuser so that he might be aware of any improper motives and bring legal action against that accuser if the prosecution is malicious.
>
> The accusation provides another important protection to the accused. It defines the scope of the proceedings against him. The evidence and argument must relate to the specific charge. It is generally not permissible, for example, to bring in evidence of other unlawful or immoral conduct on the part of the accused which does not

---

[29] Per McIntyre J., La Forest and L'Heureux-Dubé JJ. concurring. Lamer and Wilson JJ. both dissented in separate judgments.

[30] In *Heit* (1984), 11 C.C.C. (3d) 97 (Sask. C.A.), the Court favoured the view that a person served with a traffic ticket not yet sworn in Court was charged for the purposes of s. 11(a) but left the matter open. Such a view would contradict its earlier view that s. 11 could not be interpreted to protect one about to be charged.

[31] See, for example, *Morin* (1992), 12 C.R. (4th) 1 (S.C.C.) at 13.

[32] *Heit, ibid.*; *Re Warren* (1983), 35 C.R. (3d) 173 (Ont. H.C.) and *Cancor Software Corp.* (1990), 79 C.R. (3d) 22 (Ont. C.A.).

relate to the accusation which he is facing. The accused is to be tried with respect to specific alleged misconduct and not for the kind of person he is.[33]

In *Delaronde* (1997)[34] the Supreme Court of Canada adopted the view of Otis J.A. for the Quebec Court of Appeal[35] that s. 11(a) only

> protects the accused from prejudice which results from the time that is allowed to elapse before he is informed of the specific offence with which he is charged. This protection assures that the accused can make full answer and defence and, in so doing, guarantees his right to a fair trial.[36]

The Quebec Court of Appeal also adopted the view of the Ontario Court of Appeal that

> s. 11(a) does not require that an individual be charged with an offence within a reasonable time of the Crown's having knowledge of the offence. It merely requires that once a charge is laid, the accused must be provided without unreasonable delay with the information necessary to enable him to proceed appropriately with his defence.[37]

An information had been sworn charging Delaronde with several offences, including participation in a riot, 20 months prior to his arrest. The Court accepted that the delay was entirely attributable to the police. They had been reluctant to enter the reserve but could have communicated the charges through native peacekeepers. Nevertheless the Court of Appeal and the Supreme Court held that, in the absence of evidence of prejudice to a fair trial, s. 11(a) had not been breached and the trial judge had erred in staying the trial.

At face value, *Delaronde* appears to severely limit the protection of s. 11(a) to cases where there is evidence of risk to a fair trial. There is a brief addendum[38] by Lamer C.J. seeking to leave open a s. 11(a) challenge based on economic prejudice. However no other justice joined him.

It has been held[39] that the right to be informed of the specific offence under s. 11(a) refers to the substantive offence and conduct alleged. However, it does not give the accused the right to be informed in the case of a hybrid offence whether the Crown is proceeding by way of indictment or summary conviction proceedings.[40]

There are only three reported decisions in which s. 11(a) was successfully invoked in aid of a challenge to the formal sufficiency of a charge. In *Morales* (1992),[41] a complex conspiracy count laid six days before trial and two months

---

[33] "The Role of the Accused in the Criminal Process" in Tarnopolsky and Beaudouin (eds.), *The Canadian Charter of Rights and Freedoms: Commentary* (1982) p. 135.

[34] (1997), 115 C.C.C. (3d) 355 at 370 (S.C.C.). There is a brief addendum by Lamer C.J. seeking to leave open a s. 11(a) challenge based on economic prejudice.

[35] (1997), 115 C.C.C. (3d) 355 (S.C.C.).

[36] At 368.

[37] *Cancor Software*, above note 32, quoted at 368.

[38] (1997), 115 C.C.C. (3d) 355 at 370 (S.C.C.).

[39] *Warren*, above note 32, *Cancor Software*, above note 32. The charge must be understood by the accused in the language of the trial: *Simard* (1995), 105 C.C.C. (3d) 461 (Ont. C.A.).

[40] *Warren, ibid.*

[41] (1992), 12 C.R. (4th) 340 (Que. C.A.).

after the committal was quashed as violating s. 11(a). In *S.(A.)* (1998)[42] a conviction of anal intercourse was quashed on appeal because the offence had been declared unconstitutional.

In *Lucas* (1983),[43] the Nova Scotia Court of Appeal held that s. 11(a) enshrines the fundamental principle of law contained in what is now s. 581 of the Criminal Code that the charge must be in such a manner as to clearly bring home to the accused an accurate knowledge of the offence with which he is charged. An information charging an accused with a provincial motor vehicle offence but merely describing the offence as "operating overweight vehicle" without reference to the particular regulation allegedly infringed did not comply with s. 11(a). There were several means described in the regulations by which the offence could be committed. The same Nova Scotia Court of Appeal later distinguished *Lucas* in holding that a speeding charge describing the offence as "exceeding *prima facie* limit" was sufficient. There was a general speed limit posted across the province and the regulations permitted the charge by "any concise expression which sufficiently describes the offence to the accused."[44]

The lack of success and interest in utilizing s. 11(a) to enforce greater standards of particularity in the charge may well be explained by the clear judicial trend to reject so-called technical objections. Criminal Code provisions themselves obviously strive to compromise between ensuring that an accused gets adequate notice of the charge so that a defence can be prepared and avoiding undue technicalities. Under s. 581(3) which is given paramountcy under subsection (6),[45] the count must contain "sufficient detail of the circumstances of the alleged offence to give to the accused reasonable information with respect to the act or omission to be proved against him and to identify the transaction referred to." But the same section declares that the absence or insufficiency of details does not vitiate the count and a separate s. 583 lists a wide variety of details whose absence is declared not to make a count insufficient. On occasion, the Supreme Court of Canada has invalidated a charge on the basis that it does not describe the offence "in such a way as to lift it from the general to the particular."[46] But it has more frequently rejected insufficiency attacks as too technical and belonging to the "punctilio of an earlier age."[47] The Court has preferred to point to the availability of wide powers to order particulars[48] or to make amendments.[49]

This attitude is particularly evident in the decision of the Supreme Court of Canada in *B. (G.)* (1990)[50] in which, without reference to s. 11(a), it was held the

---

[42] (1998), 19 C.R. (5th) 393 (Ont. C.A.).

[43] (1983), 6 C.C.C. (3d) 147 (N.S. C.A.).

[44] *Goreham* (1984), 12 C.C.C. (3d) 348 (N.S. C.A.).

[45] "Nothing in this Part relating to matters that do not render a count insufficient shall be deemed to restrict or limit the application of this section."

[46] *Brodie*, [1936] S.C.R. 188 at 198. See especially *Wis Developments Corp.* (1984), 40 C.R. (3d) 97 (S.C.C.).

[47] *Sault Ste. Marie* (1978), 3 C.R. (3d) 30 at 38 (S.C.C.). See too *McKenzie* (1972), 16 C.R.N.S. 374 (S.C.C.) and *Cote* (1978), 40 C.R.N.S. 308 (S.C.C.).

[48] *McKenzie, ibid.*

[49] *Moore* (1988), 65 C.R. (3d) 1 (S.C.C.).

[50] (1990), 77 C.R. (3d) 347 (S.C.C.). See too *W. (A.G.)* (1992), 17 C.R. (4th) 393 (S.C.C.).

charge of sexual assault against a young child was adequate although the date of the offence specified differed from the evidence. What constituted reasonable and adequate information of necessity varied from case to case. Here, having regard to the nature of the offence and the age of the victim, the charge, which specified a period of 19 days, sufficed. Time was neither an essential element of the offence nor crucial to the defence. There should have been an amendment at trial to conform with the evidence. *B. (G.)* is consistent with a number of decisions at the level of provincial courts of appeal which have refused to force the Crown to specify the precise nature of an allegation of a sexual offence, either as to the time or the nature of the act alleged.[51]

3. SECTION 11(b): RIGHT ''TO BE TRIED WITHIN A REASONABLE TIME''

The common law knew no time limitations running against the Monarch which would bar a criminal prosecution. Prior to the enactment of s. 11(b) of the Charter, there were few statutory limitation periods on criminal prosecutions. Under the Criminal Code, there were scattered statutory exceptions[52] and a major exception in that a summary conviction proceedings cannot be instituted under s. 786(2) ''more than six months after the time when the subject-matter of the proceedings arose.''

In the criminal law context, s. 11(b) challenges have been perhaps the most frequent Charter attack. There have been literally thousands of cases. In the early years of the Charter, the Supreme Court of Canada was very badly split as to the proper approach to s. 11(b). The s. 11(b) challenge may also be the most politically charged since the Court's constitutional duty to assess court delay necessarily involves the judiciary in direct assessment of administrative and political decisions as to the deployment of scarce public resources.

(a) Forum

We have seen[53] that it was in this context of s. 11(b) that the Supreme Court settled many of the jurisdictional issues surrounding Charter challenges. A justice presiding over a preliminary inquiry is not a court of competent jurisdiction under s. 24(1) and thus cannot consider any Charter arguments.[54] Superior Courts have a jurisdiction concurrent with that of trial courts to deal with Charter issues but should normally decline jurisdiction in favour of trial courts.[55]

---

[51] See, for example, *Cook* (1985), 46 C.R. (3d) 129 (B.C. C.A.); *C. (R.I.)* (1986), 32 C.C.C. (3d) 399 (Ont. C.A.) and *German* (1989), 51 C.C.C. (3d) 175 (Sask. C.A.). See, however, *Myhren* (1985), 48 C.R. (3d) 270 (N.W.T. S.C.) but compare *Atatahak* (1986), 51 C.R. (3d) 286 (N.W.T. S.C.).

[52] In the case of treason there is a three-year limit: s. 48(1). Statutory limitations for certain sexual offences were repealed in 1987.

[53] Above, Chapter 1.

[54] *Mills* (1986), 52 C.R. (3d) 1 (S.C.C.).

[55] *Ibid.*

The Supreme Court has twice held that superior court judges properly exercised supervisory jurisdiction over s. 11(b) applications. In *Rahey* (1987),[56] the very conduct of the trial judge was alleged to be the cause of the delay. In *Smith* (1989)[57] there had been a 12-month delay since the charge of theft had been laid and 4 months remained before a preliminary inquiry, where in any case the justice would not have had jurisdiction to consider the issue.

(b) Remedy

The question of remedy for a Charter violation is here left to Chapter 12. According to a six to two majority in the Supreme Court of Canada in *Rahey* (1987),[58] the minimum remedy for a violation of s. 11(b) is a permanent stay of proceedings.

Where a violation of s. 11(b) has not yet occurred, there is authority in the judgment of Mr. Justice Martin for the Ontario Court of Appeal in *Beason* (1983)[59] that the Court may "in the exercise of its inherent power to control its own process" direct that the trial proceed at an early date and dismiss the charge if the Crown fails to proceed on that date. This power has only been touched upon by two justices in the Supreme Court who expressed "substantial agreement."[60] It has been suggested[61] that, since this jurisdiction is not based on s. 24(1) which does not contemplate remedies for anticipatory Charter breaches, not all Courts would possess this inherent jurisdiction. It seems likely, however, that the power could be utilized under a statutory adjournment power.

(c) Time Runs from Moment of Charge

Mr. Justice Lamer held in *Mills* (1986),[62] and on behalf of a full Court in *Carter* (1986)[63] over the sole dissent of Wilson J.,[64] that precharge delay is generally irrelevant to s. 11(b). He did recognize that there might be "exceptional circumstances" when it would be relevant.[65]

---

56 (1987), 57 C.R. (3d) 289 (S.C.C.).
57 (1989), 73 C.R. (3d) 1 (S.C.C.). See too *Pushie* (1990), 58 C.C.C. (3d) 38 (N.S. C.A.).
58 Above note 56. Wilson J. (Estey J. concurring) at 308, Le Dain J. (Beetz J. concurring) at 313-314 and Lamer J. (Dickson C.J. concurring) at 305-306. Lamer J. also spoke of a possibility of damages or an acquittal. La Forest J. (McIntyre J. concurring), dissented on this point, holding that a stay was not always the appropriate remedy and that the drastic remedy of stay had been counterproductive in the United States (at 321-326).
59 (1983), 36 C.R. (3d) 73 (Ont. C.A.) at 98. Martin J.A.'s preference for a dismissal rather than a stay has been overruled by the Supreme Court.
60 Lamer J. (Dickson C.J. concurring) in *Rahey*, above note 56, at 306.
61 Graeme G. Mitchell, "R. v. Smith: Old Doctrine for a New Decade" (1990), 74 C.R. (3d) 375 at 377.
62 Above note 54.
63 (1986), 52 C.R. (3d) 100 (S.C.C.).
64 Wilson J.
65 Above note 54, at 85.

In *Kalanj* (1989),[66] a majority of three judges, through McIntyre J.,[67] firmly denied that pre-charge delay can ever be relevant to whether there has been trial within a reasonable time under s. 11(b). The majority pointed to the wording of the Charter and considered its organization and structure. Remedies for pre-charge delay were to be found entirely under the right to make full answer and defence and under the doctrine of abuse of process.

This narrow majority position has since become the position of the full Court.[68] It is most unfortunate that the Supreme Court did not adopt the position of Provincial Court Judge Kopstein in *Schatkowsky* (1985).[69] His Honour's view was that a contextual construction and comparison with the wording of the right to a speedy trial under the Sixth Amendment of the United States Constitution favoured the view that pre-charge delay may be considered under the Canadian right to trial within a reasonable time. The judge reasoned that "since no trial can be formally in view until a charge is laid, the right to trial within a reasonable time *engages* only when the charge is laid."[70] Delay is one of the most pressing and difficult questions facing the criminal justice system. It seems strange to struggle to find the proper balancing approach to s. 11(b) but not apply it to a lengthy pre-charge delay case, even as long as 25 years.[71]

We have already reviewed[72] the ruling of majority of the Supreme Court in *Kalanj* that a person is charged when the information is sworn or where a direct indictment is laid where no information is sworn. *Kalanj* would deny the s. 11(b) protection given to the accused by the Quebec Court of Appeal in *Demers* (1989).[73] On his arrest in relation to a robbery, the police promised the accused that he would not be charged in exchange for his collaboration in a murder case. The accused was later charged with that murder but acquitted. Following his acquittal, the police charged him with robbery. The Quebec Court of Appeal held that time had begun to run from the first arrest and that it had been unreasonable on the laying of the murder charge for the police to postpone laying of other charges then known.

It had been expected that the Supreme Court would decide that delay during appellate proceedings could be taken into account on s. 11(b) challenges. There was a dictum of Sopinka J.[74] that the right to be tried within a reasonable time should extend to appellate proceedings. He was of the view that, given that the

---

[66] Above note 28.
[67] La Forest and L'Heureux-Dubé JJ. concurred.
[68] *Morin*, above note 31, at 14.
[69] (1985), 44 C.R. (3d) 271 at 279-280 (Man. Prov. Ct.).
[70] *Ibid.*, at 279.
[71] *Morrison* (1984), 44 C.R. (3d) 85 (Ont. C.A.), leave to appeal to S.C.C. refused 44 C.R. (3d) xxvi. Compare *L. (W.K.)* (1991), 6 C.R. (4th) 1 (S.C.C.) (30-year delay in charging abuse offences not violating ss.7 and 11(d) and not being abuse of process — discussed above, Chapter 2). See too *F. (G.A.)* (1989), 69 C.R. (3d) 92 (Ont. C.A.), *Finta* (1994), 28 C.R. (4th) 265 (S.C.C.), *H. (L.J.)* (1997), 120 C.C.C. (3d) 88 (Man. C.A.) and *Flamand* (1999), 141 C.C.C. (3d) 169 (Que. C.A.).
[72] Above note 28.
[73] (1989), 69 C.R. (3d) 66 (Que. CA.). Compare *Gelinas* (1990), 58 C.C.C. (3d) 232 (Que. C.A.), applying *Kalanj*.
[74] *Conway* (1989), 70 C.R. (3d) 209 (S.C.C.) at 247-251.

prejudice to the accused would persist until all the appeal proceedings had been finished, it would be a "shallow and illusory right" if s. 11(b) were to be limited to the trial stage. In the administration of their duties, all courts, including those at the appellate level, had to be cognizant of the need to dispose of charges against individuals in a reasonably prompt fashion.

However, Sopinka J. changed his mind. In *Potvin* (1993)[75] he lead a six-justice majority of the Supreme Court in holding that s. 11(b) does not apply to delay from appeals from conviction or acquittal. The principal reason given was that an accused person who is a party to an appeal is no longer "a person charged" under s. 11. This decision has been properly if extravagantly characterised by Graeme Mitchell[76] as interpreting the Charter with a "legalism bordering on the pharisaic". The decision seems to be a thinly disguised pragmatic decision to avoid the Supreme Court having to expand its docket to review cases of appeal delay. *Potvin* does decide that appellate delay may be the subject of review under the abuse of process doctrine. The minority through McLachlin J. find this remedy too narrow, noting that it is reserved for the clearest of cases.[77] In the event of an order of a new trial, the *Potvin* majority ruled that the s. 11(b) clock would begin to run again.

The Supreme Court has confirmed that delay in sentencing at trial *is* subject to s. 11(b) review.[78]

(d) Test for Unreasonable Delay

(i) *Barker/Ontario trilogy*

Mr. Justice Martin in his well-known 1983 trilogy of s. 11(b) judgments for the Ontario Court of Appeal in *Antoine*,[79] *Beason*[80] and *Heaslip*[81] substantially adopted the approach of the Supreme Court of the United States in *Barker v. Wingo* (1972).[82] Under an *ad hoc* balancing approach, the conduct of the prosecution and the defendant were to be weighed. Factors to be considered included the length of the delay, the reasons for the delay, the accused's assertion of his right and prejudice to the accused. A delay that was *prima facie* excessive would call for justification by the Crown. There could be an express waiver of the right by the accused, but this would have to be clear and unequivocal and with

---

[75] (1993), 23 C.R. (4th) 10 (S.C.C.).

[76] "Potvin: Charter-Proofing Criminal Appeals", (1993) 23 C.R. (4th) 37.

[77] Since *Potvin*, no Court of Appeal has been prepared to hold that an appellate delay constituted an abuse of process: see, for example, *Frazer* (1993), 83 C.C.C. (3d) 126 (S.C.C.) (16 months), *Khela* (1994), 92 C.C.C. (3d) 81 (Que. C.A.) (4 years, mostly a dispute about transcripts) and *Schlick* (1999), 140 C.C.C. (3d) 204 (B.C. S.C.) (appeal of possession of child pornography conviction to be adjourned to await appeal of declaration of unconstitutionality by B.C. C.A. to the Supreme Court).

[78] *MacDougall* (1998), 19 C.R. (5th) 275 (S.C.C.) and *Gallant* (1998), 19 C.R. (5th) 302 (S.C.C.).

[79] (1983), 34 C.R. (3d) 136 (Ont. C.A.).

[80] Above note 59.

[81] (1983), 36 C.R. (3d) 309 (Ont. C.A.).

[82] 407 U.S. 514.

full knowledge of the right. Mere silence or lack of objection would not constitute a waiver.

(ii) *Lamer approach*

Mr. Justice Lamer in *Mills* (1986),[83] and in *Rahey* (1987),[84] Chief Justice Dickson concurring, and then speaking only for himself in *Conway* (1989),[85] sought to assert an approach expressly diverging from that of the United States Supreme Court in *Barker v. Wingo*. Unlike the *Wingo* approach, s. 11(b) was seen to be an individual right whose purpose was to secure the more extensive right under s. 7 to liberty and security of the person of which no one could be deprived except in accordance with the principles of fundamental justice. No societal interest was protected even though society had an indirect interest in the prompt and effective prosecution of criminal cases. Under the Lamer approach, prejudice by delay is irrebuttably presumed. An objective standard is seen to be the only realistic means to protect the accused's security interests. Whether the accused's ability to mount full and fair defence is impaired is not relevant to the s. 11(b) inquiry but relates to the right to a fair trial. A very different balancing test was asserted. Against the accused's increasing impairment of interests with the passage of time were to be considered three factors which might justify the delay: waiver, time requirements inherent in the nature of the case and limitations on institutional resources. The assertion of the accused's right and the conduct and motives of the parties were not part of the inquiry.

The judgment of the Supreme Court in *Rahey* is notoriously difficult to analyze since there are four separate judgments, each involving two judges.[86] The Supreme Court was unanimous that an 11-month delay by a trial judge in ruling on a motion for a directed verdict in a tax evasion case, for three months over the objection of the accused, had violated the accused's rights under s. 11(b). Furthermore, it was agreed that the acquiescence in the trial judge's repeated adjournment of the defence motion for a directed verdict did not constitute a waiver. However, six judges[87] expressly held that the Court could consider the prejudice to the accused, including prejudice to the ability to make full answer and defence. Thus the fundamental underpinning of the Lamer approach was firmly rejected. These six judges favoured a balancing approach on the *Barker* lines, although this is expressed only in the judgment of Le Dain J.[88]

---

[83] Above note 54.

[84] Above note 56.

[85] Above note 74.

[86] See S.A. Cohen, "Rabey: A Fragmented Vision" (1987), 57 C.R. (3d) 333 and J.F.R. Lavesque, "Trial Within a Reasonable Time" (1988), 31 *Crim. L.Q.* 55.

[87] Wilson, Estey, Le Dain, Beetz, La Forest and McIntyre JJ.

[88] See too Cohen, above note 86, p. 338. The Lamer approach had found favour with several Courts of Appeal: see, for example, *Misra* (1986), 54 C.R. (3d) 305 (Sask. C.A.); *Fogarty* (1988), 46 C.C.C. (3d) 289 (N.S. C.A.) and *Coughlan* (1987), 81 N.B.R. (2d) 199 (N.B. C.A.).

(iii) *Askov: comparative jurisdiction test for institutional delay*

After further consideration of the proper approach to s. 11(b)[89] the Supreme Court finally settled on an approach in *Askov* (1990).[90]

Mr. Justice Cory for the majority[91] accepted the position of Lamer J. that the primary purpose of s. 11(b) was to protect the individual interest of liberty and security of the person guaranteed by s. 7 of the Charter:

> There could be no greater frustration imaginable for innocent persons charged with an offence than to be denied the opportunity of demonstrating their innocence for an unconscionable time as a result of unreasonable delays in their trial. The time awaiting trial must be exquisite agony for accused persons and their immediate family. It is a fundamental precept of our criminal law that every individual is presumed to be innocent until proven guilty. It follows that, on the same fundamental level of importance, all accused persons, each one of whom is presumed to be innocent, should be given the opportunity to defend themselves against the charges they face and to have their name cleared and reputation re-established at the earliest possible time.[92]

However, Cory J. departed from the Lamer position in holding that there was an implicit community or social interest in s. 11(b):

> That community interest has a dual dimension. First, there is a collective interest in ensuring that those who transgress the law are brought to trial and dealt with according to the law. Second, those individuals on trial must be treated fairly and justly.[93]
>
> The failure of the justice system to deal fairly, quickly and efficiently with criminal trial inevitably leads to the community's frustration with the judicial system and eventually to a feeling of contempt for court procedures. When a trial takes place without unreasonable delay, with all witnesses available and memories fresh, it is far more certain the guilty parties who committed the crimes will be convicted and punished and those that did not will be acquitted and vindicated. It is no exaggeration to say that a fair and balanced criminal justice system simply cannot exist without the support of the community. Continued community support for our system will not endure in the face of lengthy and unreasonable delays.[94]

Three justices, including Chief Justice Lamer,[95] in separate concurring judgments each registered disagreement with this notion that s. 11(b) also protected a societal interest.

Speaking for five justices, Cory J., after a detailed review of previous Supreme Court of Canada rulings on s. 11(b), concluded with a "brief summary

---

[89] *Conway*, above note 74 (majority judgment by L'Heureux-Dubé J.) and *Smith*, above note 57 (Sopinka J. for a unanimous Court), discussed by Graeme G. Mitchell, "R. v. Smith: Old Doctrine for a New Decade" (1990), 74 C.R. (3d) 375.

[90] (1990), 79 C.R. (3d) 273 (S.C.C.). See Paul Quinlan, "Askov: Lowering the Boom", C.R. *ibid.*, pp. 321-327, Graeme G. Mitchell, "Beyond Systemic Delay: The Saskatchewan Experience", C.R. *ibid.*, pp. 328-331 and Stephen G. Coughlan, "R. v. Askov — A Bold Step Not Boldly Taken" (1991), 33 *Crim. L.Q.* 247.

[91] Dickson C.J.C., La Forest, L'Heureux-Dubé and Gonthier JJ. concurred.

[92] Above note 90, at 297.

[93] *Ibid.*

[94] *Ibid.*, at 298-299.

[95] Lamer C.J.C., *ibid.*, at 277-278, Wilson J. at 281 and Sopinka J. at 284.

of all the factors which should be taken into account in considering whether the length of a delay of a trial has been unreasonable."[96] The aim of the test was to provide a method which would allow courts to balance the "applicable substantive factors in a consistent manner."[97] The factors were grouped under the headings of the length of delay, explanation for that delay, waiver and prejudice to the accused.

The only dissents registered on this test related to the issue of prejudice. The majority settles a long dispute in its holding that prejudice will usually be inferred in the case of very long delays and that it will always be open for either the Crown or the accused to lead evidence on prejudice. There are two dissents. Lamer J. continued to insist that prejudice was irrelevant to s. 11(b)[98] and Wilson J. was of the view that there should be no finding of prejudice without evidence being laid, given that the accused had the onus.[99]

Askov was the first time that the Supreme Court had considered the issue of systemic or institutional delay — delay caused by lack of resources such as courtrooms, judges and Crown counsel.

Four accused were charged with conspiracy to extort along with various weapons charges. It took about a year to complete their preliminary inquiry as it had to be rescheduled to another Court. Following a committal the first trial date was one year later. At that time the matter could not be heard and was put over for trial for another year. The Supreme Court held that, even if the delay over approximately one year prior to the preliminary could be discounted as being in large part attributable to the request for adjournments by the accused, the delay of almost two years between the preliminary and trial had been caused by a lack of facilities in Brampton, in the Ontario Judicial District of Peel. On the basis of various studies[100] the Peel District was, from the point of view of delay, the "the worst district not only in Canada but, so far as the studies indicate, anywhere north of the Rio Grande."[101] The problem in Peel was notorious, had existed at least since 1981 and was getting worse. A government delay reduction program had not been particularly successful.[102]

Cory J., speaking for the Court on this point, held that the right under s. 11(b) was of such fundamental importance to the individual and significance to the community that "the lack of institutional resources cannot be employed to justify a continuing unreasonable postponement of trials."[103] These charges had to be stayed otherwise s. 11(b) would be rendered meaningless.[104] Recognizing

---

[96] *Ibid.*, at 306.

[97] *Ibid.*, at 307.

[98] *Ibid.*, at 278-282.

[99] *Ibid.*, at 282.

[100] The Court principally relied on studies by Professor Carl Baar, Director of the Judicial Administrative Program at Brock University and the Zuber Commission Report, *Report of the Ontario Courts Inquiry* (1987).

[101] Above note 90, at 312.

[102] *Ibid.*, at 310-311.

[103] *Ibid.*, at 301.

[104] *Ibid.*, at 314.

that deference should be shown to political decisions concerning the allegation of scarce funds, the Court nevertheless asserted that "solutions must be found, as indeed they have been in many jurisdiction outside Ontario".[105] Clearly aware of the possibility of a public backlash against staying such serious charges Cory J. added that:

> Where inordinate delays do occur, it is those who are responsible for the lack of facilities who should bear the public criticism that is bound to arise as a result of the staying of proceedings which must be the inevitable consequences of unreasonable delays.[106]

As a test of whether institutional delay was unreasonably long the Court fashioned a test of comparing jurisdictions across Canada:

> [When] considering delays occasioned by inadequate institutional resources, the question of how long a delay is too long may be resolved by comparing the questioned jurisdiction to the standard maintained by the best comparable jurisdiction in the country. The comparison need not be too precise or exact. Rather, it should look to the appropriate ranges of delay to determine what is a reasonable limit. In all cases it will be incumbent upon the Crown to show that the institutional delay in question is justifiable.[107]

Although the Court clearly states that there is to be "no certain standard of a fixed time" applicable in every region of Canada it does seem to have in mind a rough comparison with the best districts of comparable geography, population and resources.[108]

In *Askov* the Court, noting that the usual delays in Peel were more than four times as long as those of busy metropolitan districts in Quebec and this delay more than eight times as long, determined that in Peel a

> period of delay in a range of some six to eight months between committal and trial must be deemed to be the outside limit of what is reasonable.[109]

The conclusion was that the figures from comparable districts demonstrated that the Peel situation was unreasonable and intolerable.

(iv) *Application of Askov in Ontario*[110]

In *Bennett* (1991),[111] Madam Justice Arbour for the Ontario Court of Appeal[112] described the impact of the *Askov* decision in Ontario as "staggering".

---

[105] *Ibid.*, at 301.

[106] *Ibid.*, at 302.

[107] *Ibid.*, at 303.

[108] *Ibid.*, at 302-303.

[109] *Ibid.*, at 313. McLachlin J. in her concurring judgment states:

> The factors to be considered will often pull in opposite directions. Thus it is impossible to dictate in advance how the balancing is to be done in each case. Yet certain parameters can be stated (at 320).

[110] For a positive review of the effect in Saskatchewan of a "nine month rule" imposed by its Court of Appeal in interpreting s. 11(b) see Mitchell, above note 90.

[111] (1991), 6 C.R. (4th) 22 (Ont. C.A.). The *Bennett* panel was originally set to hear a number of other test cases of s. 11(b) over a period of a week. Part of the list had to be reassigned to other

Statistics prepared by the Ministry of the Attorney General of Ontario disclosed that in Ontario between October 22, 1990 and April 12, 1991, 34,495 counts had been stayed, dismissed or withdrawn on the basis of *Askov*. The offence breakdown was about 8,600 impaired driving charges, 6,000 theft under $1,000, a substantial number of assaults and frauds, 500 sexual assaults and more than 1,000 drug related charges. In addition, thousands of parking tickets and over 15,000 other provincial offences had been stayed. Arbour J.A. indicated that it was time for a review given a manifest difference of opinion among trial judges, the number of cases stayed and also the nature of the remedy itself.[113]

Noting that the common law stay as an abuse of process had been granted sparingly and only in the clearest of cases,[114] the Court held that the minimum remedy of the stay in the case of a breach of s. 11(b) called for the "exercise of judgment by the individual judge."[115] The six- to eight-month period mentioned in *Askov* had wrongly been interpreted as a mechanical limitation period. The *Askov* decision required a balancing of the four factors mentioned:

> The Supreme Court decision in *Askov* makes it apparent that a skilful judgment is required to support a conclusion that there has been a violation of s. 11(b) and that a stay of proceedings must be entered. Judges must balance four factors, one of which — the reason for the delay, requires an analysis, sometimes critical of a system of which the judiciary is an integral part.
>
> *Askov* has recently been given a minimalist or reductionist interpretation. When mere lip service is paid to the required balancing of the four factors, the trial within a reasonable time issue is often resolved by the mechanical computation of the systemic time required to bring the charge to trial and the six to eight months referred to in *Askov* is then given the force of a judicially developed limitation period. This isolates and overemphasizes systemic delay and reduces the concept of reasonableness in s. 11(b) to a simplistic computation of time. This is not what the Supreme Court decision in *Askov* stands for.[116]

In his concurring opinion Chief Justice Dubin was blunt:

> The staying of so many charges has had a serious impact on the administration of justice in this province and, I fear, has eroded the public's confidence in the administration of justice. While the judgment of the Supreme Court of Canada in *Askov* must be followed, I do not read the reasons for judgment of the majority of the Court as requiring such a Draconian result.[117]

---

panels. The *Bennett* panel handed down its rulings on May 31,1991 — these included *Bennett*, and *M.(G.C.)* (1991), 6 C.R. (4th) 55 (Ont. C.A.), and *Rabba* (1991), 6 C.R. (4th) 69 (Ont. C.A.). Later other panels handed down rulings on July 6, 1991 — including *Franklin, Macmillan* and *D(S) et al*, each reported in (1991) 6 C.R. (4th). Although the July 6 rulings pay lip service to the principles asserted in *Bennett* it would seem that these other panels were far more generous to the accused in their conclusions on the facts of each case. The Ontario Court of Appeal was split on its attitude to s. 11(b).

[112] Osborne J.A. concurred. Dubin C.J.O. concurred in a separate judgment. The Chief Justice appears to have been troubled by the majority view that "in cases where dates were agreed to prior to . . . *Askov*, a flexible approach to the issue of waiver is imperative."

[113] Above note 111, at 27.

[114] *Ibid.*, at 28.

[115] *Ibid.*, at 30.

[116] *Ibid.*

[117] *Ibid.*, at 46.

In *Bennett*, a judge of the Ontario Court of Justice, General Division, had stayed a charge of assault causing bodily harm. The total period between the time of laying the information and the trial date was 13 1/2 months. There had been a delay of eight and a half months in the Provincial Court to set a trial date. The accused elected trial in District Court and the proceedings in Provincial Court had been converted into a preliminary inquiry. A further five months had resulted before the matter could be brought to trial in the District Court. The trial judge had stayed the charge on the basis of the delay in the Provincial Court. The eight and a half month period was systemic delay outside the range permissible in *Askov* and caused by a shortage of at least one judge in the Provincial Court in the district of Algoma at that time.

For the Ontario Court of Appeal, Arbour J.A. held that the trial judge had erred in translating *Askov* into a six to eight months sunset rule applicable to the provincial court rather than applying the test of delay in comparable jurisdictions. Here the overall period of some 13 1/2 months did not in itself violate s. 11(b) but did invite further scrutiny. When all the reasons for the delay were considered and weighed against the minimal prejudice suffered by the accused the systemic delay alone did not lead to a conclusion of unreasonableness. According to Arbour J.A. the methodology in *Askov* required a search for comparables and specifically rejected the notion of either a national standard or an upper limit.[118] Delays in the Provincial Court could not be compared to delays in what was now the General Division since the Provincial Court was an intake Court dealing with a much greater volume of criminal cases. Judges should not rest exclusively on judicial notice. The process of comparison contemplated by *Askov* required the processing of sophisticated information ''most of which should come in the form of admissible evidence.'' Acceptable time limits had to be set locally but adjusted periodically to reflect the comparative jurisdiction at that time to the best similar one in the country.[119] Although the current province-wide goal to schedule trial dates in the provincial courts within eight months of the laying of the charge should continue and was a desirable target, this period did not translate into a constitutional requirement since the constitutional standard was one of reasonableness.[120]

In July 1991, Mr. Justice Cory told a conference of the Canadian Institute for Advanced Legal Studies, meeting in Cambridge, England, that although the Court knew that *Askov* would have an impact, ''quite frankly . . . we were not

---

[118] *Ibid.*, at 36. Her Ladyship expressly rejected the opinion of Grange J.A. in *Carter* (1991), 62 C.C.C. (3d) 541 (Ont. C.A.) that:

> [T]he decision in *Askov* must be deemed to impose not only an outside limit of eight months between committal and trial, but also an outside limit of eight months between arrest and either committal or trial in the Provincial Court (at 546).

Grange J.A.'s judgment was a response to the narrow interpretation of Trainor J. in *Fortin* (1990), 75 O.R. (2d) 733 (Ont. Gen. Div.) that the ''*Askov* case does not apply to Provincial Court trials or preliminary hearings.'' *Bennett* confirms that s. 11(b) ''obviously applies in all courts, whatever their level'' (at 36).

[119] *Ibid.*, at 37.

[120] *Ibid.*, at 40.

aware of the extent of that impact''.[121] The justice's further remark that the Court had not been aware of the number of cases which could be affected was later challenged by the defence counsel in *Askov*,[122] who pointed to extensive statistical data filed by the Ontario Attorney-General.[123]

It was not long before the Supreme Court changed direction.

(v) *Morin: emphasis on discretion and prejudice*

In *Morin* (1992),[124] Mr. Justice Sopinka, speaking for the majority of the Supreme Court[125] restated the Court's approach to s. 11(b) in much the same language as that used in *Askov*, but with a revised emphasis on discretion and the need to establish prejudice to the accused. This prompted a commentator, Stephen Coughlan, to suggest that the right to s. 11(b) had been

> radically changed . . . to the extent that its existence in any meaningful way [has been] challenged.[126]

Case law on s. 11(b) challenges to the present date have confirmed Coughlan's analysis. The torrent of successful challenges under *Askov* has become a trickle under *Morin*. The right has been substantially curtailed.

Sopinka J. began by asserting that the general approach to s. 11(b) should not be by applying a "mathematical or administrative formula" but by a "judicial determination" balancing the interests the section was designed to protect against factors leading to delay. The individual interests protected were seen to be the right to security of the person ("seeking to minimize the anxiety, concern and stigma of exposure to criminal proceedings"[127]), the right to liberty (minimizing pre-trial incarceration and restrictive bail conditions) and the right to a fair trial (attempting to ensure trials where evidence is available and fresh). Sopinka J. also repeated the majority acceptance in *Conway* and *Askov* of a secondary societal interest in prompt trials which might well be adverse to the accused's interests in demanding that accused be brought to trial. In the balancing process, the Court saw it as now being accepted that the factors to be considered were

1. The length of the delay;
2. waiver of time periods;
3. the reasons for the delay, including

   (a) inherent time requirements or the case,
   (b) actions of the accused,

---

[121] *Lawyer's Weekly*, June 26, 1991, p. 2.

[122] Clayton Ruby and Michael Code.

[123] *Lawyer's Weekly*, August 2, 1991.

[124] (1992) 12 C.R. (4th) 1 (S.C.C.), critically reviewed by Stephen Coughlan, "Trial Within a Reasonable Time: Does The Right Still Exist?" (1992) 12 C.R. (4th) 34-44.

[125] La Forest J., Gonthier, Stevenson, and Iacobucci J. concurred. McLachlin J. delivered a concurring opinion. Lamer C.J. dissented but only on the issue of prejudice. Cory J. did not sit, presumably because his Cambridge remarks had disqualified him.

[126] Above note 124, at 34.

[127] At 12.

(c) actions of the Crown,
(d) limits on institutional resources, and
(e) other reasons for delay; and

4. prejudice to the accused.[128]

In the Court's further articulation of its approach to s. 11(b), there are four subtle but important changes from *Askov* which restrict the accused's rights:

1. The seriousness of the offence militates against granting a stay.

Curiously in the earlier lengthy and complex jurisprudence of the Supreme Court on s. 11(b) there had been no mention of the relevance of the seriousness of the offence. *Askov* only factors in the "complexity" of the case. Sopinka J. declares "seriousness" of the offence to be a relevant consideration in describing the societal interest protected by s. 11(b):

> As the seriousness of the offence increases so does the societal demand that the accused be brought to trial. The role of this interest is most evident and its influence most apparent when it is sought to absolve persons accused of serious crimes simply to clean up the docket.[129]

This recognition contradicts the Supreme Court's approach to excluding evidence under s. 24(2).[130] However, it seems realistic and justified, as very well expressed by the late Judge Peter Nasmith:[131]

> In more serious matters the jolt on victims and on the public from a stay of proceedings is likely to be greater. The public would, no doubt, want a more satisfactory basis for dismissing serious criminal charges. A stay is less harmful to the reputation of the administration of justice if charges are trivial (as so many of them are in Youth Court). In this sense I am mindful of the proportionality test reviewed at some length . . . in *Collins* . . . . The considerations would be tainted with hypocrisy if judges pretended that there were not by the influenced seriousness of the charge when they are arbitrating within the borderline area"[132].

2. The Crown no longer has the burden of proving that the delay was caused by the accused, that institutional delay was justified, not that there was any prejudice or that the accused has waived the s. 11(b) right.

In each of these instances, Cory J. spoke in *Askov* of burdens on the accused. However, Sopinka J. in *Morin* chose to regard these remarks as merely emphasizing evidentiary burdens. He fully restored the authority of his own earlier opinion for a unanimous Court in *Smith* (1989)[133] that an accused raising a s. 11(b) challenge has the "ultimate or legal burden of proof throughout".[134] The Court

---

[128] At 12-13.
[129] At 12.
[130] See below Chapter 11. Section 24: Charter Remedies.
[131] Ont. C.J. P.D., February 15, 1991, unreported.
[132] At 9.
[133] (1989), 73 C.R. (3d) 1 (S.C.C.).
[134] At 11. In *C.I.P. Inc.* (1992), 12 C.R. (4th) 237 (S.C.C.), in which the main ruling was that a corporation had no s. 11(b) right, Stevenson J. for a unanimous Court, when referring to s. 11(b), spoke of a presumption of prejudice and of the Crown having the burden of justifying institutional delay. *C.I.P. Inc.* was handed down two weeks after *Morin* and is inconsistent with *Morin* on these points. This appears to have been *per incuriam* as subsequent jurisprudence in the Supreme Court has applied *Morin*.

thus rejected the *Barker* /Ontario trilogy approach of holding that, once the accused had satisfied that the delay was "*prima facie* unreasonable", the onus shifted to the Crown to justify the delay.[135] In *Smith*, the Court did speak of a secondary or evidentiary burden of putting forth evidence or argument that would shift depending on the circumstances of each case. For example, if there had been a long period of delay following an adjournment at the request of the Crown, this would ordinarily call for an explanation from the Crown in the absence of which the Court would be entitled to infer that the delay had been unjustified. Since the Court determined that there is never a full onus on the Crown, it would appear that it thereby weakened the s.11(b) protection. However, in cases of truly excessive delay, it seems, as a practical matter, doubtful whether the Crown would have any easier time discharging its evidential burden. This scepticism seems well placed, given the Court's enigmatic conclusion that

> In all cases, the Court should be mindful that it is seldom necessary or desirable to decide this question on the basis of burden of proof and that it is preferable to evaluate the reasonableness of the overall lapse of time having regard to the factors referred to.[136]

This is a curious remark. Surely the very importance of a burden of proof is that it determines that in borderline cases where the burdenholder cannot discharge the burden that party loses. On the merits it would appear that the Crown should bear the onus in respect of most issues of delay. The Crown is in a much better position to assemble the evidence needed. Most of the evidence would be very much in its knowledge and under its control. Keeping the onus on the Crown might well encourage the Crown to keep better records as to various adjournments and the reasons therefore. In busy jurisdictions this might be onerous, but it would seem to be required if the new Charter right to be tried within a reasonable time is to be meaningful.

3. Respecting institutional delay, the Court now emphasises the need for flexible guidelines and abandons a strict comparative jurisdiction test.

Morin does not depart from the *Askov* approach of settling administrative guidelines for reasonable administrative delay. Indeed administrative guidelines are seen to be appropriate to recognize that there is a limit to the delay that can be tolerated on account of resource limitations, given that the government has a constitutional obligation to commit sufficient resources to prevent unreasonable delay, and to avoid each s. 11(b) application being turned into a trial of government budgetary policy. Indeed, Sopinka J. accepts the *Askov* guideline in the range of six to eight months for delay between committal for trial and trial and sets a new guideline of eight to 10 months for institutional delay in provincial courts. He also speaks of inherent time requirements required for particular cases depending on such factors as complexity and "intake requirements", such as time required

---

[135] In *Conway*, above note 74, L'Heureux-Dubé J. at 228 had firmly rejected this "two-stage onus requirement" over the dissent of Sopinka J.

[136] At 11-12.

for retaining counsel and disclosure.[137] Sopinka J. is at pains to emphasize the need for a flexible approach.[138] A guideline was neither a limitation period nor a fixed ceiling and should not be mechanically applied, as some trial judges had wrongly done so since *Askov*. Statistics from other jurisdictions should be applied with caution and only as a rough guide.[139] The guidelines should take into account local conditions and reflect changing circumstances. Courts of Appeal should play a supervisory role in achieving uniformity subject to special conditions and problems of different regions. The guidelines should be applied where there is no prejudice to the accused but could be shortened where there was substantial prejudice.

The Court appears to have backed off the comparative jurisdiction test on the basis that it was now convinced that the comparison made in *Askov* between delay statistics for Montreal and those for Brampton were misleading in that the manner in which criminal charges were dealt with in those jurisdictions was dissimilar. There are clearly difficulties in having such inquiries properly and fully made in each case. However, Stephen Coughlan[140] is persuasive in seeing the retraction as unfortunate. The *Askov* comparative jurisdiction test was better designed to guarantee that inefficient courts became more efficient. The Court seems to have missed the point that the 15-year history of case flow management techniques in Montreal had lead to a more efficient Court. It took the dramatic effect of *Askov* stays to force such strategies to be adopted in Brampton.

4. Prejudice to the accused becomes the key factor.

According to Sopinka J. prejudice may be inferred from the length of the delay and where prejudice is not inferred or otherwise proved

> the basis for the enforcement of the individual right is seriously undermined.[141]

In reaching this position, the Court was particularly impressed by the observation of then trial judge Doherty J., quoted with approval by Chief Justice Dubin in *Bennett*:[142]

> An accused is often not interested in exercising the right bestowed on him by s. 11(b). His interest lies in having the right infringed by the prosecution so that he can escape a trial on the merits. This view may seem harsh but experience supports its validity.[143]

---

[137] At 16. In *D.(S.)* (1992), 14 C.R. (4th) 223 (S.C.C.) the Supreme Court held that a two-year delay resulting from a Crown application to transfer a sexual assault trial to adult court was part of the inherent time requirements under the Young Offenders Act. It reversed the majority decision of the Ontario Court of Appeal to stay the proceedings.

[138] At 19-21.

[139] The Court would later dismiss the defence appeal in *Bennett*, above note 111, in a brief oral judgment applying *Morin*, adding that "We do not share the views of the appellant with respect to the emphasis placed on statistics".

[140] Above note 124 at 35-36. See too Michael Code, *Trial Within a Reasonable Time* (1992), pp. 121-125 for detailed discussion of statistical data considered in *Askov* and *Morin*.

[141] At 23.

[142] Above note 111 at 52.

[143] At 23.

Although there was no legal obligation on the accused to assert the right inaction could be relevant in assessing the degree of prejudice. It was also made clear that either the accused or the Crown could adduce evidence to show or dispel prejudice to any of the accused's security, liberty or fair trial interests.

The extent to which *Morin* makes prejudice the determining factor only becomes clear when the actual ruling is considered. The case involved a routine impaired driving trial proceeded with by way of summary conviction proceedings in provincial court. It was accepted that there had been a 14 and one-half month delay between the arrest and the trial date. The Supreme Court accepted that this delay raised the issue of reasonableness, that the accused had not waived her right at any time, that the inherent time requirements for this case were about two months and that an institutional delay of about 12 months could be inferred. Although this period exceeded the eight to 10 month guideline, the Court had just set for such trials the Supreme Court nevertheless decided that s. 11(b) had not been violated. The determining consideration seems to have been that the deviation could be justified by the absence of prejudice. On the prejudice issue the Court noted that the accused had lead no evidence of prejudice and not responded to a letter from the Crown asking the defence counsel whether he wished to have any of his cases expedited on account of prejudice.

In this ruling, the onus of proving prejudice is clearly, contrary to *Askov*, shifted to the accused. Stephen Coughlan raises troubling concerns about the apparent requirement of proving prejudice to security interests:

> it is difficult to believe the court really intends that an accused should lead evidence of prejudice to a security interest. It is easy to see how an accused would show prejudice to liberty or fair trial interests — by showing that bail conditions were onerous, or that evidence was lost due to delay. But is an accused also required to call neighbours who became stand-offish to testify about their lower opinion of the accused? Should an accused call medical evidence to show that he or she found the waiting period especially stressful? Inviting evidence on these points imports the "thin skull" doctrine into Charter litigation: a particularly nervous and sensitive accused will have greater rights. Such an approach is possible but does not immediately seem desirable.[144]

Coughlan also points out[145] that the Court is not applying its announced approach to guidelines for administrative delay. It had earlier implied that if the guidelines were exceeded there would be a breach irrespective of the issue of prejudice, evidence of prejudice only serving to shorten the guideline to be applied.

Reported case law since *Morin* makes it clear that successful s. 11(b) challenges are now rare and highly unlikely to succeed unless the accused demonstrates serious prejudice.[146] There appear to be only a handful of reported stays. In five of these cases evidence of prejudice to the accused's security interest

---

[144] Above note 124, at 40.

[145] At 40-41.

[146] See, for example, analysis of Doherty J.A. in *Allen* (1996), 1 C.R. (5th) 347 (Ont. C.A.), adopted on further appeal in (1997), 11 C.R. (5th) 296 (S.C.C.), *Rogalsky* (1994), 36 C.R. (4th) 215 (Sask. C.A.), *R. (G.W.)* (1996), 112 C.C.C. (3d) 179 (Ont. C.A.), *White* (1997), 114 C.C.C. (3d) 225 (Ont. C.A.) and *Williamson* (2000), 34 C.R. (5th) 152 (Ont. C.A.).

appears to have been determinative. This consisted respectively of medical reports of stress leading to a heart condition,[147] a bail curfew causing extreme embarrassment and the 27-month delay affecting his marriage,[148] evidence of stress and stigmatisation,[149] real prejudice in family life and employment and stigmatisation as First Nations person living on a reserve[150] and stress or damage to reputation.[151] In another the delay had impacted[152] the ability to make fair answer and defence. Stays were entered in two decisions where significant prejudice had not been proved. Two of these stays, upheld by Courts of Appeal, appear to be particularly egregious instances of institutional delay.[153]

The final reported instance of a stay since *Morin* is a decision of the Supreme Court of Canada. It seems curiously out of step with the Court's recent rulings on s.11(b). In *Collins*, (1995)[154] Sopinka J., for a 3-2 majority, upheld the stay of a new trial ordered on a murder charge. The basis for the s. 11(b) stay was that of the 23-month delay in custody before the first trial date four and one-half months had been caused by an adjournment at the request of the Crown which had been improperly investigated and the late disclosure by the Crown had lead to some part of a five and one half delay at the preliminary inquiry.[155] According to the minority, any delay caused by the delay in disclosure was minimal and the serious prejudice to the accused's liberty interest was outweighed by the societal interest in bringing the accused to trial on this most serious of charges.

Given the relatively short period of delay involved, it is difficult not to side with the minority given that *Morin* decides that the seriousness of the charge should be weighed.[156] It is doubtful that this *Collins* ruling by three justices can

---

[147] *Bisoon* (1995), 36 C.R. (4th) 235 (Ont. Gen. Div.).

[148] *Lohnes* (1992), 17 C.R. (4th) 193 (Ont. Gen. Div.).

[149] A majority decision in *White* (1998), 131 C.C.C. (3d) 33 (Nfld.C.A.) that there had been actual prejudice in addition to the prejudice to be inferred from lengthy institutional delay was confirmed on further appeal: (1998), 131 C.C.C. (3d) 32 (S.C.C.).

[150] *Maracle* (1998), 122 C.C.C. (3d) 97 (S.C.C.), with a 3-2 majority restoring a stay that had been overturned by the Ontario Court of Appeal. The majority of the delay of almost two years between committal and trial was held attributable to the busy court schedule.

[151] *Marstar Trading International Inc.* (1999), 27 C.R. (5th) 96 (Ont. C.A.). Rosenberg J.A. for the Court confirmed a stay of customs and excise charges against an arms dealer given a systemic delay of almost two years. However the charges against his one-man company had been wrongly stayed as that trial did not implicate security interests and no irremediable prejudice to a fair trial had been shown.

[152] *Padfield* (1992), 18 C.R. (4th) 364 (Ont. C.A.).

[153] *Trudel* (1992), 78 C.C.C. (3d) 169 (Que. C.A.) (20-month delay following committal partly caused by illness of trial judge without there being an attempt to replace him and by unavailability of Crown counsel and scheduling error) and *Armstrong* (1993), 22 C.R. (4th) 286 (B.C. C.A.) (reason for 23-month delay in sexual assault trial of school teacher being evolution of Crown case from five-day trial to at least five-week trial with similar fact evidence and expert testimony).

[154] (1995), 40 C.R. (4th) 273 (S.C.C.), criticised by Stephen Coughlan in an annotation, *ibid.*, pp. 274-276.

[155] Stephen Coughlan, above note 154, criticizes the majority for not applying the balancing of interests approach to consider whether the overall 23-month delay was unreasonable.

[156] Compare *Sharma* (1992), 12 C.R. (4th) 45 (S.C.C.), where Sopinka J., for the majority, held that a delay of 12 months from arrest to trial for impaired driving causing bodily harm did not violate

be applied further than its facts. It does send a strong message of consequences for Crown who do not disclose. The first trial had resulted in a directed verdict of acquittal and this, coupled with the accused's lengthy period in custody, may have coloured the determination of the majority. Even the majority emphasize that the case had nothing to do with institutional delay.

(vi) *Waiver*

One of the most difficult issues in s. 11(b) applications is the extent in which consent by an accused to an adjournment can constitute a waiver. Section 11(b) challenges are often rejected on the basis that there was no objection by the accused on the record. Prior to *Askov*, an often-quoted passage was that of Mr. Justice Grange for the Ontario Court of Appeal:[157]

> I will concede that the obligation is not upon the accused to ensure a speedy trial. That obligation is upon the Crown. But it will not enhance the appearance of justice if the accused are permitted to delay their application for relief, or indeed to conceal any claim for such relief, until any remedy other than the stay of proceedings becomes impossible to grant. The accused should not, in my opinion, be permitted to obtain an advantage in this manner — an advantage which involves the staying of proceedings in a very serious offence. Had there been the slightest indication of concern by any of the accused at the delay at any stage of the proceedings, particularly on the occasion of the last adjournment, I might have taken a quite different view of the matter.''[158]

In the Supreme Court in *Askov*, Cory J. adopted the usual high standard for a waiver for a constitutional right, asserting that the waiver must be "informed, unequivocal and freely given"[159] and that the burden of showing that a waiver is inferred is on the Crown.[160] He declares that "silence or lack of objection" is not enough and that there must be something which indicates that the accused has understood the nature of the s. 11(b) guarantee and waived it.[161]

In *Morin*, Sopinka J. adopted this position although there is no mention of the onus being on the Crown. Sopinka J. further held that

> Waiver requires advertence to the act of release rather than mere inadvertence[162]

and that, although consent to a trial date can give rise to an inference of waiver, this will not be so

> if consent to a date amounts to mere acquiescence in the inevitable.[163]

---

s. 11(b) as the accused had suffered minimal prejudice from the bail conditions and the charge was relatively serious.

[157] (1987), 60 C.R. (3d) 277 (Ont. C.A.).

[158] At 288, applied in *Hurlbert* (1988), 66 C.R. (3d) 391 (Ont. H.C.), *Askov* (1987), 59 C.C.C. (3d) 449 (S.C.C.). *Askov* and *Hurlbert* are both strongly criticised by Clayton C. Ruby, "Hurlbert — A Remedy for Delay — Now You See It, Now You Don't" (1989) 66 C.R. (3d) 395.

[159] Above note 90.

[160] *Ibid.*

[161] At 305.

[162] At 15.

[163] *Ibid.*

The application of this test has proved difficult and controversial.[164]

4. SECTION 11(c): RIGHT ''NOT TO BE COMPELLED TO BE A WITNESS IN PROCEEDINGS AGAINST THAT PERSON IN RESPECT OF THE OFFENCE''

(a) Introduction

In *Altseimer* (1982),[165] the Ontario Court of Appeal, noting that the Charter did not use the phrase principle against self-incrimination, held that what protection against self-incrimination there was, was conferred by the specific protections in s. 11(c) for an accused against being compelled to testify and in s. 13 protecting a witness from being incriminated by evidence being used in another proceeding.[166] We have seen that this view was not shared by the Supreme Court which later found a wider privilege against self-incrimination in the principles of fundamental justice guaranteed in s. 7[167] and also held that the section included a pre-trial right to silence.[168]

At common law, an accused was neither competent nor compellable as a witness. In 1893,[169] what is now s. 4(1) of the Canada Evidence Act[170] made an accused competent to testify but did not alter the fundamental position that the accused is non-compellable by the Crown. The entrenchment of s. 11(c) in the Charter established the noncompellability of the accused for the first time as a constitutional right.

(b) Testimonial Compulsion

In Canada, the privilege against self-incrimination has been consistently held to protect only against testimonial compulsion. In *Marcoux* (1975),[171] Mr. Justice Dickson held:

> As applied to an accused, the privilege is the right to stand mute. An accused cannot be asked, much less compelled, to enter the witness box or to answer incriminating questions. If he chooses to testify, the protective shield, of course, disappears. In short, the privilege extends to the accused *qua* witness and not *qua* accused. It is concerned with testimonial compulsions specifically and not with compulsion generally.[172]

---

[164] See, for example, the split decision in *Heikel* (1992), 72 C.C.C. (3d) 481 (Alta. C.A.).
[165] (1982), 29 C.R. (3d) 276 (Ont. C.A.).
[166] *Ibid.*, at 281.
[167] Discussed above, Chapter 2.
[168] *Hebert* (1990), 77 C.R. (3d) 145 (S.C.C.), discussed above, Chapter 2.
[169] See historical review in *Canada v. Amway of Canada Ltd.* (1989), 68 C.R. (3d) 97 at 104 (S.C.C.).
[170] R.S.C. 1985, c. C-5, s. 4(1):
> Every person charged with an offence, and, except as otherwise provided in this section, the wife or husband, as the case may be, of the person so charged, is a competent witness for the defence, whether the person so charged is charged solely or jointly with any other person.
[171] (1975), 24 C.C.C. (2d) 1 (S.C.C.).
[172] *Ibid.*, at 5.

The Ontario Court of Appeal soon established that s. 11(c) (and s. 13) of the Charter protected ''against testimonial compulsion and nothing else''[173] and therefore was not violated by compulsory breath tests under the Criminal Code.[174] It also held that although s. 11(c) conferred a constitutional right not to be compelled to be a witness at trial or at a preliminary inquiry,[175] it did not protect against police questioning.[176]

The Supreme Court quickly rejected s. 11(c) challenge against fingerprinting powers.[177] It also reasoned that since a corporation could not be considered a witness, it could not seek the protection of s. 11(c). It followed that the officer of a company was compellable at an examination for discovery in forfeiture proceedings against the company under the Customs Act.[178]

The Supreme Court in *Darrach* (2000)[179] also had no difficulty in holding that affidavit, *voir dire* and cross-examination requirements for an accused seeking access to prior sexual history of the complainant under s. 276 of the Criminal Code did not offend s. 11(c). This was merely tactical rather than legal compulsion.

(c) Charge ''In Proceedings Against that Person in Respect of the Offence''

This limitation has been literally construed to mean the protection only applies to protect the accused from being compelled to testify as a witness against herself in the proceedings involving a charge or charges against her.[180] Section 11(c) therefore does not stop a Crown compelling the testimony of a witness who has been charged with the same offence as the accused but is being tried separately,[181] or where the witness had previously been charged with the same

---

[173] *Altseimer*, above note 165.

[174] See too *MacDonald* (1982), 1 C.C.C. (3d) 385 (Ont. Co. Ct.) and *Gaff* (1984), 15 C.C.C. (3d) 126 (Sask. C.A.). In *Curr*, [1972] S.C.R. 889, it had been similarly held that compulsory breath tests did not offend the ''protection against self crimination'' in s. 2(d) of the Canadian Bill of Rights.

[175] In *Bird* (1990), 55 C.C.C. (3d) 441 (Sask. Q.B.), it was held that an inquiry under s. 541(1) of the Code by a justice at a preliminary inquiry as to whether the accused wished to say anything in answer to the charge did not breach s. 11(c).

[176] *Esposito* (1985), 49 C.R. (3d) 193 (Ont. C.A.); *Nelles* (1985), 46 C.R. (3d) 289 (Ont. C.A.).

[177] *Beare* (1988), 66 C.R. (3d) 97 at 120 (S.C.C.). See too *Nielsen* (1984), 16 C.C.C. (3d) 39 (Man. C.A.) (fingerprinting) and *Piché* (1999), 136 C.C.C. (3d) 217 (Que. C.A.).

[178] *Canada v. Amway*, above note 169, applied in *Nova Scotia Pharmaceutical Society* (1990), 58 C.C.C. (3d) 161 (N.S. T.D.). See criticism of Michael I. Wylie, ''Corporations and the Non-Compellability Right in Criminal Proceedings'', (1991) 33 *Crim. L.Q.* 344.

[179] (2000), 36 C.R. (5th) 223 (S.C.C.). The Court did, however, rule that s. 13 protected against incrimination at trial: see below Chapter 8.

[180] *Welton* (1986), 29 C.C.C. (3d) 226 (Ont. H.C.). For broader protections under s. 7, see above Chapter 2, under ''Principle Against Self-incrimination''.

[181] *Re Crooks* (1982), 2 C.C.C. (3d) 57 (Ont. H.C.), affirmed (1982), 2 C.C.C. (3d) 64n (Ont. C.A.) and followed in *Walters* (1982), 2 C.C.C. (3d) 512 (B.C. C.A.). Proceeding jointly where separate preliminaries have indicated antagonistic defences has been held to violate the right to fair trial: *Zurlo* (1990), 78 C.R. (3d) 167 (Que. C.A.).

offence as the accused but the proceedings had been stayed,[182] or where the accused is charged with being an accessory after the fact.[183]

(d) Adverse Inferences

It has now been determined at the level of Courts of Appeal that s. 11(c) does not prevent the trier of fact[184] or an appeal court[185] from drawing an adverse inference against an accused who did not testify.

Section 4(6) of the Canada Evidence Act[186] provides that the failure of the accused to testify "shall not be made the subject of comment by the Judge or by counsel for the prosecution." This prohibition has been held to be only against direct comment in the case of jury trials.[187] In *Boss* (1988),[188] the Ontario Court of Appeal rejected a challenge that s. 11(c) invalidated s. 4(6) such that it would be imperative to charge the jury that no adverse inference was to be drawn from the accused's failure to testify. The Court found that there was "nothing unfair" in the procedure required by s. 4(6) and that it could not be said that in the absence of a trial judge's instruction on the issue, the accused was being penalized for exercising his constitutional right. Furthermore, the tactical obligation on an accused to testify did not constitute legal compulsion to testify.

We have seen that the majority of the Supreme Court in *Noble* (1997)[189] decided that no inference should be drawn from the decision of an accused not to testify. This would suggest that s. 4(6) should now be ruled unconstitutional.

5. SECTION 11(d): RIGHT "TO BE PRESUMED INNOCENT UNTIL PROVEN GUILTY ACCORDING TO LAW IN A FAIR AND PUBLIC HEARING BY AN INDEPENDENT AND IMPARTIAL TRIBUNAL"

(a) Presumption of Innocence and Reverse Onuses[190]

The classic affirmation of the presumption of innocence principle is to be found in the words of Viscount Sankey in the English murder case of *Woolmington v. Director of Public Prosecutions* (1935):[191]

---

[182] *Welton*, above note 180.
[183] *Bleich* (1983), 7 C.C.C. (3d) 176 (Man. Q.B.).
[184] *Boss* (1988), 68 C.R. (3d) 123 (Ont. C.A.), overruling *Pelley* (1983), 34 C.R. (3d) 385 (Ont. Co. Ct.).
[185] *B. (J.N.)* (1989), 68 C.R. (3d) 145 (Man. C.A.).
[186] R.S.C. 1985, c. C-5.
[187] *Vezeau* (1977), 34 C.R.N.S. 309 (S.C.C).
[188] (1988), 68 C.R. (3d) 123 (Ont. C.A.). See too *Naglik* (1991), 65 C.C.C. (3d) 272 (Ont. C.A.) (comment by counsel for co-accused on accused's failure to testify not violating s. 11(c)).
[189] (1997), 6 C.R. (5th) 1 (S.C.C.), discussed above Chapter 2 under Right to Silence.
[190] See generally J.C. Morton and Scott C. Hutchinson, *The Presumption of Innocence* (1987) and Thomas A. Cromwell, "Proving Guilt: The Presumption of Innocence and the Canadian Charter of Rights and Freedoms" in W.H. Charles *et al.* (eds.), *Evidence and the Charter of Rights and Freedoms* (1989) chap. 2.
[191] [1935] A.C. 462 (H.L.).

> Throughout the web of the English Criminal Law one golden thread is always to be seen, that is the duty of the prosecution to prove the prisoner's guilt subject . . . to the defence of insanity and subject also to any statutory exception. If, at the end of and on the whole of the case, there is a reasonable doubt, created by the evidence given by either the prosecution or the prisoner . . . the prosecution has not made out the case and the prisoner is entitled to an acquittal. No matter what the charge or where the trial, the principle that the prosecution must prove the guilt of the prisoner is part of the common law of England and no attempt to whittle it down can be entertained.[192]

This passage was soon relied on by our Supreme Court[193] and has been cited consistently ever since.

Noting that *Woolmington* recognizes that the legislature can enact exceptions to the presumption of innocence, the majority of the Supreme Court in *Appleby* (1972)[194] held that the words ''presumed innocent until proven guilty according to law'' had to

> be taken to envisage a law which recognizes the existence of statutory exceptions reversing the onus of proof with respect to one or more ingredients of an offence in cases where certain specific facts have been proved by the Crown in relation to such ingredients.[195]

In *Oakes* (1986),[196] Chief Justice Dickson for the majority of the Supreme Court rejected the suggestion that the phrase ''according to law'' in s. 11(d) of the Charter should also be read as allowing for statutory exceptions. Such a proviso was ''not applicable''[197] to an entrenched Charter which tempered Parliamentary supremacy.

The Chief Justice saw the presumption of innocence as embodying cardinal values lying at the very heart of criminal law protected expressly by s. 11(d) but also integral to the general protection of life, liberty and security of the person in s. 7:

> The presumption of innocence protects the fundamental liberty and human dignity of any and every person accused by the state of criminal conduct. An individual charged with a criminal offence faces grave social and personal consequences, including potential loss of physical liberty, subjection to social stigma and ostracism from the community, as well as other social, psychological and economic harms. In light of the gravity of these consequences, the presumption of innocence is crucial. It ensures that, until the state proves an accused's guilt beyond all reasonable doubt, he or she is innocent. This is essential in a society committed to fairness and social justice. The presumption of innocence confirms our faith in humankind; it reflects our belief that individuals are decent and law-abiding members of the community until proven otherwise.[198]

---

[192] *Ibid.*, at 481.

[193] *Manchuk*, [1938] S.C.R. 341 at 349.

[194] [1972] S.C.R. 303.

[195] *Ibid.*, at 315-316.

[196] (1986), 50 C.R. (3d) 1 (S.C.C.). See T.A. Cromwell and A. Wayne MacKay, ''Oakes in the Supreme Court: A Cautious Initiative Unimpeded by Old Ghosts,'' (1986) 50 C.R. (3d) 34.

[197] *Ibid.*, at 19.

[198] *Ibid.*, at 15.

(i) *Oakes: Minimum content*

In *Oakes*, the majority of the Court[199] found the minimum content of the presumption of innocence in s. 11(d) of the Charter was that an individual be proven guilty beyond a reasonable doubt, that the State bear the burden of proof and that criminal prosecutions be carried out in accordance with lawful procedures and fairness. The Court went on to hold[200] that s. 8 of the Narcotic Control Act,[201] which required that an accused charged with the offence of possession of drugs for the purpose of trafficking establish that he was not in possession of the drug for that purpose, imposed a persuasive burden on the accused contrary to s. 11(d):

> In general one must, I think, conclude that a provision which requires an accused to disprove on a balance of probabilities the existence of a presumed fact which is an important element of the offence in question violates the presumption of innocence in s. 11(d). If an accused bears the burden of disproving on a balance of probabilities an essential element of an offence, it would be possible for a conviction to occur despite the existence of a reasonable doubt. This would arise if the accused adduced sufficient evidence to raise a reasonable doubt as to his or her innocence but did not convince the jury on a balance of probabilities that the presumed fact was untrue.[202]

The Court found that the rational connection test adopted in the Court below set too low a threshold for the presumption of innocence. It expressly adopted the following analysis of Professors MacKay and Cromwell:[203]

> The rational connection test approves a provision that *forces* the trier to infer a fact that may be simply rationally connected to the proved fact. Why does it follow that such a provision does not offend the constitutional right to be proved guilty beyond a reasonable doubt?[204]

It was vital to keep s. 1 and s. 11(d) analytically distinct. The appropriate stage for invoking the rational connection test was under s. 1.

In *Dubois* (1985),[205] Chief Justice Lamer linked the requirement of proof beyond reasonable doubt with the concept of a case to meet:

> Section 11(d) imposes upon the Crown the burden of proving the accused's guilt beyond a reasonable doubt as well as that of making out the case against the accused before he or she need respond, either by testifying or by calling other evidence.[206]

Chief Justice Lamer reasserted this view for a Court unanimous on this point[207] in *Pearson* (1992).[208] He also elaborated on the relationship of the

---

[199] Chouinard, Lamer, Wilson and Le Dain JJ. concurred. Estey J. (McIntyre J. concurring) preferred the approach of the Court below, the Ontario Court of Appeal.

[200] Above note 196, at 25.

[201] R.S.C. 1970, C. N-1.

[202] Above note 196, at 25.

[203] "Oakes: A Bold Initiative Impeded by Old Ghosts" (1983). 32 C.R. (3d) 221. See too Finley, "The Presumption of Innocence and Guilt: Why Carroll Should Prevail Over Oakes," (1984) 39 CR. (3d) 115.

[204] MacKay and Cromwell, *ibid.*, at 233.

[205] (1985), 48 C.R. (3d) 193 (S.C.C.).

[206] At 215.

[207] Sopinka, Iacobucci, Gonthier, and L'Heureux-Dubé JJ. concurred, as did McLachlin J. who dissented on a different point.

[208] (1992), 17 C.R. (4th) 1 (S.C.C.). *Pearson's* rulings respecting bail are considered below under s. 11(e).

presumption of innocence to principles of fundamental justice under section 7. While s. 11(d) had a special operation in its strict evidentiary sense at trial this did

> not exhaust the broader principle of fundamental justice which is enshrined in s. 7.[209]

In several rulings since *Oakes*, the Supreme Court has set out several important general principles respecting the presumption of innocence at trial.[210]

(ii) *Applicability to defences: Whyte*

Since *Oakes*, it has been accepted that any reversal of the onus of proof of an essential element is *prima facie* unconstitutional[211] and can only be saved by being demonstrably justified as a reasonable limit under s. 1. The important question was whether the Supreme Court would allow reversals of the onus of proof in respect of defences which have nothing to do with negativing an element of the conduct or fault requirement. Some lower courts had indeed been content to generalize *Oakes* to defences of justification or excuse. Most courts had not, relying on an attempted distinction that such defences, being "extraneous" or "affirmative", did not relate to the proof of an essential ingredient of the offence.

The issue was directly before the Supreme Court of Canada in *Holmes* (1988).[212] Under what is now s. 351(1) of the Criminal Code, an accused charged with the offence of possession of house-breaking implements bears the onus of proving lawful excuse. The major three to two split in the Court was over the question of the proper interpretation of this lawful excuse clause in the context of the particular offence and its legislative history. McIntyre J. holds for the majority[213] that the clause was originally inserted to allow the accused to prove the defence of innocent purpose but that a later statutory amendment imposed that obligation on the Crown and made the clause superfluous. Thus there was no conflict with s. 11(d) to consider.

In the minority on this point, Dickson C.J.C.[214] saw the "without lawful excuse" clause as casting a persuasive burden on the accused to raise a defence

---

[209] At 55. The Chief Justice remarks that s. 11(d) might not cover the proof of contested aggravated factors at a sentence hearing "the broader substantive principle in s. 7 almost certainly would" (*ibid.*).

[210] No court has yet considered the interesting view that the arbitrary assignment of an accused to a dock violates the presumption of innocence and other Charter rights: see Lynal E. Doerksen, "Out of the Dock and into the Bar: An Examination of the History and Use of the Prisoner's Dock" (1990), 32 *Crim. L.Q.* 478.

[211] See, for example, *Driscoll* (1987), 60 C.R. (3d) 88 (Alta. C.A.) (Criminal Code presumption that things obtained by NSF cheque, obtained by false pretences); *Ireco Canada II Inc.* (1988), 65 C.R. (3d) 160 (Ont. C.A.) (Customs Act requiring proof of lawful importation on balance of probabilities) and *Shisler* (1990), 53 C.C.C. (3d) 531 (Ont. C.A.) (place equipped with slot machine conclusively presumed by Criminal Code to be common gaming house). In each of these decisions, Crown arguments that the reverse onuses were justified under s. 1 of the Charter did not succeed.

[212] (1988), 64 C.R. (3d) 97 (S.C.C.).

[213] Le Dain and La Forest JJ. concurred.

[214] Lamer J. concurred.

absolving of liability despite proof of *actus reus* and *mens rea*. On the dissenting view, the clause violates s. 11(d) by requiring proof by the accused on a balance of probabilities, since it makes it possible for a conviction to occur despite the existence of a reasonable doubt:

> Any burden on an accused which has the effect of dictating a conviction despite the presence of reasonable doubt, where that burden relates to proof of an essential element of the offence or some element extraneous to the offence but nonetheless essential to verdict, contravenes s. 11(d) of the Charter.[215]

This is in flat contradiction to the view of McIntyre J. (only Le Dain J. concurring on this point) that, even if the accused were called on to establish general common law excuses or justifications such as duress and authorization by law, this would not offend s. 11(d), as such defences could be raised only where the offence had been proved.[216]

In less than two months in *Whyte* (1988),[217] the view of Chief Justice Dickson became that of majority of the Supreme Court. Beetz, Lamer, La Forest and L'Heureux-Dubé JJ., and even now McIntyre J., concurred in a unanimous judgment. The Court decided to extend the protection of the presumption of innocence beyond proof of essentials and to include defences.

At issue was the constitutionality of the Criminal Code presumption[218] in respect of offences of having care or control while impaired, which declares that a person occupying the seat normally occupied by the driver of the motor vehicle must prove an absence of an intent to set the vehicle in motion. The Crown argued that, although the section requires that the accused prove that he did not intend to set the vehicle in motion, this was not an essential element of the offence of having care and control of a vehicle while impaired and therefore did not infringe the presumption of innocence. The Chief Justice gave this short shrift:

> The short answer to this argument is that the distinction between elements of the offence and other aspects of the charge is irrelevant to the s. 11(d) inquiry. The real concern is not whether the accused must disprove an element or prove an excuse, but that an accused may be convicted while a reasonable doubt exists. When that possibility exists, there is a breach of the presumption of innocence.
>
> The exact characterization of a factor as an essential element, a collateral factor, an excuse, or a defence should not affect the analysis of the presumption of innocence. It is the final effect of a provision on the verdict that is decisive. If an accused is required to prove some fact on the balance of probabilities to avoid conviction, the provision violates the presumption of innocence because it permits a conviction in spite of a reasonable doubt in the mind of the trier of fact as to the guilt of the accused. The trial of an accused in a criminal matter cannot be divided neatly into stages, with the onus of proof on the accused at an intermediate stage and the ultimate onus on the Crown.[219]

---

[215] Above note 212, at 112.

[216] *Ibid.*, at 122.

[217] (1988), 64 C.R. (3d) 123 (S.C.C.). Compare the critical review of Jack Watson "The Golden Thread Turns Whyte: *R. v. Whyte*," (1989) 1 *J. of Motor Vehicle Law* 51.

[218] Section 258(1)(a).

[219] Above note 217, at 134-135.

Whyte clearly stands for the proposition that any type of persuasive burden of proof on the accused is *prima facie* offensive to the presumption of innocence in s. 11(d) and, to survive, must be demonstrably justified as a reasonable limit under s. 1. This is a very welcome development. The precept of the presumption of innocence is too important to be ducked by the mechanical application of an artificial dichotomy between elements of offences and defences. Commentators in Canada[220] and elsewhere[221] are agreed that the distinction cannot work and, moreover, is dangerous, in that it encourages legislative drafting to avoid the strictures of the presumption of innocence. In future there should be no need for Canadian courts to grapple with the mysteries of the English distinction between "inculpatory" and "exculpatory" elements or with the attempt to distinguish "affirmative" defences in the United States. Decisions that have refused to consider s. 11(d) merely on the basis that the persuasive burden on the accused does not relate to an essential element will now, of course, have to be revised.[222]

In both *Keegstra* (1990)[223] and *Chaulk* (1990)[224] the Supreme Court expressly confirmed that *Whyte* rather than *Holmes* is the controlling authority. Given the repudiation of *Holmes* the particular lawful excuse onus upheld in that case should now be reconsidered.

---

[220] D. Finley, "The Presumption of Innocence and Guilt: Why Carroll Should Prevail over Oakes," (1984) 39 C.R. (3d) 115; T.A. Cromwell and A. Wayne MacKay, "Oakes in the Supreme Court: A Cautious Initiative Unimpeded by Old Ghosts," (1986) 50 C.R. (3d) 34; J. Weiser, "The Presumption of Innocence in Section 11(d) of the Charter and Persuasive and Evidential Burdens," (1989) 31 *Crim. L.Q.* 318; T.A. Cromwell, "Annotation to R. v. Burge," (1986) 55 C.R. (3d) 132; R. Mahoney, "The Presumption of Innocence: A New Era," (1988) 67 *Can. Bar Rev.* 1 and Andrea Tuck-Jackson, "The Defence of Due Diligence and the Presumption of Innocence," (1990) 33 *Crim. L.Q.* 11.

[221] G. Williams, "Offences and Defences," (1982) 2 *Legal Studies* 233; Jeffries and Stephen, "Defences, Presumptions and Burdens of Proof in the Criminal Law," (1979) 88 *Yale L.J.* 1323; P. Healy, "Proof and Policy: No Golden Threads," (1987) *Crim. L. Rev.* 355; G. Williams, "The Logic of Exceptions," (1988) 47 *Camb. L.J.* 261.

[222] In a startling judgment in *Thompson* (1992), 16 C.R. (4th) 168 (Alta. C.A.), the Alberta Court of Appeal flew in the face of *Whyte*. Under s. 150.1 (2) of the Criminal Code, consent is a defence to the charge of sexual touching of one under 14. For the Court, McClung J.A. held that there should be a persuasive burden on the accused to prove the age proximity which would activate the defence. The Court gave three reasons. Firstly, the accused's age was "not an affirmative, let alone an essential element of the offence". This ignores the authority of *Whyte*. Secondly, the Court found that the evidence was "if not exclusively, at least conveniently within the knowledge of the accused". Finally the Court noted that s. 794 (2) of the Criminal Code, although referring only to summary conviction procedure, is a statutory expression of the common law rule that, in matters of pleading and proof, the Crown is not required to negative an exception. Since *Whyte*, *Thompson* cannot be considered authoritative. At an intuitive level the Court seems sensible in requiring the accused to prove age proximity to establish his consent defence. The Court points to the spectre of a middle-aged accused gaining an acquittal by remaining mute and the Crown not being able to prove age. Surely the Court went too far? All that was needed was a holding that the accused was required to point to or adduce evidence to provide the evidentiary foundation for the defence. Surely s. 794(2) is an anomaly and should be struck down? See however *G. (T.)* (1998), 123 C.C.C. (3d) 211 (N.S. C.A.) in which the Court held that the provision was saved under s. 1 when applied to a provincial offence of illegal possession of liquor.

[223] (1990), 1 C.R. (4th) 129 (S.C.C.).

[224] (1990), 2 C.R. (4th) 1 (S.C.C.).

In *Keegstra* it was held that the Criminal Code provision in what is now s. 319(3)(a) which declares that a person charged with wilfully promoting hatred against an identifiable group has a defence "if he establishes that the statements communicated were true", violated the presumption of innocence guaranteed by s. 11(d). What was of the essence, reasoned Chief Justice Dickson for the majority,[225] was not the essential nature of the crime but that the trier of fact would have to convict even where there was a reasonable doubt as to the truth of the accused's statement.[226]

In *Chaulk* the issue was the constitutionality of the provision under s. 16(4) providing as follows:

> Everyone shall, until the contrary is proved, be presumed to be and to have been sane.

Chief Justice Lamer for the majority[227] held that on the *Whyte* principles the presumption of sanity in s. 16(4) violated the presumption of innocence:

> Whether the claim of insanity is characterized as a denial of mens rea, an excusing defence or, more generally, as an exemption based on criminal incapacity, the fact remains that sanity is essential for guilt. Section 16(4) allows a factor which is essential for guilt to be *presumed*, rather than proven by the Crown beyond a reasonable doubt. Moreover, it requires an accused to disprove sanity (or prove insanity) on a balance of probabilities; it therefore violates the presumption of innocence because it permits a conviction in spite of a reasonable doubt in the mind of the trier of fact as to the guilt of the accused.[228]

Despite these strong affirmations of the presumption of innocence in *Whyte*, *Keegstra* and *Chaulk*, we shall see below that the court proceeded in each case to justify the reverse onus as a demonstrably justified reasonable limit under s. 1.

(iii) *Onus of proving certificate*

In *Schwartz* (1988),[229] the accused was charged with the Criminal Code offence of having "in his possession a restricted weapon for which he does not have a registration certificate."[230] He challenged the constitutionality of a Criminal Code provision[231] expressly placing the onus on an accused charged

---

[225] Wilson, L'Heureux-Dubé and Gonthier JJ. concurred. McLachlin and Sopinka JJ. agreed that there had been a violation but dissented on the s. 1 issue, considered below note 280.

[226] Above note 223, at 204. The Court agreed on this point with the Alberta Court of Appeal in the Court below but rejected *Andrews* (1988), 65 C.R. (3d) 320 (Ont. C.A.) where Grange J.A. (Krever J.A. concurring) had held that *Whyte* was not "governing" and that the s. 11(d) only related to proof of an essential element. See criticism of *Andrews* on this point by N. Naeem Rauf in C.R. *ibid.*, pp. 362-370.

[227] Dickson C.J.C., La Forest, Sopinka and Cory JJ. concurred. Wilson J. agreed that there was a violation but dissented on the s. 1 issue, discussed below. McLachlin J. (L'Heureux-Dubé and Gonthier JJ. concurring) viewed the presumption of sanity as a fundamental precondition of criminal responsibility which did not violate s. 11(d) (at 85-87).

[228] *Ibid.*, above note 224, at 24.

[229] (1988), 66 C.R. (3d) 251 (S.C.C.), discussed by Weiser, above note 220, pp. 332-335.

[230] Section 91(1).

[231] Section 115(1).

with various firearms offences, including this one, of proving that he was the holder of ''such firearms acquisition certificate, registration certificate or permit.'' Four of the six judges of the Supreme Court held that the provision did not reverse the onus. For the majority, Mr. Justice McIntyre[232] reasoned that, as a holder of a registration certificate cannot be made the subject of a conviction, the accused was ''not required to prove or disprove any element of the offence or for that matter, anything related to the offence.''[233] At most, he might have to produce the certificate to show that he was exempt from the offence. McIntyre J. concluded as follows:

> Although the accused must establish that he falls within the exemption, there is no danger that he could be convicted under s. 89(1), despite the existence of a reasonable doubt as to guilt, because the production of the certificate resolves all doubts in favour of the accused and in the absence of the certificate no defence is possible once possession has been shown. In such a case, where the only relevant evidence is the certificate itself, it cannot be said that the accused could adduce evidence sufficient to raise doubt without at the same time establishing conclusively that the certificate had been issued. The theory behind any licensing system is that when an issue arises as to the possession of the licence, it is the accused who is in the best position to resolve the issue. Otherwise, the issuance of the certificate or licence would serve no useful purpose. Not only is it rationally open to the accused to prove he holds a licence . . ., it is the expectation inherent in the system.[234]

In contrast, Chief Justice Dickson for the dissent[235] held that, on *Whyte*, this was a reverse onus clause which could not be justified under s. 1 of the Charter. Requiring the accused to prove the question of registration, whether this was a matter of an essential or a defence, was contrary to s. 11(d). The Charter was the occasion to review a number of reverse onus clauses which had crept into criminal law from theories of proof in civil suits. The historical influence was the Roman tradition of requiring the defendant to raise and prove exceptions to a suit. All substantive issues in a criminal trial were related to the question of guilt or innocence and should be decided by the same standard of proof of guilt beyond a reasonable doubt.[236]

The analysis of the minority seems entirely persuasive.[237] In any event, with the majority of the Ontario Court of Appeal in *Wholesale Travel* it is suggested that, despite the puzzling preoccupation in the majority opinion with whether the burden went to an element, in the result even the majority were applying the *Whyte* proposition that a statutory provision must not have the effect of allowing conviction despite a reasonable doubt as to any aspect. In any event, in *Chaulk*,[238] Chief Justice Lamer for the majority[239] goes out of his way to confine *Schwartz*

---

[232] La Forest and L'Heureux-Dubé JJ. concurred. Beetz J. concurred separately.
[233] Above note 229, at 284.
[234] *Ibid.*, at 284-285.
[235] Lamer J. concurred.
[236] Above note 229, at 267-268.
[237] See too Weiser, above note 220, pp. 334-335, Tuck-Jackson, above note 220, pp. 37-38.
[238] Above note 224.
[239] Dickson C.J.C., La Forest, Sopinka and Cory JJ. concurred.

to its facts. *Schwartz* rested on the particular factual nature of the offence and had not overruled *Whyte*.[240] Like *Holmes, Schwartz* should be re-considered.[241]

It seems clear that s. 11(d) only protects against reverse onus respecting proof of guilt or innocence. The Supreme Court has determined, with no mention of the presumption of innocence, that an accused must normally prove a Charter violation on a balance of probabilities[242] or defences relating to police or prosecutorial misconduct such as entrapment[243] and abuse of process.[244]

(iv) *Legislative avoidance by exclusion of elements or defences from offence definition*

In the case of essential elements, the Supreme Court of Canada has already spoken emphatically. In *Vaillancourt* (1987),[245] the Court struck down the constructive murder rule in s. 230(d) of the Criminal Code on the basis that s. 7 of the Charter required for a murder conviction that the Crown prove at least objective foreseeability of death. Speaking for seven members of the Court,[246] Mr. Justice Lamer stated that a legislature cannot omit an essential element of an offence if that element is required as a principle of fundamental justice under s. 7:

> Before an accused can be convicted of an offence, the trier of fact must be satisfied beyond a reasonable doubt of the existence of all of the essential elements of the offence. These essential elements include not only those set out by the legislature in the provision creating the offence but also those required by s.7 of the Charter. Any provision creating an offence which allows for the conviction of an accused notwithstanding the existence of a reasonable doubt on any essential element infringes ss. 7 and 11(d).[247]

Lamer J. also held that a legislative substitution of a different element will be constitutional only

> if upon proof beyond reasonable doubt of the substituted element it would be unreasonable for the trier of fact not to be satisfied beyond reasonable doubt of the existence of the essential element.[248]

---

[240] Above note 223, at 24-25. Wilson J. distinguishes *Schwartz* on the basis it dealt with "regulated rather than prohibited conduct" (at 57).

[241] In *Daniels* (1990), 60 C.C.C. (3d) 392 (B.C. C.A.), the Court held, relying on *Schwartz*, that requiring the accused prove that he did not have a permit for shell-fishing did not violate s. 11(d) as no presumption was involved. *Daniels* would appear to have been overruled by *Chaulk*.

[242] *Collins* (1987), 56 C.R. (3d) 193 (S.C.C.).

[243] *Mack* (1988), 67 C.R. (3d) 1 (S.C.C.).

[244] *Ibid.*

[245] (1987), 60 C.R. (3d) 289 (S.C.C.).

[246] Dickson C.J.C., Estey and Wilson JJ. concur. The concurring opinions of Beetz, Le Dain and La Forest JJ. express no reservations on this point. Only McIntyre J. dissents.

[247] Above note 245, at 326.

[248] *Ibid.*, at 327.

It was not necessary for the Court in *Vaillancourt* to speak of removal of defences, but presumably there may be constitutionally-required defences.[249]

(v) *Evidentiary burdens*

The crucial distinction between persuasive and evidentiary burdens is often misunderstood.[250] The debate is often cluttered by jargon and terminology, particularly when the word "presumption" is resorted to. The true essence of a persuasive burden is that it arises for resolution at the end of the case, never shifts, and the trier of fact *must* find against the burdenholder in borderline cases. In Canadian criminal law, when the persuasive burden is on the accused it is well accepted that the accused must prove on a balance of probabilities. *Oakes* and *Whyte* hold that in such cases an accused may be convicted while a reasonable doubt exists, contrary to the Charter presumption of innocence.

On the other hand, it is usually accepted that the essence of an evidential "burden" is that the burdenholder does not have to do any proving, that it may shift in the limited sense of diverting a "finger of suspicion"[251] and that it *may* but not must result in the trier of fact finding against the burdenholder in borderline cases. It is often said that where the accused has the evidentiary burden, he or she must "raise a reasonable doubt." This comes very close to implying that the accused must prove, usually a denial, beyond a reasonable doubt. The better view is simply to emphasize that the evidential burden can be discharged by pointing to enough evidence to put the matter in issue. Chief Justice Dickson put this very clearly:

> While any combination of phrases has its advantages and drawbacks, I prefer to use the terms "persuasive burden" to refer to the requirement of proving a case or disproving defences and "evidential burden" to mean the requirement of putting an issue into play by reference to evidence before the court. The party who has the persuasive burden is required to persuade the trier of fact, to convince the trier of fact that a certain set of facts existed. Failure to persuade means that the party loses. The party with an evidential burden is not required to convince the trier of fact of anything, only to point out evidence which suggests that certain facts existed. The phrase "onus of proof" should be restricted to the persuasive burden, since an issue can be put into play without being proven. The phrases "burden of going forward" and "burden of adducing evidence" should not be used, as they imply that the party is required to produce his or her own evidence on an issue. As we have seen, in a criminal case the accused can rely on evidence produced by the Crown to argue for a reasonable doubt.[252]

---

[249] In *Morgentaler* (1988), 62 C.R. (3d) 1 at 31 (S.C.C.), there is the enigmatic holding of Dickson C.J.C. (Lamer J. concurring) that:

> One of the basic tenets of our system of criminal justice is that, when Parliament creates a defence to a criminal charge, the defence should not be illusory or so difficult to attain as to be practically illusory.

[250] See the writers referred to in Stuart, *Canadian Criminal Law. A Treatise* (4th ed., 2001) c. 1, and Delisle, *Evidence: Principles and Problems* (5th ed., 1999) pp. 129-137.

[251] G. Williams, *Criminal Law. A General Part*, 2nd ed. (1961), p. 880.

[252] *Schwartz*, above note 229, at 270. Dickson C.J. was in dissent but the majority made no comment on this analysis.

Evidentiary burdens in the sense of pointing to evidence in the case arise continually in the ebb and flow of a trial and do not necessarily depend for their existence on statutory wording. They may arise in respect of any fact in issue and may fall on the Crown or the accused. Perhaps the most common instance is where an accused relies on a substantive defence such as self-defence. Where the defence is not put in issue by the Crown case, the accused has a duty of adducing some evidence although this does not mean that he has to proof anything or to testify. A defence must have an "air of reality" before it is put to the jury. As Cory J. put it in *Osolin* (1994):[253]

> The question is not whether there is some evidence, but rather, whether there is some evidence capable of supporting the particular defence alleged by the accused. . . . A jury should not be required to listen to instructions on defences which simply cannot be applicable to the case that they have heard.[254]

Since such evidentiary burdens on an accused do not require proof on a balance of probabilities or beyond a reasonable doubt, on the *Oakes* and *Whyte* test, there is no violation of the presumption of innocence in s. 11(d). This has been confirmed on many occasions by provincial courts[255] and *Osolin* now constitutes Supreme Court authority.[256] So too, in *Robinson* (1996),[257] the Supreme Court held that the common law rule that voluntary intoxication is a defence to specific intent crimes had to be modified to the extent that the traditional formulation has relied on drunkenness not rebutting the presumption that a man intends the natural consequences of his act. In that context, the Court insisted that the presumption of intent should only be interpreted and referred to as a common sense and logical inference that the jury can but is not compelled to make.

There is, however, the reality identified by Mr. Justice Martin in *Re Boyle* (1983):[258] not all evidentiary burdens are permissive. The issue before the Ontario Court of Appeal was a presumption created by the language of the Criminal Code "in the absence of any evidence to the contrary proof," a frequently-used legislative device.[259] The Court held that, although such presumptions can be

---

[253] (1994), 26 C.R. (4th) 1 (S.C.C.).

[254] At 30-31.

[255] *Russell* (1983), 32 C.R. (3d) 307 (N.S. C.A.) (inference arising from unexplained possession of recently stolen property); *Pye* (1984), 38 C.R. (3d) 375 (N.S. C.A.) (phrase "prima facie evidence" in provincial statute); *Cohn* (1984), 42 C.R. (3d) 1 (Ont. C.A.) (show cause proceedings for contempt).

[256] Cory J., for the majority of the Supreme Court, held that the air of reality test required for mistaken belief in consent defences against sexual assault charges did not violate ss. 11(d) or 11(j). The Court read down the Court's previous holding in *Pappajohn* (1980), 14 C.R. (3d) 243 (S.C.C.), that the air of reality had to be found in evidence independent of the accused. See further Stuart, *Treatise*, above note 250, c. 4.

[257] (1996), 46 C.R. (4th) 1 (S.C.C.).

[258] (1983), 35 C.R. (3d) 34 (Ont. C.A.).

[259] See B. Ziff, "The Presumption of Innocence and 'Evidence to the Contrary': A Comment on Re Boyle and the Queen" (1984), 22 *U. of West. Ont. L. Rev.* 29 at 143-146. In *Boyle*, the Court held that the presumption that arises under s. 354(2) on possession of a motor vehicle with an obliterated identification number, that the motor vehicle or part thereof was at some time obtained by the commission of an indictable offence, was entirely reasonable and constitutionally valid.

displaced merely by evidence which raises a reasonable doubt rather than proof on a balance of probabilities, there was a common feature in the mandatory nature of the conclusion required to be drawn. The obligation on the accused required mandatory presumptions to receive protection under the Charter presumption of innocence. Since *Oakes*, the Ontario Court of Appeal has continued[260] to assert that Charter scrutiny should be afforded to such clauses.

In *Downey* (1992)[261] the Supreme Court faced a Charter challenge to what is now s. 212 (3) of the Criminal Code which resorted to a mandatory presumption respecting the offence of living on the avails of another person's prostitution. Under that section:

> Evidence that a person lives with or is habitually in the company of prostitutes . . . is, in the absence of evidence to the contrary, proof that the person lives on the avails of prostitution.

The Supreme Court was unanimous in holding that this mandatory presumption violated s. 11(d).[262] Justice Cory for the Court on this point resorted to an analysis of different types of presumptions.[263] Some presumptions operated without the requirement of proof of basic facts. Those that required proof of a basic fact were of three types:

> (a) Permissive Inferences: Where the trier of fact is entitled to infer a presumed fact from the proof of a basic fact, but is not obliged to do so. This results in a tactical burden whereby the accused may wish to call evidence in rebuttal but is not required to do so.
>
> (b) Evidential Burdens: Where the trier of fact is required to draw the conclusion from proof of the basic fact in the absence of evidence to the contrary. This mandatory conclusion results in an evidential burden whereby the accused will need to call evidence, unless there is already evidence to the contrary in the Crown's case.
>
> (c) Legal Burdens: Similar to the burden in (b) except that the presumed fact must be disproved on a balance of probabilities instead of by the mere raising of evidence to the contrary. These are also referred to as "reverse onus clauses".[264]

The Court ruled that mandatory presumption in s. 212(3) fell into category (b) and infringed s. 11(d) because it could result in the conviction of an accused despite the existence of a reasonable doubt. The fact that someone is living with a prostitute did not lead inexorably to the conclusion that that person was living on avails.

However, the second presumption under s. 354(2), that the person found in possession knows that the vehicle or part thereof was obtained by the commission of an indictable offence, was not constitutionally valid, since it was arbitrary and hence unreasonable.

[260] *Phillips* (1988), 64 C.R. (3d) 154 (Ont. C.A.) (presumption in s. 258(1)(c) concerning alcohol concentration following breathalyzer test) (see too *Ballem* (1990), 58 C.C.C. (3d) 46 (P.E.I. C.A.)); *Nagy* (1988), 67 C.R. (3d) 329 (Ont. C.A.) (presumption of intent in s. 349(2) where Crown has proved entry without lawful excuse) and *Gosselin* (1988), 67 C.R. (3d) 349 (Ont. C.A.) (presumption in s. 252(2) that accused leaving accident without performing statutory duties had intent to escape liability (see too *T. (S.D.)* (1985), 43 C.R. (3d) 307 (N.S. C.A.)).

[261] (1992), 13 C.R. (4th) 129 (S.C.C.).

[262] The Court further ruled, but only 4-3, that the violation could be saved under s. 1, discussed below note 287.

[263] At 138.

[264] *Ibid.*

Downey is welcome in its extension of Charter protection to mandatory presumptions. However, its reasoning carries large risks of unnecessary complication and confusion. The resort to a taxonomy of presumptions is unfortunate. Many denials of the presumption of innocence do not involve any form of presumption. Confining the term evidential burden to mandatory presumptions risks confusion given that the term is so commonly used in the looser sense of pointing to evidence in the case. Professor Ron Delisle has suggested that the *Oakes* test of whether the burden on the accused might result in a conviction despite a reasonable doubt does not address the problem with mandatory presumptions: they mandate a result even if there has been no evidence on the point. He suggests a new approach, under which

> any presumptive device which compels the trier of fact to find an essential element, or the absence of any material justification or excuse, to be proved beyond a reasonable doubt, though no direct positive evidence was led concerning the existence of either, must violate the presumption of innocence.[265]

Another problem with a mandatory presumption is that it may force the accused to testify in violation of s.11(c).[266]

A disturbing decision quite at odds with this aspect of *Downey* is that of the Supreme Court in *Audet* (1996).[267] That decision concerned the offence under s. 153(1) of the Criminal Code of touching a young person for a sexual purpose while in a position of trust or authority. Mr. Justice La Forest, for a 5-2 majority,[268] holds that in the absence of evidence raising a reasonable doubt, teachers are in a position of trust and authority towards their students with the result that consent cannot be a defence. The majority further holds, in the briefest of reasons, that this mandatory presumption does not violate the presumption of innocence. According to the majority:

> As this Court has stated, a presumption that imposes an evidential burden on the accused — that is, a presumption requiring the trier of fact to draw a conclusion from proof of a basic fact if no evidence raising a reasonable doubt is adduced by either the Crown or the accused — does not violate the presumption of innocence if the unknown fact follows inexorably from the basic fact.[269]

The majority refer without discussion to the Court's previous decisions in *Downey*, *Vaillancourt* and *Whyte*. The dissenting opinion of Major J. (Sopinka J. concurring) is even briefer in reaching the conclusion that relieving the Crown of the burden of proving that a teacher accused was in a position of trust or authority violated the presumption of innocence:

---

[265] R.J. Delisle, "When Do Evidentiary Burdens Violate Section 11(d)", (1992) 13 C.R. (4th) 161 at 164.

[266] See Lamer C.J. dissenting in *Wholesale Travel Group Inc.* (1991), 8 C.R. (4th) 145 (S.C.C.). See further David Tanovich, "The Unravelling of the Golden Thread: The Supreme Court's Compromise of the Presumption of Innocence", (1993) 35 *Crim. L.Q.* 194 at 209-210, and Alan Mewett, "Compelling the Accused to Testify", (1988) 31 *Crim. L.Q.* 1.

[267] (1996), 48 C.R. (4th) 1 (S.C.C.), criticised by Anne-Marie Boisvert, "Exploitation Sexuelle, Enseignants et Présomption d'Innocence", C.R. *ibid.* 57-68.

[268] L'Heureux-Dubé, Gonthier, Cory and McLachlin JJ. concurred.

[269] At 27-28.

The accused's right in s. 11(d) of the Charter, to be presumed innocent, is paramount and should not be compromised, whether by presumption of fact or otherwise.[270]

The majority decision in *Audet* on this point is *per incuriam* in that it is not supported by the authorities on which it relies. Furthermore the Court's creation of a mandatory presumption was unnecessary and ran rough shod over the presumption of innocence.[271] Of the authorities relied upon by the majority, only *Downey* fully deals with mandatory presumptions. Contrary to the opinion of the majority in *Audet*, the Court in *Downey* was unanimous that a mandatory presumption *would* violate s. 11(d). The presumption in issue in *Downey* was only held to be constitutional by a 4-3 ruling under s. 1.[272] *Audet* never gets to s. 1. The *Downey* analysis seems equally applicable to the situation in *Audet*. Even the majority recognized that there would be situations in which there would not be a relationship of authority or trust between a teacher and student. In the *Downey* language, the fact of the relationship would not inexorably lead to the conclusion that there was a relationship of authority or trust. There was a violation of s. 11(d) and the analysis should have moved to s. 1. In *Downey*, the Supreme Court were reviewing a statutory mandatory presumption. In *Audet*, such a presumption was created out of thin air. The suspicion is that the majority did not like the acquittal and was determined to achieve a conviction. In so doing, the Court has substantially weakened the presumption of innocence. On *Audet*, mandatory presumptions can be created whenever a Court sees fit. Why wasn't it sufficient in *Audet* to allow common sense inferences to be drawn from evidence as to the relationship?

(vi) *Justifying reverse onuses and mandatory presumptions under section 1*[273]

There has been a very clear trend in Supreme Court decisions to find that reverse onus provisions and mandatory presumptions are demonstrably justified under s. 1. Until its decision in *Johnson, Laba* (1994),[274] which may be a watershed decision, the Court had not struck down a reverse onus since that considered in *Oakes*.

In the context of reverse onuses it has become particularly difficult to predict how the Supreme Court will apply the *Oakes* test.[275] In *Whyte* itself the Chief Justice decided for the unanimous Court that the persuasive burden on the accused in question was demonstrably justified by s. 1. Requiring that the accused prove some alternative reason for entering the vehicle and occupying the driver's seat

---

[270] At 3.
[271] See too Anne-Marie Boisvert, "Exploitation sexuelle, enseignants et presumption d'innocence", (1996) 48 C.R. (4th) (S.C.C.).
[272] See below note 287.
[273] See generally David Tanovich, "The Unravelling of the Golden Thread: The Supreme Court's Compromise of the Presumption of Innocence", (1993) 35 *Crim. L.Q.* 194 and John Webster, "The Proper Approach to Detection and Justification of Section 11(d) Charter Violations Since Laba", (1995) 39 C.R. (4th) 113.
[274] Discussed below note 292.
[275] See further Cromwell, above note 190, pp. 189-197.

was a restrained Parliamentary response to a pressing social problem and a minimal interference with the presumption of innocence. There is here a glaring inconsistency with the Chief Justice's earlier minority judgment in *Holmes*. In that case, a major reason for holding that reversing the onus of proving lawful excuse did not impair "as little as possible" was that Parliament could have merely imposed an evidentiary burden.[276] This consideration was never raised in the reasons in *Whyte*. If this was the price to be paid to obtain a unanimous court the price was too high.

In *Keegstra* (1991),[277] the Supreme Court held four to two that the requirement in s. 319(3)(a) that an accused prove a truth defence to a charge of wilfully promoting hatred against an identifiable group was a demonstrably justified reasonable limit on the presumption of innocence. Chief Justice Dickson for the majority[278] carefully reasoned[279] that because the harm was created by statements promoting hatred, whether true or not, the defence of truth could not be too easily available. Out of caution Parliament had made a concession to the importance of truth in allowing an accused to benefit from the possibility that his or her statements, while intended to promote hatred, might have some utility as part of a public dialogue. Any alternative method of incorporating an issue of truth into the offence would skew the equilibrium and excessively compromise the effectiveness of the offence. The reverse onus represented a minimal impairment of the presumption of innocence.

In contrast, McLachlin J. for the minority[280] held that the infringement could not be justified under s.1. The section did not impair as little as possible. The fact that Parliament intended that falsehood would be an important element of the offence, coupled with the centrality of the presumption of innocence, suggested that only a countervailing State interest of the most compelling kind justify the infringement.[281]

In *Chaulk* (1991),[282] the Supreme Court held five to one that the presumption of sanity in s. 16(4) of the Criminal Code, requiring the accused to prove a defence of insanity on a balance of probabilities, was a violation of the presumption of innocence that was demonstrably justified as a reasonable limit. We have already considered and criticized how the majority of the Supreme Court substituted for the *Oakes* test of intrusion as little as possible the far less stringent test of whether the lesser intrusive means would achieve the same objective as effectively.[283] For the majority, Chief Justice Lamer[284] saw the object of s. 16(4) as to avoid placing on the Crown the impossibly onerous burden of disproving insanity. Many of the parties had identified potential difficulties the Crown would face if it was required

---

[276] Above note 217, at 116.

[277] Above note 223.

[278] Wilson, L'Heureux-Dubé and Gonthier JJ. concurred.

[279] Above note 223, at 205-208.

[280] Sopinka J. concurred.

[281] Above note 223, at 262-263.

[282] Above note 224.

[283] *Ibid.*, at 32, discussed above, Chapter 1

[284] Dickson C.J.C., La Forest, Sopinka and Cory JJ. concurred.

to prove sanity. Reducing the burden to the accused to a mere evidentiary burden to raising a reasonable doubt would not achieve the objective as effectively. It would be very easy for the accused to "fake" insanity and to raise a reasonable doubt. In enacting s. 16(4) Parliament may not have chosen the absolutely least intrusive means of meeting its objective, but it had chosen from a range of means impairing s. 11(d) as little as reasonable possible.[285]

In *Chaulk* the lonely but persuasive dissent on this point was by Madam Justice Wilson.[286] The objective of the reverse onus was to prevent perfectly sane persons who had committed crimes from escaping criminal liability on tenuous insanity pleas. However, the Government had not adduced evidence to show that this was a real social problem of sufficient importance to warrant overriding one of the most, if not the most, fundamental tenet of our criminal justice system. There was no historic experience in our jurisdiction with the purely evidential burden to show that such a burden was not adequate to achieve the Government's objective. The American experience with an evidentiary burden did not support the contention that such a standard of proof would result in more people being acquitted by reason of insanity. This was not a case for relaxing the minimum intrusion test. This might be done where a legislature, mediating between competing groups of citizens or allocating scarce resources, had to compromise on the basis of conflicting evidence. But here the State was acting as "singular antagonist" of a very basic legal right of an accused and the strict standard of review in Oakes should be applied. The government's objective could be quite easily met by a burden on the accused to adduce evidence that made insanity "a live issue fit and proper to be left to the jury".

In *Downey* (1992),[287] a 4-3 majority of the Supreme Court held that the violation of the presumption of innocence by a mandatory presumption that persons living with or habitually in the company of prostitutes are living on avails was a demonstrably justified reasonable limit under s. 1. According to Cory J. for the majority,[288] the section was aimed at a cruel and pervasive social evil of pimping and the presumption met the rational connection and proportionality tests. There was often a connection between maintaining close ties to prostitutes and living off avails. Parliament did not have to choose the least intrusive alternative. The issue was whether Parliament could have reasonably chosen an alternative means which would have achieved the identified objective as effectively. For the minority the presumption was too broad in that it caught many people who were innocent of the exploitive activity at which the section was aimed. According to McLachlin J.,[289] this overbreadth rendered the presumption "arbitrary, unfair" and ultimately irrational. There had to be a very high degree

---

[285] Above note 224, at 28-34.

[286] *Ibid.*, at 57-75. For a fine pre-*Chaulk* criticism of the reversal of the burden of proof of insanity and call for re-evaluation of the whole defence, see Anne-Marie Boisvert, "Psychoanalysis of a Defence: Reflections on the Insanity Defence" (1990), 66 *Can. Bar Rev.* 46.

[287] Above note 261. See critical comments by Tanovich, above note 273, and R.J. Delisle, "When Do Evidentiary Burdens Violate Section 11(d)", (1992) 13 C.R. (4th) 161.

[288] L'Heureux-Dubé, Sopinka and Gonthier JJ. concurred.

[289] Iacobucci J. concurred. La Forest J. also dissented in a separate opinion.

of internal rationality between the substituted and presumed facts. At a minimum proof of the substituted fact "must make it *likely* that the presumed fact is true".[290]

The Supreme Court is still confusingly inconsistent. In its controversial decision in *Daviault* (1994),[291] the Court took but a few lines to hold that section one could demonstrably justify an onus on the accused of proving the defence of extreme intoxication akin to automatism or insanity. There was no discussion of what minimum intrusion test was being applied or of whether an evidentiary burden would have sufficed. The majority was content to draw a quick analogy to its decision in *Chaulk*.

Within two months, in *Laba* (1994),[292] the full Court through Sopinka J. adopted an approach to a reverse onus clause substantially similar to that of the minority opinion of Wilson J. in *Chaulk*. For the first time since *Oakes*, the Court held that a reverse onus clause could not be saved by s. 1. Under s. 394(1)(b) of the Criminal Code, an accused is prohibited from selling or purchasing precious metal "unless he establishes that he is the owner or agent of the owner or is acting under lawful authority". Despite a great deal of evidence establishing that theft of ore was a serious problem in Ontario, Quebec and the Yukon and difficult to prove, the Court held that shifting the persuasive burden could not pass the minimum intrusion test of whether the measure impaired the presumption of innocence as little as reasonably possible. Although Parliament should be accorded some leeway, this was a case where the government could be characterised as the singular antagonist of an individual attempting to assert a legal right fundamental to the criminal justice system. The Crown had not demonstrated that an evidentiary burden would not be sufficient. The remedy for the unconstitutional reverse onus in question was to read it down as an "evidentiary burden". The section was in future to be read as deleting "unless he establishes" and inserting "in the absence of evidence which raises a reasonable doubt".

The *Laba* approach mirrors much but not all of the dissenting opinion of Wilson J. in *Chaulk*. One can only hope that the Supreme Court has at last settled on a tougher approach to section one justification in the context of criminal law.[293] Hopefully, the Court will in the future be consistent in its *Laba* view that reverse onuses cannot be saved without consideration of the alternatives. If so the Court will have embarked on a new course much more protective of the presumption of innocence and for less receptive to arguments of law enforcement expediency. Many previous decisions of the Supreme Court may no longer be authoritative or at least should be reconsidered.

Signs are not encouraging. When *Keegstra* reached the Supreme Court for the second time in 1996[294] the Court refused to reconsider its earlier ruling that

---

At 157.

[290] At 157.

[291] (1994), 33 C.R. (4th) 165 (S.C.C.), discussed below Chapter 6, "Incapacity".

[292] (1994), 34 C.R. (4th) 360 (S.C.C.). See comments by Tanovich, above note 273, and R.J. Delisle, "Confusion on Evidentiary Burdens", (1995) 34 C.R. (4th) 402.

[293] See further Chapter 1.

[294] (1996), 48 C.R. (4th) 118 (S.C.C.).

the reverse onus in question was saved under s. 1. A brief oral judgment asserted *Laba* was distinguishable. In *Stone* (1999)[295] a 5-4 majority[296] placed the persuasive burden of proof for the defence of sane automatism on the accused even though the issue of onus had not been raised by any counsel in the case. There was furthermore no discussion of Charter issues even though the dissenting opinion strongly urged that they were engaged.

However, a major problem with *Laba* is the remedy adopted. The Court substituted for a persuasive burden an "evidentiary burden" which the Court, consistent with its terminology in *Downey*, found to require a mandatory presumption. No consideration was given to simply striking the provision down so that the normal evidential burden would arise such that the accused would merely have to point to evidence in the case sufficient to pass the air of reality test. This was the approach of Wilson J. in *Chaulk* and has commendably been adopted by the Ontario Court of Appeal since *Laba*.[297]

In its s. 1 decisions on reverse onuses, the Supreme Court appears to have been inconsistent with the minimum intrusion test and also far too accepting of arguments of law enforcement expediency. On the test of effectiveness it seems likely that any type of reverse onus will be saved under s. 1. If this is so, the fine analytic effort made by the Supreme Court Canada in *Whyte* will have come to naught. It seems fundamental that in any borderline case involving penal responsibility the accused should receive the benefit of the doubt. The Court in *Whyte* and *Chaulk* was too cavalier in its acceptance of arguments of difficulty of law enforcement.

The Supreme Court appears too wedded to reverse onuses and mandatory presumptions. Both should violate s. 11(d) and engage a rigorous s. 1 analysis. What is required is evidence and/ or convincing argument relating to the need to violate the presumption of innocence.[298] To pass the *Oakes* proportionality test in this context, the Court should always be satisfied that less intrusive means such as the normal evidentiary burden or, failing that, a mandatory presumption, are

---

[295] (1999), 24 C.R. (5th) 1 (S.C.C.). For criticism of *Stone* see R.J. Delisle "Stone: Judicial Activism Gone Awry to Presume Guilt", (1999) 24 C.R. (5th) 91 and David Pacciocco, "Death by Stoneing: The Demise of the Defence of Simple Automatism", (1999) 26 C.R. (5th) 273.

[296] Per Bastarache J. (L'Heureux-Dubé, Gonthier, Cory and McLachlin JJ. concurring). Binnie J. (Lamer C.J., Iacobucci and Major JJ. concurring) dissented.

[297] *Fisher* (1994), 28 C.R. (4th) 63 (Ont. C.A.) (striking down persuasive burden in s. 121(1)(c) of Criminal Code concerning civil service corruption requiring that accused prove written consent by head of government department). See too *Curtis* (1998), 14 C.R. (5th) 328 (Ont. C.A.) (striking down the reverse onus for proving lawful excuse for failing to provide necessaries of life). Compare however Bastarache J. as he then was in *Wilson* (1997), 11 C.R. (5th) 347 (N.B. C.A.) (a provincial vicarious liability provision imposed liability on the owner of a vehicle subject to the owner establishing no consent: the Court struck it down but retained a presumption the driver was the owner).

[298] John Webster, "The Proper Approach to Detection and Justification of Section 11(d) Violations Since Laba", (1995) 39 C.R. (4th) 113, suggests that "The courts must be diligent in their scrutiny of the objective. The Crown should have to prove that there is a significant problem securing convictions. A reverse onus is not justified simply on proof that some people who commit offences are avoiding conviction. . . . The problem with securing convictions must be *real* and not merely hypothetical or theoretical" (at 124).

not reasonable alternatives. Canada and the Criminal Code in particular is conspicuous for its overuse of reverse onus causes. It is time to hold most of them unconstitutional or to read them down to burdens to point to evidence in the case.

(vii) *Reverse onus for due diligence defences for regulatory offences*

The record is quite clear that the Supreme Court's reversal of the onus of proof of the new due diligence defence to the accused in *City of Sault Ste. Marie* was based on misinterpretations of common law authority in the United Kingdom and Australia.[299] Without addressing this problem, the Supreme Court in *Wholesale Travel Group Inc.* (1991)[300] determined by a narrow 5-4 majority that in the case of regulatory offences there is nothing unconstitutional about placing a persuasive burden of proving the due diligence defence on the accused. The majority unfortunately rejected the views of the Ontario Court of Appeal and the Ontario Law Reform Commission[301] that the accused should only face a mandatory presumption.

Chief Justice Lamer for the dissenting minority in *Wholesale Travel* (Sopinka, McLachlin and La Forest JJ. concurring), is entirely convincing in holding that here the persuasive burden on the accused to establish due diligence violated s. 11(d) and could not be saved under s. 1. The object of the onus was to ensure that misleading advertising convictions were not lost due to evidentiary problems. However, the means did not infringe the protected right as little as reasonably possible under s. 1 because Parliament clearly had the option of employing a mandatory presumption of negligence as recently recommended by the Ontario Law Reform Commission. The Chief Justice acknowledged that a mandatory presumption could operate to indirectly force the accused into the stand and would also thereby violate the s. 11(c) protection against testimonial compulsion.[302]

The two judgments for the five-judge majority on this point are quite different. Mr. Justice Iacobucci J. (Gonthier and Stevenson JJ. concurring) agree that there is a reverse onus violating the presumption of innocence in s. 11(d) but hold that the persuasive burden can be demonstrably justified under s. 1. Their disagreement with the position of the Chief Justice lies in their holding on the "minimum intrusion" part of the *Oakes* test for s. 1. In the view of Iacobucci J., an approach of a mandatory presumption of negligence in which the accused would not have to establish due diligence on a balance of probabilities but merely raise a reasonable doubt would not achieve the objective "as effectively nor would it go a long way in achieving it". In his view

---

[299] See Stuart, *Treatise*, above note 250, c. 3.

[300] (1991), 8 C.R. (4th) 145 (S.C.C.).

[301] *Report on the Basis of Liability for Provincial Offences* (1990). This author was the principal consultant. The report was favourably reviewed by Bruce P. Archibald in (1991) *Dalhousie L.J.* but considered by Kent Roach in (1990) *Can. Bar Rev.* to be "a combination of misplaced criminal law orthodoxy and abstract analysis . . . which significantly reduces the chances for successful deterrence and prosecution of harmful social and corporate behaviour".

[302] At 217.

such an alternative would in practice make it virtually impossible for the Crown to prove public welfare offences such as the one in question and would effectively prevent governments from seeking to implement public policy through prosecution. It would also not provide effective inducement for those engaged in regulated activity to comply strictly with the regulatory scheme including adopting proper procedures and record-keeping and might even have a contrary effect. Though such a result would be clearly advantageous to an accused, it would not be effective in avoiding the loss of convictions because the Crown could not prove facts within the particular knowledge of the accused.[303]

The trouble with these arguments of law enforcement expediency is that they could demonstrably justify any reverse onus clause for any type of crime. Iacobucci J. expressly relies on the majority decision in *Chaulk*.

In *Wholesale Travel*, the other two majority judges for the position that the onus of proving due diligence defences in regulatory offences is constitutional were Mr. Justice Cory, with Madam Justice L'Heureux-Dubé J. concurring. Mr. Justice Cory's judgment is extraordinary and utterly unconvincing on this point. He rests heavily on the unruly distinction between real and regulatory[304] offences and is of the view that the Charter must be applied differently in the case of regulatory offences. Cory J. asserts without evidence that a reverse onus on the accused would make it virtually impossible for the Crown to prove regulatory offences and would effectively prevent governments from seeking to implement public policy through regulatory means. There was furthermore nothing unfair about imposing the onus on the accused to show on a balance of probabilities that they took reasonable precautions, no violation of the presumption of innocence and no need to proceed to a s. 1 justification.

As the minority point out in *Wholesale Travel*, it is clear that s. 11 Charter rights are available to anybody charged with a provincial offence. Mr. Justice Cory does not come close to justifying why, in the case of regulatory offences, perhaps the most important s. 11 right, the presumption of innocence, does not apply.

The result of the distinct positions of Iacobucci and Cory JJ. is that all accused charged with regulatory offences must prove lack of fault. Why, in a borderline case involving State punishment, should there be a presumption of guilt? Is it satisfactory that an accused goes to gaol where the trier of fact can only say "The accused was probably at fault". The *Wholesale* ruling applies not just to corporations, large or small, but to any individual, weak or strong.

In *Ellis-Don* (1990),[305] the Ontario Court ruled that an onus under statute or common law requiring an accused charged with an Occupational Health and Safety Act offence to prove the defence of due diligence on a balance of probabilities violates the presumption of innocence under s. 11(d) and had to be read down to require the accused to satisfy an evidentiary rather than persuasive burden. When the matter reached the Supreme Court,[306] the Court, in contrast to

---

[303] At 191.
[304] For an argument that such a distinction is invalid see Stuart, *Treatise*, above note 299.
[305] (1990), 2 C.R. (4th) 118 (Ont. C.A.).
[306] (1992), 71 C.C.C. (3d) 63 (S.C.C.).

Chaulk and *Wholesale Travel*, were presented with complete empirical data as to enforcement options and patterns seeking to show that the reverse onus could not be justified under section one. However, in a brief oral judgment, the Court refused to reconsider or distinguish its *Wholesale* ruling.

The justification of the reverse onus in *Wholesale Travel* rests on the characterization of the offence as regulatory. There is no Supreme Court authority for applying the due diligence standard and the reverse onus to a crime.[307]

The upholding of the reverse onus for the due diligence defence for regulatory offences by a bare majority of the Court should be revisited.[308] The ruling rests in part on resort under the s. 1 enquiry to a mere assertion that the law would otherwise be ineffective. The authority of the ruling should be considered suspect since the Supreme Court ruling in *Laba*. There is a reasonable alternative of a mandatory presumption of negligence, favoured by the minority of the Supreme Court, the Ontario Court of Appeal and the Ontario Law Reform Commission.[309] The prospect that the accused may have to call evidence adequately responds to arguments of law enforcement efficacy. This alternative has the advantage that, in a borderline case, the accused will not be convicted simply because the persuasive burden has not been discharged. "Probably guilty" is not enough to justify state punishment.

(b) Independent and Impartial Tribunal

(i) *Valente test*

The leading pronouncement on the meaning of "an independent and impartial tribunal" under s. 11(d) of the Charter is the decision of the Supreme Court in *Valente* (1985).[310] For a unanimous seven-judge panel Mr. Justice Le Dain held that a judge of the Provincial Court (Criminal Division) of Ontario, as then appointed under the Provincial Courts Act,[311] met the test.

Although there was "obviously a close relationship" between independence and impartiality they were "separate and distinct values or requirements":[312]

> Impartiality refers to a state of mind or attitude of the tribunal in relation to the issues and the parties in a particular case. The word "impartial" . . . connotes absence of

---

[307] In *Metro News Ltd.* (1986), 53 C.R. (3d) 289 (Ont. C.A.), Martin J.A. read in a due diligence defence for a Criminal Code obscenity offence, but held that the persuasive burden had to remain with the Crown. See similarly *Smillie* (1998), 20 C.R. (5th) 179 (B.C. C.A.) (Criminal Code offence in s. 86(3) of storage of firearm contrary to federal regulations).

[308] *Wholesale Travel* was distinguished in *Bergeron v. Quebec (P.G.)* (1995), 41 C.R. (4th) 261 (Que. C.A.). The Quebec Court of Appeal accepted the authority of *Strasser v. Roberge*, [1979] 2 S.C.R. 953, that a provincial offence of participating in an illegal strike required proof of intent by the accused. However, this was interpreted to require an evidentiary burden. According to the Quebec Court, a persuasive burden on the accused would violate s. 11(d) even though this was a regulatory offence.

[309] Above note 301.

[310] (1985), 49 C.R. (3d) 97 (S.C.C.).

[311] R.S.O. 1980, c. 298, as amended by S.O. 1983, c. 18.

[312] Above note 310, at 105.

bias, actual or perceived. The word "independent" in s. 11(d) reflects or embodies the traditional constitutional value of judicial independence. As such, it connotes not merely a state of mind or attitude in the actual exercise of judicial functions, but a status or relationship to others, particularly to the executive branch of government, that rests on objective conditions or guarantees.[313]

The Court further held that the test for independence, as that for impartiality, was whether the tribunal might be "reasonably perceived as independent."[314] The perception had to be of

whether the tribunal enjoys the essential objective conditions or guarantees of judicial independence, and not a perception of how it will in fact act, regardless of whether it enjoys such conditions or guarantees.[315]

Noting that public concern about judicial independence had increased with the new power and responsibility given to courts by the Charter, the Supreme Court however held that it "would not be feasible" to apply under s. 11(d) the "most rigorous and elaborate conditions of judicial independence."[316] The essential conditions of judicial independence had to bear some reasonable relationship to the wide variety of Canadian tribunals trying persons charged with an offence. The standard of judicial independence under s. 11(d) could not be uniform.[317]

Here, the Court held, the Provincial Court judges were not entitled to the highest degree of constitutional guarantees of security of tenure, salary and pension afforded superior courts under the Constitution Act of 1867.[318] Provincial judges could be reasonably perceived to meet the essential conditions of judicial independence which related to security of tenure, financial security and independence respecting matters of court administration bearing directly on the exercise of the judicial function.[319] The Court noted that provincial judges are removable prior to retirement only for cause, subject to independent review at which the judge affected is afforded a full opportunity to be heard. However, the Court did hold that a post-retirement reappointment procedure at the pleasure of the executive would not make the tribunal independent within s. 11(d), despite a tradition of the executive always acting on the recommendations of the Chief Justice.[320]

In a lengthy and controversial ruling in 1997[321] the Supreme Court intervened to strengthen the independence of provincially appointed judges. For the Court Chief Justice Lamer[322] determined that under s. 11(d) it was unconstitutional for provincial governments and legislatures to reduce the salaries of Provincial Court

---

[313] *Ibid.*
[314] *Ibid.*, at 108.
[315] *Ibid.*, at 108-109.
[316] *Ibid.*, at 111.
[317] *Ibid.*, at 112.
[318] Sections 99 and 100.
[319] Above note 310, at 112-128.
[320] *Ibid.*, at 119.
[321] *Campbell* (1997), 118 C.C.C. (3d) 193 (S.C.C.). See editorial by Kent Roach, "Beyond Salary Commissions for Provincial Courts", (1999) 43 *Crim. L.Q.* 1.
[322] La Forest J. dissented.

judges without prior recourse to independent, effective and objective commissions. The recommendations of the commissions were not binding but might have to be justified if need be in a court of law. The Court also held that governments had offended judicial independence by negotiating salaries with judges, not guaranteeing salaries, changing judges' residences after appointment and in dictating court sitting days. However judicial independence had not been infringed by providing discretionary benefits, designating places of residence on appointment and controlling budget on matters outside matters essential to administrative independence.

The military tribunal system did not survive Charter review under s. 11(d). In *Genereux* (1992),[323] the majority of the Supreme Court ruled that the structure and constitution of General Courts Martial at the time did not meet the conditions of judicial independence under *Valente*. The convening military authorities appointed both the members of the Court Martial and the prosecutor from officers of the armed forces. So too the Court Martial Appeal Court later held[324] that the Standing Court Martial was not an independent tribunal because of its lack of guarantee of financial security of members and its process of appointment. The declaration of invalidity was suspended for one year.

Even where judicial independence has been damaged, the Supreme Court has sometimes been reluctant to halt the proceedings. In *Lippé* (1991)[325] the Court held that a stay of a break and entry charge because of highly disparaging remarks about a witness by Premier Rene Levesque had been premature. In *Tobiass* (1997)[326] it ruled that a citizen revocation hearing for a suspected war criminal should not have been stayed despite judicial interference by the Chief Justice at the behest of an Assistant Deputy General.

(ii) *Part-time judges*

In *Quebec (A.G.) v. Lippé* (1990),[327] the majority of the Quebec Court of Appeal,[328] in a lengthy judgment, carefully applied *Valente* in holding that part-time municipal judges in Quebec were *not* impartial within the meaning of s. 11(d). Such judges are entitled to practice law or engage in other provincial or business activities while holding and exercising judicial office. The majority reasoned that the public could not put the same confidence in such judges who might perceive their judgments could affect their other careers. There was a reasonable apprehension of a conflict of interest, not only financial but possibly

---

[323] (1992), 70 C.C.C. (3d) 1 (S.C.C.). L'Heureux-Dubé J. dissented.
[324] *Lauzon* (1998), 18 C.R. (5th) 288 (Can. Crt. Martial App. Ct.). See too *Bergeron* (1999), 136 C.C.C. (3d) 327.
[325] (1991), 64 C.C.C. (3d) 513 (S.C.C.).
[326] (1997), 10 C.R. (5th) 163 (S.C.C.), considered more fully below in Chapter 7 under "Abuse of Process". See too *Benoit* (1999), 134 C.C.C. (3d) 203 (Nfld. C.A.) (Chief Justice's ruling that a trial judge's order of transcript was unnecessary to result in mistrial rather than stay).
[327] (1990), 60 C.C.C. (3d) 34 (Que. C.A.); (1990), 80 C.R. (3d) 1 (Que. C.A.) (French).
[328] Per Proulx J.A. (Rothman J.A. concurring). Tourigny J.A. dissented.

also moral, psychological or professional. The Supreme Court of Canada, however, soon granted an expedited appeal and reversed.[329]

Chief Justice Lamer for the Court held that the system of part-time Municipal Court judges in Quebec did give rise to a reasonable apprehension of bias in a substantial number of cases and was *per se* incompatible with the functions of a judge. Constitutional requirements of impartiality were, however, met having regard to safeguards in place, such as the requirement of an oath, judicial immunity and the judicial Code of Ethics requiring municipal judges to avoid potential conflicts of interest.

In *Valente*, the Supreme Court makes a powerful case for flexible Charter standards of independence and impartiality given the section's applicability to a wide variety of tribunals. However, its ruling in *Lippé* seems surprisingly expedient and quite inconsistent with the Court's resolve to use the Charter to improve the criminal justice system. Compare the Court's attitude to the issue of institutional delay respecting the right to be tried within a reasonable time[330] and its ruling in *Hunter v. Southam Inc.* (1984)[331] that somebody issuing a search warrant must be capable of acting judicially with neutrality and the detachment necessary to balance the interests involved. The Quebec Court of Appeal should be applauded for having taken the test of reasonable perception of bias seriously.

The decision of the majority of the Newfoundland Court of Appeal in *Hart* (1986)[332] was equally disappointing. The majority[333] held that a system of prosecution of summary conviction matters by police officers properly appointed by a provincial Attorney General did not offend the guarantee under s. 11(d). The majority put its faith in the control by the trial judge and the integrity of the police officer. The dissenting judge, Mr. Justice Mahoney, is persuasive in seeing the practice as a dangerous one which overlooks the importance to the accused of the distinct role of a Crown prosecutor.[334]

(iii) *Justices of the Peace*

There have been several s. 11(d) challenges against systems of justices of the peace. Few have succeeded.

---

[329] (1991), 64 C.C.C. (3d) 513 (S.C.C.). *Vermette* (1988), 41 C.C.C. (3d) 523 (S.C.C.) (stay of break and entry charge because of Premier's highly disparaging remarks about a key defence witness being premature) is discussed below, Chapter 11.

[330] Above note 90 *et seq.*

[331] (1984), 41 C.R. (3d) 97 at 117-118 (S.C.C.), discussed in Chapter 3 under "Minimum Constitutional Standards for a Search Warrant". See too *Baylis* (1988), 65 C.R. (3d) 62 (Sask. C.A.) (justice of peace issuing search warrant not being impartial as subject to control of airport police).

[332] (1986), 26 C.C.C. (3d) 438 (Nfld. C.A.).

[333] Per Mifflin C.J.N. (Morgan J.A. concurring).

[334] See too *Joyal* (1990), 55 C.C.C. (3d) 233 (Que. C.A.) (s. 11(d) not being violated where prosecutor having previously defended accused) and *Cohn*, above note 255 (trial of contempt in face of court by same judge not necessarily violating s. 11(d)).

Mr. Justice Ewaschuk of the Ontario Supreme Court in *Currie* (1984)[335] did grant an order of prohibition against all justices of the peace in Ontario. He held that justices of the peace were not independent in view of the fact that they are appointed at the pleasure of the government, their differential schemes for salary, their functions being dependent on administrative directions, control by the Attorney General and their low status.[336] However, these positions were each rejected by the Ontario Court of Appeal on the appeal.[337]

For the Court, MacKinnon A.C.J.O. held that it was important not only to look at the legislation but to consider the practice and tradition of judicial independence, the acceptance of that tradition by succeeding Attorneys General and the oath of office taken by justices of the peace. If there was any doubt, the matter had been laid to rest by subsequent amendments to the Justices of the Peace Act[338] which had, for example, abolished the ''piece-work'' fee system. Justices of the peace were subject to the direction of provincial court judges, who had themselves been declared impartial and independent.

In *Davies* (1990),[339] Provincial Court Judge Young held that the current Ontario system for the appointment, training and supervision of justices of the peace was adequate to ensure an accused charged with a provincial offence a trial before an independent and impartial tribunal, even if the justice was not a lawyer. The Court concluded by adopting a dictum of MacKinnon A.C.J.O.:

> It might be better if all justices of the peace were legally trained with so many years at the bar so that when they are appointed it is clear that they are, on the surface at least competent to deal with all legal issues. But that involves policy considerations which a court cannot force on a Legislature. The fact that such appointments might be preferable even though much of what they are called on to do would not require such training, does not make the present practice improper.[340]

In 1996[341] the Ontario Court of Appeal quickly rejected a challenge that the accused charged with violations of the Occupational Health and Safety Act of Ontario[342] were entitled to a trial before a provincial court judge rather than a justice of the peace because the latter lacked competence. The Court, noting revised methods of appointment, training, supervision and education, held that the system was not institutionally and structurally flawed as to lead to an unfair trial. The Court added that the co-ordinate jurisdiction did not give rise to an inference that there was a different level of competence although it made administrative sense to have more complex cases heard by justices more senior

---

[335] (1984), 13 C.C.C. (3d) 35 (Ont. H.C.).

[336] Ewaschuk J.'s ruling was followed by de Weerdt J. in *Walton* (1984), 15 C.C.C. (3d) 65 (N.W.T. S.C.).

[337] (1984), 16 C.C.C. (3d) 193 (Ont. C.A.), applied in *Re St. Marys Cement Corp.* (1996), 106 C.C.C. (3d) 21 (Ont. C.A.). See too similarly *Valois* (1986), 33 C.C.C. (3d) 535 (Que. C.A.) and *Isaac* (1989), 47 C.C.C. (3d) 353 (B.C. S.C.).

[338] S.O. 1984, c. 8.

[339] (1990), 56 C.C.C. (3d) 321 (Ont. Prov. Ct.).

[340] *Ibid.*, at 329.

[341] *Eton Construction Co.* (1996), 106 C.C.C. (3d) 21 (Ont. C.A.).

[342] R.S.O. 1980, c. 321.

in the hierarchy. The end result here is a most pragmatic acceptance that a trial of a serious provincial matter could well be judged by a non-lawyer. Even if there is no Charter protection, the situation is surely far from satisfactory. The rule of law demands more.

Especially given the difficulty of making valid distinctions between criminal and penal law, it is disappointing that the courts have not seized the opportunity under s. 11(d) to ensure that there can be no possibility of trials taking place before judges who lack training in fundamental legal principles. Professor Alan Mewett has suggested that the provinces should be moving to a goal of having all judges trying offences legally qualified. In the meantime

> it would not be difficult and not impossibly expensive to give all accused persons, charged with provincial offences the right to be tried before a judge who is legally trained — in practice, one assumes, a provincial court judge, until such time as justices of the peace are either required or encouraged to be so trained.[343]

6. SECTION 11(e): RIGHT "NOT TO BE DENIED REASONABLE BAIL WITHOUT JUST CAUSE"

In 1971 the term "bail" was removed from the Criminal Code with the passage of substantial new provisions relating to release from custody entitled the Bail Reform Act.[344] The principal aim of this major Parliamentary effort was to encourage release of those arrested pending trial. It had been well documented that few of those arrested were in fact released until their first court appearance.[345] Arresting officers and officers in charge of the lock-up were given express and wide powers to release.[346] For those accused still detained there was no longer a bail hearing in which the accused applied and sought to persuade the justice to release. Under the new provisions there are show cause hearings at which there is under s. 515 an onus on the Crown to show cause why the accused should not be released.

(a) Grounds for Release

Under the Bail Reform Act provisions, detention could only be justified at a show cause hearing upon either a specified primary or secondary ground. Under s. 515(10) of the Criminal Code:

> For the purposes of this section, the detention of an accused in custody is justified only on either of the following grounds:

---

[343] Editorial, "Legally Trained Judges" (1990), 33 *Crim. L.Q.* 1 at 2. See Anthony Dool, Patricia Baranek and Susan Addario, *Understanding Justices — A Study of Canadian Justices of the Peace* (1991).

[344] S.C. 1970-71-72, c. 37. See generally Gary Trotter, *The Law of Bail in Canada* (2nd ed., 1999).

[345] M. Friedland, *Detention Before Trial* (1965) had found the figure for Toronto to be 84% of those arrested. At the time the police power to release was unclear: *Debot* (1987), 54 C.R. (3d) 120 at 137-138 (Ont. C.A.).

[346] Sections 495(2), 497-499.

(a) on the primary ground that his detention is necessary to ensure his attendance in court in order to be dealt with according to law; and

(b) on the secondary ground (the applicability of which shall be determined only in the event that and after it is determined that his detention is not justified on the primary ground referred to in paragraph (a)) that his detention is necessary in the public interest or for the protection or safety of the public, having regard to all the circumstances including any substantial likelihood that the accused will, if he is released from custody, commit a criminal offence or an interference with the administration of justice.

In *Pearson* (1992),[347] Lamer C.J., speaking for the Supreme Court,[348] announced important new Charter standards for bail. Section 11(e) was held to guarantee separate rights to

1. "Reasonable bail" : the terms of bail such as quantum and restrictions must be reasonable; and

2. No denial of bail without "just cause": denials must be only in a narrow set of circumstances, necessary to promote the proper functioning of the bail system and not undertaken for a purpose extraneous to that system.[349]

There is a dearth of authority applying the first aspect of *Pearson*, although the dicta should be powerful allies to defence counsel. However, long before *Pearson* and shortly after the Charter was proclaimed, District Court Judge Vannini decided in *Fraser* (1982)[350] that imposing a condition of release which the accused would be unable to meet was a denial of his constitutional right to reasonable bail. In that case a condition requiring a sister to post a bond of $1,000 cash was changed to require no deposit of surety.

In practice, most contested show cause hearings turned on the primary ground that detention was justified to ensure attendance in court or on the secondary ground referring to the safety of the public, having regard to the substantial likelihood that the accused would commit a criminal offence or interfere with the administration of justice. On occasion, usually as a last ditch stand, the Crown came to rely on the much more general secondary ground that detention is necessary in the "public interest." Reliance was often based on a strong passage by an Ontario High Court Judge, Lerner J. in *Powers* (1972):[351]

"Public interest" involves many considerations, not the least of which is the "public image" of the Criminal Code, the Bail Reform Act amendments, the apprehension and conviction of criminals, the attempts at deterrence of crime, and ultimately the protection of that overwhelming percentage of citizens of Canada who are not only socially conscious but law-abiding. This cannot be emphasized too strongly. Much has been written in the public press about the attitude of citizens, juries, law

---

[347] (1992), 17 C.R. (4th) 1 (S.C.C.). See discussion by Gary Trotter, "Pearson and Morales: Distilling the Right to Bail", (1993) 17 C.R. (4th) 150.

[348] Sopinka, Iacobucci, Gonthier, and L'Heureux-Dubé JJ. concurred. McLachlin J.'s dissent is confined to the question of onus, discussed below note 386.

[349] At 57, 60.

[350] (1982), 38 O.R. (2d) 172 (Dist. Ct.).

[351] (1972), 20 C.R.N.S. 23 (Ont. H.C.).

enforcement officers (who some seem to forget are also citizens in our society) concerning accused persons being released and subsequently arrested on allegations of commission of further offences. When weighing the *rights* of the accused in the context that he should not be improperly detained or discriminated against, one is also mindful of the *rights* of the community and remember that in the "public interest" the scales not be tipped in the other direction to the extent that the citizen may, in wonderment and bewilderment, feel that the application of our criminal laws (bail provisions) is a mockery or at least not being administered realistically or in the public interest.[352]

Mr. Justice Baudouin for the Quebec Court of Appeal in *Lamothe* (1990)[353] turned in part to both the presumption of innocence and s. 11(e) to assert a quite different view of the public interest:

With respect to the perception of the public, as we know, a large part of the Canadian public often adopts a negative and even emotional attitude towards criminals or powerful criminals. The public wants to see itself protected, see criminals in prison and see them punished severely. To get rid of a criminal is to get rid of crime. It perceives the judicial system harshly and the administration of justice in general as too indulgent, too soft, too good to the criminal. This perception, almost visceral in respect of crime, is surely not the perception which a judge must have in deciding the issue of interim release. ... [The] perception of the pubic must be situated at another level, that of a public reasonably informed about our system of criminal law and capable of judging and perceiving without emotion that the application of the presumption of innocence, even with respect to interim release, has the effect that people, who may later be found guilty of even serious crimes, will be released for the period between the time of their arrest and the time of their trial. In other words, the criterion of the public perception must not be that of the lowest common denominator. An informed public understands that there exists in Canada a constitutionally guaranteed presumption of innocence (*s. 11(d) of the Charter*) and the right not to be denied reasonable bail without just cause (*s. 11(e) of the Charter*).[354]

When the Supreme Court came to consider the "public interest" ground of detention in *Morales* (1992),[355] it did not choose between these interpretations of s. 515(10)(b). Instead Chief Justice Lamer, for a 5-2 majority,[356] decided that this ground of detention violated s.11(e) because it did not meet the Court's test for vagueness.[357] According to the majority the term "public interest" was incapable of framing the legal debate in any meaningful way or structuring discretion. "Public interest" permitted a

standardless sweep, as the court can order imprisonment whenever it sees fit[358]

and no amount of judicial interpretation

---

[352] *Ibid.*, at 36.
[353] (1990), 58 C.C.C. (3d) 530 (Que. C.A.).
[354] *Ibid.*, at 541-542. Monet and McCarthy JJ.A. concurred. Baudouin J.A. also invoked in aid the Supreme Court of Canada's ruling in *Collins*, above note 242 concerning disrepute of the justice system for the purposes of s. 24(2) — see below, Chapter 11.
[355] (1992), 17 C.R. (4th) 74 (S.C.C.).
[356] La Forest, Sopinka, McLachlin and Iacobucci JJ. concurred. Gonthier J. (L'Heureux-Dubé J. concurring) dissented.
[357] The ruling is discussed above Chapter 2.
[358] At 95.

would be capable of rendering it a provision which gives any guidance for legal debate.[359]

The ruling appears surprising,[360] given the Court's conservatism on claims of vagueness[361] and the Quebec Court of Appeal's interpretation, which was in line with Charter values. The striking down of the public interest ground for denial of bail in *Morales*[362] was welcome. The problem with pre-trial detention on the ground of public interest is that detention can so easily be based on a judge's personal abhorrence for a particular crime or the manner in which it was committed. However five years later Parliament chose to re-enact a revised version of such a ground.[363] Section 515(10) no longer uses the terms primary and secondary grounds and now includes a new independent ground for detention in s. 515(10)(c):

> (c) on any other just cause being shown and, without limiting the generality of the foregoing, where the detention is necessary in order to maintain confidence in the administration of justice, having regard to all the circumstances, including the apparent strength of the prosecution's case, the gravity of the nature of the offence, the circumstances surrounding its commission and the potential for a lengthy term of imprisonment.

On the issue of vagueness, commentators[364] agree that this provision is inconsistent with *Morales* and should be struck down. Professor Gary Trotter suggests, after examining judicial interpretations of the new s. 515(10)(c), that the criterion of public confidence is as vague as that of public interest. He further suggests that the umbrella phrase "on any other cause being shown, and without limiting the generality of the foregoing" makes this tertiary ground even broader.[365]

The vagueness challenge has however already been rejected by two Courts of Appeal. In *McDougal* (1999)[366] the B.C. Court of Appeal held that Parliament had not left the legal profession and the judiciary without a road map to use in the interpretation of the section. By delineating the list of relevant factors to be considered in the section under review, Parliament had provided sufficient direction to afford guidance for informed legal debate. The provision was neither vague nor overbroad. The Court added that if the phrase "any other just cause",

---

[359] *Ibid.*

[360] See too Trotter, above note 344. Trotter also criticises the outcome, noting that justices are under a duty to act fairly and in the public interest and can be reviewed.

[361] See Chapter 2.

[362] (1992), 17 C.R. (4th) 74 (S.C.C.).

[363] *Criminal Law Improvement Act*, S.C. 1996-1997, c. 18. This was part of an omnibus bill. This amendment had been requested by various provinces at a 1993 Uniform Law conference: see *Hall*, reported below note 367. There appears to be no record of evidence that the bail system was working badly without the public interest ground.

[364] Gary Trotter, *The Law of Bail in Canada* (2nd ed., 1999) pp. 23-26, 159-165; Trotter, "Pearson and Morales: Distilling the Right to Bail", (1993) 17 C.R. (4th) 150 and Louis Strezos, "Section 515(10)(c) of the Criminal Code: Resurrecting the Unconstitutional Denial of Bail", (1998) 11 C.R. (5th) 43.

[365] At pp. 161-164.

[366] (1999), 27 C.R. (5th) 340 (B.C. C.A.).

divorced from what follows in the section, was overbroad, the simple remedy would be to read down the section so that only the stipulated considerations could or would result in a finding of "just cause" for ordering detention. The Court could not however envisage a situation of "just cause" that would not need to be underpinned by the listed considerations in s. 515(10)(c).

In the first degree murder case of *Hall* (2000)[367] the Ontario Court of Appeal similarly ruled that s. 515(10)(c) was neither vague nor overbroad. The expression "confidence in the administration of justice" in s. 515(10)(c) is seen to provide a workable standard especially since Parliament has identified specific factors to be considered. The Court refused to consider the umbrella phrase "any other just cause" because that part of the section had not been relied on by the judge in detaining the accused.

Both the B.C. and Ontario Courts gloss over the ruling in *Heywood*[368] that an overbreadth challenge is distinct from one of vagueness. This is important because the *Heywood* overbroad test of whether a measure is wider than necessary to achieve its objective is much easier to satisfy than the *Nova Scotia Pharmaceutical Society*[369] test for vagueness of whether there is sufficient room for legal debate.

The reticence in both Courts of Appeal to strike down at least the umbrella clause seems to show a reluctance to uphold Charter standards declared by the Supreme Court. Surely, if the issue is vagueness or overbreadth, the whole section is to be considered otherwise the consideration is blinkered and distorted. On the narrow approach of the Ontario Court, the umbrella clause will only be reviewable where a bail judge expressly rests on it. Reasons given at show cause hearings are often enigmatic and the approach in *Hall* may well insulate the section from proper review. Courts are the guardians of the Constitution and should not be bending over backwards to sidestep fully developed and presented Charter challenges. The process of review is difficult, as illustrated in *Hall*, which involved a *habeas corpus* application and an appeal.

In *Hall*, the Ontario Court of Appeal also rejected an alternate Charter challenge that s. 515(10)(c) was unconstitutional because *Morales* and *Pearson* had implicitly decided that the only constitutional bases for detention were those of a risk of not attending and public safety now set out in subsections (a) and (b). The grounds of just cause for detention, held the Court, were not frozen and Parliament had clearly intended there to be three grounds for detention. Section 515(c) met the *Pearson* tests. The ground was confined to a narrow set of circumstances and maintaining the confidence of the public in the administration of justice was not a purpose extraneous to the proper functioning of the bail system.

It is most unfortunate that the Court in *Hall* was largely content with linguistic analysis and chose not to address broader bases presented to it on this further Charter challenge. The Court, which had reserved for over five months, had before

---

[367] (2000), 35 C.R. (5th) 201 (Ont. C.A.).
[368] (1994), 34 C.R. (4th) 133 (S.C.C.).
[369] (1992), 15 C.R. (4th) 1 (S.C.C.).

it material[370] to indicate that there is nothing in the legislative history of the Bail Reform Act, the common law or the jurisprudence of other countries, including the United States, that would support grounds of detention other than those respecting the risk of non-attendance or the maintenance of public safety. The Court also had before it mounting empirical studies of negative effects of pre-trial detention in Canada,[371] which include serious allegations of systemic racism in the operation of the bail system in Toronto. That the Court chose to not even refer to such material does no credit to the institution of the Court of Appeal of Ontario. The studies were surely significant to an assessment of the validity of both Charter challenges.

In the case of applications for bail following conviction and pending appeal under s. 679(3)(c) of the Criminal Code, "public interest" is one of the criteria for release. Several Courts of Appeal have held that for these purposes the test is *not* unconstitutionally vague.[372] *Morales* has been distinguished on the basis the constitutional right to bail under s. 11(e) rests on the presumption of innocence which is spent by conviction.[373] Any protection is to be found in s. 7. At this point "public interest" is seen to be an intelligible standard under which to maintain confidence in the administration of justice. The Saskatchewan Court of Appeal,[374] however, held that s. 679(7) of the Criminal Code was unconstitutional as a result of *Morales* to the extent it made "public interest" the ground of detention where a conviction had been quashed and a new trial ordered.

(b) Reverse Onuses[375]

After only four years experience with the Bail Reform Act, Parliament introduced a number of changes. It specifically provided in what is now s. 522 that an accused charged with murder has the burden of showing cause why detention and custody is not justified on the primary or secondary grounds.

In *Pugsley* (1982),[376] the Nova Scotia Court of Appeal saw this reverse onus on the accused as a very substantial burden to show cause on a balance of probabilities. The Court read s. 11(e) as making it clear that an accused was entitled to reasonable bail unless the Crown could show just cause for detention.

---

[370] The Court was referred to Trotter's comprehensive text and Strezos, the author of the article referred to above, was counsel for an intervenor, the Criminal Lawyer's Association of Ontario.

[371] See especially Trotter, pp. 31-50, and *Report of the Commission on Systemic Racism in the Ontario Criminal Justice System* (1995) ch. 55. See now too Report of the National Council of Welfare, *Justice and the Poor* (2000) pp. 28-50, documenting disadvantages experienced by low income Canadians in every aspect of our bail system. This was the very reason Parliament passed the Bail Reform Act in 1972.

[372] *Farinacci* (1993), 25 C.R. (4th) 350 (Ont. C.A.), and *Branco* (1993), 25 C.R. (4th) 370 (B.C. C.A.).

[373] Section 11(e) does apply after conviction but before sentencing: *Hrynkiw* (1999), 134 C.C.C. (3d) 349 (Ont. Gen. Div.) and to one cited for *in facie* contempt: *Rudko* (1999), 28 C.R. (5th) 375 (Alta. Q.B.).

[374] *Sutherland* (1994), 30 C.R. (4th) 265 (Sask. C.A.).

[375] See further Trotter, pp. 207-221.

[376] (1982), 31 C.R. (3d) 217 (N.S. C.A.).

The reverse onus was a "glaring inconsistency" with s. 11(e) and had to be declared of no force or effect.[377]

Pugsley was not followed by the Ontario Court of Appeal in *Bray* (1983).[378] Mr. Justice Martin for the Court held that s. 11(e) "does not address the issue of onus and says nothing about onus."[379] If there had been a conflict with s. 11(e), the reverse onus would have been demonstrably justified as a reasonable limit under s. 1. The reverse onus only required the accused to satisfy the judge on a balance of probabilities that detention was justified on either the primary or secondary ground, a burden which was rationally in the accused's power to discharge.[380]

Although the *Bray* view has been followed in Quebec[381] its premises seem suspect. Professor Ron Delisle has put this well:

> Although s. 11(e) does not explicitly refer to onus, is there not by implication a logical requirement that the person who charges another with an offence should have the onus of establishing just cause for his detention? By the Court's literal reading of s. 11(e), the effect of the section is changed from "no person shall be detained without just cause" to "a person can be detained unless there is just cause for his release."[382]

In the 1976 amendments[383] Parliament also enacted four other reverse onus clauses in what is now s. 515(6). The accused must show cause for release when charged with an indictable offence or a bail abuse offence allegedly committed while at large awaiting trial on another offence (subsections (a) and (c)), or where the charge is an indictable offence and the accused is not ordinarily resident in Canada (subsection (b)) and finally when the accused is charged with certain offences under the Narcotics Control Act (subsection (d)).

Two of these reverse onus provisions have been upheld as constitutional by the Supreme Court of Canada. In *Morales* (1992),[384] the Court was unanimous in upholding s. 515(6)(a) (applying to accused committing indictable offences while on bail) and in *Pearson* (1992)[385] a 5-2 majority held that the reverse onus for narcotics traffickers in s. 515(6)(d) also survived Charter review.

Chief Justice Lamer for the Court decided in *Pearson* that s. 11(d) did not exhaust the presumption of innocence. That presumption was a principle of fundamental justice applying at all stages of the trial. However, here the reverse onus challenges fell to be considered under s. 11(e) which offered a "highly specific guarantee" which covered the complaint.[386] Both reverse onuses were

---

[377] *Ibid.*, at 222.

[378] (1983), 32 C.R. (3d) 316 (Ont. C.A.).

[379] *Ibid.*, at 320.

[380] *Ibid.*, at 321.

[381] *Dubois (No. 2)* (1983), 8 C.C.C. (3d) 344 (Que. S.C.) and see *Lamothe*, above note 353, where the Quebec Court of Appeal accepted the reverse onus as a given.

[382] "Annotation to *R. v. Bray*" (1983), 32 C.R. (3d) 317.

[383] S.C. 1974-75-76, c. 93, s. 47.

[384] Above note 355.

[385] Above note 347.

[386] At 56. The ruling in *Bray* is overruled to the extent that it denies that s. 11(e) engages the presumption of innocence.

justified as narrow and necessary special bail rules where the normal system did not function properly.[387]

The ruling in *Pearson* is particularly disappointing.[388] It proceeded in the face of an extraordinarily conscientiousness judgment of Mr. Justice Proulx of the Quebec Court of Appeal in the Court below. The Quebec Court had noted that no discretion was given to the judge to consider the circumstances of the case, such as the quantity of the drugs involved or the degree of participation. It was arbitrary, unjust and discriminatory to require that every person accused of trafficking in narcotics had to establish that detention was not necessary. Lamer C.J.[389] recognized that the onus also applied to "soft" drugs, "small fry" drug dealers and the "generous smoker". However, such persons would normally have no difficulty justifying their release.[390] Pointing to evidence from the United States and Australia, the Chief Justice nevertheless held that the special rule was justified as drugs offences had special characteristics. Trafficking in narcotics was often a highly sophisticated commercial operation which would create incentives for offenders to continue criminal behaviour even after arrest and release on bail. McLachlin J., with the concurrence of La Forest J., persuasively find the data provided by the majority provide no justification for denying bail to the many "small-time" drugs traffickers. The violation of s. 11(e) could not be justified as it did nothing to promote the objectives of the section, which was aimed at repeat or absconding offenders.

The 1995 *Report of the Commission on Systemic Racism in the Ontario Criminal Justice System* found[391] that the practical effect of the reverse onus to show cause for pre-trial release for accused charged with trafficking or importing narcotics is to imprison small-scale offenders and also to result in racism. The black pre-trial admission rate for drug trafficking/importing charges was 27 times higher than the white rate. The Report persuasively suggests that the majority ruling in *Pearson* that the reverse onus was constitutional was based on incomplete data and should be reconsidered.

Unless reconsidered, *Pearson* stands as a strong precedent for the reversal of the onus at show cause hearings for a particular offence. Given *Pearson*, it is not surprising that the Nova Scotia Court of Appeal reversed its previous decision in *Pugsley* to reinstate the reverse onus for murder.[392] If a reverse onus is justifiable for narcotics and murder, why stop there? What, for example, of domestic assault or even all violent offences? In 1997, Parliament, far from responding to the above documentation of systemic racism, pressed on with a reverse onus for all drug

---

[387] *Morales* at 104; *Pearson* at 60.

[388] See too Trotter, above note 364, and Rosemary Cairns Way, "Developments in Criminal Law and Procedure. The 1992-93 Term", (1994) 5 *Sup. Ct. Rev.* 113 at 159-165, and Graeme G. Mitchell, "Significant Developments in Criminal Charter Jurisprudence in 1992," (1993) 57 *Sask. L. Rev.* 59 at 94-95.

[389] At 60-64.

[390] Trotter, above note 364, retorts, "This may be so, but the point is that they should not be required to do so" (at 152).

[391] At p. 158.

[392] *Sanchez* (1999), 24 C.R. (5th) 330 (N.S. C.A.).

traffickers[393] and another for those charged with the new offence of participating in a criminal organisation.[394] With each addition the Bail Reform Act is fundamentally weakened. The Supreme Court should reverse itself and be much more resistant to arguments for exceptions. A further consideration is that there was insufficient evidence placed before Parliament in 1976 to justify any of the reverse onuses.[395]

(c) Procedure at Show Cause Hearing

Under what is now s. 518(1)(b) an accused at a show cause hearing

> shall not be examined or cross-examined by the justice or any other person respecting the offence with which he is charged, and no inquiries shall be made of him respecting that offence.

This prohibition has, not surprisingly, been held[396] to apply to the defence counsel as well as to prosecutors and justices. One can well understand the need to protect an accused at this early stage, where guilt is not in issue, from the risk of giving incriminating answers at a stage where the accused might not have had an opportunity for full consultation with counsel. However, the reason for the absolute ban on questions by defence counsel is obscure.

Potential unfairness to the accused increased when s. 518(1)(c)(iv) was added to make it clear that the prosecutor may lead evidence

> to show the circumstances of the alleged offence, particularly as they relate to the probability of conviction of the accused.

Although the strength of the case may be crucial on the very issue of whether the accused is to be released, the accused cannot testify as to the weakness of the case.

In *Millar* (1983),[397] Barrett-Joncas J. of the Quebec Superior Court held that s. 518(1)(b) was invalid as "it clearly contravenes the *audi alteram partem* rule which is an elementary principle of fundamental justice"[398] guaranteed by s. 7 of the Charter. The defence counsel (but presumably still not the justice or the prosecutor) could examine the accused as to the offence. *Millar* concerned a murder show cause hearing where there was a reverse onus. A reverse onus would appear to make the unfairness of s. 518(1)(b) more palpable. However, it is difficult to see why the *Millar* ruling should not also apply to the normal case where there is no reverse onus.

Millar was indeed applied in *T.B.B.* (1988),[399] which did not involve a reverse onus situation. The Court held that s. 518(1)(b) was a valid protection to the

---

[393] Section 515(6)(d), with the passage of the Controlled Drugs and Substances Act.
[394] Section 515(6)(a)(ii).
[395] See further Trotter, above note 364.
[396] *Paonessa* (1982), 27 C.R. (3d) 179 (Ont. C.A.).
[397] (1983), 36 C.R. (3d) 102 (Que. S.C.).
[398] *Ibid.*, at 104.
[399] (1988), 62 C.R. (3d) 306 (Ont. Prov. Ct.).

accused against inquiry by the justice or Crown. However it was inoperative where the accused waived the protection and sought to introduce the evidence.

7. SECTION 11(f): RIGHT "EXCEPT IN THE CASE OF AN OFFENCE UNDER MILITARY LAW TRIED BEFORE A MILITARY TRIBUNAL TO THE BENEFIT OF TRIAL BY JURY WHERE THE MAXIMUM PUNISHMENT FOR THE OFFENCE IS IMPRISONMENT FOR FIVE YEARS OR A MORE SEVERE PUNISHMENT"

This right is a new constitutional right. There was no counterpart under the Canadian Bill of Rights. Although our courts frequently refer in glowing terms to the fundamental nature of the right to a jury trial[400] decisions under s. 11(f) have, in general, been most conservative.

(a) Non-Applicability

The Charter confers s. 11 rights to "any person" charged with an offence. In *P.P.G. Industries* (1983),[401] the majority of the British Columbia Court of Appeal held that a corporation did not have a right to a jury trial under s. 11(f). According to Chief Justice Nemetz, in the context of s. 11(f) "person" had to be interpreted as a "natural person" since it was only such natural persons who could be subjected to imprisonment for five years or more. Since ss. 7, 8, 9, 10 and 12 used the word "everyone" and ss. 13 and 14 "witness" or "party and witness",[402] it must have been intended that the words "any person" in s. 11 had a more restricted meaning.[403] Mr. Justice Anderson also applied a contextual rather than literal approach to interpretation in holding that the jury clause was not intended to include artificial persons and only applied to persons who might upon conviction be actually sentenced to a term of imprisonment for five years or more.[404] In dissent, Mr. Justice Seaton saw no need to tamper with the "straightforward" words of the Charter. Section 11(f) addressed the harm of persons being convicted of serious offences without trial by jury. The rights should be held equally applicable to corporate persons.[405]

Section 11(f) specifically removes the right to a jury trial from those charged with "an offence under military law tried before a military tribunal." The exemption has survived Charter challenge.[406] It makes it quite clear that other

---

[400] See, for example, *Sherratt* (1991), 3 C.R. (4th) 129 (S.C.C.) and *Bryant* (1984), 16 C.C.C. (3d) 408 (Ont. C.A.) (a generous ruling on s. 11(f), now overruled: see *Lee,* below note 439).

[401] (1983), 3 C.C.C. (3d) 97 (B.C. C.A.).

[402] *Ibid.,* at 103-104.

[403] *Ibid.,* at 113.

[404] *Ibid.,* at 108-109.

[405] *Ibid.,* at 108.

[406] *Brown* (1995), 35 C.R. (4th) 318 (Court Martial Appeal Court). The Court also rejected a challenge based on the presumption of innocence against the Court Martial being able to each a verdict by a simple majority. Both rulings are criticized in an annotation by Guy Cournoyer, C.R. (4th), *ibid.,* pp. 319-321.

Charter rights apply to such military trials. In *Macdonald* (1983),[407] a Court Marshal Appeal Court[408] held that an "offence under military law" under s. 11(f) had to fall within the letter of the National Defence Act[409] and have a "real military *nexus*."[410] A charge of trafficking in marijuana based on the sale by the accused serviceman to another did have such a military *nexus* as illegal drug use by service personnel entailed serious disciplinary considerations. It was of little moment that the serviceman had been off-duty and the sale was off the base.

No authority is given for the nexus requirement. It probably stems from a constitutional doctrine that where military and civilian justice systems overlap the civilian criminal courts are paramount. The leading decision is that of the Supreme Court of Canada in *MacKay* (1980).[411] The widely applied *nexus* theory actually rests on the minority judgment of Mr. Justice McIntyre.[412] It has been soundly criticized.[413]

In *Genest* (1990),[414] the Quebec Court of Appeal thankfully held that s. 11(f) had not fixed the composition of the jury at 12 *men*, as was the case at common law. Section 644(2) of the Criminal Code allowing the trial judge to discharge up to two jurors and continue the trial did not violate s. 11(f).

(b) Five Years or More Punishment

In *B. (S.)* (1982),[415] Bouck J. of the British Columbia Supreme Court found the Juvenile Delinquents Act[416] unconstitutional to the extent that it denied a juvenile's right under s. 11(f) to a jury trial. A juvenile, aged 12, was charged with the delinquency of having committed break and entry, wilfully setting fire and wilful damage to property. The judge pointed out that the juvenile could be committed to an industrial school until he was 21 years of age and therefore faced a potential nine years of incarceration. This ruling was, however, reversed by the British Columbia Court of Appeal.[417] For the Court, Mr. Justice Anderson held that a commitment to an industrial school for five years or more did not mean that the juvenile was subject to *punishment* by way of imprisonment. The whole purpose of the Act was not to punish but to provide treatment. The child was not be dealt with as an offender but as a delinquent requiring help and guidance.

---

[407] (1983), 6 C.C.C. (3d) 551 (Ct. Martial App. Ct.).

[408] Per Mahoney J. Rutherford and Goodridge JJ. concurred.

[409] R.S.C. 1970, C. N-4.

[410] Above note 407, at 555.

[411] (1980), 54 C.C.C. (2d) 129 (S.C.C.).

[412] Dickson J. concurred.

[413] See Kenneth W. Watkin, *Canadian Military Justice: Summary Proceedings and the Charter* (1990), unpublished LL.M. thesis, Queen's University, chap. 4.

[414] (1990), 61 C.C.C. (3d) 251 (Que. CA.). For consideration of successful s. 15 challenges against Criminal Code provisions for six-person juries in the Yukon and in the Northwest Territories, see below, Chapter 10.

[415] (1982), 30 C.R. (3d) 226 (B.C. S.C.).

[416] R.S.C. 1970, c. J-3 (repealed S.C. 1980-81-82-83, c. 110).

[417] (1983), 33 C.R. (3d) 33 (B.C. C.A.).

The reasoning of the British Columbia Court of Appeal was adopted by its counterpart in Ontario.[418] It is, however, most unconvincing.[419] That a process of labelling should not be used to avoid a serious question of the civil rights of a child was well addressed by Justice Fortas, for the United States Supreme Court in *Re Gault* (1987):[420]

> It is of no constitutional consequence — and of limited practical meaning — that the institution to which he is committed is called an Industrial School. The fact of the matter is that, however euphemistic the title, a "receiving home" or an "industrial school" for juveniles is an institution of confinement in which the child is incarcerated for a greater or lesser time. His world becomes "a building with whitewashed walls, regimented routine and institutional hours. . ." Instead of mother and father and sisters and brothers and friends and classmates, his world is peopled by guards, custodians, state employees, and "delinquents" confined with him for anything from waywardness to rape to homicide.[421]

Equally impressive, the trial judge in *B. (S.)* said simply "a jail is a jail."[422]

The Juvenile Delinquents Act[423] has now been replaced by the Young Offenders Act,[424] under which the maximum disposition is normally three years in custody. There is therefore no Charter right to a jury trial in a youth court, although a youth will have a right to a jury trial if transferred to adult court.[425] Although the Charter issue is moot there is still an important issue of whether young offenders, so broadly defined under the Act as those under 18, should be deprived of the right to be tried before their peers, even in the case of serious offences.

Although it is now usually accepted[426] that a citation for contempt of court amounts to a charge of an offence which will trigger s. 11 rights, it would appear that the right to a jury trial under s. 11(f) will only apply if the contempt is proceeded with by way of indictment rather than by way of summary conviction proceedings. According to the Ontario Court of Appeal,[427] s. 11(f) does not apply to contempt proceeded with by way of summary conviction since at common law it is not an offence punishable by a sentence of five years or more. The Manitoba Court of Appeal[428] however excludes s. 11(f), and indeed all of s. 11, on a much broader basis:

---

[418] *T. (D.)* (1984), 39 C.R. (3d) 95 (Ont. C.A.).

[419] Nick Bala "Jury Trial for Juveniles? No Charter Right," (1984) 37 C.R. (3d) 30 also criticizes the reasoning of the British Columbia Court of Appeal but supports the decision on the basis of practical considerations and other legal barriers to jury trials within the J.D.A.

[420] 387 U.S. 1(1987).

[421] *Ibid.*, at 27.

[422] Above note 415, at 232. See similarly the overruled trial judge, Beaulieu P.J., in *T. (D.)* (1983), 37 C.R. (3d) 19 (Ont. Fam. Ct.).

[423] Above note 416.

[424] R.S.C. 1985, c. Y-1. Confirmed by *B. (S.)* (1989), 72 C.R. (3d) 117 (Sask. C.A.).

[425] In *L. (R.)* (1986), 52 C.R. (3d) 209 (Ont. C.A.), it was held that the denial of the right to jury in youth court did not violate the right to equality under s. 15. See below, Chapter 10 and criticism of R.E. Charney, "R.L. Bootstrap Equality", C.R. *ibid.*, p. 232.

[426] *Sed contra Laurendeau* (1983), 9 C.C.C. (3d) 206 (Que. S.C.), appeal dismissed on jurisdictional grounds (1983), 9 C.C.C. (3d) 206 (Que. C.A.).

[427] *Cohn*, above note 255.

[428] *Manitoba (A.G.) v. Groupe Quebecor Inc.*, above note 4.

A contempt of court may well involve an interruption of court proceedings which must be dealt with immediately and expeditiously by the presiding judge. When a witness refuses to respond to legitimate questions, the threat of contempt is to persuade the witness to co-operate so that the business of the court may proceed. To hold that the reluctant witness is entitled to a jury trial to determine whether he has committed contempt of court, would frustrate the inherent power of the court to control the proper administration of the criminal justice system. In my view, s. 11 of the Charter was not meant to include contempt proceedings.[429]

(c) Criminal Code Restrictions on Right to Trial By Jury

Under the Criminal Code the accused only has a right to elect trial by jury in the case of proceedings on indictment not in the absolute jurisdiction of the provincial court.[430] The Charter right to a jury under s. 11(f) is not applicable to proceedings by way of summary conviction (where the maximum imprisonment sentence is usually six months)[431] or proceedings on indictment where the maximum penalty is less than five years' imprisonment. In the case of hybrid offences the Crown has an unfettered discretion to proceed by way of indictment or summary conviction proceedings. Where the Crown chooses to proceed by way of summary conviction proceedings the accused no longer has a right to choose trial by jury.

In *Desroches* (1985)[432] the accused was charged with a hybrid offence where the indictable alternative had a maximum penalty of five years in jail. The Crown elected to proceed by way of summary conviction. Ontario Provincial Court Judge Clendenning held that the accused had a s. 11(f) right to choose trial by jury. Noting that the Interpretation Act[433] deemed an offence to be indictable "if the enactment provides that the offence may be prosecuted for the offence by indictment" and referring to the wide dictionary definition of "charge", he held the legislation conferring the prosecutorial discretion in the particular case had to be declared inoperative. This order was, however, quashed by a judge of the Ontario Supreme Court,[434] a ruling confirmed by the Ontario Court of Appeal.[435] The Court of Appeal reasoned that s. 11(f) "arises from and is based upon the potential penalty" and that election to proceed by indictment "at the time of arraignment crystallizes that right." Peter Rosenthal[436] has argued cogently that the right under s. 11(f) is conferred immediately on being charged and that the Ontario Court of Appeal's interpretation is not "generous" in measuring the potential penalty at a point later than that specified in the Charter. There is,

---

[429] *Ibid.*, at 428 (per Huband J.A.).

[430] Section 536.

[431] Section 787. In 1994, Parliament raised the maximum for certain offences, including assault causing bodily harm and sexual assault to 18 months.

[432] Ont. Prov. Ct., April 11, 1985, unreported, reviewed by Peter Rosenthal, "Crown Election Offences and the Charter," (1990) 33 *Crim. L.Q.* 84 at 117-119.

[433] R.S.C. 1985, c. I-21, s. 34(1)(a).

[434] Ont. H.C., May 24, 1985, unreported (per Fitzpatrick J.), reviewed by Rosenthal, above note 432, at 119.

[435] Ont. C.A., January 30, 1986, unreported, reviewed by Rosenthal, above note 432, at 119.

[436] Above note 432, pp. 120-121.

however, a pragmatic consideration: the more generous interpretation would give an accused an entitlement to a trial by jury in cases where, even if there were proceedings by indictment, there would in reality be no possibility whatsoever of anything approaching a five year prison sentence.[437]

Some Criminal Code provisions expressly remove the accused's right to elect trial by jury. Examples are some provisions restricting reelections[438] and s. 598, which declares that one who absconds from a jury trial may not later choose trial before judge and jury unless the accused establishes that there was a legitimate excuse for his failure to appear or to remain at his previous trial.

In *Lee* (1989),[439] the Supreme Court of Canada determined that s. 598 violated s. 11(f)[440] but the majority went on to hold that the restriction was a demonstrably justified reasonable limit under s. 1. The Court agreed that the purpose of the section extended beyond punishment to ''protect the administration of justice from delay, inconvenience, expense and abuse, and to secure the respect of the public for the criminal trial process.''[441]

For the majority, Mr. Justice Lamer[442] held that this purpose was of sufficient importance to warrant overriding the constitutionally protected right and that the legislative provision was proportionate to its objective. He concluded as follows:

> There is only a limited amount of goodwill, confidence and respect in the public for our system of criminal justice. Therefore there is a corresponding limit to the amount of that public goodwill that all participants in the system, including accused persons, can spend before respect and confidence in the system significantly diminishes. In my view, the accused in the case at bar have spent their share of goodwill in the public as regards the civic duty of serving on juries. Only those accused who both fail to appear and can offer no legitimate excuse are deprived of the second chance to be tried by a jury.[443]

Madam Justice Wilson, for the minority,[444] examined court statistics relating to absconding accused in Vancouver and concluded that the Crown had not met its onus of establishing that the section met a pressing and substantial concern:

> It has not been shown that the non-appearing accused is a major problem. There is accordingly nothing to support the purpose of the legislation as sufficiently compelling to justify the violation of a guarantee right under the Charter. The objective is mainly concerned with efficiency and the operation of the criminal justice system and the expense incurred for jury trials. Many of the rights in the

---

[437] See too Anderson J.A. in *P.P.G. Industries*, above note 401, at 114.

[438] For example, s. 561(2) reads:

> An accused who elects to be tried by a provincial court judge may, not later than fourteen days before the day first appointed for the trial, re-elect as of right another mode of trial, and may do so thereafter with the written consent of the prosecutor.

In *Mohammed* (1990), 60 C.C.C. (3d) 296 (Man. Q.B.) the Court refused to interfere with the Crown exercise of such a discretion.

[439] (1989), 73 C.R. (3d) 257 (S.C.C.).

[440] Gonthier J. held that s. 11(f) was not offended. To exercise that right the accused had to appear in court at the requisite time.

[441] Above note 439, at 261, 306.

[442] Dickson C.J., La Forest and Cory JJ. concurred.

[443] Above note 439, at 262-263.

[444] Sopinka J. concurred.

Charter and other legal rights run counter to this concern about efficiency and cost. But reducing the administrative inconvenience and reducing expense are not, in my view, sufficient objectives to override such a vital constitutional right.[445]

(d) Waiver

The Supreme Court in *Lee* (1989) [446] did agree that the failure of an accused to attend court might properly lead to the inference that the accused had waived his or her right to be present but did not amount to a waiver of the constitutionally guaranteed right to a jury trial. The Court had previously determined that a high standard was necessary for waiver of Charter rights.[447] A waiver had to be clear and unequivocal and the accused fully aware of the consequences of waiver. The only way to truly waive the right to be tried by jury was to re-elect, elect differently or enter a guilty plea.[448]

(e) Right to Non-Jury Trial

In *Turpin* (1989),[449] the Supreme Court ruled that s. 11(f) could not be interpreted as a constitutional right to a non-jury trial. At the time of the accused's first degree murder trial in Ontario, Criminal Code provisions[450] provided that the trial had to be before a judge and jury. Only in Alberta was it possible for an accused charged with a murder to elect trial by judge alone.[451] The trial judge had allowed the accused to elect trial by judge alone on the basis that the Criminal Code provisions in question violated s. 11(f).[452]

For a unanimous Court, Madam Justice Wilson held that s. 11(f) guarantees an accused the benefit of a jury trial where a jury trial is in fact from the accused's perspective a benefit, but does not impose it upon the accused when it is not. It is a matter for the accused whether the benefit should be waived. Here the accused had clearly and unequivocally waived their right to a jury trial but that waiver did not defeat the operation of the Criminal Code, which required that they be tried by a judge and jury. Nothing in s. 11(f) gave the accused a constitutional right to elect their mode of trial such that the mandatory jury trial provision of the Criminal Code was unconstitutional.

---

[445] Above note 439, at 285.

[446] Above note 439.

[447] Wilson J., *ibid.*, at 277 relied on *Clarkson* (1986), 50 C.R. (3d) 289 (S.C.C.) — discussed above, Chapter 1, and *Turpin*, below note 449, where it was held that the accused had knowingly waived his right to a jury trial.

[448] Lamer J., *ibid.*, at 261. This may make suspect the ruling in *Switzer* (1985), 22 C.C.C. (3d) 60 (B.C. S.C.) that an accused originally tried by judge alone had waived his right to a jury and could not choose trial by jury following an order of a new trial before judge alone.

[449] (1989), 69 C.R. (3d) 97 (S.C.C.).

[450] Sections 469-471.

[451] Section 473.

[452] The Court also held that there had been a violation of s. 15. This ruling was also rejected by the Supreme Court: see below, Chapter 10.

The particular issue in *Turpin* is now moot since, in 1985,[453] the Criminal Code was amended to allow murder trials in all provinces to take place before a judge alone on the consent of the accused and the Attorney General.

(f) Right to Twelve-Person Jury

At common law the petit jury has long been set at 12. In the Yukon Territory and the Northwest Territories the Criminal Code used to mandate six-person juries. This provision was repealed in 1985 after it was found to violate equality rights under s. 15.[454]

(g) No Right to Representative Jury

Reported cases have mostly involved challenges to the composition of jurors brought on behalf of aboriginal person. Few challenges have been brought under s. 11(f). By far the most detailed consideration of the issues is to be found in the judgment of Justice Stach of the Ontario Court of Justice, General Division, in *F. (A.)* (1994).[455]

The accused, a member of the Nishnawbe-Aski nation, was committed to stand trial on various counts of sexual assault, aggravated sexual assault and anal intercourse. The preliminary inquiry took place in Sandy Lake, a small First Nations community about 400 kilometres north of Kenora. The jury trial was to take place in Kenora where only 17.7% of those selected for jury panels would be aboriginal. The accused asserted a constitutional right under ss. 7, 11(d), 15, 25 and 27 of the Charter to be tried in Sandy Lake by a jury of his cultural peers. The complainant had been shunned by the Sandy Lake community since her allegations and wanted the trial in Kenora.

Justice Stach delivered a very lengthy judgment dismissing the Charter arguments. The trial was to be held in Kenora. The Charter did not extend to aboriginal accused the right to the extraordinary composition of jury sought. Fair trial interests had to be measured against societal concerns. Language issues and problems in comprehension could be satisfied by interpreters. With respect to cultural disparity, there was no empirical or other evidence to indicate that the values of Canadian aboriginal societies, as they relate to family abuse and child abuse, differed from that of the Canadian community at large. A jury should reflect the diverse community as a whole and should not be restricted to persons of the same race, culture and language. If the cultural affinity of the accused predominated, this would ignore the perspective of the complainant and the interests of the public. Counsel could address cultural disparity by calling expert evidence to explain any relevant cultural idiosyncrasies, philosophy, behaviour,

---

[453] R.S.C. 1985, c. 27 (1st Supp.).
[454] *Emile* (1988), 65 C.R. (3d) 135 (N.W.T. C.A.).
[455] (1994), 30 C.R. (4th) 333 (Ont. Gen. Div.). See too *Redhead* (1995), 42 C.R. (4th) 252 (Man. Q.B.).

speech patterns or mannerisms. Any issue of racial or cultural bias could be addressed through the challenge for cause process.[456]

In *Church of Scientology of Toronto* (1997)[457] Justice Rosenberg held for the Ontario Court of Appeal that the exclusion of non-citizens from the jury roll did not violate the accuseds' rights under s. 11(f) or s. 11(d) of the Charter.[458] The right to a representative jury roll was not absolute in the sense that the accused was entitled to a roll representative of all of the many groups that make up Canadian society. This level of representativeness would be impossible to obtain. There were a number of practical barriers inherent in the selection process that made complete representativeness impossible. The roll is selected from a discrete geographical district which itself may or may not be representative of the broader Canadian society. Further, the critical characteristic of impartiality in the petit jury was ensured, in part, by the fact that the roll and the panel are produced through a random selection process. What was required is a process that provides a platform for the selection of a competent and impartial petit jury, ensures confidence in the jury's verdict, and contributes to the community's support for the criminal justice system. There is no characteristic that persons bring to the fact-finding process of the jury based solely on their immigration status. According to Rosenberg J.A., exclusion of non-citizens does not infringe the representativeness or fair-cross section requirement. Citizens, at least in Metropolitan Toronto, are of all races, colours and national origin.

8. SECTION 11(g): RIGHT "NOT TO BE FOUND GUILTY ON ACCOUNT OF ANY ACT OR OMISSION UNLESS, AT THE TIME OF THE ACT OR OMISSION, IT CONSTITUTED AN OFFENCE UNDER CANADIAN OR INTERNATIONAL LAW OR WAS CRIMINAL ACCORDING TO THE GENERAL PRINCIPLES OF LAW RECOGNIZED BY THE COMMUNITY OF NATIONS"

The common law presumption against retrospective affect is a corollary of the *nullum crimen sine lege, nulla poena sine lege* principle that there must be no crime or punishment except in accordance with fixed, predetermined law.[459] The non-retrospectivity presumption is not universal. It has not been applied to judge-made law. In the case of statute law, our courts have followed the English common law position that the presumption against retrospectivity applies only to substantive law.[460] New substantive provisions are prospective while procedural provisions are generally retrospective.[461]

---

[456] Stach J. relies on the controversial challenge for cause procedure to protect against racial bias in jury selection involving black accused adopted by Mr. Justice Doherty for the Ontario Court of Appeal in *Parks* (1993), 24 C.R. (4th) 81. This approach is not based on the Charter. It was later largely accepted by the Supreme Court in *Williams* (1998), 15 C.R. (5th) 227 (S.C.C.).

[457] (1997), 7 C.R. (5th) 267 (Ont. C.A.).

[458] Paras. 146-162.

[459] See generally Stuart, *Treatise*, above note 291, c. 1.

[460] See especially *Howard Smith Paper Mills*, [1957] S.C.R. 403.

[461] For analysis of common law distinctions and intricate non-retrospectivity provisions in Interpretation Acts, see Stuart, *Treatise*, above note 459.

Section 11(g) provides constitutional protection against new crimes being applied retrospectively to conduct legal at the time it occurred. The wide words used might also be applied to the taking away of a former defence.[462] However, the Supreme Court[463] determined that s.11(g) has nothing to do with the question of how law is made known. It provided no authority for the publication of the terms and conditions of bingo licenses.

The legislative history of the enactment of the Charter shows that the exemption for conduct constituting "an offence under Canadian or international law" or a crime "according to the general principles of law recognized by the community of nations" was inserted to ensure that the rule against non-retrospectivity would not prevent the prosecution in Canada of past war crimes.[464]

In *Finta* (1994),[465] the Supreme Court held that war crimes provisions in the Criminal Code[466] did not violate s. 11(g) (or s. 7). According to the three justices,[467] they fitted within an exception to the rule against *ex post facto* laws. This allowed for retroactive law providing individual punishment for acts which were illegal but not criminal at the time they were committed. Three other justices, dissenting on other issues,[468] found no violation of s. 11(g) on the basis that the provisions were not retroactive. The accused was not being charged or punished for an international offence, but a Canadian criminal offence which was in the Criminal Code when the offence occurred.

9. SECTION 11(h): RIGHT "IF FINALLY ACQUITTED OF THE OFFENCE, NOT TO BE TRIED FOR IT AGAIN AND, IF FINALLY FOUND GUILTY AND PUNISHED FOR THE OFFENCE, NOT TO BE TRIED OR PUNISHED FOR IT AGAIN"

(a) Non-Charter Protection Against Double Jeopardy and Double Punishment

A leading author in this area, Professor Martin Friedland, writes:

The history of the rule against double jeopardy is the history of criminal procedure. No other procedural doctrine is more fundamental or all pervasive.[469]

According to the United States Supreme Court:

The underlying idea, one that is deeply ingrained in at least the Anglo American system of jurisprudence, is that the State with all its resources and power should not be allowed to make repeated attempts to convict an individual for an alleged offence, thereby subjecting him to embarrassment, expense and ordeal and compelling him

---

[462] Compare *Angus v. Hart* (1988), 52 D.L.R. (4th) 193 at 201 (S.C.C.).

[463] *Furtney* (1991), 8 C.R. (4th) 121 (S.C.C.).

[464] See *Finta* (1989), 50 C.C.C. (3d) 236 (Ont. H.C.), at 246-247.

[465] (1994), 28 C.R. (4th) 265 (S.C.C.).

[466] Now s. 7(3.1), as enacted in R.S.C 1985, c. 30 (3rd Supp.), s. 1.

[467] Cory J. (Gonthier J. and Major J. concurring) at 343-344. Lamer C.J. saw this issue as moot.

[468] La Forest J. (L'Heureux-Dubé and McLachlin JJ. concurring) at 387.

[469] *Double Jeopardy* (1969), p. 3.

to live in a continuing state of anxiety and insecurity, as well as enhancing the possibility that even though innocent he may be found guilty.[470]

Under existing Canadian law there is certainly no one rule on double jeopardy. The subject is one of the utmost complexity and subtlety and is certainly in need of clarification.[471] The law provides protection against harassment of multiple trials for the same act[472] but also protection against multiple punishment.[473] The concern to do something about double punishment stems from a distinct consideration based far more squarely on the fairness of proportionate punishment. There are at least four separate doctrines to consider.

(i) *Pleas of autrefois acquit or autrefois convict*

These special pleas that the accused has been previously convicted or acquitted are set out in the Criminal Code.[474] In *Van Rassel* (1990),[475] McLachlin J. for a unanimous Supreme Court paraphrased the Code requirements as follows:

(1) the matter must be same, in whole or in part; and
(2) the new count must be the same as at the first trial, or be implicitly included in that of the first trial, either in law or on account of the evidence presented if it had been legally possible at that time to make the necessary amendments.[476]

The accused R.C.M.P. officer, a member of an international drug enforcement team, had been acquitted in the United States on a charge of soliciting and accepting bribes in exchange for information given to him by American authorities Based on the same evidence he was subsequently charged in Canada with breach of trust under the Criminal Code.[477] The Supreme Court held that the plea of *autrefois acquit* did not apply. Even though the Code did not require that the charges be absolutely identical, here the accused could not have been convicted at the first trial of the offence with which he was charged. The Canadian charge was limited to events occurring in Canada and the conduct involved was different in that the Canadian charges made no reference to any exchange of money and required that the accused be a Canadian official.

In *Moore* (1988),[478] the Supreme Court determined that a plea of *autrefois acquit* would only be available where the accused was previously "put in jeopardy" and there was a "final determination equivalent to an acquittal."[479] Notwithstanding this test the line has proved difficult to draw. The Supreme Court

---

[470] *Green v. United States*, 355 U.S. 184 at 187-188(1957).
[471] See Law Reform Commission of Canada, *Working Paper 63. Double Jeopardy, Pleas and Verdicts* (1991), which provides a most helpful review of the present law: see pp. 1-18.
[472] This reflects the often quoted Latin maxim "*nemo debet bis vixari pro una et eadem cause.*"
[473] Here the Latin tag is "*nemo debet bis puniri pro una delicto.*"
[474] Sections 606, 607, 610.
[475] (1990), 75 C.R. (3d) 150 (S.C.C.).
[476] *Ibid.*, at 169.
[477] Now s. 122.
[478] (1988), 65 C.R. (3d) 1 (S.C.C.).
[479] *Ibid.*, at 23.

has held that the plea was available where a judge had refused to adjourn proceedings and no evidence was presented[480] and where a judge had wrongly quashed a defective count[481] but not where the Crown had withdrawn the charge before evidence had been led.[482]

(ii) *Rule against multiple convictions*

This rule was developed by the Supreme Court in its famous judgment in *Kienapple* (1974).[483] For the majority,[484] Mr. Justice Laskin (as he then was) ruled that the accused had been wrongly convicted of both counts of rape and unlawful carnal knowledge of a female under 14 stemming from one event as this would offend the doctrine of *res judicata*. One of the dissenting judges, Martland J., saw this as an "academic exercise," since the sentences on each charge were exactly the same and concurrent.[485]

The tests set out in *Kienapple* proved highly ambiguous. In particular, the issue litigated in countless cases over the next 12 years[486] was whether there was a wide rule preventing multiple convictions from a single act or whether there was a narrow protection which would only be available if the offences had substantially common elements.

In *Prince* (1986),[487] Chief Justice Dickson, for a unanimous Court, set out to clarify the jurisprudence and, in so doing, clearly adopted the narrow approach. The Court ruled that the *Kienapple* principle could only be applied where the offences had both a factual *nexus* (the offences arose from the same transaction) but also an adequate legal nexus. The requirement of sufficient proximity between the offences would only be satisfied

> if there is no additional and distinguishing element that goes to guilt contained in the offence for which a conviction is sought to be precluded by the *Kienapple* principle.[488]

The Court gave three illustrations of where offences would be not sufficiently distinct so that the *Kienapple* doctrine might apply: cases where there might be a particularization in one offence of an element of another,[489] where in reality a single delict was embodied in more than one offence[490] and, third, where in the

---

[480] *Riddle*, [1980] 1 S.C. R. 380. See too *Peterson*, [1982] 2 S.C.R. 493.

[481] *Moore*, above note 478 — a majority ruling.

[482] *Selhi*, [1990] 1 S.C.R. 277. See too *Burrows* (1983), 6 C.C.C. (3d) 54 (Man. C.A.) (Crown stay).

[483] (1974), 26 C.R.N.S. 1 (S.C.C.).

[484] Judson, Spence, Pigeon and Dickson JJ. concurred.

[485] The other dissenters were Ritchie, Abbott JJ. and Fauteux C.J.C.

[486] See especially D.R. Klinck, " 'The Same Cause or Matter': The Legacy of Kienapple" (1983-84), 26 *Crim. L.Q.* 280 and the Law Reform Commission, above note 471, pp. 10-12.

[487] (1986), 54 C.R. (3d) 97 (S.C.C.).

[488] *Ibid.*, at 112.

[489] *Ibid.*, at 113. The example given was the offence of pointing a firearm (s. 86) and using a firearm while committing an indictable offence (s. 85(1)(a)).

[490] *Ibid.*, at 114. He refers to perjury (s. 132) and giving evidence in judicial proceedings contrary to previous testimony (s. 136).

case of an offence Parliament had eased the proof of the same wrongful act embraced in another offence.[491] The Chief Justice added that these examples were subject to "the manifestation of a legislative intent to increase punishment in the event that two or more offences overlap."[492]

In *Prince*, the accused had stabbed a pregnant woman, causing her child's premature birth and death. The Supreme Court held that the accused's conviction of causing bodily harm to the mother did not prevent trial on the charge of manslaughter of the child. *Kienapple* was not applicable. Although a single act grounded both charges, the elements of the two offences did not sufficiently correspond. The Court further added, pragmatically, that at least insofar as crimes of personal violence were concerned the rule against multiple convictions was inapplicable when the convictions related to different victims.[493]

Since *Prince* it has been clear that the rule against multiple convictions provides very little protection to an accused. As a practical matter *Prince* appears to have been a *de facto* reversal of *Kienapple*. That this is so is clear on consideration of subsequent Supreme Court of Canada rulings that there could be convictions of breaking and entering and committing robbery and also attempted murder based on the same incident[494] and that a conviction for a police service offence of using unnecessary violence towards a prisoner did not preclude a Criminal Code prosecution for assault arising from the same event.[495] So too provincial Courts of Appeal have upheld convictions based on evidence from one incident for impaired driving causing bodily harm and criminal negligence causing bodily harm,[496] breach of recognizance and breach of probation,[497] aggravated assault and using a firearm while committing aggravated assault,[498] and trafficking in narcotics and possession of the proceeds of narcotic trafficking.[499]

(iii) *Issue estoppel*

Since the decision of the Supreme Court in *Gushue* (1980)[500] it has been recognized that an accused may defend a charge on the basis that the Crown is estopped from re-litigating an issue previously determined in the accused's favour at a previous trial. The limits of this doctrine are "problematic".[501] The defence will often founder on the difficulties of deciphering a general verdict of not guilty.

---

[491] *Ibid.*, at 115. He refers to impaired driving and driving "over 80" (s. 253(a) and (b)).
[492] *Ibid.*, at 113.
[493] *Ibid.*, at 118.
[494] *Wigman* (1987), 56 C.R. (3d) 289 (S.C.C.).
[495] *Wigglesworth*, discussed below note 510.
[496] *Andrew* (1990), 78 C.R. (3d) 239 (B.C. C.A.).
[497] *Furlong* (1993), 81 C.C.C. (3d) 449 (Nfld. C.A.).
[498] *Osbourne* (1994), 94 C.C.C. (3d) 435 (Ont. C.A.).
[499] *Khouri* (1995), 97 C.C.C. (3d) 223 (Sask. C.A.).
[500] [1980] 1 S.C.R. 798. See K.L. Chasse, "A Note on Issue Estoppel" (1980) 16 C.R. (3d) 357.
[501] See the discussion by the Law Reform Commission, above note 471, pp. 13-14.

In *Verney* (1993),[502] the Ontario Court of Appeal rejected an argument of issue estoppel on the basis that the finding on the relevant issue must be the only rational explanation of the previous verdict. In criminal matters the doctrine of issue estoppel has rarely proved to be of much use against multiple trials.

(iv) *Judicial stay as abuse of process*

We have seen[503] that there is a general doctrine that a judge can stay a criminal trial as an abuse of process but that this is a power which is only exercised in "the clearest of cases." In *Keyowski* (1988),[504] the Supreme Court held that a series of trials could *per se* constitute an abuse of process. Thus far this remedy has rarely proved successful to stop multiple trials. Consider, for example, the ruling of the Ontario Court of Appeal that the trial judge had improperly stayed an incest charge laid two days after an acquittal on a charge of sexual assault against the accused's daughter.[505]

(b) Section 11(h) Narrower

Section 11(h) has had little impact on the protection of the accused against double jeopardy and double punishment. This may not be surprising since it is so narrowly drafted.[506] The double jeopardy provision of the Fifth Amendment of the United States Constitution is much more generously phrased, reading:

> nor shall any person be subject for the same offence to be twice put in jeopardy of life and limb.[507]

The relationship between s. 11(h) and the existing doctrines protecting double jeopardy and double punishment cannot be considered to have been determined. In *Thibault* (1988)[508] the Supreme Court seems to suggest that s. 11(h) does no more than to constitutionalize the plea of *autrefois acquit*:

> Section 11(h) guarantees the accused the right to plead autrefois acquit if the prosecution attempts to have him tried again for an offence of which he has been acquitted.[509]

On the other hand, in *Wigglesworth* (1987)[510] s. 11(h) was applied as if it was the same as the rule against multiple convictions.

---

[502] (1993), 87 C.C.C. (3d) 363 (Ont. C.A.). Compare, however, *Padfield* (1992), 79 C.C.C. (3d) 53 (Ont. C.A.) (*obiter* recognition that a Crown would be estopped from making an argument given its failure to appeal).

[503] Above, Chapter 2.

[504] (1988), 62 C.R. (3d) 349 (S.C.C.).

[505] *B. (K.R.)* (1986), 53 C.R. (3d) 216 (Ont. C.A.).

[506] See criticism of M.L. Friedland, "Legal Rights Under the Charter" (1981-82), 24 *Crim. L.Q.* 430 at 448-449.

[507] This was pointed out by Borins C.C.J. in *Shettler* (1983), 33 C.R. (3d) 57 at 61 (Ont. Co. Ct.).

[508] Above note 4.

[509] *Ibid.*, at 292 (Lamer J. for a unanimous Court).

[510] Above note 2, see below note 512. *Sed contra* the majority in *Travers* (1984), 41 C.R. (3d) 339 (N.S. C.A.).

Given the wording of s. 11(h) if — and on their past record it is a substantial if — the courts wish to expand the protection against double jeopardy and/or punishment the vehicle may be the broader principles of fundamental justice under s. 7. In *Krug* (1985),[511] La Forest J. for the Court left open the question of

> [w]hether Parliament would in certain circumstances be prevented by s. 7 from defining or redefining a single transaction so as to create a series of offences for no obvious reason.[512]

The broad question was held not to arise since "fundamental justice" within the meaning of s. 7 had not been breached. Parliament had made it possible by the enactment of what is now s. 85 to convict an accused already convicted of robbery of a second offence punishable by mandatory imprisonment for the use, as distinct from being armed with, a firearm in committing that robbery. It had in effect created an aggravated form of robbery in response to a proliferation of firearm-related crimes.

(c) "Finally Acquitted" or "Finally Found Guilty and Punished"

In *Morgentaler* (1988),[513] the Court held that these words had to be construed to mean "after the appellate procedures have been completed, otherwise there would be no point or meaning in the word 'finally'."[514] The Court had little difficulty in rejecting the argument that the Crown's right of appeal against an acquittal under the Criminal Code[515] violated s. 11(h).

However, in *Thibault* (1988),[516] Mr. Justice Lamer for the Supreme Court held that "finally acquitted" under s. 11(h) means "acquitted by a judgment containing no error."[517] The accused had been acquitted on counts of unlawfully practicing medicine contrary to the Medical Act of Quebec.[518] Relying on provisions of the Summary Convictions Act of Quebec[519] the Crown appealed by way of trial *de novo*. The Supreme Court characterized this as not a true appeal as it could raise questions of fact as well as law. It was of right and the prosecutor did not have to allege errors committed by the justice. The prosecutor might repeat or add evidence. This was the type of abuse that s. 11(h) sought to prevent. The Court held that the provisions of the Summary Convictions Act to the extent that they allowed a prosecutor or complainant to appeal by way of trial *de novo* from an acquittal were inconsistent with s. 11(h) and of no force or effect. The Court dismissed the Crown's submission that the accused would not have been finally acquitted until he had had two trials and exhausted all his appeals. That

---

[511] (1985), 48 C.R. (3d) 97 (S.C.C.).
[512] *Ibid.*, at 109. This possibility is reviewed by Allan Manson in an annotation, C.R. *ibid.*, pp. 98-100. The s. 7 issue was left open in *Wigglesworth*, above note 2, at 212.
[513] (1988), 62 C.R. (3d) 1 (S.C.C.).
[514] *Ibid.*, at 95 (per McIntyre J. for the Court on this point).
[515] Section 676(1)(a).
[516] Above note 4. See Annotation by Louise Viau, (1988) 63 C.R. (3d) 273.
[517] *Ibid.*, at 292.
[518] L.R.Q. 1977, c. M-9.
[519] L.R.Q. 1977, c. P-15.

interpretation would deprive the word "finally" of all meaning and be contrary to the spirit of s. 11(h).[520]

It has been held[521] that the discretionary power of a trial judge under the Criminal Code[522] in the event that a jury is unable to agree does not offend s. 11(h). No verdict has been reached and the accused not yet finally acquitted.

The usual probation order under the Criminal Code is that pursuant to s. 731(l)(a), under which the sentence is suspended and the accused released on conditions prescribed in the probation order. The express Criminal Code power under s. 732.2(5) to sentence on the original charge in the event of proof of breach of probation has withstood s. 11(h) challenge on the basis that the accused has not yet been finally punished[523] and also, far less persuasively, on the basis that some probation orders are not punishment.[524]

These decisions are inconsistent with those respecting a controversial provision of the now repealed Juvenile Delinquents Act.[525] Under s. 20(3) of that Act one found delinquent and placed on probation could be brought back to the court at any time before the delinquent reached the age of 21 and re-sentenced, whether or not there had been a breach, or even transferred to adult court. The weight of authority[526] was that s. 20(3) violated s. 11(h). It was sometimes read down to authorize only responses to changed circumstances or to reduce the severity of the original disposition. Now under the review provisions of the Young Offenders Act[527] it is not possible to impose a more onerous disposition so the s. 11(h) issue does not arise.

(d) Charge of Offence

Like any other s. 11 right, before s. 11(h) can apply there must be a charge of an offence. We have earlier examined the Supreme Court's narrow test asserted in *Wigglesworth* (1987):[528] s. 11 applies to a charge of a public nature (including all criminal and provincial offences) and also to matters which are private, domestic or disciplinary but only where such proceedings involve true penal consequences.

Several s. 11(h) challenges have foundered on this triggering test. We have already examined the Supreme Court of Canada's extraordinary ruling in *Shubley*

---

[520] Above note 4, at 292.
[521] *Misra* (1985), 44 C.R. (3d) 179 (Sask. Q.B.).
[522] Section 653.
[523] *Elendiuk* (1986), 27 C.C.C. (3d) 94 (Alta. C.A.).
[524] *Linklater* (1983), 9 C.C.C. (3d) 217 (Y.T. C.A.).
[525] Above note 416.
[526] See *W. (S.); L. (W.)* (1983), 34 C.R. (3d) 90 (Ont. H.C.), adopting *M. (D.)* (1982), 30 C.R. (3d) 210 (Ont. Fam. Ct.). *Sed contra R. (T.) (No. 2)* (1984), 11 C.C.C. (3d) 49 (Alta. Q.B.) (compulsory admission to psychiatric unit being treatment not punishment). See generally Nick Bala, "Constitutional Challenges Mark Demise of Juvenile Delinquents Act" (1983), 30 C.R. (3d) 245 at 249-255.
[527] R.S.C. 1985, c. Y-1, s. 32.
[528] Above note 2.

(1990)[529] that prison disciplinary proceedings do not involve true penal consequences. In *Lavers* (1989),[530] the British Columbia Court of Appeal held, four to one,[531] that penalty assessments issued by the Minister of Revenue under appropriate Federal and Provincial Income Tax Acts did not meet either *Wigglesworth* test and therefore did not give rise to a s. 11(h) challenge to the conviction and punishment for the offence of income tax evasion respecting the same taxes. For similar reasons the British Columbia Court of Appeal has held that customs forfeiture proceedings do not bar an accused conviction for a customs offence[532] and that a 24-hour licence suspension under a provincial Highway Traffic Act does not ground a s. 11(h) challenge to subsequent impaired driving charges.[533]

(e) "Not to be Tried or Punished for it Again"

The "it" in s. 11(h) clearly refers back to the offence. A literal construction would be that the protection only applies to prevent double proceedings or double punishment for exactly the same offence. If this were so the protection of s. 11(h) would be even less than the Criminal Code *autrefois acquit* or *convict* pleas since they allow the protection against *substantially* similar charges.[534] Thus far the Supreme Court has indeed applied that literal interpretation to s. 11(h).

In *Wigglesworth* (1987),[535] the issue was whether a conviction of a major service offence by a police officer for using unnecessary violence to a prisoner precluded a subsequent prosecution for assault in the criminal courts, based on the same evidence. For the Court, Madam Justice Wilson, having decided that s. 11 applied since the disciplinary proceedings in question carried a possible prison sentence, however held that s. 11(h) had not been violated because the accused was "not being tried and punished for the same offence."[536] The Court without further explanation adopts the *Prince*[537] test for the rule against multiple convictions:

> The "offences" are quite different. One is an internal disciplinary matter. The accused has been found guilty of a major offence and has, therefore, accounted to his profession. The other offence is the criminal offence of assault. The accused must now account to society at large for his conduct. He cannot complain, as a member

[529] Above note 22.
[530] (1989), 74 C.R. (3d) 21 (B.C. C.A.). See too *Yes Holdings Ltd.* (1987), 40 C.C.C. (3d) 30 (Alta. C.A.), in which Stevenson J.A. (as he then was) acknowledged that the accused risked being twice penalized for the same conduct but held that "s. 11(h) does not provide a free-standing prohibition against double punishment" (at 36).
[531] Lambert J.A. dissented.
[532] *Luchuk* (1987), 39 C.C.C. (3d) 567 (B.C. C.A.). See too *Re Green* (1983), 5 C.C.C. (3d) 95 (Ont. H.C.) (forfeiture under Narcotic Control Act).
[533] *Art* (1987), 61 C.R. (3d) 204 (B.C. C.A.).
[534] In *Genaille* (1983), 35 C.R. (3d) 315 (Man. Q.B.), s. 11(h) was held applicable to the assault causing bodily harm and unlawfully causing bodily harm, despite "slight differences."
[535] Above note 2.
[536] *Ibid.*, at 214.
[537] Above note 487.

of a special group of individuals subject to private internal discipline, that he ought not to account to society for his wrongdoing. His conduct has a double aspect as a member of the R.C.M.P. and as a member of the public at large. To borrow from the words of the Chief Justice [in *Prince*], I am of the view that the two offences were "two different 'matters', totally separate one from the other and not alternative one to the other". While there was only one act of assault there were two distinct delicts, causes or matters which would sustain separate convictions.[538]

Just how narrow the protection becomes is evident in the Supreme Court's subsequent ruling in *Van Rassell* (1990).[539] It was determined that s. 11(h) did not preclude the trial in Canada of a charge of breach of trust against a police officer previously acquitted of soliciting or accepting bribes in the United States based on the same facts and circumstances. The Court was content to point out that the offences were based on different duties — one owed by an official to the Canadian public and the other to the American public.[540]

10. SECTION 11(i): RIGHT "IF FOUND GUILTY OF THE OFFENCE AND IF THE PUNISHMENT FOR THE OFFENCE HAS BEEN VARIED BETWEEN THE TIME OF COMMISSION AND THE TIME OF SENTENCING TO THE BENEFIT OF THE LESSER PUNISHMENT"

If the punishment for a particular offence is increased or decreased before the time of sentencing, s. 11(i) makes it crystal clear that the accused has a right to the lesser punishment. Clearly any attempt at transitional legislation would have to give way to this Charter protection.

Does this mean at the time of sentencing by the trial judge or at the time of an appeal against sentence? Decisions of Courts of Appeal conflict. Some read the section literally to require any change to have taken place before the sentence at trial.[541] Others are content to give an accused within the system the s. 11(i) benefit respecting legislative changes to penalties occurring after trial but before appeal.[542] It seems the antithesis of a purposeful interpretation not to allow the accused within the appeal system to take advantage of reductions in penalty. All that is required is an interpretation that sentence is not finally imposed until appeal remedies have been exhausted. Such an interpretation would be consistent with the determination of the Supreme Court[543] that under s. 44(e) of the Interpretation

---

[538] Above note 2, at 214-215.

[539] (1990), 75 C.R. (3d) 150 (S.C.C.).

[540] *Ibid.*, at 173. *Van Rassell* was applied in *Sillipp* (1995), 42 C.R. (4th) 381 (Alta. Q.B.), in a ruling that s. 11(h) did not prevent the charging of the Criminal Code offence of criminal harassment under s. 264 after a conviction for civil contempt based on the same facts.

[541] *Luke* (1994), 28 C.R. (4th) 93 (Ont. C.A.), followed in *B. (G.)* (1994), 94 C.C.C. (3d) 97 (Alta. C.A.).

[542] *Lusignan* (1993), 79 C.C.C. (3d) 572 (N.S.C.A.) (accused having benefit of Criminal Code amendment since the trial to give a trial judge a discretion to refuse to impose a firearms prohibition order). See too *Anderson* (1996), 104 C.C.C. (3d) 215 (B.C. C.A.).

[543] *R. (R.A.)* (2000), 140 C.C.C. (3d) 523 (S.C.C.) at 533, allowing accused within the system to argue for the new conditional sentence option.

Act[544] an accused is entitled to the benefit of any sentencing amendments in force at the time of an appeal.[545]

Section 11(i) only deals with the situation of a changed punishment for a particular offence. It gives no protection to an accused properly charged with an offence which, by the time of his trial, has been replaced by another with different elements and lesser penalties. Thus it has been held[546] that an accused charged with statutory rape carrying a life sentence could not be sentenced on the new 10-year maximum applicable under the new regime of various forms of sexual assault. The Saskatchewan Court of Appeal[547] has held that ''punishment'' in s. 11(i) is to be construed to mean punishment fixed by Parliament rather than any range of sentences emerging from court sentences. A sexual offender could not benefit by a more lenient attitude to sexual assault existing at the time he committed the offences.

Section 11(i) uses the term ''punishment'' which suggests a reach wider than changes in maximum penalties. Courts of Appeal[548] have accepted that s. 11(i) applies to new judicial powers under what is now s. 743.6(1) of the Criminal Code to declare periods of parole ineligibility for certain offences. Such declarations could not therefore be retrospectively applied to conduct before the provisions came into force. In this context, Mr. Justice Steele, for the Newfoundland Court of Appeal, held that the term ''punishment'' had to be interpreted in addition to the formal sentence to include

> any other ''severe handling'' or ''harsh or injurious treatment'' . . . [and] may also encompass any coercive or punitive treatment likely to discourage or deter an accused (and sometimes others) from a repetition of criminal activity.[549]

The Ontario Court of Appeal did declare[550] a Criminal Code provision lengthening parole ineligibility for a convicted murderer from 20 to 25 years inoperative under s. 11(i) in a case where an accused had been convicted of first degree murder but not yet sentenced. However, that Court had earlier been far less generous[551] in holding that a 16-year-old accused tried in ordinary court for several offences could not have the benefit of the lesser punishment regime subsequently put in place for 16 and 17 year olds under the Young Offenders Act.[552]

---

[544] R.S.C. 1985, c. I-21. Under s. 44(e)

> where any punishment, penalty or forfeiture is reduced or mitigated by the new enactment, the punishment, penalty or forfeiture if imposed or adjudged after the repeal shall be reduced or mitigated accordingly.

[545] Such an interpretation had previously been rejected by the Ontario Court of Appeal in *Luke*, above note 541.

[546] *B. (J.W.)* (1989), 51 C.C.C. (3d) 35 (P.E.I. T.D.). See too *R. (E.)* (1992), 77 C.C.C. (3d) 193 (B.C. C.A.).

[547] *D. (R.)* (1996), 48 C.R. (4th) 90 (Sask. C.A.).

[548] *Lambert* (1994), 93 C.C.C. (3d) 88 (Nfld. C.A.), *Ferris* (1994), 35 C.R. (4th) 52 (N.B. C.A.) and *Richard* (1994), 94 C.C.C. (3d) 285 (N.S. C.A.).

[549] *Lambert*, at 93.

[550] *Logan* (1986), 51 C.R. (3d) 326 (Ont. C.A.).

[551] *L. (R.D.)* (1985), 47 C.R. (3d) 378 (Ont. C.A.).

[552] S.C. 1980-81-82-83, c. 110.

In *Molloy* (1990)[553] the issue was whether the accused charged with impaired driving was entitled to a discharge for curative treatment. That penalty was authorized by the Criminal Code[554] but the provision had not been proclaimed in force in Ontario. Prior to sentencing the accused sought the benefit of a ruling of the Ontario Court of Appeal[555] that had declared that the non-proclamation had violated the accused's right to equality under s. 15. However, three days before sentencing the Ontario Court of Appeal reversed its previous equality ruling,[556] with the result that a discharge was no longer available in Ontario for such an offence. Ontario Provincial Court Judge MacDonnell held that s. 11(i) did not apply because the decisions of the Ontario Court of Appeal did not amount to varying sentence within the meaning of s. 11(i). The situation would have been different had the section been proclaimed in force in Ontario.

---

[553] (1990), 76 C.R. (3d) 371 (Ont. Prov. Ct.).
[554] Section 255(5).
[555] *Hamilton* (1986), 54 C.R. (3d) 193 (Ont. C.A.).
[556] *Alton* (1989), 74 C.R. (3d) 124 (Ont. C.A.).

7

Section 12: Protection Against Cruel and Unusual Treatment or Punishment

Under s. 12 of the Charter:

Everyone has the right not to be subjected to any cruel and unusual treatment or punishment.

1. HISTORICAL ORIGINS

The protection dates back to s. 10 of the English Bill of Rights of 1688,[1] which declared that

excessive bail ought not to be required, nor excessive fines imposed; nor cruel and unusual punishments inflicted.

The modern extension of protection to include "treatment" is reflected in Article 7 of the International Covenant on Civil and Political Rights (1966),[2] under which

no one shall be subjected to torture or to cruel, inhuman or degrading treatment or punishment.[3]

The outlawing of cruel and unusual punishment by the English Bill of Rights came at a time when there were still a substantial number of capital offences in that jurisdiction. Indeed, more capital offences were added until 1823 after which

---

[1] I Will. & Mar. sess. 2, C. 2. The eighth amendment to the U.S. Constitution (1791) provides "Excessive bail shall not be required, nor excessive fines imposed, nor cruel and unusual punishment inflicted."

[2] Res. 2200A (XXI), 21 UN GAOR, Supp. No. 16, p. 52, UN Doc. A/6316.

[3] See similarly article 3 of the European Convention for the Protection of Human Rights and Fundamental Freedoms, 213 U.N.T.S. 222 (1950) and article 5 of the Universal Declaration of Human Rights, GA Res. 217A (III), p. 71, UN Doc. A/810 (1948).

the British Parliament began a gradual process towards the abolition of the death penalty. This only occurred in 1975.[4]

2. CANADIAN BILL OF RIGHTS

The 1960 Bill[5] declared in s. 2(b) that

[N]o law of Canada shall be construed or applied so as to . . .

(b) impose or authorize the imposition of cruel and unusual treatment or punishment.

The judicial record in interpreting s. 2(b) is one of deference to Parliament. Courts followed rather than led. No judicial sentence authorized by statute was finally determined to be cruel and unusual punishment. In 1964,[6] the Manitoba Court of Appeal found that whipping was not cruel and unusual punishment. That sentencing alternative was abolished by Parliament in 1972.[7] An Ontario Provincial Court judge held in 1970[8] that preventive detention of habitual criminals, through which a number of "nuisance offenders" were sentenced to life imprisonment subject to parole, did not offend s. 2(b). That penalty was abolished by Parliament in 1977,[9] but maintained for dangerous offenders. The Ontario Court of Appeal held in *Shand* (1975)[10] that the minimum seven-year jail sentence for importing or exporting a narcotic under the Narcotic Control Act, including marijuana, did not amount to cruel and unusual punishment.

When the Canadian Bill of Rights was enacted in 1960 the death penalty was still prescribed for treason, piracy and murder. Executions continued until 1962. Capital murder was defined more restrictively in 1961 and even more restrictively in 1967. In 1976 Parliament abolished the death penalty.[11]

Prior to the historic abolition vote, the Supreme Court in *Miller* (1977)[12] had heard an argument that the death penalty for the murder of a policeman constituted cruel and unusual punishment contrary to s. 2(b). Notwithstanding abolition the Supreme Court later ruled that the death penalty *was* constitutional. The majority through Mr. Justice Ritchie[13] rested largely on the interpretive nature of the Bill of Rights and on the view that questions of morality were policy matters for

---

[4] The impetus was the comprehensive *Report of the Royal Commission on Capital Punishment, 1949-1953* (1953).

[5] 8-9 Eliz. II, C. 44 (Can.).

[6] *Dick*, [1965] 1 C.C.C. 171 (Man. C.A.).

[7] S.C. 1972, C. 13, s. 70.

[8] *Buckler*, [1970] 2 C.C.C. 4 (Ont. Prov.Ct.).

[9] S.C. 1976-77, C. 53, s. 14.

[10] (1976), 30 C.C.C. (2d) 23 (Ont. C.A.).

[11] S.C. 1974-75-76, C. 21. For a review of the legislative history see Allan Manson, "The Easy Acceptance of Long Term Confinement in Canada" (1990), 79 C.R. (3d) 265.

[12] [1977] 2 S.C.R. 680. In the Court below ((1975), 33 C.R.N.S. 129 (B.C. C.A.)) the dissenting judge McIntyre J.A. (as he then was) had strongly asserted the view that the death penalty was cruel and unusual punishment.

[13] Martand, Judson, Pigeon and de Grandpre JJ. concurred. Beetz J. concurred separately.

Parliament and not the courts. Chief Justice Laskin for the minority[14] agreed in the result, largely based on the gravity of the offence of killing a police officer. He did indicate that the death penalty for theft and probably other offences would be cruel and unusual punishment.

The only decision finding a treatment or punishment to be cruel and unusual not reversed on appeal was that of Heald J. of the Trial Division of the Federal Court in *McCann* (1976).[15] Extensive evidence was led as to the particularly severe prison conditions to which certain prisoners were subjected in the solitary confinement unit of the British Columbia Penitentiary. These conditions included 24-hour light, a half hour of exercise per day and guards pointing rifles at them. Heald J. held this regime constituted cruel and unusual punishment or treatment. It served no "positive penal purpose" and was, in any case, "not in accord with public standards of decency and proprietary." There were "adequate alternatives" that would remove the cruel and unusual aspects of administrative dissociation.[16]

3. GROSS DISPROPORTIONALITY TEST: SMITH

The first Supreme Court of Canada ruling on the protection afforded by s. 12 of the Charter clearly encouraged courts to show less deference to legislatures. In *Smith* (1987),[17] the Court declared that the minimum seven-year sentence provided by s. 5(2) of the Narcotic Control Act for importing narcotics breached s. 12 and had to be declared of no force or effect.

Five separate judgments were delivered. The Court was unanimous in accepting the view of Chief Justice Laskin in the pre-Charter decision in *Miller*[18] that the words "cruel and unusual" should not have a disjunctive meaning but should be considered as a "compendious expression of a norm." Both the leading judgments of Lamer and McIntyre JJ. quoted the following Laskin dictum from *Miller*:

> The various judgments in the Supreme Court of the United States, which I would not discount as being irrelevant here, do lend support to the view that "cruel and unusual" are not treated there as conjunctive in the sense of requiring a rigidly separate assessment of each word, each of whose meanings must be met before they become effective against challenged legislation, but rather as interacting expressions

---

[14] Spence and Dickson JJ. concurred.

[15] (1976), 29 C.C.C. (2d) 337 (Fed.T.D.).

[16] *Ibid.*, at 368-370.

[17] (1987), 58 C.R. (3d) 193 (S.C.C.). See Allan Manson, "Answering Some Questions About Cruel and Unusual Punishment", C.R. *ibid.*, pp. 247-252, and Kent Roach, "Case Commentary" (1989), 11 *Sup. Ct. L. Rev.* 433. See too earlier Manson, "Fresh Approaches to Defining Cruel and Unusual Treatment or Punishment" (1984), 35 C.R. (3d) 262. *Smith* has overruled *Guiller* (1985), 48 C.R. (3d) 226 (Ont. Dist. Ct.) (seven year minimum for conspiracy to import narcotics not violating s. 12). Ironically the judge in *Guiller*, Borins J., had earlier held in *Shand*, above note 10, that such a minimum violated s. 2(b) of the Bill of Rights. In *Guiller* he was accepting that his position in *Shand* had been overruled.

[18] Above note 12.

colouring each other, so to speak, and hence to be considered together as compendious expression of a norm.[19]

Both Lamer and McIntyre JJ. adopted the test of Chief Justice Laskin in *Miller* that punishment will be cruel and unusual when "the punishment prescribed is so excessive as to outrage standards of decency."[20] Lamer J. further defined a gross disproportionality test:

> In assessing whether a sentence is grossly disproportionate, the court must first consider the gravity of the offence, the personal characteristics of the offender and the particular circumstances of the case in order to determine what range of sentences would have been appropriate to punish, rehabilitate or deter this particular offender or to protect the public from this particular offender. The other purposes which may be pursued by the imposition of punishment, in particular the deterrence of other potential offenders, are thus not relevant at this stage of the inquiry. This does not mean that the judge or the legislator can no longer consider general deterrence or other penological purposes that go beyond the particular offender in determining a sentence, but only that the resulting sentence must not be grossly disproportionate to what the offender deserves.[21]

He stressed that merely disproportionate or excessive sentences should not be characterized as unconstitutional and should be left to the usual sentencing appeal process to review the fitness of a sentence.[22] Some guidelines were whether the punishment was necessary to achieve a valid penal purpose, whether it was founded on recognized sentencing principles, whether there were valid alternatives and comparison with punishments imposed by other crimes in the same jurisdiction.[23]

McIntyre J. considered American authorities and academic opinion[24] and concluded that a punishment will be cruel and unusual contrary to s. 12 where it has any one or more of three characteristics:

(1) the punishment is of such character or duration as to outrage the public conscience or be degrading to human dignity;

(2) the punishment goes beyond what is necessary for the achievement of a valid social aim, having regard to the legitimate purposes of punishment and the adequacy of possible alternatives; or

(3) the punishment is arbitrarily imposed in the sense that it is not applied on a rational basis in accordance with ascertained or ascertainable standards.[25]

Disagreement as to the proper approach only occurs when McIntyre lists this third factor of arbitrariness. According to McIntyre J. even if a punishment is proportionate to the offence it will be cruel and unusual if it is imposed "arbitrarily, unevenly and without reason upon some people and not others."[26]

---

[19] *Ibid.*, at 689-690.

[20] *Ibid.*, at 688.

[21] Above note 17, at 235.

[22] *Ibid.*

[23] Some reliance was placed on the views of Walter Tarnopolsky, "Just Deserts or Cruel and Unusual Treatment or Punishment" (1978), 10 *Ottawa L. Rev.* 1.

[24] McIntyre J. relies heavily on Tarnopolsky, *ibid.*

[25] Above note 17, at 212.

[26] *Ibid.*, at 216.

In this regard the most important consideration is seen to be whether the punishment is authorized by law and imposed under "standards or principles which are rationally connected to the purposes of the legislation."[27] In contrast Lamer J. found that arbitrariness was a "minimal factor,"[28] suggesting that it had been developed in the United States to ensure equality under the law and that it should not be transported into s. 12 of our Charter. On this difference of opinion Lamer J. was in the minority. Chief Justice Dickson concurred. However Wilson J., in her concurring judgment, specifically found that the arbitrary nature of a minimum sentence was relevant.[29] So did Le Dain J., who on this point concurred with McIntyre J.[30] La Forest J. considered it unnecessary to decide this question.[31]

Allan Manson has suggested[32] that there does not seem to be a meaningful difference between the approach of Lamer J. and McIntyre J. even on this question of arbitrariness. He points out that Mr. Justice Lamer's ultimate conclusion respecting s. 5(2) of the Narcotic Control Act rested on the "certainty"[33] that there would be cases in which, in light of the circumstances of the offender and the offence, the seven-year minimum would be grossly disproportionate. This notion of "certainty" takes into account the arbitrariness of a mandatory imposition. Lamer J.'s view that legal rights under ss. 7 to 14 should be compartmentalized and not allowed to overlap, with the exception of the general right under s. 7, has been clearly rejected by the majority of the Court in the context of s. 11(b).[34]

In *Lyons* (1987),[35] Mr. Justice La Forest for a Supreme Court unanimous on this point held that provisions in what is now Part XXIV of the Criminal Code providing for the indeterminate detention of dangerous offenders do *not* violate s. 12. He adopts Lamer J.'s judgment in *Smith* as setting the parameters of what amounts to cruel and unusual punishment but simply ignores any reference to the difference of opinion on arbitrariness.[36] However, part of the Court's conclusion is that the legislative classification of the target group of offenders met "the highest standard of rationality."[37] Since rationality is the flipside of arbitrariness *Lyons* seemed to decide that arbitrariness is a crucial factor in the determination under s. 12.

The *Lyons* judgment is also important for the observation of La Forest J. that inquiring into the presence or absence of less restrictive means might be incompatible with the *Smith* test of gross disproportionality. The word "grossly" reflected

---

[27] *Ibid.*
[28] *Ibid.*, at 216.
[29] *Ibid.*, at 243.
[30] *Ibid.*, at 245.
[31] *Ibid.*, at 246.
[32] *Ibid.*, at 248-249.
[33] *Ibid.*, at 246.
[34] Above, Chapter 6.
[35] (1987), 61 C.R. (3d) 1 (S.C.C.).
[36] *Ibid.*, at 29-30.
[37] *Ibid.*, at 31.

this Court's concern not to hold Parliament to a standard so exacting, at least in the context of s. 12, as to require punishments to be perfectly suited to accommodate the moral nuances of every crime and every offender. [38]

4. SECTION 12 CHALLENGE NOT DEPENDENT ON INDIVIDUAL CASE

Smith is a most important authority for the view that a Charter challenge against a law can be considered independently of whether particular facts support the claim.[39] The trial judge in *Smith* held that the minimum sentence was of no effect since it violated s. 12, but nevertheless sentenced this particular accused to eight years in the penitentiary.[40]

Prior to *Smith* some judges had avoided Charter challenges based on hypothetical cases not before the courts. For example, Mr. Justice Watt of the Ontario High Court said in *Moore* (1984):[41]

> In assessing Charter applications, it is generally socially unrealistic to consider only the possible worst case where such case is not before the Court. Indeed, it is only too easy for the creative legal imagination to concoct bizarre examples that never come to court. Where the worst case comes before the court, then the preferable practice is not to invalidate otherwise valid legislation but to hold it inoperative in the particular case.[42]

In the Supreme Court five justices over the objections of only McIntyre J.[43] agreed that an accused may challenge the constitutional validity of a statutory punishment structure even if the facts of the particular case do not support the claim. This was best put by Le Dain J.:

> . . . I am of the opinion that an accused should be recognized as having standing to challenge the constitutional validity of a mandatory minimum sentence, whether or not, as applied to his case, it would result in cruel and unusual punishment. In such a case the accused has an interest in having the sentence considered without regard to a constitutionally-invalid mandatory minimum sentence provision.[44]

5. EFFECTS OF SENTENCE PROTECTED

The Court in *Smith* applies the holding in *Big M Drug Mart Ltd.* (1985)[45] that a law can be unconstitutional because of its purpose *or* its effect.[46] This is

---

[38] *Ibid.*, at 35. For a view that La Forest J. improperly collapsed the *Oakes* two-stage inquiry of determining the breach and then and only then justifiability under s. 1 see Morris Manning "Lyons: A One-Stage Approach to the Charter and Undue 'Constitutional Notice' " (1988), 61 C.R. (3d) 72.

[39] The authority of *Smith* on this point is still intact but has been substantially undermined by the Court's later application in *Goltz*, discussed below note 97.

[40] Above note 17, described by Lamer J. at 223.

[41] (1984), 10 C.C.C. (3d) 306 (Ont. H.C.).

[42] *Ibid.*, at 312.

[43] "The test of proportionality must be applied generally and not on an individual basis" (above note 17, at 207).

[44] *Ibid.*, at 246. Le Dain J. agreed with McIntyre J.'s general approach but not on this point. See further discussion by Manson, above note 17, p. 250.

[45] [1985] 1 S.C.R. 295 at 331, 334.

[46] Lamer J., above note 17, at 234.

particularly significant in this context. Prisoners can now claim the protection against cruel and unusual punishment or treatment given that the section applies to the manner in which a punishment is carried out after sentencing. Strong *obiter* in the Supreme Courts point to an expanded range of protection. McIntyre J. suggests that the inclusion of the word "treatment" has extended the protection to allow a wide variety of possible challenges:

> Solitary confinement as practised in certain circumstances affords an example: see *McCann*. . . . Section 12 might also be invoked to challenge other kinds of treatment, such as the frequency and conditions of searches within prisons, dietary restrictions as a disciplinary measure, corporal punishment, surgical intervention including lobotomies and castration, denial of contact with those outside the prison, and imprisonment at locations far distant from home, family and friends, a condition amounting to virtual exile which is particularly relevant to women, since there is only one federal penitentiary for women in Canada.[47]

Lamer J. also seems to envisage greater Charter scrutiny:

> Sometimes it will be the result of the combination of factors which, when considered in isolation, would not in and of themselves amount to gross disproportionality. For example, 20 years for a first offence against property would be grossly disproportionate, but so would three months of imprisonment if the prison authorities decide it should be served in solitary confinement. Finally, I should add that some punishments or treatments will always be grossly disproportionate and will always outrage our standards of decency: for example, the infliction of corporal punishment, such as the lash, irrespective of the number of lashes imposed, or, to give examples of treatment, the lobotomization of certain dangerous offenders or the castration of sexual offenders.[48]

These express promises of greater rights for prisoners have not materialized in the judicial record since *Smith*.

In *Milne* (1987),[49] the Supreme Court held that continued indeterminate detention under the dangerous offender provisions in Part XXIV of the Criminal Code did not amount to cruel and unusual punishment, even though the triggering offence in question had since been removed from the Criminal Code. Only one justice dissented on this point.[50]

In *Steele v. Mountain Institution* (1990),[51] the Supreme Court did intervene in the case of a person declared a "criminal sexual psychopath" in 1953, after pleading guilty to attempted rape, and still in custody after 37 years. After most careful examination of the prisoner's parole and revocation record over the years,

---

[47] *Ibid.*, at 204. In *Daniels*, [1990] 4 C.N.L.R. 51 (Sask. Q.B.), Wedge J. held it was cruel and unusual treatment to require native women from Saskatchewan to serve life sentences for murder in the federal Prison for Women in Kingston, Ontario. On appeal, the Saskatchewan Court of Appeal, [1991] 5 W.W.R. 340, reversed on jurisdictional grounds, holding that the application should have been brought in Federal Court.

[48] *Ibid.*, at 236. Lamer J. had earlier suggested that international covenants, above note 3, may "on occasion be of assistance" in interpreting s. 12 (at 226).

[49] (1987), 61 C.R. (3d) 55 (S.C.C.), followed by the majority in *Collin* (1990), 58 C.C.C. (3d) 553 (Que. C.A.) (continued detention under unconstitutional murder law not violating s. 12).

[50] Estey J., *ibid.*, at 60-61.

[51] (1990), 80 C.R. (3d) 257 (S.C.C.).

Mr. Justice Cory held for the Court that the continued indeterminate detention violated s. 12 because the National Parole Board had erred in denying him parole on relatively minor and explicable breaches of discipline, rather than focusing on the crucial issue of undue risk.[52] However, at the end of the judgment, the Court adds that in the future such challenges should be by way of judicial review of the National Parole Board decision rather than, as in *Steele*, an application for *habeas corpus*. Cory J. wished to avoid the establishment of a "costly and unwieldy parallel system" for challenging parole decisions and was, furthermore, of the opinion that release of such long-term inmates should be supervised by parole experts.

Allan Manson has suggested[53] that this jurisdictional restriction undercuts developing protections for prisoners under the law relating to *habeus corpus* and that judicial review is unlikely to provide adequate protection for cases such as *Steele*.

This view appears to be shared by the Ontario Court of Appeal. In *Gallichon v. Canada (Commissioner of Corrections)* (1995),[54] the Court determined that where the prisoner's complaint is neither with parole nor with the terms of parole, but rather with the continuation of the original sentence, the proper procedure is not judicial review but by way of action or by *habeas corpus* with *certiorari* in aid with an application for relief under the Charter. The Court determined that the continued detention of an "habitual offender" after 26 years in prison of one who had been no more than a social nuisance and was not a danger to the public, surpassed all bounds of treatment or punishment and was so excessive as to outrage standards of decency. Particularly disturbing aspects of this case were that the applicant had never met the criteria to be declared an habitual offender and that he should have been released in 1986 when he satisfied conditions laid down by a judicial review of the status of habitual offenders following the abolition of that designation.

In *Olson* (1987),[55] the Ontario Court of Appeal held that the administrative segregation of an inmate for five years following his conviction on 11 counts of first degree murder would not constitute cruel and unusual punishment. Segregation to a prison within a prison was not *per se* contrary to s. 12.[56] There was held to be no adequate alternative to administrative segregation given the inmate's criminal record, the need to maintain order and discipline in the prison and good reason to fear for the protection of the staff, other inmates and the accused himself, if he were to be allowed into the general population.[57]

---

[52] *Ibid.*, at 281.

[53] Allan Manson, "The Effect of Steele on Habeas Corpus and Indeterminate Confinement" (1991), 80 C.R. (3d) 282.

[54] (1995), 43 C.R. (4th) 187 (Ont. C.A.). See annotation by Allan Manson, C.R. (4th) *ibid.* 189-190 who sees the decision as having confirmed the continuing vitality of the remedy of *habeas corpus* and also its potential flexibility.

[55] (1987), 38 C.C.C. (3d) 534 (Ont. C.A.).

[56] *Ibid.*, at 550.

[57] *Ibid.*

Earlier in *Soenen v. Director of Edmonton Remand Centre* (1983),[58] Mr. Justice D.C. McDonald of the Alberta Queen's Bench had dismissed a s. 12 claim based on a number of grievances: a limitation of contact visits, reduction of open air exercises, visual rectal searches, the application of pesticide lotion upon re-entering the prison and the conduct of an internal investigation. Since the *obiter* in *Smith* such challenges should be re-instituted.

On occasion, trial judges faced with allegations of improper treatment in custody have found s. 12 breaches. Charges against young offenders as a result of damage to holding cells were stayed by Ontario Provincial Division Judge King where it was determined[59] that the offences were linked to violations of ss. 10(b) and 12. The usual holding cells for young offenders had become unavailable. The young offenders had been handcuffed in transit to other holding cells, mixed irrespective of age, the cells were bare and they had no privacy. The cells were overcrowded, hot and dirty, permeated by a putrid smell and with no fresh air. A psychiatrist testified that in this environment many youths, especially the young ones, would feel "intimidated and frightened" and "devalued and, perhaps, humiliated". New Brunswick Queen's Bench Judge McLellan[60] held that videotaped evidence that the accused was strapped by guards to a stretcher when he banged on his cell door requesting a lawyer showed unreasonable and excessive use of force in violation of ss. 10(b) and 12. The applicant for *habeas corpus* was serving a short sentence in a provincial gaol. The Court ordered a number of remedies, including reduction of sentence to time served and the right to sue for damages.[61] On the other hand, in Ontario, Judge O'Connor[62] had little difficulty in dismissing a claim that a smoking ban on a provincial gaol violated s. 12. Even it amounted to treatment, it was far short of being cruel and unusual.

In *Rodriguez* (1993),[63] the Supreme Court rejected a claim of a terminally ill patient that the Criminal Code prohibition against assisting suicide violated her s. 12 right not to be subjected to any cruel or unusual treatment or punishment. Even assuming that "treatment" could include that imposed by the state in contexts other than that of a penal or quasi-penal nature, State prohibition of action without more could not constitute treatment. There would have to be some more active state process involving an exercise of control over the individual.[64]

---

[58] (1983), 35 C.R. (3d) 206 (Alta. Q.B.).

[59] *M. (T.), M.L.* and *J.H.* (1991), 7 C.R. (4th) 55 (Ont. Prov. Ct.).

[60] *McPherson* (1996), 48 C.R. (4th) 122 (N.B. Q.B.).

[61] In her report arising out of videotaped strip-searches at a penitentiary for women, Madam Justice Arbour, then of the Ontario Court of Appeal, recommends a mechanism be developed to permit a court to reduce a sentence if it appeared that the circumstances in which the sentence was actual served was by reason of "illegalities, gross mismanagement or unfairness" harsher than the court intended: see *Commission of Inquiry into Certain Events at the Prison for Women at Kingston* (1996), pp. 183-185.

[62] *McNeil v. Ontario (Ministry of Solicitor General & Correctional Services)* (1998), 126 C.C.C. (3d) 466 (Ont. Gen. Div.).

[63] (1993), 24 C.R. (4th) 281 (S.C.C.).

[64] At 313-314.

6. CAN SECTION 12 VIOLATIONS BE SAVED UNDER SECTION 1?

In *Smith*, McIntyre J. views s. 12 as an "absolute right" to be protected from excessive punishment and treatment that would outrage standards of decency.[65] Le Dain J. flatly asserts that a punishment found to be cruel and unusual could not be justified under s. 1.[66] However, Lamer J., for a majority on this point,[67] had no apparent qualms in turning to the issue of whether the Crown could discharge its burden under s. 1 of salvaging the legislation held to have been a *prima facie* violation of s. 12. Although the fight against the importing of hard drugs was seen to be an object of sufficient importance to warrant overriding a Charter right, the seven-year minimum did not meet the minimum impairment part of the *Oakes* proportionality test:

> Clearly there is no need to be indiscriminate. We do not need to sentence the small offenders to seven years in prison in order to deter the serious offender. Indeed, the net cast by s. 5(2) for sentencing purposes need not be so wide as that cast by s. 5(1) for conviction purposes. The result sought could be achieved by limiting the imposition of a minimum sentence to the importing of certain quantities, to certain specific narcotics of the schedule, to repeat offenders, or even to a combination of these factors.[68]

The advantage of the usual two-stage approach to the Charter[69] is that Charter protections are not diluted by balancing State interests at the point of defining the content of the right. This is left to the s. 1 inquiry, where the State must discharge a heavy burden of justification.[70] Nevertheless, the notion that cruel and unusual punishment or treatment could ever be justified in a free and democratic society is troubling.[71] Given that the test is one of gross disproportionality and outraging public decency, it seems highly unlikely that violations of s. 12 will be saved under s. 1. As in *Smith*, such arguments should founder under the minimum intrusion test.

7. MINIMUM PUNISHMENT FOR MURDER

The 1976 Bill to abolish the death penalty would not have passed without a key political compromise negotiated on the floors of the House of Commons.[72] A new distinction was drawn between first and second degree murder. While the sentence for murder remained fixed at mandatory life imprisonment, the distinction between first and second degree determined minimum periods of

---

[65] Above note 17, at 207.
[66] *Ibid.*, at 245.
[67] Dickson C.J.C. concurred. Wilson and La Forest JJ. would appear to have agreed with the resort to s. 1 and Lamer J.'s analysis. The majority in *Goltz*, below note 97, also accept the possibility of s. 1 justification.
[68] Above note 17, at 241.
[69] Above, Chapter 1.
[70] See too *Soenen*, above note 58.
[71] See too Manson, above note 17, p. 251.
[72] See further Manson, above note 11.

parole ineligibility. Criminal Code provisions[73] provide that persons convicted of first degree murder are not eligible for release under parole until 25 years have elapsed, although there can be a review of that period of ineligibility by a jury after 15 years. In the case of one convicted of second degree murder the trial judge sets the parole eligibility between 10 and 25 years, taking into consideration, but not being bound by, the recommendation of the jury. Section 231 declares murder to be first degree murder where it is planned and deliberate (subsection (2)), a contract killing (subsection (3)), where the victim is a police officer or jail guard (subsection (4)), or where the murder is caused by that person while committing or attempting to commit a certain list of offences, including sexual assault and kidnapping (subsection (5)).

Luxton (1990)[74] concerned a challenge to the constructive first degree murder category under s. 231(5) of murder during a kidnapping. Chief Justice Lamer for a unanimous Supreme Court spent less than two pages in dismissing the argument that the penalty of life imprisonment and 25 years before parole eligibility violated s. 12.[75] The punishment was not excessive and did not clearly outrage our standards of decency. The Criminal Code provided for punishment of the most serious crime in criminal law, that of first degree murder. Since *Martineau* (1990),[76] it carried the most serious level of moral blameworthiness, namely subjective foresight of death. The penalty was deservedly severe to reflect society's condemnation of one who had exploited a position of power and dominance to the gravest extent possible by murdering the person being forcibly confined.[77]

Professor Allan Manson[78] has powerfully pointed to the barrenness of this reasoning. Under the logic that it is constitutionally acceptable to impose the most severe punishment for the most serious offence, mandatory terms of 30, 40 or 50 years would survive. The test of outraging decency was not the sole consideration in the judgment in *Smith* but in *Luxton* it was the sole criterion applied. There was no consideration or evidence adduced as to the human impact of such long term confinement. The actual punishment was "not assessed in real, human terms."[79]

Mr. Justice Lamer suggests that Parliament has been sensitive to the particular circumstances of each offender through various provisions allowing for the royal prerogative of mercy, escorted absences from custody for humanitarian and rehabilitative purposes and for early parole.[80] Manson responds by documenting that in reality these indulgences are very rarely exercised.[81]

---

[73] Sections 742-745.

[74] (1990), 79 C.R. (3d) 193 (S.C.C.).

[75] The Court also dismissed challenges based on arbitrariness under ss. 7 and 9, discussed above and criticized in Chapter 2.

[76] (1990), 79 C.R. (3d) 129 (S.C.C.), discussed above, Chapter 2.

[77] Above note 74, at 203.

[78] Allan Manson, above note 11.

[79] *Ibid.*, p. 269.

[80] Above note 74, at 203.

[81] Above note 11, at 270.

Given *Luxton*, it would appear highly likely that the Supreme Court will accept lower court decisions rejecting attacks on minimum life sentences,[82] the discretion to set parole eligibility dates in the case of second degree murders,[83] and the 25 year minimum periods of parole ineligibility in the cases of planned and deliberate murders[84] and the murders of police officers.[85]

Smith stands for the proposition that punishment might be cruel and unusual in its impact on a particular individual. *Luxton* does not preclude an individual convicted of first degree murder from attempting to challenge the application of the mandatory sentence in his or her particular case. Clearly this would be an uphill battle, given *Luxton*. It would be highly advisable to compile a thorough empirical record and all available evidence on such matters as the impact of long-term incarceration. Since *Luxton* was heard in the absence of a proper factual record the Supreme Court should be prepared to re-consider. In the meantime it is most unfortunate that a hasty Parliamentary compromise in 1976 has so easily become the "constitutional benchmark."[86]

Were Canada to re-introduce the death penalty, would it survive the s. 12 test of gross disproportionality? There are indications that the Supreme Court might reverse its previous Bill of Rights ruling in *Miller*. In *Kindler v. Minister of Justice of Canada* (1991),[87] a four to three majority of the Supreme Court held that it should not interfere with the extradition of a prisoner facing the death penalty in the United States. The majority justices saw the issue not as the constitutionality of the death penalty but whether an extradition to face the death penalty in another country offended fundamental principles of justice under s. 7. They held that it did not. Mr. Justice Cory for the minority held that the surrender would violate s. 12 and could not be justified under s. 1 The death penalty was *per se* cruel and unusual punishment because it was the ultimate denial of human dignity. A further three members of the Court through La Forest J., in the course of s. 7 analysis, comment that:

> There is strong ground for believing that having regard to the limited extent to which the death penalty advances any valid penological objectives and the serious invasion of human dignity it engenders, that the death penalty cannot, except in exceptional circumstances, be justified in this country.[88]

---

[82] *LeBlanc* (1989), 68 C.R. (3d) 164 (Que. S.C.).

[83] *Mitchell* (1987), 39 C.C.C. (3d) 141 (N.S. C.A.) and *Sidoruk* (1993), 25 C.R. (4th) 126 (B.C.S.C.)

[84] *Cairns* (1989), 51 C.C.C. (3d) 90 (B.C. C.A.).

[85] *Bowen* (1990), 2 C.R. (4th) 225 (Alta. C.A.) (appeal dismissed: (1991), 5 C.R. (4th) 124 (S.C.C.)) and *Lefebvre* (1992), 72 C.C.C. (3d) 162 (C.A. Qué.). For the Court, Cote J.A. noted that "15 years before parole will always be much milder than what the accused did to the police officer he killed" (at 233). However, he left open the issue of liability as a party under s. 21 (*ibid.*).

[86] Manson, above note 11, p. 268.

[87] (1991), 8 C.R. (4th) 1 (S.C.C.). The majority judgments were delivered by La Forest and McLachlin JJ. L'Heureux-Dubé and Gonthier JJ. concurred with each opinion. Lamer C.J. concurred in the separate dissenting opinions of Sopinka and Cory JJ. See the critical review by Allan Manson, "Kindler and the Courage to Deal with American Convictions", (1992) 8 C.R. (4th) 68.

[88] At 27. See too Huggesson J.A., dissenting in the Court below: (1988), 69 C.R. (3d) 38 (Fed. C.A.) (the death penalty violates s. 12 because it was founded on "no recognized sentencing principle").

Confusingly, two of these majority justices also express agreement with McLachlin J. who, at one point of her s. 7 analysis, observes that

> There is no clear consensus in this country that capital punishment is morally abhorrent and absolutely unacceptable.[89]

However recently in *U.S.A. v. Burns* (2001)[90] the court was unanimous in deciding the Minister of Justice should not have agreed to the extradition of Canadian citizens on aggravated first degree murder charges in the state of Washington without obtaining assurances the death penalty would not be imposed. The issue was decided under s. 7. However the Court added the following comment:

> We are not called upon in this appeal to determine whether capital punishment would, if authorized by the Canadian Parliament, violate s. 12 of the *Charter* ("cruel and unusual treatment or punishment"), and if so in what circumstances. It is, however, incontestable that capital punishment, whether or not it violates s. 12 of the *Charter,* and whether or not it could be upheld under s. 1, engages the underlying values of the prohibition against cruel and unusual punishment. It is final. It is irreversible. Its imposition has been described as arbitrary. Its deterrent value has been doubted. Its implementation necessarily causes psychological and physical suffering. It has been rejected by the Canadian Parliament for offences committed within Canada. Its potential imposition in this case is thus a factor that weighs against extradition without assurances.[91]

8. OTHER MINIMUM PENALTIES

No judge in *Smith,* suggests that minimum punishments are *per se* contrary to s. 12. However, Lamer J. finds support in the Report of the Canadian Sentencing Commission,[92] which had recommended the abolition of mandatory minimum penalties except for murder and high treason. He quoted the Commission's view that

> existing mandatory minimum penalties, with the exception of those prescribed for murder and high treason, served no purpose that can compensate for the disadvantages resulting from their continued existence.[93]

There are few minimum sentences under the Criminal Code. The usual pattern is one of a high discretionary maximum. The most important example of a minimum is the life imprisonment sentence for all murderers. Other instances are the scale of minimum punishments for impaired driving offences,[94] the minimum sentence of one year imprisonment for someone using a firearm while committing or attempting to commit an indictable offence[95] and a four-year minimum imposed by the 1995 Firearms Act,[96] for ten listed offences where committed by a firearm.

---

[89] At 21.

[90] (2001), 151 C.C.C. (3d) 97 (S.C.C.).

[91] At 132.

[92] *Sentencing Reform: A Canadian Approach* (1987).

[93] *Ibid.,* at 188, quoted above note 17, at 242.

[94] Under s. 255 the mandatory minimum penalties are, for a first offence, a fine of $300, a second offence, 14 days imprisonment and, for each subsequent offence, 90 days imprisonment.

[95] Section 85.

[96] S.C. 1995, c. 39.

In *Goltz* (1991),[97] a 6-3 majority of the Supreme Court determined that a mandatory minimum sentence of seven days' imprisonment for driving while prohibited prescribed by s. 88(1)(c) of the British Columbia Motor Vehicle Act[98] did not violate s. 12. The Court purported to be applying *Smith*, but in so doing may have eviscerated its authority.

Mr. Justice Gonthier, for the majority,[99] reviewed dicta suggesting that under s. 12, the Courts should not be quick to invalidate sentences crafted by legislators given the need to balance the deterrent and protective aspects of punishment. The test for whether a sentence was disproportionate was "very properly stringent and demanding".[100] The majority opted for the Lamer view in *Smith* that the arbitrariness of the sentence did not necessarily mean that s. 12 had been violated.[101] The *Smith* approach was seen to involve two aspects.[102] Firstly, the penalty must be considered from the point of view of the actual offender. The gravity of the offence must be balanced with the particular circumstances and the personal characteristics of the offender. The penalty will *prima facie* violate s. 12 if the sanction in the particular case would be so excessive or grossly disproportionate as to outrage decency. Secondly, if the particular facts do not support such a conclusion, there may be a finding of gross disproportionality

> as evidenced in *reasonable hypothetical circumstances*, as opposed to far-fetched or marginally imaginable cases.[103]

On the majority approach, the challenged provision did not violate s. 12. In the particular circumstances, the sentence was not grossly disproportionate. The offence of knowingly driving while prohibited is grave and involved risks to other users of the roads by persons identified as bad drivers. Reasonable hypothetical examples did not support the conclusion that the provision would likely result in cruel and unusual punishment. The system of points and discretionary review guaranteed that the prohibition of a "small offender" would be rare. Other infractions which might lead to a prohibition and subsequent s. 88(1)(c) penalty, especially those not linked to bad driving, might result in grossly disproportionate punishment but their constitutionality was not at issue in this appeal.

According to Madam Justice McLachlin, for the dissenting three justices,[104] the minimum penalty provision should be reviewed in all its potential applications and this lead to a conclusion that it violated s. 12. The majority approach of applying a more limited focus amounted to reading the provision down or using a doctrine of constitutional exemption, which the Court had hitherto not applied.[105] The majority approach left the constitutional status of the provision uncertain, to

---

[97] (1991), 8 C.R. (4th) 82 (S.C.C.).
[98] R.S.B.C. 1979, c. 288.
[99] La Forest, L'Heureux-Dubé, Sopinka, Cory and Iacobucci JJ. concurred.
[100] At 97.
[101] At 95.
[102] At 99-100.
[103] At 100 (emphasis by Gonthier J.).
[104] Lamer C.J. and Stevenson J. concurred.
[105] McLachlin J. referred to her majority judgment in *Seaboyer* (1991), 7 C.R. (4th) 117 (S.C.C.), reviewed later here on this point in Chapter 11.

be determined by other judges in future cases. Looking at the entire range of prohibitions which could generate the mandatory sentence, together with a modest amount of human experience applied to unlimited numbers of offence and personal circumstances, support should be given to the conclusion of Mr. Justice Wood of the British Columbia Court of Appeal, the Court below, that a grossly disproportionate penalty was inevitable.[106]

In *Morrisey* (2000),[107] as Allan Manson, the indefatigable commentator in this area, puts it, the "narrow lens of *Goltz* was made even smaller".[108] The Court holds that the mandatory minimum sentence of four years for criminal negligence causing death with a firearm under s. 220(a) did not violate s. 12. There was agreement that a four-year sentence was not grossly disproportionate for this particular accused.[109] While intoxicated he had jumped up onto to a camp bunk bed occupied by a friend, the gun had discharged and the friend had been killed. He had dragged the body into the bushes and tried to hide it. The offence was very serious and the accused had shown wanton and reckless disregard for life and safety.

However there is a sharp division on the issue of the reasonable hypothetical test which is dramatically narrowed by the majority. Gonthier J., speaking for five justices,[110] rejected the applicability of examples even from actual cases as the proper test was one of common examples of the particular offence:

> *Goltz* requires that hypotheticals be "common" rather than "extreme" or "far-fetched". It is sufficient when dealing with a rare and uncommon crime that the hypotheticals be common examples of the crime rather than examples of common occurrences in day-to-day life.[111]

> [T]he proper approach is to develop imaginable circumstances which could commonly arise with a degree of generality appropriate to the particular offence.[112]

According to Gonthier J., the reasonable hypothetical cases to be considered in this case were the actual reported cases of two types: individuals playing with a loaded gun that goes off, and people on hunting trips where a shot is fired at an

---

[106] At 117-120.

[107] (2000), 36 C.R. (5th) 85 (S.C.C.).

[108] "Morrisey: Observations on Criminal Negligence and s. 12 Methodology", (2000) 36 C.R. (5th) 121 at 124.

[109] The sentence was reduced to three years to take into account pre-trial custody. The Court had ruled in *Wust* (2000), 32 C.R. (5th) 58 (S.C.C.) that this was possible in minimum sentence cases on the basis of statutory interpretation of s. 719(3). It adopted the reasoning of Rosenberg J.A. in *McDonald* (1998), 17 C.R. (5th) 1 (Ont. C.A.) in preference to decisions of other Courts of Appeal. The Firearms Act, S.C. 1995, c. 39 imposed a four-year minimum for ten listed offences where committed by a firearm. Prior to *Morrisey* a number of these provisions had survived s. 12 challenges: see, for example, s. 344(a): robbery (e.g., *McDonald*, above); s. 279(1.1)(a): kidnapping (*Mills* (1999), 133 C.C.C. (3d) 451 (B.C. C.A.)); s. 244(b): discharging firearm with intent to endanger life (*Roberts* (1998), 125 C.C.C. (3d) 471 (N.B. C.A.)). However in *Bill* (1997), 13 C.R. (5th) 103 (B.C. S.C.) the minimum sentence of four years for manslaughter under s. 236(a) was held by Low J. to violate s. 12.

[110] Iacobucci, Major, Bastarache and Binnie JJ.A. concurred.

[111] Para. 33.

[112] Para. 50.

object in the woods. In both situations, a four-year sentence was not cruel and unusual. The sentence did not violate s. 12 and there was no need to consider a constitutional exemption given the accused's concession that the sentence was not personally grossly disproportionate.

Justice Arbour, joined only by McLachlin J., concurred in the result in this case. However she differed sharply in her further view[113] that it could not be said that the four-year sentence was not grossly disproportionate for any reasonable hypothetical offender. It was inappropriate and unworkable to restrict the reasonable hypothetical test to imaginable circumstances which could commonly arise with a degree of generality appropriate to the particular offence. There was no difference between a s. 220(a) offence and manslaughter under s. 222(5)(b). Manslaughter could occur in a great variety of circumstances and appropriate sentences could range from a suspended sentence to life imprisonment. Even within the sub-category of criminal negligence with a firearm, there was a great variation of conduct which could attract liability. To limit the Charter analysis to two types of hypotheticals, playing with a loaded gun and hunting cases, contradicted the very nature of the offence. Real cases had to be considered as reasonable hypotheticals no matter how unusual they appear. A different approach was called for. The constitutional validity of s. 220(a) generally should be upheld but it should be indicated that it may not be applied in a future case, if the minimum penalty was found to be grossly excessive for that future offender. The various kinds of circumstances which might arise in the future[114] should not be prejudiced by a determination now of constitutionality.

There seems little doubt that while Gonthier J. in *Goltz* and *Morrisey* paid lip service to the gross disproportionality test of *Smith*, he has substantially narrowed the reasonable hypothetical test. The views of Arbour J. are compelling in that the majority were pre-empting challenges in worse cases arising in the future. But she did not carry the day. It appears that the authority of *Smith* to impose protection against the harshness and inflexibility of minimum prison sentences has been significantly weakened. This appears most unfortunate as few judges or criminologists see wisdom and justice in mandatory sentencing. The seven-year minimum sentence struck down in *Smith* had often been criticised, but it took the intervention of the Supreme Court under the Charter to remove it.

Perhaps the Court will re-consider its approach when it comes to review the growing Parliamentiary trend to declare that sentences be served consecutively. Signs are not encouraging. In *Brown* (1994),[115] the Court took but a few lines to reverse the decision of the Manitoba Court of Appeal that s. 85(2) of the Criminal Code violated s. 12 in requiring consecutive sentences for the offence of using a weapon in the commission of indictable offences. The Supreme Court was content, in applying *Goltz*, to hold that the provision did not violate s. 12 where the underlying offence was armed robbery.

---

[113] Paras. 68-90.

[114] Examples suggested were killings by a woman of her abuser or by a police officer. What too of accessory liability where the party had no knowledge of the gun or played a minor role?

[115] (1994), 34 C.R. (4th) 24 (S.C.C.).

Hope may lie in the Arbour solution which appears to be one of allowing for constitutional exemptions in exceptional cases,[116] although she never resorts to those controversial words. Although this was the minority position in *Morrisey*, Justice Gonthier expressly indicates the issue of constitutional exemption did not arise given the concession that the sentence was not grossly disproportional in the particular case.

Courts are even less likely to strike down minimum sentences where recognition is given to the concept that a Court may grant a constitutional exemption in a particular case. This was the basis upon which the British Columbia Court of Appeal in *Kumar* (1993)[117] rejected challenges under ss. 7 and 12 to the minimum Criminal Code sentence of 14 days' imprisonment for a second drinking and driving offence. The Court accepted that there might be very unusual cases where the second offence involved a technical violation and a 14-day sentence would be grossly disproportionate. However, the Court read *Goltz* as not precluding resort to constitutional exemptions.

Somewhat unsatisfactorily, the Supreme Court left the issue of constitutional exemptions open in the context of a one line rejection of a s. 12 challenge against the mandatory firearms ban in s. 100.[118] The Court may have wished to avoid addressing the difficult exemption issue in that context given that Parliament has since revised the provision to allow for discretion.[119]

The earlier conflicting jurisprudence on the mandatory firearms prohibition is still instructive.

In *Chief* (1990),[120] the majority of the Yukon Territory Court of Appeal[121] found such an order to be cruel and unusual treatment or punishment contrary to s. 12 in its application to a trapper who depended significantly on the sale of furs to support his family and who hunted to supply meat for his family. The accused had been convicted of an assault on his wife and possession of a weapon for a purpose dangerous to the public peace. It was the latter offence that had resulted in the prohibition order. The trial judge had found that the mandatory prohibition order violated s. 12 and had imposed a less restrictive order, prohibiting the accused from possessing firearms in his residential property for a period of five years. The majority of the Court of Appeal agreed that the application of the mandatory prohibition in s. 100 to this particular accused was grossly disproportionate to a degree which would outrage standards of decency and be considered shocking.[122] The Court added that not every mandatory sentence offended the Charter and that even this mandatory sentence could in some cases withstand Charter scrutiny. A firearms prohibition against a trapper with a proven

---

[116] See too Manson, above note 108, who points to *Steele* as an example of a constitutional exemption.

[117] (1993), 85 C.C.C. (3d) 417 (B.C. C.A.).

[118] *Sawyer et al* (1992), 78 C.C.C. (3d) 191 (S.C.C.).

[119] S.C. 1991, c. 40, s. 12. The amended s. 100 was interpreted in *Austin* (1994), 36 C.R. (4th) 241 (B.C. C.A.).

[120] (1990), 74 C.R. (3d) 57 (Y.T. C.A.). *Chief* was adopted in *Johnson* (1994), 31 C.R. (4th) 262 (Yuk. C.A.), but distinguished on the facts.

[121] Per McEachern C.J.Y.T. and Esson J.A. in separate opinions. Locke J.A. dissented.

[122] Above note 120, at 67.

disposition to violence could, for example, be constitutional.[123] The Court, however, held that the trial judge had erred in the remedy of reading down the prohibition. The appropriate remedy was to declare the section inoperative with respect to the accused and to amend the probation order to prohibit the accused from possessing any firearm in his residence for a period of three years.[124] In dissent, Locke J.A. considered that the effect of the prohibition on the trapper was "unhappy, regrettable, and perhaps even tragic" but did not amount to being cruel and unusual under s. 12.[125]

Chief was applied by the Saskatchewan Court of Appeal in *McGillivary* (1991),[126] where that Court similarily held that a treaty Indian dependent on hunting and trapping for livelihood should receive a constitutional exemption from the prohibition.

On the other hand, the Ontario Court of Appeal in *Kelly* (1990)[127] refused to follow *Chief*. For the Court, Mr. Justice Finlayson[128] saw the real complaint as being that the mandatory penalty did not fall with equal severity on all to whom it applied. This was nothing unusual in such cases. A conviction of impaired driving might be inconsequential to an irresponsible teenager while it might mean a loss of employment to a truck driver or be fatal to the career of a person in public office. Section 100 was not an example of casting the net too wide. The prohibition was narrowly focused on persons who had committed violent crimes against the person and were the very persons who should not be in possession of instruments of violence. It could not be that a mandatory prohibition directed against a person convicted of crime was unconstitutional because it precluded that person from continued employment in a particular trade or calling. The Court further suggested that a remedy of constitutional exemption would be inappropriate in the case of a minimum sentence.[129]

9. CONSTITUTIONAL EXEMPTION FOR LATIMER?

The issue of a constitutional exemption arose for consideration in the controversial context of the murder trial of *Latimer* (2001).[130] A father was on trial before a jury charged with the first degree murder of his severely disabled 12-year-old daughter, Tracy. While his wife and other children were at church, he killed her by placing her into his pickup truck and using a hose to divert carbon monoxide fumes from the exhaust pipe. He took her back to her bed and feigned

---

[123] *Ibid.*, at 68.

[124] For consideration of the remedial issue see Allan Manson, "The Charter and Declarations of Invalidity" (1990), 74 CR. (3d) 95 and below, Chapter 11, in the section on "Declarations of Invalidity".

[125] Above note 120, at 77.

[126] (1991), 62 C.C.C. (3d) 407 (Sask. C.A.), followed in *Netser* (1992), 70 C.C.C. (3d) 477 (N.W.T. C.A.).

[127] (1990), 80 C.R. (3d) 185 (Ont. C.A.). *Kelly* was reasserted in *Luke* (1994), 28 C.R. (4th) 93 (Ont. C.A.).

[128] McKinlay and Catzman JJ.A. concurred.

[129] Above note 127, at 200-201.

[130] (2001), 39 C.R. (5th) 1 (S.C.C.). For an array of differing comments see C.R. *ibid,* for comments by Archie Kaiser, Allan Manson, Barney Sneiderman and Don Stuart.

that she had died in her sleep. He later confessed that he had killed her to put her out of her pain. The tragic context has been described by Professor Barney Sneiderman as follows:

> Gravely affected since birth by cerebral palsy, Tracy Latimer was a "totally body-involved spastic quadriplegic", whose constant muscle spasms and seizures had wrenched her body into a twisted frozen position. She had the mental age of a two- or three- month old baby, weighed 38 pounds, wore diapers, often needed suppositories to unplug her bowels, had impaired vision, and could not sit up, talk, or feed herself. Her parents kept a bucket at hand when feeding her as she had difficulty in swallowing and would constantly vomit. She spent her days either in bed or propped in a wheelchair, tightly fitted to prevent her thrashing about during her daily seizure episodes.
>
> Tracy had undergone a number of surgical procedures to relieve the painful muscular tension afflicting her grossly contorted body; muscles had been cut at the top of her legs, her toes, her heel cords, and knees. There was also surgery on her spine; stainless steel rods were inserted on each side to relieve the cramping of her stomach and lungs. Because Tracy was on anticonvulsant medication to control her seizures, her parents were fearful that using narcotics to control her pain could prove fatal by depressing her respiration (a concern shared by Tracy's orthopaedic surgeon). She was in constant pain from a dislocated hip, and Latimer was appalled at the prospect of impending surgery that would involve the removal of part of her hip and thigh bone. And there would be more surgery to come.[131]

At the first trial the trial judge withdrew the defence of necessity from the jury. The jury returned a verdict of second degree murder. The sentence was life imprisonment with no parole eligibility for 10 years. The Saskatchewan Court of Appeal dismissed Latimer's appeal against conviction.[132] A majority, over the dissent of Chief Justice Bayda, also rejected the argument for a constitutional exemption from the mandatory sentence. Chief Justice Bayda carefully considered public outrage expressed against the sentence and four other mercy killing cases, two involving consent, where the charges were reduced from murder and the sentences were probation.

At the second trial,[133] ordered by the Supreme Court,[134] the charge was second degree murder. The trial proceeded on the basis the accused had been motivated by concern for his daughter's present and future pain. For very similar reasons to those offered in the first trial, the trial judge, Noble J., withdrew the defence of necessity but only after the addresses by counsel. The jury again convicted but

---

[131] "The Latimer Mercy-Killing Case: A Rumination on Crime and Punishment", (1997) 5 *Health L.J.* 1 at 1-2. His sources are the reported decision in (1995), 41 C.R. (4th) 1 (Sask. C.A.), the trial transcript and newspaper accounts. The notion Tracy was in constant pain has been disputed: see Ruth Enns, *A Voice Unheard. The Latimer Case and People with Disabilities* (1999). An appendix at pp. 166-170 shows that Tracy's mother's communication books had multiple entries as to her happiness and smiles.
[132] Above note 131.
[133] *Latimer* (1997), 12 C.R. (5th) 112 (Sask. Q.B.).
[134] *Latimer* (1997), 4 C.R. (5th) 1 (S.C.C.). The new trial was ordered given a "flagrant abuse" by a Crown Attorney. He had conducted a police-administered questionnaire to 30 prospective jurors about their possible attitudes without disclosure to the defence counsel. Five had served on the jury. The Crown was later charged with wilful obstruction of justice but was acquitted: *Kirkham* (1998), 17 C.R. (5th) 250 (Sask. Q.B.).

were visibly upset when asked to made a recommendation whether parole eligibility should be set at more than 10 years. They recommended one year! This reality was a factor Noble J. took into account in opting for a constitutional exemption. The murder was a compassionate homicide, committed for caring and altruistic reasons. If a cruel and unusual punishment is one which is so excessive that it outrages standards of decency, then the hundreds of letters protesting the harshness of the mandatory sentence represented considerable evidence that the sentence was seen as an outrage. Examples from other provinces where compassionate homicides did not result in murder prosecutions or life sentences, showed the inequality of the penalty Latimer was facing. The imposition of the mandatory minimum sentence would be unjust, unfair and excessive. This conclusion relates only to this accused in respect of this crime. This was a unique set of facts warranting a constitutional exemption. Judge Noble imposed a sentence of one year followed by probation for one year less one day.

The Saskatchewan Court of Appeal[135] again upheld the conviction and also confirmed its previous decision that a constitutional exemption was not available. The Supreme Court also rejected the conviction appeal.[136] The Court found no violation of s. 12. the gravity of the offence was not outweighed by the individual circumstances and there was a need for denunciation. There was thus no need to consider the issue of constitutional exemption.

Latimer is clearly a hard case. It engages the emotions of disabled persons who understandably feel vulnerable if the accused was not punished for deliberately taking an innocent life without consent and at the possibility this would encourage other similar actions and moves to decriminalise assisted suicide and euthanasia. Not putting the defence of necessity betrays a lack of confidence in the jury system. It is clear at the second trial that the twelve jurors who listened to the evidence wanted compassion to be exercised. Failing legislation to deal with mercy killings and euthanasia, there was much to be said for the notion of a constitutional exemption to avoid disproportional punishment in this heartwrenching case.

10. OTHER SECTION 12 CHALLENGES

In *Joe* (1993),[137] the Manitoba Court of Appeal held that the penalty of imprisonment in default of payment of a parking offence under the Summary Convictions Act of Manitoba (a penalty since repealed) was cruel and unusual punishment contrary to s. 12 of the Canadian Charter of Rights and Freedoms. Mr. Justice Twaddle[138] held that the punishment was grossly disproportionate and

---

[135] *Latimer* (1998), 22 C.R. (5th) 380 (Sask. C.A.).

[136] Above note 130. For full consideration of the ruling that there was no air of reality to the defence of necessity, see Stuart, *Treatise*, ch. 7.

[137] (1993), 27 C.R. (4th) 79 (Man. C.A.).

[138] Huband J.A. concurred. In his concurring judgement, Scott C.J.M. held that the legislative scheme also violated s. 7 in subjecting an offender to the risk of imprisonment for which he may have no notice and no opportunity to be heard. According to the Chief Justice, the issue of whether the Manitoba fine option program contravened s. 7 of the Charter should not be dealt with due to a lack of an evidentiary foundation respecting the overall workings of the current procedure.

so excessive as to outrage standards of decency. It was preposterous that imprisonment was even a possible penalty for such a petty crime. Imprisoning a parking offender served no valid penal purpose. It was used as a means to coerce payment of a debt. Imprisonment for wilful default might be justified but could not be presumed in the absence of an inquiry into ability to pay. There was an alternative punishment in that the Manitoba Legislature had since eliminated imprisonment as a possible consequence of a parking conviction and had provided for the possibility of a lien. The Court held that the violation could not be justified under s. 1 of the Charter. Imprisonment did not achieve the objective of the collection of fines and was totally disproportionate. There were many other equally if not more effective remedies.

Courts of Appeal[139] have rejected s. 12 challenges against a provision in the Excise Act[140] that provides for a minimum fine for sale of contraband tobacco determined by a mathematical formula according to the quantity of tobacco involved. However Provincial Court Judge Bigelow[141] granted a constitutional exemption against a mandatory fine provision in the Income Tax Act.[142] There was no allowance made for considering ability to pay constituted a grossly disproportionate penalty contrary to s. 12.

---

[139] *Calvin* (1996), 3 C.R. (5th) 96 (Que. C.A.) and *MacFarlane* (1997), 121 C.C.C. (3d) 211 (P.E.I. C.A.).
[140] R.S.C. 1985, c. E-14, s. 240.
[141] *Piscione* (1997), 12 C.R. (5th) 131 (Ont. Prov. Div.).
[142] R.S.C. 1985, c. 1 (5th Supp.), s. 238(1).

8

Section 13: Right of Witness Not to Have Incriminating Evidence Used in Subsequent Proceedings

Under s. 13:

> A witness who testifies in any proceeding has the right not to have any incriminating evidence so given used to incriminate that witness in any other proceedings, except in a prosecution for perjury or for the giving of contradictory evidence.

Section 11(c) of the Charter[1] only protects a person charged with an offence from being compelled to testify against him or herself in that proceeding. The Supreme Court of Canada has determined that there is a wider protection against self-incrimination than that expressly provided in ss. 11 (c) and 13. The principles against fundamental justice under s. 7 are held to guarantee a ''principle against self-incrimination''[2] and a pre-trial right to silence.[3]

The impact of s. 13 cannot be meaningfully assessed without first considering its common law and legislative context.[4]

1. COMMON LAW RIGHT NOT TO ANSWER INCRIMINATING QUESTIONS

Professor David Paciocco describes the principle against self-incrimination as it relates to admissibility of evidence, as requiring that

---

[1] Above, Chapter 6.

[2] Above, Chapter 2.

[3] *Hebert* (1990), 77 C.R. (3d) 145 (S.C.C.), discussed above Chapter 2.

[4] There is a wealth of Canadian research. See especially E. Ratushny, *Self-Incrimination in the Canadian Criminal Process* (1979) and D.M. Paciocco, *Charter Principles and Proof in Criminal Cases* (1987). See too Paciocco, ''Self-Incrimination: Removing the Coffin Nails'' (1989), 35 *McGill L.J.* 73 and Alan Whitten, ''The Privilege Against Self Incrimination'' (1987), 29 *Crim. L.Q.* 66.

no persons shall be required to respond (in the sense of providing information as opposed to real evidence) to an allegation made against him by the state until the Crown has established on evidence that there is a case to meet.[5]

At common law, part of this protection allowed a witness to claim privilege respecting any evidence which would expose the witness to the risk of criminal conviction or a penalty or forfeiture.[6] This rule and other protection against self-incrimination were established by the common law courts in the seventeenth century in response to the excesses of the Court of Star Chamber. The original concern was actually rooted in the lack of particularity of charges that led to fishing expeditions to discover some form of guilt rather than any concern that the accused had to testify.[7] The privilege not to answer incriminating questions was well described by Stephen J. in *Lamb v. Munster* (1882):[8]

> The extent of the privilege is I think this: the man may say, "If you are going to bring a criminal charge, or if I have reason to think a criminal charge is going to be brought against me, I will hold my tongue. Prove what you can, but I am protected from furnishing evidence against myself out of my own mouth."[9]

2. SECTION 5 OF CANADA EVIDENCE ACT[10]

In Canada, the common law privilege to refuse to answer incriminating questions was repealed by the passage of the Canada Evidence Act of 1893.[11] Under what is now s. 5(1),

> No witness shall be excused from answering any question on the ground that the answer to the question may tend to criminate him or maintain to establish his liability to a civil proceeding at the instance of the Crown or any person.

The trade-off was to declare qualified immunity for that witness against incriminating answers being used against that witness in subsequent criminal proceedings. That immunity was, however, only available if the witness first objected to answer on the ground that his answer might be incriminating or establish civil liability. What is now s. 5(2) reads as follows:

> Where with respect to any question a witness objects to answer on the ground that his answer may tend to criminate him, or may tend to establish his liability to a civil proceeding at the instance of the Crown or of any person, and if but for this Act, or the Act of any provincial legislature, the witness would therefore have been excused from answering the question, then although the witness is by reason of this Act or the provincial Act compelled to answer, the answer so given shall not be used or admissible in evidence against him in any criminal trial or other criminal proceeding against him thereafter taking place, other than a prosecution for perjury in the giving of that evidence or for the giving of contradictory evidence.

---

[5] *McGill L.J.*, above note 4, p. 75.

[6] *Phipson on Evidence*, 13th ed. (1962), pp. 15-36, is frequently cited for this proposition.

[7] See Ratushny, above note 4, chap. 4.

[8] (1882), 10 Q.B.D. 110.

[9] *Ibid.*, at 113.

[10] R.S.C. 1985, c. C-5.

[11] S.C. 1893, c. 31.

Our courts have repeatedly held[12] that the protection under s. 5(2) is not available where a witness did not in some way register an objection at the earlier proceedings. This requirement clearly operates unfairly[13] where a witness was simply ignorant of the immunity protection. There is, furthermore, no obligation on the court or tribunal to inform the witness of the immunity, even if the witness is unrepresented.

3. GREATER PROTECTION UNDER SECTION 13

The broad impact of s. 13 is very well described by Mr. Justice McIntyre in the leading Supreme Court of Canada decision in *Dubois* (1985):[14]

> Section 13 of the Charter provides a much wider protection. In the clearest terms it gives the right to a witness who testifies in any proceeding not to have any incriminating evidence so given used to incriminate him in any other proceedings. This is a protection going far beyond that accorded by s. 5(2) of the Canada Evidence Act. It does not depend on any objection made by the witness giving the evidence. It is applicable and effective without invocation and even where the witness in question is unaware of this rights. It is not limited to a question in respect of which a witness would have been entitled to refuse to answer at common law and its prohibition against the use of incriminating evidence is not limited to criminal proceedings. It confers a right against incrimination by the use of evidence given in one proceeding in any other proceedings.[15]

4. PURPOSE OF SECTION 13

In *Dubois*, the majority judgment was delivered by Mr. Justice Lamer with five justices concurring.[16] Section 13 had to be considered in the light of two closely related rights: the right under s. 11(c) of an accused not to be compelled to testify and the presumption of innocence under s. 11(d), which included the concept of the Crown having to make out a case against the accused before he or she had to respond by testifying or calling other evidence.[17] This concept of the "case to meet" was common to ss. 11(c), 11(d) and 13. Lamer J. continued:

> In the context of ss. 11(c) and 13, it means specifically that the accused enjoys "the initial benefit of a right of silence" . . . and its corollary protection against self-incrimination. Section 13, like s. 11(c), is a recognition of the principle (Wigmore on Evidence . . .) that:
>
>> . . . the individual is sovereign and that proper rules of battle between government and individual require that the individual not be bothered for less than good reason and not be conscripted by his opponent to defeat himself . . .
>
> Hence the purpose of s. 13, when the section is viewed in the context of s. 11(c) and (d), is to protect individuals from being indirectly compelled to incriminate

---

[12] The leading discussion is *Tass*, [1947] S.C.R. 103 at 105.

[13] See G.A. Martin, "Self-Incrimination in Canada" (1961), 3 *Crim. L.Q.* 431 at 442.

[14] (1985), 48 C.R. (3d) 193 (S.C.C.).

[15] *Ibid.*, at 205. McIntyre J. dissented on a different point: see below note 20.

[16] Dickson C.J.C., Estey, Chouinard, Wilson and La Dain JJ.

[17] Above note 14, at 215, expressly relying on the views of Professor Ed Ratushny.

themselves, to ensure that the Crown will not be able to do indirectly that which s. 11(c) prohibits. It guarantees the right not to have a person's previous testimony used to incriminate him or her in other proceedings.[18]

Louise Arbour, now a Justice of the Supreme Court, provided a blunt critique of the Lamer approach:

> It is almost cynical to suggest that s. 13 of the Charter is another recognition of the sound and clear principle of Canadian law that an accused cannot be conscripted to defeat himself. . . . Much can be said of the right of an accused not to testify, but, with a few exceptions, everything an accused has ever said, in just about any circumstances, can be used in evidence against him, against his will, even if it was obtained without his knowledge, through official wiretapping or various forms of trickery.[19]

She sees the purpose of s. 13 having been much more convincingly expressed by Mr. Justice McIntyre in his dissenting judgment. McIntyre J. saw the purpose of s. 13, like s. 5(2) of the Canada Evidence Act, as lying in the "social interest in encouraging people to come forward to give evidence" not only in court but in proceedings before various commissions, boards and tribunals.[20] Even if they were compelled to testify, the witnesses would be reluctant to be forthright if they risked incriminating themselves in subsequent proceedings. The immunity provisions were to facilitate getting at the truth in the earlier proceedings.

5. BENEFICIARY OF RIGHT

In *Dubois*, the majority clearly determines that s. 13, like s. 5(2) of the Canada Evidence Act, does not apply to the original proceedings where the testimony was taken and only inures when the former witness has become an accused in subsequent proceedings and an attempt is made to incriminate that witness with the former testimony.[21]

The Court further held that, given the nature and purpose of the right which is essentially protection against self-incrimination, the question of whether the earlier testimony was given voluntarily or under compulsion was "irrelevant".[22] Dubois had testified at his first trial that he had killed the deceased but that there were circumstances of justification. He was convicted but the conviction was subsequently quashed on appeal on the basis of non-direction on the defences raised by his evidence. At the new trial, the Crown read in as part of its case 60 pages of transcript of the testimony given by the accused at his earlier trial. The trial judge rejected the accused's objection that this was contrary to s. 13. There was a conviction. On further appeal the Supreme Court quashed the second conviction and ordered a new trial. Under s. 13, the Crown ought not to have been allowed to tender incriminating evidence as part of its case.

---

[18] *Ibid.*, at 215-216.
[19] "Annotation to Dubois", C.R. *ibid.*, pp. 194-196.
[20] Above note 14, at 209-210.
[21] *Ibid.*, at 216-219.
[22] *Ibid.*, at 219.

Although the law is therefore quite clear that s. 13 protects even where the prior testimony was entirely voluntary it is of interest that several commentators[23] regard this aspect of the *Dubois* ruling as an extension of the privilege against self-incrimination that is not warranted given its historical roots.

6. INCRIMINATING EVIDENCE

The majority in *Dubois* also rejected the literal interpretation of s. 13 that the evidence had to be incriminating in both the first and second proceedings. The proper time to decide whether evidence was incriminating was at the subsequent proceedings when the Crown sought to make use of the previous evidence.[24] According to Lamer J. any evidence the Crown tendered as part of its case against an accused would be incriminating evidence for the purpose of s. 13:

> The Crown tenders evidence to support its case and obtain a conviction; it knows best what is incriminating. In a sense, the Crown could be said to be estopped from arguing that the evidence it tenders to that end is not incriminating.[25]

In *Mannion* (1986),[26] s. 13 protection, as interpreted in *Dubois*, was extended by the Supreme Court to preclude cross-examination of an accused on an inconsistent statement given at a previous trial for the same offence where the purpose was to incriminate the accused. Mannion had been convicted of rape but, on appeal, a new trial had been ordered. He was convicted again on the second trial and the issue was whether there had been a violation of s. 13. The Crown had introduced evidence at both trials that prior to the accused's arrest no police officer had told him that they were investigating his involvement in a rape. At his first trial, the accused had testified that he knew a rape was involved. At his second trial, the Crown did not introduce the accused's testimony from his early trial in chief but confronted him with it under cross- examination when he testified. The Crown position in both trials was that the accused's flight from the city where the rape occurred was because he was aware that the police wanted to see him and that this displayed a consciousness of guilt. The Supreme Court held that, in the circumstances, s. 13 excluded the incriminating use of evidence of these contradictory statements.[27]

Both the Saskatchewan[28] and British Columbia[29] Courts of Appeal subsequently read *Mannion* as limited to the situation of a cross-examination for the purpose of incrimination and not precluding Crown cross-examination of an accused on prior testimony for the purposes of impugning credibility. However, Mr. Justice Martin for the Ontario Court of Appeal in *Kuldip* (1988)[30] held that

---

[23] See, for example, David Doherty (as he then was) "Annotation to Dubois", C.R. *ibid.*, pp. 196-197 and Paciocco, *McGill L.J.*, above note 4, pp. 92-94.

[24] Above note 14, at 220-221.

[25] *Ibid.*, at 221.

[26] (1986), 53 C.R. (3d) 193 (S.C.C.).

[27] *Ibid.*, at 194.

[28] *B. (W.D.)* (1987), 38 C.C.C. (3d) 12 (Sask. C.A.).

[29] *Johnstone v. Law Society (British Columbia)*, [1987] 5 W.W.R. 637 (B.C. C.A.).

[30] (1988), 62 C.R. (3d) 336 (Ont. C.A.). Howland C.J.O. and Grange J.A. concurred.

Mannion could not be distinguished. Section 13 protected an accused from the use of that accused's testimony at the first trial both for incrimination and attacking credibility at the second trial. Martin J.A. pointed to the difficulty of drawing a clear line between these types of cross-examination.[31] He further suggested that, since it had been well established that s. 5(2) of the Canada Evidence Act would not allow use of prior testimony for the purposes of attacking credibility,[32] an interpretation limiting s. 13 would revive the unfairness of s. 5(2). Only the sophisticated witness could obtain the benefit of a blanket protection by registering an objection at the first proceedings.

On the appeal in *Kuldip* (1990),[33] a narrow four to three majority of the Supreme Court of Canada reversed the ruling of the Ontario Court of Appeal and ruled that using a prior inconsistent statement from a former proceeding during cross-examination to impugn the credibility of an accused does *not* incriminate the accused person contrary to s. 13. There had been no violation of s. 13 where, in a re-trial on a charge of failing to remain at the scene of the accident, the accused had been cross examined as to why he had identified a particular officer at the first trial, which officer the accused now knew had not been on duty that day.[34]

For the majority,[35] Chief Justice Lamer agreed with the Ontario Court of Appeal that it might sometimes be difficult to distinguish cross-examination of the accused's prior testimony for the purpose of incrimination from that for the purpose of impeaching credibility.[36] A trial judge's instructions to the jury as to the proper use of prior testimony would have to be clear. The Court reasoned that, even though the distinction might be somewhat troublesome, the need for a jury to have all relevant information clearly outweighed the benefits of simplicity.[37] No unfairness arose concerning s. 5(2) of the Canada Evidence Act as, properly interpreted,[38] that section did not protect against subsequent use of evidence where the purpose was to impeach the accused's credibility. Sections 5(2) and 13, held the Court, offered virtually identical protection. The only difference was that s. 5(2) required an objection in the first proceedings. Above all it seems quite clear that the Chief Justice was concerned that a ruling that s. 13 had been violated would unduly hamstring the Crown:

> An accused has the right to remain silent during his or her trial. However, if an accused chooses to take the stand, that accused is implicitly vouching for his or her credibility. Such an accused, like any other witness, has therefore opened the door

---

[31] *Ibid.*, at 347.

[32] The Court (*ibid.*, at 345) referred to *Wilmot* (1940), 2 W.W.R. 401 (Alta. C.A.) and *Quebec (A.G.) v. Côté* (1979), 8 C.R. (3d) 171 (Que. C.A.) and noted they had been cited with approval by the Supreme Court in *Mannion*.

[33] (1990), 1 C.R. (4th) 285 (S.C.C.).

[34] For *Kuldip* applications allowing cross-examination on prior testimony to attack credibility see *Richards* (1997), 6 C.R. (5th) 154 (B.C. C.A.) and *Ross* (1998), 131 C.C.C. (3d) 114 (Que. S.C.).

[35] Dickson C.J.C., Gonthier and McLachlin JJ. concurred. Wilson J. (La Forest and L'Heureux-Dubé JJ. concurring) dissented, adopting the reasons of the Ontario Court of Appeal.

[36] Above note 33, at 303.

[37] *Ibid.*

[38] It seems clear that the Court was in fact re-interpreting s. 5(2).

to having the trustworthiness of his/her evidence challenged. An interpretation of s. 13 which insulates such an accused from having previous inconsistent statements put to him/her on cross-examination where the only purpose of doing so is to challenge that accused's credibility, would, in my view, "stack the deck" too highly in favour of the accused.[39]

Kuldip has been criticized[40] on the basis that the distinction between cross-examination on a prior statement to challenge credibility rather than incriminate is "artificial in the extreme" and would have a "devastatingly incriminating effect."

Kuldip was distinguished in *Calder* (1996),[41] in which the majority rejected the argument that it should allow Crown cross-examination on a statement by the accused excluded under s. 24(2) for impeachment purposes. The test for the repute of the administration of justice was different. The "reasonable well-informed citizen who represents community values" would likely find admission of the statement no less fair because it was only used to destroy credibility. The majority's distinction of *Kuldip* is not compelling and *Calder* has been criticized on this and other bases.[42]

The Ontario Court of Appeal[43] ordered a new trial where the Crown had been allowed to cross-examine the accused on his knowledge of the protection provided by s. 13. The minimum probative value was outweighed by the evidence's prejudicial effect.

7. ANY OTHER PROCEEDING

Dubois expressly declared that a re-trial of the "same offence or one included" ordered by a Court of Appeal is considered as "other proceedings" entitled to the protection of s. 13.[44] To allow the prosecutor to use the accused's previous testimony as part of the case would allow the Crown to indirectly violate the s. 11(c) protection against compelling the accused to testify and also the presumption of innocence in s. 11(d) by conscripting the accused to help it discharge its burden of a case to meet. Section 13 should not be interpreted in a way which would violate other Charter rights.[45]

The dissenting judge, Mr. Justice McIntyre, would have determined that "proceedings in s. 13 included in a criminal case all judicial steps taken upon one charge to resolve and reach a final conclusion of the issue therein raised

---

[39] Above note 33, at 303.
[40] Naeem Rauf, "Section 13 of the Charter and the Use of an Accused's Prior Testimony: A Reply to David Doherty and Ronald Delisle" (1991), 4 C.R. (4th) 42.
[41] (1996), 46 C.R. (4th) 133 (S.C.C.), discussed below Chapter 11.
[42] See Ian D. Scott, "Calder. The Charter Trumps the Truth Seeking Tool of Impeaching the Accused with a Prior Inconsistent Statement", (1996) 46 C.R. (4th) 161 and David Rose, "Calder Applications Will Rarely Succeed and the Procedure is Unclear", (1996) 46 C.R. (4th) 151. *Calder* is discussed further, below Chapter 11.
[43] *Swick* (1997), 118 C.C.C. (3d) 33 (Ont. C.A.).
[44] Above note 14, at 222.
[45] *Ibid.*

between the same party and the Crown."[46] He would have included the preliminary hearing, the trial, an appeal and a new trial but not a *voir dire* held during the trial, since that did not resolve any issue raised in the charge but merely determined what could be introduced into the proceedings.[47]

David Doherty (now a member of the Ontario Court of Appeal) strongly criticizes *Dubois*[48] on the basis that it was an unjustified extension of the right against self-incrimination to limit the Crown's ability to adduce evidence, through witnesses other than the accused, of prior statements of the accused even if they had been voluntary. He sees "absolutely no unfairness" in using the type of evidence that was prohibited in *Dubois*, noting that such statements under oath are more reliable and cogent then other statements by an accused. He underlines his concern with a powerful example:

> Assume that the accused testifies and admits the actus reus at the initial trial. He is convicted, appeals, and the Court of Appeal orders a new trial. At the retrial he does not testify but through other witnesses advances an alibi defence. If the Crown cannot adduce his prior evidence, the trier of fact is left to assess the alibi defence without the knowledge that the accused had voluntarily under oath at an earlier time, in an effort to secure an acquittal, admitted doing the deed. An acquittal on the retrial in these circumstances might test the faith of even the most ardent civil libertarian. It is hoped that *Dubois* will represent an anomaly rather than the seminal case in the interpretation of s. 11(c) of the Charter.[49]

The Supreme Court's ruling in *Kuldip* should assuage many of Mr. Justice Doherty's law enforcement concerns.

The Ontario Court of Appeal has held[50] that the evidence of an accused at a preliminary inquiry may be admitted at the trial as part of the Crown's case as the trial does not constitute "other proceedings" within the meaning of s. 13. The Saskatchewan Court of Appeal has similarly held[51] that s. 13 does not prevent a Crown at a sentence hearing from relying on the accused's testimony at trial that he had previously been convicted of impaired driving. Both these decisions pre-date *Dubois* and seem inconsistent with the Supreme Court's approach.[52] On

---

[46] *Ibid.*, at 211.

[47] *Ibid.*, at 212.

[48] "Annotation to Dubois", above note 23.

[49] *Ibid.*, at 197. See similarly criticism of Paciocco, above note 4, and Whitten, above note 4, pp. 86-89.

[50] *Yakeleya* (1985), 46 C.R. (3d) 282 (Ont. C.A.).

[51] *Protz* (1984), 13 C.C.C. (3d) 107 (Sask. C.A.).

[52] This was the view adopted by Hrabinsky J. in *Lucas and Lucas* (1995), 97 C.C.C. (3d) 89 (Sask.Q.B.) in holding that s. 13 prevented the Crown from introducing a transcript of the accused's testimony at the preliminary inquiry as part of its case.

the other hand, it has been held that *Dubois* prohibits the use of testimony to incriminate an accused at trial from an earlier *voir dire*,[53] a Charter application,[54] a bail hearing[55] and a wrongful conviction hearing respecting another party.[56]

8. "EXCEPT IN A PROSECUTION FOR PERJURY OR FOR THE GIVING OF CONTRADICTORY EVIDENCE"

Section 5(2) of the Canada Evidence Act used to exempt only perjury from its protection. The Ontario Court of Appeal ruled[57] that the protection of s. 5(2) still applied to a case of giving contradictory evidence. Given that the protection under ss. 5(2) and 13 seems designed to encourage witnesses to be truthful, the broader exemption under s. 13 was sensible. Parliament has now[58] amended s. 5(2) to add the "giving of contradictory evidence" as an exemption. Section 5(2) and s. 13 are now identical in this respect.

There is much to be said for the purposeful interpretation of the Saskatchewan Court of Appeal in *Staranchuk* (1983),[59] adopted by the Supreme Court on appeal,[60] that s. 13 cannot be applied to "those occasions where a person makes false statements, while on oath, as a result of which he is charged with giving false evidence," cases in which the "very essence" of the offence is the giving of false testimony.[61]

9. BROADER PROTECTION AGAINST SELF-INCRIMINATION

Professor Ed Ratushny has long argued that the protection of ss. 11(c) and 13 is deficient:

> The basic problem is that many of the protections provided by the criminal process may be subverted by calling the suspect or accused as a witness at some other proceeding prior to his criminal trial.
> It is true that such a witness may prevent his testimony being introduced at any subsequent criminal trial. However, the damage may be done in other ways. The earlier hearing might be used as a "fishing expedition" to subject the witness to extensive questioning with a view to uncovering possible criminal conduct. The

[53] *Darrach* (2000), 36 C.R. (5th) 223 (S.C.C.) (evidence of accused at *voir dire* to determine admissibility of past sexual history of complainant not admissible to incriminate at trial though possibly admissible under *Kuldip* to impeach credibility). See too *Tarafa* (1989), 53 C.C.C. (3d) 472 (Que. S.C.).
[54] *Gordon* (1998), 130 C.C.C. (3d) 129 (Ont. Gen. Div.). Hill J. held s. 24(1) provided jurisdiction to prevent a threatened violation and stopped the use of a s. 11(b) application to provide voice identification evidence.
[55] *Sicurella* (1997), 14 C.R. (5th) 166 (Ont. Prov. Div.). Compare *Richards* where such evidence was admitted to attack credibility.
[56] *Fisher* (1999), 139 C.C.C. (3d) 418 (Sask. Q.B.) (testimony and D.N.A. samples provided on consent).
[57] *Chaperon* (1979), 52 C.C.C. (2d) 85 (Ont. C.A.).
[58] S.C. 1997, c. 18, s. 116.
[59] (1983), 36 C.R. (3d) 285 (Sask. C.A.).
[60] (1985), 47 C.R. (3d) 192 (S.C.C.).
[61] Above note 59, at 288 (per Cameron J.A., Hall and Talus JJ.A. concurring).

questioning might also be used to investigate a particular offence. For example, the accused might be required to reveal possible defences, the names of potential defence witnesses and other evidence. Moreover, the publicity generated by the hearing may seriously prejudice the likelihood of a fair trial.

The problem is that the initial hearing is likely to have none of the protections guaranteed by the criminal process. There will be no specific accusation, no presumption of innocence, no protection against prejudicial publicity, no right to counsel and no rules of evidence. The person presiding at the hearing may not have any legal training or any sense of impartiality. Indeed he may consider himself to be an arm of law enforcement!

What is the integrity of the protection in s. 11(c) if the actual laying of the charge can be delayed while the person, who is intended to be charged, is called as a witness at some other proceeding in order to further the investigation against him?[62]

In *Starr v. Houlden* (1990),[63] the Supreme Court has addressed some of these concerns under the rubric of an interpretation of the criminal law power under s. 91(27) of the Constitution Act of 1867, rather than through the mechanism of enhanced Charter protection. For the majority Mr. Justice Lamer, with five judges concurring,[64] held that, although the Supreme Court had consistently upheld the constitutionality of provincial commissions of inquiry granting fairly broad powers of investigation, which might incidently impact on the federal criminal law power, the powers of the provinces to establish such commissions were not constitutionally unlimited.[65] A province could not use the public inquiry process with all its coercive powers as a substitute for a police investigation and a preliminary inquiry into the alleged commission of specific criminal offences by named individuals.[66] This would interfere with the federal interests in protecting an individual according to the system of criminal justice established by the Criminal Code and would therefore be *ultra vires* the province as a matter under the federal criminal law power in s. 91(27). The inquiry in question had been set up to deal with the relationship between named individuals and corporations and elected and unelected public officials. Although the terms of reference of the Commission[67] prohibited it from expressing any conclusion of law regarding the civil or criminal responsibility of any individual or organization, it was asked *inter alia* to inquire into and report if there was sufficient evidence that a benefit, advantage or reward of any kind had been conferred upon an elected or unelected public official. The inquiry was in pith and substance a substitute police

---

[62] "Emerging Issues in Relation to the Legal Rights of a Suspect Under the Canadian Charter of Rights and Freedoms" (1983), 61 Can. Bar Rev. 177 at 186. He had earlier extensively documented his thesis: *Self Incrimination in the Canadian Criminal Process* (1979) pp. 78-87, 347-404.

[63] (1990), 55 C.C.C. (3d) 472 (S.C.C.). See criticism by S.G.M. Grange, "A Requiem for the Royal Commission", (1994) 43 *U.N.B.L.J.* 381 and further contributions to the *U.N.B.L.J.* forum on public inquiries, *ibid.*, by H. Archibald Kaiser, David H. Orr, Kent Roach and M. Anne Stalker.

[64] Dickson C.J.C., La Forest, Sopinka, Gonthier and Cory JJ. concurred. L'Heureux-Dubé J. dissented.

[65] Above note 63, at 489.

[66] *Ibid.*, at 505.

[67] *Ibid.*, at 477-478.

investigation and preliminary inquiry into a specific offence defined under s. 121 of the Criminal Code. It was unconstitutional.[68]

---

[68] *Ibid.*, at 497.

9

Section 14: Right to an Interpreter

Under s. 14:

> A party or witness in any proceedings who does not understand or speak the language in which the proceedings are conducted or who is deaf has the right to the assistance of an interpreter.

Section 14 was the subject of comprehensive consideration by Chief Justice Lamer for a unanimous Supreme Court in *Tran* (1994).[1] The accused, a native of Vietnam, had been convicted of sexual assault. The Supreme Court held that the failure to provide the accused with full and contemporaneous translation of all the evidence at trial, in particular during the questioning and testimony of the interpreter, breached the accused's s. 14 right and necessitated a new trial.

The Chief Justice took the opportunity to fully explore and interpret[2] s. 14. It was seen to confer upon

> all accused, irrespective of the gravity of the offence charged and its classification, a constitutionally guaranteed right to the assistance of an interpreter where the accused does not understand or speak the language of the court.[3]

It was made express that the judgment covered all accused in criminal proceedings, whether proceeded with on indictment or by way of summary conviction proceedings. The Court expressly left open the possibility that different rules might apply in other situations such as civil or administrative proceedings.[4] Although the issue is not addressed, *Tran* should surely extend to charges of

---

[1] (1994), 32 C.R. (4th) 34 (S.C.C.).

[2] Particular reliance was placed on *Lee Kun*, [1916] 1 K.B. 337 (C.A.), on two previous decisions on s. 14, namely *Petrovic* (1984) 41 C.R. (3d) 275 (Ont. C.A.) and *Tsang* (1985), 27 C.C.C. (3d) 365 (B.C. C.A.), and Graham J. Steele, "Court Interpreters in Canadian Criminal Law" (1992) 34 *Crim. L.Q.* 218. See further the comprehensive consideration of David J. Heller, "Language Bias in the Criminal Justice System", (1995) 37 *Crim. L.Q.* 344.

[3] At 42.

[4] At 43.

provincial offences. Section 14 speaks broadly of "any proceedings" and there is no limiting triggering requirement, such as that of a charge of an offence required for s. 11 rights.

1. PURPOSES OF SECTION 14

To Chief Justice Lamer in *Tran:*

> The right of an accused person who does not understand or speak the language of the proceedings to obtain the assistance of an interpreter serves several important purposes. First and foremost, the right ensures that a person charged with a criminal offence hears the case against him or her and is given a full opportunity to answer it. Second, the right is one that is intimately related to our basic notions of justice, including the appearance of fairness. As such, the right to interpreter assistance touches on the very integrity of the administration of criminal justice in this country. Third, the right is one which is intimately related to our society's claim to be multicultural, expressed in part through s. 27 of the Charter.[5]

The magnitude of these interests favoured a purposive and liberal interpretation of s. 14. The underlying principle was that of linguistic understanding. The level of understanding would necessarily have to be high although those with difficulty communicating or comprehending the language of the proceeding, whether English or French, should not be given an unfair advantage.[6]

2. ESTABLISHING VIOLATION

The Court in *Tran* accepts that the accused has the usual burden of proof in establishing a Charter violation. A finding that section had been breached required either (1) proof that he or she was in need of an interpreter in that he or she did not understand or speak the language of the Court or (2) proof that there was a material deficiency in the interpretation actually provided.

The Court sets special parameters for how a s. 14 violation is to be established. Although the Chief Justice holds that there is no requirement that courts inform all accused of the right to interpreter assistance or inquire as a matter of course into every accused's capacity to understand, there is

> no absolute requirement on an accused that the right be formally asserted or invoked as a pre-condition to enjoying it.[7]

The explanation for this is that the Courts are seen to have an independent responsibility to ensure that their proceedings are fair and in accordance with principles of fundamental justice. This onus on the judge respecting s. 14 appears unique[8] and should, in the interests of consistency, have implications for other

---

[5] At 55.

[6] At 56.

[7] At 58.

[8] Under present jurisprudence, both the right to disclosure under s. 7, discussed above Chapter 2, and the right to be tried within a reasonable time under s. 11(b), discussed above Chapter 6, require assertions by accused.

Charter rights such as the right to counsel at trial and the right to make full answer and defence.

Later, the Court also determines[9] that whether the violation of the right prejudiced the accused in that the outcome of the case would have been different, is not material to the issue of whether there was a breach. Prejudice is only material to remedy. This is a position markedly at odds with the Supreme Court's determination that the establishment of prejudice is key to the determination of whether the accused's right to be tried within a reasonable time has been violated.[10]

3. GENERAL STANDARDS FOR INTERPRETATION

The *Tran* ruling deals elaborately[11] with the standard to be required for interpretation. The standard is to be high although not one of perfection. Criteria include those of continuity, precision, impartiality, competency and contemporaneousness. The Court accepts that the lapse in interpretation must be respecting a material part of the proceedings

> involving the vital interests of the accused, and... not merely in respect of some collateral or extrinsic matter, such as an administrative issue relating to scheduling.[12]

The Manitoba Court of Appeal in *R. (A.L.)* (1999)[13] held that no formal training was necessary to meet these tests. The Court also held that s. 14 did not cover interpretation for communication between the accused and lawyer since s. 14 referred to "proceedings". The Court added that any protection would have to be found in the right to instruct counsel under s. 10(b), the right to a fair trial under s. 11(d) or the right to full answer and defence under s. 7. The majority held there had been no air of reality to such arguments on the facts. The request for a second interpreter had been a delaying tactic after a challenge to the court interpreter had failed.

4. WAIVER

The Supreme Court in *Tran* confirms that the threshold for waiver is "very high"[14] and that the Crown must show a valid and effective waiver on a balance of probabilities.[15] Given the very real potential for misunderstanding through language difficulties the Court further imposes for s. 14 a special requirement of a personal waiver.

> The Crown must not only show that the waiver was clear and unequivocal and made with a knowledge and understanding of the right, but also that it was made personally by the accused or with defence counsel's assurance that the right and the effect on that right of waiving it were explained to the accused in language in which the accused is fully conversant.[16]

---

[9] At 68-69.
[10] Discussed above Chapter 6.
[11] At 61-65.
[12] At 65.
[13] (1999), 29 C.R. (5th) 320 (Man. C.A.).
[14] At 69.
[15] At 71.
[16] At 71.

5. REMEDY

The Supreme Court in *Tran* holds that a denial of the interpreter right under s. 14 can never be characterised as minor or harmless, and therefore cannot be made subject to Criminal Code no substantial wrong or miscarriage of justice provisos.[17] The normal s. 24(1) remedy is held to be a re-hearing of the issue or proceeding in which the violation occurred. Thus, there might be an order for a new trial or, where the violation occurred in a discrete part of the proceedings, such as a bail or sentence hearing, a re-hearing of that issue.[18] The Court emphasizes that s. 24(1) remedies are flexible. Damages could be ordered where financial prejudice is established.[19]

Tran appears to be a *tour de force* judgment and it is difficult to imagine how accused or witnesses who have language comprehension problems could have been better protected. Whether the *Tran* standards are in practice in place is another matter. The 1995 *Report on the Commission on Systemic Racism in the Ontario Criminal Justice System* (1995) found that interpreters, as well as judges, lawyers and representatives of community agencies involved in criminal justice in Ontario, had

> serious concerns about the guarantees of court interpreter competence, impartiality and accountability for mistakes.[20]

---

[17] At 79.

[18] In *Haskins* (1995), 44 C.R. (4th) 335 (Alta. C.A.), a deaf accused, who was relying on sign language, was charged with theft. The defence counsel indicated that it was not necessary to swear the interpreter. However, the accused objected to this procedure after the examination-in-chief of the first Crown witness. The trial judge attempted to remedy the problem by summarizing the testimony. The interpreter was sworn and the trial proceeded. The accused was convicted. On appeal, the Alberta Court of Appeal held that the summary provided by the trial judge was not an adequate remedy for the breach of s. 14 and a new trial was necessary.

[19] At 80.

[20] At 243-244.

10

Section 15: Equality Rights

Under s. 15(1) of the Charter:

> Every individual is equal before and under the law and has the right to the equal protection and equal benefit of the law without discrimination and, in particular, without discrimination based on race, national or ethnic origin, colour, religion, sex, age or mental or physical disability.

Section 15(2) provides constitutional protection for affirmative action programs:

> Subsection (1) does not preclude any law, program or activity that has as its object the amelioration of conditions of disadvantaged individuals or groups including those that are disadvantaged because of race, national or ethnic origin, colour, religion, sex, age or mental or physical disability.

In contrast to the remainder of the Charter the guarantee of equality in s. 15 was deferred for three years. Section 15 came into force on April 17, 1985.[1]

There is also an express guarantee in s. 28 that Charter rights are guaranteed equally to both sexes:

> Notwithstanding anything in this Charter the rights and freedoms referred to in it are guaranteed equally to male and female persons.

1. CANADIAN BILL OF RIGHTS

Under s. 1(b) of the Bill

> It is hereby recognized and declared that in Canada there have existed and shall continue to exist without discrimination by reason of race, national origin, colour, religion or sex, the following human rights and fundamental freedoms, namely . . . the right of the individual to equality before the law and the protection of the law.

---

[1] Constitution Act, 1982 [en. Canada Act 1982 (U.K.), c. 11, sched. B], s. 32(2).

In its landmark decision in *Drybones* (1970),[2] the Supreme Court ruled that a provision of the Indian Act[3] making it an offence for an Indian to be intoxicated off a reserve denied equality before the law in terms of s. 1(b). However, *Drybones* was subsequently distinguished by the Court in two controversial decisions. In *Canada (A. G.) v. Lavell* (1974)[4] it was held that another provision of the Indian Act depriving women of their membership in Indian Bands if they married non-Indians did not constitute inequality before the law. In *Bliss v. Canada (A.G.)* (1979)[5] the Court decided that provisions of the Unemployment Insurance Act,[6] which denied a pregnant woman unemployment benefits to which she would have been entitled had she not been pregnant, did not violate s. 1(b) because any inequality had not been created by legislation ''but by nature.''[7]

The Canadian Bill of Rights does not have the equivalent of s. 1 of the Charter under which rights can be qualified. In *MacKay* (1980)[8] the Supreme Court held that some legislative distinctions contrary to the concept of equality before the law could be justified by the courts. The test asserted was

> whether it is a necessary departure from the general principle of universal application of the law for the attainment of some necessary and desirable social objective.[9]

2. PURPOSE OF SECTION 15

The Supreme Court of Canada asserted its approach to s. 15 in *Andrews v. Law Society of British Columbia* (1989).[10] The challenge was against a provision of the Barristers and Solicitors Act of British Columbia[11] barring entry to the legal profession of one who had met all the requirements for admission except that of Canadian citizenship. The Court found that it violated s. 15(1) and did not constitute a demonstrably justified reasonable limit under s. 1. Mr. Justice McIntyre wrote the majority judgment on the meaning of s. 15(1) and the relationship between s. 15(1) and s. 1,[12] but dissented on the facts.[13]

The *Andrews* test was embellished by Madam Justice Wilson for a unanimous Court in *Turpin* (1989).[14] The Court there held that a former Criminal

---

[2] [1970] S.C.R. 282.
[3] R.S.C. 1970, C I-6.
[4] [1974] S.C.R. 1349.
[5] [1979] 1 S.C.R. 183.
[6] S.C. 1970-71-72, C. 48.
[7] Above note 5, at 190.
[8] [1980] 2 S.C.R. 370.
[9] *Ibid.*, at 407.
[10] [1989] 1 S.C.R. 143. See the critical review by William Black and Lynn Smith, ''Canadian Citizenship and the Right to Practice Law'', (1989) 68 *Can. Bar Rev.* 591, and Marc Gold, ''Andrews v. the Law Society of British Columbia'', (1989) 34 *McGill L.J.* 1063.
[11] R.S.B.C. 1979, C. 26, s. 42.
[12] Lamer J. concurred, Wilson J. (Dickson C.J. and L'Heureux-Dubé J. concurring) expressly agreed with the approach of McIntyre J., except for his application of s. 1 to the particular case (above note 10, at 150). That was also the position of La Forest J. in a separate concurring opinion (at 193).
[13] Only Lamer J. joined McIntyre J. on this issue.
[14] (1989), 69 C.R. (3d) 97 (S.C.C.). See Tom Fitzgerald, ''Turpin and Equality: A New Approach to an Old Problem'', (1989) 70 C.R. (3d) 331.

Code provision[15] allowing an accused to elect a non-jury murder trial, but only in Alberta, did not violate s. 15.

In *Andrews*, McIntyre J. held that it was "readily apparent" that the much broader language of s. 15 had been deliberately chosen to remedy perceived defects under the Canadian Bill of Rights.[16] The clear purpose of s. 15 was to "ensure equality in the formulation and application of the law."[17] Section 15(1) was not, however,

> a general guarantee of equality; it does not provide for equality between individuals or groups within society in a general or abstract sense, nor does it impose on individuals or groups an obligation to accord equal treatment to others.[18]

The concept of equality was an "elusive concept which more than any other Charter right lacked precise definition".[19] It was a "comparative concept" which required comparison with the conditions of others in the social and political setting in question. McIntyre J. hastened to point out that

> every difference in treatment between individuals under the law will not necessarily result in inequality and, as well, that identical treatment may frequently produce serious inequality.[20]

A law expressed to bind all should not "because of irrelevant personal differences have a more burdensome or less beneficial impact on one than another".[21] Section 15 was seen to have a much more specific goal than the mere elimination of distinctions. The evil against which s. 15 provided a guarantee was that discriminatory measures should not have the force of law.[22]

3. REJECTION OF "SIMILARLY SITUATED" TEST

In *Andrews*, McLachlin J.A. (as she then was) had asserted in the British Columbia Court of Appeal that

> The essential meaning of the constitutional requirement of equal protection and equal benefit is that persons who are "similarly situated be similarly treated" and conversely, that persons who are "differently situated be differently treated."[23]

The Supreme Court, through McIntyre J., noting that this test had been widely accepted with various modifications in both trial and appeal courts,[24] nevertheless flatly rejected it:

---

[15] Section 430, repealed by R.S.C. 1985, C. 27 (1st Supp.), s. 63.
[16] Above note 10, at 170.
[17] *Ibid.*, at 171.
[18] *Ibid.*, at 163-164.
[19] *Ibid.*, at 164.
[20] *Ibid.*
[21] *Ibid.*, at 165.
[22] *Ibid.*, at 172.
[23] (1986), 27 D.L.R. (4th) 600 at 605 (B.C. C.A.).
[24] See, for example, *Ertel* (1987), 58 C.R. (3d) 252 (Ont. C.A.) and *Turpin* (1987), 60 C.R. (3d) 63 (Ont. C.A.). In *Turpin* the Court held:
> To establish a s. 15 infringement, the one challenging the law must: (1) identify the class of individuals who are alleged to be treated differently; (2) demonstrate that the class purported to be treated differently from another class is similarly situated to that other class in relation to the purposes of the law; and (3) show that the difference in treatment is discriminatory, in the sense of there being a pejorative or invidious purpose or effect of the impugned law (at 69-70).

> The test as stated, however, is seriously deficient in that it excludes any consideration of the nature of the law. If it were to be applied literally, it could be used to justify the Nuremburg laws of Adolf Hitler. Similar treatment was contemplated for all Jews.[25]

McIntyre J. noted that the similarly situated test would justify the formalistic and long rejected "separate but equal" doctrine of the United States Supreme Court[26] and could lead to results like those in *Bliss*.

In the context of criminal law many s. 15 challenges have foundered at least in part on this "similarly situated" test. This occurred, for example, in unsuccessful s. 15 challenges against the denial of the right to choose a jury trial under the Young Offenders Act,[27] against release on mandatory supervision in the case of federal but not provincial inmates[28] and against the process of empanelling the jury.[29] Given *Andrews*, such rulings can no longer be considered authoritative.

4. ANDREWS/TURPIN TEST OF EQUALITY[30]

In *Swain* (1991),[31] Chief Justice Lamer for a 5-1 majority[32] held that a common law rule that would allow the Crown to raise evidence of insanity only where the accused's own defence had put mental capacity for criminal intent into issue or where the accused's defence had been concluded, did not infringe s. 15(1). According to the Chief Justice, *Andrews* and *Turpin* conveyed a "basic framework" within which s. 15(1) claims could be analyzed:

> The Court must first determine whether the claimant has shown that one of the four basic equality rights has been denied (i.e., equality before the law, equality under the law, equal protection of the law and equal benefit of the law). This inquiry will focus largely on whether the law has drawn a distinction (intentionally or otherwise) between the claimant and others, based on personal characteristics. Next, the Court must determine whether the denial can be said to result in "discrimination". This second inquiry will focus largely on whether the differential treatment has the effect of imposing a burden, obligation or disadvantage not imposed upon others or of withholding or limiting access to opportunities, benefits and advantages available to others. Furthermore, in determining whether the claimant's s. 15(1) rights have been infringed, the Court must consider whether the personal characteristic in question

[25] Above, note 10, at 166.

[26] *Plessy v. Ferguson*, 163 U.S. 537 (1896).

[27] R.S.C. 1985, C. Y-1: *L. (R.)* (1986), 52 C.R. (3d) 209 (Ont. C.A.), criticized by Robert E. Charney, "R.L.: Bootstrap Equality", C.R. *ibid.*, pp. 232-239.

[28] *Dempsey* (1987), 34 C.C.C. (3d) 95 (Fed. C.A.).

[29] *Stoddart* (1987), 59 C.R. (3d) 134 (Ont. C.A.).

[30] See Tom Fitzgerald "Turpin and Equality: A New Approach to An Old Problem", (1989) 70 C.R. (3d) 331. For comprehensive review of equality issues see Dale Gibson, *The Law of the Charter: Equality Rights* (1989) and Anne Bayefsky and Mary Eberts (eds.), *Equality Rights and the Canadian Charter of Rights and Freedoms* (1985).

[31] (1991), 63 C.C.C. (3d) 481 (S.C.C.).

[32] Sopinka and Cory JJ. concurred. Gonthier J., La Forest J. concurring on this issued in a separate opinion. Wilson J. dissented, holding that the common law rule would violate s. 15 and could not be saved by s. 1. L'Heureux-Dubé J. in dissent did not consider the s. 15 issue.

falls within the grounds enumerated in the section or within an analogous ground, so as to ensure that the claim fits within the overall purpose of s. 15; namely, to remedy or prevent discrimination against groups subject to stereotyping, historical disadvantage and political and social prejudice in Canadian society.[33]

The Chief Justice clearly envisages a two-stage process of first determining whether there has been a denial of an equality right and, second, whether there has been discrimination. It is also quite clear that if the Court decides there has been a breach there is a third stage of balancing interests under s. 1. Here these three stages will be considered in turn.

(a) Breach of Equality Rights

In contrast to the Canadian Bill of Rights, which only protects equality before the law, s. 15(1) of the Charter provides a much broader protection of four basic rights: the right to equality before the law, the right to equality under the law, the right to equal protection of the law and the right to equal benefit of the law. In *Andrews*, McIntyre J. sees the inclusion of the last three additional rights as an attempt to remedy the shortcomings of the Canadian Bill of Rights and reflecting an expanded concept of discrimination being developed under various Human Rights Codes.[34] He holds that principles applied under the Human Rights Acts are equally applicable to the Charter, subject to the normal two-stage approach to the Charter under which consideration of limiting factors on a right is to be made under s. 1:

> Any justification of an infringement which is found to have occurred must be made, if at all, under the broad provisions of s. 1. It must be admitted at once that the relationship between these two sections may well be difficult to determine on a wholly satisfactory basis. It is, however, important to keep them analytically distinct if for no other reason than the different attribution of the burden of proof. It is for the citizen to establish that his or her Charter right has been infringed and for the state to justify the infringement.[35]

Similarly, in *Turpin*, Wilson J. emphasized that in defining the four basic equality rights

> it is important to ensure that each right be given its full independent content, divorced from any justificatory factors applicable under s. 1 of the Charter.[36]

She soon enters a caveat to the interpretation of equality rights:

> [In] these early days of interpreting s. 15 it would be unwise, if not foolhardy, to attempt to provide exhaustive definitions of phrases which by their nature are not susceptible of easy definition and which are intended to provide a framework for the ''unremitting protection'' of equality rights in the years to come.[37]

The value protected by s. 15 is seen to be rooted in the rule of law:

---

[33] Above note 31, at 520-521.
[34] Above note 10, at 170.
[35] *Ibid.*, at 178.
[36] Above note 14, at 121.
[37] *Ibid.*

The guarantee of equality before the law is designed to advance the value that all persons be subject to the equal demands and burdens of the law and not suffer any greater disability in the substance and application of the law than others. This value has historically been associated with the requirements of the rule of law that all persons be subject to the law impartially applied and administered.[38]

The minimal content of the right to equality in s. 15 was that "no individual or group of individuals is to be treated more harshly than another under that law."[39] The accused in *Turpin* had been denied equality before the law since the Criminal Code provisions in question treated them more harshly than those charged with the same offence in Alberta who had the opportunity to be tried by judge alone.[40]

In his summary of principles in *Swain*, Chief Justice Lamer suggests that the focus in this first stage is on whether there is a distinction based on a personal characteristic. This focus is not evident in *Turpin* and seems more applicable to the second stage determination of whether there has been discrimination.

(b) Amounting to Discrimination

In *Andrews*, McIntyre J. adopted an "enumerated and analogous approach" to the interpretation of s. 15. The words "without discrimination" within s. 15 were a form of qualifier built into s. 15, which required more than a mere finding of a distinction between the treatment of groups or individuals:[41]

A complainant under s. 15(1) must show not only that he or she is not receiving equal treatment before and under the law or that the law has a differential impact on him or her in the protection or benefit accorded by law but, in addition, must show that the legislative impact of the law is discriminatory.[42]

Discrimination would generally be expressed by the enumerated grounds but also extended to analogous grounds. The Court appears to have adopted the following approach of Mr. Justice Hugessen in *Smith, Kline and French Laboratories Ltd v. Canada (A.G.)* (1987):[43]

As far as the text of section 15 itself is concerned, one may look to whether or not there is "discrimination", in the pejorative sense of that word, and as to whether the categories are based upon the grounds enumerated or grounds analogous to them. The inquiry, in effect, concentrates upon the personal characteristics of those who claim to have been unequally treated. Questions of stereotyping, of historical disadvantagement, in a word, of prejudice, are the focus and there may even be a recognition that for some people equality has a different meaning than for others.[44]

Relying on the modern approach to discrimination under Human Rights Acts, McIntyre J. sought to define discrimination:

[38] *Ibid.*, at 123.
[39] The Court was applying a dictum of Ritchie J. in *Drybones*, above note 2, at 297.
[40] Above note 14, at 124.
[41] Above note 10, at 180-181.
[42] *Ibid.*, at 182.
[43] [1987] 2 F.C. 359 (C.A.).
[44] Above note 10, at 180.

[Discrimination] may be described as a distinction, whether intentional or not but based on grounds relating to personal characteristics of the individual or group, which has the effect of imposing burdens, obligations, or disadvantages on such individual or group not imposed upon others, or which withholds or limits access to opportunities, benefits, and advantages available to other members of society.[45]

McIntyre J. had little difficulty in holding that a rule barring persons from being able to become lawyers solely on the basis of lack of citizenship status infringed s. 15. Non-citizens permanently resident in Canada were "a good example of a 'discrete and insular minority'[46] who came within the protection of s. 15."[47]

In *Andrews*, McIntyre J. rejected two other approaches. Professor Peter Hogg[48] had suggested that s. 15 should be interpreted as requiring the universal application of every law such that any distinction between individuals would breach s. 15 and move the constitutional issue to s. 1. To McIntyre J. this position would trivialize the Charter, deprive the words "without discrimination" of content and virtually deny any role for s. 1.[49] The other jettisoned view was that of McLachlin J. in the Court below, shared by many other courts,[50] that the courts should ask whether "the legislative means adopted are unreasonable or unfair."[51] Such a view, held McIntyre J., would involve a "radical" departure from the Court's analytic approach to the Charter in that the determination would be made under s. 15(1) with "virtually no role" left for s. 1.[52]

In *Turpin*, Wilson J. emphasized that whether the differential treatment was discriminatory was "determinative" of whether there has been a violation of s. 15.[53] She determined for the Court that it was important to look beyond the particular legal distinction being challenged and to examine the "larger social, political and legal contexts."[54] Whether a group fell into a category analogous to those specifically enumerated in s. 15 was not to be made in the context of the law being challenged but "in the context of the place of the group in the entire social, political and legal fabric of our society."[55] If this was not done the s. 15 analysis would become "a mechanical and sterile categorization process" likely to result in the "same kind of circularity" that had characterized the "similarly situated, similarly treated" test rejected in *Andrews*.[56]

The s. 15 challenge failed in *Turpin* because it would be "stretching the imagination" to hold that persons accused of crimes listed in s. 469 of the Criminal Code in all provinces but Alberta were members of a "discrete and insular

[45] *Ibid.*, at 174, adopted in both *Turpin* and *Swain*.
[46] These words were taken from *United States v. Carolene Products Co.*, 304 U.S. 144 at 152-153 (1938).
[47] Above note 10, at 182.
[48] *Constitutional Law of Canada*, 2nd ed. (1985) pp. 800-801.
[49] Above note 10, at 181.
[50] For the similar Ontario Court of Appeal approach, see above note 24.
[51] Above note 23, at 610.
[52] Above note 10, at 181-182.
[53] Above note 14, at 125.
[54] *Ibid.*
[55] Wilson J. was re-asserting views she had first expressed in *Andrews*.
[56] Above note 14, at 126.

minority.'' Wilson J. added that this categorization was not an end in itself but merely an analytical tool to help determine whether the interest claimed was the kind of interest protected by s. 15.[57] The provision in question in *Turpin* was held to have little to do with remedying or preventing discrimination against groups suffering social, political and legal disadvantage.[58]

In *Swain*, Chief Justice Lamer, for the majority, accepted that the common law rule in question distinguished between individuals on the basis of a personal characteristic which fell within the enumerated ground of mental disability. However, the differential treatment was not discriminatory. A rule which allows the Crown to move an accused from the category of one who will surely be convicted and sentenced to one who may be acquitted on the grounds of insanity did not impose a burden or a disadvantage on that individual.[59] Wilson J. was the sole dissenter on the basis that the new common law rule of the majority also conferred on the prosecution the right to raise the issue of insanity where the accused had put his mental capacity in issue. This denied the mentally disabled, a ''negatively stereotyped and historically disadvantaged'' group, the control over their defences and was discriminatory and contrary to s. 15.[60]

5. RE-CONSIDERATION IN M.E.T. TRILOGY[61]

In 1995, the Supreme Court handed down three s. 15 rulings, none involving criminal law, in which the Court revealed itself to be remarkably divided on the proper approach to the determination of whether the s. 15 guarantee has been breached.

In *Miron v. Trudel* (1995),[62] the Court decided 5-4 that the failure to include common law spouses in the definition of ''spouse'' in a provincial Insurance Act violated s. 15 and could not be demonstrably justified under s. 1. An unmarried partner had been denied accident benefits available to a married partner and the majority[63] held that marital status is an analogous ground of discrimination for purposes of s. 15(1). The minority was of the view that there had been no discrimination.[64]

---

[57] In *Hess* (1990), 79 C.R. (3d) 332 (S.C.C.), discussed below, McLachlin J. in dissent rejected an interpretation that a group (in that case men) could only be protected under s. 15 if it constituted a ''discrete and insular minority'' disadvantaged independently of the legislation under challenge (at 361).

[58] Above note 14, at 127.

[59] Above note 31, at 521.

[60] *Ibid.*, at 552.

[61] In considering these very complex decisions I have derived considerable assistance from an unpublished paper by a Queen's L.L.B. graduate, Laurie Lacelle, ''Section 15 Under the M.E.T. Trilogy and Its Implications for the Interests of Women and Victims in Criminal Law''. See too L. Trakman, ''Section 15: Equality? Where?'', (1995) 6:4 *Constitutional Forum* 112.

[62] [1995] 2 S.C.R. 418.

[63] Sopinka, Cory, and Iacobucci JJ. concurred in the judgment of McLachlin J. L'Heureux-Dubé J. delivered a separate concurring judgment.

[64] Gonthier J. (Lamer C.J., La Forest and Major JJ. concurring) dissented.

In *Egan v. Canada* (1995),[65] the challenge was also to the definition of
"spouse", this time under the federal Old Age Security Act.[66] The plaintiffs were
a homosexual couple who had lived together in a spousal-like relationship since
1948. They had been denied the benefit on the basis that the spousal relationship
had to be heterosexual. The Court unanimously held that sexual orientation was
an analogous ground of discrimination under s. 15. However, the Court decided
5-4 that the section 15 claim could not succeed. Four of the majority justices held
that the definition did not constitute discrimination because it satisfied a test of
relevance.[67] The four dissenting justices[68] found discrimination that could not be
justified under s. 1. The ninth justice, Sopinka J., was the swing vote in deciding
that there was discrimination, but it could be saved under s. 1:

> Given the fact that equating same-sex couples with heterosexual spouses, either
> married or common law, is still generally regarded as a novel concept, I am not
> prepared to say that by its inaction to date the government has disentitled itself to
> rely on s. 1 of the Charter.[69]

In *Thibaudeau v. R.* (1995),[70] a 5-2 majority[71] held that a provision of the
federal Income Tax Act requiring a divorced women to include in her taxable
income amounts received from her former husband as alimony for child
maintenance did not violate s. 15. The majority held that the provision did not
impose a benefit or withhold a benefit within the meaning of s. 15.

Can a general approach to s. 15 be gleaned from this intricate series of split
opinions? There appear to be three competing tests. McLachlin J. (Cory J.,
Iacobucci J. and Sopinka J. concurring) adopt a two-step approach:

> The analysis under s. 15 (1) involves two steps. First, the claimant must show a
> denial of "equal protection or equal benefit of the law", as compared with some
> other person. Second, the claimant must show that the denial constitutes
> discrimination. At this second stage, in order for discrimination to be made out, the
> claimant must show that the denial rests on one of the grounds enumerated in s. 15
> (1) or an analogous ground and that the unequal treatment is based on the stereotypical
> application of presumed group or personal characteristics. If the claimant meets the
> onus under this analysis, violation of s. 15 (1) is established. The onus then shifts to
> the party seeking to uphold the law, usually the state, to justify the discrimination as
> "demonstrably justified in a free and democratic society" under s. 1 of the Charter.[72]

This approach appears similar to that in *Andrews*, with the s. 1 inquiry kept
separate. However, the definition of discrimination appears to have been narrowed
to one requiring proof of a "stereotypical application of presumed group or
personal characteristics".

---

[65] [1995] 2 S.C.R. 513.

[66] R.S.C. 1985, c. O-9, ss. 2 and 19(1).

[67] La Forest J. (Lamer C.J., Gonthier and Major JJ. concurring).

[68] Separate opinions were delivered by Cory J. (Iacobucci J. concurring), L'Heureux-Dubé J. and
McLachlin J.

[69] At 576.

[70] [1995] 2 S.C.R 627.

[71] Separate majority opinions were delivered by Sopinka J. (La Forest J. concurring), Cory and
Iacobucci JJ., and Gonthier, McLachlin and L'Heureux-Dubé JJ. dissented in separate opinions.

[72] *Miron*, para. 128 at 485.

Gonthier J. (Lamer C.J., La Forest and Major JJ. concurring), also purporting to rely on *Andrews*, articulates a three step approach:.

> The first step looks to whether the law has drawn a distinction between the claimant and others. The second step then questions whether the distinction results in disadvantage, and examines whether the impugned law imposes a burden, obligation or disadvantage on a group or persons to which the claimant belongs which is not imposed on others, or does not provide them with a benefit which its grants others... It is at this second step that the direct or indirect effect of the legislation is examined. The third step assesses whether the distinction is based on an irrelevant personal characteristic which is either enumerated in s. 15 (1) or one analogous thereto.... This third step...comprises two aspects: determining the personal characteristic shared by a group and then assessing its relevancy having regard to the functional values underlying the legislation.[73]

The ninth justice, L'Heureux-Dubé J., would adopt a new approach to discrimination which focuses

> on *impact* (i.e. discriminatory effect) rather than on *constituent elements* (i.e. the grounds of the distinction).[74]

On her approach:

> A distinction is discriminatory within the meaning of s. 15 where it is capable or either promoting or perpetuating the view that the individual adversely affected by this distinction is less capable, or less worthy of recognition or value as a human being or as a member of Canadian society, equally deserving of concern, respect, and consideration.[75]

Strictly speaking, there is therefore no majority approach to s. 15 that emerges from the *M.E.T.* trilogy. However, there is a strong case for the view that adopting the two-step McLachlin test better reflects the majority consensus. The most controversial aspect of the Gonthier approach is the resort in his step three to the test of relevance. This aspect is strongly attacked by L'Heureux-Dubé J.[76] on the basis that it is far too narrow in not being able to consider discriminatory effects and is to be considered under s. 1. The broader L'Heureux-Dubé approach clearly has much more affinity with the McLachlin approach than with that of Gonthier.

Similar criticisms of the Gonthier requirement of relevance are expressed in varying degrees in judgments by the McLachlin group. McLachlin J. puts the criticism well:

> If the basis of the distinction on an enumerated ground is clearly irrelevant to the functional values of the legislation, then the distinction will be discriminatory. However, it does not follow from a finding that a group characteristic is relevant to the legislative aim, that the legislator has employed that characteristic in a manner which does not perpetuate limitations, burdens and disadvantages in violation of section 15 (1).[77]

---

[73] *Miron*, paras. 13-15 at 435.
[74] *Egan*, para. 39 at 549.
[75] *Ibid.*, para. 56 at 552-553.
[76] *Ibid.*, paras 43-45.
[77] *Miron*, para. 133 at 488.

Cory J. and Iacobucci J. point out that the analytical separation of the ss. 1 and 15(1) inquiries is important as the claimant only has the burden of showing a discriminatory distinction while the onus of justifying a breach is on the government.[78]

6. CONSOLIDATED TEST IN LAW DECISION

The Court was at this point clearly in disarray as to its approach to s. 15. In *Law v. Canada (Minister of Employment & Immigration)*[79] the Court dismissed a s. 15 claim of age discrimination respecting survivor benefits under the Canada Pension Plan.[80] Justice Iacobucci, for a unanimous Court, set out to describe basic principles, for which there was consensus in the Supreme Court, under which courts are to analyze s. 15 challenges. He was at pains to describe these as mere guidelines, points of reference, not a rigid test, which would depend on context analysis and might well be the subject of further elaboration and modification in later cases.[81]

Subject to this caveat, the Court laid out an elaborate ten-part test:

General Approach

(1) It is inappropriate to attempt to confine analysis under s. 15(1) of the *Charter* to a fixed and limited formula. A purposive and contextual approach to discrimination analysis is to be preferred, in order to permit the realization of the strong remedial purpose of the equality guarantee, and to avoid the pitfalls of a formalistic or mechanical approach.

(2) The approach adopted and regularly applied by this Court to the interpretation of s. 15(1) focuses upon three central issues:

(A) whether a law imposes differential treatment between the claimant and others, in purpose or effect;

(B) whether one or more enumerated or analogous grounds of discrimination are the basis for the differential treatment; and

(C) whether the law in question has a purpose or effect that is discriminatory within the meaning of the equality guarantee.

The first issue is concerned with the question of whether the law causes differential treatment. The second and third issues are concerned with whether the differential treatment constitutes discrimination in the substantive sense intended by s. 15(1).

(3) Accordingly, a court that is called upon to determine a discrimination claim under s. 15(1) should make the following three broad inquiries:

(A) Does the impugned law (a) draw a formal distinction between the claimant and others on the basis of one or more personal characteristics, or (b) fail to take into account the claimant's already disadvantaged position within Canadian society resulting in substantively differential treatment between

---

[78] *Egan*, para. 136 at 586.
[79] [1999] 1 S.C.R. 497.
[80] R.S.C. 1985, c. C-8.
[81] Para. 88.

the claimant and others on the basis of one or more personal characteristics?

(B) Is the claimant subject to differential treatment based on one or more enumerated and analogous grounds?

and

(C) Does the differential treatment discriminate, by imposing a burden upon or withholding a benefit from the claimant in a manner which reflects the stereotypical application of presumed group or personal characteristics, or which otherwise has the effect of perpetuating or promoting the view that the individual is less capable or worthy of recognition or value as a human being or as a member of Canadian society, equally deserving of concern, respect, and consideration?

Purpose

(4) In general terms, the purpose of s. 15(1) is to prevent the violation of essential human dignity and freedom through the imposition of disadvantage, stereotyping, or political or social prejudice, and to promote a society in which all persons enjoy equal recognition at law as human beings or as members of Canadian society, equally capable and equally deserving of concern, respect and consideration.

(5) The existence of a conflict between the purpose or effect of an impugned law and the purpose of s. 15(1) is essential in order to found a discrimination claim. The determination of whether such a conflict exists is to be made through an analysis of the full context surrounding the claim and the claimant.

Comparative Approach

(6) The equality guarantee is a comparative concept, which ultimately requires a court to establish one or more relevant comparators. The claimant generally chooses the person, group, or groups with whom he or she wishes to be compared for the purpose of the discrimination inquiry. However, where the claimant's characterization of the comparison is insufficient, a court may, within the scope of the ground or grounds pleaded, refine the comparison presented by the claimant where warranted. Locating the relevant comparison group requires an examination of the subject-matter of the legislation and its effects, as well as a full appreciation of context.

Context

(7) The contextual factors which determine whether legislation has the effect of demeaning a claimant's dignity must be construed and examined from the perspective of the claimant. The focus of the inquiry is both subjective and objective. The relevant point of view is that of the reasonable person, in circumstances similar to those of the claimant, who takes into account the contextual factors relevant to the claim.

(8) There is a variety of factors which may be referred to by a s. 15(1) claimant in order to demonstrate that legislation demeans his or her dignity. The list of factors is not closed. Guidance as to these factors may be found in the jurisprudence of this Court, and by analogy to recognized factors.

(9) Some important contextual factors influencing the determination of whether s. 15(1) has been infringed are, among others:

(A) Pre-existing disadvantage, stereotyping, prejudice, or vulnerability experienced by the individual or group at issue. The effects of a law as they relate to the important purpose of s. 15(1) in protecting individuals or groups who are vulnerable, disadvantaged, or members of "discrete and insular minorities" should always be a central consideration. Although the claimant's association with an historically more advantaged or disadvantaged group or groups is not *per se* determinative of an infringement, the existence of these pre-existing factors will favour a finding that s. 15(1) has been infringed.

(B) The correspondence, or lack thereof, between the ground or grounds on which the claim is based and the actual need, capacity, or circumstances of the claimant or others. Although the mere fact that the impugned legislation takes into account the claimant's traits or circumstances will not necessarily be sufficient to defeat a s. 15(1) claim, it will generally be more difficult to establish discrimination to the extent that the law takes into account the claimant's actual situation in a manner that respects his or her value as a human being or member of Canadian society, and less difficult to do so where the law fails to take into account the claimant's actual situation.

(C) The ameliorative purpose or effects of the impugned law upon a more disadvantaged person or group in society. An ameliorative purpose or effect which accords with the purpose of s. 15(1) of the *Charter* will likely not violate the human dignity of more advantaged individuals where the exclusion of these more advantaged individuals largely corresponds to the greater need or the different circumstances experienced by the disadvantaged group being targeted by the legislation. This factor is more relevant where the s. 15(1) claim is brought by a more advantaged member of society.

and

(D) The nature and scope of the interest affected by the impugned law. The more severe and localized the consequences of the legislation for the affected group, the more likely that the differential treatment responsible for these consequences is discriminatory within the meaning of s. 15(1).

(10) Although the s. 15(1) claimant bears the onus of establishing an infringement of his or her equality rights in a purposive sense through reference to one or more contextual factors, it is not necessarily the case that the claimant must adduce evidence in order to show a violation of human dignity or freedom. Frequently, where differential treatment is based on one or more enumerated or analogous grounds, this will be sufficient to found an infringement of s. 15(1) in the sense that it will be evident on the basis of judicial notice and logical reasoning that the distinction is discriminatory within the meaning of the provision.[82]

This hugely complex *Law* approach confirms previous jurisprudence that there is in fact no Charter guarantee of equality *per se*. The guarantee is against discrimination within the meaning of s. 15. On the key test of discrimination the Court adopts in its (3)(A) criterion McLachlin J.'s workable test of discrimination as the "stereotypical application of presumed group or personal characteristics". However it also cuts and pastes to adopt as an alternative the L'Heureux-Dubé J. test of

---

[82] Para. 88.

[having] the effect of perpetuating or promoting the view that the individual is less capable or worthy of recognition or value as a human being or as a member of Canadian society, equally deserving of concern, respect, and consideration.[83]

The L'Heureux-Dubé extension seems extraordinarily wide and unlike any definition of discrimination in normal discourse. If this was the price of consensus, it was too high.[84] Since the test has changed, presumably some rejected s. 15 claims should be re-asserted. The Court in *Law* also stresses careful identification of "one or more relevant comparators", discrimination on an enumerated or analogous ground and the consideration of context.[85] Given that the tests are so woolly and the stress on the need for flexibility based on context, it seems highly unlikely that *Law* will re-focus s. 15 jurisprudence in a meaningful way.

In the context of establishing s. 15 rights for complainants in sexual assault cases in *Mills* (1999),[86] we have seen that the Court proceeded by mere assertion and did not even cite the new *Law* guidelines! It is not explained why the Court in *Mills* did not apply any of the *Law* analysis. In *Law*, Iacobucci J. did indicate that they were only guidelines and not to be interpreted as a rigid test. He certainly didn't suggest they could be ignored. It would clearly be an error of law for lower courts to do so.

Is the comparator group in *Mills* all other victims of crime or is it male victims of sexual assault? It surely couldn't be the accused, given that the context is a criminal trial where the issue is punishment rather than compensation. Is the violation discrimination by gender or age or is it an analogous ground because complainants in sexual assault cases have been discriminated against through myths and stereotypical views? The Court abandoned a principled approach in this context and left a number of uncertainties.[87]

There have been two important applications of the *Law* approach in the criminal law context. The first turns on its tests of discrimination and the second on the meaning of analogous grounds.

In *Winko v. Forensic Psychiatric Institute* (1999)[88] the Supreme Court held that Part XX.1 of the Criminal Code respecting the disposition of offenders found not criminally responsible by reason of mental disorder did not violate s. 15.[89] Although there was differential treatment on the enumerated ground of mental disability under section 15(1) this did not constitute discrimination under *Law*. Part XX.1 did not reflect the application of presumed group or personal characteristics. Indeed Part XX.1 had been adopted to eliminate the stereotyping and stigmatisation that mentally ill accused had historically suffered from:

The stereotype of the "mad offender" too often led to the institutionalization of an acquitted accused or worse, incarceration in prisons where they were denied the

---

[83] Para. 88.

[84] See, however, support for the L'Heureux-Dubé J. approach by Douglas Kropp, "Categorial Failure: Canada's Equality Jurisprudence — Changing Notions of Identity and Legal Subject", (1997) 23 *Queen's L.J.* 201.

[85] *Ibid.*, in points (2)B, 6 and 7.

[86] (1999), 28 C.R. (5th) 207 (S.C.C.). See full discussion above Chapter 1.

[87] See further Chapter 1.

[88] (1999), 25 C.R. (5th) 1 (S.C.C.).

[89] The Court also found no violation of s. 7: see above Chapter 2.

medical attention they required and were subjected to abuse. By forcing an accused to face indefinite detention at the pleasure of the Lieutenant Governor in Council, on the assumption that such confinement was necessary for purposes of public safety, it encouraged the characterization of mentally ill people as quasi-criminal and contributed to the view that the mentally ill were always dangerous, a view we now know to be largely unfounded. In many cases, indeed, it treated people who had committed no crime and were indeed not capable of criminal responsibility worse than true criminals, sometimes using jails as the places of detention.[90]

At every stage of Part XX.1 the assessment was based on the individual's situation and needs and was subject to the overriding rule of the least restrictive avenue and annual review.[91] Part XX.1 was not discriminatory in the sense of perpetuating or promoting the view that individuals falling under its provisions were less worthy of respect and recognition.

Rather than denying the dignity and worth of the mentally ill offender, Part XX.1 recognizes and enhances them.[92]

The Court did however add that had s. 672.54 been read as raising a presumption of dangerousness, allowing courts and Review Boards to restrict the liberty of the NCR accused without a finding that the person posed a significant threat to public safety, would have been an argument for a discriminatory effect. For a 7-2[93] majority McLachlin J. read s. 672.54 restrictively to require an unconditional discharge if there was no finding that the individual posed a "significant risk of committing a serious criminal offence":[94]

To engage these provisions of the *Criminal Code*, the threat posed must be more than speculative in nature; it must be supported by evidence... The threat must also be "significant", both in the sense that there must be a real risk of physical or psychological harm occurring to individuals in the community and in the sense that this potential harm must be serious. A miniscule risk of grave harm will not suffice. Similarly, a high risk of trivial harm will not meet the threshold. Finally, the conduct or activity creating the harm must be criminal in nature.[95]

In *Sauve v. Canada (Chief Electoral Officer)* (1999)[96] the Federal Court of Appeal rejected a s. 15 challenge to s. 51(e) of the Canada Elections Act.[97] This provision prohibits prisoners serving sentences of two years or more from voting in federal elections. Justice Linden for the majority[98] pre-empted the s. 15 enquiry

---

[90] Para 85.

[91] At 41. Inexplicably the Court did not confront the effect of the capping provisions not having been proclaimed. This had prompted the Manitoba Court of Appeal to declare that s. 672.54 and 672.81(1) violated s. 7 and were of no force or effect: *Hoeppner* (1999), 25 C.R. (5th) 91 (Man. C.A.). In *Winko* McLachlin J., in the course of deciding that the new scheme was not overbroad, indicated baldly that "I cannot agree with the contrary decision" in *Hoeppner* (at para. 36).

[92] Para. 82.

[93] Lamer C.J., Cory, Iacobucci, Major, Bastarache and Binnie JJ. concurred. Gonthier J. (L'Heureux-Dubé J. concurring) dissented as to this interpretation (at paras. 112-148).

[94] Para 57.

[95] *Ibid.*

[96] (1999) 29 C.R. (5th) 242 (Fed. C.A.).

[97] R.S.C. 1985, c. E-2.

[98] Isaac C.J. concurred. Deschenes J.A. dissented on the further ruling of the majority that a violation of s. 3 of the Charter could be demonstrably justified under s. 1.

on the consideration that the status of prisoner does not constitute an analogous ground for the purposes of the section. The definition of analogous grounds had been provided subsequent to *Law* by McLachlin and Bastarache JJ. for the Supreme Court in *Corbiere v. Canada (Minister of Indian & Northern Affairs)* (1999).[99] This referred to

> a personal characteristic that is immutable or changeable only at unacceptable cost to personal identity...or that the government has no legitimate interest in expecting ...change to receive equal treatment under the law.[100]

7. DEMONSTRABLY JUSTIFYING INEQUALITY UNDER SECTION 1

Andrews makes it quite clear that the Court envisages that some violations of s. 15 might be saved under s. 1.

McIntyre J., with Lamer J. concurring, was of the view that the first step of the *Oakes* test of establishing whether the objective related to concerns that were "pressing and substantial" was too stringent for application in s. 15 cases.[101] However, Wilson J. for the majority on this point[102] determined that the *Oakes* standard need not be modified under s. 15, in the course of ruling that the violation could not be justified under s. 1.

Since *Andrews*, s. 15 challenges have, on several occasions, floundered in the Supreme Court on the basis of s. 1 justification.[103]

In *Rodriguez* (1993)[104] Sopinka J. for the majority held that any violation of equality rights of the terminally ill by the Criminal Code offence against assisting suicide would be saved under s. 1. Lamer C.J. was of the minority view that the provision indirectly discriminated against those with physical disabilities. McLachlin J. (L'Heureux-Dubé J. concurring) held that this was not discrimination under s. 15 and to hold otherwise might deflect equality jurisprudence from the true focus of s. 15: to remedy or prevent discrimination against groups subject to stereotyping, historical disadvantage and political and social prejudice in Canadian society. It is not clear why those with physical disabilities did not meet this test.

8. REJECTION OF GEOGRAPHIC EQUALITY FOR CRIMINAL LAW

Prior to *Turpin* the most frequently successful s. 15 challenge in the context of criminal law was on the basis of regional disparity in application.

---

[99] [1999] S.C.R. 203.

[100] *Corbiere*, para 13. See too *McNeil v. Ontario (Ministry of Solicitor General & Correctional Services)* (1998), 126 C.C.C. (3d) 466 (Ont. Gen. Div.), dismissing an inmate's s. 15 argument against a prison ban on smoking.

[101] Above note 10.

[102] Dickson C.J.C. and L'Heureux-Dubé JJ. concurred. La Forest J. concurred in a separate opinion.

[103] See, for example, *Egan*, above note 65.

[104] (1993), 24 C.R. (4th) 281 (S.C.C.).

The leading authority was the decision of the Ontario Court of Appeal in *Hamilton* (1986).[105] In 1976,[106] Parliament created a sentencing option for those convicted of drinking and driving offences of a discharge for curative treatment rather than the mandatory minimum sentence otherwise prescribed. However, the new penalty option was only to come into force in any province if proclaimed to be in force in that province. By the time of *Hamilton* the penalty had been proclaimed in force in Alberta, the Northwest Territories, Prince Edward Island and in New Brunswick but not in Ontario. Mr. Justice Dubin (as he then was) for the Court[107] held that the uneven proclamation of the law had denied individuals in Ontario the right to the equal protection and the equal benefit of the law without discrimination. Although there might be circumstances which would permit a lack of uniform application of the criminal law such circumstances were held to be exceptional. As a general rule it was fundamental that the criminal law treated all individuals in like circumstances equally. Once enacted the equal application of the criminal law could not depend on the acquiescence of provincial Attorneys General.[108] *Hamilton* had been followed by some[109] but by no means all courts of appeal.[110]

In *Turpin*,[111] Wilson J. for the Court expressly rejected the proposition that it was a fundamental principle under s. 15 that the criminal law apply equally through the country.[112] Such a proposition could not be stated in bald and absolute form for the purposes of s. 15. Section 15 required a case-by-case analysis to determine whether the distinction violated one of the equality rights and, if so, whether the distinction was discriminatory in purpose or effect. The Court did not preclude the possibility that some provincial variations in criminal law and procedure could give rise to discrimination in the sense defined in *Andrews*.[113] Wilson J. also noted that s. 7 had not been pleaded and added:

> I make no comment on whether equal application of the criminal law to all persons in Canada constitutes a principle of fundamental justice within the meaning of that section.[114]

---

[105] (1986), 54 C.R. (3d) 193 (Ont. C.A.).

[106] S.C. 1974-75-76, c. 93.

[107] Cory and Krever JJ.A. concurred.

[108] Above note 105, at 218-219.

[109] See *Hardiman* (1987), 35 C.C.C. (3d) 226 (N.S. C.A.) (non-proclamation of curative discharges); *Frohman* (1987), 56 C.R. (3d) 130 (Ont. C.A.) (non-proclamation of roadside breath test provisions) and *Emile* (1988), 65 C.R. (3d) 135 (N.W.T. C.A.) (provision for six-person juries in Northwest Territories imposing real injustice as discriminating on arbitrary geographic basis).

[110] *Ellsworth* (1988), 46 C.C.C. (3d) 442 (Que. C.A.) and *Van Vliet* (1988), 45 C.C.C. (3d) 481 (B.C. C.A.) (both non-proclamation of curative discharges); *White* (1988), 41 C.C.C. (3d) 236 (Nfld. C.A.) (practice of police prosecutors in rural areas) and *Buchanan* (1989), 46 C.C.C. (3d) 468 (N.S. C.A.) (differing provincial lengths of licence suspensions for Criminal Code driving offences).

[111] In *Cornell* (1988), 63 C.R. (3d) 50 (S.C.C.), the Court had held that non-universal proclamation of Criminal Code roadside testing provisions did not infringe the right to equality before the law under s. 1(b) of the Canadian Bill of Rights.

[112] Above note 14, at 127.

[113] *Ibid.*, at 128.

[114] *Ibid.*

Notwithstanding these two small windows of opportunity it seems highly unlikely that geographical disparity in the application of the criminal law across Canada will in future result in a successful Charter challenge. The Ontario Court of Appeal moved quickly to reverse *Hamilton*[115] and *Turpin* has already been used on several occasions to reject geographical discrimination arguments.[116] Such claims are even less likely to succeed since the Supreme Court of Canada ruling in *S. (S.)* (1990).[117]

In *S. (S.)*, a Youth Court judge and the Ontario Court of Appeal had held that Ontario's failure to designate "alternative measures programs" within the meaning of s. 4 of the Young Offenders Act[118] had violated the youth's rights under s. 15. Section 4 provides that such alternative measures may be used to deal with a young person instead of judicial proceedings under the Act, provided certain conditions are met. The trial judge found that the Ontario government, unlike governments of other provinces, had not implemented such a program as the Ontario Attorney General was philosophically opposed and reluctant to extend public funds and cope with the administrative difficulties in setting up such a program.

For a unanimous Supreme Court, Chief Justice Dickson reversed. The Attorney General's decision had been made in accordance with the permissive terms of s. 14. That section rather than the discretionary determination by the Attorney General was "the law" for the purpose of the s. 15 challenge. The Court further held that, had s. 4 been challenged, there would have been no violation of s. 15. While the accused had established that the absence of the benefit of an alternative measures program was a legal disadvantage that violated s. 15, he had not established that s. 4 was discriminatory. The Court agreed with Wilson J. in *Turpin* that a case-by-case approach was necessary to decide whether province-based distinctions in the application of federal law violated s. 15(1).[119] However, the Chief Justice went much further and held that accepting geographical discrimination challenges under s. 15 would undermine the division of powers, which he saw as rooted in the value of diversity:[120]

> Obviously, the federal system of government itself demands that the values underlying s. 15(1) cannot be given unlimited scope. The division of powers not only permits differential treatment based upon province of residence, it mandates and encourages geographical distinction. There can be no question, then, that unequal treatment which stems solely from the exercise, by provincial legislators, of their

---

[115] *Alton* (1989), 74 C.R. (3d) 124 (Ont. C.A.), followed in *Jackson* (1993), 80 C.C.C. (3d) 22 (Nfld. C.A.). See too *Furtney* (1989), 73 C.R. (3d) 242 (Ont. C.A.).

[116] *Ushkowski* (1989), 51 C.C.C. (3d) 15 (Man. C.A.) and *Schell* (1990), 57 C.C.C. (3d) 227 (Sask. C.A.) (both non-universal proclamation of roadside testing provisions).

[117] (1990), 77 C.R. (3d) 273 (S.C.C.).

[118] R.S.C. 1985, c. Y-1.

[119] Above note 117, at 300.

[120] *Ibid.*, at 299. The Chief Justice appears to have seized the opportunity to assert his minority position in *Hauser*, [1979] 1 S.C.R. 984 and *Canada (A.G.) v. C.N. Transport Ltd.* (1984), 38 C.R. (3d) 97 (S.C.C.). In these decisions, Laskin C.J.C. led the majority in a strong assertion of federal criminal power. See J. Whyte, "The Administration of Criminal Justice and the Provinces" (1984), 38 C.R. (3d) 184.

legitimate jurisdictional powers cannot be the subject of a s. 15(1) challenge on the basis only that it creates distinctions based upon province of residence.[121]

9. DISCRIMINATORY LAW ENFORCEMENT

At the moment our courts seem in no mood to accept the challenge of Professors Boyd, Lowman and Mosher[122] that it is time to place the rhetoric of the Charter's equality provisions against the realities of Canadian law. Those researchers carefully collate statistics relating to Canadian drug law, enforcement and sentencing patterns and find them characterized by inequality by jurisdiction, sex, age and type of drug:

> To be more specific, there are substantial differences across Canadian provinces in the use of withdrawals, stays and drug charges *per capita*, and in the use of fines, discharges, and imprisonment. These are not differences that can be explained by provincial variations in rates of use, nor by provincial variations in the nature or logic of illegal drug use or distribution. These are, rather, variations in criminal law and procedure, variations that seem difficult to reconcile with s. 91(27) of the B.N.A. Act and s. 15 of the Charter of Rights and Freedoms.[123]

The 1995 *Report of the Commission on Systemic Racism in the Ontario Criminal Justice System* appears to document systemic racism against black accused on the basis of extensive original empirical investigations, for example as to police stops, pre-trial detention and increased incarceration rates, especially respecting drugs offences.

Thus far courts have been resistant to attempts to use the s. 15 equality guarantee as a protection against discriminatory law enforcement in a particular case.[124] Clearly an argument that enforcement was discretionary will not be enough. There will have to be evidence of discrimination under the *Law* test. Discrimination does not have to be intentional. On McLachlin J.'s test picking on someone on the basis of a stereotypical assumption, for example that black persons commit the drugs offences, would establish the violation.

In *Smith* (1993),[125] the Nova Scotia Court of Appeal appears to have accepted the trial judge's propositions that s. 15 protection includes inequality in the administration of law by police or prosecutors, that intention is not relevant in determining whether discrimination exists and that discrimination can be established by racial differences in treatment or neutral treatment that results in adverse effects based on race. Here, the Court of Appeal agreed with the Courts below that there had been no evidence of discrimination in the investigation and prosecutions stemming from several days of racially motivated fights at a high school. Although the Court accepted that much more could have been done by

---

[121] *Ibid.*

[122] "Case Law and Drug Convictions: Testing the Rhetoric of Equality Rights" (1987), 29 *Crim. L.Q.* 487.

[123] *Ibid.*, at 505.

[124] See, for example, *Paul Magder Furs Ltd.* (1989), 49 C.C.C. (3d) 267 (Ont. C.A.) and *Bridges* (1989), 58 C.C.C. (3d) 1 (B.C. S.C.).

[125] (1993), 23 C.R. (4th) 164 (N.S. C.A.).

446 / Charter Justice in Canadian Criminal Law

the police, it held that it did not necessarily follow that more whites would have been charged and convicted as a result. There appears to be no reported decision where such a s. 15 claim has succeeded.

In *White* (1994),[126] the Nova Scotia Court of Appeal brushed off a challenge that police enforcement of street prostitution laws through exclusive use of a "decoy" system constituted gender discrimination. Statistics indicated that five times more females than males were being prosecuted by Halifax police. The reason why this did not amount to gender discrimination, reasoned the Court, was that it had not been established that as many men committed the offence as women. The major flaw in the accused's argument was the assumption that every time an offence was committed under the communicating for prostitution offence there were two parties, usually a male and a female. In the absence of evidence to the contrary, it could be assumed that many street solicitations by female prostitutes did not attract an answer from a potential customer that contravened s. 213. The offence was committed more often by prostitutes than by customers. There was no evidence that male customers regularly approached women who were not prostitutes. If the offence was committed more often by females, it was not surprising that more females were charged.

It may be that courts are fearful of being deluged by such claims. The United States Supreme Court has clearly accepted the principle that discriminatory enforcement by police or prosecutors violates equal protection guarantees in that jurisdiction. In *U.S.* v. *Armstrong* (1996),[127] the Court confirmed that:

> To establish a discriminatory effect in a race case, the claimant must show that similarly situated individuals of a different race were not prosecuted.[128]

However, the Court appears to have place virtually unsurmountable obstacles to such a remedy by requiring a very high threshold of evidence before the defence may even be considered. In *Armstrong*, the Court discounted the accused's attempt to demonstrate racial discrimination in drugs law enforcement. The majority held that an affidavit that all crack and cocaine prosecutions in a particular jurisdictions involved black accused did not even make the threshold test for ordering discovery.

In Canada, we have seen, under the heading of stay as abuse of process,[129] that the present Supreme Court envisages court review of Crown behaviour to be ill-advised as a matter of policy and violating an established notion of separation of powers. However, the Court in the leading decision of *O'Connor* (1996)[130] does still recognize the possibility of stay as an abuse of process and a "residual category" of abuse of process where the integrity of the process is affected. Especially where the trial would not have occurred but for discrimination, or continuation will extend it, this is surely the "clearest of cases" for a stay? Hopefully, any court faced with proven evidence of discrimination under s. 15

---

[126] (1993), 35 C.R. (4th) 88 (N.S. C.A.).
[127] 116 S. Ct. 1480 (1996).
[128] At 1487.
[129] Above Chapter 2.
[130] (1995), 44 C.R. (4th) 1 (S.C.C.).

would be prepared to act either against police or Crown misconduct. Our Courts have not shied away from racism as the basis for findings of unreasonable search under s. 8[131] or arbitrary detention under s. 9.[132] The more direct and educative approach would be to adopt a remedy expressly based on a finding of discrimination under s. 15.

10. SEXUAL OFFENCES

Many of the s. 15 challenges in criminal law have occurred in the highly gendered context of sexual offences. We earlier examined how the Supreme Court has recognised a s. 15 equality right for complainants in sexual assault cases in *Mills* (1999),[133] respecting access to therapeutic records, and *Darrach* (2000),[134] concerning rape shield laws.

Section 15 challenges against various sexual offence laws have largely[135] involved male accused relying on gender discrimination arguments. The reason for this is not only that the vast proportion of those charged with sexual offences are male. It is also that the few gender specific offences remaining have been directed at males. We shall also see very few such challenges have succeeded.

Under the former s. 146(1) of the Criminal Code it was an indictable offence punishable by a maximum of life imprisonment for a male to have sexual intercourse with a female under the age of 14 who was not his wife. It was clearly a gender-specific offence directed at males. In 1985[136] the offence was replaced by a new range of gender neutral sexual offences.

There was a considerable difference of views amongst lower courts as to whether the statutory rape offence offended the guarantee of equality under s. 15. In *Hess* (1990),[137] the Supreme Court finally resolved that s. 146(1) did *not* violate equality before the law under s. 15. Madam Justice Wilson, for the majority,[138] held that the offence did not infringe s. 15 at all. Madam Justice McLachlin, for the minority,[139] was of the view that it did infringe s. 15 but was a demonstrably justified reasonable limit under s. 1.

According to the majority whether a distinction on the basis of sex violates s. 15 must, in the context of criminal law, depend on the nature of the offence in issue. Section 146(1) addressed an offence of penetration which ''as a matter of biological fact can only be committed by males.''[140] Accepting that a female does not commit a physical act that could be readily equated with that by the male, the

---

[131] Above Chapter 3.
[132] Above Chapter 4.
[133] (1999), 28 C.R. (5th) 207 (S.C.C.). See above and Chapters 1 and 7.
[134] (2000), 36 C.R. (5th) 223 (S.C.C.). See Chapter 7.
[135] For an example of an unsuccessful gender discrimination argument by female accused see *White*, discussed above note 126.
[136] R.S.C. 1985, c. 19 (3rd Supp.).
[137] Above note 57. See above, Chapter 2 for discussion of the majority view that s. 146(1) violated s. 7 of the Charter in denying a defence of mistake of fact as to age.
[138] Lamer C.J.C., La Forest and L'Heureux-Dubé JJ. concurred.
[139] Gonthier and Sopinka JJ. concurred.
[140] Above note 57, at 351.

issue of whether a female should be punished for that act was a policy matter best left for the legislature and not discriminatory within the meaning of s. 15(1).[141]

This reasoning is deeply troubling and quite extraordinary coming from the distinguished justice who stressed in *Turpin* that under s. 15 the large social, political and legal contexts had to be examined. Professors William Black and Isabel Grant[142] put the dangers very well:

> Her reasoning contains no mention of the social context of sexual relations between men and women and particularly between males and girls under fourteen years of age. Further, she seems to ignore the fact that biological differences between the genders have historically been used to disadvantage women. We should be cautious about legal reasoning that uses biological differences in a way that benefits men or that creates disadvantage for women. Yet the reasoning of Wilson J. opens up this possibility.[143]

The majority position cannot be distinguished from the discredited reasoning of male judges in *Bliss*[144] that laws discriminating against pregnant women did not amount to inequality before the law because only women get pregnant. Indeed, in *Brooks v. Canada Safeway Ltd.* (1989),[145] the Court unanimously reversed *Bliss*. The reasoning of the majority in *Hess* on the s. 15 issue was *obiter* and should be reconsidered.[146]

McLachlin J. for the minority had little difficulty in finding that s. 146(1) constitutes discrimination contrary to s. 15:

> It makes distinctions on the enumerated ground of sex. It burdens men as it does not burden women. It offers protection to young females which it does not offer to young males. It is discriminatory.[147]

She found that the violation was saved under s. 1. The object of the provision was to protect female children from the harms associated with premature sexual intercourse and to protect society from the social problems which sexual intercourse with children may produce.[148] The means were proportionate and justified. Only females risked pregnancy and the argument that it was unjust to blame only the male for sexual activity by females under 14 was met by "enforceability considerations."[149]

---

[141] *Ibid.*, at 351-352.

[142] "Equality and Biological Differences" (1990), 79 C.R. (3d) 372.

[143] *Ibid.*, at 373.

[144] Above note 5.

[145] [1989] 1 S.C.R. 1219.

[146] Black and Grant, above note 142, search for ways to reconcile *Hess* with Wilson J.'s important other pronouncements on equality (at 377-378).

[147] Above note 57, at 362.

[148] *Ibid.*, at 364.

[149] She notes that this consideration had persuaded the majority of the U.S. Supreme Court to uphold a statutory rape law applying to females under 18: *M. (M.) v. Superior Court of Sonoma County*, 450 U.S. 464 (1981). McLachlin J. thus relies on an efficiency standard for s. 1 adopted by a majority in *Chaulk* (1990), 2 C.R. (4th) 1 (S.C.C.), discussed and criticized in Chapter 1.

Not considered in *Hess* was the view of the Saskatchewan Court of Appeal in *Morin* (1989).[150] According to the Saskatchewan Court, on examining the larger social, political and legal contexts according to *Andrews*, it was not possible to characterize either adult males generally or adult males potentially accused under the statutory rape provision as a "discrete and insular minority." For the Court, Chief Justice Bayda suggested that to speak of such males as a disadvantaged group in need of society's protection or nurture "borders on the alarming if not the preposterous".[151] One can accept the Court's characterization in the case of the particular accused, who was 39 years of age. However, the Saskatchewan Court does not address the fact the offence also prohibited consensual sexual intercourse by young boys.

We earlier considered a troubling ruling of a unanimous Supreme Court in *Weatherall v. Canada (Attorney General)* (1993),[152] dismissing a s. 8 claim by a male penitentiary inmate against cross-gender touching that might occur during a frisk search by a female guard and against the possibility that a female guard could see the inmates undressing or using the toilet during scheduled and unscheduled counts. The Court was also unanimous in quickly rejecting a s. 15 claim of gender discrimination against male inmates based on the reality that at the time[153] female penitentiary inmates were not similarly subject to such cross-gender frisk searches and surveillance. According to Mr. Justice La Forest for the Court, it was "doubtful" whether s. 15(1) had been violated and the practices were in event saved under s. 1.[154] Equality did not require identical treatment and different treatment might be called for to promote equality. The Court explained its view as follows:

> Given the historical, biological and sociological differences between men and women, equality does not demand that practices which are forbidden where male officers guard female inmates must also be banned where female officers guard male inmates. The reality of the relationship between the sexes is such that the historical trend of violence perpetrated by men against women is not matched by a comparable trend pursuant to which men are the victims and women the aggressors. Biologically, a frisk search or surveillance of a man's chest area conducted by a female guard does not implicate the same concerns as the same practice by a male guard in relation to a female inmate. Moreover, women generally occupy a disadvantaged position in society in relation to men. Viewed in this light, it becomes clear that the effect of cross-gender searching is different and more threatening for women than for men.

---

[150] (1989), 73 C.R. (3d) 383 (Sask. C.A.).

[151] *Ibid.*, at 390.

[152] (1993), 23 C.R. (4th) 1 (S.C.C.).

[153] The law and regulations for cross-gender searching in penitentiaries were subsequently made gender neutral: see Allan Manson, Annotation, (1993), 23 C.R. (4th) 2-6. Videotaped strip searches of female penitentiary inmates by a male C.S.C. emergency response team was severely criticised by Madam Justice Arbour then of the Ontario Court of Appeal in her *Commission of Inquiry into Certain Events at the Prison for Women* (1996).

[154] The Court's very brief reasoning on s. 1 included a reference to Parliament's ideal of achieving employment equity here through the employment of female guards. See criticism by Manson, above note 153.

The different treatment to which the appellant objects thus may not be discrimination at all.[155]

In *M. (C.)* (1995),[156] the Ontario Court of Appeal declared that s. 159 of the Criminal Code prohibiting anal intercourse where a participant was under the age of 18, despite consent violated s. 15 and should be declared of no force or effect. The Court differed as to the basis. For Goodman and Catzman JJ.A., it was sufficient to decide that the section constituted age discrimination that was not justified under s. 1 for reasons given by Abella J.A. The particular charge of anal intercourse involved a 23-year-old man and a 13-year-old female complainant.

Madam Justice Abella saw the real constitutional vice as discrimination on the basis of the analogous ground of sexual orientation.[157] She emphasised that not all distinctions are discriminatory, not all differences are irrelevant and not all disadvantage is inequality. Only those distinctions which perpetuate disadvantage based on differences which are irrelevant or arbitrarily ascribed to group membership are discriminatory and therefore violative of the equality guarantee. Here, s. 159 arbitrarily disadvantaged gay men by denying until they were 18 their choice of sexual expression with a consenting partner. Unmarried heterosexual adolescents aged 14 and over could participate in consensual anal intercourse without criminal penalty. The violation of s. 15 could not be justified under s. 1. The measure chosen in s. 159 to protect young persons from health risks from unprotected anal intercourse were arbitrary and unfair when compared to measures used to protect against health risks for individuals who prefer other forms of sexual conduct. There was no rational connection between such aim and imprisonment. There was no proportionality between the objective and the draconian criminal means chosen.

We have seen that in *Egan* (1995),[158] a 5-4 majority of the Supreme Court of Canada recognized sexual orientation as an analogous ground of discrimination protected by the equality guarantees of s. 15 of the Canadian Charter of Rights and Freedoms. A differently composed 5-4 majority, however, upheld the constitutionality of the particular provision in question: old age security legislation not extending an allowance for a homosexual partner.

Under s. 151.1 of the Criminal Code, where an accused is charged with certain sexual offences respecting a complainant under the age of 14, consent is not generally a defence. However, subsection (2) specifies that consent is a defence where the complainant is 12 years of age or more but under the age of 14 and the accused is less than two years older. Such provisions have been attacked

---

[155] At 8.

[156] (1995), 41 C.R. (4th) 134 (Ont. C.A.).

[157] In *Roy* (1998), 125 C.C.C. (3d) 442 (Que. C.A.) the Court struck down s. 159 on the basis it violated s. 15 through discrimination based on age, sexual orientation and marital status. In *Halm v. Minister of Employment and Immigration* (1995), 28 Imm. L.R. (2d) 25 (Fed. T.D.), Reed J. declared s. 159 as an unconstitutional violation of s. 15 as it discriminates on the grounds of sexual orientation and age. A deportation order based on a conviction for such an offence outside Canada was quashed.

[158] Above note 65.

on the basis of age discrimination. In *Le Gallant* (1985),[159] then trial judge McLachlin J. held that such a provision constituted age discrimination contrary to s. 15 which could not be demonstrably justified under s. 1. It could not be justified by the rationale of deterring exploitation by older persons or by the assertion that objectional sexual activities were not objectional where the ages of the persons involved were more similar.

McLachlin J.'s ruling in *LeGallant* was, however, reversed by the British Columbia Court of Appeal.[160] The Court reasoned that the provision in question reflected Parliament's intention to distinguish between sexual exploitation by adults of adolescents and consensual sexual activity between adolescents. The view of the British Columbia Court of Appeal has been followed[161] but has also been found unconvincing by a Prince Edward Island Supreme Court judge.[162]

In *Hann* (1992),[163] the Newfoundland Court of Appeal held that the denial in s. 150.1 of the Criminal Code of the excuse of consent to a person in a position of trust and authority for sexual assault towards adolescents, 14 and 18 years of age, did not violate s. 15. The distinction for teachers was an occupational distinction and there had been no discrimination based on irrelevant personal differences.

In *S. (M.)* (1996)[164] the B.C. Court of Appeal had little difficulty in rejecting a s. 15 challenge to the incest prohibition in s. 155 of the Criminal Code. Any analogy to the position of homosexuals was strained beyond credulity and the accused's desire to mate with his daughter was not a group or individual characteristic bearing any resemblance to the anti-discriminatory purpose of s. 15.[165]

11. OTHER SECTION 15 CHALLENGES IN CRIMINAL LAW

In *Kent* (1986),[166] the Manitoba Court of Appeal held that s. 15 could not be resorted to in order to require that a jury be composed of a particular racial group:

> The equality provisions of s. 15 do not require a jury composed entirely or proportionally of persons belonging to the same race as the accused. An accused has no right to demand that members of his race be included on the jury. To so interpret the Charter would run counter to Canada's multicultural and multiracial heritage and the right of every person to serve as a juror (unless otherwise disqualified). It would mean the imposition of inequality.[167]

---

159 (1985), 47 C.R. (3d) 170 (B.C. S.C.).

160 (1986), 54 C.R. (3d) 46 (B.C. C.A.).

161 *Halleran* (1987), 39 C.C.C. (3d) 177 (Nfld. C.A.).

162 *M. (R.S.)* (1990), 78 C.R. (3d) 39 (P.E.I. T.D.).

163 (1992), 15 C.R. (4th) 355 (Nfld. C.A.).

164 (1996), 4 C.R. (5th) 113 (B.C. C.A.).

165 At 129.

166 (1986), 27 C.C.C. (3d) 405 (Man. C.A.). See too *Chipesia* (1991), 3 C.R. (4th) 169 (B.C. S.C.).

167 *Ibid.*, at 421. See similarly, and for the most detailed consideration of the issues, the judgment of Justice Stach of the Ontario Court, General Division, in *F. (A.)* (1994), 30 C.R. (4th) 333 (Ont. Gen. Div.), discussed above Chapter 6.

The accused, a Canadian Indian, had not been denied his s. 15 rights where only three Canadian Indians were on the array from which the jury was chosen. The juror's list was racially neutral and had to be presumed to provide a fair cross-section of the community and to be reasonably representative.[168]

In *Bob* (1991),[169] the majority of the Saskatchewan Court of Appeal held the administrative act of a registrar of bingos in refusing licences to members of an Indian band who would not pay a licence fee (because they were exempt under the Indian Act) *did* amount to inequality before the law contrary to section 15.

The usual basis for rejection of s. 15 challenges is a lack of proof of discrimination as, for example, in unsuccessful challenges against the protection of s. 4 of the Canada Evidence Act against compellability of spouses not applying to common law spouses[170] or against the power of wildlife officers to seize firearms invoked against a hunter.[171]

In *Campbell* (1996)[172] the Manitoba Court of Appeal held that a by-law offence passed by an Indian band under s. 85.1 of the Indian Act[173] prohibiting intoxication and intoxicants on a reserve was not discriminatory under s. 15 for three reasons. It was passed under s. 91(24) of the Constitution Act, 1867, for the governance of Indians and reserves, it was freely adopted by band members and it was applicable to all persons on the reserve.

According to the British Columbia Court of Appeal in *Pearson* (1994),[174] in considering the requirements of necessity and reliability for admitting hearsay evidence, persons with mental and physical disabilities have to receive equal protection of the law under s. 15. Hearsay evidence of the complainant in a sexual assault case and evidence as to what the complainant had told his mother was necessary as his credibility could not, because of his mental disabilities, be assessed in the normal way.

12. CORPORATIONS EXCLUDED

Section 15 equality rights are only made available to "every individual." It has been held that s. 15 protection is thus not available to corporations.[175]

Similarly a corporate accused had no standing to challenge the constitutional validity of exclusion of non-citizens from the jury pool on the basis of s. 15 rights of others.[176]

---

[168] *Ibid.*, at 422.
[169] (1991), 3 C.R. (4th) 348 (Sask. C.A.).
[170] *Thompson* (1994), 32 C.R. (4th) 143 (Alta. C.A.).
[171] *Brown* (1991), 66 C.C.C. (3d) 97 (Nfld. C.A.).
[172] (1996), 5 C.R. (5th) 133 (Man. C.A.).
[173] R.S.C. 1985, c. I-5.
[174] (1994), 36 C.R. (4th) 343 (B.C. C.A.).
[175] *Paul Magder Furs Ltd.* (1989), 49 C.C.C. (3d) 267 (Ont. C.A.).
[176] *Church of Scientology of Toronto* (1996), 7 C.R. (5th) 267 (Ont. C.A.) at paras. 127-128.

11

Section 24: Charter Remedies

1. RIGHT TO REMEDY

Under Article 8 of the Universal Declaration of Human Rights (1948):[1]

Everyone has the right to an effective remedy by the competent national tribunals for acts violating the fundamental rights granted him by the constitution or by law.

Similarly Article 2(3) of the International Covenant on Civil and Political Rights (1966)[2] provides

Each State Party to the present Covenant undertakes:

(a) To ensure that any person whose rights or freedoms as herein recognized are violated shall have an effective remedy, notwithstanding that the violation has been committed by persons acting in an official capacity:

(b) To ensure that any person claiming such a remedy shall have his right thereto determined by competent judicial, administrative or legislative authorities, or by any other competent authority provided for by the legal system of the State, and to develop the possibilities of judicial remedy . . .

Unlike the Canadian Bill of Rights or the United States Constitution, the Canadian Charter entrenches remedial powers for breaches. A "court of competent jurisdiction" under s. 24 has power to grant "appropriate and just remedies" (subsection 1) and to exclude evidence where it is established that admission would bring the administration of justice into disrepute (subsection 2):

24(1) Anyone whose rights or freedoms, as guaranteed by this Charter, have been infringed or denied may apply to a court of competent jurisdiction to obtain such remedy as the court considers appropriate and just in the circumstances.

(2) Where, in proceedings under subsection (1), a court concludes that evidence was obtained in a manner that infringed or denied any rights or freedoms guaranteed by this Charter, the evidence shall be excluded if it is established that, having regard

---

[1] G.A. Res. 217A (III), 3 U.N. GAOR, Pt. 1 at 71, U.N. Doc. A/8b10 (1948).

[2] 2200, 21 U.N. GAOR, Supp. (No. 16) 52, U.N. Doc. A/6316 (1966).

to all the circumstances, the admission of it in the proceedings would bring the administration of justice into disrepute.

In *Mills* (1986),[3] Mr. Justice Lamer viewed s. 24(1) as establishing the "right to a remedy as a foundation stone for the effective enforcement of Charter rights" consistent with Canada's international obligations.[4] The large impact that the Charter has had on the criminal justice system in Canada is due in no small measure to these remedial provisions and in particular to the possibility of exclusion of evidence under s. 24(2). In our earlier consideration of issues of jurisdiction and procedure[5] we saw that, in the context of criminal law, trial courts are usually the "courts of competent jurisdiction" for the purpose of granting s. 24 remedies.

A third remedial power is derived from the supremacy clause in s. 52:

> The Constitution of Canada is the supreme law of Canada and any law that is inconsistent with the provisions of the Constitution is, to the extent of the inconsistency, of no force or effect.

In *Big M Drug Mart* (1985),[6] the Supreme Court established that under s. 52 any accused can defend a criminal charge by arguing that the law under which the charge has been brought is unconstitutionally invalid and should be declared inoperative.

2. SECTION 24(1): JUST AND APPROPRIATE REMEDIES

(a) Legislative History[7]

Section 24 had a chequered history. The first Federal Government Draft introduced into Parliament in June of 1978,[8] but never passed, sought to strengthen the Charter with a remedies section. It read:

> Where no other remedy is available or is provided by law, any individual may, in accordance with the applicable procedure of any court in Canada of competent jurisdiction, request the court to define or enforce any of the individual rights and freedoms declared by this Charter, as they extend or apply to him or her, by means of a declaration of the court or by means of an injunction or similar relief, accordingly as the circumstances require.

---

[3] (1986), 52 C.R. (3d) 1 (S.C.C.), discussed above, Chapter 1.

[4] *Ibid*, at 35. Lamer J. (Dickson C.J.C. concurring) was in the minority on many jurisdictional points. This issue was not considered in any of the separate judgments delivered by McIntyre, La Forest and Wilson JJ.

[5] Above, Chapter 1 See especially *Mills*, above note 3. See further Kent Roach, *Constitutional Remedies in Canada* (1994).

[6] (1985), 18 C.C.C. (3d) 385 (S.C.C.), discussed above Chapter 1.

[7] In this section I have relied heavily on Anne McLellan and Bruce Elman, "The Enforcement of the Canadian Charter of Rights and Freedoms: An Analysis of Section 24" (1983), 21 *Alta. L. Rev.* 205 at 206-208. See too Dale Gibson, "Enforcement of the Canadian Charter of Rights and Freedoms (Section 24)" in Tarnopolsky and Beaudoin (eds.), *The Canadian Charter of Rights and Freedoms* (1982), chap. 16, pp. 492-493.

[8] Bill C-60 introduced by the Liberal Government of Prime Minister Pierre Trudeau.

The specification of only a very narrow range of remedies was strongly criticized by various civil liberties groups.[9]

By the summer of 1980 the Federal government proposed a more general version:

> Where no other effective recourse or remedy is available or provided for by law, anyone whose rights or freedoms as declared by this Charter have been infringed or denied to his or her detriment, has the right to apply to a court of competent jurisdiction to obtain such relief or remedy as the court deems appropriate and just in the circumstances.

However, some provincial governments voiced concerns that this might lead to the adoption of the American exclusionary rule excluding illegally obtained evidence, which was contrary to our tradition.[10] As a result, a companion section was added to make it clear that this was *not* the intent:

> 26. No provision of this Charter, other than section 13, affects the laws respecting admissibility of evidence in any proceedings or the authority of Parliament or a legislature, to make laws in relation thereto.

The Federal Government later dropped clause 26 as a result of strong criticism during the hearings of the Special Joint Committee of the Senate and House of Commons, which sat from December 1980 to February 1981. In withdrawing the clause the Minister of Justice[11] referred to the opposition of the Canadian Bar Association, the Canadian Civil Liberties Association, the Chief Commissioner of the Canadian Human Rights Commission and others.[12] Professor Walter Tarnopolsky (later of the Ontario Court of Appeal) had argued that:

> Section 24 enshrines the rule that evidence, even if illegally obtained, is admissible if relevant and I cannot imagine a Bill of Rights that we would want to hold up proudly in the world having that kind of provision specifically protected.[13]

The final and present versions of s. 24(1) and (2) resulted from the further urgings and work of the members of the minority parties on the Committee.[14]

(b) Exclusion of Evidence Not Being Remedy Under Section 24(1)

In *Therens* (1985),[15] Mr. Justice Le Dain for the Supreme Court,[16] dissenting on the facts, determined that the remedy of exclusion of evidence was exclusively that set out in s. 24(2). He could have based this ruling on the legislative history of s. 24(2) but instead rested on linguistic construction:

---

[9] See McLellan and Elman, above note 7, p. 207.
[10] *Ibid.* See discussion below note 99 *et seq.*
[11] The Hon. Jean Chretien.
[12] McLellan and Elman, above note 7, p. 208, note 14.
[13] *Ibid.*, quoting Committee *Minutes of Proceedings and Evidence* of November 18, 1980.
[14] *Ibid.*, p. 208. See further below note 168 *et seq.*
[15] (1985), 45 C.R. (3d) 97 (S.C.C.).
[16] Dickson C.J.C. and Lamer J. would have left the issue open.

It is clear, in my opinion, that in making explicit provision for the remedy of exclusion of evidence in s. 24(2), following the general terms of s. 24(1), the framers of the Charter intended that this particular remedy should be governed entirely by the terms of s. 24(2). It is not reasonable to ascribe to the framers of the Charter an intention that the courts should address two tests or standards on an application for the exclusion of evidence — first, whether the admission of the evidence would bring the administration of justice into disrepute and, if not, secondly, whether its exclusion would nevertheless be appropriate and just in the circumstances. The inevitable result of this alternative test or remedy would be that s. 24(2) would become a dead letter. The framers of the Charter could not have intended that the explicit and deliberately adopted limitation in s. 24(2) on the power to exclude evidence because of an infringement or a denial of a guaranteed right or freedom should be undermined or circumvented in such a manner.[17]

This reversed the opinion of four of the five judges of the Saskatchewan Court of Appeal,[18] in the Court below, that there should be an additional discretion to exclude evidence under s. 24(2) where necessary to do justice. Even subsequent to *Therens*, Mr. Justice Lambert in *Gladstone* (1985)[19] made a last ditch plea for such a discretion, arguing that the ruling in *Therens* was *obiter* and that

[i]f the denial of [Charter] rights works an injustice to an individual, but in such a way that the public interest in the general administration of justice is unaffected, surely the Charter rights would be meaningless, and the purpose of the Charter would be frustrated, unless the evidence were excluded.[20]

Whatever the merits of this position the Supreme Court of Canada has since regarded the issue as having been determined in *Therens*.[21] However this is subject to recently developed jurisprudence on a general power to exclude to ensure a fair trial.

(c) Exclusion of Evidence to Ensure Fair Trial

There is now clear authority in the Supreme Court that there is a discretion under the Charter and at common law to exclude evidence to ensure trial fairness distinct from the power under s. 24(2). Unfortunately it is not clear when and how that power should be exercised.

In *Harrer* (1995)[22] the Court unanimously held that an interrogation of a Canadian by United States authorities in the United States in violation of the s. 10(b) requirement[23] could not ground a s.10(b) challenge when a statement

---

[17] Above note 15, at 128-129.
[18] Bayda C.J.S., Talus, Hall and Cameron JJ. Brownridge J.A. took the view ultimately adopted by the Supreme Court.
[19] (1985), 47 C.R. (3d) 289 (B.C. C.A.).
[20] *Ibid.*, at 300.
[21] *Collins* (1987), 56 C.R. (3d) 193 at 204 (S.C.C.). See, however, *Harrer*, below note 22.
[22] (1995), 42 C.R. (4th) 269 (S.C.C.).
[23] Under s. 10(b) of the Charter a person arrested or detained must be re-advised of the right to counsel when the reason for the detention changes. No such requirement exists in U.S. jurisprudence concerning *Miranda* warnings. In *Harrer,* U.S. officials had arrested the accused for illegal entry. When the investigation turned to the crime of assisting her boyfriend escape lawful custody in Vancouver, she had not been re-advised of her *Miranda* rights.

obtained thereby was subsequently tendered in a trial in Canada. The Charter could not govern authorities outside Canada.[24] The majority noted that the situation would be different if the Canadian was being interrogated in the United States by Canadian authorities[25] or by United States officials acting as agents for Canada.[26]

The startling further majority ruling of Mr. Justice La Forest in *Harrer* is that, even where no evidence has been obtained by a Charter breach to trigger s. 24(2), a trial judge has a discretion to exclude evidence to ensure a fair trial. This could be under common law or as an adjunct to the right to a fair trial under s. 11(d) or as a principle of fundamental justice under s. 7 rather than under s. 24(1). The minority through McLachlin J. recognized the same discretion, but found it under the common law or s. 24 (1). These remarks were *obiter*. Both justices found that admission would not render the trial unfair in the circumstances. However in *White* (1999)[27] Iacobucci J. for a 6-1 majority exercised[28] the *Harrer* discretion not to admit evidence to ensure a fair trial and even expressly adopted the minority McLachlin view:

> Although I agree with the majority position in *Harrer*... that it may not be *necessary* to use s. 24(1) in order to exclude evidence whose admission would render the trial unfair, I agree also with McLachlin J.'s finding in that case that s. 24 (1) may appropriately be employed as a discrete source of a court's power to exclude such evidence.[29]

The recognition of a discretion to exclude evidence on the basis of ensuring trial fairness is not in itself surprising or new.[30] What is startling is that the discretion in *Harrer* and *White* was recognized respecting evidence obtained by unfair police methods.[31] In *Therens* (1985)[32] the Supreme Court expressly rejected the view that there should be a discretion to exclude evidence obtained in breach

---

[24] *Harrer* was applied on this point in *Terry* (1996), 48 C.R. (4th) 137 (S.C.C.). McLachlin J. for the majority reviewed authority for the proposition that a state is only competent to enforce laws within its own territorial boundaries.

[25] This was confirmed by the majority in *Cook* (1998), 19 C.R. (5th) 1 (S.C.C.). The Charter was applicable under s. 32 (1) to an interrogation by Canadian police in the United States respecting crimes committed in Canada and to be prosecuted in Canada. This would not interfere with the sovereign authority of a foreign state and thereby generate an objectionable extraterritorial effect.

[26] In *Cobb* (1996), 46 C.R. (4th) 355 (Que. C.A.) this remark was applied to authorize the application of the Charter to the interrogation and search of U.S. Marines on a U.S. ship at anchor in Quebec City harbour respecting a sexual assault in Quebec City. The U.S. officers were acting as agents of the Quebec police.

[27] (1999), 24 C.R. (5th) 201 (S.C.C.).

[28] The Court excluded, from a criminal trial, motor vehicle accident reports made by an accused under the honest and reasonable belief they were required by law. This would violate the principle against self-incrimination under s. 7. See discussion in Chapter 2.

[29] At 235.

[30] See above Chapter 2 for discussion of Supreme Court jurisprudence.

[31] The *Harrer* discretion has been used to exclude the use of physical coordination tests prior to being advised of the right to counsel at an impaired driving trial: *Milne* (1996), 48 C.R. (4th) 182 (Ont. C.A.), or a roadside test to impeach evidence to the contrary on charges of over 80: *Coutts* (1999), 136 C.C.C. (3d) 225 (Ont. C.A.).

[32] Above note 15.

of the Charter other than that found in s. 24(2). The majority in *Harrer* and six justices in *White* recognize a discretion to exclude in the interests of trial fairness unfettered by complex s. 24(2) tests and jurisprudence[33] or the wording of s. 24(1) which gives remedies where "rights have been infringed or denied" rather than prospective remedies.

The only attempt to address what is meant by "fair trial"[34] for this purpose was by McLachlin J. in her minority opinion in *Harrer*:

> Evidence may render a trial unfair for a variety of reasons. The way in which it was taken may render it unreliable. Its potential for misleading the trier of fact may outweigh such minimal value it might possess. Again, the police may have acted in such an abusive fashion that the court concludes the admission of the evidence would irremediably taint the fairness of the trial itself.[35]

The Court also indicated in *United States v. Dynar* (1997)[36] that

> the fact that evidence was obtained in the foreign jurisdiction in a way that does not comply with our *Charter* is not enough on its own to render the proceeding so unfair that the evidence should be excluded.[37]

Although the Court has not spoken to the point, it seems likely that criminal courts will continue to employ the s. 24(2) tests exclusively in most cases where evidence has been obtained by Charter violations. The *Harrer/White* power to exclude may be more appropriate to fair trial arguments under ss. 7 and 11(d) and where the Charter does not otherwise apply. It is not clear why the Court did not limit it to the latter situation. It has certainly created a "can of worms".[38]

(d) Range of Just and Appropriate Remedies

In *Mills* (1986),[39] the Supreme Court unanimously held that all criminal trial courts as defined by s. 2 of the Criminal Code were courts of competent jurisdiction for s. 24 purposes. There was also a concurrent supervisory jurisdiction of superior courts, which those courts should normally decline.[40] Mr. Justice McIntyre determined that trial courts had such jurisdiction because they already had

---

[33] See below note 216 *et seq.*

[34] See further Michael Davies, "Using s. 24(1) of the Charter to Exclude Evidence: It's Just Not Fair!", (2000) 29 C.R. (5th) 225.

[35] At 288. Major J. concurred.

[36] [1997] 2 S.C.R. 462.

[37] At 521. In *Riel* (2000), 37 C.R. (5th) 72 (B.C. C.A.) the Court applied this *dictum* to admit electronic surveillance evidence legally obtained by a consent intercept in Nevada contrary to the *Duarte* authorizations requirement. This may well have been *per incuriam* as it appears that the U.S. police were acting as agents of Vancouver police who had requested the Nevada police to assist their investigations of a murder committed in Vancouver. This was surely a case of agency specifically distinguished in *Harrer*, above note 26.

[38] Davies at 241.

[39] Above note 3.

[40] See discussion above, Chapter 1.

jurisdiction conferred by statute over the offences and persons and power to make the order sought.[41]

Clearly the Supreme Court decided that in criminal law new Charter issues are to be considered within the confines of preexisting jurisdictional and remedial regimes — new wine in old bottles. Even if a Charter violation is established, a criminal court is limited to its normal arsenal of remedies such as adjournment, dismissal, judicial stay or reduction of sentence. The remedy of allowing the Charter breach to be a ground for mitigation of sentence appears to be a useful compromise and has been accepted by Courts of Appeal.[42] However, in *Glykis* (1995),[43] Chief Justice Dubin held for the Ontario Court of Appeal that a breach of a Charter guarantee should not be considered in imposing sentence unless it mitigated the seriousness of the offence or constituted a form of punishment or undue hardship. It is not clear what this means and why the Ontario Court put such roadblocks in the path of what might well be a just remedy.[44] So too there is reason to doubt the wisdom of the rigid majority ruling of the Newfoundland Court of Appeal in *Collins* (1999)[45] that a Charter violation cannot mitigate penalty if the s. 24(2) application did not result in exclusion.

The usual Charter remedy in criminal courts is dismissal following a ruling that key evidence is to be excluded under s. 24(2) because admission would bring the administration of criminal justice into disrepute. It has been confirmed that both superior courts as part of their inherent jurisdiction,[46] and provincial division courts under s.24(1),[47] can award costs against the Crown as a remedy for Charter breach. Most courts have insisted on a yardstick of serious misconduct. The remedy is becoming routine for non-disclosure in breach of the right to make full answer and defence.[48] Civil claims for compensation, including any claim for

---

[41] Above note 3, at 19. See similarly Lamer J. at 53.

[42] *Charles* (1987), 59 C.R. (3d) 94 (Sask. C.A.), *Stannard* (1989), 52 C.C.C. (3d) 544 (Sask. C.A.) and *Dennison* (1990), 80 C.R. (3d) 78 (N.B. C.A.).

[43] (1995), 41 C.R. (4th) 310 (Ont. C.A.). In *Leaver* (1996), 3 C.R. (5th) 138 (Ont. C.A.) the Court held that excessive delay not amounting to a s.11(b) breach could be a factor considered in mitigation of sentence. This appears inconsistent with *Glykis* which was not, however, referred to.

[44] See too criticism by Allan Manson, "Charter Violations in Mitigation of Sentence", (1995) 41 C.R. (4th) 318. In her report arising out of videotaped strip-searches at a penitentiary for women, Madam Justice Arbour of the Ontario Court of Appeal recommends a mechanism be developed to permit a court to reduce a sentence if it appears that the circumstances in which the sentences are actually served are by reason of "illegalities, gross mismanagement or unfairness" harsher than the court intended: see *Commission of Inquiry into Certain Events at the Prison for Women at Kingston* (1996), pp. 183-185.

[45] (1999), 22 C.R. (5th) 269 (Nfld. C.A.).

[46] *Pawlowski* (1993), 20 C.R. (4th) 233 (Ont. C.A.) and *Robinson* (1999), 142 C.C.C. (3d) 303 (Alta. C.A.).

[47] *Pang* (1994), 35 C.R. (4th) 371 (Alta. C.A.).

[48] See, for example, *Pang, ibid., Dostaler* (1994), 32 C.R. (4th) 172 (N.W.T. S.C.) and *L. (S.V.)* (1995), 42 C.R. (4th) 241 (Ont. Prov. Ct.). See too the full review by Judge Fairgrieve in *Di Fruscia*, Ont. C.J.P.D., December 8, 1995, not yet reported and *Greganti* (2000), 142 C.C.C. (3d) 77 (Ont. S.C.J.) (costs of $11600 awarded for preliminary inquiry, pre-trial preparation and abuse of process application).

punitive damages, have to be pursued separately in the appropriate forum.[49]

The power to grant a remedy which is "appropriate and just" in the circumstances clearly allows for considerable discretion.[50] The Supreme Court has not yet squarely addressed the question of what remedies are appropriate for the criminal law. There are *dicta* suggesting that the Court might go further than lower courts. Even McIntyre J. in *Mills* expresses the hope that trial judges will devise "imaginative remedies to serve the needs of individual cases."[51] In *Gamble* (1988),[52] Madam Justice Wilson held for the majority that the purposive approach was equally applicable to the issue of Charter remedies and that the courts should display "creativity and flexibility" in considering a Charter argument on an *habeas corpus* application.[53] The Supreme Court has also demonstrated its flair by, on several occasions, ordering a transition period before new Charter rulings come into effect.[54]

The Supreme Court has determined that judicial stays of proceedings are appropriate remedies for abuse of process[55] and breach of the s. 11(b) right to be

---

[49] Lamer J. in *Mills*, above note 3, suggests criminal courts are "not staffed and equipped" to cope with such issues as the determination of damages (at 39). In *Chabot* (1992), 77 C.C.C. (3d) 371 (C.A. Qué.) it was held that a judge has no power to award damages in a criminal case. In *Tran* (1994), 32 C.R. (4th) 34 (S.C.C.) at 80, Lamer C.J. spoke of a remedy of damages for breach of the s. 14 right to an interpreter where financial prejudice is established. This appears to be referring to an award of costs. See K.D. Cooper-Stephenson, "Tort Theory for the Charter Remedy" (1988), 52 *Sask. L. Rev.* 1, M. Pilkington, "Monetary Redress for Charter Infringement", in R. Sharpe (ed.), *Charter Litigation* (1987) p. 322 and Paul Bourque, "Constitutional Torts and Criminal Prosecutions", (1995) 37 *Crim. L.Q.* 428. There are thus far few reported civil cases: see, for example, *Crossman* (1984), 12 C.C.C. (3d) 547 (Fed. T.D.) (exemplary damages of $500 and costs awarded for police violation of right to counsel resulting in assault conviction and imprisonment) and *Chrispen* v. *Kalinowski* (1997), 117 C.C.C. (3d) 176 (Sask. Q.B.) (special damages of $300 and compensatory damages of $500 awarded for armed entry at 4 a.m. contrary to s. 8). In *Turigan* v. *Alberta* (1988), 45 C.C.C. (3d) 136 (Alta. C.A.), a class action on behalf of persons convicted of offences since declared unconstitutional to recover their fines was held to be barred by the doctrine of *res judicata*. See too *Bertram S. Miller Ltd.* (1985), 18 D.L.R. (4th) 600 (Fed T.D.) and *Collin* v. *Lussier*, [1983] 1 F.C. 218 (Fed. T.D.) (in each the trial judge awarded damages for Charter breach but was overturned on appeal on the basis there had been no breach: see respectively (1986), 69 N.R. 1 (Fed. C.A.) and [1985] 1 F.C. 124 (Fed. C.A.)). In *Simpson* v. *The Attorney-General* (1994), 3 N.Z.L.R. 667 (C.A.), the majority of New Zealand's highest court awarded $70,000 damages to a plaintiff whose home had been searched for drugs as a result of wrong address on a search warrant.

[50] See David P. Cole and Allan Manson, *Release From Imprisonment* (1990) pp. 151-157, for discussion of the possibilities in cases of Charter challenges to public institutions such as prisons.

[51] Above note 3, at 19.

[52] (1988), 66 C.R. (3d) 193 (S.C.C.).

[53] *Ibid.*, at 230. Lamer and L'Heureux-Dubé JJ. concurred. Dickson C.J.C. (Beetz J. concurred) dissented on the basis that the Charter should not be applied retrospectively.

[54] See, for example, *Brydges* (1990), 74 C.R. (3d) 129 at 150 (S.C.C.) (right to counsel), *Mills*, above note 3 (trial within reasonable time — but only express in case of Lamer J. (Dickson C.J.C. concurring)), and *Swain* (1991), 63 C.C.C. (3d) 481 (S.C.C.) (automatic detention for one found not guilty by reason of insanity violating ss. 7 and 9). For an account of a successful Crown application to obtain such an order see Paul Moreau and Bart Rosborough, "*R.* v. *Cobham* — Obtaining a Transition Period*", (1995) 35 C.R. (4th) 310.

[55] See above Chapter 2.

tried within a reasonable time.[56] However in both cases its recent jurisprudence has emphasized that this remedy is to be reserved for rare cases and, in the case of s. 11(b) breaches, where prejudice has been established.

(e) Remedy for Arbitrary Detention Contrary to Section 9

The Supreme Court needs to confront the difficult issue of the proper remedy for a breach of s. 9. If the arbitrary detention occurred prior to the obtaining of the evidence against the accused the issue can be determined in the normal way under s. 24(2).[57] However, the remedy issue is much more difficult where the arbitrary detention occurs after the incriminating evidence has been obtained and thus there is no possibility of arguing under s. 24(2) that the evidence upon which guilt rests was obtained in violation of the Charter.[58] What then is the appropriate and just remedy under s. 24(1)?

A tendency for trial judges to enter stays in such cases has now been scotched by decisions of three Courts of Appeal.[59]

In *Erickson* (1984),[60] the trial judge had stayed a Criminal Code counterfeiting charge where it came to light that the accused had been detained in custody for four days and not brought before a justice within 24 hours as required by the Criminal Code.[61] The police and Crown had mistakenly believed that this was not necessary in view of his parole status. The British Columbia Court of Appeal held that, even if there had been a violation, there had been no malice or negligence on the part of the authorities and that the "most sweeping and drastic remedy" of stay was neither just nor appropriate.[62] For the Court, Mr. Justice Esson added now frequently-quoted remarks:

> The source of the error may be the view of the trial judge, which is implicit in his decision, that having found that, in connection with the charges before him there had been a breach of the rights of the accused, he must grant some remedy. I will assume that for every breach of a Charter right there is some remedy. It simply does not follow that every breach must lead to some remedy being granted at trial. The purpose of the trial is, as it was before the Charter, to decide whether the accused is guilty. Breaches of Charter rights do not become a proper subject of inquiry at trial simply because they occurred in relation to the charge being tried.[63]

---

[56] See above Chapter 6.

[57] See, for example, *Duguay*, considered below, notes 192 and 287.

[58] See however *Strachan*, considered below note 224, concerning a relaxed causal link requirement under s. 24(2).

[59] See Vittorio C. Toselli, "Arbitrary Detention and Judicial Stay of Proceedings" (1991), 80 C.R. (3d) 86, for a full review of reported and unreported rulings. For a comprehensive critique of the stay power see Gary Trotter, "Judicial Termination of Criminal Proceedings Under the Charter" (1988-89), 31 *Crim. L.Q.* 409.

[60] (1984), 13 C.C.C. (3d) 269 (B.C. C.A.).

[61] Section 503.

[62] Above note 60, at 275.

[63] *Ibid.* Taggart and Anderson JJ.A. concurred. However, Anderson J.A. added that if the police had acted "maliciously, deliberately or carelessly" an acquittal might have been appropriate (at 275).

In *Cutforth* (1987)[64] the Alberta Court of Appeal took *Erickson* much further. A trial judge had stayed impaired driving on the basis that there had been arbitrary detention not when the accused had been detained overnight in a drunk tank cell but when he had been detained for an additional five hours the next morning. Acknowledging that there was no nexus between the breach and the evidence of the offence, the trial judge nevertheless held that there had to be a remedy "as a right without a remedy . . . is, in effect, no right at all."[65] Mr. Justice McClung for the Court[66] reversed. The criminal trial remained an inquiry into guilt and should not be the occasion for an open-ended review of all aspects of the arrest and detention.[67] The remedy was to pursue damages in the appropriate court. To engage the attention of a criminal court the Charter breach would have to "equate to a recognized defence in law,"[68] not be "foreign to the issues raised by the indictment"[69] or else fall within the jurisdiction to exclude under s. 24(2). Furthermore, any stay should be confined to those "clearest of cases" contemplated by the law of abuse of process.[70]

This interpretation of the Alberta Court of Appeal is the antithesis of purposeful and imaginative protection of Charter rights and has been persuasively criticized.[71] *Cutforth* was indeed rejected by the Nova Scotia Court of Appeal in *Davidson* (1988).[72] Mr. Justice Jones for the Court[73] held that it was open to the accused to raise Charter issues in the broadest terms. However, the Court went on to adopt *Erickson* and affirm that not every Charter violation requires a remedy at the criminal trial. The remedy had to be "appropriate and just in the circumstances" and, where there was no reasonable connection between the violation and the offence charged, a stay or dismissal might not be the appropriate remedy.[74] The trial judge had rightly denied a motion to stay based on an unsubstantiated allegation that an impaired driver had been abused by the police while in custody.

Mr. Justice McDonald of the Alberta Court of Queen's Bench in *Germain* (1984)[75] accepted that the accused's incarceration had been oppressive but refused to stay aggravated assault charges. In the context of criminal law, a just remedy had to be as far as possible one that did not "offend the reasonable expectations of the community for the enforcement of the criminal law."[76] Here the closing of

---

[64] (1987), 61 C.R. (3d) 187 (Alta. C.A.), strongly criticized by M. Naeem Rauf, "Annotation", C.R. *ibid.*, pp. 188-191.

[65] *Ibid.*, at 195.

[66] Laycraft C.J.A. and Berger J. (*ad hoc*) concurred.

[67] Above note 64, at 197.

[68] *Ibid.*, at 198.

[69] *Ibid.*, at 199.

[70] *Ibid.*, at 203.

[71] See Rauf, above note 64.

[72] (1988), 67 C.R. (3d) 293 (N.S. C.A.).

[73] Macdonald and Pace JJ.A. concurred.

[74] Above note 74, at 303.

[75] (1984), 53 A.R. 264 (Q.B.). See too McDonald J.'s further judgment in *Hay*, [1987] 2 W.W.R. 270 (Alta. Q.B.).

[76] *Ibid.*, at 276.

the door to the possibility of conviction on serious charges would be out of proportion to the violation in question.[77]

Gary Trotter,[78] while acknowledging that *Cutforth* goes too far, suggests that the courts are rightly cautious before staying criminal trials. Before courts can terminate proceedings under s. 24(1) they should consider the full range of considerations they apply under s. 24(2) and,

> before the termination remedy is invoked, the applicant must establish a nexus between the Charter infringement and the propriety of allowing the case to continue, such that the remedy is qualitatively responsive to the Charter infringement. The remedy should also be quantitatively sound in that it must reflect an element of proportionality by functioning as a truly reparative measure, and not as a ''windfall''.[79]

It is not at all clear why the special test under s. 24(2) for the exclusion of evidence, which turns on the public interest in the repute of the justice system, should be imported to the discretionary remedy to give an appropriate and just remedy to an individual under s. 24(1).[80] It is suggested that the courts have gone too far in avoiding the remedy of stay. There seems no reason to import the abuse of process criterion of the clearest cases of unfairness and oppression.[81] Under the Charter, issues *do* arise in the criminal trial independent of guilt. In the case of a breach of the important protection against arbitrary detention the courts should be receptive to a meaningful remedy such as a stay or, in some cases, a reduction in sentence. It is disingenuous to rely on the availability of a civil remedy for damages given the difficulty and cost of bringing such actions against authorities and the sparse record of success both before and after the Charter.[82]

A frank assessment of the effectiveness of other remedies should sometimes result in a stay. This was the case in *Pithart* (1987).[83] Judge Leggatt of the British Columbia County Court had held that the blanket police policy of arrest and overnight detention on charges of communicating for the purpose of prostitution without consideration of Criminal Code provisions constituted arbitrary detention. His Honour distinguished *Erickson* on the basis that here the violation was not isolated and could be fairly described as ''flagrant''. The offence was not serious and the proper remedy was a stay. An award of damages was the only possible alternative but the criminal court would appear to be condoning the unconstitutional police action. To allow the case to proceed would be to ''participate in the wrong.''[84]

---

[77] *Ibid.*

[78] Above note 41.

[79] *Ibid.*, at 411.

[80] See too Kent Roach, ''Section 24(1) of the Charter: Strategy and Structure'' (1986-87), 29 *Crim. L.Q.* 222 at 256.

[81] See too R. Grondin, ''Une Doctrine d'abuse de Procedure Revigore en Droit Penal Canadien'' (1983), 24 *C. de D.* 673.

[82] See above note 49 and below note 160.

[83] (1987), 57 C.R. (3d) 144 (B.C. Co. Ct.).

[84] *Ibid.*, at 160.

Similarly in *Rudko* (1999),[85] Johnstone J. of the Alberta Court of Queen's Bench decided that a stay and motion of prohibition was the most appropriate remedy. The accused had been cited for *in facie* contempt and detained without consideration of bail within 24 hours contrary to s. 9.

In *Simpson* (1995),[86] a 21-year-old accused was arrested on Sunday afternoon on charges of assault causing bodily harm and public mischief alleging a false allegation of assault.The incidents giving rise to the charges occurred some 7 or 8 months prior to her arrest. The officer wanted to release her but only on condition that she would stay away from certain persons. Such a condition could under the Criminal Code only be imposed by a justice. No justices of the peace trained to handle show cause hearings were available. At the time of arrest, the officer knew that under the local system the accused would remain in custody until the first court day in Provincial Court following the arrest. Since the Monday was a Provincial holiday, the officer knew that this day would be Tuesday and that there would be a breach of s. 503(1) of the Criminal Code which requires an accused to be brought before a justice without unreasonable delay and, in any event, within 24 hours after the arrest, or, if no justice was available, as soon as possible. The accused was detained in custody until the Tuesday, when she was released on the conditions requested by the police.The trial judge held that the failure of the police to bring the accused before a justice within the Criminal Code time limits resulted in arbitrary detention contrary to s. 9 of the Charter and that the appropriate remedy was a stay of proceedings. A majority of the Newfoundland Court of Appeal allowed the Crown appeal.[87] Although there had been a major violation of a statutory provision protecting the fundamental right of the accused to be free unless properly detained by law and the violation was serious, a stay of proceedings was a special remedy reserved for very special occasions and the violation had no relation to the charges. The accused had been unlawfully imprisoned and her remedy was a civil proceeding for civil or constitutional tort. On the further appeal as of right, the Supreme Court[88] restored the stay with a terse remark that there was no reason to interfere with the trial judge's discretion. It is unfortunate that the Court was not more expansive in rejecting a majority position of the Nova Scotia Court of Appeal which recognised that the police, administrative and judicial system had failed the accused but simply refused to give an effective remedy. The dissenting judge had pointed out that an action for civil damages would require an application in the Supreme Court with increased legal fees, delay and inconvenience.

(f) Restoration of Property Seized in Violation of Section 8

This is an important remedial issue which deserves the attention of the Supreme Court. Lower courts are in agreement that once a court has determined

[85] (1999), 28 C.R. (5th) 375 (Alta. Q.B.).
[86] (1995), 95 C.C.C. (3d) 96 (S.C.C.).
[87] (1994), 29 C.R. (4th) 274 (Nfld. C.A.) *per* Goodridge C.J.N. (Gushue J.A. concurring, O'Neill J.A. dissenting).
[88] *Ibid.*, note 86.

that property has been seized by the authorities in violation of s. 8 it has a remedial power under s. 24(1) to order that the property be returned to the lawful owner or possessor. There is, however, little agreement on when and how that power is to be exercised.

Mr. Justice Boilard of the Quebec Superior Court has asserted, in a series of decisions,[89] that the remedy is automatic:

> The only sanction that may be truly effective when faced with an illegal search is to order the return of the things unlawfully seized. Any other solution seems to me to be inadequate.[90]

On the other hand, in *Dobney Foundry Ltd.* (1985),[91] Mr. Justice Esson, then of the British Columbia Court of Appeal, saw the Court as having a wide discretion. The interests of the community required a reasonable balance between individual rights and the community interest. A court could refuse to order a return if the Crown showed that the things seized were required for the purposes of a prosecution either under an already laid charge or one intended to be laid in respect of a specified offence.[92] Factors to be considered included the conduct of the Crown, the seriousness of the offence, the potential cogency of the evidence, the nature of the defect in the warrant and the potential prejudice to the owner.[93]

In *Lagiorgia* (1987),[94] the Federal Court of Appeal asserted a much narrower discretion. Mr. Justice Hugessen for the Court[95] saw the "vast discretion" in the words of s. 24(1) being a discretion to "fashion a remedy, not to deny it altogether":[96]

> In our view, it would be difficult to think of any more appropriate remedy for the unreasonable and therefore illegal seizure of property than to order its immediate return to its rightful owner and lawful possessor. Anything less negates the right and denies the remedy. The only circumstances which suggest themselves to us as justifying a court in refusing such an order would be where the initial possession by the person from whom the things were seized was itself illicit, e.g., in the case of prohibited drugs or weapons. While there may be other cases, there can be no doubt in our minds that when the Crown seeks, as in effect it does here, to profit from a Charter barred seizure it bears a very heavy burden indeed. . . . With due respect to those who appear to hold the opposite view. . . . we do not think that burden can be satisfied today by a simple assertion that the things seized are needed for a prosecution.[97]

---

[89] *Gillis* (1982) 1 C.C.C. (3d) 545 (Que. S.C.) and *Evdokias v. Clerk of the Crown and Peace* (1985), 46 C.R. (3d) 179 (Que. S.C.) (quashing search warrants). See too *Batsos v. City of Laval* (1983), 9 C.C.C. (3d) 438 (Que. S.C.) and *Landry v. Desmarais* (1983), 37 C.R. (3d) 86 (Que. S.C.) (ordering return of goods seized without warrant).

[90] *Gillis, ibid.,* at 556.

[91] (1985), 19 C.C.C. (3d) 465 (B.C. C.A.), applied by the majority in *Commodore Business Machines Ltd.* (1988), 41 C.C.C. (3d) 232 (Ont. C.A.).

[92] *Ibid.,* at 474.

[93] *Ibid.*

[94] (1987), 57 C.R. (3d) 284 (Fed. C.A.).

[95] MacGuigan and Lacombe JJ. concurred.

[96] Above note 94, at 287.

[97] *Ibid.*

3. SECTION 24(2): EXCLUSION OF EVIDENCE[98]

(a) Common Law Rules on Excluding Illegally Obtained Evidence

(i) *Canada: Wray*

Prior to the Charter, a series of decisions from the Supreme Court had carefully mapped out the position that whether evidence had been illegally obtained was simply no business of the criminal courts.

In *Quebec (A.G.) v. Begin* (1955),[99] the Supreme Court unanimously held, without exploring policy considerations, that the results of a blood test were admissible to prove intoxication even if the blood test had been illegal. On behalf of the Court, Mr. Justice Fautaux held:

> Without doubt, the method used in obtaining certain of this evidence can, in certain cases, be illegal and even give rise to appeals of civil or even criminal order against those who have used it, but the proposition will not be discussed, since in this case, illegality tainting the method of obtaining the evidence does not affect *per se* the admissibility of this evidence in the trial.[100]

In their much debated decision in *Wray* (1970),[101] the majority of the Court went out of their way to narrowly confine any discretion in the trial judge to exclude technically admissible evidence. The victim had been shot through the heart in the front office of a gas station. Fifty dollar bills were missing from the cash register. A man carrying a rifle was seen running from the scene. Following a lengthy *voir dire* the trial judge excluded the accused's signed confession on the basis that it had not been voluntary. It has been "procured by trickery, duress and improper inducements."[102] Most of this had occurred during a lengthy and abusive interrogation accompanying a lie detector test.[103] The police had also refused access to a lawyer.[104] At the end of the confession the accused had

---

[98] In this area of the Charter, academic writing is particularly rich. See especially Roach, above note 5; Keith B. Jobson, "The Canadian Charter of Rights and Freedoms: Section 24(2)" in Charles et al. (ed.) *Evidence and the Charter of Rights and Freedoms* (1989) chap. 3; McLellan and Elman, above note 7; Gibson, above note 7; Yves-Marie Morissette, "The Exclusion of Evidence Under the Canadian Charter of Rights and Freedoms: What To Do and What Not To Do" (1984), 29 *McGill L.J.* 521; Peter Mirfield, "The Early Jurisprudence of Judicial Disrepute" (1988), 30 *Crim. L.Q.* 434; Gerard E. Mitchell, "Exclusion from on High" (1989), 70 C.R. (3d) 118 and David M. Paciocco, "The Judicial Repeal of s. 24(2) and the Development of the Canadian Exclusionary Rule" (1990), 32 *Crim. L.Q.* 326.

[99] [1955] S.C.R. 593.

[100] *Ibid.*, at 602 [Tr.].

[101] (1970), 11 D.L.R. (3d) 673 (S.C.C.).

[102] The characterization of the Ontario Court of Appeal: (1970), 3 C.C.C. 122 at 123 (Ont. C.A.).

[103] The interrogation was surreptitiously recorded. The verbatim transcript is reviewed by E.L. Greenspan, "The Exclusionary Rule" (1982), 16 *Law Soc. Upper Can. Gaz.* 107. The tone is illustrated by one of the polygraphist's "questions":

> Now for Christ sake John, if you did it see, if you did it and if you think for one Goddam minute you can live with this all your life without telling, you'll never make it. You'll never ever make it. It will haunt you and in about five years' time you will be in the Goddam with the rubby dubs trying to hide it, you'll be trying to get in behind some curtains, you'll be trying to pull a shroud around you but you'll never make it . . .

[104] *Ibid.*

indicated that he had thrown the gun in a swamp and that he would try to show the police where the spot was. He indeed later directed the police to an area where a rifle, which turned out to be the murder weapon, was found. The prosecutor sought to link the accused to the gun by admitting, under the accepted common law rule in the *St. Lawrence* case (1949),[105] that part of the confession that had been confirmed by the finding of the fact that the gun was in the swamp. The trial judge, however, exercised a discretion to disallow this evidence and directed a verdict of acquittal.

The Ontario Court of Appeal upheld the trial judge's ruling and confirmed that there was a discretion to exclude. In an oral judgment Mr. Justice Aylesworth described it as follows:

> In our view, a trial Judge has a discretion to reject evidence, even of substantial weight, if he considers that its admission would be unjust or unfair to the accused or calculated to bring the administration of justice into disrepute, the exercise of such discretion, of course, to depend upon the particular facts before him. Cases where to admit certain evidence would be calculated to bring the administration of justice into disrepute will be rare, but we think the discretion of a trial Judge extends to such cases.[106]

The Supreme Court of Canada, however, reversed and directed a new trial.[107] For the majority, Mr. Justice Martland held that there was no authority in Canada or in England for a discretion to exclude evidence on the basis that it bring the administration of justice into disrepute and that a discretion to reject "unfair" evidence was narrowly limited:

> [T]he exercise of a discretion by the trial Judge arises only if the admission of the evidence would operate unfairly. The allowance of admissible evidence relevant to the issue before the Court and of substantial probative value may operate unfortunately for the accused, but not unfairly. It is only the allowance of evidence gravely prejudicial to the accused, the admissibility of which is tenuous, and whose probative force in relation to the main issue before the Court is trifling, which can be said to operate unfairly.[108]

In *Hogan* (1975),[109] the Supreme Court by a majority of seven to two refused to fashion a wider discretion to exclude in the case of violations of the Canadian Bill of Rights. Hogan had been convicted of driving a motor vehicle with excessive alcohol in his blood and argued that he should have been acquitted because the test had been taken after he had been denied his right to counsel under s. 2(c)(ii). He had requested to see his counsel, who had in fact been in the police station, but the request had been denied.

In dissent, Mr. Justice Laskin characterized the Bill of Rights as a "quasi-constitutional" instrument and would have provided a remedy of exclusion for the breach of the right to counsel:

---

[105] (1949), 7 C.R. 464 (Ont. H.C.).

[106] Above note 102, at 123.

[107] The accused was convicted at the new trial. His defence counsel is on record suggesting Wray was innocent: Robert J. Carter, "Regina v. Wray" (1977), 10 *Crim. Lawyers Assoc. Newsletter* 28.

[108] Above note 101, at 689-690. Cartwright C.J., Hall and Spence JJ. dissented.

[109] (1975), 48 D.L.R. (3d) 427 (S.C.C.).

There being no doubt as to such denial and violation, the Courts must apply a sanction. We would not be justified in simply ignoring the breach of a declared fundamental right in letting it go merely with words of reprobation. Moreover, so far as denial of access to counsel is concerned, I see no practical alternative to a rule of exclusion if any serious view at all is to be taken, as I think it should be, of this breach of the *Canadian Bill of Rights*.[110]

However, the majority through Mr. Justice Ritchie, would have none of this:

Whatever view may be taken of the constitutional impact of the *Canadian Bill of Rights*, and with all respect for those who may have a different opinion, I cannot agree that, wherever there has been a breach of one of the provisions of that Bill, it justifies the adoption of the rule of "absolute exclusion" on the American model which is in derogation of the common law rule accepted in this country.[111]

There seems little doubt that it was the majority decision in *Hogan* that ensured that the Bill of Rights had virtually no impact on the criminal justice system.

In *Rothman* (1981),[112] the year before the passage of the Charter, the majority of the Supreme Court refused to expand the traditional voluntary confession rule.[113] Rothman, arrested on a drug charge, refused to give a statement to the police. A short time later he confessed in a cell to a disguised undercover officer, who told him he was a fisherman arrested for failing to pay a traffic ticket. The trial judge found that the officer was a person in authority and excluded the statements on the basis that the police disguise was an improper way of obtaining the statements. Mr. Justice Martland, speaking for five other justices,[114] bluntly held that a trial judge could not reject a confession "solely because he disapproved of the method by which it was obtained."[115] The issue was one of voluntariness[116] to which the privilege against self-incrimination was irrelevant.[117] In any event, the majority held, the test for a person in authority was subjective so the rule did not apply here since the accused did not believe that the person in the cell was a police officer. In dissent, Mr. Justice Estey[118] would have applied an "exclusionary rule" under which confessions are not admissible

where to admit them would bring the administration of justice into disrepute, or, to put it another way, would prejudice the public interest in the integrity of the judicial process.[119]

---

[110] *Ibid.*, at 443-444. Spence J. concurred.

[111] *Ibid.*, at 434. Fauteux C.J.C. Abbott, Martland, Judson and Dickson JJ. concurred. Pigeon J. concurred in a separate judgment.

[112] (1981), 59 C.C.C. (2d) 30 (S.C.C.).

[113] For consideration of jurisprudence since the Charter on the voluntary confession rule, see above Chapter 2.

[114] Ritchie, Dickson, Beetz, McIntyre and Chouinard JJ.

[115] Above note 112, at 38.

[116] *Ibid.*

[117] *Ibid.*, at 37.

[118] Laskin C.J. concurred.

[119] *Ibid.*, at 52. The approach of Lamer J. is similar except that he applied a narrower "community shock" test under which he agreed with the majority on the facts. Under Lamer J.'s test:

There first must be a clear connection between the obtaining of the statement and the conduct; furthermore that conduct must be so shocking as to justify the judicial branch of the criminal

Estey J. had invoked in aid the powerful views of Manitoba Chief Justice Freedman as follows:

> Undoubtedly, as already stated, the main reasons for excluding them is the danger that they may be untrue. But there are other reasons, stoutly disclaimed by some judges, openly professed by others, and silently acknowledged by still others — the last perhaps being an instance of an "inarticulate major premise" playing its role in decision-making. These reasons, all of them, are rooted in history. They are touched with memories of torture and the rack, they are bound up with the cause of individual freedom, and they reflect a deep concern for the integrity of the judicial process.[120]

(ii) *Other Commonwealth countries*

In *Sang* (1980),[121] the House of Lords in the course of deciding that a trial judge has no discretion to exclude evidence on the basis that it was obtained as a result of police entrapment, agreed in separate speeches[122] with two propositions:

> (1) A trial judge in a criminal trial has always a discretion to refuse to admit evidence if, in his opinion, its prejudicial effect outweighs its probative value.
> (2) Save with regard to admissions and confessions and generally with regard to evidence obtained from the accused after commission of the offence, he has no discretion to refuse to admit relevant admissible evidence on the ground that it was obtained by improper or unfair means.[123]

Subsequently, the English courts cautiously developed the notion in the second proposition that there could be a discretion to exclude on a basis wider than the rule excluding involuntary confessions.[124]

The extremely limited discretion to exclude recognized in *Wray* was even more out of step with much wider discretions recognized in Scotland, Australia and New Zealand. In often-quoted words the Scottish High Court of Justiciary in *Lawrie v. Muir* (1950)[125] attempted to balance the interests of civil liberties against those of effective law enforcement:

> From the standpoint of principle it seems to me that the law must strive to reconcile two highly important interests which are liable to come into conflict — (a) the interest of the citizen to be protected from illegal or irregular invasions of his liberties

---

> justice system in feeling that, short of disassociating itself from such conduct through rejection of the statement, its reputation and, as a result, that of the whole criminal justice system, would be brought into disrepute (at 74).

The present Supreme Court recently undertook a major review of the common law voluntary confession rule. See *Oickle* (2000), 36 C.R. (5th) 129 (S.C.C.), fully reviewed above Chapter 2 under "New Common Law Voluntary Confessions Rule". The Court adopts a new approach to voluntariness and also the community shock test.

[120] "Admission and Confessions" in Salhany and Carter (ed.), *Studies in Canadian Criminal Procedure* (1972), chap. 4.

[121] [1980] A.C. 402 (H.L.).

[122] J.C. Smith in a casenote on *Sang* (1975), *Crim. L. Rev.* 655, suggests the various qualifications in each speech leaves the scope of discretion as uncertain as before.

[123] Above note 121, at 437.

[124] See Mirfield, above note 98, pp. 436-437.

[125] (1950) S.C. (J.) 19.

by the authorities, and (b) the interest of the State to secure that evidence bearing upon the commission of crime and necessary to enable justice to be done shall not be withheld from Courts of law on a merely formal or technical ground. Neither of these objects can be insisted upon to the uttermost. The protection of the citizen is primarily protection for the innocent citizen against unwarranted, wrongful and perhaps high-handed inference, and the common sanction is an action in damages. The protection is not intended as a protection for the guilty citizen against the efforts of the public prosecutor to vindicate the law. On the other hand the interest of the State cannot be magnified to the point of causing all the safeguards for the protection of the citizen to vanish, and of offering a positive inducement to the authorities to proceed by irregular methods. It is obvious that excessively rigid rules as to the exclusion of evidence bearing upon the commission of a crime might conceivably operate to the detriment and not the advantage of the accused, and might even lead to the conviction of the innocent; and extreme cases can easily be figured in which the exclusion of a vital piece of evidence from the knowledge of the jury because of some technical flaw in the conduct of the police would be an outrage upon common sense and a defiance of elementary justice.[126]

In deciding to exclude evidence obtained by an illegal search the Court focused on the nature and explanation for the illegality and all the particular circumstances.

The New Zealand Bill of Rights adopted in 1990 contains no express remedy of exclusion of evidence for breaches of rights. The New Zealand Court of Appeal[127] nevertheless held that evidence obtained in violation of rights is prima facie inadmissible subject to a broad discretion to include.[128]

In *Ireland* (1970),[129] the Australian High Court accepted that a trial judge should have a discretion to reject unlawfully or unfairly obtained evidence. For the Court, Chief Justice Barwick held that

the competing public requirements must be considered and weighed against each other. On the one hand there is the public need to bring to conviction those who commit criminal offences. On the other hand there is the public interest in the protection of the individual from unlawful and unfair treatment. Convictions obtained by the aid of unlawful or unfair acts may be obtained at too high a price. Hence the judicial discretion.[130]

Recognition of such discretions does not mean that they are regularly exercised. It is, for example, well documented in the United Kingdom that it was only when a discretion was put into statutory form by the Police and Criminal Evidence Act of 1984[131] that the courts began to exercise it. Parliament had in s. 76(2) of that Act reconstructed the voluntary confession rule to read that a confession would be inadmissible where it had been obtained by "oppression"[132] or

---

126 *Ibid.*, at 26-27.
127 *See, e.g., Goodwin* (1993), 3 N.Z.L.R. 153 (C.A.).
128 The Court rejected the test in s. 24(2) of the Canadian Charter.
129 (1970), 125 C.L.R. 321 (Austl. H.C.).
130 *Ibid.*, at 324-325, applied in *Bunning v. Cross* (1978), 19 A.L.R. 641 (Aust. H.C.).
131 1984 (U.K.), c. 60.
132 Under s. 76(8), " 'oppression' includes torture, inhuman or degrading treatment or the use or threatened use of violence (whether or not amounting to torture)."

in consequence of anything said or done which was likely in the circumstances existing at the time, to render unreliable any confession which might be made by him in consequence thereof.[133]

Parliament had, in a last minute compromise, also declared in s. 78(1) a discretion to exclude

if it appears to the Court that, having regard to all the circumstances, in which the evidence was obtained, the admission of the evidence would have such an adverse effect on the fairness of the proceedings that the court ought not to admit it.

The prediction of commentators was that this was a narrow and vague formula that would, like the common law discretion, be rarely used. The commentators were wrong. The courts soon developed a pattern of exclusion, particularly in cases where there had been breaches of the new Home Secretary's Code of Practice for the Detention, Treatment and Questioning of Persons by Police Officers.[134]

(iii) *Exclusionary rule in United States*

In *Weekes v. United States,*[135] the United States Supreme Court held that evidence seized in violation of the Fourth Amendment should not be admitted in a criminal trial. This was soon expanded[136] to evidence derived from the initial violation, the doctrine becoming known as the "fruit of the poisonous tree" doctrine.

In *Wolf v. Colorado* (1949),[137] the Supreme Court refused to extend the exclusionary rule to state prosecutions through the "due process" clause of the Fourteenth Amendment. At that time 30 states rejected the *Weekes* case doctrine, while 17 states accepted it. The Court reasoned that minimum standards of due process could be achieved by the remedies of civil action for damages and through internal police discipline proceedings.

However, in *Mapp v. Ohio* (1961),[138] the Supreme Court decided that the time had come to apply the exclusionary rule to the states, thereby vastly expanding its application to criminal trials. Justice Clark for the Court wrote:

To hold otherwise is to grant the right but in reality to withhold its privilege and enjoyment. . . . [The] purpose of the exclusionary rule "is to deter — to compel respect for the constitutional guarantee in the only effectively available way — by removing the incentive to disregard it".[139]

The change of course was seen to be necessary as other remedies were seen to have completely failed to secure compliance with the Constitution. The

---

[133] See M. Zander, *The Police and Criminal Evidence Act*, 2nd ed. (1990).

[134] Zander analyzed 72 reported cases between January 1986 and June 1990 and found that evidence was excluded in 46 cases (26 out of 28 at trial and 20 out of 44 on appeal). See, for example, *Keenan* (1989), *Crim. L. Rev.* 720 and *Canale* (1990), *Crim. L. Rev.* 329.

[135] 232 U.S. 383 (1914).

[136] *Silverthorne Lumber Co. v. United States*, 251 U.S. 385 (1920).

[137] 338 U.S. 25 (1949).

[138] 367 U.S. 643 (1961).

[139] *Ibid.*, at 656, quoting *Elkins v. United States*, 364 U.S. 206 (1960).

exclusionary rule now applies to evidence obtained in violation of any of the accused constitutional rights.

The exclusionary rule is automatic in the sense that once a constitutional violation has been found the evidence obtained directly or indirectly must be excluded irrespective of the seriousness and circumstances of the violation. In this sense there is no discretion. There is, of course, considerable discretion at the earlier stage of deciding on the scope of the constitutional right and whether there has been a violation.

In recent years various members of the United States Supreme Court have expressed, to say the least, strong reservations about the automatic operation of the exclusionary rule. In *Stone v. Powell* (1976),[140] for example, Chief Justice Burger referred to the rule as a "draconian, discredited device in its present absolutist form."[141] The majority opinion by Powell J. sees the rationale of the exclusionary rule as deterring future police misconduct.

> The *Mapp* majority justified the application of the rule to the States on several grounds, but relied principally upon the belief that exclusion would deter future unlawful police conduct. Although our decisions have often alluded to the "imperative of judicial integrity", they demonstrate the limited role of this justification in the determination whether to apply the rule in a particular context.[142]

Powell J. then articulated serious concerns about the automatic operation of the rule:

> The costs of applying the exclusionary rule even at trial and on direct review are well known: the focus of the trial, and the attention of the participants therein, are diverted from the ultimate question of guilt or innocence that should be the central concern in a criminal proceeding. Moreover, the physical evidence sought to be excluded is typically reliable and often the most probative information bearing on the guilt or innocence of the defendant . . .
>
> Application of the rule thus deflects the truthfinding process and often frees the guilty. The disparity in particular cases between the error committed by the police officer and the windfall afforded a guilty defendant by application of the rule is contrary to the idea of proportionality that is essential to the concept of justice. Thus, although the rule is thought to defer unlawful police activity in part through the nurturing of respect for Fourth Amendment values, if applied indiscriminately it may well have the opposite effect of generating disrespect for the law and administration of justice.[143]

---

[140] 428 U.S. 465 (1976).

[141] *Ibid.*, at 500.

[142] *Ibid.*, at 484-485.

[143] *Ibid.*, at 489-91.

Although the exclusionary rule is still intact in the United States the Supreme Court has now, in a series of decisions, qualified its operation. Of particular interest to criminal law are rulings

1. restricting the types of proceedings and searches to which it can apply;[144]
2. creating a good faith exception for now narrowly confined to situations where police officers have used a technically defective warrant believing it to be valid;[145]
3. allowing a statement of an accused obtained in violation of the Constitution to be used for the purpose of cross-examination;[146]
4. including evidence where the connection with the illegality was too remote,[147] obtained by an independent source[148] or which would have been inevitably discovered by the authorities;[149] and
5. applying the doctrine of "harmless error" on appeal, even now to coerced confessions.[150]

The academic debate in the United States continues to rage.[151] Since the United States Supreme Court focuses on the deterrence rationale much of the energy has been spent on an empirical debate as to whether the rule in fact deters police violations of the Constitution. Some have suggested that police are encouraged to bypass the criminal justice system and resort to vigilante justice.

---

[144] Bass, "The Erosion of the Exclusionary Rule Under the Burger Court" (1981), 33 *Baylor L. Rev.* 363.

[145] *United States v. Leon*, 104 S. Ct. 3405 (1984) and *Massachusetts v. Sheppard*, 104 S. Ct. 3423 (1984).

[146] *Harris v. New York*, 401 U.S. 222 (1971); *Oregon v. Hass*, 420 U.S. 714 (1975).

[147] *Nardone v. United States*, 308 U.S. 338 (1939); *Wong Sun v. United States*, 371 U.S. 471 (1963); *United States v. Ceccolini*, 435 U.S. 268 (1978).

[148] *Silverthorne Lumber Co.*, above note 136 (*dictum* of Holmes J.); *United States v. Crews*, 445 U.S. 463 (1980).

[149] *Brewer v. Williams*, 430 U.S. 487 (1977); *Nix v. Williams*, 467 U.S. 471 (1984).

[150] *Arizona v. Fulminante*, 11 S.Ct. 1246 (1991). The doctrine of "harmless error" is comparable to the Canadian "no substantial wrong or miscarriage of justice" proviso. The U.S. doctrine has been strongly attacked. Goldberg, "Harmless Error: Constitutional Sneak Thief" (1980), 71 *J. of Crim. L.C. & P.S.* 421 writes:

> The doctrine is unmatched as a tool for the secret theft of constitutional rights. A finding that a constitutional error is harmless is almost beyond question on review. . . . If a state or federal appellate court chooses to use the harmless constitutional error as a tool to emasculate a constitutional right through a consistent finding of harmlessness in a series of cases, it is likely to succeed without question (at 436).

and

> the effect of the doctrine upon precedents defining constitutional criminal procedure — their creation, maintenance and change — is devastating (at 441).

[151] See especially Paulsen, "The Exclusionary Rule and Misconduct by the Police" in Sowle (ed.), *Police Power and Individual Freedom* (1962), p. 87 and the dialogue between two leading protagonists, Kamisar and Wilkey (1978-79) 62 *Judicature* 70, 215, 337 and 351. See also Wilkey, "Enforcing the Fourth Amendment by Alternatives to the Exclusionary Rule" (1982), 95 *F.R.D.* 211 and Kamisar, "Search and Seizure of America" (1982), 10 *Human Rights* 14. See now Harry M. Caldwell and Carol Chase, "The Unruly Exclusionary Rule: Heeding Justice Blackmaun's Call to Examine the Rule in Light of Changing Judicial Understanding About Its Effects Outside the Courtroom", (1994) 78 *Marq. L.R.* 45.

The central study by Oakes[152] found no significant difference but has been severely attacked on the grounds of methodology[153] and rebutted by other empirical studies.[154] It is generally conceded that the empirical debate in the United States is at a stalemate. The focus is now on the question of who bears the onus of justifying that the exclusionary does or does not deter police misconduct. Some writers[155] make the important point that the efficacy of alternative methods of controlling the constitutionality of law enforcement should also be assessed and compared.

Other writers and judges have long since abandoned the attempt to justify the exclusionary rule on such utilitarian grounds. For them the question is indeed rooted in the principle of the integrity of the criminal justice system. A much quoted dictum is of the dissenting opinion of Brennan J. in *United States v. Calandra* (1974),[156] advancing the

> twin goals of enabling the judiciary to avoid the taint of partnership in official lawlessness and of ensuring the people ... all potential victims of unlawful government conduct that ... the government would not profit from its lawless behaviour, thus minimizing the risk of seriously undermining popular trust in government.[157]

(b) Canadian Complacency

Prior to the Charter there was precious little Canadian interest in importing anything like the exclusionary rule. In 1961 G. Arthur Martin wrote:

> The problem of deliberate violation of the rights of the citizen by the police in their efforts to obtain evidence has not been as pressing in Canada as in some other countries ... In addition, the remedy in tort has proved reasonably effective; Canadian juries are quick to resent illegal activity on the part of the police and to express that resentment by a proportionate judgment for damages.[158]

Although this statement was not supported by reference to authority or empirical data it came to be relied upon in the United States by opponents of the exclusionary rule, such as Oakes,[159] until it was pointed out that the Canadian reality was in fact different:

> An American commentator, James E. Spiotto, has written 'Canada's experience with the tort remedy suggests that viable alternatives to the exclusionary rule do exist.''

---

[152] "Studying the Exclusionary Rule in Search and Seizure" (1967), 37 *U. Chi. L. Rev.* 665.

[153] See, for example, "On the Limitations of Empirical Evaluations of the Exclusionary Rule: A Critique of the Spiotto Research and *U.S. v. Calandra*", (1975) 69 *N.W.U.L. Rev.* 740.

[154] Canon, "The Exclusionary Rule: Have Critiques Proven That It Doesn't Deter Police?", (1979) 62 *Judicature* 398 and Loewenthal, "Evaluating the Exclusionary Rule in Search and Seizure" (1980), 9 *Anglo-Amer. L. Rev.* 238. See now too Richard Leo, (1996) 86 *J.Crim. L. & Crim.* 266, Cassell and Hayman, (1996) 43 *U.C. L.Rev.* 839 and George Thomas, (1996) 43 *U.C. L.Rev.* 933.

[155] Gary S. Goodpaster, "An Essay on Ending the Exclusionary Rule", (1982) 33 *Hastings L.J.* 1065.

[156] 414 U.S. 338 (1974).

[157] *Ibid.*, at 357.

[158] "The Exclusionary Rule Under Foreign Law" (1961), 52 *J. Crim. L.C. & P.S.* 271.

[159] Above note 152, at 174.

Mr. Spiotto offered that conclusion despite his survey of Canadian law which turned up no appellate case involving a tort action against police officers for illegal searches and seizures in the Province of Ontario, only two appellate cases in other Canadian provinces, and a statement from a police commissioner that he could not remember any illegal search and seizure tort suits since the 1950's. In fact, the only suit which the commissioner could remember from the 1950's resulted in a finding against the police officers but the award of damages was only one dollar. Perhaps that damage award is the best explanation for the paucity of torts suits.[160]

In response to academic criticism of *Wray* the Law Reform Commissions of both Canada[161] and Ontario[162] recommended the statutory declaration of a discretion to exclude. The Law Reform Commission of Canada recommended a discretion to exclude in terms similar to the second prong of the discretion fashioned by Aylesworth J.A. in the Ontario Court of Appeal in *Wray*.[163] The Commission also set out guidelines as to how that discretion should be exercised:

> 15. (1) Evidence shall be excluded if it was obtained under such circumstances that its use in the proceedings would tend to bring the administration of justice into disrepute.
>
> (2) In determining whether evidence should be excluded under this section, all the circumstances surrounding the proceedings and the manner in which the evidence was obtained shall be considered, including the extent to which human dignity and social values were breached in obtaining the evidence, the seriousness of the case, the importance of the evidence, whether any harm to an accused or others was inflicted wilfully or not, and whether there were circumstances justifying the action, such as a situation of urgency requiring action to prevent the destruction of loss of evidence.[164]

The Commission expressed intent was not to incorporate an absolute exclusionary rule but to give the judges the right "in exceptional cases" to exclude unfairly obtained evidence.[165]

The political realities of the day and sentiments of Attorneys General were clearly represented by the majority recommendation of the federal/provincial Task Force on Uniform Rules of Evidence[166] which recommended against any such discretion to exclude illegally obtained evidence. It would have been content to codify the *Wray* discretion to exclude

> evidence the admissibility of which is tenuous, the probative force of which is trifling in relation to the main issue and the admission of which would be gravely prejudicial to a party.[167]

---

[160] Katz, "Reflections on Search and Seizure and Illegally Obtained Evidence in Canada and the United States" (1980), 3 *Can.-U.S. L.J.* 103 at 128-129.

[161] *Report on Evidence* (1975) p. 22.

[162] *Report on the Law of Evidence* (1976) p. 72. The Ontario Law Reform Commission preferred a formula of excluding where the Court "is of the opinion that because of the nature of the illegal means by which it was obtained its admission would be unfair to the party against whom it is tendered."

[163] Above note 101.

[164] Above note 161, at 22. This was supported by the McDonald Royal Commission, *Freedom and Security Under the Law* (2nd Report) 1981 p. 1045.

[165] *Ibid.*, at 62.

[166] *Report on Evidence* (1982).

[167] *Ibid.*, at 549.

(c) Drafting of Section 24(2)

The addition of s. 24(2) was an accident of history in the sense that it arose[168] because the federal government had sought to include an express provision to make it clear that there was no remedy of exclusion of evidence for a Charter breach. This prompted various civil liberties groups to appeal to the sterility of the Canadian Bill of Rights once the courts had indicated that there was no remedy to exclude. Professor Joseph Magnet, Special Advisor to the Canadian Jewish Congress put it clearly:

> ... [T]he *Hogan* case in the Supreme Court of Canada recognized the violation of legal rights under the Diefenbaker Bill of Rights, the court said: Well, we see no remedy clause here, we cannot grant a remedy ... [w]e think that to deal with problems like this, as well as the panoply of rights which would be entrenched in the Charter, an enforcement clause is crucial, that the Charter would be hollow without it, and we think that this is in conformity with our international obligation under the Covenant on Civil and Political Rights.[169]

The actual drafting of s. 24(2) seems to have been a hasty adoption of the Aylesworth approach in the Ontario Court of Appeal in *Wray*. That the government drafters intended exclusion to be rare is crystal clear from the following exchange during the Committee proceedings:

> Senator Austin: Mr. Chairman, one question of Mr. Ewaschuk, could you provide the committee with the general definition of the test "bring the administration of justice into disrepute?". Is there a general principle that you could articulate that would give us a dividing line?

> Mr. Ewaschuk: (Q.C., Director Criminal Law Amendment Section, Department of Justice) Well, somebody told me today — I am on a task force to revise rules of evidence — and Dr. Tollefson from the Federal Department of Justice is the head of it and he says the test is as articulated by the former Justice Black of the United States, that the admission of this evidence would make me vomit, it was obtained in such a reprehensible manner. I said to Dr. Tollefson, it might be a little tough writing that in, but that is the type of case, he is saying, where the conduct is very blameworthy, repugnant, very reprehensible, what the police did in the circumstances and therefore although, and this is the other argument, they had been lawbreakers allow another lawbreaker, an accused, to go free. Once it has reached this certain level of reprehensibility it should be excluded.[170]

(d) Early Disagreement in Courts of Appeal

Given subsequent and firm new direction from the Supreme Court of Canada it is no longer necessary to review in detail earlier attempts by trial courts and Courts of Appeal to arrive at a proper interpretation of s. 24(2). It is still, however, most pertinent to highlight fundamental disagreements on the wisdom of excluding evidence under s. 24(2).

---

[168] Above note 9.

[169] Special Joint Committee on the Constitution of Canada Proceedings. 32nd Parl. sess. 1 (1980-81) No. 7. at 99-100, as quoted by McLellan and Elman, above note 7.

[170] *Ibid.*, cited in the Crown's *factum* to the Supreme Court in *Duguay*, below note 287.

The British Columbia Court of Appeal set out to ensure that the exclusion of evidence under s. 24(2) would be rare. In *Collins* (1983),[171] the Court held that a throat search on suspicion rather than reasonable belief that the suspect had drugs in her mouth violated s. 8[172] but that the evidence of heroin found in her hand should not be excluded under s. 24(2) since the police conduct would not shock the community.[173] According to Mr. Justice Seaton[174] under s. 24(2) a court in Canada could not exclude evidence to discipline the police. Improperly obtained evidence was under that section *prima facie* admissible.[175] Section 24(2) had adopted a "middle ground" between the "extreme answers" of admitting all evidence regardless of the means it had been obtained and, on the other hand, excluding all improperly obtained evidence.[176] However, the middle ground did not involve a discretion[177] as under s. 24(2) "the evidence shall be excluded" if it was established that the admission of the evidence would bring the administration of justice into disrepute. Canada could learn from the recent experience of the exclusionary rule in the United States. Seaton J.A. considered the United States debate in *Stone v. Powell*[178] and other authorities and concluded that the lesson is that if evidence is regularly excluded the admission of justice will not be held in high regard.[179] Canadian courts were "not badly regarded" even though they had regularly admitted illegally obtained evidence. Furthermore,

> Canadians may feel that in most cases it is illogical to abandon the trial's primary purpose, to find the truth, and veer off on another inquiry with another purpose. Wigmore in a Treatise on the Anglo-American System of Evidence in Trials at Common Law thought that to be so, and gave this illustration:
>
>> The indirect and unnatural method is as follows: "Titus, you have been found guilty of conducting a lottery; Flavius, you have confessedly violated the Constitution. Titus ought to suffer imprisonment for crime, and Flavius for contempt. But no! We shall let you *both* go free. We shall not punish Flavius directly, but shall do so by reversing Titus' conviction . . . Our way of upholding the Constitution is not to strike at the man who breaks it, but to let off somebody else who broke something else."[180]

In *Hamill* (1984),[181] the British Columbia Court of Appeal, in deciding not to exclude evidence of drugs obtained under the authority of a writ of assistance,

---

[171] (1983), 33 C.R. (3d) 130 (B.C. C.A.). There was a companion judgment in *Cohen* (1983), 33 C.R. (3d) 151 (B.C. C.A.). Six separate judgments were delivered. Only Anderson J.A., dissenting in *Cohen*, would have excluded on the basis of a test of police conduct tending to "prejudice the public interest in the integrity of the judicial process" (at 187).

[172] Seaton J.A. also doubted the trial judge's ruling on s. 8.

[173] See below the Supreme Court's rejection of Seaton J.A.'s views on the need to shock and his definition of community.

[174] Taggart J.A. expressly adopted Seaton J.A.'s approach in *Cohen*.

[175] Above note 171, at 144.

[176] *Ibid.*, at 143.

[177] *Ibid.*, at 145. Surely Seaton J.A. was setting up a straw person? Section 24(2) is a discretionary exercise and so the American experience with automatic exclusion was, and is, of marginal relevance.

[178] Above note 140.

[179] Above note 171, at 149.

[180] *Ibid.*

[181] (1984), 41 C.R. (3d) 123 (B.C. C.A.).

accepted the Seaton position. For the Court Mr. Justice Esson added[182] that the
argument that evidence obtained in violation of any Charter breach should be
excluded rested on the faulty premises that "our police forces lack integrity,
professional pride and respect for law" and that other forms of relief such as civil
remedies for damages would not provide an effective remedy.[183] The remedy of
exclusion was a drastic and inherently dangerous tool" which would "suppress
the truth" and should be used with caution.[184]

In marked contrast the Ontario Court of Appeal soon embraced the remedy
of exclusion with enthusiasm. In *Manninen* (1983),[185] the Court held that an
incriminating statement made by an accused in an armed robbery case to a police
officer following his arrest should be excluded as it had been obtained in violation
of his right to counsel under s. 10(b).[186] For the Court, Associate Chief Justice
MacKinnon[187] characterized the breach as "wilful and deliberate."[188] The police
had read the accused his rights twice but had nevertheless questioned him even
though he said he wanted to speak to his lawyer. Even though the offence was
serious and guilt clearly established by his answer, the statement would have to
be excluded:

> I conclude that, in view of the open and flagrant disregard of the appellant's
> rights without any justification being attempted or available to allow the appellant's
> answers to be admitted into evidence, under all the circumstances, would bring the
> administration of justice into disrepute. To exclude the evidence under s. 24(2) is
> the only meaningful sanction in this case, if the exercise of the appellant's rights is
> not to become an empty one.[189]

In *Simmons* (1984),[190] Chief Justice Howland for the Ontario Court of Appeal
rejected the community shock test:

> In my opinion it is preferable to consider every case on its merits as to whether it
> satisfies the requirements of s. 24(2) of the Charter and not to substitute a
> "community shock" or any other test for the plain words of the statute.[191]

In *Duguay* (1985),[192] the Ontario Court of Appeal however split dramatically
on the issue of s. 24(2). MacKinnon A.C.J.O. for the majority[193] determined that
placing three youths in a police cruiser on mere suspicion that they had been
involved in a residential burglary in order to obtain inculpatory statements and
fingerprints constituted arbitrary detention within the meaning of s. 9 of the

---

[182] *Ibid.*, at 147.
[183] *Ibid.*, at 148.
[184] *Ibid.*
[185] (1983), 37 C.R. (3d) 162 (Ont. C.A.).
[186] The Supreme Court later confirmed the ruling that there had been a violation: (1987), 58 C.R.
 (3d) 97 (S.C.C.), discussed above, Chapter 5. The Court also confirmed the exclusion.
[187] Martin and Blair JJ.A. concurred.
[188] Above note 188, at 173.
[189] *Ibid.*, at 174.
[190] (1984), 39 C.R. (3d) 223 (Ont. C.A.).
[191] *Ibid.*, at 252.
[192] (1985), 45 C.R. (3d) 140 (Ont. C.A.).
[193] Martin J.A. concurred.

Charter.[194] After considering the circumstances[195] the majority decided to exclude the statements, the stereo set recovered as a result of one of the statements, and the evidence of the fingerprints. According to the majority:

> If the Court should turn a blind eye to this kind of conduct, then the police may assume that they have the court's tacit approval of it. I do not view the exclusion of the evidence as a punishment of the police for their conduct, although it is to be hoped that it will act as a future deterrent. It is rather an affirmation of fundamental values of our society, and the only means in this case of ensuring that the individual's Charter rights are not illusory.[196]

Duguay is conspicious for the vigorous dissent of Mr. Justice Zuber. In holding that the evidence should not have been excluded he reworks the views of Mr. Justices Seaton and Esson into a number of principles that should be considered under s. 24(2).[197]

1. The compromise of s. 24(2) "tilts the balance in favour of truth, so that evidence, even though obtained as a result of constitutional violation, is *prima facie* admissible."[198]
2. It is not necessary for courts to turn a blind eye to Charter violations by admitting the evidence since they have a wide range of other remedies.
3. Canadian courts should be wary of moving in the direction of the American exclusionary rule.
4. The reliability of the evidence cannot defeat the effect of s. 24(2) but is an important consideration.

> The question becomes whether the admission of the truth (albeit discovered as a result of a Charter violation) will bring the administration of justice into disrepute. The converse question is: What will the suppression of the truth do to the repute of the administration of justice?[199]

5. The criminal justice system until 1982 regularly admitted evidence despite the fact that it was illegally obtained and was held in high regard.

> Granted that the Charter has changed the law but it has not overnight transformed the healthy repute of the administration of justice into a fragile flower ready to wilt because of the admission of evidence obtained as a result of a violation of the Charter rights of an accused. The regard of the Canadian public for the administration of justice prior to the Charter, despite the fact that evidence illegally obtained was admitted as a matter of course, was, in my view, very high. The repute of the administration of justice has not now suddenly become highly vulnerable.[200]

---

[194] This ruling is discussed above, Chapter 4.

[195] MacKinnon A.C.J.O. suggests that the trial judges condemnation of the police action may have been "somewhat excessive" but nevertheless himself observes that "the manner in which the police proceeded suggested a somewhat incipient Star Chamber attitude" (above note 192, at 149).

[196] Above note 192, at 152.

[197] *Ibid.*, at 156-158.

[198] Zuber J.A. adopted the words of Ewaschuk J. in *Gibson* (1983), 37 C.R. (3d) 175 at 185 (Ont. H.C.).

[199] Above note 192, at 157.

[200] *Ibid.*, at 158.

6. Exclusion of evidence to control the police has no place under s. 24(2) and has not been proved to be an effective remedy.
7. Disrepute must rest on the view of the whole community rather of the few ''no matter how knowledgeable or expert.''
8. Evidence should be excluded in ''highly exceptional cases.''

> Frequent resort to the exclusion of evidence will create a perception by the public that the criminal justice system is a sort of legalistic game in which a misstep by the police confers immunity upon the accused. This perception will most certainly bring the administration of justice into disrepute.[201]

Although Mr. Justice Zuber's judgment was in dissent it clearly struck a responsive cord amongst many trial judges and was indeed adopted by other Courts of Appeal.[202] The Zuber perspective and that of the British Columbia Court of Appeal was, however, soon largely rejected by the Supreme Court.

(e) Interventionist Perspective of Supreme Court

Although there were a complex series of splits in the five separate judgments delivered in *Therens* (1985),[203] the Supreme Court's message in its first ruling on s. 24(2) was to encourage the remedy of exclusion. An overwhelming majority of six to two of the Court[204] decided to exclude a breathalyzer reading obtained after a violation of the right to counsel. The minority judges through Le Dain J.[205] would also have excluded the evidence had it not been for the determination that the violation was a result of good faith reliance by the police on existing jurisprudence in the Supreme Court of Canada.[206] The Court agreed that the definition of detention under s.10 of the Charter should be broadened from its Canadian Bill of Rights interpretation such that it would now include those subjected to breathalyzer demands and thus entitle them to a right to counsel.[207] The court's rejection of this special type of good faith claim was clearly a powerful blow against the strongly held views of Mr. Justice Zuber and the British Columbia Court of Appeal that exclusion of evidence should be rare.

As Kerans J.A. put it for the Alberta Court of Appeal in *Perras* (1986):[208]

> [T]he majority of the Supreme Court of Canada simply has refused to condone a ''wait-and-see'' attitude on the part of the police about the giving of advice about the right to counsel, no doubt in part because the giving of such advice offers no great difficulty or cost to the police, in part because, if there is a detention, the giving

---

[201] *Ibid.*, at 159.
[202] *Strachan* (1986), 49 C.R. (3d) 289 at 313 (B.C. C.A.); *Brown* (1987), 33 C.C.C. (3d) 54 (N.S. C.A.) and *Spence* (1988), 62 C.R. (3d) 293 (Man. C.A.) (per Lyon J.A. dissenting at 303).
[203] Above note 15.
[204] The majority judgments were by Estey J., Beetz, Chouinard and Wilson JJ. concurring and Lamer J. and Dickson C.J.C. concurring.
[205] McIntyre J. concurred in a short judgment, emphasizing that exclusion was not ''automatic'' (at 108).
[206] *Ibid.*, at 133.
[207] It reversed *Chromiak* (1980), 12 C.R. (3d) 300 (S.C.C.). See above, Chapter 5.
[208] [1986] 1 W.W.R. 429 (Alta. C.A.).

of the advice is mandatory, and in part also, perhaps, because the underlying right protected by s. 10(b) of the Charter is considered by some to be 'the right most valued by civilized man': Brandeis J. in *Olmstead v. U.S.* 277 U.S. 438 at 478, 72 L. Ed. 944, 48 S. Ct. 564 (1928). I accept that a ''wait-and-see'' attitude is, after all, not far from a ''wait-to-be-told'' attitude, and the court might fear that police would otherwise be encouraged always to take a lax attitude about Charter issues.[209]

Ambiguity in the judgment in *Therens* stemmed from the fact that Mr. Justice Estey, writing for half the Court, surprisingly announced that the Court need not expand on the meaning of ''administration of justice.'' Instead, he simply held that the police had ''flagrantly'' violated a Charter right and the evidence directly obtained as a result had to be excluded otherwise the police officers would be invited to disregard Charter rights ''with an assurance of impunity.''[210] Mr. Justice Le Dain in his minority judgment did carefully advance a possible interpretation of s. 24(2), holding that there would be a different balancing of factors in the case of a denial of a right to counsel:

> In my opinion, the right to counsel is of such fundamental importance that its denial in a criminal law context must *prima facie* discredit the administration of justice. That effect is not diminished but, if anything, increased by the relative seriousness of the possible criminal law liability.[211]

Some Courts of Appeal tried to avoid the rigor of the message of *Therens* by distinguishing it to its facts.[212] However, this exercise became impossible after the Supreme Court's dramatic decision in *Clarkson* (1986).[213] The police found the accused crying and screaming, hysterical and very drunk, near the body of her husband, who laid sprawled in a living room chair with a bullet hole in his head. Several hours later the police interrogated her at the police station even though a blood sample obtained at the hospital had shown her blood-alcohol level to be .21. The accused was advised of her right to counsel but indicated that there was ''no point'' in having counsel. The interrogation continued in spite of the efforts of an aunt to have it postponed and to convince the accused to stop talking until counsel was present. The Supreme Court had little difficulty in holding that the accused had been rightly acquitted of murder. Her confession had been obtained in violation of her right to counsel and should be excluded under s. 24(2). For the Court on this point, Madam Justice Wilson[214] found that the police interrogation had been clearly aimed at extracting a confession from someone

---

[209] *Ibid.*, at 436.

[210] Above note 203, at 108.

[211] *Ibid.*, at 133.

[212] In *Strachan*, above note 202, for example, the B.C. Court of Appeal held that exclusion on *Therens* would only flow from a denial of the right to counsel in impaired driving and related cases!

[213] (1986), 50 C.R. (3d) 289 (S.C.C.), strongly criticized by Bruce Duncan, ''Clarkson: Some Unanswered Questions'', C.R. *ibid.*, pp. 305-314. See too Duncan earlier, ''The Blind Eye Argument and a Modest Proposal'' (1985), 47 C.R. (3d) 16. Compare, however, a vehement reply to Duncan by Timothy W. White, ''The Exclusion of Evidence Pursuant to S. 24(2) of the Charter: A View From the Moat'' (1986), 52 C.R. (3d) 388.

[214] Estey, Lamer, Le Dain and La Forest JJ. concurred. McIntyre and Chouinard JJ. concurred in the result without considering the Charter issue.

they feared would not confess when she later sobered up and appreciated the need for counsel. In surprisingly terse reasons, given the enormity of the result, the Court applied the approach of the Estey wing in *Therens* and held that this "flagrant exploitation" by the police of the fact that the accused was in no condition to insist on her rights had to be the kind of violation giving rise to the remedy of exclusion.[215]

It was only in *Collins* (1987)[216] that the Supreme Court of Canada through a majority judgment of Mr. Justice Lamer[217] (as he then was) carefully articulated an approach to s. 24(2), which has been influential ever since.

(f) Onus

We have seen[218] that it was decided in *Collins* that an applicant has to prove on a balance of probability that a Charter right has been breached before being entitled to the remedy of exclusion under s. 24(2). Under s. 24(2) the evidence "shall be excluded" where (1) the evidence was obtained in a manner that infringed or denied any Charter right or freedom and (2) "if it is established" that having regard to all the circumstances admission would bring the administration of justice into disrepute. In the case of the second prerequisite, it was confirmed[219] in *Collins* that the phrase "if it is established" places the burden of persuasion on the accused — a civil standard of a balance of probabilities. According to Lamer J. the applicant must "make it more probable then not that the admission of the evidence would bring the administration of justice into disrepute."[220]

It is unfortunate that the word "established" in s. 24(2) has led the Supreme Court to conclude that there is some burden of proof on the accused.[221] The language of burdens of proof is more appropriate to matters of establishing facts rather than to an issue of whether evidence should be excluded. One never speaks, for example, of the burden of proving that evidence was inadmissible hearsay. As a practical matter many of the issues under s. 24(2) such as issues of the seriousness of the offence and the seriousness of the violation are questions of value to be assessed by the court rather than proved.[222] Where issues of facts have

---

[215] Above note 213, at 304. For discussion of Clarkson on "waiver" see above, Chapter 1 and, on the right to counsel issue, see above, Chapter 5.

[216] (1987), 56 C.R. (3d) 193 (S.C.C.).

[217] Dickson C.J.C., Wilson and La Forest JJ. concurred. Le Dain J. concurred separately. McIntyre J. dissented.

[218] Above, Chapter 1.

[219] At 208. The Court in *Brydges*, above note 54, did hold that the accused need not "demonstrate" a causal link between the Charter breach and the evidence obtained thereby (at 145), applying *Strachan*, discussed below note 224.

[220] *Ibid.* The Court later interprets the word "would" as "could". See Kenneth Jull, "Exclusion of Evidence and the Beast of Burden" (1988), 30 *Crim. L.Q.* 178 at 180-181 for discussion of resulting logical problems.

[221] See too R.J. Delisle, "Annotation to Manninen" (1983), 37 C.R. (3d) 163-164.

[222] See too Mirfield, above note 98, at 452.

to be determined, the Supreme Court has repeatedly made it quite clear that whoever bears the burden must lay the evidential foundation at trial.[223]

(g) Evidence "Obtained in a Manner that Infringed or Denied" Charter Rights or Freedoms

This is one of the few issues under s. 24(2) not addressed in *Collins*. The controlling authority is *Strachan* (1988).[224] Chief Justice Dickson for a Court unanimous on this point[225] held that "obtained in a manner" did not require a strict causal connection between the violation and the evidence. The focus should be on the "entire chain of events"[226] A temporal link between the violation and the discovery of the evidence would be sufficient provided only that it was not too remote:

> [T]he first inquiry under s. 24(2) would be to determine whether a Charter violation occurred in the course of obtaining the evidence. A temporal link between the infringement of the Charter and the discovery of the evidence figures prominently in this assessment, particularly where the Charter violation and the discovery of the evidence occur in the course of a single transaction. The presence of a temporal connection is not, however, determinative. Situations will arise where evidence, though obtained following the breach of a Charter right, will be too remote from the violation to be "obtained in a manner" that infringed the Charter. In my view, these situations should be dealt with on a case-by-case basis. There can be no hard and fast rule for determining when evidence obtained following the infringement of a Charter right becomes too remote.[227]

This is a slight recasting of a view first expressed by Le Dain J. in his majority judgment in *Therens*:[228]

> In my opinion the words "obtained in a manner that infringed or denied any rights or freedoms guaranteed by this Charter" particularly when they are read with the French version, "obtenus dans des conditions qui portent atteinte aux droits ou libertes garantis par la presente charte", do not connote or require a relationship of causation. It is sufficient if the infringement or denial of the right or freedom has preceded, or occurred in the course of the obtaining of the evidence. It is not necessary to establish that the evidence would not have been obtained but for the violation of the Charter. Such a view gives adequate recognition to the intrinsic harm that is caused by a violation of a Charter right or freedom, apart from its bearing on the obtaining of evidence. I recognize, however, that in the case of derivative evidence,

---

[223] See discussions of *Collins* and other rulings on this point by Gerard E. Mitchell, "Trial Counsel and the Facts on S. 24(2) Applications" (1990), 76 C.R. (3d) 304.

[224] (1988), 67 C.R. (3d) 87 (S.C.C.).

[225] Beetz, McIntyre, Lamer, Wilson, La Forest, and L'Heureux-Dubé JJ. concurred.

[226] Above note 224, at 107.

[227] *Ibid.* This implicitly overrules a brief oral judgment in *Upston* (1988), 63 C.R. (3d) 299 (S.C.C.) suggesting that the Court was applying a causal test.

[228] Above note 203.

which is not what is in issue here, some consideration may have to be given in particular cases to the question of relative remoteness.[229]

Under *Strachan* there is no but-for causal test. In *Black* (1989),[230] Wilson J. for a unanimous Court however interpreted *Strachan* as not precluding a causal connection test where the connection was clearly present and the evidence obtained clearly derivative. Furthermore, in *Strachan* itself Chief Justice Dickson goes on to hold that the presence of a "causal link" will be a factor for consideration under the "more important" branch of the s. 24(2) inquiry into whether the admission of the evidence would bring the administration of justice into disrepute.[231]

The Chief Justice's approach in *Strachan* is expressly justified on pragmatic and policy considerations. A strict causal test was seen to involve the Court in the "highly artificial" test of speculating whether the evidence would have been obtained without a Charter violation and focusing the inquiry too narrowly on the actions most directly responsible for the discovery of the evidence rather than considering the whole picture.[232] Dickson C.J. sees the majority approach of the British Columbia Court of Appeal in *Cohen* (1983)[233] as "overly narrow." Drug squad officers had subjected the accused to an unreasonable choke hold contrary to s.8 of the Charter. They had immediately frisked her and found cocaine in her purse. The majority of that Court held that the evidence could not be excluded under s. 24(2) as the evidence had not been directly obtained by the choke hold. The Supreme Court agreed with the dissenting opinion of Mr. Justice Anderson that this would "render almost nugatory" the purposes sought to be obtained by s. 24(2).[234] The Supreme Court was also much swayed by the consideration that a causation requirement in s. 24(2) would generally exclude from consideration much real evidence obtained following a violation of the right to counsel.[235]

Professor David Paciocco[236] vehemently complains that the Court had no business in reading out the causal requirement from s. 24(2) which requires that the evidence be obtained in an unconstitutional manner. This is not clear on a

---

[229] *Ibid.*, at 130. McIntyre J. concurred. In *Therens* Lamer J. disagreed, holding that a mere temporal relationship was not enough and that there would have to be a "nexus" (above note 203, at 109-110). In *Strachan* Lamer J. noted that he has changed his position. On the strength of the Chief Justice's reasoning he now saw the Le Dain approach as "from a practical point of view, the better one" and his "nexus" requirement "too difficult a test to apply" (above note 224, at 109-110). The other judges in *Therens* did not consider this issue, holding that the breathalyzer evidence had been directly obtained by the violation.

[230] (1989), 70 C.R. (3d) 97 at 115 (S.C.C.).

[231] Above note 224, at 107.

[232] *Ibid.*, at 104.

[233] Above note 171. Just how limited s. 24(2) would become under a strict causal test is illustrated by an early ruling in *Watchel* (1983), 32 C.R. (3d) 264 (B.C. Prov. Ct.). The Court refused to exclude breathalyzer evidence obtained after a violation of the right to counsel as the accused had provided the sample "because he was compelled to do so by statute, not because he was not advised of his rights" (at 270).

[234] *Ibid.*, at 105.

[235] *Ibid.*

[236] Above note 98, at 345-350.

consideration, as did Le Dain J. of the French text — "dans des conditions" that infringed rights. The *Strachan* interpretation is expansive but the Court makes a compelling case for its activism. A causal test would often derail a court from the essence of s. 24(2): an inquiry into all the circumstances to consider whether admission of the evidence would bring the administration of justice into disrepute. The Court's position rightly rests on the assumption that the Charter would be sterilized in its impact in criminal law if the remedy of exclusion of evidence were to be too curtailed.

A cynic might suggest that the Court's resort to a "case by case" approach is a counsel of despair at finding an appropriate test. The record of the Supreme Court indicates that the causal link requirement *is* a low level one.

It has decided that s. 24(2) governs the admissibility of drugs seized pursuant to a valid and constitutional search warrant but during which search the right to counsel was violated[237] and of drugs found under a search warrant based on an unconstitutional warrantless perimeter search of a building on mere suspicion.[238] The Court has also applied s. 24(2) to exclude evidence of a murder weapon recovered as a result of a confession obtained in violation of the right to counsel[239] and a subsequent statement by the accused to his girlfriend that he had taken the police to the gun.[240]

In *Goldhart* (1996),[241] the Supreme Court may have adopted a stricter approach to the requirement of causal connection. At a trial on a charge of cultivating marihuana, the trial judge excluded evidence obtained by a search warrant on the basis that it was tainted by a warrantless perimeter search that had been in violation of s. 8. However, the accused was convicted on the basis of the testimony of a witness who was present at the time of the execution of the warrant. The majority of the Ontario Court of Appeal substituted an acquittal on the basis that the testimony was causally connected with the unconstitutional search and should be excluded under s. 24(2). However, Sopinka J., for a 8-1 majority of the Supreme Court, held that the evidence should not be excluded as the testimony had not been obtained by the Charter violation within the meaning of *Strachan*. The connection between the securing of the evidence and the breach was too remote. Sopinka J. held that the concept of remoteness applied to both the temporal and causal connections:

> If both the temporal connection and the causal connection are tenuous, the court may very well conclude that the evidence was not obtained in a manner that infringes a right or freedom under the Charter. On the other hand, the temporal connection may

---

[237] *Strachan* itself.

[238] *Kokesch* (1990), 1 C.R. (4th) 62 (S.C.C.).

[239] *Black* (1989), 70 C.R. (3d) 97 (S.C.C.), and *Burlingham.* In *Timm* (1998), 131 C.C.C. (3d) 306 (Que. C.A.) the majority held that no such causal link had been established where police had seized a murder weapon as a result of information provided by a co-conspirator. But compare *Robinson* (2000), 32 C.R. (5th) 342 (B.C. C.A.) (causal link between s. 10(b) violation and statements).

[240] *Burlingham* (1995), 38 C.R. (4th) 265 (S.C.C.).

[241] (1996), 107 C.C.C. (3d) 481 (S.C.C.).

be so strong that the Charter breach is an integral part of a single transaction. In that case, a causal connection that is weak or even absent will be of no importance.[242]

Here, the pertinent event to find the temporal link was the decision of the witness to cooperate. The existence of a link between the illegal search and the arrest was of virtually no significance. Moreover any temporal link was greatly weakened by the intervening events of the witness's voluntary decision to cooperate with the police and to plead guilty and to testify. The decision to testify had been

> an expression of his own free will, a product of detached reflection and a sincere desire to co-operate, largely brought about by his recent conversion as a born-again Christian.[243]

The causal connection was equally extremely tenuous.

In sole dissent, La Forest J. saw the majority as departing from the generous approach to causal connection set out in *Strachan*. There was a sufficient causal link for the matter to proceed to the inquiry as to whether admission would bring the administration of justice into disrepute. The witness's exercise of free will could not be viewed separately from the arrest pursuant to the illegal search. This view is persuasive. Wasn't the witness's decision to confess as much related to the Charter breach as the girlfriend's evidence in *Burlingham*?

There is a common law rule on the issue of whether a second confession following a confession ruled involuntary must also be excluded. This is variously known as the "contaminated", "tainted" or "derived" confession rule. The leading authority is *I. (L.R.)* (1993)[244] where Sopinka J. concluded that

> a subsequent confession would be involuntary if either the tainting features which disqualified the first confession continued to be present or if the fact that the first statement was made was a substantial factor contributing to the making of the second statement.[245]

In *G. (B.)* (1999)[246] Bastarache J. for a 6-3 majority held that a statement made to a psychiatrist when confronted with an inadmissible confession to police had been wrongly admitted under the s. 672.21(3)(f) Criminal Code exception allowing admission to challenge credibility. That exception[247] had to be read subject to the contaminated confession rule set out in *I. (L.R.)*. According to Bastarache J.:

> This interpretation also meets the requirements of the *Charter*, which entrenched certain aspects of the confessions rule in s. 7. A confession found to be inadmissible could not be introduced indirectly without affecting the right to silence and the principle against self-incrimination.[248]

---

[242] At 495.
[243] *Ibid.*
[244] [1993] 4 S.C.R. 504 (S.C.C.).
[245] At 526.
[246] (1999), 24 C.R. (5th) 266 (S.C.C.). See too *McIntosh* (1999), 30 C.R. (5th) 161 (S.C.C.).
[247] For an argument that the exception for protected statements should be declared unconstitutional see Jonathan D. Gray, "Protected Statements and Credibility Under Section 672.21(3) of the Criminal Code", (2000) 44 *Crim. L.Q.* 71.
[248] At 283.

The authority of *G. (B.)* may be in doubt now that the Supreme Court has decided in *Oickle* (2000)[249] that the voluntary confession rule is a matter of common law, not the Charter.

(h) Purpose of Section 24(2)

In *Collins*, Lamer J. accepts that s. 24(2) adopts an "intermediate position" between the American rule excluding all unconstitutionally obtained evidence and the common law rule admitting all evidence irrespective of police methods.[250] He very clearly states that s. 24(2) is "not a remedy for police misconduct."[251] The section could have been drafted in that way but instead focused on whether the admission of the evidence would in the long-term bring the administration of justice into disrepute:

> [T]he purpose of s. 24(2) is to prevent having the administration of justice brought into *further dispute* by the admission of the evidence in the proceedings. This further disrepute will result from the admission of evidence that would deprive the accused of a fair hearing, or from judicial condonation of unacceptable conduct by the investigatory and prosecutorial agencies. It will also be necessary to consider any disrepute that may result from the exclusion of the evidence . . .. It is the long-term consequences of regular admission or exclusion of this type of evidence on the repute of the administration of justice which must be considered.[252]

Collins confirms that s. 24(2) turns on the repute of the justice system. It seems clear that deterrence of police misconduct is not the main rationale. This has the pragmatic advantage that efforts to decide empirically whether police conduct is in fact changed to the better by the exclusion of evidence would in Canada, as opposed to the United States, be of marginal value.

L'Heureux-Dubé J., in dissenting opinions,[253] suggests that since *Collins* "it is generally not proper for a court to exclude evidence with a view to controlling the police."[254] This would appear to overstate *Collins* given Lamer J.'s express recognition that exclusion might occur where judges wish not to condone police or prosecutorial misconduct.

The doublespeak evident in *Collins* on this point has continued. According to Chief Justice Dickson in *Genest* (1989):[255]

> While the purpose of s. 24(2) is not to deter police misconduct, the courts should be reluctant to admit evidence that shows the signs of being obtained by an abuse of common law and Charter rights by the police.[256]

Similarly Mr. Justice Sopinka for the majority in *Kokesch* (1990)[257] writes:

---

[249] (2000), 36 C.R. (5th) 129 (S.C.C.).
[250] Above note 216, at 208.
[251] *Ibid.* He had earlier held: "It is not open to the courts in Canada to exclude evidence to discipline the police, but only to avoid having the administration of justice brought into disrepute" (at 204).
[252] *Ibid.*
[253] *Duguay* (1989), 67 C.R. (3d) 252 (S.C.C.) and *Burlingham*, below note 259.
[254] *Ibid.*, at 276.
[255] (1989), 45 C.C.C. (3d) 385 (S.C.C.); (1989), 67 C.R. (3d) 224 (S.C.C.) (in French).
[256] *Ibid.*, at 409.
[257] Above note 238.

This Court must not be seen to condone deliberate unlawful conduct designed to subvert both the legal and constitutional limits of police power to intrude on individual privacy.[258]

In *Burlingham* (1995),[259] the majority judgment of Iacobucci J. repeatedly uses language that includes a focus on the need to deter police misconduct by the state. Consider, for example, the following statements:

The purpose of [the *Collins* test] is to oblige law enforcement authorities to respect the exigencies of the Charter and to preclude improperly obtained evidence from being admitted to the trial process when it impinges upon the fairness of the trial.[260]

[The] goals of preserving the integrity of the criminal justice system as well as promoting the decency of investigatory techniques are of fundamental importance in applying s. 24(2).[261]

Once the emphasis shifts from the repute of the justice system to that of deterring police misconduct exclusion is likely to be more common.

(i) Rejection of Community Shock Test

Le Dain J., in his minority judgment in *Therens*, held that the Court should not substitute for the words of s. 24(2) from the different voluntary confession context in *Rothman* (1981)[262] either the Lamer J. test of what would shock the community or the Estey J. formula of what would be prejudicial to the public interest in the integrity of the judicial process.[263] In *Collins*, Lamer J. agreed and thereby abolished the community shock test intended by the drafters[264] and applied by many lower courts. Mr. Justice Lamer held that the threshold for exclusion under s. 24(2) was lower than the common law since there would have been a violation of the "most important law in the land."[265] The second reason provided was that, since one of the purposes of s. 24(2) was to protect the right to a fair trial, the accused should have the benefit of the more favourable French text of s. 24(2) — "est susceptible de déconsidérer l'administration de la justice" — such that the question should be whether the admission "could" rather than "would" bring the administration of justice into disrepute.[266]

The Supreme Court of Canada clearly rejected the proposition that exclusion under s. 24(2) should be rare. In abandoning the community shock test the Court might have invoked in aid the powerful passage of Provincial Court Judge Merredew in *Texaco Canada Inc.* (1984):[267]

---

[258] *Ibid.*, at 73-74.
[259] (1995), 38 C.R. (4th) 265 (S.C.C.).
[260] At 283.
[261] At 290.
[262] Above note 112.
[263] Above note 15, at 131-132.
[264] See too Ewaschuk J. in *Gibson*, above note 198.
[265] *Ibid.*, at 213.
[266] *Ibid.*, at 213-214.
[267] (1984), 13 C.E.L.R. 124 (Ont. Prov. Ct.).

The concept of "shock" is that of an immediate, sudden, unreflective, possibly emotional and almost certainly uninformed response: it smacks of the response we have to a startling headline, or sudden tragedy, or seeing or hearing, without warning, something tragic, disgusting or degrading. I am not sure that is the appropriate test if it is the long term repute of our system of justice which is in question.

In accepting the concept of innocence until proven guilty and requiring a very high standard of proof for the Crown to surmount before finding against that innocence, our common law/criminal law has had to accept the premise that some persons who might otherwise have been found guilty of crime will not be so found, even if charged, because of the inability of the Crown to meet the required standards of proof. When someone has been charged and the circumstances reported are such that it seems likely to the public that the accused is guilty, but he is not found guilty, for whatever reason, most often the public, including the victim or victims and their associates, have an immediate response to shock and outrage; the journalists describe the event using descriptions which suggest that the accused has "got off" on a technicality, or the like, or has subverted the course of justice through nefarious and unpalatable means, or the like. It is human nature to respond in this way; such a response is the kind of response which could be described as a "shocked" response. With respect to the apparently developing jurisprudence to the contrary, if the tradition of our common law is to be maintained, it is exactly this kind of response which should not be established as the test for application of the Charter.[268]

(j) Disrepute in Eyes of Judges Not Public

Mr. Justice Seaton in the British Columbia Court of Appeal in *Collins*[269] saw s. 24(2) as requiring an assessment of values of the wide community:

Disrepute in whose eyes? That which would bring the administration of justice into disrepute in the eyes of a policeman might be the precise action that would be highly regarded in the eyes of a law teacher. I do not think that we are to look at this matter through the eyes of a policeman or a law teacher, or a judge, for that matter. I think that it is the community at large, including the policeman and the law teacher and the judge, through whose eyes we are to see this question.[270]

This approach did not, however, find favour in the Supreme Court. In *Therens*, Le Dain J. had already offered the opinion that the question of whether evidence must be excluded because its admission would bring the administration of justice into disrepute was a question of law which had to be determined by a court without evidence of the effect of exclusion on public opinion. The Court was held to be the best judge and opinion polls were rejected on the basis that they could not be specific enough and would be too costly.[271]

Collins made Le Dain's position that of the Court but for slightly different reasons. Although public opinion polls could be used to assess the level of community tolerance in the case of obscenity it would be unwise to use them for this Charter issue. The public only became conscious of the importance of Charter

---

[268] See further "Annotation to Gibson" (1983), 37 C.R. (3d) 177.

[269] Above note 171.

[270] *Ibid.*, at 144-145. See too Zuber J.A. dissenting in *Duguay*, note 197.

[271] Above note 15, at 133, rejecting the suggestion of D. Gibson, "Determining Disrepute: Opinion Polls and the Canadian Charter of Rights and Freedoms" (1983), 61 *Can. Bar Rev.* 377. See further the criticism of Morissette, above note 98, pp. 537-538.

rights where they were affected personally or through the experience of friends or family. As Lamer J. bluntly put it:

> The Charter is designed to protect the accused from the majority, so the enforcement of the Charter must not be left to that majority.[272]

The Court adopted the reasonable person test of Professor Morissette[273] according to whom the relevant question is "would the admission of the evidence bring the administration of justice into disrepute in the eyes of a reasonable man, dispassionate and fully apprised of the circumstances of the case?" However, Lamer J. added that the reasonable person is "usually the average person in the community, but only when that community's current mood is reasonable."[274]

This aspect of the *Collins* approach has been vehemently criticized as a unjustifiable resort by the courts to the expediency of exclusion despite the language of s. 24(2) and irrespective of what the public might think about it.[275] On the other hand, Professor Jobson[276] has supported the approach on the basis that s. 24(2) requires a professional understanding of our complex system of criminal justice and the democratic ideals of the Charter. Ordinary citizens may too easily sacrifice long- term goals "for a felt need to stamp out crime and support police illegality."[277] The argument is very like that of Provincial Court Judge Merredew in rightly rejecting the community shock test. The Canadian system of justice both before and after the Charter should be a dignified process of asserting principles.

Professor Bryant and colleagues have a made a most careful attempt to ascertain what the public would think of exclusion of evidence under the Charter.[278] Groups of citizens were confronted with detailed vignettes mostly based on actual Supreme Court decisions, such as that in *Therens*. While the social research documented a gap between public and judicial opinion in a number of contexts, notably in the case of drinking and driving and the right to counsel, the researchers were guarded in their conclusions. They suggest it is not at all clear that the gap will remained fixed and that the relationship between public opinion and moral legitimacy of the system is complex. It was premature to conclude that the apparent gap between judicial and public opinion endangers public confidence in our justice system.

---

[272] Above note 216, at 209.

[273] Above note 98, p. 538.

[274] Above note 216, at 209. This pragmatic qualification was too much for McIntyre J., who dissented on the basis that the common law reasonable person test should be applied. He did not, however, favour polls.

[275] Paciocco, above note 98, pp. 342-345. The Pacciocco position was adopted by L'Heureux-Dubé J. dissenting in *Burlingham*. However, the *Collins* approach was strongly defended by Sopinka J., with three justices concurring: see below note 473.

[276] Above note 98, pp. 272-273.

[277] *Ibid.*, at 273.

[278] A. Bryant, M. Gold, H.M. Stevenson and D. Northrup, "Public Attitudes Towards the Exclusion of Evidence: Section 24(2) of the Canadian Charter of Rights and Freedoms", (1990) 69 *Can. Bar Rev.* 1.

The same researchers in another report of their work[279] doubt that the gap between public and judicial opinion is substantial over a broad range of cases and conclude that

> any argument for or against how judges apply section 24 (2) that relies upon a supposedly monolithic ''public opinion'' clearly must be rejected.[280]

(k) "Shall Exclude" — Discretion or Duty?

In *Collins* Lamer J. expressly agrees with the statement of Mr. Justice Seaton that s. 24(2) ''does not confer a discretion on the judge but a duty to admit or exclude as a result of his finding.'' Similarly, Le Dain J. in *Therens*[281] had concluded that s. 24(2) involved the application of the ''broad test or standard'' which necessarily gave the Court some latitude but ''not, strictly speaking, a discretion.''[282]

This view that s. 24(2) does not involve an exercise of discretion seems formalistic.[283] Section 24(2) does say ''the evidence shall be excluded'' but it also declares that this shall only happen if the Court finds that it has been established ''having regard to all the circumstances'' that admission would bring the administration of justice into disrepute. It is strange to deny a discretion when the bulk of the judgment carefully assesses how various factors should be weighed in the balance. This is clearly a discretionary exercise, which the present Supreme Court no longer denies.[284]

The real reason that the courts wish to avoid the characterization of a discretion may lie in the concern of appellate courts that a wide discretion is not subject to review.[285] Even this explanation is not particularly compelling because courts of appeal have traditionally intervened to review discretionary exercises by trial judges in glaring cases. In any event, *Collins* clearly holds that the trial judge's discretion as to whether to exclude under s. 24(2) is a question of law from which an appeal will generally lay except where the trial judge's decision was based on assessment of credibility.[286]

In *Duguay* (1989),[287] in which the Supreme Court refused to address Zuber J.A.'s concerns, the Court also announced a policy of caution for its own exercise of review jurisdiction:

> It is not the proper function of this court, though it has jurisdiction to do so, absent some error as to the applicable principles or rules of law, or absent a finding that is

---

[279] ''Public Support for the Exclusion of Unconstitutionally Obtained Evidence'', (1990) 1 *Sup. Crt. L.R.* (2d) 555.

[280] At 587, relied on by Sopinka J. in *Burlingham* at 323.

[281] Above note 15. See too similarly the Ontario Court of Appeal in *Manninen*, above note 185, at 172.

[282] *Ibid.*, at 134.

[283] See further Delisle, ''Annotation to Manninen'', C.R. *ibid.*, p. 163.

[284] *Burlingham*, above note 259.

[285] See Jobson, above note 98, pp. 250-251.

[286] Above note 216, at 204.

[287] (1989), 67 C.R. (3d) 252 (S.C.C.). See similarly Lamer J. at 53.

unreasonable, to review findings of the courts below under s. 24(2) of the Charter and substitute its opinion of the matter for that arrived at by the Court of Appeal.[288]

(l) Three Collins Factors for What Brings the Administration of Justice into Disrepute

In *Collins* Mr. Justice Lamer, in considering how the judge was to "consider all the circumstances" under s. 24(2), found it as "a matter of personal preference" useful to group the factors according to the way in which they affected the repute of the administration of justice.[289] His personal approach was applied like a boilerplate. A clear summary of *Collins* by Chief Justice Dickson for the majority in *Jacoy* (1988)[290] was frequently[291] relied upon:

> First, the court must consider whether the admission of evidence will affect the fairness of the trial. If this inquiry is answered affirmatively, 'the admission of evidence would *tend* to bring the administration of justice into disrepute and, subject to a consideration of other factors, the evidence generally should be excluded' (at p. 284). One of the factors relevant to this determination is the nature of the evidence; if the evidence is real evidence that existed irrespective of the Charter violation, its admission will rarely render the trial unfair.
>
> The second set of factors concerns the seriousness of the violation. Relevant to this group is whether the violation was committed in good faith, whether it was inadvertent or of a merely technical nature, whether it was motivated by urgency or to prevent the loss of evidence, and whether the evidence could have been obtained with Charter violation.
>
> Finally, the court must look at factors relating to the effect of excluding the evidence. The administration of justice may be brought into disrepute by excluding evidence essential to substantiate the charge where the breach of the *Charter* was trivial. While this consideration is particularly important where the offence is serious, if the admission of the evidence would result in an unfair trial, the seriousness of the offence would not render the evidence admissible.[292]

This approach distinguishes between evidence which affects the fairness of the trial and evidence that does not. If it does affect the fairness of the trial there is in effect a presumption that the evidence be excluded under s. 24(2). This may suggest a presumption that other types of evidence obtained in violation of the Charter be admitted. Under the *Collins* test each factor — fairness of the trial, seriousness of the violation and effect of exclusion on repute of system — must be considered in all cases. We here consider each factor in turn as we examine the ten years of jurisprudence from the Supreme Court prior to the Court's reconsideration of its approach in *Stillman* (1997).[293] This journey will be arduous as the Supreme Court jurisprudence on s. 24(2) over this period has been overly complex and subtle, divided in its opinions and seemingly inconsistent.

---

[288] *Ibid.*, at 256. *Kokesch* and *Burlingham* are examples of intervention by the Supreme Court.
[289] Above note 216, at 211.
[290] (1988), 66 C.R. (3d) 336 (S.C.C.).
[291] *Jacoy* was adopted as recently as *Evans* (1996), 104 C.C.C. (3d) 23 (S.C.C.).
[292] *Ibid.*, at 344-345.
[293] (1997), 5 C.R. (5th) 1 (S.C.C.).

(i) *Fairness of trial*

According to Lamer J. in *Collins*:

> If the admission of the evidence in some way affects the fairness of the trial, then the admission of the evidence would *tend* to bring the administration of justice into disrepute and, subject to a consideration of the other factors, the evidence generally should be excluded.[294]

The Court makes it quite clear that evidence that goes to the fairness of the trial will usually but not always be excluded. It is also clear that even in such cases there must be a consideration of the other factors grouped under the heading of seriousness of violation and effect on the system. This is how *Collins* was applied by courts at all levels until the Supreme Court's ruling in *Elshaw*.

In *Elshaw* (1991),[295] Mr. Justice Iacobucci, for the majority[296] held that the first and second group of factors (trial fairness and seriousness of violation) are

> alternative grounds for the exclusion of evidence, and not alternative grounds for the admission of evidence.[297]

The Iacobucci position has been criticized as unnecessarily precluding the discretionary consideration of all factors.[298] On *Elshaw*, once it has been determined that the evidence obtained in violation of the Charter has rendered the trial unfair, there is no reason to consider the second group of factors relating to the seriousness of the violation.

This aspect of *Elshaw* was adopted by Chief Justice Lamer for a 7-2 majority of the Supreme Court in *Bartle* (1994).[299] In *Borden* (1994),[300] in which the Supreme Court excluded D.N.A. evidence because the sample had been obtained in violation of ss. 8, 10 (a) an 10(b) of the Charter, Iacobucci J., for the majority, explained his own judgment in *Elshaw* as holding that:

> While the bad faith of the police would operate to strengthen the case for exclusion, the good faith of police could not support the admission of evidence in circumstances where the admission had been found to render the trial unfair.[301]

Despite the *Elshaw* approach, in practice the Supreme Court has usually still addressed the seriousness of the violation inquiry even where it has characterised the evidence as making the trial unfair.[302]

In *Collins*, Mr. Justice Lamer indicated that he was distinguishing evidence relating to the fairness of the trial as trials were a key part of the administration

---

[294] Above note 216, at 211.

[295] (1991), 7 C.R. (4th) 333 (S.C.C.), *obiter*, adopting the minority position of Sopinka J. in *Hebert* (1990), 77 C.R. (3d) 145 (S.C.C.) at 167.

[296] Lamer C.J., Sopinka, Gonthier, McLachlin and Stevenson JJ. concurred.

[297] At 167.

[298] See, for example, Stuart, Annotation to *Elshaw*, (1991) 7 C.R. (4th) 335-336 and Delisle, "*Mellenthin*: Changing the Collins Test", (1993) 16 C.R. (4th) 286.

[299] (1994), 33 C.R. (4th) 1 (S.C.C.).

[300] (1994), 33 C.R. (4th) 147 (S.C.C.).

[301] At 162-163.

[302] See, for example, *Elshaw*, *Mellenthin*, *Bartle*, *Harper* and *Burlingham*.

of justice and their fairness a major source of the repute of the system. In a passage explaining the distinction between real evidence and evidence where an accused is conscripted against himself, it becomes clear that this distinction is mostly rooted in an expanded right against self-incrimination:

> It is clear to me that the factors relevant to this determination will include the nature of the evidence obtained as a result of the violation and the nature of the right violated and not so much the manner in which the right was violated. Real evidence that was obtained in a manner that violated the Charter will rarely operate unfairly for that reason alone. The real evidence existed irrespective of the violation of the Charter and its use does not render the trial unfair. However, the situation is very different with respect to cases where, after a violation of the Charter, the accused is conscripted against himself through a confession or other evidence emanating from him. The use of such evidence would render the trial unfair, for it did not exist prior to the violation and it strikes at one of the fundamental tenets of a fair trial, the right against self-incrimination.[303]

As predicted in *Collins*, evidence obtained following a violation of the right to counsel will usually give rise to evidence affecting the fairness of the trial, as in the case of breathalyzer evidence[304] or a confession to the police.[305]

In *Leclair* (1989),[306] Lamer J. for the majority of the Court[307] confirmed that the expression "emanating from him" used in *Collins* was not an attempt to limit to statements the kind of evidence capable of rendering a trial unfair.

> I am of the opinion that the use of any evidence that could not have been obtained for the participation of the accused in the construction of the evidence for the purposes of the trial would tend to render the trial process unfair.[308]

The accused had been denied their right to counsel[309] and had participated in a police identification parade held in the middle of the night. The majority held that this evidence went to the fairness of the trial and should be excluded. The minority view was that this would go too far. The identity of the accused and the perceptions of the witness to the crime existed prior to the violation and could not be considered to have emanated from the accused. Given the strength of the Crown case and that the line-up itself had been carried out fairly, the minority were of

---

[303] Above note 216, at 211-213. In *Elshaw* the majority suggest the test for admissibility of self-incriminating evidence under s. 24(2) is "more stringent" as this evidence is "directly related to the Charter violation and its admission would dramatically affect the presumption of innocence of the accused and also affect his or her right not to testify" (at p. 21).

[304] *Therens*, above note 15. In *Bartle*, the majority expressly reversed the ruling of the Ontario Court of Appeal in *Jackson* (1993), 15 O.R. (3d) 709 (C.A.) which had sought to distinguish and admit breathalyzer evidence obtained in violation of s. 10(b) on the basis that the accused was under a Criminal Code duty to provide a breathalyzer sample.

[305] *Clarkson*, above note 213; *Manninen*, above note 186 and *Brydges*, above note 54.

[306] (1989), 67 C.R. (3d) 209 (S.C.C.).

[307] Beetz, Wilson, and La Forest JJ. concurred. L'Heureux-Dubé J. (McIntyre J. concurring) dissented.

[308] Above note 306, at 220-221.

[309] See above, Chapter 5.

the view that admission of the evidence could not bring the administration of justice into disrepute.[310]

In a most dramatic ruling the Nova Scotia Court of Appeal in *Nugent* (1988)[311] held that a video re-enactment of a murder by an accused who had been denied his right to counsel was to be excluded under s. 24(2). The majority held that the evidence was self-incriminating and the use of the evidence would render the trial unfair.[312] The ruling was prior to *Leclair* but consistent with it.

There has been an overwhelming tendency for our courts to characterise any tangible evidence such as weapons or drugs as real evidence not going to the fairness of the trial and hence, under the *Collins* regime, more likely to be admitted. The Supreme Court itself has usually made this characterisation where such evidence was found as a result of a search or seizure contrary to s.8[313] or other non s. 10(b) Charter violation.[314]

In *Mellenthin* (1992)[315] the Court however excluded real evidence of drugs found following a random vehicle search in the accused's duffle bag on the basis that the accused himself turned out the contents and was thus conscripted against himself. In its short judgment in *Pohoretsky* (1987)[316] one of the reasons the Court gave for excluding a blood sample, taken at the hospital from an unconscious impaired driver at the request of the police, was that the effect of the police conduct had been to conscript the accused against himself. On the other hand, in both *Duarte (Sanelli)* (1990)[317] and *Wong* (1991),[318] the majority classified the unconstitutional video surveillances in question as not going to the fairness of the trial and, in both cases, admitted the evidence.[319]

Black (1989)[320] determines that where some of the unconstitutional evidence is real evidence and some relates to the fairness of the trial, the different *Collins* approaches should be applied separately to each. In the middle of the night an

---

[310] Above note 306, at 233-224, supported by Michael Brown, ''Annotation to Leclair and Ross'', C.R. *ibid.*, pp. 211-212.

[311] (1988), 63 C.R. (3d) 351 (N.S. C.A.).

[312] *Ibid.*, at 380 (per Jones J.A.). Clarke C.J.N.S., Pace and Matthews JJ.A. concurred. Chipman J.A. dissented.

[313] See, for example, *Genest, Jacoy* and three perimeter search cases: *Grant* (1993), 24 C.R. (4th) 1 (S.C.C.), *Plant* (1993), 24 C.R. (4th) 47 (S.C.C.) and *Wiley* (1993), 24 C.R. (4th) 34 (S.C.C.). In *Pohoretsky* (1987), 58 C.R. (3d) 113 (S.C.C.), one of the reasons the Court gave for excluding a blood sample, taken at the request of the police, was that the effect of the police conduct had been to conscript the accused against himself. In *Colarusso* (1994), 26 C.R. (4th) 289 (S.C.C.), blood and urine samples already in existence prior to seizure by the state were classified as real evidence. The samples had originally been taken on consent for medical purposes (at 316).

[314] *Greffe* (1990), 75 C.R. (3d) 257 (S.C.C.) at 263, 283 (concerning a s. 10(a) violation).

[315] (1992), 16 C.R. (4th) 273 (S.C.C.). The holding that the vehicle search had violated s. 8 is discussed above in Chapter 3.

[316] (1987), 58 C.R. (3d) 113 (S.C.C.). This issue was not addressed when the Court later more fully considered the constitutionality of blood samples: *Dyment* (1988), 66 C.R. (3d) 348 (S.C.C.).

[317] (1990), 74 C.R. (3d) 281 (S.C.C.).

[318] (1991), 1 C.R. (4th) 1 (S.C.C.).

[319] In *Wong*, Wilson J. dissented on the basis that the evidence was analogous to a confession, went to trial fairness, and should be excluded (at 26-31).

[320] Above note 239, discussed above, Chapter 5.

accused previously arrested on a charge of attempted murder and now charged with first degree murder had, before she had an opportunity to speak to the lawyer of her choice, been asked about the location of the knife and to tell him the whole story. She had confessed and later been taken to her apartment where she had pulled a knife out of the kitchen drawer and indicated that it was the murder weapon. Madam Justice Wilson, for a unanimous Supreme Court, characterized the evidence relating to the conduct in retrieving the knife as well as any words she may have uttered as, on *Leclair*, evidence going to the fairness of the trial, that should be excluded. However, the knife itself was real evidence which existed whether or not the police had breached the accused's rights and should not be excluded. Since the admission of the knife itself would not in any way affect the jury's determination of the only issue — whether the stabbing was intentional — the proper verdict as returned by the jury was that of manslaughter.[321]

Black was distinguished by the majority of the Court in *Burlingham*. Following what was held to be a serious violation of the right to counsel, the accused, already having confessed to one murder, lead the police to the murder weapon in another case. He also told his girlfriend that he had done so. Iacobucci J., for the Court held that, contrary to the situation in *Black*, the police would not otherwise have found the evidence. The real evidence of the gun and the evidence of the girlfriend were characterised as conscripted evidence going to the fairness of the trial and excluded.

The consideration that the evidence should be excluded because the police would not otherwise have found the evidence is an application of what has become known as the "discoverability doctrine". In *Mellenthin*, one of the reasons given by Cory J. for exclusion was that

> the evidence (the marihuana) would not have been discovered without the compelled testimony (the search) of the appellant.[322]

Ron Delisle[323] has traced how this notion of discoverability is a muddled version of a distinction attempted by La Forest J. Justice La Forest had expressed the view that the real/conscripted distinction is not all that useful and the better distinction is that a trial would be unfair where the evidence was created by the violation as opposed to just being discovered or located.[324]

In *Bartle*, Chief Justice Lamer held that conscripted evidence going to the fairness of the trial will not be excluded where the Crown discharges a burden of proof on a balance of probabilities[325] that the evidence would have been obtained irrespective of the breach:

> In my view, the Crown should bear the legal burden (the burden of persuasion) of establishing, on the evidence, that the s. 24(2) applicant would not have acted differently had his s. 10(b) rights been fully respected, and that, as a consequence, the evidence would have been obtained irrespective of the s. 10(b) breach.[326]

---

[321] *Ibid.*, at 116-118.
[322] At 284.
[323] Above note 298.
[324] See especially *Wise* (1992), 11 C.R. (4th) 253 (S.C.C.) and *Colarusso*, above note 313.
[325] This standard of proof was specified in *Pozniak* (1994), 33 C.R. (4th) 49 (S.C.C.) at 56.
[326] At 32.

This reversal of an onus to the Crown in *Bartle* was quite new and not to be found in *Collins*. *Bartle* involved a breach of the right to counsel and the Court held that any uncertainty as to what the accused would have done was to be resolved in the accused's favour. The Crown only discharged this burden in one of the companion cases: *Harper* (1994),[327] a domestic assault case where, according to Lamer C.J. for the Court, the accused understood the warnings but had an "almost irresistible desire to confess". Significantly the burden was held to have been discharged in the absence of the accused's testimony at the *voir dire*. *Harper* suggests that the accused would be well advised to testify at the exclusion hearing.

Following *Mellenthin* and *Burlingham*, some Courts of Appeal viewed the Supreme Court as having decided that any evidence, including real evidence, can be determined to effect trial fairness and to be excluded simply on the basis that the evidence would not otherwise have been obtained. That view has been asserted on several occasions in the Ontario Court of Appeal.[328] However, in *Belnavis and Lawrence* (1996),[329] the Ontario Court changed course. For the Court, Mr. Justice Doherty carefully reviewed recent Supreme Court jurisprudence and rejected the view that discoverability relates to trial fairness. It can only be the participation of the accused in the obtaining of the evidence which gives that evidence a self-incriminatory quality such that it can effect trial fairness.

Madam Justice McLachlin, writing for the Supreme Court in three rulings, has stressed probative worth as a test for deciding whether the evidence went to the fairness of the trial.

In *Hebert* (1990),[330] the confession to the undercover officer in the cell in violation of the accused's right to silence recognized under s. 7 was held to go to the fairness of the trial since he had been conscripted against himself by an unfair trick and also because the statement was the "only evidence against him."[331] In *Smith* (1991)[332] it was held that a statement obtained as a result of a breach of the accused's right to be informed of the reasons for his arrest under s. 10(a) of the Charter had been properly admitted by the trial judge. In the course of her judgment McLachlin J. notes that under *Collins* two related factors which may make a statement unfair are that the statement was self-incriminating and that the evidence would not have been available but for the breach.[333] Here these two factors were held not compelling. The accused's statement was neither incriminating[334] nor prejudicial in that it did not present evidence not otherwise

---

[327] (1994), 33 C.R. (4th) 61 (S.C.C.).
[328] See, for example, *Simpson* (1993), 20 C.R. (4th) 1 (Ont. C.A.), *Acciavatti* (1993), 80 C.C.C. (3d) 109 (Ont. C.A.) and *Zammit* (1993), 21 C.R. (4th) 86 (Ont. C.A.), reviewed and criticised by R.J. Delisle, "Excluding Evidence under Section 24(2): *Mellenthin Re-incarnated*", (1996), 42 C.R. (4th) 61. See too the majority decision in *Richard* (1995), 99 C.C.C. (3d) 441 (N.S. C.A.).
[329] (1996), 107 C.C.C. (3d) 195 (Ont. C.A.).
[330] Above note 295, discussed above, Chapter 2.
[331] *Ibid.*, at 192.
[332] (1991), 4 C.R. (4th) 125 (S.C.C.), discussed above, Chapter 5.
[333] *Ibid.*, at 141.
[334] R.J. Delisle, "Annotation to Smith", C.R. *ibid.*, pp. 127-129, suggests that the statement only

available, except insofar as it assisted the accused. There was ample independent evidence as to the shooting and the events that preceded it. In *Evans* (1991)[335] McLachlin J. held that confessions of a youth of subnormal mental capacity should be excluded on a charge of first degree murder, resulting in an acquittal, where they had been obtained in violation of his right to counsel. In the course of her judgment she reasons that here the statements went to the fairness of the trial since they were highly incriminatory and provided evidence not otherwise available. Furthermore, it would be unfair to use the statements against the accused as the circumstances cast significant doubt on their reliability.[336]

Professor Ron Delisle[337] persuasively criticized this aspect of the judgment in *Smith* on the basis that it seems to say that a trial judge, applying *Collins*, should admit evidence of an incriminating statement of the accused following a violation of Charter rights if there is other independent, compelling evidence implicating the accused. Surely the strength of the rest of the case is independent of the question of the remedy of exclusion of evidence for a particular Charter violation? Delisle also points out the judgment in *Smith* applied rigorously would produce a very difficult task for a trial judge who would have to postpone the final decision on the admissibility at the *voir dire* until the rest of the evidence is known. He suggests that Her Ladyship has misread *Collins* in that Lamer J. in *Collins* was emphasizing that the use of an incriminating statement following a Charter violation would make the trial unfair since it did not exist prior to the violation. On the other hand, McLachlin J. asks the very different question of whether the statement is evidence of a matter which would not otherwise be proved. *Smith* may be viewed more as an instance where an appellate court was looking back at the trial to decide whether the no substantial wrong or miscarriage of justice proviso should be applied to avoid a new trial. Even if this is true there is a danger. If appeal courts too readily apply the proviso important Charter rights may become emasculated.[338]

The Supreme Court has now clearly held in *Burlingham*[339] that an appeal court should not lightly use the proviso where evidence should have been excluded under s. 24(2).[340] Iacobucci J. further suggests,[341] referring to a note by David Tanovich,[342] that the Court might be prepared to adopt a standard of only applying

---

reproduced in the Court below ((1990), 53 C.C.C. (3d) 97 (N.S. C.A.)) was incriminating as it would have had a negative effect on his defence of intoxication.

[335] (1991), 4 C.R. (4th) 144 (S.C.C.), discussed above, Chapter 5.

[336] *Ibid.*, at 167.

[337] Above note 334.

[338] See the strong criticism by Goldberg of the similar "harmless error" doctrine in the United States, above note 150. Compare now *Elshaw*, above note 295, where the majority held that the no substantial wrong or miscarriage of justice proviso should generally not be invoked where evidence should have been excluded under s. 24(2).

[339] Applying *Elshaw*.

[340] At 291.

[341] *Ibid.*

[342] "Can the Improper Admission of Evidence Under the Charter Ever be Cured?", (1994) 32 C.R. (4th) 82.

the proviso where the Crown proves beyond a reasonable doubt that the evidence to be excluded would not have contributed at all to the original verdict.

Even if reliability can determine whether evidence relates to the fairness of the trial, this should by no means end the s. 24(2) inquiry. It is quite clear that the Supreme Court has on numerous occasions excluded reliable evidence on the basis that a Charter right has been seriously violated and that admission would bring the system of justice into disrepute.

(ii) *Seriousness of violation*

In *Kokesch* (1990),[343] Mr. Justice Sopinka writing for the majority[344] saw the purpose of considering factors relating to the seriousness of the Charter violation as being to assess the disrepute the administration of justice would suffer if judges were to accept evidence obtained through a serious Charter breach. The Court had "refused to condone, and must disassociate itself from, egregious police conduct.''[345]

The leading dictum of the factors to be considered under this grouping is still that of Lamer J. in *Collins*:

> As Le Dain J. wrote in *Therens* at p.652:
>> The relative seriousness of the constitutional violation has been assessed in the light of whether it was committed in good faith, or was inadvertent or of a merely technical nature, or whether it was deliberate, wilful or flagrant. Another relevant consideration is whether the action which constituted the constitutional violation was motivated by urgency or necessity to prevent the loss of destruction of the evidence.
>
> I should add that the availability of other investigatory techniques and the fact that the evidence could have been obtained without the violation of the Charter tend to render the Charter violation more serious. We are considering the actual conduct of the authorities and the evidence must not be admitted on the basis that they could have proceeded otherwise and obtained the evidence properly. In fact, their failure to proceed properly when that option was open to them tends to indicate a blatant disregard for the Charter, which is a factor supporting the exclusion of the evidence.[346]

In *Strachan* (1988),[347] Chief Justice Dickson for the Court emphasized that another factor to be considered was whether the violation was "part of a larger pattern of disregard for Charter rights.''[348] The Court went on to admit the evidence found during a search of the accused's apartment despite a violation of the accused's right to counsel. In initially denying the accused's request for counsel the police had acted out of a desire to stabilize an uncertain situation. They should have allowed him to call a lawyer once the position had become

---

[343] Above note 238.
[344] Wilson, La Forest and McLachlin JJ. concurred. Dickson C.J., L'Heureux-Dubé and Cory JJ. concurring, did not comment on this passage in his dissent.
[345] Above note 238, at 67.
[346] Above note 216, at 212. See too, *Elshaw*, above note 295.
[347] Above note 238.
[348] *Ibid.*, at 108.

stable but this was an isolated error of judgment and not part of a desire to trap the accused into talking.

In *Genest* (1989)[349] Chief Justice Dickson, again speaking for the Court, held that the Court could consider whether the circumstances of the case showed a real threat of violent behaviour, directed at the police or third parties. The Court added an important caveat:

> The consideration of the possibility of violence must, however, be carefully limited. It should not amount to a *carte blanche* for the police to ignore completely all restrictions on police behaviour. The greater the departure from the standards of behaviour required by the common law and the Charter, the heavier the onus on the police to show why they thought it necessary to use force in the process of an arrest or a search. The evidence to justify such behaviour must be apparent in the record, and must have been available to the police at the time they chose their course of conduct. The Crown cannot rely on *ex post facto* justifications.[350]

The Court later made it clear that the Crown was not required to prove a tendency to violence beyond a reasonable doubt and was not precluded from referring to past conduct. However, there would have to be an evidentiary framework laid at the beginning of the trial.[351] The Court went on to exclude the real evidence of weapons found at the accused's dwelling house in an abortive drugs raid pursuant to a search warrant. A large group of police officers had broken open the door of the house without any advance warning. The search had been a serious breach of s. 8. The police had a facially defective warrant and had used an excessive amount of force. Well-established common law limits on the powers of the police to search had been ignored and there was strong reason to believe that the search was a part of a continuing abuse of search powers.[352]

In *Collins* itself, the Court was clearly disturbed by the possibility of unnecessary violence. It ordered a new trial because the Crown had been improperly prevented from establishing whether there were reasonable grounds for the search. However, Lamer J. commented that had the search been conducted on a mere suspicion that the violation would have been a flagrant and serious one which should result in exclusion. He added:

> Indeed, we cannot accept that police officers take flying tackles at people and seize them by the throat when they do not have reasonable and probable grounds to believe that those people are either dangerous or handlers of drugs.[353]

In the case of real evidence it seems clear that the Court's determination as to the seriousness of the violation will be determinative. Evidence will only be excluded if the Court is prepared to brand the police conduct in terms such as "deliberate", "flagrant" or "blatant".

This is well demonstrated by the split decision of the Supreme Court in *Greffe* (1990).[354] Relying on "confidential information received and background

---

[349] Above note 255.
[350] *Ibid.*, at 407-408.
[351] *Ibid.*, at 409.
[352] *Ibid.*
[353] Above note 216, at 214.
[354] (1990), 75 C.R. (4th) 273 (S.C.C.). See too *Kokesch*, above note 238.

investigation'' that the accused was bringing back drugs police alerted airport customs officials. There officials detained him and subjected him to a strip search without informing him of the reason for the detention or his right to counsel under s. 10(a) and (b). The police then arrested him providing, the trial judge found, the spurious reason of outstanding traffic warrants. He was told he would be the subject of a body search at the hospital. The hospital sigmoidoscope examination recovered two condoms of heroin of a street value of approximately $225,000. Mr. Justice Lamer for the majority[355] held that real evidence of heroin found by rectal search had to be excluded under s. 24(2) given the seriousness of a cumulative effect of Charter violations. According to Lamer J., the trial judge had erred by concluding through *ex post facto* reasoning that the police had reasonable and probable grounds because drugs had been found. The record revealed no evidence to support the existence of such grounds. The premise therefore had to be that the search had proceeded as incident to an arrest for outstanding traffic warrants and not on the basis of reasonable and probable grounds for belief that the accused was in possession of heroin. The violations of the accused's rights under s. 10 by the customs inspectors went to the very reasonableness of the subsequent search by the police. The fact that the rectal examination was conducted as incident to an arrest for traffic warrants, absent any evidence on the record of reasonable and probable grounds for the belief that the accused was in possession of heroin, made the unreasonable search an extremely serious violation of the accused's Charter rights. On the assumption that the police were acting on suspicion, the Court had to disassociate itself from the police conduct given the flagrant and serious violation of the rights of the accused. The Charter breaches were not isolated errors of judgments but rather part of a larger pattern of disregard.[356]

In marked contrast, Chief Justice Dickson for the minority[357] would not have excluded the evidence. The Charter violations were technical in nature and an example of ''minor police stupidity.'' The failure to arrest for the proper offence had been a trivial violation of the accused's Charter rights. The finding of the trial judge that the police had reasonable and probable grounds should not be reversed. Nor should there be any inference drawn that the police had acted in bad faith in arresting the accused for outstanding traffic violations. There was no evidence of malice on the part of the authorities towards the accused and no evidence of mistreatment.[358]

The Supreme Court has made it clear that violations of the protection against unreasonable search and seizure under s. 8 will be considered very serious in the case of intrusive searches of the person. In *Pohoretsky* (1987),[359] Lamer J. for the Court held that a ''violation of the sanctity of a person's body is much more serious than that of his office or even of his home.''[360] The Court excluded the

---

[355] La Forest, Wilson and Gonthier JJ. concurred.
[356] Above note 354, at 285-292.
[357] L'Heureux-Dubé and Cory JJ. concurred.
[358] Above note 354, at 264-268.
[359] Above note 316.
[360] *Ibid.*, at 116.

evidence of a blood sample in an impaired driving trial. The sample had been taken from the accused by a doctor at the request of a police officer at the time when he was lying in a hospital bed in an incoherent, delirious state. The Court added that the violation was wilful and deliberate and that there was no suggestion that the police acted inadvertently or in good faith.[361] The *Pohoretsky* dictum was extended in *Dyment* (1988)[362] to exclude evidence of a sample of free-flowing blood taken originally for medical purposes and then offered to the police by the doctor.[363]

In *Collins*, Lamer J. lists as one of the factors to be considered "was it deliberate, wilful or flagrant, or was it inadvertent or committed in good faith?"[364] The issue of police "good faith" is amorphous. It is usually addressed indirectly, as is the case whenever a court decides that a breach by the police was wilful or flagrant. Where the Supreme Court has directly addressed the issue of "good faith", its decisions appear inconsistent.

In *Kokesch* (1990)[365] Mr. Justice Sopinka for a majority of the Supreme Court[366] determined that evidence of marihuana discovered in the search of a residence pursuant to a search warrant should be excluded since the evidence had been obtained as a result of an unconstitutional perimeter search of the building on mere suspicion. Good faith was here not capable of mitigating the seriousness of the s. 8 violation. On the evidence, the police knew they had insufficient grounds to either search without a warrant or to obtain a search warrant under the Narcotic Control Act. Even if the officers had honestly but mistakenly believed that they had the power to search they could not be said to have been proceeding in "good faith" as that term was understood under s. 24(2). Either they knew they were trespassing "or they ought to have known."[367] Sopinka J. did not wish to be seen as imposing upon the police a burden of "instant interpretation of court decisions" and left open the question of the length of time permitted to pass after a judgment before knowledge was "attributed to the police for the purposes of assessing good faith."[368]

In contrast, Chief Justice Dickson in dissent[369] would not have excluded the evidence and found that there was evidence of good faith on the part of the authorities. The police officer's error as to the scope of authority to engage in the perimeter search was not unreasonable. An opinion that such a search would not offend the Charter had been shared by the British Columbia Court of Appeal.

---

[361] *Ibid.*
[362] Above note 316.
[363] *Ibid.*, at 367-368. McIntyre J. dissented.
[364] Above note 216.
[365] Above note 238.
[366] Wilson, La Forest and McLachlin JJ. concurred.
[367] Above note 365, at 72. Sopinka J. relied on *Genest*, above note 349, where Dickson C.J. asserted that police officers "should have noticed" serious defects in the search warrant. See too *Dyment*, above note 316, where La Forest J. for the majority refused to condone a "lax procedure" in accepting a blood sample.
[368] *Ibid.*, at 72.
[369] L'Heureux-Dubé and Cory JJ. concurred.

Here the police motivation was to obtain evidence in a situation where other avenues appeared to have been foreclosed. They had obtained a search warrant prior to the actual search of the dwelling house.[370]

The majority in *Kokesch* found a "world of difference"[371] between claim of good faith in that case and previous Supreme Court of Canada rulings where evidence was not excluded on the consideration that police had in good faith relied on the constitutionality of search powers. Referring to previous decisions of the Supreme Court to this effect in the case of writs of assistance[372] and consensual electronic surveillance without prior judicial authorization,[373] Sopinka J. sees an important distinction:

> The police cannot be expected to predict the outcome of Charter challenges to their statutory search powers, and the success of a challenge to such a power does not vitiate the good faith of police officers to conduct a search pursuant to the power. Where, however, police powers are already constrained by statute or judicial decisions, it is not open to a police officer to test the limits by ignoring the constraint and claiming later to have been "in the execution of my duties."[374]

In three warrantless perimeter drug search cases reaching the Supreme Court in 1993,[375] Sopinka J., writing for the majority, distinguished *Kokesch* on the basis that in these cases the police had had reasonable grounds and were not merely acting on suspicion as in *Kokesch*. Reliance on a statutory power in s. 10 not declared unconstitutional had been in good faith such that the evidence should not be excluded. Furthermore, the search warrants subsequently issued for the premises were valid as, excising from consideration evidence obtained from the unconstitutional perimeter search, there were sufficient reasonable grounds to justify issuance of the warrant.

Silveira (1995)[376] is now the leading authority on good faith. Its 6-1 ruling not to exclude on that basis is clearly a windfall for the Crown. Cory J. for the majority held that the police entry into a dwelling house to secure the drugs evidence in violation of the warrant requirement under the Narcotic Control Act was a very serious violation of s. 8. Indeed, he observed that:

> It is hard to imagine a more serious infringement of an individual's right to privacy.[377]

Notwithstanding this rhetoric the majority nevertheless decided that the evidence should *not* be excluded under s. 24(2). The real evidence existed prior to the

---

[370] Above note 365, at 90.

[371] *Ibid.*, at 72.

[372] *Hamill* (1987), 56 C.R. (3d) 220 (S.C.C.); *Sieben* (1987), 56 C.R. (3d) 225 (S.C.C.).

[373] *Duarte (Sanelli)* (1990), above note 317, according La Forest "The police acted entirely in good faith. They were acting in accordance with what they had good reason to believe was the law — as it had been for many years before the advent of the Charter . . . In short, the Charter breach stemmed from an entirely reasonable misunderstanding of the law" (at 303). This dictum was followed in *Thompson* (1990), 80 C.R. (3d) 129 at 184 (S.C.C.) to allow evidence by electronic interceptions at pay telephones and residences contrary to s. 8.

[374] Above note 365, at 73.

[375] *Grant, Plant* and *Wiley*, above note 313.

[376] (1995), 38 C.R. (4th) 330 (S.C.C.).

[377] At 378.

search and would inevitably have been discovered in the search and therefore admission would not render the trial unfair. The seriousness of the violation was mitigated by exigent circumstances given the nature of the crime, the publicity of the arrests and the police belief that they needed to enter to preserve evidence. The police had acted in good faith as they could not reasonably have been expected to consider other investigative techniques such as obtaining a search warrant prior to the arrests on more limited information. However, the Court noted that in future cases, which would be decided on a case by case basis, admission of the evidence would be "rare"[378] as the police would have difficulty in establishing good faith.

It seems unjust that Silveira persuaded the Court that there had been a major Charter violation but could not himself benefit from it. The dissenting judgment of La Forest J. is compelling. He carefully makes the case[379] for exclusion, concluding that the police conduct showed bad faith or ineptitude and a pattern of disregard of Charter values. However, he was in a minority of one. As a practical matter *Silveira* confirms that even in the Supreme Court exclusion of real evidence *is* usually handled differently and will likely be admitted.[380] Since *Silveira* in drugs cases where the accused was not conscripted the Supreme Court has consistently admitted evidence obtained in violation of s. 8, usually on the basis of good faith and that drugs offences are serious. At least the majority in *Silviera* confirm that good faith is not to be tested subjectively but by asking what could reasonably have been expected of the police. That is also the approach to the controversial good faith exception to the exclusionary rule in the United States.[381]

One would have thought that the Supreme Court's repeated acceptance of good faith reliance on statutory powers subsequently declared unconstitutional[382] had impliedly overruled its early ruling in *Therens*.[383] In that decision a majority of six to two, in excluding a breathalyzer certificate obtained in violation of the right to counsel, had refused to admit it on the basis that police had relied on a pre-Charter definition of detention in the Supreme Court which would have made the right to counsel unavailable. However, the authority of *Therens* on this point is still alive. In *Hebert* (1990)[384] police had placed an informer in the cell relying on authorization to do so in a pre-Charter ruling of the Supreme Court in *Rothman*.[385] All Courts of Appeal had subsequently ruled that to do so would not violate the Charter. However, the Supreme Court found that there was a pre-Charter right to silence under s. 7 and went on to exclude the confession. For the

---

[378] At 383.

[379] At 349-363.

[380] See *Patriquen* (1995), 43 C.R. (4th) 134 (S.C.C.), *Evans*, above note 145, and *Martin* (1996), 104 C.C.C. (3d) 224 (S.C.C.).

[381] See above note 291. The *Leon* good faith exception has been rejected by the highest courts of eight States and accepted by eleven: L.A. Morrissey, "State Courts Reject *Leon* on State Constitutional Grounds: A Defense of Reactive Rulings", (1994) 47 *Vanderbilt L. Rev.* 916. See also "The Exclusionary Rule", (1995) 83 *The Georgetown Law Review* 824.

[382] See too *Simmons*, above note 190 and *Jacoy*, above note 290.

[383] Above note 15.

[384] Above note 295.

[385] Above note 112.

Court on this point, Madam Justice McLachlin flatly rejected the good faith argument on the basis that

> ignorance of the effect of the Charter does not preclude application of s. 24(2) of the Charter (*Therens*) nor does it cure an unfair trial.[386]

It may be that good faith should never cure an unfair trial but the notion that good faith based on ignorance of the Charter cannot lead to inclusion is belied by the other Supreme Court of Canada decisions we have been considering both before and after *Hebert*.

Professor Stephen Coughlan[387] has suggested that the Supreme Court has confusingly used ''good faith'' in both a broad and narrow sense. The broad sense refers to ''an absence of malice and an honest belief by the police in the guilt of the accused''. Coughlan suggests such good faith should be of very little significance under s. 24(2) since we expect the best of our police. The narrow sense describes ''reliance on an investigative technique which is later declared unconstitutional''. Coughlan further questions the trend to admit such evidence, pointing out that Charter rights of accused might well be jeopardized where there is little practical incentive to establish a new Charter standard.

(iii) *Effect of exclusion on repute of system*

In *Collins* Lamer J. considered that since the repute was the test it would be necessary to consider any disrepute that might result from the exclusion of the evidence. In his view the administration of justice would be brought into disrepute by an acquittal because of exclusion of essential evidence where the breach of the Charter was ''trivial''.[388] He then gauges the effect of the seriousness of the offence:

> Such disrepute would be greater if the offence was more serious. I would thus agree with Professor Morissette that evidence is more likely to be excluded if the offence is less serious. .... I hasten to add, however, that if the admission of the evidence would result in an unfair trial, the seriousness of the offence could not render that evidence admissible. If any relevance is to be given to the seriousness of the offence in the context of the fairness of the trial, it operates in the opposite sense: the more serious the offence, the more damaging to the system's repute would be an unfair trial.[389]

Given that the criterion in s. 24(2) is repute, one can understand that courts might be more ready to exclude evidence obtained in violation of the Charter where the offence is less serious. However, the converse proposition that in the case of serious offences where the violation relates to the fairness of the trial repute will suffer more if the evidence is admitted, seems highly questionable.[390]

---

[386] Above note 295, at 193, applied in *Elshaw*, above note 295.
[387] ''Good Faith and Exclusion of Evidence under the Charter'', (1992) 11 C.R. (4th) 304
[388] Above note 216, at 212.
[389] *Ibid.*
[390] See too, for example, Mirfield, above note 98, p. 462.

The Supreme Court has nevertheless consistently applied it. In *Evans* (1991),[391] for example, Madam Justice Southin in the Court below — the British Columbia Court of Appeal — had held that the admission of a confession in a double murder case was required since there was nothing more detrimental to the repute of the criminal justice system "than letting the accused, a self-confessed killer, go free to kill again on the basis of such infringements." However, Madam Justice McLachlin, for a unanimous Supreme Court, flatly rejected this reasoning. It was seen to rest on the questionable assumption that the particular confession was reliable and true and further:

> To justify the fairness of his trial by presuming his guilt is to stand matters on their head and violate that most fundamental of rights, the presumption of innocence. Few things could be more calculated to bring the administration of justice into disrepute than to permit the imprisonment of a man without a fair trial. Nor, as a practical matter, can it be said that such imprisonment would achieve the end sought by Southin J.A., namely, the prevention of further murders by the killer of [these victims). Only a conviction after a fair trial based on reliable evidence could give the public that assurance.[392]

It would appear that the consideration of the third group of factors under *Collins* is largely formalistic. One gets the impression that once a court reaches the third group the decision to include or exclude has already been made. Reference to the repute occurring from inclusion or exclusion merely bolsters that opinion. If this is true[393] it is ironic. Only the third group of factors concern the issue of "disrepute", which is what s. 24(2) is expressed to be about!

(m) Automatic Exclusion?

In *Strachan* (1988),[394] Chief Justice Dickson for the Court clearly set out to reject a commonly asserted view since *Therens* and *Collins* that evidence obtained in violation of the Charter which went to the fairness of the trial, typically confessions following a violation of the right to counsel, was to be automatically excluded. Chief Justice Dickson could not have been clearer:

> Routine exclusion of evidence necessary to substantiate charges may itself bring the administration of justice into disrepute. Any denial of a Charter right is serious, but s. 24(2) is not an automatic exclusionary rule. Not every breach of the right to counsel will result in the exclusion of evidence.[395]

Chief Justice Dickson asserted an equally important corrective against the trend not to exclude real evidence in *Genest* (1989).[396] For the Court, he held that consideration of the impact of exclusion in the particular case should not be

---

[391] Above note 335. See too *Clarkson, Manninen,* and *Black.*

[392] At 168.

[393] There appears to be renewed interest by provincial Court of Appeal in the third group of factors: see, for example, *Makwaychuk* (1993), 22 C.R. (4th) 103 (Man. C.A.), *Kennedy* (1995), 103 C.C.C. (3d) 161 (Nfld. C.A.) and *Belnavis and Lawrence* (1996), 48 C.R. (4th) 320 (Ont. C.A.).

[394] Above note 224.

[395] *Ibid.,* at 109. Compare similarly *Elshaw,* above note 295.

[396] Above note 255.

determinative otherwise exclusion of evidence under s. 24(2) would be ''very rare'':

> While the purpose of the rule is not to allow an accused to escape conviction, neither should it be interpreted as available only in those cases where it has no effect at all on the result of the trial. The consideration whether to exclude evidence should not be so closely tied to the ultimate result in a particular case. Justice Lamer for the majority in *Collins* held that a court should consider the effect on the administration of justice of excluding evidence but that factor alone should not decide the case.[397]

In *Burlingham* (1995),[398] the majority of the Supreme Court through Iacobucci J. acknowledged that when evidence obtained in violation of the Charter affects the fairness of the trial exclusion is ''virtually certain.''[399] This is certainly sounds close to an automatic rule of exclusion. L'Heureux-Dubé J. indeed has no doubts and vigorously dissents on the basis that the majority approach has wrongly ''dug a hole''[400] by creating a rigid rule of exclusion.[401] However, Sopinka J. responds in a concurring opinion[402] that it is ''not accurate'' to characterise the first branch of the *Collins* test as an automatic rule of exclusion respecting all self-incriminating evidence on the basis that the Court must first conclude that ''in all the circumstances'' admission of the evidence would render the trial unfair.

The upshot of this complex jurisprudence, at this point, is that the Supreme Court approach still demands exclusion of conscripted evidence going to the fairness of the trial in most cases. The Supreme Court itself has only rarely admitted such evidence.[403] On the other hand real evidence that cannot be said to have conscripted the accused is usually admitted. There are, however, Supreme Court precedents for exclusion [404]and clearly no rule of automatic inclusion.

Lower courts too now regularly emphasize that exclusion under s. 24(2) is not automatic. Thus the Ontario Court of Appeal has held that the violation of the accused's right to consult counsel in private will not in every case require that the evidence obtained thereafter be excluded.[405] On the other hand, the Saskatchewan Court of Appeal has, in a series of decisions, rejected the view that exclusion of real evidence obtained in violation of the Charter should be rare.[406]

---

[397] *Ibid.*, at 403.

[398] (1995), 38 C.R. (4th) 265 (S.C.C.).

[399] At 284, the Court adopts this characterisation from Sopinka, Lederman and Bryant, *The Law of Evidence in Canada* (1992) p. 407.

[400] At 312.

[401] The L'Heureux-Dubé position is discussed below notes 472 *et seq.*

[402] Further discussed below note 473.

[403] *Strachan, Tremblay* (1987), 60 C.R. (3d) 59 (S.C.C.) (impaired driver ''violent, vulgar and obnoxious'') and *Mohl* (1989), 69 C.R. (3d) 399 (S.C.C.) (impaired driver too drunk to understand right to counsel), and *Harper*, above note 327.

[404] See, for example, *Genest, Dyment, Pohoretsky* and *Kokesch.*

[405] *Olak* (1990), 55 C.C.C. (3d) 257 (Ont. C.A.).

[406] *Baylis* (1988), 65 C.R. (3d) 62 (Sask. C.A.); *Pastro* (1988), 42 C.C.C. (3d) 485 (Sask. C.A.); *Nielson* [1988] 6 W.W.R. 1 (Sask. C.A.) and *Cheecham* (1989), 51 C.C.C. (3d) 498 (Sask. C.A.). See too *MacDonald* (1988), 66 C.R. (3d) 189 (P.E.I. C.A.). *Salamon* (1989), 72 C.R. (3d) 355 (Ont. Dist. Ct.) and *Ferguson* (1990), 1 C.R. (4th) 53 (Ont. C.A.) (strip search at side of highway).

(n) Stillman: Conscripted Evidence Generally to be Excluded Except where Discoverable

Those hoping for a re-consideration of the Court's s. 24(2) approach were encouraged when the Supreme Court in *Stillman* (1997)[407] heard arguments before seven justices, then pointedly ordered a re-hearing before the full Court to re-consider s. 24(2) principles.[408] However hopes were dashed after that full re-hearing when some ten months later a 6-3 majority[409] largely confirmed the *status quo*.[410]

After a lengthy review of recent s. 24(2) jurisprudence, Justice Cory for the majority summarized his views and then provided the following short summary of the proper approach:

> 1. Classify the evidence as conscriptive or non-conscriptive based upon the manner in which the evidence was obtained. If the evidence is *non*-conscriptive, its admission will not render the trial unfair and the court will proceed to consider the seriousness of the breach and the effect of exclusion on the repute of the administration of justice.
>
> 2. If the evidence is conscriptive and the Crown fails to demonstrate on a balance of probabilities that the evidence would have been discovered by alternative non-conscripted means, then its admission will render the trial unfair. The Court, as a general rule, will exclude the evidence without considering the seriousness of the breach or the effect of exclusion on the repute of the administration of justice. This must be the result since an unfair trial would necessarily bring the administration of justice into disrepute.
>
> 3. If the evidence is found to be conscriptive and the Crown demonstrates on a balance of probabilities that it would have been discovered by alternative non-conscriptive means, then its admission will generally not render the trial unfair. However, the seriousness of the Charter breach and the effect of exclusion on the repute of the administration of justice will have to be considered.[411]

---

[407] (1997), 5 C.R. (5th) 1 (S.C.C.).

[408] The adjournment on May 23, 1996, was accompanied by the following reasons:
"In view of the importance of the issues raised on the facts of this appeal which, in some aspects, invite a re-consideration of established principles as regards the application of s. 24(2) of the Canadian Charter of Rights and Freedoms, and in view of the fact that this appeal was heard by a bench of seven justices without representations from any intervenors, a re-hearing is ordered, to be heard in the fall session."

[409] Per Cory J., with Lamer C.J., La Forest, Sopinka, Iacobucci and Major JJ. concurring on the s. 24(2) issue. L'Heureux-Dubé J. in dissent found no Charter violation and did not consider s. 24(2). McLachlin J. (Gonthier J. concurring) dissented in part on s. 24(2). See below note 475.

[410] For critical reviews of *Stillman* see David Paciocco, "Stillman, Disproportion and the Fair Trial Dichotomy under Section 24(2)", (1997) 2 *Can. Crim. L.R.* 163 and *Getting Away With Murder* (1999) pp. 224-244; Carol Brewer, "Stillman and Section 24(2): Much Ado About Nothing", (1997) 2 *Can. Crim. L.R.* 240, Stuart, "Stillman: Limiting Search Incident to Arrest, Consent Searches and Refining the Section 24(2) Test", (1997) 5 C.R. (5th) 99, Stephen Coughlan," Criminal Procedure Cases in the Supreme Court of Canada", (1997) 13 *Supreme Court Review*, Grace Hession, "Is Real Evidence Still a Factor in the Assessment of Trial Fairness under s. 24(2)", (1998) 41 *Crim. L.Q.* 93, Richard Mahoney "Problems with the Current Approach to s. 24(2) of the Charter: An Inevitable Discovery", (1999) 42 *Crim. L.Q.* 443 and J.A.E. Potlow, "Constitutional Remedies in the Criminal Context: A Unified Approach to Section 24 (Part II)", (2000) 44 *Crim. L.Q.* 34.

[411] Para. 119.

As with most summaries the danger may be that key aspects of the full analysis may be missed. The majority's approach to s. 24(2) refines the approach to the trial fairness factor and adopts a new approach to the issue of "discoverability".

(i) *Conscripted/non-conscripted dichotomy*

According to the majority the first task is to decide whether the evidence was conscripted. This depends on the way the evidence was obtained rather than any categorisation of the evidence as a statement or real evidence. The *Stillman* test for conscription is whether the accused was compelled to participate in the creation or discovery of the evidence.[412] Stillman was conscripted by being forced to provide the bodily samples without lawful authority contrary to ss. 7 and 8. The unauthorized use of his body was as much compelled testimony as compelling a statement.[413] Cory J. also determines that real evidence derived from the conscripted evidence, like the finding of the gun in *Burlingham* (1995),[414] should also be classified as conscripted.[415]

This extended classification of what constitutes conscripted evidence is good news for accused and those favouring the remedy of exclusion of evidence for Charter violations, especially as the *Stillman* majority further determines that the Court will "as a general rule" exclude such evidence without considering the other *Collins* factors, such as seriousness of the breach or the effect on the repute of the administration of justice.

The significance of the majority allowing for exceptional cases where evidence affecting trial fairness may be admitted is unclear given that the issues of seriousness and repute are not to be considered. What other factors would be material? The minority are surely correct in characterising the majority approach as one of erecting an automatic exclusion rule. There is often a circular tone to the majority position: since the compelled testimony makes the trial unfair, the evidence must be excluded to ensure a fair trial. The Court never says *why* compelled testimony makes the trial "unfair". The majority are on stronger ground in justifying their position on the Court's commitment to the fundamental principle that the state cannot compel the accused to incrimination.[416]

---

[412] The Court implicitly rejects the sometimes expressed view that evidence obtained by a Charter violation necessarily goes to the fairness of the trial, as did the Ontario Court of Appeal in *Belnavis*, above note 393.

[413] There is an ambiguous reference to a procedure that "may be so unobtrusive and so routinely performed it is accepted without question by society" such that it comes under the "rare exception for merely technical or minimal violations" (para. 90). It is not clear whether this refers to the issue of Charter violation or that of s. 24(2). See further Paciocco, above note 410, 178-179. The view of Duncan J. that this meant that the Supreme Court had changed the rule that breathalyser evidence obtained in violation of s. 10(b) affects trial fairness for s. 24(2) purposes was reversed on appeal: *McKenzie* (1999), 28 C.R. (5th) 394 (Ont. S.C.). The Court could not have intended a major change in the law without adverting to its prior jurisprudence.

[414] (1995), 38 C.R. (4th) 265 (S.C.C.).

[415] Paras. 78, 100. This aspect of the ruling led to an order of a new trial in *Robert* (1996), 104 C.C.C. (3d) 480 (B.C. C.A.) and an acquittal in *Ricketts* (2000), 144 C.C.C. (3d) 152 (Ont. C.A.).

[416] Para. 81.

The majority's line between conscripted and non-conscripted evidence seems to hinge on the aspect of compulsion but seems problematic. Cory J. points to *Evans* (1996)[417] and *Wijesinha* (1995)[418] as examples where the accused was *not* conscripted. In *Evans*, drug squad officers, relying on a tip, decided to obtain reasonable grounds to obtain a search warrant by employing a "knock on" procedure. They knocked on the door which the accused opened. The smell of marihuana was relied on to get the warrant. The majority of the Court held that there was a violation of s. 8 but that the evidence had not been conscripted and should be admitted.[419] In *Wijesinha* a police officer wearing a body pack surreptitiously recorded a conversation with the accused to obtain evidence that a lawyer was seeking referrals from police officers for a fee. There was a violation of s. 8 because the search had been without a warrant. The Supreme Court nevertheless admitted the evidence holding that the evidence did not affect trial fairness because the accused could not "by any stretch of the imagination be said to have been conscripted into incriminating himself in these conversations".[420]

How is it that both Evans and Wijesinha did not meet the *Stillman* test of being compelled to participate in the creation or discovery of evidence? Like Stillman they had no real choice but to comply.

Since *Stillman*, an issue has arisen as to whether conscription under *Stillman* is to be limited to a narrow approach of whether the evidence fits into one of three categories of compelled evidence: statements,[421] use of the body and bodily samples. This is based on a remark by Cory J. in *Stillman*:

> Evidence will be conscriptive when an accused, in violation of his *Charter* rights, is compelled to incriminate himself at the behest of the state by means of a statement, the use of the body or the production of bodily samples.[422]

The wider interpretation is that such a closed category approach is inconsistent[423] with Cory J.'s view that

> if the accused was not compelled to participate in the creation or discovery of the evidence (i.e., the evidence existed independently of the *Charter* breach in a form useable by the state), the evidence will be classified as non- conscriptive.[424]

He had been at pains to establish that the question is how the evidence was obtained rather than whether the evidence was real or otherwise.

[417] (1996), 45 C.R. (4th) 210 (S.C.C.).
[418] [1995] S.C.R. 422.
[419] In *Vu* (1999), 23 C.R. (5th) 302 (B.C. C.A.) the Court applies *Evans* but expresses dissatisfaction with its ruling that there was a s. 8 violation.
[420] Para. 55, quoted by Cory J. at para. 97. This was followed in *Pope* (1998), 20 C.R. (5th) 173 (Alta. C.A.) (for purposes of trial fairness under s. 24(2) element of compulsion requiring more than State passive observation or eavesdropping).
[421] In *Cook* (1998), 19 C.R. (5th) 1 (S.C.C.) the majority made it clear that a statement that is largely or wholly exculpatory will be considered conscripted where an accused is compelled in breach of Charter rights to provide evidence which can later be used against him (at 31).
[422] Para. 80.
[423] See Vaso Maric, "The Aftermath of Stillman: Should Courts Pigeonhole The Right to a Fair Trial?", (1999) 25 *Queen's L.J.* 95. Compare David Tanovich, "Making Sense of the Meaning of Conscriptive Evidence Following Stillman", (1999) 20 C.R. (5th) 233.
[424] Para. 75.

It is true that in *Belnavis* (1997),[425] Cory J., in deciding for the majority of six justices that the stolen property found in a vehicle in violation of s. 8 was not conscripted evidence, starts by quoting the category passage from his judgment in *Stillman*. However Justice Cory immediately returns to the basic *Stillman* test in holding that the evidence in question was not conscripted:

> There is no doubt that the evidence in this case was not conscriptive. The merchandise, allegedly stolen, was not obtained through any compelled participation ... and the evidence in question was not a statement of any kind.[426]

In *Davies* (1998)[427] the Yukon Territory Court of Appeal felt bound by an *ex cathedra* speech of Cory J. at a Federated Law Societies meeting to accept the narrow view. A police officer saw the accused and another, who were known to him, acting suspiciously in an empty street early one morning. There had been a rash of break and enters in the area. When speaking to one of the males the accused walked quickly by with a backpack. The officer asked what was in the backpack and the accused said nothing or it was empty. The officer said, "Then you would not object if I saw what was in it?" The accused opened it and the officer saw bolt cutters. At the accused's trial on a charge of possession of a break-in instrument contrary to s. 351(1) of the Criminal Code, the trial judge found that the seizure was contrary to s. 8 of the Charter as it was on mere suspicion and not consensual. However she admitted the evidence under s. 24(2), finding that the evidence was real and non-conscripted. The only issue on the appeal was whether the evidence should have been excluded as conscripted evidence. The Yukon Territory Court of Appeal would have allowed the appeal on the ground that the discovery of the evidence involved the participation of the accused in the course of a Charter breach. The Crown had not established that the evidence was discoverable without a Charter breach. However the Court was somewhat reluctantly persuaded to adopt the narrow category approach reflected in Judge Cory's extrajudicial paper explaining *Stillman* and adopted by the Ontario Court of Appeal in *Lewis* (1998).[428] There was a reference in the paper to a hypothetical remarkably close to the circumstances of the instant case. The ruling on admissibility therefore had to be reversed although the narrow category sense was more restrictive than the language of *Stillman*.[429]

This is extraordinary. Cory J. spoke for a majority of the Supreme Court after full argument by counsel but at the conference he spoke only for himself. The doctrine of precedent would mean very little if made subject to *ex cathedra* glosses. The Yukon Territory Court of Appeal should have stuck to its own interpretation, which would properly have left any review of *Stillman* for the

---

[425] (1997), 10 C.R. (5th) 65 (S.C.C.).
[426] Para. 36. However in a later s. 24(2) ruling in *Cook*, above note 421, Cory and Iacobucci J. for the majority only refer to the category definition of conscripted evidence (at 11).
[427] (1998), 18 C.R. (5th) 113 (Y.T. C.A.).
[428] (1998), 13 C.R. (5th) 34 (Ont. C.A.).
[429] The narrow interpretation adopted in *Davies* was followed by the B.C. Court of Appeal in *Yamantha*, August 18, 1998, and *Ellrodt*, September 23, 1998.

Supreme Court. Even more extraordinary is that the Supreme Court later refused leave to appeal.[430]

The Ontario Court of Appeal in *Lewis* in fact only partly adopted Cory J.'s *ex cathedra* statement. Justice Doherty for the Ontario Court first seized on the category remarks in *Stillman* and *Belnavis*. However this was not seen as determinative. The Court did refer to the *ex cathedra* comment in rejecting the defence counsel's argument that when the accused opened the bag for the police in the course of a search at an airport contrary to s. 8, he was conscripted to assist in obtaining the evidence in the bag. However Doherty J. decided the case on the basis that the accused was not used against himself "in any relevant sense".

Even if the conscripted/non-conscripted distinction is to be maintained, it is obviously in urgent need of clarification.

(ii) *Discoverability*

The *Stillman* majority introduces new nuances on the issue of "discoverability". Here the pronouncements favour the Crown and those reluctant to exclude evidence obtained in violation of the Charter.

Under *Stillman* if the Crown can demonstrate on a balance of probabilities that the evidence would have been lawfully discovered by alternative non-conscripted means, admission will generally not render the trial unfair. In such cases the seriousness of the Charter breach and the effect of exclusion on the repute of the administration of justice must be considered.

Once again the use of the word "generally" produces untamed uncertainty. Cory J. refers to this issue of discoverability in slightly different ways at different points of his judgment. He distinguishes between evidence which would have been obtained from an independent source and evidence which would have been inevitably discovered.[431] Then he seems to acknowledge that these notions are one and the same.[432] There are important qualifications in that the other means must be non-conscriptive[433] and constitutional.[434]

When the Crown shows discoverability in the above sense all the *Collins* factors must be considered. Surely the dissenters are correct in suggesting this is how it should be in all cases, as s. 24(2) was designed as a discretionary decision based on all the circumstances. It is odd that seriousness and repute are ever irrelevant.

The last consideration of discoverability seems highly speculative. Instead of asking whether the evidence was obtained by a Charter breach, ask whether

---

[430] Surprisingly Cory J. was a member of the panel.
[431] Paras. 102, 116.
[432] Para. 106.
[433] Para. 106.
[434] Paras. 76, 109. Sopinka J. in *Feeney* later introduced another nuance that in the case of derivative evidence the discoverability question becomes whether the evidence would have been obtained, not whether it would have been constitutionally obtained. The change was not justified and adds another layer of unnecessary subtlety.

the police could have got the evidence without the violation. Why gloss over the reality that the police chose a method that violated the Charter?

The Court has never sought to justify its position on discoverability. David Paciocco sees it as pragmatic:

> Discoverability is a prudent criterion, but it is entirely pragmatic and not the least principled. It is born of the realization that to exclude evidence that the police would have had in any event is to give the accused a windfall, and to require the state to overcompensate....This has nothing to do with whether the trial is fair.[435]

Similarly Kent Roach writes that

> the State, as well as the accused, should not be put in a worse position than if the violation had occurred.[436]

These views are not persuasive. Surely, as Richard Mahoney puts it,

> a proper enquiry under s. 24(2) should never be stultified by any purported rule that the state should never be worse off as a result of having breached one of the accused's Charter rights. There are times when the state should be worse off to the extent of seeing a guilty accused acquitted.[437]

Discoverability should not be a controlling factor. The inquiry seems quite perverse. If the issue is seriousness of the breach, discoverability makes the violation worse and should point to exclusion. As Carol Brewer has put it,[438] it should be a Catch-22 for the Crown. The fact that the police could have discovered the evidence without breaching the Charter should make the violation more serious and should point to exclusion. This consideration appears largely absent from the jurisprudence in non-conscripted cases.[439]

According to Cory J. the fact that there was no lawful means of obtaining the evidence cannot excuse or justify a Charter violation.[440] This appears totally at odds with the discoverability exception.

(iii) *Inclusionary rule for non-conscripted evidence*[441]

In contrast to the mountain of criticism against the automatic exclusion rule for conscripted evidence, there has been very little adverse comment on the strong tendency before and after *Stillman* to *admit* non-conscripted evidence obtained in violation of the Charter.

It is particularly instructive to consider s. 8 cases where the evidence is normally characterised as non-conscripted.[442] What appears to be a virtually

---

[435] Above note 410, at 170.

[436] "The Evolving Fair Trial Test Under Section 24(2) of the Charter", (1996) 1 *Can. Crim. L.R.* 117 at 123.

[437] Above note 410, at 472.

[438] Above note 410, at 250.

[439] It was relied on by Justice Sopinka in *Feeney,* below note 444.

[440] Para. 125, relying on Sopinka J. in *Kokesch*, [1990] 3 S.C.R. 3 at 28.

[441] These views were first and more fully expressed in "Eight Plus Twenty-Four Two Equals Zero", (1998) 13 C.R. (5th) 50.

[442] See recent full analysis in *Collins* (1999), 22 C.R. (5th) 269 (Nfld. C.A.).

automatic *inclusionary* rule is reducing the pronouncement of s. 8 standards to meaningless rhetoric. There is a troubling paradox under present Supreme Court s. 24(2) jurisprudence. Conscripted evidence obtained in violation of the Charter is excluded in murder and sexual assault cases, like *Burlingham*, *Borden* and *Stillman*, whereas non-conscripted evidence, locating drugs in violation of the Charter as in *Evans*, is admitted because the police could have done it right and drug offences are serious.

Stillman itself provides an illustration of how quickly the Court will admit evidence of non-conscripted evidence. Having decided that the seizure of the abandoned tissue violated s. 8, the Supreme Court had no difficulty in deciding to nevertheless admit the evidence. The evidence was not conscripted because the accused blew his own nose, there was no loss of dignity and the police "could and would" have discovered the evidence by a lawful search warrant.[443]

Since *Stillman* there has only been one s. 8 case where the Supreme Court excluded non-conscripted evidence — that in *Feeney* (1997).[444] In *Feeney* the majority held that the entry into the trailer home on suspicion of murder and without warrant violated Charter rights including s. 8. The statements in the trailer, at the detachment, and the fingerprints had to be excluded as affecting trial fairness because they were conscriptive and not discoverable without violating Charter rights. However Justice Sopinka held that although the evidence of the bloody shirt, the shoes, the cigarettes and the money were not conscripted evidence nor derived from conscripted evidence, that evidence also had to be excluded. The violations were serious, the police were not acting in good faith, there were no exigent circumstances, there was a pattern of disregard for Charter rights and the admission of the evidence would bring greater harm to the repute of the administration of justice than its exclusion. According to the majority, any price to society occasioned by the possible loss of a conviction was fully justified in a free and democratic society governed by the rule of law.[445]

In the subsequent s. 8 decisions in *Belnavis* (1997)[446] and *Caslake* (1998)[447] the Court admitted the non-conscripted evidence. In *Belnavis* the trial judge's finding that the breach was serious was held to have been unreasonable. The Supreme Court decided that the accused had a greatly reduced expectation of privacy because her claim was in relation to a vehicle and her expectation was further reduced because her relative privacy interest in this particular vehicle was low. There was no ongoing disregard for Charter rights. The breach was in no way deliberate, wilful or flagrant. The officer acted entirely in good faith. The presence of reasonable and probable grounds mitigated the seriousness of the breach. The administration of justice would be brought into disrepute if the evidence was excluded. The evidence was essential to substantiate the charge and

---

[443] Para. 128.

[444] (1997), 7 C.R. (5th) 101 (S.C.C.).

[445] Para. 47. On the new trial evidence was sought and admitted under the new D.N.A. warrant procedure: *Feeney* (1999), 23 C.R. (5th) 74 (B.C. S.C.). The accused was convicted of second degree murder. The appeal was dismissed (January 24, 2001) (B.C. C.A.).

[446] (1997), 10 C.R. (5th) 65 (S.C.C.).

[447] (1998), 13 C.R. (5th) 1 (S.C.C.).

the breach, if any, was minimal. The evidence was reliable and the quantity of merchandise suggested more than a random act of theft.

In *Caslake*, the Court ruled that evidence of cocaine found in an inventory search of an impounded vehicle in violation of the right to search incident to arrest should not be excluded under s. 24(2). The breach was not sufficiently serious to justify exclusion. The search was not especially obtrusive. There was a lesser expectation of privacy in a car than in one's home or office, or with respect to the physical person. Although the officer did not know that he had reasonable and probable grounds to conduct a search, objectively speaking, he did. The search was conducted in good faith reliance on an R.C.M.P inventory search policy. Finally, excluding the evidence would have a more serious impact on the repute of the administration of justice than admitting it. That the prosecution had no case without the evidence weighed in favour of admission.

In post-*Stillman* s. 8 cases involving drugs, the Ontario Court of Appeal has usually firmly rejected applications to exclude drugs found in violation of s. 8 where the evidence is found to be not conscripted.[448]

The impression left by these recent Supreme Court and Ontario Court of Appeal rulings, especially in drug cases, is that those courts seem generally determined not to exclude real evidence found in violation of s. 8 . Those courts tend to ratchet up the rhetoric respecting the third *Collins* factor about the seriousness of the offence and the effect on the repute of the system if exclusion of reliable evidence were to result in acquittals. If this is the major reason for admitting the evidence, it points to an irony and inconsistency with the *Stillman* approach in that the seriousness of the offence and reliability are *not* relevant factors where evidence is characterised as going to trial fairness. Canadian criminal trials under the Charter are no longer exclusively concerned with determining guilt or innocence. It betrays respect for the Charter to argue a return to the pre-Charter days where police conduct was not a material consideration. Particular abhorrence of drug offences may well have coloured consideration of the second *Collins* factor, such that seriousness of the violation is unduly de-emphasised. The Courts as guardians of the Charter should be above the war against drugs. This one category of offences does not require special and reduced Charter standards.

If Charter standards for police behaviour are to mean anything, judges should be cautious lest they too easily discount the seriousness of a Charter breach. When such a vigilant attitude is evident, as in Justice Sopinka's judgment in *Feeney*,[449] the factor of seriousness of the offence becomes far less significant.

By contrast what message are police officers to take from the ruling of the Ontario Court of Appeal in *Polashek* (1999)?[450] There was a systemic problem in that police were not being instructed to read accused their s. 10(b) rights on

[448] See, for example, *Lauda* (1998), 13 C.R. (5th) 20 (Ont. C.A.) and *Lewis* (1998), 13 C.R. (5th) 34 (Ont. C.A.).
[449] Above note 144.
[450] (1999), 25 C.R. (5th) 183 (Ont. C.A.).

detention but the real evidence of drugs found shortly after the breach should not be excluded as the evidence was not conscripted and the breach not too serious.[451]

The strong trend not to include non-conscripted evidence after s. 8 violations have been established, especially in drug cases, carries the special freight of making s. 8 rulings empty. It will be little comfort to an accused that he or she has established that the evidence was obtained in violation of a major Charter standard when it will nevertheless be used to convict because the violation wasn't in a home, the police were in good faith ignorance and/or the offence is considered serious. Charter rights will only have bite if there are meaningful remedies. In this context there must be a real risk that investigations that violate Charter rulings may result in exclusion of evidence and acquittal, even in serious cases, in the long-term interests of the integrity of the justice system. There are, however, recent strong signs that courts are becoming more receptive to arguments that serious violations must result in exclusion especially where the police were ignoring or ignorant of established Charter rights.[452]

In *Fowler* (1990),[453] Mr. Justice Lyon of the Manitoba Court of Appeal suggested that excluding truthful evidence was a remedy "which should be seldom sought, even more infrequently granted and then only when all the circumstances including the interests of justice absolutely required the withholding of evidence."[454] He indicated that no one could maintain that the application of the exclusionary evidence rule leading to the supression of truth had been one of the major purposes of the drafters of s. 24 of the Charter. Mr. Justice Lyon was, of course, a signatory to the Charter as the then Premier of Manitoba. However, a colleague on the Manitoba Court of Appeal in *Fowler*, O'Sullivan J.A., seems justified in his strong rebuke.

> Truth is one of the grand objectives of the criminal justice system; it is not the only objective. The common law has recognized over the ages that truth may come at too great a price to warrant its reception into evidence. That is the reason why we have rules of evidence . . .. In applying the Charter we are bound by the interpretations given to it not by its framers, but by the majority of the Supreme Court of Canada. We may have a duty, as we certainly have the right, to subject the Supreme Court's views to vigorous criticism, but in the end, if the rule of law and hierarchy of courts is to prevail, we are bound by the guidelines set by that court.[455]

(o) Stillman Approach Should Be Re-considered

Although the majority stuck to its guns in *Stillman*, the composition of the Supreme Court is now radically altered. Only two justices of the *Stillman* majority

[451] The Court ordered a new trial to determine whether a conscripted statement should be excluded. It needed to be determined whether the Crown could discharge its burden of showing that the accused would not have behaved differently had he been read his rights.
[452] See decisions to exclude non-conscripted evidence in *Damianakos* (1997), 13 C.R. (5th) 64 (Man. C.A.), *West* (1998), 12 C.R. (5th) 106 (B.C. C.A.), *Flintoff* (1998), 16 C.R. (4th) 248 (Ont. C.A.), *Hosie* (1996), 49 C.R. (4th) 1 (Ont. C.A.), *Fry* (1999), 29 C.R. (5th) 337 (Nfld. C.A.), *Price* (2000), 33 C.R. (5th) 278 (Ont. C.A.), *Bohn* (2000), 33 C.R. (5th) 265 (B.C. C.A.) and *Sutherland* (2000), 150 C.C.C. (3d) 231 (Ont. C.A.).
[453] (1990), 3 C.R. (4th) 225 (Man. C.A.).
[454] *Ibid.*, at 243.
[455] *Ibid.*, at 236.

remain but the three dissenters are still on the Court. It seems on the cards that there will be a further re-consideration of s. 24(2) principles. Should there be changes?

The notion that there should be a virtually automatic exclusion for conscripted evidence seen to affect trial fairness has troubled most writers.[456] The majority of the Supreme Court have consistently subscribed to the view that what the Court now calls the "principle against self-incrimination"[457] is particularly fundamental. A breach is likely to require exclusion. In this sense the Court recognises a hierarchy of rights despite the Court's recent pronouncements to the contrary.[458] The idea germinated with the opinion of Le Dain J. in *Therens* that the right to counsel is of pre-eminent importance. This is certainly debatable. A person whose dwelling has been ransacked by a drug squad in violation of s. 8 may, for example, suggest that the protection of privacy is more important than the right to speak with a lawyer.

Most commentators are troubled by the consequences for exclusion of the distinction between self-incriminating and other evidence. This will continue to lead to odd results. Thus Ron Delisle questions whether it make sense to admit the evidence in a vehicle search case like *Mellenthin*, had the officer, instead of asking Mellenthin to open the bag, picked up the bag himself and looked inside.[459] Should it make a difference in drug search cases that the suspect was conscripted in that he or she was asked where the drugs were or otherwise assisted in the search?

Professor David Pacciocco[460] has gone further in his criticism. He complains that the Supreme Court has fashioned an "extremely aggressive exclusionary remedy"[461] by departing from the words and intent of s. 24(2). He suggests that exclusion should be rare and that

> the exclusionary philosophy of the Court is not driven a wit by what are almost certainly the views of the average Canadian on the matter.[462]

He has sharpened his attack since *Stillman*. A major theme of his book[463] is that the criminal justice system should put a higher value on truth. He provides a fine exploration of the history and justification of the rule of law[464] and is at pains to justify the presumption of innocence and standard of proof beyond reasonable doubt, especially in the emotive context of sexual assault.[465] He is, however,

---

[456] See, for example, R.J. Delisle, "Collins: An Unjustified Distinction", (1987) 56 C.R. (3d) 216, Mirfield, above note 98, pp. 452-453, and writers referred to above note 410. However Kent Roach, above note 436, is supportive.

[457] See above Chapter 2.

[458] See above Charter 1.

[459] "Mellenthin: Changing the Collins Test", (1993) 16 C.R. (4th) 286 at 290.

[460] "The Judicial Repeal of s. 24(2) and the Development of the Canadian Exclusionary Rule", (1990) 32 *Crim. L.Q.* 326.

[461] At 342.

[462] At 365.

[463] *Getting Away With Murder, The Canadian Criminal Justice System* (1999).

[464] Chapter 5.

[465] Chapter 8.

inconsistent on the issue of exclusion of relevant evidence. Paciocco justifies[466] many common law rules of exclusion on the basis that there are sometimes more compelling reasons of policy than getting at the truth or because experience has shown that the particular kind of proof being offered is likely to stand in the way of accurate decisions.[467] This leads him to stout defences of the rule that involuntary confessions should be excluded as "garbage" to guard against unjust convictions. So too with evidence of bad character and similar fact evidence showing that the accused is the sort of person likely to have committed the crime charged.[468] However, when he comes to the Supreme Court's virtually automatic exclusion of conscripted evidence[469] obtained by a Charter violation, his sole concern is with the truth. He excoriates the Court for excluding such evidence in the high profile murder investigations in *Feeney* and *Burlingham*. In *Burlingham*, where the police interrogation involved a major violation of the accused's right to counsel, Paciocco supports the automatic exclusion of the induced confession at common law but not the Court's further ruling that the confession that lead to the finding of the gun by the accused had also to be excluded under the Charter. According to Paciocco:

> The principle of proportionality requires courts to make the decision whether to exclude evidence by comparing the severity of the breach and the seriousness of the consequences of excluding the evidence, given all of the circumstances and the long-range interests of the administration of justice...
>
> The majority has never attempted to explain why proportionality is crucial in non-conscriptive evidence cases but not even relevant where the evidence is conscriptive, other than repeating the empty truism that evidence that would undermine the fairness of the trial must be excluded to keep the trial fair.[470]

It seems ironic that the very David Paciocco, who wrote a book on expanding self-incriminating protections under the Charter,[471] would here take such a strong position. Many writers, including this one, and many judges, also oppose an automatic exclusion interpretation under s. 24(2). But it is surprising that the author does not recognize the strength of the counter policy argument that if Charter rights are to be taken seriously, there must be a real risk of exclusion of evidence obtained in violation of the Charter, even in serious cases and even at the cost of determining the truth.

In dissent in *Burlingham*,[472] L'Heureux-Dubé J. adopts Paciocco's earlier views and launches a blistering attack of her own. She would have replaced the approach by one stressing what she calls the principles of reliability and fairness.

---

[466] Chapter 9.
[467] At 203.
[468] At 203-204.
[469] Chapter 10 at 229-242.
[470] At 172-173.
[471] *Charter Principles and Proof in Criminal Cases* (1987).
[472] Above note 398.

This is seen to be more faithful to the original *Collins* approach and to find its roots in the judgment of Lamer J. in *Rothman* (1981).[473]

This prompted a pointed reply by Justice Sopinka. [474] According to Sopinka J., the L'Heureux-Dubé solution, and particularly the stress on reliability, cannot be found in *Collins* or earlier common law. He is certainly on a sound footing in not finding a reliability focus in *Collins* although reliability *was* indeed the exclusive focus of the majority of the Supreme Court in the pre-Charter voluntary confession ruling in *Rothman*. Sopinka J. appears unfair in suggesting that L'Heureux-Dubé J. seeks a return to the *Wray*[475] position that illegally obtained evidence should not be excluded. The L'Heureux-Dubé position is not as radical a departure as it first seems as she supports the *Collins* approach. Her major complaint is that all three factors should always be considered. There is indeed much to be said for this point of view. It seems clear, however, that Madam Justice L'Heureux-Dubé *would* seek to ensure that the exclusion of evidence is very rare in her further view that under the third group of factors the test should be whether exclusion would shock the community. To this extent she would reverse *Collins*. If there is no real possibility of exclusion of evidence obtained in violation of a Charter right, those rights would have little meaning as Justices Iacobucci and Sopinka eloquently point out. It seems fortunate that this aspect of the L'Heureux-Dubé and Paciocco views were so clearly rejected. Twenty years of careful development of Charter rights for accused could be rendered nugatory.

In *Stillman* McLachlin J. for the first time enters a strong dissent to the majority position. The framers of the Charter did not intend s. 24(2) to act as an automatic exclusionary or quasi-exclusionary rule. The view of the majority that any evidence which affects the fairness of the trial must be excluded should be resisted. First, it runs counter to the spirit and wording of s. 24(2) which requires that judges in all cases balance all factors which may affect the repute of the administration of justice and elevates the factor of trial fairness to a dominant and in many cases conclusive status. Second, it rests on an expanded and erroneous concept of self-incrimination or conscription which equates any non-consensual participation by, or use of, the accused's body in evidence gathering with trial fairness. Third, it erroneously assumes that anything that affects trial fairness automatically renders the trial so fundamentally unfair that other factors can never outweigh the unfairness, so that it becomes unnecessary to consider other factors.

It seems likely that there is in the now Chief Justice's judgment the seeds of a restatement. Fortunately it is much more flexible than that of Justice L'Heureux Dubé. The conscripted/non-conscripted distinction should indeed be abandoned. It has proved too difficult to draw. It has produced the unacceptable result that seriousness of the violation and effect of exclusion on the repute of the system are sometimes not to be considered. It is of particular concern that the *Stillman* majority has arrived at an arbitrary bright line rule where evidence compelled by

---

[473] (1981), 20 C.R. (3d) 97 (S.C.C.).
[474] Three of the majority judges concur but for some reason La Forest J. does not add his imprimatur. Surprisingly Gonthier J. agrees with both L'Heureux-Dubé J. and Sopinka J.
[475] [1971] S.C.R. 272.

a Charter violation is almost always excluded whereas all other evidence obtained in violation of the Charter will almost always be admitted. The decision under s. 24(2) should always be discretionary and there should be no categories of cases where there is a presumption of exclusion or inclusion.

The doctrine of discoverability has the advantage of weakening the rigour of an exclusionary rule for conscripted evidence said to affect a fair trial. But it seems to add a complexity and perverseness to the proper analysis. The Court should abandon it as well.

Much of the *Collins* approach would and should remain, including its considered approach to public opinion and its rejection of the visceral community shock test. The shock test advocated by L'Heureux-Dubé J. would put in place an approach far too complacent if entrenched rights of accused are to be taken seriously.[476] Every case should involve a consideration of all the facts, with a focus on the second and third factors of seriousness of the violation and effect of exclusion on the repute of the system. The Court should stand back and consider lessons from the overwhelming trend to include non-conscripted evidence. It should declare that the seriousness of the violation is the key determinant and that taking rights seriously requires the real risk of exclusion of evidence obtained in violation of the Charter even if the evidence is reliable and probative and even if the offence is serious. Exclusion has proved to be an effective vehicle for holding agents of the State accountable.[477] Courts can and should be more demanding of police in their considerations of the second *Collins* factor of seriousness of the violation and place less weight on the seriousness of the offence when considering the third factor of effect on repute.

(p) Admissible for Another Purpose such as Credibility?

Can evidence held inadmissible under s. 24(2) of the Charter nevertheless be used for another purpose in the same trial?

In *Rousseau* (1990),[478] Ontario District Court Judge Clarke held that the Crown could not tender evidence of blood samples excluded at the trial at the sentence hearing. He reasoned that a sentence hearing was not a separate proceedings and that to admit the same evidence against the same accused in the same proceedings would "garble the clear message of the inviolability of rights and freedoms which the Charter was intended to convey" and be "repugnant to common sense."[479]

In *Kuldip* (1990),[480] a majority of the Supreme Court held that confronting an accused with a prior inconsistent statement from a former proceeding during

---

[476] However in *Oickle* (2000), 36 C.R. (5th) 129 (S.C.C.), fully reviewed above, Chapter 2 under "New Common Law Voluntary Confessions Rule" the Court returns to the shock test in the course of its review of the common law voluntary confessions rule.

[477] The option of a civil action for a constitutional tort is undeveloped, costly, difficult and, if successful, is presently resulting in low damages awards: see above notes 49 and 160.

[478] (1990), 54 C.C.C. (3d) 378 (Ont. Dist. Ct.).

[479] *Ibid.*, at 383.

[480] (1990), 1 C.R. (4th) 285 (S.C.C.), discussed above, Chapter 8.

cross-examination to impugn credibility did not incriminate the accused contrary to s. 13 of the Charter. Professor Ron Delisle[481] suggested that the logic of *Kuldip* should also allow a Crown to cross-examine an accused on an earlier inconsistent statement excluded because of a violation of the Charter. Presumably, there would have to be a new *voir dire*. Delisle also points out that the United States Supreme Court has held since *Harris v. New York* (1971)[482] that, while statements of an accused in custody obtained by the police in violation of the Fifth Amendment[483] standards of *Miranda v. Arizona* (1966)[484] are inadmissible against the accused in the prosecutor's case in chief, this does not bar admission in cases where the story changes and the evidence is used to attack credibility.

A Crown counsel tried the argument in *Calder* (1996).[485] A police officer was charged with procuring the sexual services of a person under 18 and breach of trust. There was evidence in the form of an independent witness and the officer's own notebook that he had met a prostitute late one evening . When senior officers questioned the accused, he denied the meeting. On a pre-trial motion, this statement, tendered as evidence of consciousness of guilt, was excluded as it had been obtained in violation of s. 10(b). At trial, the officer testified that he had met with the prostitute but he provided an innocent explanation. The Crown's motion to be permitted to cross-examine on the statement for impeachment purposes was rejected.

The Crown received a measure of success in the Ontario Court of Appeal.[486] The majority decided that there could be circumstances in which *Kuldip* could be relied upon to cross-examine the accused based on a statement previously ruled inadmissible under s. 24(2). Mr. Justice Doherty (McKinlay J.A. concurring) set out a number of restricted conditions, including that the statement would have to be voluntary. Labrosse J.A. strongly disagreed. The purpose to which the statement was put was immaterial. Whether used directly to incriminate the accused or to impeach credibility the evidence was only in existence because of a Charter breach and admission would render the trial unfair. McKinlay J.A. agreed with Doherty J.A. that there could be cases where cross-examination could be allowed but held that here the facts were not extreme enough.

The further Crown appeal to the Supreme Court closed the Crown's window of opportunity even further. For the 6-1 majority[487] Sopinka J. rejected the analogy to *Kuldip*. The test under 24(2) as to the effect of admission on the repute of the administration of justice was different. The "reasonable well-informed citizen who represents community values" would likely find admission of the statement not less fair because it was only used to destroy credibility.

---

481 "Annotation to Kuldip" (1991), 1 C.R. (4th) 286 at 287.
482 401 U.S. 222 (1970). See too *Oregan v. Hass*, 420 U.S. 714 (1975).
483 "[no] person shall be compelled in any criminal case to be a witness against himself."
484 384 U.S. 436 (1966).
485 (1996), 46 C.R. (4th) 133 (S.C.C.).
486 (1992), 32 C.R. (4th) 197 (Ont. C.A.). See David Tanovich, "Calder: Using Unconstitutionally Obtained Evidence to Impeach", (1995) 35 C.R. (4th) 82.
487 Gonthier, Cory, Iacobucci, and Major JJ. concurred as did La Forest J. in a separate opinion. McLachlin J. dissented.

The sole dissenting opinion was by McLachlin J.:

> The same concern for getting at the truth may weigh in favour of using the same statement in cross-examination to test the accused's credibility and uncover any inaccuracies or fabrications in his evidence in chief. From the perspective of the individual case, it is important to permit the jury to fairly judge the truthfulness of the witness. From the perspective of the trial process as a whole, it is equally important not to permit witnesses to take the stand and fabricate lies free from fear that they may be cross-examined on earlier contradictory statements.[488]

The majority's distinction of *Kuldip* is indeed not compelling. The *Calder* decision has been criticized on this and other bases.[489] In *Calder*, Sopinka J. for the majority did leave upon the possibility of "very limited circumstances" in which a material change of circumstances would warrant reopening the issue of exclusion of evidence under s. 24(2). Given the ruling on the facts in *Calder*, it is very difficult to imagine any special circumstances that would warrant a departure from the majority approach.[490] This scepticism is voiced in a concurring opinion of La Forest J. and by commentators.[491]

The *Calder* approach may have become even more rigid with the rulings of the majority in *Cook* (1998)[492] that those special circumstances would be "very rare indeed" and further that there was no difference in the s. 24(2) test when the purpose was to impeach credibility.[493]

In *Hanneson* (1989),[494] the Ontario Court of Appeal determined that a violation of the right to counsel under s. 10(b) could not insulate the detainee from subsequent criminal responsibility based in whole or part on the statements given. Even if the accused in question had been denied their right to counsel when they gave statements to their superiors during an investigation of an assault by another police officer, those very statements could be the basis for subsequent convictions of attempting to obstruct justice. The statements were the *actus reus*.

4. SECTION 52: DECLARATIONS OF INVALIDITY

(a) Only Remedy?

The supremacy clause in s. 52 provides that any law inconsistent with the Constitution is "to the extent of the inconsistency" of "no force or effect." This

---

[488] At 149-150.

[489] See Ian D. Scott, "Calder. The Charter Trumps the Truth Seeking Tool of Impeaching the Accused with a Prior Inconsistent Statement", (1996) 46 C.R. (4th) 161 and David Rose, "Calder Successes Will Be Rare and the Procedure is Uncertain" (1996), 46 C.R. (4th) 151.

[490] See however view of Peter Sankoff, "Carter Should Not Preclude the Re-admission of Real Evidence", (1998) 14 C.R. (5th) 283 suggesting that, where an accused misleads a Court about previously excluded real evidence, judges should be more favourable to a *Calder* application. No such distinction was recognised in *Bisko* (1998), 14 C.R. (5th) 283 (Ont. C.A.).

[491] *Ibid.*

[492] Above note 421.

[493] *Cook* was applied on this point in *Coutts*, above note 31, for the proposition that conscripted evidence that was not discoverable cannot be admitted for impeachment purposes (at 235-236).

[494] (1989), 49 C.C.C. (3d) 467 (Ont. C.A.).

suggests that once it has been established that a law violates the Charter it must be struck down and declared inoperative. In *Big M Drug Mart Ltd.* (1985)[495] Chief Justice Dickson sees s. 52 as imposing a duty to make such declarations:

> If a court or tribunal finds any statute to be inconsistent with the constitution, the overriding effect of the Constitution Act, 1982, s. 52(1), is to give the court not only the power, but the duty to regard the inconsistent statute to the extent of the inconsistency, as being no longer 'of force or effect'.[496]

In *Seaboyer* (1991),[497] Madam Justice McLachlin, for the majority,[498] specifically left open the question whether a court could declare legislation found to have violated the Charter "valid in part by techniques such as reading down and constitutional exemption."[499]

In *Hunter v. Southam Inc.* (1984),[500] it was very much a part of Mr. Justice Dickson's purposive view of the Charter that the Charter was to "constrain governmental action" inconsistent with Charter rights and freedoms and not "in itself an authorization for governmental action."[501] Given this perspective it is not surprising that, having declared minimum standards under s. 8 for a valid search and seizure,[502] Dickson J. refused to read them into the particular search and seizure power in question:

> While the courts are guardians of the Constitution and of individual's rights under it it is the legislature's responsibility to enact legislation that embodies appropriate safeguards to comply with the Constitution's requirements. It should not fall to the courts to fill in the details that will render the legislative lacunae constitutional.[503]

Similarly in *Wong* (1991),[504] La Forest J., for the majority, firmly held that it was not the function of the Court to craft procedures authorizing the deployment of new technologies at the disposal of the State, such as that of video surveillance. This was a function for "Parliament, and Parliament alone."[505]

If the Supreme Court were to hold that there is no way around the duty of declaring unconstitutional legislation invalid under s. 52 the responsibilities of courts and Parliaments would be more clearly demarcated. The courts would be measuring laws against minimum constitutional standards and avoiding a legislative function. Legislature would be left to arrive at solutions which met those standards. On the other hand the legislative process is slow. Lower courts have often proved resistant to the notion that it is not the function of the court to

---

[495] [1985] 1 S.C.R. 295.

[496] *Ibid.*, at 353.

[497] *Seaboyer* (1991), 7 C.R. (4th) 117 (S.C.C.).

[498] Lamer C.J.C., La Forest, Sopinka, Cory, Stevenson and Iacobucci JJ. concurred. L'Heureux-Dubé J. (Gonthier J. concurring) did not address this point in her dissent.

[499] Above note 497, at 141.

[500] (1984), 41 C.R. (3d) 97 (S.C.C.).

[501] *Ibid.*, at 111, discussed above, Chapter 1.

[502] See above, Chapter 3 for the *Hunter v. Southam* rulings on search and seizure.

[503] Above note 500, at 121.

[504] (1991), 1 C.R. (4th) 1 (S.C.C.) discussed above, Chapter 2.

[505] *Ibid.*, at 18.

patch up legislation. They have sought to preserve an otherwise valid and valuable legislative initiative.

As we turn to a consideration of techniques courts have thus far employed we should bear in mind a comprehensive statistical study of all federal and provincial appeal decisions from 1982 to 1988 where statutes were declared in violation of the Charter.[506] The researchers found that the nullification rate was twice as great for provincial as opposed to federal statutes and suggest that there are major variations between courts of appeal in terms of their willingness to declare statutes invalid.

(b) Reading In and Reading Down

The Supreme Court appears to be increasingly prepared to read in. In *Grant* (1993),[507] the Supreme Court decided that s. 10 of the Narcotic Control Act violated s.8 in so far as it authorized warrantless searches of places other than a dwelling-house in circumstances in which it would be practicable to obtain a warrant because it authorized warrantless searches. There was no exception in the provision for exigent circumstances. Writing for a unanimous court, Justice Sopinka relied on *Schachter v. Canada* (1992),[508] for guidance as to remedy:

> A court has flexibility in determining what course of action to take following a violation of the Charter which does not survive s. 1 scrutiny. Section 52 of the Constitution Act, 1982 mandates the striking down of any law that is inconsistent with the provisions of the Constitution, but only ''to the extent of the inconsistency''. Depending upon the circumstances, a court may simply strike down, it may strike down and temporarily suspend the declaration of invalidity, or it may resort to the techniques of reading down or reading in. ... In choosing how to apply s. 52 ... a court will determine its course of action with reference to the nature of the violation and the context of the specific legislation under consideration.[509]

The appropriate remedy here, held Sopinka J., was to ''read down'' s. 10 so as not to authorize warrantless searches where it is feasible to obtain a warrant.

The remedy in *Grant* looks very much like an exercise of ''reading in.''[510] Clearly Mr. Justice Sopinka had no qualms about reading in in his decision for the Court in *Johnson, Laba et al* (1994).[511] The remedy for the unconstitutional reverse onus in question was to read it as an evidentiary burden. The section was in future to be read as deleting ''unless he establishes'' and inserting ''in the absence of evidence which raises a reasonable doubt''. This seems very much like a job of legislative drafting in which the Supreme Court should not be

---

[506] F.L. Morton, G. Solomon, J. McNish and D.W. Poulton, ''Judicial Nullification of Statutes under the Charter of Rights and Freedoms, 1982-88'' (1990), 28 *Alta. L. Rev.* 396.

[507] (1993), 24 C.R. (4th) 1 (S.C.C.).

[508] [1992] 2 S.C.R. 679.

[509] At 695-696.

[510] The majority of the Court appears to refuse to adopt the *Grant* reading in approach in a subsequent s. 8 ruling in *Silveira*, above note 376, and see discussion of this point in Chapter 3.

[511] (1994), 34 C.R. (4th) 360 (S.C.C.), discussed concerning s. 1 in Chapter 1 and respecting the presumption of innocence in Chapter 6.

engaged. There is much to be said for the early vision of Chief Justice Dickson in *Hunter v. Southam* that it is for the courts to review legislation but for the legislators to respond to deficiencies.

Mr. Justice Beetz in *Manitoba (A.G.) v. Metropolitan Stores (MTS) Ltd.* (1987),[512] speaking for the Court, rejected any formal presumption that duly enacted legislation meets the requirements of the Charter:

> In my view, the presumption of constitutional validity understood in the literal sense . . . and whether it applied to laws enacted prior to the Charter or after the Charter, is not compatible with the innovative and evolutive character of this constitutional instrument.[513]

However, Beetz J. left open the issue of

> the rule of construction under which an impugned statute ought to be construed, whenever possible, in such a way as to make it conform to the Constitution.[514]

In recent decisions, the Court has grown comfortable with such a rule of construction and now speaks of a presumption of constitutionality.[515]

This distinction between ''reading down'' and ''reading in'', which is also made by authors,[516] is not clear. Here ''reading down'' will be taken to refer to those cases where courts decide not to strike down the whole law but instead decide to remove an offensive part. ''Reading in'' will be taken to refer to those instances where courts have avoided a declaration of invalidity by interpreting a legislative provision in such a way that it conforms to new Charter standards not addressed in the section itself.

''Reading down'' in this sense seems far less likely to be improper judicial legislating. Furthermore, it seems to be directly authorized by s. 52's recognition that there must be a declaration of invalidity only ''to the extent of the inconsistency.'' Lower courts have indeed frequently been content to declare that a part of the legislation is inoperative through a violation of the Charter but that the remnant will continue to apply. For example, the Ontario Court of Appeal held that a Criminal Code provision providing for a mandatory order banning publicity of the identity of a sexual assault complainant on mere application of the complainant or the prosecutor should be severed from the rest of the section leaving all such applications subject to judicial discretion and validity.[517] The Ontario Court has on a number of occasions declared particular reverse onus clauses inoperative while accepting that the substantive provision itself is still in force.[518]

---

[512] [1987] 1 S.C.R. 110.

[513] *Ibid.*, at 124.

[514] *Ibid.*, at 125.

[515] See, for example *Mills* (1999), 28 C.R. (5th) 207 (S.C.C.) at 243.

[516] See further David M. Paciocco, *Charter Principles and Proofing Criminal Cases* (1987) pp. 16-18; Dale Gibson, *The Law of The Charter: General Principles* (1986) p. 191.

[517] *Cdn. Newspapers Co. v. Canada (A.G.)* (1985), 44 C.R. (3d) 97 (Ont. C.A.) (reversed by the Supreme Court on the basis the section was valid under s. 1 (1988), 65 C.R. (3d) 50).

[518] Above, Chapter 6. See too the minority of the Supreme Court in *Holmes* (1988), 64 C.R. (3d) 97 (the majority held there was no reverse onus).

It seems clear that excision is subject to the common law notion of severability. Ontario has applied the test of severability of Viscount Simon for the Judicial Committee of the Privy Council in *Alberta (A.G.) v. Canada (A.G.)* (1947):[519]

> The real question is whether what remains is so inextricably bound up with the part declared invalid that what remains cannot independently survive or, as it has sometimes been put, whether on a fair review of the whole matter it can be assumed that the legislature would have enacted what survives without enacting the part that is ultra vires at all.[520]

(c) Constitutional Exemptions

Some support for a ''constitutional exemption'' approach can be found in Chief Justice Dickson's obiter in *Edwards Books & Art Ltd.* (1986).[521] The Chief Justice observed that had he found the Sunday Observance legislation in question offensive he would have been faced with the question of whether to strike it down or rule that it was ''ineffective or inapplicable with respect to a limited class of persons.''[522] However, the matter is still expressly left open by the Supreme Court.[523]

In criminal cases lower courts have resorted to a notion of constitutional exemption in three contexts.

The first is as a remedy against the formerly mandatory firearms prohibition order under s. 100 of the Criminal Code respecting one convicted of indictable offences involving violence to the person.[524] Although holding that s. 100 does not *per se* constitute cruel and unusual punishment contrary to s. 12, the Courts of Appeal of the Yukon Territories[525] and Saskatchewan[526] have held that an accused dependent on hunting and trapping for a livelihood should receive a constitutional exemption from the prohibition. The prohibition remains valid for others. On the other hand the Ontario Court of Appeal[527] has held that a constitutional exemption is an inappropriate remedy in the case of such a minimum sentence.

---

[519] [1947] A.C. 503.
[520] *Ibid.*, at 518 applied by the Ontario Court of Appeal, above note 517 and see too Wilson J. in *Edwards Books & Art Ltd.* (1986), 55 C.R. (3d) 193 at 255 (S.C.C.).
[521] Above note 520.
[522] *Ibid.*, at 245.
[523] *Sawyer* (1992), 78 C.C.C. (3d) 191 (S.C.C.), *Corbiere v. Canada (Minister of Indian & Northern Affairs)*, [1999] 2 S.C.R. 203 and *Morrisey* (2000), 36 C.R. (5th) 85 (S.C.C.). See Manson "Morrisey: Observations on Criminal Negligence and s. 12 Methodology", (2000) 36 C.R. (5th) 121 and discussion of *Morrisey* above Chapter 7. See also Rosenberg J.A. in *Parker* (2000), 146 C.C.C. (3d) 193 (Ont. C.A.) at 265-268.
[524] See further, above, Chapter 7.
[525] *Chief* (1990), 74 C.R. (3d) 57 (Y.T. C.A.).
[526] *McGillivary* (1991), 62 C.C.C. (3d) 407 (Sask. C.A.), followed in *Nester* (1992), 70 C.C.C. (3d) 477 (N.W.T. C.A.).
[527] *Kelly* (1990), 80 C.R. (3d) 185 (Ont. C.A.). *Kelly* was reasserted in *Luke* (1994), 28 C.R. (4th) 93 (Ont. C.A.).

In the controversial context of Charter challenges to the Criminal Code provision in s. 276 restricting evidence of sexual conduct by the complainant with others[528] the Ontario Court of Appeal favoured the remedy of a constitutional exemption. For the majority of the Ontario Court in *Seaboyer* (1987),[529] Mr. Justice Grange, for the majority,[530] held that the evidentiary restriction in s. 276 was not on its face contrary to the Charter. In certain rare instances a trial judge might rule the section inoperative and create a "constitutional exemption" when to foreclose the evidence would deny the accused a fair trial. If the defence was legitimate and the evidence had real probative force on the fact in issue it should be admitted.[531]

In dissent Mr. Justice Brooke[532] rejected a case-by-case approach and held that s. 276 should be struck down. It was doubtful that cases would be rare and accused charged with a sexual offence should be treated as an accused charged with any other offence by applying the general rules with respect to relevancy and admissibility of evidence. Requiring the accused to satisfy a judge that he had a legitimate defence and that the evidence had real probative force would impose a substantial restriction on the right to make full answer and defence. This dissenting view carried the day in the Alberta Court of Appeal in *Wald* (1989)[533] where both judgments delivered held that the "constitutional exemption" approach would place too high a burden on the accused.[534]

When this matter reached the Supreme Court of Canada in *Seaboyer* (1991)[535] the majority of the Court who found a violation also rejected the remedy of constitutional exemption. For the majority,[536] Madam Justice McLachlin reasoned that a constitutional exemption would not be appropriate as the importing of the discretion of the trial judge would not achieve the end of substantially upholding the law which Parliament had enacted. It would set up a regime based on common law notions of relevancy. In delegating to trial judges the task of determining when the legislation should not be applied it would be difficult to apply. However, she expressly sought not to foreclose the possibility that a constitutional exemption might be appropriate in some other case.[537]

Perhaps the most controversial use of a constitutional exemption by lower courts occurred in the mercy killing case of *Latimer* (2001),[538] in which a trial judge sought unsuccessfully to avoid having to impose the mandatory minimum sentence of life imprisonment with no parole eligibility for ten years.

---

[528] See above, Chapter 2.

[529] (1987), 58 C.R. (3d) 289 (Ont. C.A.), affirmed (1991), 7 C.R. (4th) 117 (S.C.C.).

[530] Martin and Thorson JJ.A. concurred.

[531] Above note 529, at 308-312.

[532] *Ibid.*, at 294-298.

[533] (1989), 68 C.R. (3d) 289 (Alta. C.A.).

[534] Harradence J.A. at 304; Hetherington J.A. at 318.

[535] Above note 497.

[536] Above note 498.

[537] *Ibid.*, at 41-44. Compare her position in *Morrisey*, above note 523, where she appears, with Arbour J., to contemplate a constitutional strategy in some cases of mandatory minimum punishments.

[538] (2001), 39 C.R. (5th) 1 (S.C.C.), discussed above in Chapter 7, respecting the cruel and unusual protection in s. 12.

(d) Possible Compromise?

Professor Allan Manson[539] has suggested that techniques for avoiding a declaration of invalidity should be only occasionally resorted to and only where an agency or process will be significantly disempowered by a declaration of invalidity:

> If forms of constitutional exemption or limited declarations of invalidity are permissible, they should be used only exceptionally. The balance should usually tip towards striking down a provision and leaving questions of criteria, procedural safeguards and limitations for the legislature. The problem of situating protections on the plane above minimum constitutional standards is a matter for the legislature. Still, courts should consider the extent to which invalidation disempowers a legitimate process. Exemptions, declarations of limited invalidity and excision should be restricted to situations where the intrusive legislative provision is ordinarily, and in most circumstances, exercised in a constitutionally valid and beneficial manner. This approach gives effect to both the dictates of s. 52(1) and the expanded mandate of s. 24(1) by imposing the remedy which is "appropriate and just" to the accused and the process.[540]

---

[539] "The Charter and Declarations of Invalidity" (1990), 74 C.R. (3d) 95.
[540] *Ibid.*, at 104.

Index